D1345269

COASTAL, SUPPORT

SUPPORT

—AND—

SPECIAL

SQUADRONS

OF THE RAF AND THEIR AIRCRAFT

COASTAL, SUPPORT
AND
SPECIAL
SQUADRONS
OF THE RAF AND THEIR AIRCRAFT

JOHN D. R. RAWLINGS

JANE'S

Copyright © John D. R. Rawlings, 1982

First published in the United Kingdom in 1982 by
Jane's Publishing Company Limited
238 City Road, London EC1V 2PU

ISBN 0 7106 0187 5

All rights reserved. No part of this publication may be
reproduced, stored in a retrieval system, transmitted in
any form by any means electrical, mechanical or
photocopied, recorded or otherwise without prior
permission of the publisher

Typesetting by
D.P. Media Limited
Hitchin, Hertfordshire

Printed in the United Kingdom by
Biddles Limited
Guildford, Surrey.

CONTENTS

ACKNOWLEDGEMENTS

A book such as this is the culmination of nearly fifty years of interest and enthusiasm for RAF history and during that time the collation of information and photographs has been fed and assisted most ably by a host of friends and colleagues almost too numerous to record without whom this book would be immeasurably poorer.

Chronologically, I must start by mentioning, as in *Fighter Squadrons of the RAF*, the late Joe Fletcher, with whom I kept company as a schoolboy around the hedges of many airfields and, later, within the RAF itself. Our joint enthusiasm led each other on in those heady days of the thirties and forties. Michael Bowyer of Cambridge has been another stalwart with whom much information has been shared happily over the years, and Gordon Swanborough generally introduced me to the joys of publishing Squadron Histories way back in the old *Aeroplane Spotter* days and has been a great and friendly help in many ways through the years, as has David Dorrell, editor of *Air Pictorial*. Many other friends, too, have participated over many years – Chris Ashworth, Chaz Bowyer, Alan Hall, Chris Cole, Peter Green, Jim Halley, Ray Sturtivant, Geoff Thomas and Richard Leask Ward being foremost amongst them, contributing on a grand scale over the years to building up a comprehensive collection of photographs and information on the squadrons.

No such book as this could be published without official help for the Operational Record Books are the primary sources from which the history of each unit starts. So I am indebted to both the Air Historical Branch of the Ministry of Defence, and in particular Humphrey Wynn and Eric Turner, and to the Public Record Office and particularly Freddie Lambert, for the opportunity to browse unhindered through these vital documents and for other help to plug gaps and answer inconsistencies in the records. The Imperial War Museum, too, has been another of those official sources where the researcher is greeted with friendship, co-operation and understanding and to Messrs Goulding and Hine I express my thanks. New upon the scene compared with these other institutions is the Royal Air Force Museum at Hendon but here, too, with the doyen of RAF researchers, Jack Bruce, a colleague down the years, and his dedicated helpers in the Photographic Department I have found so much help and interested encouragement towards making this as worthy a tribute to the Royal Air Force as time and money can accomplish.

Also I would like to thank all those many, many people, not a few of them serving officers on the Squadrons concerned, who share my keenness for the recording and preservation of the history and traditions of the Royal Air Force. Many of them have gone to considerable lengths and some expense to answer my questions or supply suitable photographs and whilst I cannot mention them all in this book I hope they will feel, when they see it, a sense of satisfaction at having played a part in its production.

Finally, my thanks go to the staff at Jane's Publishing Company who, in these dark days of recession, have had the courage to go forward with this book and have given me so much assistance; particularly thanking Alex Vanags-Baginskis whose enthusiasm, dedication and sheer hard work has been such a factor in the eventual outcome of the book.

Very many of the photographs come from private individuals and helpers along the way and for this reason, that they may know my indebtedness, I list below the photo credits, as far as I can ascertain, to the originators of the photographs in this book. If I have misaligned or omitted any credits I apologise for it is not always possible to trace certain pictures back to their origin; it is certainly not my intention or wish so to omit anyone.

F/Lt Adams (136), *The Aeroplane* (3, 19, 28, 53, 102, 119, 150, 203), *Aeroplane Photo Supply* (200, 202), R. Arbery (184), R. C. B. Ashworth (17, 33, 48, 50, 69, 107, 173, 239), W. Baker (185), W. E. Barefoot (188), P. C. M. Bashford (64), D. Batchelor (105), J. Beedle (158, 230), Howard Bell (103), Chaz Bowyer (4, 16, 83), M. J. F. Bowyer (149, 162, 163). A. J. Broker (77), R. A. Brown (157), V. Cells (177), Central Press (66), T. R. Collick (182), R. J. S. Dudman (24, 91, 113, 180, 231), H. Edmondson (127), J. Edwards (198), J. E. H. Fail (196), J. K. Fletcher (31, 118), *Flight* (14, 122, 134), Fox (81), D. S. Glover (25), B. Goulding (161), P. H. T. Green (208, 222, 237), L. J. Greenham (229), A. S. Griffin (147), S. Harding (11, 190), T. Harrison (227), R. Hayward (145, 193), E. Hemingway (62), R. A. Higham (114, 218), M. Hodgson (212), J. Howes (234), Imperial War Museum (7, 108, 135, 146, 155, 159, 183, 187, 194, 215, 225), R. C. Jones (206), G. S. Leslie (156), Howard Levy (117, 132, 197, 211), Brian Lowe (61, 70), C. H. Luke (110), A. S. C. Lumsden (207), Peter March (88), C. J. Marchant (140), T. Mason (13), I. W. Matthews (232), Ministry of Defence (2, 27, 35, 79, 80, 84, 144, 224), D. H. Newton (174), G. Nielson (45), Arthur Pearcy Jr. (219), C. Pearson (128), Brian Pickering (137), Alfred Price (55), RAAF (205, 210), RAF Museum (8, 101, 109, 151, 152, 160, 178, 209, 213), Heather Rawlings (23), RCAF (201), D. S. Rees (40), E. J. Riding (112, 191, 204), Short Bros (195), G. Simister (186), Squadron Records (9, 18, 20, 43, 44, 46, 47, 59, 68, 75, 78, 89, 96, 97, 98, 106, 121, 123, 130, 141, 165, 169, 172, 228), SAAF (52), R. C. Sturtivant (72, 111), Gordon Swanborough (29, 37, 143, 216), Tate Collection (58), A. S. Thomas (26), G. J. Thomas (34, 238, 240), C. A. Vass (115), R. L. Ward (6, 132), J. S. Wood (233), R. C. Woolven (116, 138), RAF Wyton (65).

SELECT BIBLIOGRAPHY

Bruce, Jack M., *British Aeroplanes, 1914–1918*
Barfield, Norman, *Vickers-Armstrong Warwick.*
Bowyer, Chaz, *Beaufighter at War.*
Chartres, John, *Helicopter Rescue.*
Franks, Norman L. R., *First in Indian Skies.*
Hall, Alan W. and Taylor, Eric, *The Avro Anson.*
Hallam, T. D., *The Spider's Web.*
Halley, James J., *The Squadrons of the Royal Air Force.*
—— *Famous Maritime Squadrons of the RAF.*
Hunt, Leslie, *Twenty-One Squadrons.*
Jackson, A. J., *Blackburn Aircraft.*
Kinsey, Gordon, *Seaplanes–Felixstowe.*
Kostenuk, S. and Griffin, J., *RCAF.*

Mason, T., *9 Squadron, Leads the Field.*
Merrick, K. A., *Halifax.*
Mitchell, Alan W., *New Zealanders in the Air War.*
Nesbit-Dufois, J., *Black Lysander.*
Pearcy, Arthur Jr., *Dakota.*
Ranson, Derek, *Battle Axe.*
Roberson, N. J., *A History of No.15 Squadron.*
Russel, Wilfred, *The Friendly Firm.*
Sharp, C. Martin and Bowyer, Michael J. F., *Mosquito.*
Shorrick, N., *Lion in the Sky.*
Southall, Ivan, *They Shall not Pass Unseen.*
Thetford, Owen G., *Aircraft of the Royal Air Force.*

INTRODUCTION

Any modern student of air warfare might be forgiven if he believed that the core of an Air Force's activities comprised its fighter and bomber strength. But it was not ever thus and when the aeroplane first impinged on the military mind no such operations were envisaged. To the generals this new-fangled machine could only be seen to be of any use as a reconnaissance tool – to see behind the enemy's lines and discover what he was up to. Likewise, the admirals considered that it might be the thing to enable them to see over the horizon and trace the whereabouts of enemy ships, or see below the surface for the lurking submarine.

So the aeroplane first entered His Majesty's Services for the reconnaissance task alone and all efforts went to perfect it in this role. Since then reconnaissance has come on apace through two wars but the aeroplane is still a vital device for this purpose, satellites notwithstanding. Great developments enabled high-level photo reconnaissance to cover large areas of enemy territory with impunity in World War II and since then aircraft have switched into the electronic intelligence field.

But the Army, once World War I broke out, found that the aeroplane was good for much more – for Corps recce, for artillery co-operation, for supply dropping and so on. The Army Co-operation aeroplane was soon born and it is interesting to see, from the records, that those rather prosaic Corps squadrons, flying B.Es and R.Es in World War I, had an operational sorties rate day by day far in excess of the more glamorous scout squadrons. By the end of the war in 1918 those squadrons attached to the Army were flying a wide variety of duties never envisaged four years before as the following pages will testify.

The admirals, too, soon saw the aeroplane diversifying. One purpose was to put aeroplanes on board ship but this took longer than realised and forms no part of this story. The other was to develop large seaplanes and flying boats which could fly out over the oceans and not only find but also attack any enemy in its path. Such beginnings grew on the East Coast Naval Air Stations and eventually blossomed into the Coastal Command of World War II which played such an indispensable part in the war. Whilst we rightly give credit where it is due to Fighter Command for its victory in the Battle of Britain in actual fact Hitler came nearer to defeating this country with his U-boat war, and in this field Coastal Command played an indispensable part in the country's salvation – a lesson that should be taken greater heed of in these present dangerous days when the run-down of our Navy and RAF in the face of the huge preponderance of Soviet submarines is a criminal folly.

From Coastal Command sprang the vast organisation known now as Search and Rescue, whose helicopters save so many lives year by year, as well as the squadrons which spent hours sampling the upper air to give us better weather information until the Metsats took over this task.

As aircraft became larger between the wars a viable transport force grew up and in due course this had proved invaluable to the RAF, enabling them to transport and supply vast crowds of people, to drop great armies in enemy territory and keep them supplied by air, to evacuate servicemen and civilians alike from disasters and areas of danger. Many are the diverse tasks of the transport aircraft down the years, supplemented by the arrival of the helicopter and the many avenues of operation that this has opened up for the Royal Air Force.

As far as space permits these diverse activities are recorded in the pages that follow, detailing Squadrons which have served faithfully down the years in many unsung but vital operational tasks. Initially one might think they do not have the glamour of the fighter and bomber squadrons but this is a notion born of ignorance. Think for a minute of the majestic Sunderland, hundreds of miles out over the Atlantic rollers, out of touch with every friendly force, battling it out with a U-boat which is staying on the surface to fight; or the thrill of the front cockpit of a Beaufighter diving in to a forest of ships' masts with flak bursting all around and companions darting all over the sky as the targets loom large in the face of the pilot and the torpedo drops away. Or again, imagine a moonlit night, a small black Lysander plodding over the fields of France with no navaids looking for the shining of a torch to throttle back and glide into a small field, the pilot trusting it is big enough to drop off an agent and get out again before the Gestapo arrives. Or again think of an unwieldly Dakota breaking cloud just over the steaming dense jungle of Burma, searching for a clearing and then weaving frantically around with the wingtips brushing the hillside to try and drop the supplies where they can be picked up by the soldiers relying on them for their very survival. Are these not stirring exploits indeed? Yet these were the bread and butter duties, and many more besides of the Squadrons chronicled in this book.

This therefore becomes a very satisfying volume, both to write and to have completed for, in company with its predecessors it now presents a chronicle, in standard format, on all the operational squadrons of the Royal Air Force. At the end of this book will be found also, in brief form, information of all the other numbered squadrons, under role headings, which nominally have been non-operational but even so have involved, as the Search and Rescue units for example, many flights of daring and courage. Space has not permitted a fuller treatment of these units.

As already said, I have attempted to maintain a format in this book consistent with the two previous volumes on the Bomber Squadrons and the Fighter Squadrons so that the serious student will in effect have the total operational spectrum covered. Unfortunately, the time differential between those previous volumes and this has so escalated the costs of book production that I have been unable, for cost reasons alone, to include the great number of illustrations that were a feature of the predecessors. In selecting the photographs in this book, therefore, I have followed three guidelines:

1) I have attempted to provide at least one photograph of each squadron of which illustrations are obtainable.
2) I have endeavoured to provide a balanced selection of all the major, and many of the minor types used by the Squadrons concerned.
3) Wherever possible I have endeavoured to use photographs which have either never been published before or have only had a limited exposure to publication, thus giving a freshness to the book. I do believe that even hardened students of Squadron illustrations will find one or two to open their eyes a little wider.

It is my great regret that we have had to omit the Squadron badges from this volume owing to the disproportionate reproduction fees now charged.

In these days it is not fashionable to enthuse about the exploits of our Armed Services but yet it remains a fact that we rely on them for our ultimate stability and peace as a nation and it is the fostering of this spirit of selfless service that brought us through the last two conflicts (Kipling wrote a very good poem about this theme). It is encouraging to find that, even though the RAF of today is a very different place to that of yore, the same spirit is apparent in the few crew rooms still open.

It is my hope that these pages will not only be used as a work of reference by all those seeking information on the traditions and past activities of the Royal Air Force but will be a source of pleasant nostalgia to past members of the Squadrons and a source of inspiration to today's young men to follow in what is an illustrious tradition. If this book accomplishes these goals I shall be satisfied.

John D. R. Rawlings

No. 1 SQUADRON

BADGE
The numeral '1' winged

MOTTO
'In omnibus princeps'
('Foremost in everything')

The badge is an adaptation of No. 1's first
unofficial badge which comprised a figure '1'
on the national marking within a laurel wreath
between two wings.

When the Royal Flying Corps was formed on 13 May, 1912 it
acquired the aeronautical equipment belonging to the Royal
Engineers. All the lighter-than-air material was formed into No. 1
Squadron, RFC at Farnborough on that date. Soon after forming
the Squadron received its third airship from the factory alongside
which the Squadron lived. It flew two airships in the army manoeuvres that year, using W/T in one of them. It continued to explore
the possibilities of airship recce in wartime until 1 January, 1914
when all lighter-than-air craft were handed over to the Admiralty
and No. 1 Squadron became a unit without aircraft until 1 May
when a new CO was posted in. With the advent of war, however, the
other aeroplane squadrons went to France and No. 1 was hard put
to accomplish anything until 15 August when it moved to Brooklands and received some aircraft. Training went on slowly and on 3
March the Squadron flew to France for the battle of Neuve
Chapelle. On 12 March, No. 1 dropped its first bombs (20 lb)
without any observable effect and lost its first pilot. Then No. 1
began co-operating with the army before moving to Bailleul. At this
time the Squadron flew four different types of aircraft over the
Ypres salient day by day. In May the Squadron had its first aerial
engagements and soon it was encountering Fokker Scouts, with
ensuing casualties. Most of the sorties flown were reconnaissance of
the German lines and spotting for the guns, though to the end of
1915 more bombing attacks were made. In 1916 the arrival of
Moranes enabled longer recce flights to be made; these were just
what the German Fokker pilots wanted and No. 1's casualties
mounted. To remedy this the Squadron received some Nieuport
Scouts in March for escort duties. These were also used for attacking German observation balloons. After a heavy summer on the
Somme the Squadron went over to the fighter role completely in
January, 1917 and has flown in that role ever since.

Disbanding in January, 1920 No. 1 was re-formed as a Home
Defence squadron at Tangmere in February, 1927, fought in the
Battle of Britain in 1940 with Hurricanes after having to move out of
France a second time at Dunkirk, and flew Hurricanes until 1942
when it converted to Typhoons, and, subsequently, Spitfires. After
World War II it became a Meteor fighter squadron at Tangmere
once more, following these with Hunters before becoming the
world's first VTO fighter squadron with the Harrier.

Bases etc.

Formed at Farnborough on 13 May, 1912.

Farnborough	May 1912—Aug 1914
Brooklands	Aug 1914—Nov 1914
Netheravon	Nov 1914—Feb 1915
St. Omer	Feb 1915—Mar 1915
Bailleul	Mar 1915—Jan 1917

Became a fighter squadron on 1 January, 1917.

Main Equipment

Lighter-than-air Craft (May 1912—Jan 1914)
  Beta II; Gamma; Delta; Eta; Zeta
Farman Longhorn (May 1914—Feb 1915)
  19
Caudron (May 1914—Aug 1915)
  1884; 1885; 1891
Avro 504A (Aug 1914—Jul 1915)
  752; 769; 773; 2859
B.E.8 (Aug 1914—May 1916)
  2130
Bristol Scout C (Apr 1915—Oct 1915)
  1603; 4672
Martinsyde S.1 (Apr 1915—Aug 1916)
  748
Morane Parasol (Dec 1915—Jan 1917)
  1894; 1897; 5006; 5080
Morane Biplane (Jan 1916—Jan 1917)
  5160

Commanding Officers

Maj E. M. Maitland	May 1912—May 1914
Maj C. A. H. Longcroft	May 1914—Jan 1915
Maj W. G. H. Salmond	Jan 1915—Aug 1915
Maj P. B. Joubert de la Ferte	Aug 1915—Nov 1915
Maj G. F. Pretyman, DSO	Nov 1915—Dec 1916
Maj G. C. St. P. de Dombasle	Dec 1916—Jan 1917

Aircraft Insignia

As far as is known no distinctive squadron insignia was carried on the aircraft
at this early stage.

(See also *Fighting Squadrons of the RAF*, pp. 11–18)

No. 2 SQUADRON

BADGE
Three concentric circles, all over a wake knot

MOTTO
'Hereward'

The three concentric circles represent the
RAF, and the wake knot comes from the arms
of Hereward the Wake and signifies the
guardian of the Army.

No. 2 Squadron formed out of the Air Battalion of the Royal
Engineers at Farnborough on 13 May, 1912, equipped with the
early B.E. biplanes. Exactly nine months later the Squadron began
an epic (for those days) when it set out to fly to its new base at
Montrose; they all arrived finally after thirteen days' flying. Here it
remained until August, 1914 when it went to France with the BEF,
equipped with no fewer than seven different types of aeroplane. It
began reconnaissances that month and on 25th forced down the
RFC's first enemy aircraft. It soon specialised in artillery co-
operation duties and in 1915 used wireless-equipped B.Es in the
battle of Neuve Chapelle for this task, flying anything up to 2 hour
sorties over the lines. In the same battle it also began ground attack,
using 100 lb bombs; whilst doing this at Ypres Lt W. B. Rhodes
Moorhouse posthumously won the first air VC. By the summer of
1915 the Squadron had standardised on B.E.2Cs with a few scouts
for defence until specific scout squadrons were formed later in the
war (1916). The Squadron was now flying intensively on recce,
artillery shoots and photo work, with the occasional bombing raid
(283 sorties were flown in May, 1916). The B.E.2s lasted until May,
1917, being by then hopelessly outclassed and causing many casualties amongst the crews. The Armstrong-Whitworth F.K.8 was a
much better proposition which the Squadron flew until the war
ended. During 1917 these were flown on quite a number of night
bombing raids in addition to the Army work. That the 'Big AckW',
as the F.K.8 was known, was better in combat is shown by the
action in which 2nd Lt MacLeod won the Squadron's second VC, in
March 1918. Whilst ground strafing he was attacked by eight Fokker Triplanes; he manoeuvred to enable his gunner to shoot down
three of them before his petrol tank was set on fire. He managed to

sideslip the aircraft to the ground, although wounded five times, and got his wounded observer out. During the final offensive the Squadron flew as much in ground attack as on artillery work. After the war it returned to the UK and was disbanded at Weston-on-the-Green on 20 January, 1920.

However, on 1 February, 1920 No. 2 was re-formed at Oranmore in S. Ireland with Bristol Fighters, supporting the troops dealing with the riots there. It flew on this task until withdrawal in 1922, setting up base at Digby and then, after another spell in Belfast, moved to Farnborough, Andover and then Manston in the 'twenties. Basically an army co-operation unit once more it also went overseas with HMS *Hermes* in 1927, flying from Shanghai Racecourse to help quell the disturbances there from May to September. Bristol Fighters were replaced by Atlas and then Audax aircraft in the inter-war period, No. 2 setting up permanent base at Hawkinge in December, 1935. After a few months on Hectors it re-equipped with Westland Lysanders with which it entered World War II.

In October, 1939 it flew to Abbeville and began taking photos of its local area, then tactical recces of the 3rd British Division positions. It was engaged on exercises until May, 1940 threw it into action with the German advance. It now flew Tac/R duties as intensively as possible and it was soon found that the Lysander was as helpless against German air opposition as the B.E's had been previously. Casualties began to mount but No. 2 fought on until having to move back to the UK on 19 May. From here it continued Tac/R duties over the BEF retreating on Dunkirk. It also flew sorties to drop supplies to beleagured garrisons, eight aircraft going to Calais on 27 May. By the end of the month No. 2's action was over and it retired inland to re-equip. Its next task was to fly dawn and dusk patrols around a sector of the East Coast as an anti-invasion tactic. This task was maintained throughout the year. In November, 1940, with no other action, the Lysanders were used for radar calibration duties. 1941 saw the beginning of frequent army exercises, at first preparing for German landings. In August the first Tomahawks arrived alongside the Lysanders for Tac/R but they were not at all satisfactory and it was not until April, 1942 that No. 2 had an aircraft suitable for operations once more. This was the Mustang I and after a lengthy work-up the Squadron became operational in November, 1942 flying low-level photo sorties of radar sites on the French coast, followed by more general PR along the coast. Sporadic sorties were flown during the winter but in spring 1943 No. 2 began *Lagoon* operations, flying shipping recces off the Dutch coast in pairs; in April 76 sorties were flown, and the following month *Populars* (photo recce) and *Rangers* were also flown, amounting to 110 sorties. Throughout the year this type of activity was maintained; with 1944 came attention to the V1 sites which took an increasing proportion of the Squadron's effort. By May, though, the Squadron was more fully committed to the Second Front and from D-Day onwards was operating with the forward troops; 308 sorties were flown that month. Moving to the Continent at the end of July enabled No. 2 to increase its effort and in August 632 Tac/R sorties were flown with the loss of but two aircraft. It had now received Spitfire XIs as well as the Mustangs. As the year moved on Spitfires took over, the Squadron receiving FR.14s in November flying high and low-level work but with Tac/R predominating still. The last Mustangs left in January, 1945 with the Squadron then in Holland. Despite the winter the Squadron maintained about 300 sorties per month until the end of the war in Europe. One of the newer tasks of the Squadron was Flak spotting and this was put to good use at the Rhine crossing on 24 March.

The end of the war still gave the Squadron plenty to do and its usefulness was increased when re-formed on a two flight basis with Spitfire 19s from No. 4 Squadron joining its own Mk.14s. It remained in RAF Germany after the war, flying high and low-level PR until the end of 1950 brought the first Meteors to replace Spitfires. These were FR.Mk.9s for low-level Tac/R and the Squadron continued in this role in RAF Germany for the next two decades. In this time No. 2 flew Meteors until 1956, then Swifts until 1961, and then Hunters from 1961 until changing the emphasis of its role in March, 1971. At that time Phantom FGR.2s replaced the Hunter FR.10s and, whilst retaining a Tac/R commitment, became also a fighter ground attack squadron. Since then the Phantoms have been replaced by Jaguar GR.1s; the Squadron is still part of RAF Germany.

Bases etc.

Formed at Farnborough 13 May, 1912.

Farnborough	May 1912	Feb 1913
Montrose	Feb 1913	Aug 1914
Amiens	Aug 1914	Aug 1914
Maubeuge	Aug 1914	Aug 1914
Berlaimont	Aug 1914	Aug 1914
Le Cateau	Aug 1914	Sep 1914
Juilly	Sep 1914	Sep 1914
Serris	Sep 1914	Sep 1914
Pezearches	Sep 1914	Sep 1914
Melun	Sep 1914	Sep 1914
Pezearches	Sep 1914	Sep 1914
Coulommiers	Sep 1914	Sep 1914
Fere en Tardenois	Sep 1914	Sep 1914
Vieul Aroy	Sep 1914	Nov 1914
Merville, det. St. Omer	Nov 1914	Jun 1915
Hesdigneul	Jun 1915	Jun 1918
Floringhem	Jun 1918	Oct 1918
Mazingarbe	Oct 1918	Oct 1918
Genech	Oct 1918	Feb 1919
Bicester	Feb 1919	Sep 1919
Weston-on-the-Green	Sep 1919	Jan 1920

Disbanded at Weston-on-the-Green on 20 January, 1920. Re-formed at Oranmore on 1 February, 1920.

Oranmore, det. Castlebar, Fermoy	Feb 1920	Feb 1922
Digby	Feb 1922	May 1922
Aldergrove	May 1922	Sep 1922
Farnborough	Sep 1922	Sep 1923
Andover	Sep 1923	Mar 1924
Manston	Mar 1924	Apr 1927
HMS *Hermes*	Apr 1927	May 1927
Shanghai Racecourse	May 1927	Sep 1927
HMS *Hermes*	Sep 1927	Oct 1927
Manston	Oct 1927	Dec 1935
Hawkinge	Dec 1935	Oct 1939
Bertangles	Oct 1939	Oct 1939
Abbeville	Oct 1939	May 1940
Bethune, det. Weveghem	May 1940	May 1940
Lympne	May 1940	May 1940
Bekesbourne	May 1940	Jun 1940
Hatfield, det. Sawbridgeworth	Jun 1940	Jun 1940
Teversham	Jun 1940	Oct 1940
Sawbridgeworth	Oct 1940	Feb 1943
Bottisham, det. Fowlmere	Feb 1943	Apr 1943
Sawbridgeworth	Apr 1943	Jul 1943
Gravesend	Jul 1943	Aug 1943
Odiham	Aug 1943	Sep 1943
Hutton Cranswick	Sep 1943	Oct 1943
Odiham	Oct 1943	Nov 1943
North Weald	Nov 1943	Nov 1943
Sawbridgeworth	Nov 1943	Feb 1944
North Weald, det. Benson	Feb 1944	Feb 1944
Sawbridgeworth	Feb 1944	Mar 1944
Dundonald	Mar 1944	Mar 1944
Sawbridgeworth	Mar 1944	Apr 1944
Gatwick	Apr 1944	Jun 1944
Odiham	Jun 1944	Jul 1944
Plumetot	Jul 1944	Aug 1944
Beny-sur-Mer	Aug 1944	Sep 1944
Boisney	Sep 1944	Sep 1944
Fresnoy	Sep 1944	Sep 1944
Fort Rouge	Sep 1944	Oct 1944
St. Denis-Westrem	Oct 1944	Nov 1944
Deurne	Nov 1944	Mar 1945
Gilze-Rijen	Mar 1945	Apr 1945
Mill	Apr 1945	May 1945
Twente	May 1945	Jun 1945
Celle	Jun 1945	Sep 1945
Hustedt	Sep 1945	Apr 1947
Celle	Apr 1947	Jun 1948
Wunstorf	Jun 1948	Sep 1949
Wahn	Sep 1949	Jun 1950
Wunstorf	Jun 1950	May 1952
Bückeburg	May 1952	Jul 1953
Gütersloh	Jul 1953	Oct 1955
Wahn	Oct 1955	Oct 1957
Geilenkirchen	Oct 1957	Oct 1961
Jever	Sep 1961	Dec 1970
Gütersloh	Dec 1970	Mar 1971
Brüggen		

On 12 March, 1971 the Squadron became a fighter ground attack Squadron with a fighter-reconnaissance commitment and re-equipped with Phantom FGR.2s at RAF Brüggen.

Main Equipment

B.E. Prototype (May 1912—Jan 1915)
30
B.E.2 (1912—1914)
205; 217; 218; 222; 225
Farman S.7 Longhorn (Jan 1913—   1914)
214; 215; 223; 224; 266
Bréguet Biplane (Feb 1913—Aug 1914)
212; 211
R.E.1 (Aug 1914—   1914)
607 and/or 608
Bleriot XI (1914—   1915)
297; 323
B.E.2a/B.E.2b (1914—   1915)
(B.E.2a's)
226; 230; 235; 267; 272; 317; 368; 386
(B.E.2b's)
396; 492; 687; 733
Farman S.11 Shorthorn (1914—Aug 1915)
1846; 1850; 1851
R.E.5 (Sep 1914—   1915)
No serials known
B.E.2c (Nov 1914—May 1917)
1655; 1686; 1707; 1719; 2019; 2101; 2496; 2503; 2604; 2673; 4074; 4495; 7331; B702
Bristol Type C & D (1915—   1916)
4667; 5327
B.E.2d (Jul 1916—Apr 1917)
5730; 5741; 5789; 5825; 6232; 6250; 6736; 6746
B.E.2e (1917—May 1917)
A1363; A1819; C7086
A.K. F.K.8 (Apr 1917—Feb 1919)
A2627; A2681; A2724; A9984; A9998; B210'12'; B246'13'; B288; B304; B5758; B5773; C3372; C3530; C3553; C3782; D5005
Bristol F.2B Fighter (Feb 1920—Jan 1930)
B1223; B1329; C767; F4360; F4484; F4537; F4854; H1526; J6696; J6703; J7652; J7699; J8245; J8265; J8269
A.W. Atlas I (Jan 1930—Sep 1934)
J9951; J9952; J9954; J9956; J9958; J9964
Hawker Audax I (Sep 1934—Nov 1937)
K2002; K2003; K2029; K3056; K3058; K3061; K3066; K3086; K3088; K3090; K3111; K3126; K3718
Hawker Hector I (Nov 1937—Sep 1938)
K9700; K9715; K9737; K9739; K9740; K9755; K9770
Westland Lysander I (Sep 1938—Feb 1940)
L4687; L4692; L4694; L4699; L4702; L4705, KO:D; L4706; L4711
Westland Lysander II (Jan 1940—   1942)
L4780; L4810; L4815; L6847; L6852; N1203, KO:M; N1217; N1242; N1262; N1318; P1686; P1721; P9067; P9107; P9132; R2030
Boulton Paul Defiant I (Aug 1940—Aug 1941)
N1571; N1572
Westland Lysander III (Jan 1941—Apr 1942)
T1528; T1532, KO:D; T1613
Curtiss Tomahawk I, IIA, IIB (Aug 1941—Apr 1942)
(Mk. I)
AH857
(Mk. IIA)
AH899; AH908; AH916, XV:U; AH934, XV:W; AH942, XV:S
(Mk. IIB)
AK144; AK146
North American Mustang I (Mar 1942—Feb 1944)
AG370, XV:D; AG465, G; AG574, XV:X; AG593, XV:U; AG630, R; AG638, XV:F; AL969, K; AL995, XV:S; later S; AM112, XV:X; AM234, A; AP203, P; AP245, D
North American Mustang IA (Feb 1944—Jun 1944)
FD444; FD477; FD480; FD501; FD529; FD547; FD552; FD567, A
North American Mustang II (Jun 1944—Jan 1945)
FR891; FR898; FR906; FR915; FR922; FR930; FR938
Vickers-Supermarine Spitfire XI (Aug 1944 & Sep 1945 only)
PA837; PL831
Vickers-Supermarine Spitfire XIV (Nov 1944—Jan 1951)
MV270, OI:D; MV348, OI:S; NH646; NH903, OI:Q; NM821, OI:L; RM822; RM851; RM878, OI:C; RM920, OI:C; RM939; RN113; SM827, OI:C; SM883, OI:H; TZ112, OI:G
Vickers-Supermarine Spitfire PR.19 (Nov 1945—Mar 1951)
PM549, OI:F; PM555, OI:K; PM616, OI:T; PM628, OI:P; PM660, OI: ; PS832; PS915;

Gloster Meteor FR.9 (Dec 1950—Jun 1956)
VW361; VW371; VZ577; VZ605, B:S, later S; VZ611, B:Z; WB115, K; WB133, R; WB143, B:U; WH542, B:K, later K; WH546, B:A, later A; WL255, C; WX965, Z; WX986, H
Gloster Meteor PR.10 (Mar 1951—Aug 1951) (B Flight only)
VS974; VS987; VW379; WB154; WB155, B:A; WB156
Vickers-Supermarine Swift FR.5 (Apr 1956—   1961)
WK277, N; WK295, G; WK307, C; WK314, H; WN124, S; XD908, A; XD912, C; XD927, N; XD959, V; XD962, L
Hawker Hunter FR.10 (Apr 1961—Mar 1971)
WW596, N; XE456, W; XE625, L; XF422, H; XF458, W; XG127, Y; XJ694, Z

Commanding Officers

Maj C. J. Burke	May 1912	Nov 1914
Maj G. W. P. Dawes	Nov 1914	Mar 1915
Maj T. I. Webb-Bowen	Mar 1915	Jun 1915
Maj J. H. W. Becke	Jun 1915	Sep 1915
Maj C. F. de S. Murphy	Sep 1915	Apr 1916
Maj R. A. Cooper, DSO	Apr 1916	Aug 1917
Maj W. R. Snow, DSO, MC	Aug 1917	Aug 1918
Maj P. G. Ross-Hume	Aug 1918	Jan 1920
S/Ldr B. F. Moore	Feb 1920	
S/Ldr F. W. Stent		
S/Ldr H. J. Butler		
S/Ldr L. E. Forbes		Mar 1925
S/Ldr R. E. Saul	Mar 1925	Oct 1926
S/Ldr L. W. Sowrey, DFC	Oct 1926	Mar 1928
S/Ldr H. M. Probyn, DSO	Apr 1928	Sep 1930
S/Ldr S. E. Toomer, DFC	Sep 1930	Jan 1933
S/Ldr P. F. Fullard, DSO, MC	Jan 1933	Dec 1933
S/Ldr J. H. Green	Dec 1933	Jul 1935
S/Ldr N. L. Desoer	Jul 1935	Jan 1938
S/Ldr W. A. Opie	Jan 1938	Apr 1939
W/Cdr A. J. W. Geddes, OBE	Apr 1939	Oct 1941
S/Ldr D. I. C. Eyres	Oct 1941	Jan 1942
W/Cdr P. J. A. Riddell	Jan 1942	Feb 1943
W/Cdr P. W. Stansfeld	Feb 1943	Jun 1943
S/Ldr B. O. C. Egan-Wyer	Jun 1943	Aug 1943
S/Ldr M. Gray, DFC	Aug 1943	Sep 1944
S/Ldr C. E. Maitland	Sep 1944	Mar 1945
S/Ldr R. J. F. Mitchell, DFC	Apr 1945	Apr 1945
S/Ldr D. W. Barlow, DFC	Apr 1945	Dec 1945
S/Ldr G. Collinson	Dec 1945	Oct 1948
S/Ldr W. A. Newenham, DFC	Oct 1948	Feb 1950
S/Ldr L. H. Bartlett, DFC	Feb 1950	Nov 1950
S/Ldr R. M. Pugh, AFC	Nov 1950	May 1953
S/Ldr R. H. G. Weighill, DFC	May 1953	Nov 1955
S/Ldr R. S. Mortley, AFC	Nov 1955	May 1958
S/Ldr C. A. Wade	May 1958	Sep 1960
S/Ldr C. S. MacDonald	Sep 1960	Feb 1962
S/Ldr D. L. F. Thornton	Feb 1962	Dec 1964
S/Ldr N. J. R. Walpole	Dec 1964	Jun 1967
S/Ldr T. Barrett	Jun 1967	Nov 1969
S/Ldr R. J. M. David	Nov 1969	Dec 1970
W/Cdr B. A. Stead	Dec 1970	Dec 1972

Aircraft Insignia

No Squadron markings were carried until April, 1916 at which time No. 2 Squadron was allotted a marking of a triangle to be painted on the sides of the fuselage aft of the roundels, black on clear-doped aircraft, white on khaki aircraft. In August, 1917 this was changed to a white zigzag which was maintained on the A.W. F.K.8s until the war's end. The Bristol Fighters originally carried red/blue/red bands around the rear fuselage but by 1925 this had been dropped and by 1929 the black triangle had re-appeared, this time on the fin with a white figure '2' on it. No markings were carried on the Atlas but the triangle was moved to its original position on the Audax, on the fuselage side. The Squadron badge was also painted on the fins. This was retained on the Hectors. With the Lysander came also the era of code letters and No. 2 used 'KO' from 1938 until ca. 1941, being replaced by 'XV'. This was used until 1943 when identity markings were dropped until 1945, the new code combination being 'OI', carried on Spitfire 14s and 19s. With the advent of the Meteor a single letter code was used, in No. 2's case it was 'B', and the squadron emblem was painted on the nacelle sides. However in the mid-fifties an official marking was approved for the Squadron comprising a black rectangle each side of the fuselage roundel with a white triangle on each side. This marking was perpetuated on the Swifts and Hunters.
(See also *Fighter Squadrons of the RAF*, p. 559)

11

No. 3 SQUADRON

BADGE

On a monolith a cockatrice

MOTTO

'Tertius primus erit'
('The third shall be first')

The first badge was five monoliths, having been introduced in reference to the unit's connection with Stonehenge. In the official badge it was decided to use only one and to place thereon a cockatrice, representing a very early form of flying creature.

It falls to No. 3 Squadron to claim being the first aeroplane squadron in the Royal Air Force. The original No. 3 Squadron, Royal Flying Corps, was formed from 2 Company (Heavier-than-air), Air Battalion, Royal Engineers at Larkhill on Salisbury Plain on 13 May, 1912. On that date it was the only unit to have aeroplanes and it literally pioneered the use of such craft for army purposes, using many different types as different roles were explored. In 1913 it moved to Netheravon and on 13 August, 1914 to Amiens ready for war. First operations (reconnaissances) were flown on 19 August. This was their prime task although they were also intended to patrol on anti-Zeppelin sorties with bombs and revolvers. During the retreat from Mons No. 3 distinguished itself with valuable recces. To this was added photography, in preparation for the Neuve Chapelle battle, and, when fighting on the ground was fierce, the Squadron loaded up small bombs and went strafing. The Squadron also took part in 'shoots' co-operating with the artillery before specialised squadrons took on this role. By the summer of 1915 the Squadron had standardised on one type of aircraft, the Morane Parasol, for its army co-operation duties and with these it became increasingly involved in scout flying (air fighting). Eventually, in October 1917, it was re-constituted as a fighter squadron with Sopwith Camels, continued flying them until the war ended, eventually disbanding on 27 October, 1919. A short spell with Sopwith Snipes ensued in India from 1920 to 1921 then on 1 October, 1921 it took on the task of coastal recce at Leuchars. It was given Westland Walrus and D.H.9A aircraft for this task, which was properly a Fleet Air Arm duty, and on 1 April, 1923 was disbanded once more. From then onwards No. 3 has served primarily as a fighter squadron, at Upavon and Kenley between the wars, as a Hurricane squadron in France at Dunkirk and then in home defence duties in 1940, including night fighting in 1941. Ground attack followed, with Hurricanes, Typhoons, and eventually Tempests, the Squadron moving over to Holland in September, 1944. After World War II it has remained in RAF Germany, at first on ground attack duties until disbanding on 15 June, 1957, then from January, 1959 until January, 1961 as an all-weather fighter squadron. From January, 1961 until January, 1972 No. 3 operated as a Canberra intruder squadron and, since then, as part of the Harrier Force in Germany.

Bases etc.

Formed at Larkhill on 13 May, 1912.

Larkhill	May 1912—Jun 1913
Netheravon	Jun 1913—Aug 1914
Amiens	Aug 1914—Aug 1914
Mauberge	Aug 1914—Aug 1914
Le Cateau	Aug 1914—Aug 1914
St. Quentin	Aug 1914—Aug 1914
La Fere	Aug 1914—Aug 1914
Compiegne	Aug 1914—Aug 1914
Senlis	Aug 1914—Aug 1914
Juilly	Aug 1914—Sep 1914
Serris	Sep 1914—Sep 1914
Pezearches	Sep 1914—Sep 1914
Melun	Sep 1914—Sep 1914
Touquin	Sep 1914—Sep 1914
Coulommiers	Sep 1914—Sep 1914
Fere-en-Tardenois	Sep 1914—Oct 1914
Amiens	Oct 1914—Oct 1914
Abbeville	Oct 1914—Oct 1914
Bienfay	Oct 1914—Oct 1914
St. Omer	Oct 1914—Nov 1914
Houges	Nov 1914—Jun 1915
Auchel	Jun 1915—Mar 1916
Bruay	Mar 1916—Apr 1916
Bertangles	Apr 1916—Apr 1916
La Houssoye	Apr 1916—Jan 1917
Lavieville	Jan 1917—Jul 1917
Longavesnes	Jul 1917—Aug 1917
Lechelle	Aug 1917—Oct 1917

In October, 1917 the Squadron became a scout squadron with Sopwith Camels, serving in this role until 1 October, 1921. It then re-formed at Leuchars in the coastal recce role.

Leuchars	Oct 1921—Apr 1923

Disbanded at Leuchars on 1 April, 1923. Re-formed on 1 April, 1924 at Manston as a fighter squadron in which role it has predominantly served ever since.

Main Equipment

Bleriot XI (May 1912—Apr 1915)
219; 221; 292; 374; 389; 810; 1825
B.E.2/2a (1913— 1913)
205; 220; 227; 273; 299; 387
B.E.4 (1913— 1913)
204
B.E.3 (1913— 1914)
203
Farman F.20 Shorthorn (1913—Apr 1915)
274; 277; 286; 295; 350; 708
Farman S.7 (1913—Apr 1915)
214; 216; 269; 270; 356
B.E.8 (Aug 1914— 1914)
209
S.E.2a (Mar 1914—Apr 1915)
609
Bristol Scout B (Sep 1914— 1915)
633
Avro 500 (1915— 1915)
285; 288; 289; 290; 291
Avro 504K (1915—Mar 1915)
A1979
Morane Parasol (Mar 1915—Oct 1917)
1849; 1862; 1866; 1875; 5021; 5034; 5045; 5055; 5087; A6607; A6635; A6706; A6710; B1521; B1612; B3451
D.H.9A (Oct 1921— 1922)
E8765; E8767; H3512; H3515; H3518; H3539; H3540
Westland Walrus (Oct 1922—Apr 1923)
No serials known

Commanding Officers

Maj H. R. M. Brooke-Popham	Mar 1912—Aug 1914
Maj J. M. Salmond, DSO	Aug 1914—Apr 1915
Maj D. S. Lewis, DSO	Apr 1915—Nov 1915
Maj E. R. Ludlow-Hewitt	Nov 1915—Feb 1916
Maj H. D. Harvey Kelly	Mar 1916—Sep 1916
Maj E. E. Stodart	Sep 1916—Apr 1917
Maj E. D. Horsfall	Apr 1917—Jun 1917
Maj J. A. G. de C. Courcy	Sep 1917—Sep 1917
Maj R. Raymond Barker	Sep 1917—Oct 1917
S/Ldr D. G. Donald	Oct 1921—Jan 1923
S/Ldr C. C. Miles	Jan 1923—Apr 1923

Aircraft Insignia

During the two periods in the Squadron history covered by this volume it appears that no Squadron insignia was carried by the Squadron aircraft. (See also *Fighter Squadrons of the RAF*, pp. 18–25 and *Bomber Squadrons of the RAF*, pp. 9 & 386.)

No. 4 SQUADRON

BADGE
A sun in splendour divided per bend by a flash
of lightning
MOTTO
'In futurum videre'
('To see into the future')

The divided sun (red and black) indicates
round the clock operations; the lightning flash
denotes speed and also refers to early wireless
use.

No. 4 Squadron originally formed three months after the formation of the Royal Flying Corps itself. Farnborough was the place and sometime in August, 1912 was the time when it came into being, equipped with one of Cody's Biplanes, some Bréguet Biplanes and some B.E.2As. It took ten months to become a complete unit and then moved to Netheravon. Its task in the development of military aviation was to develop night flying and aerial photography. At the end of July, 1914 it was seconded to the RFC Naval Wing (known in the Navy as the RNAS) at Eastchurch and began the war flying Zeppelin patrols over the Thames Estuary. A month later it moved to France as part of the BEF and shared with No. 3 Squadron the honour of flying the first operations of the war, a recce on 19 August. It was using the B.E.s and Farmans and these were soon augmented by Sopwith and Martinsyde scouts. Much of its task was reconnaissance but it also indulged in ground attack, first such sorties being on 31 October, 1914. On operations, No. 4 was still trying out new devices, such as using field glasses to spot for the guns. 100 lb bombs were carried for use against suitable targets and first steps in artillery co-operation took place but the main task was still reconnaissance. By mid-1915 the Squadron had virtually standardised on the B.E.2c which it was to fly for the next two years, at great cost to itself, as the German aircraft found the B.E.2 an easy target. 1916 saw much more in the way of contact patrols (with infantry) and these led into more general ground attack work, although a more light-hearted task was the occasional bombing of observation balloons. At last in June, 1917 the B.E.s were replaced by R.E.8s and for a while No. 4 had a Flight of Bristol Fighters in addition. The Squadron was expanded into an additional unit, known as 4A Squadron, which flew with the Portuguese elements on the Western Front. The Squadron fought on, mainly in recce and artillery co-operation duties, until the Armistice and eventually returned to the UK in February, 1919; it was disbanded at Northolt on 20 September, 1919.

On 30 April, 1920 No. 4 was re-formed, again for co-operation with the Army, and given Bristol Fighters at Farnborough. In November it sent A Flight to Ireland where it supported the troops involved in the fighting there until January, 1922 when it returned to Farnborough. The whole Squadron then embarked on HMS *Ark Royal* and went to Turkey to support the British Army of Occupation. It spent a year there, mostly combating muddy airfields before returning to Farnborough in September, 1923. It now set about the task of army co-operation refinement, flying many detachments for army exercises and becoming adept in using any fields that were alongside the particular units. In 1925 the Squadron was detached to Turnhouse to patrol railway lines during the General Strike as sabotage was expected. Between the wars the Squadron flew the various army co-op types of aircraft produced for the RAF, Atlas, Audax and Hector. Each year consisted of many army exercises, a few displays (No. 4 took part at Hendon in 1930 and 1936) and the annual armament practice camp. In 1936 No. 4 was given an Air Laison Officer, an army officer who maintained contact with the armies in the field with which the Squadron was operating. In 1937 No. 4 left Farnborough for Odiham and there re-equipped with Lysanders in 1939. On 22 September, 1939 the Squadron flew to France to join 50 Wing, BEF. There was little to do except battle with bad winter conditions until May, 1940 when the Germans broke through; on 10 May No. 4 began recces with the British

troops in action. Three days later fighting became intense and it was found that the Lysander was no match for the Luftwaffe. Nevertheless, intensive Tac/R sorties were flown and the Squadron began retreating, losing about two aircraft a day to the enemy. On 24th the situation was so bad that remaining aircraft flew back to Hawkinge and then on to Ringway. In two weeks of action 106 sorties had been flown and 9 aircraft and crews shot down.

The Squadron was now effectively non-operational and began a lengthy period of training with the army once more. It did fly coastal dawn and dusk patrols from June, 1940 to watch out for invasion forces, and in October it established a detachment at Manston for ASR duties. In 1941 it took on an additional role of training glider pilots.

The routine did not change until April, 1942 when Tomahawks and Mustangs arrived, the Squadron eventually re-equipping with the latter. By October, 1942 it was ready for operations once more and began coastal patrols from Gatwick followed by photo recce sorties over the French coast. In November it practised *Rhubarbs* and on 27th attacked marshalling yards in France at low-level. In 1943 these *Rhubarbs* and *Populars* were gradually increased; in April *Lagoons* began – these were shipping recces off the Dutch coast – and *Rangers* as far as North-West Germany. The latter part of 1943 saw many moves for the Squadron and in 1944 a fundamental change: A Flight was re-equipped with Spitfire XIs and XIIIs for high-level PR and B Flight with Mosquito XVIs for high and low-level PR. First operations with these types were flown on 7 March, photo-recces of Continental *Noball* sites (V1 bases). These were high priority but so was the preparations of up-to-date mosaics of northern France, so the Squadron was very busy. The Mosquito was phased out in May, No. 4 consolidating on Spitfires. That month 115 sorties were flown. The Squadron was now concentrating on high-level work in support of the invading armies. In August the Squadron moved to a bridgehead airstrip and for the next two months continued a high intensity of operations. In October it received some Typhoons to develop a low-level PR role alongside the Spitfires, and by December it was flying both (eg 22 low-level and 152 high-level PR sorties in the month).

This was the pattern into 1945 but by the end of February the Typhoons were phased out. By then No. 4 was based in Holland and continued its high-level task until the war ended in Europe. On 31 August, 1945 it disbanded at Celle, becoming the high-level flight of No. 2 Squadron. On the same day a new No. 4 Squadron was re-formed by re-numbering No. 605 Squadron at Volkel. It now took on a bomber role with Mosquito FB. VIs which it maintained until July, 1950 when it became a fighter ground attack squadron with Vampire FB.5s, still in RAF Germany, following these with Sabres and Hunters before disbanding again in January, 1961.

On the same day (1 January, 1961) No. 4 re-formed in the fighter-recce role once more at Gütersloh by re-numbering No. 79 Squadron. It briefly flew their Swift FR.5s whilst re-equipping with Hunter FR.10s. With these it acquired a high reputation, taking part in the AAFC recce competitions and gaining 2nd place in 1961 and first place from 1962 to 1968. In March, 1970 it relinquished this role once more, temporarily re-equipping with Hunter FGA.9s and then with Harrier GR.1s. These it took to Wildenrath and whilst there it maintained a reconnaissance commitment, the only Harrier Squadron to do so, which is retained to this day.

Bases etc.

Formed at Farnborough in August, 1912.

Farnborough	Aug 1912—Jun 1913
Netheravon	Jun 1913—Jul 1914
Eastchurch, det. Dover	Jul 1914—Aug 1914
Dover	Aug 1914—Aug 1914
Mauberge, det. Dover	Aug 1914—Aug 1914
Le Cateau	Aug 1914—Aug 1914
St. Quentin	Aug 1914—Aug 1914
La Fere	Aug 1914—Aug 1914

Compiegne	Aug	1914—Aug	1914
Juilly	Aug	1914—Sep	1914
Serris	Sep	1914—Sep	1914
Pezearches	Sep	1914—Sep	1914
Melun	Sep	1914—Sep	1914
Touquin	Sep	1914—Sep	1914
Coulommiers	Sep	1914—Sep	1914
Fere-en-Tardenois	Sep	1914—Oct	1914
Amiens	Oct	1914—Oct	1914
Abbeville	Oct	1914—Oct	1914
Moyenville	Oct	1914—Nov	1914
Poperinghe, det. St. Omer	Oct	1914—Nov	1914
St. Omer	Nov	1914—Apr	1915
Bailleul	Apr	1915—Jul	1915
Vert Galand	Jul	1915—Aug	1915
Baizieux	Aug	1915—Nov	1915
Allonville	Nov	1915—Feb	1916
Baizieux	Feb	1916—Feb	1916
Marieux	Feb	1916—Mar	1916
Baizieux	Mar	1916—Feb	1917
Warloy/Baillon	Feb	1917—May	1917
Abeele	May	1917—Nov	1917
Chocques	Nov	1917—Apr	1918
Treizennes	Apr	1918—Apr	1918
St. Omer	Apr	1918—Sep	1918
St. Marie-Cappel	Sep	1918—Oct	1918
Linselles	Oct	1918—Nov	1918
Ascq	Nov	1918—Dec	1918
Linselles	Dec	1918—Feb	1919
Northolt	Feb	1919—Sep	1919

Disbanded at Northolt 20 September, 1919. Re-formed at Farnborough on 30 April, 1920 in the army co-operation role with a detached Flight at Stonehenge.

Farnborough, det. Stonehenge	Apr	1920—Nov	1920
Farnborough, det. Stonehenge and Aldergrove	Nov	1920—Jan	1921
Farnborough, det. Stonehenge and Baldonnel	Jan	1921—Jan	1922
HMS Ark Royal	Jan	1922—Sep	1922
Kilia	Sep	1922—Nov	1922
Kilid el Bahr	Nov	1922—Sep	1923
Farnborough, det. Turnhouse	Sep	1923—Feb	1937
Odiham	Feb	1937—Sep	1939
Mons-en-Chaussee	Sep	1939—Oct	1939
Monchy-Lagache	Oct	1939—May	1940
Aspelaere	May	1940—May	1940
Lille/Ronchin	May	1940—May	1940
Hawkinge	May	1940—May	1940
Ringway	May	1940—Jun	1940
Linton-on-Ouse	Jun	1940—Aug	1940
Clifton, det. Manston, Detling	Aug	1940—Mar	1943
Bottisham, det. Detling	Mar	1943—Jul	1943
Gravesend	Jul	1943—Aug	1943
Odiham	Aug	1943—Sep	1943
Funtington	Sep	1943—Oct	1943
Odiham	Oct	1943—Nov	1943
North Weald	Nov	1943—Nov	1943
Sawbridgeworth	Nov	1943—Jan	1944
Aston Down	Jan	1944—Mar	1944
Sawbridgeworth	Mar	1944—Apr	1944
Gatwick	Apr	1944—Jun	1944
Odiham	Jun	1944—Aug	1944
Beny-sur-Mer (B.4)	Aug	1944—Sep	1944
Boisney (B.27)	Sep	1944—Sep	1944
Fresnoy Folny (B.31)	Sep	1944—Sep	1944
Fort Rouge (B.43)	Sep	1944—Sep	1944
St. Denis Westrem (B.61)	Sep	1944—Oct	1944
Antwerp/Deurne (B.70)	Oct	1944—Nov	1944
Gilze-Rijen (B.77)	Nov	1944—Mar	1945
Mill (B.89)	Mar	1945—Apr	1945
Twente (B.106)	Apr	1945—May	1945
Celle (B.118), det. Hustedt (B.150)	May	1945—Aug	1945

Disbanded at Celle on 31 August, 1945. On the same day No. 605 Squadron at Volkel was re-numbered No. 4 Squadron, in the light bomber role. It again re-formed in the fighter-reconnaissance role at Gütersloh on 1 January, 1961.

Gütersloh	Jan	1961—Mar	1970

Disbanded at Gütersloh in March, 1970, being re-formed in the fighter ground attack role at the same time.

Main Equipment

Cody Biplane (Aug 1912—   1912)
301
Bréguet Biplane (Aug 1912—Aug 1914)
No serials known
B.E.2a (Aug 1912—Nov 1914)
206; 234; 299; 314; 336; 368; 465; 612
B.E.2b
493; 705; 746

Farman S.7 Longhorn (1913—Apr 1915)
233; 533
Martinsyde S.1 (Oct 1914—Apr 1915)
2449
Caudron G.3 (Jan 1915—Apr 1915)
1900; 5003
Voisin (Jan 1915—Apr 1915)
1856; 1860; 1864; 1890; 1898; 5025; 5028
Morane Monoplane (1915—Aug 1915)
587
Bristol Scout (Apr 1915—   1915)
Type B
648
Type C
4666; 4678
B.E.2c (Apr 1915—Jun 1917)
1655; 1658; 1668; 1678; 1686; 1698; 1701; 1726; 1781; 2001; 2035; 2061; 2073; 4073
R.E.8 (Jun 1917—Feb 1919)
A3445; A3628; A3720; A3817; A3830; B785; B2252; B3405; B5071; B5893; B6482; C5036
4A Squadron:
A4691; A4724; C2491; C7721
Bristol F.2B Mk.IIIA (Apr 1920—Oct 1929)
E2624, A:4; F4944; H1415, A:2; H1486; H1526, A:2; J6715, A:1; J6760; J7654; J7686; J8271; J8275
Armstrong Whitworth Atlas I (Oct 1929—Feb 1932)
J9537; J9538; J9541; J9544; J9549; J9549; J9983
Hawker Audas I (Feb 1932—   1937)
K1997; K1999; K2002; K2007; K2014; K2022; K3065; K3076; K3093; K3124; K3689; K3708; K3710
Hawker Hector I (Feb 1937—   1938)
K8091; K8095; K8099; K8109; K8121; K9687; K9714
Westland Lysander II (dec 1938—   1940)
L4742, TV:H; L4746, TV:L, later FY:L; L4753, FY:W; L4814; L6852; N1203; N1216; N1226; N1257; N1298; P1699; P1711; P1734; P9061; P9101; P9184; R1990; R2025; R2042
Westland Lysander III (Nov 1940—Jun 1942)
R9013; R9029; R9075; R9118; T1442; T1583; T1686
Westland Lysander IIIA (May 1941—Jun 1942)
V9305; V9339; V9426; V9449; V9485; V9556; V9676
Curtiss Tomahawk II (Apr 1942—Jul 1942 & Jan 1942—May 1943)
AH791; AK101; AK155
North American Mustang I (Apr 1942—Jun 1944)
AG361; AG398; AG426; AG487; AG519; AG599; AG664; AM127; AM153; AM207; AM223; AP158; AP247, A; AP255, P
de Havilland Mosquito PR.XVI (Jan 1944—Jun 1944)
MM273, P; MM299, Q; MM303, N; MM313, T; MM361, W
Vickers-Supermarine Spitfire PR.XI (Jan 1944—Aug 1945)
EN680; MB949; PA852, E; PA884, A; PA897, G; PA931, K; PL759, H; PL764, T; PL786, X; PL787, Y; PL831, S; PL843, J; PL897; PM132
Hawker Typhoon IB (Oct 1944—Feb 1945)
EK180; EK247; EK436; JP272; JP373; JP389
Vickers-Supermarine Swift FR.5 (Jan 1961—Jan 1961)
WK293, N; XD921, G
Hawker Hunter FR.10 (Jan 1961—Mar 1970)
WW595, G; XE580, D; XE585, A; XE625, F; XF459, F; XJ633, H; XJ714, B

Commanding Officers

Maj G. M. Raleigh	Sep	1912—Jan	1915
Maj H. R. P. Reynolds	Jan	1915—Jan	1915
Maj C. A. M. Longcroft	Jan	1915—Jul	1915
Maj F. F. Waldron	Jul	1915—Sep	1915
Maj G. E. Todd	Sep	1915—Feb	1916
Maj V. A. Barrington-Kennett	Feb	1916—Mar	1916
Maj T. W. C. Carthew	Mar	1916—Sep	1916
Maj L. Jenkins	Sep	1916—Dec	1917
Maj R. E. Saul	Dec	1917—Jan	1919
Maj H. B. Prior	Jan	1919—Feb	1919
S/Ldr C. H. B. Blount	Mar	1920—Apr	1925
S/Ldr J. C. Slessor	Apr	1925—Oct	1928
S/Ldr N. H. Bottomley	Oct	1928—Jan	1930
S/Ldr C. E. H. Medhurst	Jan	1930—Jan	1931
S/Ldr L. P. Simpson	Jan	1931—Oct	1933
S/Ldr F. M. F. West	Oct	1933—Jan	1936
S/Ldr E. J. Kingston-McLoughry	Jan	1936—May	1937
S/Ldr G. H. Loughman	May	1937—Jan	1938
S/Ldr J. O. B. MacGregor	Jan	1938—Aug	1939
S/Ldr G. P. Charles	Aug	1939—Sep	1940
S/Ldr P. L. Donkin	Sep	1940—Sep	1940
W/Cdr G. P. Charles	Sep	1940—Oct	1940
S/Ldr Maffett	Oct	1940—Dec	1940
W/Cdr P. H. R. Saunders	Dec	1940—Feb	1941
W/Cdr G. P. Charles	Feb	1941—Jun	1941
W/Cdr P. H. R. Saunders	Jun	1941—Oct	1942
W/Cdr G. E. Macdonald	Oct	1942—Mar	1943

S/Ldr R. H. D. Rigall	Mar 1943—Dec 1943
S/Ldr R. J. Hardiman	Dec 1943—May 1944
S/Ldr W. Shepherd	May 1944—May 1945
S/Ldr C. D. Harris-St. John	May 1945—Aug 1945
S/Ldr R. T. J. Buchanon	Jan 1961—Nov 1961
S/Ldr R. J. Bannard	Nov 1961—Dec 1963
S/Ldr W. J. Milner	Dec 1963—Nov 1964
S/Ldr E. J. E. Smith	Nov 1964—Jun 1967
S/Ldr A. J. Hopkins	Jun 1967—Sep 1969
S/Ldr R. M. Austin	Sep 1969—Mar 1970

Aircraft Insignia

Markings were introduced in 1916 and No. 4's aircraft carried a white band around the fuselage, forward of the roundels; No. 4A Squadron carried three such bands aft but these were only on the lower fuselage panels.

Post-war the Bristol Fighters originally carried a white band around the fuselage aft of the roundels but when the aircraft were re-sprayed silver no identity markings were carried until the arrival of the Audax. This carried the number '4' on the fuselage side. The Hawker Hectors carried the squadron badge in a six-pointed star on the fin and this was perpetuated on the Lysanders until September, 1939. The Lysanders also carried code letters; at first 'TV', later changed to 'FY'. On the outbreak of war this was changed again, reverting to 'TV'. Code letters were dropped in 1943 and as far as is known no identity markings were carried again. With the Hunter FR.10s an official marking was carried each side of the roundels on the fuselage. It comprised a rectangle, half red, half black bisected diagonally by a gold lightning flash and edged in gold. This was repeated on the nose each side of the squadron emblem.
(See also *Fighter Squadrons of the RAF*, pp. 25–26 & 560 and *Bomber squadrons of the RAF*, pp. 9–10.)

No. 5 SQUADRON

BADGE
A maple leaf

MOTTO
'Frangas non Flectas'
('Thou mayest break but shall not bend me')

The maple leaf in the badge reflects the Squadron's close association with the Canadian Corps in 1917–18.

On 26 July, 1913 No. 5 Squadron was formed at South Farnborough and was pressed into the 1913 army manoeuvres soon after its formation with four Maurice Farmans, three Avros and a Caudron, to which were soon added Sopwiths and the S.E.2. Training continued until war broke out when the Squadron moved to France, taking Avros and Henri Farmans, adding B.E.8s en route. It became operational on 21 August, flying reconnaissance over Namur and losing the RFC's first war casualty when one aircraft was shot down. Four days later an inconclusive combat took place with a German aircraft, and in September the Squadron took the first operational aerial photographs. In addition the Squadron played a key role in the development of W/T for corps work. During the next year the RFC in general and No. 5 in particular, worked out all the necessary types of operation for army co-operation work including low bombing attacks on German troops. By 1916 it was entirely B.E.2c-equipped and embarked on night operations; at this time bombing was occupying much of its time, particularly during the battle of the Somme (July–October) when the Squadron largely flew diversionary raids outside the battle area. Then it returned to its original task of artillery observation with the 5th Brigade. By then the B.E.2c was an easy target for enemy fighters and 5 Squadron was re-equipped in May, 1917 with the R.E.8. This aircraft enabled it to carry out a full task in the battles of Arras and Messines after which it reverted to night bombing, returning to army co-operation for the spring retreat in 1918 and the heavy fighting which turned the Germans back. From then on No. 5 flew its R.E.8s on a variety of corps tasks until the war ended. Afterwards it remained in the Army of Occupation in Germany until September, 1919, returning to the UK and disbanding in January, 1920.

Twelve days after disbanding it was re-formed, on 1 February, at Quetta in India by re-numbering No. 48 Squadron. Now equipped with Bristol Fighters No. 5 became a general purpose squadron, although officially on army co-operation duties. Not only did it operate with army units but it flew re-supply sorties to isolated forts and patrolled the North-West Frontier, particularly flying over areas where dissident tribes were operating. This flared up into outright fighting at times and the Squadron's CO, S/Ldr Capel, earned both DSO and DFC for his work in the mid-twenties, which included being captured and directing operations though a prisoner! In 1931 the Wapiti succeeded the weary Brisfits. These were used, in 1935, for rescue work when the earthquake hit Quetta in May, No. 5 losing some personnel in the disaster. In August, however, No. 5 was back in action on the frontier from its new base

at Risalpur, moving to Chaklala in 1936. The Squadron remained on this task, unaffected by rumours of wars for the NW Frontier had been and still was an intermittent war zone. Wapitis remained the equipment until 1940 when No. 5 moved to Lahore and re-equipped with Harts as a light bomber squadron, augmenting them with Audaxes. In February, 1941 its role was again changed to that of a fighter squadron (still with Audaxes) and as such it flew throughout the Burma campaign, at first with Mohawks and then Hurricanes and Thunderbolts. After the war it re-equipped with Tempest F.2s but was disbanded on 1 August, 1947.

No. 5 re-formed as a fighter squadron at Wunstorf in Germany on 1 March, 1952, having had a brief existence in between on AAC duties in the UK, and flew Vampires and Venoms as a fighter-bomber squadron until October, 1957 when it was again disbanded. Two years later, on 21 January, 1959, No. 5 was again re-formed in RAF Germany, this time as a night-fighter squadron with Meteor NF.11s, followed by Gloster Javelins until disbanding at Geilenkirchen in October, 1965. The Squadron was re-formed the same month at Binbrook with Lightnings in defence of the UK, a role it has maintained ever since.

Bases etc.

Formed at Farnborough on 26 July, 1913.

Farnborough	Jul 1913—May 1914	
Netheravon	May 1914—Jul 1914	
Gosport	Jul 1914—Aug 1914	
Amiens	Aug 1914—Aug 1914	
Mauberge	Aug 1914—Aug 1914	
Le Cateau	Aug 1914—Aug 1914	
St. Quentin	Aug 1914—Aug 1914	
La Fere	Aug 1914—Aug 1914	
Compiegne	Aug 1914—Aug 1914	
Senlis	Aug 1914—Aug 1914	
Juilly	Aug 1914—Sep 1914	
Serris	Sep 1914—Sep 1914	
Pezearches	Sep 1914—Sep 1914	
Melun	Sep 1914—Sep 1914	
La Boisserotte	Sep 1914—Sep 1914	
Touquin	Sep 1914—Sep 1914	
Rebais	Sep 1914—Sep 1914	
Coulommiers	Sep 1914—Sep 1914	
Fere-en-Tardenois	Sep 1914—Oct 1914	
Abbeville	Oct 1914—Oct 1914	
Moyenville	Oct 1914—Oct 1914	
St. Omer	Oct 1914—Oct 1914	
Bailleul	Oct 1914—Apr 1915	
Abeele	Apr 1915—Mar 1916	
Droglandt	Mar 1916—Oct 1916	
Marieux	Oct 1916—Mar 1917	
La Gorgue	Mar 1917—Apr 1917	
Savy	Apr 1917—Jun 1917	
Ascq	Jun 1917—May 1918	
Le Hameau	May 1918—Aug 1918	
Bovelles, det. Moeres	Aug 1918—Aug 1918	
Le Hameau, det. Moeres	Aug 1918—Sep 1918	
Le Hameau	Sep 1918—Oct 1918	
Pronville	Oct 1918—Oct 1918	
Enerchicourt	Oct 1918—Nov 1918	
Aulnoy	Nov 1918—Nov 1918	
Pecq	Nov 1918—Nov 1918	

Disbanded at Bicester on 20 January, 1920. Re-formed at Quetta on 1 February, 1920 by re-numbering No. 48 Squadron.

Quetta	Feb 1920—	1921
Hinaidi	1921—	1923
Ambala	1923—	1924
Dardoni	1924—	1925
Kohat	1925—	1925
Tank	1925—Oct 1925	
Risalpur	Oct 1925—	1928
Quetta	1928—Jun 1935	
Karachi	Jun 1935—Sep 1935	
Risalpur	Sep 1935—Oct 1935	
Chaklala, det. Julalpur Oct.—Dec, 1935	Oct 1935—Apr 1936	
Chaklala, det. Miranshah Apr 1936—Apr 1937	Apr 1936—Apr 1937	
Risalpur	Apr 1937—Oct 1939	
Fort Sandeman	Oct 1939—Jun 1940	
Lahore	Jun 1940—Dec 1941	

20 February, 1941 re-designated as a fighter squadron.

Main Equipment

Maurice Farman S.11 Shorthorn (Jul 1913—   1914)
342; 742; 369

Avro 504 (Jul 1913—   1915)
383; 568; 683; 750; 782; 785; 4225

S.E.2a (1914—   1914)
609

Caudron (1913—   1914)
311; 312

Henri Farman (1913—May 1915)
284; 341

B.E.8 (Aug 1914—Aug 1914)
391

Martinsyde S.1 (Aug 1914—   1915)
749; 2823

B.E.2a (Sep 1913—Dec 1913)
202; 220; 228; 232; 267

Vickers F.B.5 (Feb 1915—   1915)
1637; 1651; 2873; 2878

Blériot Parasol (Mar 1915—   1915)
576; 577; 578; 616

Bristol Scout (1915—Feb 1916)
648, (Model B); 1603, (Model C); 4671, (Model C)

B.E.2c (1915—Apr 1917)
1728; 1775; 1784; 2043; 2129; 2509; 2523; 2588; 2603; 2616; 2684; 2755; 4085; 4114; 4413; 4501; 7327

B.E.2d (Jun 1916—   1917)
5742; 5755; 5781; 6254; 6277; 6284

B.E.2f/2g (Apr 1917—May 1917)
2551, (2F); 2557, (2F); 7156, (2G); 7204, (2G); A2786, (2G); A2828, (2G)

F.E.8 (Jan 1916—May 1916)
7457

D.H.2 (Feb 1916—May 1916)
5917

R.E.8 (May 1917—Sep 1919)
A69; A3236; A3422; A3571; A3601; A3736; A4246; A4340; A4455; A4712; B5027; B5062

A.W. F.K.8 (Aug 1917—   1917)
B210; B240; B248

Bristol F.2B (Dec 1918 & Feb 1920—May 1931)
C801, A; C1039, B; D8035, A; F4616, M; F4766, H; H1546, O; J6634, V; J6759, L

Westland Wapiti IIA (May 1931—Jun 1940)
J9401, D; J9482, G; J9509, C; K1294, D; K1303, M; K1309, F

Hawker Hart (India) (Jun 1940—Dec 1941)
K2084, OQ:O; K2129, OQ:P; K4380

Commanding Officers

Maj J. F. A. Higgins	Jul 1913—Nov 1914	
Maj A. C. H. Mclean	Nov 1914—Apr 1915	
Maj A. G. Board	Apr 1915—Dec 1915	
Maj J. G. Hearson	Dec 1915—May 1916	
Maj R. M. Vaughan	May 1916—Jul 1916	
Maj F. J. L. Cogan	Jul 1916—Jan 1917	
Maj G. L. P. Henderson	Jan 1917—Feb 1917	
Maj R. E. Lewis	Feb 1917—May 1917	
Maj E. J. Tyson	May 1917—Mar 1918	
Maj C. H. Gardner	Mar 1918—Nov 1918	
Maj G. Knight	Nov 1918—Mar 1919	
Maj D. F. Stevenson	Mar 1919—Sep 1919	
S/Ldr P. C. Maltby	Feb 1920—Jan 1924	
S/Ldr A. J. Capel, DSO, DFC	Jan 1924—Nov 1928	
S/Ldr O. C. Bryson	Nov 1928—Oct 1931	
S/Ldr W. K. Mercer	Oct 1931—Dec 1932	
S/Ldr A. B. Ellwood	Dec 1932—Nov 1933	
S/Ldr C. N. Ellen, DFC	Nov 1933—Jul 1935	
S/Ldr P. F. Fullard, DSO, MC, DFC	Jul 1935—Feb 1936	
S/Ldr H. R. McL. Reid	Feb 1936—Apr 1937	
S/Ldr L. W. Cannon	Apr 1937—Dec 1937	
S/Ldr H. J. G. E. Proud	Dec 1937—Nov 1938	
S/Ldr W. T. N. Nichols	Nov 1938—Jan 1940	
S/Ldr N. F. Simpson	Jan 1940—Aug 1940	
S/Ldr E. T. T. Nelson	Aug 1940—Nov 1940	
S/Ldr A. J. Young	Nov 1940—Feb 1941	
S/Ldr J. R. Maling	Feb 1941—Dec 1941	

Aircraft Insignia

No distinctive insignia was carried on the aircraft until April, 1916 when squadron markings were issued to Corps squadrons. No. 5 Squadron's markings consisted of a band round the fuselage forward of the roundel and another band forward of the tailplane, painted black on clear-doped aircraft and white on khaki aircraft. These were retained until the end of the war. The post-war Bristol Fighters, which were painted silver, carried a black aircraft letter forward of the roundels and, at one stage, a black '5' on the fin. Wapitis carried the aircraft letter on the nose and a black band around the fuselage aft of the roundels. In April, 1939 the code letters 'QN' were allotted but it is not known whether these were carried. On the Harts the letters 'OQ' were painted on the fuselage side forward of the roundels with the aircraft letters aft.

(See also *Fighter Squadrons of the RAF*, pp. 26—29 & 561)

No. 6 SQUADRON

BADGE
An eagle, wings elevated, preying on a serpent

MOTTO
'Oculi exercitus'
('The eyes of the Army')

The badge is based on a previously used design consisting of a bird sitting within the figure '6'.

No. 6 Squadron, RFC, was formed on 31 January, 1914 at South Farnborough and as well as receiving two aircraft also inherited the Kite Flight from No. 1 Squadron. As it built up to squadron strength it became largely an experimental unit, including a Wireless and Photographic Flight as well as testing new types of aircraft. By June it had worked up sufficiently to join the Concentration Camp at Netheravon but when war came in August it relinquished most of its strength to enable No. 2 Squadron to go to France. A new No. 6 was then formed and this squadron went to France on 7 October, 1914. Its task was originally strategic recce but by November had turned to artillery co-operation, spotting for the guns of the British 5th Div. During the 1st Battle of Ypres it was largely involved in this role but also flew photo recces and trench mapping. In 1915 it had its own Scout Flight for a while, in which Capt L. G. Hawker gained the VC for attacking three enemy aircraft on one flight and shooting one (an Aviatik) down in flames. The Squadron's main task from now on was co-operating with the artillery although it tried its hand at bombing from time to time and also flew the first, unsuccessful, sortie to land an agent behind the enemy lines. By the end of the year it had re-equipped with B.E.2c's and 2e's, and during 1916 flew many bombing sorties with these types. Casualties increased as German scouts became more prolific but it was not until 1917 that a suitable replacement, the R.E.8 arrived. With this No. 6 fought for the rest of the war on corps work, contact patrols and ground strafing, towards the end of hostilities co-operating with the Cavalry Corps and earning the GOC's commendation.

After the war No. 6 was deployed to Basra and a year later was re-equipped with Bristol Fighters for general purpose duties, policing Iraq. For eleven years it flew the Brisfits, at first against the Turks and then against dissident tribesmen in Kurdistan. In October, 1929 it moved to Ismailia, with a detachment in Palestine and two years later was re-designated a bomber squadron. Flying Gordons and then Harts the Squadron was continuously engaged in the Arab–Jewish conflicts in Palestine.

In February, 1940 the Squadron was re-designated an army co-operation squadron once more, equipped with Hawker Hardys and some Gloster Gauntlet fighters. The Hardys were soon replaced by Westland Lysanders and the Squadron sent detachments into the Western Desert in September, 1940, flying recces to keep track of the advancing Italian forces. These detachments were involved operationally until the end of the year. For a while the Squadron was off operations but when A Flight received Hurricanes these were used for tactical recces at the front. With the German advance from April, 1941 the whole squadron was involved in recce duties, moving into the Tobruk perimeter and fighting desperately there in April and May.

Here, in addition to being harassed by German fighters whilst on recce and gun spotting flying, the Squadron was shelled and bombed at its base. It left Tobruk on 10 May when it was withdrawn, having suffered many casualties. After a rest it returned to the fray with Lysanders and Gladiators largely replacing the Hurricanes temporarily. Based at Kufra Oasis it was not very active for the rest of 1941 and in early 1942 the Squadron was transferred to the fighter role with the advent of the 40 mm-cannon Hurricane IID. This was specifically designed for tank-busting and No. 6 used it effectively in this role. The Squadron retained Hurricanes on fighter duties throughout the N. African campaign and on into Sicily and Italy. In 1945 it was flying from Yugoslav airfields in support of the partisans and kept its Hurricanes until January, 1947 (in Cyprus). Until 1957 it remained a Middle East fighter squadron, converting to Canberra bombers in 1957 as part of the Near East Bombing Wing with which it flew for twelve years. It then re-formed as a fighter ground attack squadron in the UK with Phantoms and later Jaguars.

Bases etc.

Formed at S. Farnborough on 31 January, 1914.

Farnborough	Jan 1914	May 1914
Netheravon	May 1914	Jul 1914
Farnborough	Jul 1914	Sep 1914
Netheravon	Sep 1914	Oct 1914
Farnborough	Oct 1914	Oct 1914
Ostende	Oct 1914	Oct 1914
St. Pol	Oct 1914	Oct 1914
St. Omer	Oct 1914	Nov 1914
Bailleul	Nov 1914	Mar 1915
Poperinghe	Mar 1915	Apr 1915
Abeele	Apr 1915	Oct 1916
Droglandt	Oct 1916	Nov 1916
Abeele	Nov 1916	Nov 1917
Bertangles	Nov 1917	Mar 1918
St. Andre aux Bois	Mar 1918	Mar 1918
Le Crotoy (det. Treizennes, Rely, Auxi-le-Chateau)	Mar 1918	Jul 1918
Fienvillers	Jul 1918	Aug 1918
Bovelles	Aug 1918	Aug 1918
Auxi-le-Chateau	Aug 1918	Aug 1918
Ascq	Aug 1918	Sep 1918
Moislains	Sep 1918	Oct 1918
Longavesnes	Oct 1918	Oct 1918
Bertry West	Oct 1918	Oct 1918
Marchy	Oct 1918	Nov 1918
Gondecourt	Nov 1918	Nov 1918
Pecq	Nov 1918	Dec 1918
Gerpinnes	Dec 1918	Mar 1919
Sart	Mar 1919	Apr 1919
en route to Iraq	Apr 1919	Jul 1919
Basra	Jul 1919	Oct 1919
Mosul (det. Hinaidi (1923), Shaibah (1924–25))	Oct 1919	Oct 1929
Ismailia (det. Ramleh)	Oct 1929	Apr 1931

1 April, 1931 the Squadron was re-designated No. 6 (Bomber) Squadron at Ismailia.

1 February, 1940 the Squadron was re-designated No. 6 (army co-operation) Squadron at Ramleh.

Ramleh (det. Gaza & Qasaba 1940)	Feb 1940	Feb 1941
Aqir (det. Agedabia & Barce)	Feb 1941	Feb 1941
Heliopolis (det. M'sus)	Feb 1941	Mar 1941
Barce	Mar 1941	Apr 1941
Maraua	Apr 1941	Apr 1941
Derna, El Adem	Apr 1941	Apr 1941
El Gubbi (Tobruk) (det. Maaten Bagush)	Apr 1941	May 1941
Maaten Bagush (det. Qasaba)	May 1941	Jul 1941
Tel Aviv	Jul 1941	Aug 1941
Wadi Hafra (det. Kufra)	Aug 1941	Jan 1942
Helwan	Jan 1942	Jan 1942
LG.224	Jan 1942	Apr 1942

In April, 1942 the Squadron transferred to the fighter role.

Main Equipment (in the Army co-operation role)

Bleriot XI (Jan 1914—Oct 1914)
No known serials
B.E.2a (Jan 1914—Apr 1915)
206; 241; 368; 488
Farman S.7 Longhorn (Jan 1914—Apr 1915)
270; 322
Farman S.11 Shorthorn (Jan 1914—Apr 1915)
1869; 653
R.E.1 (Jan 1914—   1914)
607; 608
R.E.5 (Jan 1914—   1914)
380
B.E.8 (Jan 1914—Apr 1915)
373; 632; 636
Martinsyde S.1 (1914—   1915)
1601
B.E.2c (Mar 1915—   1916)
1680; 1718; 1781; 2031; 2113; 2674
Farman F.40 (1915—   1916)
9156; 9157; 9165; 9173
B.E.2e (Sep 1915—Dec 1917)
6241
R.E.8 (Apr 1917—Jul 1920)
A3198; A3214; A3849; A4210; A4316; B5013; H7038
Bristol Fighter F.2B Mk. IIIA (Jul 1920—Jun 1931)
C766; C4683; D7874; DR8056; E2529; F4691; F4727; FR4925; H1464; H1677; JR6635; J6742; J7676; J8281
Gloster Gauntlet I & II (Feb 1940—Jun 1940)
K4091; K4104; K5290; K5315; K7792; K7881
Westland Lysander I & II (Feb 1940—Feb 1942)
L4675, (I); L4709, (I); L4793; L6874; L6887; JV:E; N1307; N1319; P1676, (I); P1740; P9054; P9073; P9189; R2037
Hawker Hurricane I (Feb 1941—Feb 1942)
P2646; P3067; P3967; V6737; V7806; Z4263; AS989
Gloster Gladiator II (Jul 1941—Feb 1942)
N5822; N5828; N5851

Commanding Officers

Maj J. H. W. Becke	Jan 1914	Mar 1915
Maj G. S. Shephard	Mar 1915	Dec 1915
Maj R. P. Mills	Dec 1915	Sep 1916
Maj A. S. Barratt, MC	Sep 1916	Jun 1917
Maj A. W. H. James, MC	Jun 1917	Jul 1918
Maj G. C. Pirie, MC	Jul 1918	Feb 1920
S/Ldr W. Sowrey	Feb 1920	May 1920
S/Ldr E. A. B. Rice	May 1920	Apr 1922
S/Ldr E. R. Manning, DSO, MC	Apr 1922	Jan 1924
S/Ldr D. S. K. Crosbie, OBE	Jan 1924	Nov 1925
S/Ldr D. F. Stephenson, DSO, MC	Nov 1925	Nov 1926
S/Ldr C. N. Lowe, MC, DFC	Nov 1926	Jan 1928
S/Ldr C. H. Keith	Jan 1928	Feb 1930
S/Ldr C. R. Cox, AFC	Feb 1930	Feb 1931
S/Ldr W. N. McKechnie, EGM	Feb 1940	Sep 1940
S/Ldr E. R. Weld	Sep 1940	Apr 1941
S/Ldr P. Legge	Apr 1941	Feb 1942

Aircraft Insignia

In World War I no squadron insignia was carried until April, 1916 when No. 6 Squadron was allotted the official marking of three bands around the fuselage, one each side of the roundel and one just forward of the tailplane. This was painted black on clear-doped aircraft and white on khaki drab aircraft. The Bristol Fighters originally carried a star on the fin with a white '6' therein. This was later modified to an unofficial badge on the fin comprising an eagle preying on a serpent in the shape of a '6', and eventually this badge was carried on a shield background. During World War II the Lysanders and Hurricanes carried the identity letters 'JV', although for much of the time no letters at all were carried.

(See also *Bomber Squadrons of the RAF*, pp. 10–12 and *Fighter Squadrons of the RAF*, pp. 30–33, 561–562)

No. 7 SQUADRON

BADGE
On a hurt seven mullets of six points forming a
representation of the constellation Ursa Major

MOTTO
'Per diem per noctem'
('By day, by night')

The constellation Ursa Major has formed part
of a device used by the Squadron since 1926,
the introduction of seven stars in such a
constellation being appropriate to this
Squadron.

The original No. 7 Squadron RFC lasted only three months and was disbanded a few days after World War I had begun. It had been formed at Farnborough on 1 May, 1914 to work up with Sopwith Scouts and a B.E.8 but with the outbreak of war its members were posted to build up the operational squadrons in France and it was not until 28 September, 1914 that No. 7 was re-formed and got into its stride. Again at Farnborough it served at first in a training role but at the same time gradually equipped with the R.E.5 and took this type, together with Vickers F.B.5s, to France on 8 April, 1915. It began operations on 16 April, flying reconnaissance sorties towards the end of the Second Battle of Ypres. The R.E.5s flew the recce and bombing sorties with the Vickers providing fighter cover. On 31 July Capt J. A. Liddell brought his R.E.5 home although his right thigh was broken and saved the life of his observer. For this he received the VC. B.E.2c's replaced the other types during the summer of 1915 and in the autumn No. 7 flew mainly bombing sorties, but in the New Year it was back to artillery observation duties and photo recce. Now the casualties began to mount and this continued until the arrival of the R.E.8 in June, 1917, enabling the Squadron to hit back at its attackers. Night bombing raids were undertaken as were many different tasks during the final offensive in 1918 which the Squadron flew in support of the Belgians in the north of the Front, using R/T for the first time during October, 1918. After the war No. 7 had a year serving in the Army of Occupation before returning to the UK and disbandment back at Farnborough on 31 December, 1919.

No. 7 was re-formed at Bircham Newton on 1 June, 1923 as a heavy bomber squadron and has served most of its existence in this role. Between the wars it flew biplane Vimys, Virginias and Heyfords, and after a short spell on Whitleys became the first squadron to fly and then operate the new generation of four-engined bombers, receiving its Short Stirlings in August, 1940. It pioneered this type in service eventually re-equipping with Lancasters in 1943 to continue the night offensive against Germany. After World War II it remained in Bomber Command until October, 1962 when it disbanded as a Vickers Valiant unit.

On 1 May, 1970 No. 7 re-formed at St. Mawgan with various marks of English Electric Canberra in the target facilities role, in which it now serves.

Bases etc.

Formed at Farnborough on 1 May, 1914.

Farnborough	May 1914	Aug 1914

Disbanded at Farnborough on 8 August, 1914 to send personnel to France.
Re-formed at Farnborough on 28 September, 1914.

Farnborough	Sep 1914	Oct 1914
Netheravon	Oct 1914	Apr 1915

St. Omer (det. Boulogne Apr 1915—May 1915)	Apr 1915	Sep 1915
Droglandt	Sep 1915	Dec 1915
Bailleul	Dec 1915	Jul 1916
Warloy	Jul 1916	Feb 1917
Moreuil	Feb 1917	Apr 1917
Maligny	Apr 1917	May 1917
Proven East	May 1917	Apr 1918
Droglandt	Apr 1918	Sep 1918
Proven East	Sep 1918	Oct 1918
Bisseghem	Oct 1918	Nov 1918
Staceghem	Nov 1918	Nov 1918
Menin	Nov 1918	Nov 1918
Staceghem	Nov 1918	Nov 1918
Peronnes	Nov 1918	Nov 1918
Cognelee	Nov 1918	Dec 1918
Elsenborn	Dec 1918	Dec 1918
Bickendorff	Dec 1918	Dec 1918
Spich	Dec 1918	Jul 1919
Buckheim	Jul 1919	Sep 1919
Eastleigh	Sep 1919	Nov 1919
Farnborough	Nov 1919	Dec 1919

Disbanded at Farnborough on 31 December, 1919. Re-formed as a bomber squadron at Bircham Newton on 1 June, 1923. Served in this role until 4 April, 1940 when it was disbanded into No. 16 OTU at Upper Heyford. Re-formed again in the bombing role at Leeming on 7 August, 1940 and served until further disbandment at Upwood on 2 January, 1956. Re-formed again as a bomber squadron at Honington on 8 October, 1956 and served until disbandment on 30 September, 1962. Re-formed in the target role at St. Mawgan on 1 May, 1970.

Main Equipment (in the army co-operation role)

Sopwith Tabloid & B.E.8 (May 1914—Aug 1914)
No serials known
R.E.5 (Oct 1914—Sep 1915)
631; 674; 678; 2457; 2458
Vickers F.B.5 Gun Bus (Oct 1914—Apr 1915)
No serials known
Morane, Blériot XI, B.E.2, Voisin (Oct 1914—Apr 1915)
No serials known
Bristol Scout D (Jun 1915—Jun 1916)
4669; 4676
B.E.2c (Jul 1915—Apr 1917)
2750
B.E.2e (Oct 1916—Jul 1917)
5782; 5869; A2800; A2801
R.E.8 (Jul 1917—Dec 1919)
A3615; A4381; E1207 L

Commanding Officers

Maj J. M. Salmond	May 1914	Aug 1914
Capt A. G. Board	Sep 1914	Apr 1915
Maj C. G. Hoare	Apr 1915	Nov 1915
Maj F. L. J. Cogan	Nov 1915	Jul 1916
Maj R. M. Vaughan	Jul 1916	Sep 1916
Maj A. T. Whitlock	Sep 1916	Oct 1917
Maj B. E. Sutton	Oct 1917	Jan 1919
Maj R. E. Saul	Jan 1919	Dec 1919

Aircraft Insignia

No insignia was carried until April, 1916 when No. 7's aircraft were given official recognition markings of two bands, one around the rear fuselage and one down the forward end of the fin. This was to be black on clear-doped aircraft and white on khaki drab aircraft and was carried on the B.E.2c and B.E.2e aircraft. With the re-equipment with R.E.8s the marking was modified to two white bands around the rear fuselage just forward of the tailplane. It is believed that the marking was discontinued at some time in 1918.

(See also *Bomber Squadrons of the RAF*, pp. 12–15 & 386) and Appendix in this volume.

No. 8 SQUADRON

BADGE
An Arabian dagger sheathed
MOTTO
'*Uspiam et Passim*'
('Everywhere unbounded')

The dagger commemorates the Squadron's long sojourn in South-west Arabia. Its being sheathed denotes the Squadron's long policing role.

No. 8 Squadron was formed on the first day of 1915 and became the first RFC squadron to equip with one single type of aircraft, the B.E.2c. It moved to Gosport to work up and went to France on 15 April, 1915. Here its task was a hazardous one for it was given the role of strategic reconnaissance, and later on in the year this developed into long-distance flights up to 100 miles behind the enemy lines, no mean feat in a B.E.2c. After moving to La Bellevue in February, 1916 the recces were abandoned and the Squadron became an army co-operation unit, flying contact patrols and 'shoots' for the artillery during the battles of the Somme and Arras. A photo section was formed to facilitate its work with the army and in addition bombing raids were made when necessary on communications immediately behind the German lines. The B.E.2c, and its successor the B.E.2e, were soon outclassed and the Squadron suffered many casualties in 1916 and early 1917. It had originally had a fighter flight but later relied on the scout squadrons for protection.

At last in the summer of 1917 the R.E.8 replaced the B.E.s and the Squadron had a new aircraft more suited to its corps duties which were continued and intensified; in 1917 over 100,000 prints were made of enemy positions. In addition it flew night and dawn recces with the aid of flares, and indulged in ground attack sorties at times. In June, 1918, by which time it was flying Armstrong-Whitworth F.K.8s as well, it was allocated to the Tank Corps and, after a short while of experimentation, began contact patrols with the army's tanks. This developed into patrols against counter-tank attacks and specialising in knocking out the German anti-tank guns, all of which involved very low-level flying in the thick of the battle. Whilst engaged in tank contact patrol Lt F. M. F. West of No. 8 Squadron was awarded the VC for his bravery. This work was continued right up until the Armistice after which the Squadron was re-equipped with Sunbeam Arab-engined Bristol Fighters. Eight months later it returned to the UK and was disbanded.

No. 8 re-formed on 18 October, 1920 at Helwan in Egypt as a bomber squadron and was used for policing duties in Iraq from 1921 to 1927 and in Aden from 1927 until May, 1942, being instrumental in the peaceful policing of the Aden Protectorate until this time. From 1940 to 1942 it flew coastal recce flights and was also in action against the Italians in Somaliland.

In May, 1942 its role changed to that of maritime reconnaissance in view of the increased U-boat activity in the Indian Ocean and on the convoy routes. It was equipped with Blenheim IV bombers originally for this task and maintained regular Red Sea patrols, escorted convoys in the north-east Indian Ocean and maintained such anti-submarine search as was possible. In October, 1942 Blenheim Vs supplemented the Mk. IVs but the first real GR type to join the Squadron was the Hudson in February, 1943. Now No. 8 had search radar and could make a viable anti-submarine force. July, 1943 brought the first sub action with sightings on the 8th, 10th and 14th. All three were depth-charged and the last occasion resulted in the submarine sinking and oil appearing, establishing the Squadron's first kill. For the rest of the year no more submarines were sighted and in January, 1944 the Hudsons were replaced by Wellingtons and these took up the endless patrols over No. 8's area. In May, 1944 the Squadron found and attacked *U.852* but it was finished off by No. 621 Squadron, also flying Wellingtons. The patrolling continued but there was no further action until the Squadron disbanded on 1 May, 1945. Ten days later No. 8 was re-formed at Jessore, India by re-numbering No. 200 Squadron. It

was now equipped with Liberators. The new No. 8 soon moved to Ceylon and was engaged on special duties, flying supply drops to guerillas in Malay and later Sumatra. Between fifty and sixty drops were made each month from June through to September but with the collapse of hostilities in the Far East operations ceased on 17 October and the Squadron was again disbanded on 15 November, 1945.

It was re-formed at Aden on 1 September, 1946 by re-numbering No. 114 Squadron, and was now at its traditional base in its traditional bomber role. It remained there for 21 years, in the fighter role from 1952. In 1967 it moved to the Arabian Gulf and disbanded there in 1971.

On 8 January, 1972 No. 8 re-formed once more in a maritime role. The base was Kinloss and the equipment was the Avro Shackleton AEW.2. It was originally allocated the task of replacing much of the maritime early-warning coverage that had been given by the Gannets of the FAA before the Royal Navy was reduced to one aircraft carrier, but No. 8 principally used its radar-equipped aircraft to provide an early-warning picket line for the defence of the UK and the sea lanes around Britain. As such it co-operates with 11 Fighter Group, acting as an airborne control post for its Lightning and Phantom fighters. The Shackleton will be replaced by the Nimrod AEW.3 when this comes into service in the near future.

Bases etc.

Formed at Brooklands on 1 January, 1915.

Brooklands	Jan	1915—Jan	1915
Gosport	Jan	1915—Mar	1915
Farnborough	Mar	1915—Apr	1915
Hill 62	Apr	1915—May	1915
Oxelaere	May	1915—Jul	1915
Ferme du Rosel	Jul	1915—Aug	1915
Marieux	Aug	1915—Feb	1916
La Bellevue	Feb	1916—Feb	1917
Soncamp	Feb	1917—May	1917
Boiry St. Martin	May	1917—Oct	1917
Longavesnes	Oct	1917—Oct	1917
Mons-en-Chaussée	Oct	1917—Mar	1918
Templeux la Fosse	Mar	1918—Mar	1918
Chipilly	Mar	1918—Mar	1918
Poulainville	Mar	1918—Mar	1918
Vert Galand	Mar	1918—Apr	1918
Auxi-le-Château (det. Bruay & Poulainville)	Apr	1918—Jul	1918
Avesnes	Jul	1918—Jul	1918
Vignacourt	Jul	1918—Aug	1918
La Bellevue	Aug	1918—Sep	1918
Foucaucourt	Sep	1918—Sep	1918
Estrees-en-Chaussée	Sep	1918—Oct	1918
Hervilly	Oct	1918—Oct	1918
Malincourt	Oct	1918—Nov	1918
La Bellevue	Nov	1918—May	1919
Sart	May	1919—Jul	1919
Duxford	Jul	1919—Jan	1920

Disbanded at Duxford on 20 January, 1920. Re-formed at Helwan on 18 October, 1920 in the bomber role. Role changed to that of general reconnaissance at Khormaksar in May, 1942.

Khormaksar	May	1942—May 1945

Disbanded at Khormaksar on 15 May, 1945. Re-formed at Jessore on 15 May, 1945 by re-numbering No. 200 Squadron.

Jessore	May	1945—May 1945
Minneriya	May	1945—Nov 1945

Disbanded at Minneriya on 15 November, 1945. Re-formed in the bomber role at Khormaksar on 1 September, 1946 by re-numbering No. 114 Squadron. Disbanded at Muharraq in 1971. Re-formed in the early-warning role at Kinloss on 8 January, 1972.

Kinloss	Jan	1972—Aug 1973
Lossiemouth	Aug	1973—

Main Equipment

B.E.2c (Jan 1915—Apr 1917)
    1665; 1711; 2008; 2124; 2530; 4197
Fighter Flight (May 1915—early 1916)
B.E.8
    740; 2130
B.E.9
    1700
Bristol Scout C
    1608; 1613; 4666

B.E.2e (Apr 1917—ca Aug 1917)
5748; 5784; 5811; 6252; 7248
Armstrong Whitworth F.K.8 (Aug 1917—Nov 1918)
B4170; B4194; C3684; C8507; D5196; F3487
Bristol F.2B. Fighter (May 1919—Jan 1920)
No known serials
Bristol Blenheim IV (May 1942—Dec 1942)
L9316; V6246; V6325; V6502; Z6379; Z7794; Z7845; Z9648; Z9750
Bristol Blenheim VA (Oct 1942—Jan 1944)
AZ862; AZ884; AZ896; BA108; BA255; BA386; BA447; BA594; BA620; BA685; BA718; BA884; BA927
Lockheed Hudson IIIA, VI (Feb 1943—Dec 1943)
FH285; FK625; FK628; FK664
Vickers Wellington XIII (Dec 1943—May 1945)
HZ703, B; HZ705, F; HZ956; JA109; JA271, A:E; JA356, A:N; JA413, G; MP767, X
Consolidated Liberator GR.VI (May 1945—Nov 1945)
KG854, L; KG912, F; KG990, Y; KH127, B; KH142, T; KH144, U; KH331, W
Avro Shackleton AEW.2 (Apr 1972—   )
WL741; WL756; WL790; WL795; WR960; WR965

Commanding Officers

Maj L. E. O. Charlton	Jan 1915—Aug 1915	
Maj A. C. H. McLean	Aug 1915—Jan 1916	
Maj P. H. L. Playfair	Jan 1916—Aug 1916	
Maj E. L. Gossage	Aug 1916—Nov 1917	
Maj T. L. Leigh-Mallory	Nov 1917—Nov 1918	
W/Cdr R. H. Humphries	May 1942—Aug 1942	
W/Cdr D. W. Reid, DFC	Aug 1942—Jul 1944	
W/Cdr M. G. L. Foster, DFC	Jul 1944—May 1945	
W/Cdr J. M. Milburn	May 1945—Nov 1945	
W/Cdr G. Moores	Jan 1972—Jan 1973	
	—Mar 1978	
W/Cdr P. J. F. Burton	Mar 1978—	

Aircraft Insignia

No. 8 Squadron's identity marking in the 1914–18 war consisted of a horizontal bar painted along the top longeron from the front of the rear cockpit to the rudder post, black on clear-doped aircraft, white on khaki aircraft. It first came into use in April, 1916. As far as is known no specific markings were carried on the Blenheims and Hudsons in Aden but the Wellingtons, later in their careers, carried a letter 'A' to denote the Squadron, in addition to the individual aircraft letters. On the Shackleton AEW.2s the Squadron badge is carried on the nose of the aircraft and each side of the fuselage roundel is carried the marking originated on the Vampires consisting of three horizontal bars, sand, blue and red from top to bottom.
(See also *Bomber Squadrons of the RAF*, pp. 16–17, and *Fighter Squadrons of the RAF*, pp. 34–5.)

No. 9 SQUADRON

BADGE
A bat

MOTTO
'Per noctem volamus'
('Throughout the night we fly')

The badge, which is based on a device previously used by the Squadron, denotes the night role of the Squadron.

The origins of No. 9 Squadron are to be found in the Wireless Flight attached to RFC HQ in France in September, 1914. Its task was to develop wireless for use in communicating between aircraft and ground forces for Corps duties. On 8 December, 1914 this Flight was designated No. 9 Squadron with its HQ at St. Omer. It provided two, later three, Flights which were attached to other RFC squadrons to provide wireless aircraft, A Flight having B.E.2a's, B Flight Maurice Farmans and C Flight Blériots. However, in February, 1915 these Flights were incorporated into the various squadrons with which they flew, and the HQ at St. Omer became part of the Aircraft Park; the remnants of No. 9 Squadron were a Capt H. C. T. Dowding and six men.

Dowding was promoted to Major and formed a new No. 9 Squadron at Brooklands on 1 April, 1915; it was effectively the first wireless school in the RFC. In July it moved to Dover for coastal defence, having a go at the odd Zeppelin, and in December 1915 moved to France once more. Here it served the 3rd British Army on long-range reconnaissance duties until the spring when, flying from Allonville, it was involved in recce flying for the Somme battles to come. When the fighting began No. 9 was heavily involved on counter-battery patrols, contact patrols, trench flights, photography and kite balloon attacks; on the first day 69 hours were flown. In working with the guns during this battle No. 9 lost more aircraft by being hit by artillery shells than by enemy aircraft. Until the end of the offensive in September the Squadron was heavily involved then weather reduced flying during the winter. In 1917 the Squadron again became busy with the advance on the Hindenburg Line and then, whilst the Arras battle was on, flew diversionary bombing raids to the south.

In June, 1917, now re-equipped with R.E.8s, the Squadron moved north for Ypres where it was largely involved in artillery co-operation. Now it was standard practice to carry 20 lb bombs on all flights, to be used on targets of opportunity. In the German advance of March, 1918 No. 9 flew many offensive patrols before being pulled out for a rest. Returning to action in June it now had a roving commission and flew many bombing raids on targets behind the lines; it also developed a method of supplying troops with ammunition from the air and flew many such sorties during the summer. It also flew recces for crashed aircraft. In September, 1918 it joined IX Corps for the final offensive then moved into the Army of Occupation after the Armistice. In July, 1919 it returned to the UK and was disbanded on the last day of that year.

When No. 9 Squadron re-formed at Upavon on 1 April, 1924 it was as a heavy bomber squadron with Vickers Vimy aircraft. It has served as such ever since, flying Virginias and Heyfords in the 'twenties and 'thirties, becoming the first squadron with Wellingtons in 1939. Throughout World War II it flew with 3 Group, Bomber Command with Wellingtons and then 5 Group with Lancasters, being one of the squadrons to fly the shuttle raids to and from the Soviet Union against the *Tirpitz*. It has remained a bomber squadron since, flying Lincolns, Canberras and Vulcans. With the latter it was part of the Near East Bomber Wing at Akrotiri in Cyprus from 1969 to 1975.

Bases etc.

Formed on 8 December, 1914 at St. Omer from Headquarters, Wireless Flight.

St. Omer	Dec 1914—Feb 1915	

February, 1915 absorbed into other units. Re-formed at Brooklands on 1 April, 1915.

Brooklands	Apr 1915—Jul 1915	
Dover	Jul 1915—Dec 1915	
St. Omer	Dec 1915—Dec 1915	
Bertangles	Dec 1915—Mar 1916	
Allonville	Mar 1916—Jul 1916	
Chipilly	Jul 1916—Sep 1916	
Mourlancourt (det. Mons-en-Chaussée Apr 1917)	Sep 1916—Apr 1917	
Nurlu	Apr 1917—May 1917	
Estrées-en-Chaussée	May 1917—Jun 1917	
Proven	Jun 1917—Apr 1918	
Calais	Apr 1918—Jun 1918	
Argenvilliers	Jun 1918—Jul 1918	
Quevauvilliers	Jul 1918—Aug 1918	
Amiens	Aug 1918—Sep 1918	
Proyart	Sep 1918—Sep 1918	
Athies	Sep 1918—Oct 1918	
Montigny Farm	Oct 1918—Oct 1918	
Premont Farm	Oct 1918—Oct 1918	
Tarcienne	Oct 1918—Dec 1918	
Cognellée	Dec 1918—Jan 1919	
Ludendorf	Jan 1919—Jul 1919	
Castle Bromwich	Jul 1919—Dec 1919	

Disbanded at Castle Bromwich on 31 December, 1919. Re-formed at Upavon on 1 April, 1924 in the bomber role.

Main Equipment

B.E.2a (Sep 1914—Mar 1915)
231; 238; 317; 336; 368; 470
(B.E.2b)
484
Blériot XI (Dec 1914—Mar 1915)
576; 578; 616; 1825; 1838
Farman Shorthorn (Nov 1914—Mar 1915)
1839; 1841; 1846; 1851; 1869
Bristol Scout C (Dec 1915—Jun 1916)
4679; 5291; 5297; 5306
B.E.2c (Nov 1915—Oct 1916)
2018; 2084; 2102; 2500; 2518; 2615; 2689; 2733; 2764; 4088; 4132; 4178; 4206; 4513; 5391; 5441; 7321
B.E.2d (Jun 1916—Sep 1916)
5751; 5817; 5842; 5851; 6235; 6250; 6744
B.E.2e (Aug 1916—Jun 1917)
5733; 5860; 6265; 6279; 6750; 7076; 7084; 7103; 7163; 7198; 7255; A1852; A2784; A2833; A2887; A2916; A3055; A3164
R.E.8 (May 1917—May 1919)
A103; A3475; A3721; A4262; A4366; 21; A4634; B765; B2263; B4105; B5039; B5100; B6451; B8885; C2379; C2735; D4844; D4938; E16; E134; E1161; F1667; F6010; H7048; H7139
Bristol F.2b (Jul 1918—Oct 1918 & Feb 1919—Jul 1919)
B1347; C917; C9950; D7947; E2271; E9602; F5139

Commanding Officers

Maj H. Musgrave	Dec 1914	Feb 1915
Maj H. C. T. Dowding	Apr 1915	Sep 1915
Maj J. A. Wanklyn	Sep 1915	Mar 1916
Maj A. B. Burdett	Mar 1916	Dec 1916
Maj J. A. E. Edwards	Dec 1916	May 1917
Maj H. C. F. Hunter	May 1917	Nov 1917
Maj J. T. Rodwell	Nov 1917	Dec 1919

Aircraft Insignia

When squadron identity markings were introduced in April, 1916 No. 9 Squadron's aircraft carried a band around the fuselage just aft of the roundels, black on clear-doped aircraft and white on khaki aircraft. This was worn by the B.E.2s and R.E.8s but it is not known whether the other aircraft (Bristols) also carried it.
(See also *Bomber Squadrons of the RAF*, pp. 17–20 & 38y)

No. 10 SQUADRON

BADGE
A winged arrow
MOTTO
'Rem acu tangere'
('To hit the mark')

On the first day of 1915 No. 10 Squadron was formed from a nucleus of No. 1 Reserve Squadron at Farnborough. Six months later it went to France with B.E.2c's on reconnaissance work and was soon to extend this work into artillery 'shoots'. The Squadron was prominent in the Battle of Loos that autumn, flying for the Indian Corps. It became a corps squadron in 1916 co-operating closely with the army, mainly in artillery work but also dropping message bags, the occasional bombing raid (carrying 2 × 112 lb bombs) and recces. On some of these it took photographs for the army as well. As the war progressed the bombing task became more fully defined and a special flight of the Squadron was allocated to strategic bombing. In July, 1917 the B.E.2s were replaced by Armstrong-Whitworth F.K.8s, more ideal for the corps duties, which included trench recces, contact patrols, counter battery patrols, artillery 'shoots', photo and flash recces and plain ground strafing. This latter became the main task in early 1918, but when the German offensive had been halted and the Allies at last launched the final offensives the Squadron was engaged in the full range of duties. After the war No. 10 returned to the UK in February, 1919 and was disbanded at Ford on 31 December, 1919.

No. 10 re-formed on 3 January, 1928 at Upper Heyford as a heavy bomber squadron and served in that role throughout World War II, flying Whitleys and Halifaxes with 4 Group, Bomber Command. With the war over it was transferred to Transport Command. The Squadron soon re-equipped with Dakotas and made its way to India, arriving just after the VJ-Day. However, it remained there, flying army support transport duties and various transport routes (and acquiring some Halifaxes for heavy duties) until again disbanding at Chaklala on 20 December, 1947.

Just under a year later No. 10 was again re-formed, on 5 November, 1948 at Oakington, to swell the numbers on the Berlin Airlift, flying into the city out of Lübeck on this task of mercy. Thus it was again disbanded after Operation Plainfare had finished on 20 February 1950, having flown the last airlift sortie on 23 September, 1949.

When No. 10 re-formed again it was as a bomber squadron and in fact flew two existences in the bomber role, the first from January, 1953 to January, 1957 with Canberras and the second from April, 1958 to March, 1964 with Victors.

Its current phase began on 1 July, 1966 when No. 10 re-formed at Brize Norton as the only RAF squadron to fly the Vickers (BAC) VC10 in the long-range strategic transport role. As well as flying specific regular tasks, linking RAF units in different parts of the world, the Squadron maintains a high state of mobility for meeting emergencies and such tasks as evacuating families and refugees out of Cyprus at the same time taking UN troops in at the time of the Turkish invasion: this was a typical example. It also undertakes the VIP role for long-distance, having carried the Queen and other members of the royal family and ministers of state, being the first RAF squadron to enter Communist China. July, 1975 brought No. 10's biggest evacuation yet with the Angolan troubles, flying over 5,500 refugees out to Lisbon. Its regular routes were increased in 1976 with the withdrawal of the Britannia from the RAF, No. 10 remaining the only Squadron in the long-range strategic transport role.

Bases etc.

Formed on 1 January, 1915 at Farnborough.

Farnborough	Jan 1915	Jan	1915
Brooklands	Jan 1915	Apr	1915
Hounslow	Apr 1915	Apr	1915
Netheravon	Apr 1915	Jul	1915
St. Omer	Jul 1915	Jul	1915
Aire	Jul 1915	Aug	1915
Chocques	Aug 1915	Nov	1917
Abeele West	Nov 1917	Apr	1918
Droglandt	Apr 1918	Sep	1918
Abeele West	Sep 1918	Oct	1918
Menin	Oct 1918	Nov	1918
Staceghem	Nov 1918	Nov	1918
Menin	Nov 1918	Dec	1918
Reckem	Dec 1918	Feb	1919
Ford	Feb 1919		

Disbanded at Ford on 31 December 1919. Re-formed in the bomber role on 3 January, 1928 at Upper Heyford. Served in this role in 4 Group Bomber Command until 7 May, 1945 when transferred to transport duties at Melbourne.

Melbourne	May 1945	Aug	1945
Broadwell	Aug 1945		1945
St. Mawgan	1945	Sep	1945
Bilaspur	Sep 1945	Sep	1945
Poona, det. Chaklala, Mauripur	Sep 1945		1947
Chaklala	1947	Dec	1947

Disbanded at Chaklala on 20 December, 1947. Re-formed at Oakington from No. 238 Squadron on 5 November, 1948.

Oakington, det. Lübeck	Nov 1948	Feb	1950

Disbanded at Oakington on 20 February, 1950. Re-formed at Scampton on 15 January, 1953 as a bomber squadron. Disbanded at Cottesmore on 1 March, 1964. Re-formed on 1 July, 1966 at Brize Norton in the long-range strategic transport role.

Brize Norton	Jul 1966		

Main Equipment (in the Army co-operation and transport roles)
B.E.2c (Jan 1915—Apr 1917)
1702; 1737; 2009; 2036; 2128; 2589; 2601; 2732; 4172; 4325; 4547;
(also 1 Bristol Scout) 5295)
B.E.2d (Jul 1916—Dec 1916)
5777; 5862; 6250; 6253; 6742
B.E.2e (Dec 1916—Jul 1917)
6286; 7153
Armstrong-Whitworth F.K.8 (Jul 1917—Feb 1919)
A2685; B227; B324; B3328; B5759; B5791; C3522; C3548; C8597;
C8634; D5071; D5159; F616; F5808
Bristol 14 F.2B (Jun 1918—Oct 1918)
B1234; C967; C984; E2426
R.E.8 (Oct 1918—Jan 1919)
C2547; C2912; D6737
Douglas Dakota C.3, C.4 (May 1945—Dec 1947 & Nov 1948—Feb 1950)
KN516, ZA:M; KN555, ZA:V; KN651, ZA:T; KP245, ZA:S;
(1945—1947); KJ900, C; KJ989, N; KK130; KN235, Q; KN318, G;
KN525, H; KN603, A; KN691, T; KP245, S; KP273, F
Handley Page Halifax A.7 (1946—Dec 1947)
PN258
BAC VC 10 C.1 (Jul 1966—   )
XR806 *George Thompson, VC*
XR807 *Donald Garland, VC, Thomas Gray, VC*
XR808 *Kenneth Campbell, VC*
XR809 *Hugh Malcolm, VC*
XR810 *David Lord, VC*
XV101 *Lanoe Hawker, VC*
XV102 *Guy Gibson, VC*
XV103 *Edward Mannock, VC*
XV104 *James McCudden, VC*
XV105 *Albert Ball, VC*
XV106 *Thomas Mottershead, VC*
XV107 *James Nicholson, VC*
XV108 *William Rhodes-Moorhouse, VC*
XV109 *Arthur Scarf, VC*

Commanding Officers

Maj G. S. Shepherd	Jan 1915	—Mar 1915
Maj U. J. D. Bourke	Mar 1915	—Jun 1916
Maj W. G. S. Mitchell	Jun 1916	—Dec 1916
Maj G. B. Ward	Dec 1916	—Sep 1917
Maj K. D. P. Murray	Sep 1917—	1919
W/Cdr A. C. Dowden	May 1945—	1946
W/Cdr J. A. Chorlton	1946—	1946
W/Cdr A. J. Ogilvie	1946—	Dec 1947
S/Ldr T. F. C. Churcher	Nov 1948	—Sep 1949
S/Ldr I. D. N. Lawson	Sep 1949	—Feb 1950
W/Cdr M. G. Beavis	Jul 1966	—Oct 1968
W/Cdr D. E. B. Dowling	Oct 1968	—Feb 1971
W/Cdr R. L. Lamb	Feb 1971	—Dec 1972
W/Cdr R. I. C. Howden	Jan 1973	—Mar 1975
W/Cdr A. J. Richards	Mar 1975	—Feb 1977
W/Cdr R. G. Peters	Feb 1977—	

Aircraft Markings

When markings were introduced in 1916 No. 10's identity was displayed by a disc painted on the fuselage sides aft of the roundels, black on clear-doped aircraft and white on the khaki-drab machines. This was later altered to a horizontal white bar along the lower edge of the aircraft fuselage and this remained the Squadron's markings until 1918.

With the transport aircraft the Dakotas at first continued to use the two-letter code carried on the bombers in World War II, 'ZA'. This was later discontinued and only aircraft letters carried. VC.10s carried the names of the RAF's VCs.
(See also *Bomber Squadrons of the RAF*, pp. 20–4)

No. 12 SQUADRON

BADGE
A fox's mask

MOTTO
'Leads the Field'

The Squadron was at one time equipped with the Fairey Fox which was a great step forward in daylight bombing capability and the badge recalls this period.

The Squadron was formed at Netheravon on 14 February, 1915 out of a Flight of No. 1 Squadron. The original intention was that one Flight should have Avro 504s and the other Moranes. The Avros arrived but by April the Squadron was completely equipped with B.E.2cs, using the Avros for training. Work-up for France commenced and on 6 September, and No. 12 arrived at St. Omer where it became Headquarters squadron for long-range reconnaissance, flying its first operation, a photo-recce, on 9 September. Three days later Capt L. A. Strange, B Flight commander, drove down a German aircraft over Comines. But now the Squadron concentrated on bombing railways targets preparatory for the Loos offensive, Capt Laurence scoring a most effective attack on a troop train on 25 September. In addition reconnaissance flights were still flown and after the bombing period intensified, together with offensive and defensive patrols over the front. The Squadron had been allocated a few scouts for defence but casualties with the vulnerable B.E.2c mounted and it was soon necessary to have escorts from the new scout squadrons.

In February, 1916 No. 12 was transferred to VI Corps with whom it served out the 1914–18 war. It was now a corps squadron and initially trained in its new role of artillery co-operation and infantry patrols. Many accidents were now taking place as pilots were arriving on the squadron with only twenty hours' training. Operationally the greatest dangers were AA fire although the occasional air combat took place. But largely No. 12 now spotted for artillery 'shoots' or made contact patrols along the front lines. When the Somme offensive began No. 12 again flew some bombing sorties, now with scout escorts, against railways and airfields. Before Arras the whole sector

of the front was photographed by No. 12, and by the end of 1916 the Squadron had re-equipped with B.E.2e's. These lasted until June, 1917 when R.E. 8s took over; now No. 12 had a reasonable corps aircraft with which to fight in the Cambrai and Ypres offensives. By September, 1917 the Squadron was trying its hand at night bombing with some success in addition to the corps work. During the German offensive of March, 1918 No. 12 was busily engaged in contact flying with the troops, resulting in heavy losses, although at least eight enemy aircraft were also destroyed. As the offensive was stopped and the Allies counter-attacked the Squadron returned to its more normal tasks, receiving some Bristol Fighters for long-range gunnery 'shoots'. In the summer and autumn offensives of 1918 the Squadron was heavily involved with many and varied tasks, including ammunition dropping, ground attack and combats in addition to the normal tasks, No. 12 ending the war with 45 enemy aircraft to its credit.

After the Armistice it became part of the Army of Occupation, re-equipped completely with Bristol Fighters. Flying photo sorties and army co-op it remained the last operational squadron in Germany, disbanding at Bickendorff on 22 July, 1922. When it re-formed at Northolt on 1 April, 1923 it was as a day-bomber squadron and after a period with D.H.9As and Fawns it received the revolutionary Fairey Fox, faster than any fighter. These were replaced in 1931 by Harts. No. 12 entered World War II with Fairey Battles with which F/O Garland and Sgt Gray won VCs during the hectic Battle of France. On return to the UK in 1940 it took up night bombing with Wellingtons, then Lancasters in 1 Group. After the war No. 12 remained as a UK bomber squadron with Lincolns, Canberras, Vulcans and finally Buccaneers, being the first RAF squadron with this type.

Bases etc.

Formed at Netheravon on 14 February, 1915.

Netheravon	Feb 1915	—Sep 1915
St. Omer	Sep 1915	—Feb 1916
Vert Galand	Feb 1916	—Mar 1916
Avesnes-le-Comte	Mar 1916	—May 1917
Wagonlieu	May 1917	—Jul 1917

Ablainzeville	Jul 1917—Aug 1917
Courcelles-le-Comte	Aug 1917—Dec 1917
Boiry St. Martin	Dec 1917—Mar 1918
Soncamp	Mar 1918—Sep 1918
Mory	Sep 1918—Oct 1918
Estourmel	Oct 1918—Nov 1918
Gerpinnes	Nov 1918—Dec 1918
Clavier	Dec 1918—Dec 1918
Düren	Dec 1918—May 1919
Heumar	May 1919—Nov 1920
Bickendorff	Nov 1920—Jul 1922

Disbanded at Bickendorff on 22 July, 1922. Re-formed at Northolt on 1 April, 1923 in the bomber role.

Main Equipment

Avro 504 (May 1915—Sep 1915)
759; 760; 763; 794
B.E.2c (Apr 1915—Feb 1917)
1742; 1781; 2014; 2079; 2106; 2521; 2646; 2731; 4090; 4202; 4401
(B.E.2d)
5787; 6229
B.E.2e (Dec 1916—Aug 1917)
7062; 7129; 7255; A2738; A2769; A2787; A2807; A2844
Scout Aircraft (Sep 1915—May 1916)
Bristol Scout
1606; 4669; 5301
Voisin
5066
R.E.5
2458
R.E.7
2289

F.E.2b
5201; 6330; 6356
R.E.8 (Aug 1917—Jul 1919)
A3579; A3633; A3676; A3750; A3773; A3864; A4440; B832; B2273; B5030; B6512; B6653; B7715; C2298; C2783; D6803; E270
Bristol F.2B (Mar 1918—Jul 1922)
D7914, C3; D8095, B5; E2506, A2; F4402, B3; F4661, B6; F4893, C1; H1568, C6

Commanding Officers

Maj C. L. N. Newall	Feb 1915—Jan 1916
Maj J. C. Halahan	Jan 1916—Oct 1916
Maj C. S. Burnett	Oct 1916—Sep 1917
Maj J. A. G. de Courcy, MC	Sep 1917—Jul 1918
Maj H. S. Lees-Smith	Jul 1918—Aug 1918
Maj T. Q. Back	Aug 1918—Mar 1919
Maj G. H. B. McCall	Mar 1919—Apr 1919
Maj J. G. Selby, MC	Apr 1919—Sep 1919
S/Ldr R. E. Saul, DFC	Sep 1919—Mar 1921
S/Ldr H. J. F. Hunter, MC	Mar 1921—May 1922
F/Lt P. F. Fullard, DSO, MC, AFC	May 1922—Jul 1922

Aircraft Insignia

At first no squadron insignia was carried though it appears that during the latter half of 1916 some at least of the aircraft carried a black patch on the engine with the Flight letter on in white. An official marking had been issued in April, 1916 but it has been reported that this was not applied until the end of 1917. The marking consisted of a white strip painted along the lower side of the fuselage from the roundel to the rudder post. It is believed that it lasted only until March, 1918.
(See also *Bomber Squadrons of the RAF*, pp. 27–30 & 386–387)

No. 13 SQUADRON

BADGE
In front of a dagger a lynx's head
MOTTO
'*Adjuvamus tuendo*'
('We assist by watching')

The dagger had been used as the Squadron's unofficial badge for some time; the lynx's head denotes vigilance.

No. 13 Squadron was formed at Gosport on 10 January, 1915 being one of the first with one basic type of aircraft, the B.E.2c. After work-up it went to France in October, 1915 though having spent a week's detachment at Sutton's Farm on home defence duties just previously. In France it served on army co-operation duties (recce and artillery 'shoots') but in the following year it became more offensive with bombing raids during the Somme fighting, being one of the first squadrons to bomb in formation. Its foremost contribution, though, was in artillery spotting, working in the main with XVII Corps. R.E.8s came in 1917 as a welcome relief to the outmoded B.E.s and with these the accent was on photographic duties although contact patrols became the norm in the hectic fighting in the spring of 1918. In March, 1919 it returned to the UK and was disbanded at Sedgeford on 31 December, 1919.

On 1 April, 1924 No. 13 was re-formed at Kenley as an army co-operation squadron with Bristol Fighters, moving to Andover later that year. Its tasks were to develop the techniques of direct air support with front-line troops and for this the Squadron was almost continuously having detachments with army formations in different parts of the country. In 1927 the A.W. Atlas Is replaced the Bristols for tactical recce, as the Squadron's main task. Between the wars it flew the standard army co-op types, Audax and Hector, and took part in the RAF Displays at Hendon in 1927, 1934 and 1937. When war came again it was equipped with Lysanders which it took to France as part of the Air Component of the BEF. First task in France was to map the local area. It was May, 1940 when No. 13 was again thrown into action and its Lysanders were heavily involved in tactical recce and contact patrols during the retreat to Dunkirk. It

eventually returned to UK having been severely mauled in France. It now took up two ancillary tasks which became its most operational duties, one of these being ASR for which it maintained a detachment at Warmwell and the other anti-invasion coastal patrols which were flown at dawn and dusk. For a year it was stationed in N.W. England with a Flight in N. Ireland (which became No. 231 Squadron in September, 1940), then it moved to its old base of Odiham in July, 1941, re-equipping with Blenheim IVs. It was now involved in many army exercises, the accent being on invasion and attack, although the Blenheim was not suitable for close range Tac/R. From May, 1942 it returned to specific operational duties, flying night intruder sorties, and also took part in the Dieppe raid in August. Its role here was to drop 100 lb phosphorus bombs on AA sites to blind them. In September it received Blenheim VAs and worked up for overseas, moving to Gibraltar in November and on to Blida airfield, Algiers, as soon as Algeria had fallen. From here, in 1943, it was heavily involved in tactical bombing in support of the advancing 1st Army troops. This was tough flying and fighting and casualties were incurred. In May, 1943 a complete change of role came about and No. 13 transferred to N.W. African Coastal Air Force, flying convoy patrols along the Algerian and Tunisian coasts to keep the U-boats at bay. For the most part these patrols were boring and unproductive but during this period (May–December, 1943) No. 13 claimed two U-boats attacked, one probably destroyed and one damaged.

In December, 1943 the Squadron began conversion to the pure bomber role, settling on to Martin Baltimores. These it took to Italy in 1944, flying as part of the Desert Air Force. This task was maintained until the war's end, with Bostons from October, 1944 onwards, the Squadron ending its operational service in Greece and disbanding there on 19 April, 1946. On 1 September, 1946 No. 680 Squadron at Ein Shemer in the Canal Zone was re-numbered No. 13 Squadron. It was equipped with Mosquitoes which it flew in the photo-recce role. Now that it was peacetime the Squadron's primary function was survey and it flew many miles about the Near East photo-surveying for making up-to-date maps of Africa, Arabia and the Eastern Mediterranean, going as far south as Southern Rhodesia. At the end of 1951 this task was taken up with Meteor

PR.10s which continued flying from Egypt until moving to Cyprus in 1956. Here No. 13 re-equipped with PR Canberras which it used operationally in the Suez campaign later that year. For nine years No. 13 remained in Cyprus using various marks of PR Canberra before transferring to Malta. More and more the Squadron's task became the tracking of Soviet warships through the Mediterranean and this work was continued, together with other PR and survey duties until October, 1978 when the British presence in Malta ceased and No. 13 returned to the UK to take up PR duties there.

Bases etc.

Formed at Gosport on 10 January, 1915.

Gosport, det. Sutton's Farm	Jan 1915—Oct 1915
St. Omer	Oct 1915—Oct 1915
Vert Galand	—Mar 1916
Le Hameau	Mar 1916—Mar 1916
Savy	Mar 1916—May 1917
Etrun	May 1917—Mar 1918
Izel-le-Hameau	Mar 1918—Sep 1918
Mory	Sep 1918—Oct 1918
Carnières	Oct 1918—Dec 1918
Vert Galand	Dec 1918—Jan 1919
St. Omer	Jan 1919—Mar 1919
Sedgeford	Mar 1919—Dec 1919

Disbanded at Sedgeford on 31 December, 1919. Re-formed at Kenley from the Signals Co-operation Flight on 1 April, 1924.

Kenley	Apr 1924—Jun 1924
Andover	Jun 1924—Sep 1929
Netheravon	Sep 1929—May 1930
Odiham	May 1930—Sep 1930
Netheravon	Sep 1930—May 1935
Old Sarum	May 1935—Feb 1937
Odiham	Feb 1937—Sep 1939
Mons-en-Chaussée	Sep 1939—Apr 1940
Flamincourt	Apr 1940—May 1940
Deva	May 1940—May 1940
Abbeville Woods	May 1940—May 1940
Châteaubriant	May 1940—May 1940
Cherbourg	May 1940—May 1940
Hawarden	May 1940—Jun 1940
Speke	Jun 1940—Jun 1940
Hooton Park, det. Newtownards, Warmwell	Jun 1940—Jul 1941
Odiham, det. Detling, Wattisham, Macmerry	Jul 1941—Nov 1942
Gibraltar	Nov 1942—Nov 1942
Blida	Nov 1942—Dec 1942
Canrobert	Dec 1942—Feb 1943
Oulmene	Feb 1943—May 1943
Blida	May 1943—Sep 1943
Protville	Sep 1943—Oct 1943
Sidi Ahmed	Oct 1943—Oct 1943
Sidi Amor	Oct 1943—Dec 1943
Kabrit	Dec 1943

In December, 1943 the Squadron converted to Baltimores and transferred to the bomber role which it maintained until disbanding at Hassani on 19 April, 1946. On 1 September, 1946 No. 13 Squadron was re-formed at Ein Shemer by re-numbering No. 680 Squadron.

Ein Shemer	Sep 1946—Dec 1946
Kabrit	Dec 1946—Feb 1947
Fayid	Feb 1947—Jan 1955
Abu Sueir	Jan 1955—Feb 1956
Akrotiri	Feb 1956—Sep 1965
Luqa	Sep 1965—Jan 1972
Akrotiri	Jan 1972—Oct 1972
Luqa	Oct 1972—Oct 1978
Wyton	Oct 1978—Jan 1982

Disbanded at Wyton on 1 January 1982.

Main Equipment

B.E.2c (Jan 1915—   1916)
2017; 2043; 2045; 4079; 4084; 4510; 4595
Bristol Scout D (1916—   1916)
8988
B.E.2d (1916—Apr 1917)
5770; 5787; 5841; 5848; 5851
B.E.2e (1916—Apr 1917)
7089; 7150; 7221; A1841; A1843
R.E.8 (Apr 1917—Mar 1919)
B5070
Bristol F.2B (Apr 1924—Dec 1927)
C1042; F4369; F4488; F4572; H1623; J6594; J7460
A.W. Atlas I (Aug 1927—Jun 1932)
J8783; J9526; J9980; K1005; K1025; K1528; K1542
Hawker Audax I (Feb 1932—May 1937)
K2009; K2014; K2027; K2033; K3081; K3103; K7433
Hawker Hector I (May 1937—Feb 1939)
K8091; K8093; K8107; K8140; K8159; K9737; K9759

Westland Lysander II (Jan 1939—Nov 1940)
L4759, OO:T; L4767, OO:F; L4772, OO:L; L4792; L4812; L6851; L6886; N1219; N1260; P1713; P9056; R2028
Westland Lysander III (Nov 1940—May 1941)
R9135; T1439, OO:C; T1466, OO:E; T1516, OO:A; T1582, OO:B; T1620; T1621
Westland Lysander IIIA (May 1914—Aug 1941)
V9288, OO:D
Bristol Blenheim IV (Aug 1941—Sep 1942)
N3545; N3616, OO:P; N6143; R3879; T2184, OO:T; T2254; V5380; V5467, OO:B; Z5811; Z5882; Z6089; Z6357, OO:D; Z6358, OO:G
Bristol Blenheim VA (Sep 1942—Dec 1943)
BA730, G; BA755, B; BA807, J; BA873, Y; BB172, P; EH322, H; EH463, W
Transferred to bomber role
de Havilland Mosquito PR.16 (Sep 1946—   1947)
No serials known
de Havilland Mosquito PR.34 (1946—Feb 1952)
PF633, D; PF678, H; RG242, A; RG293, F; RG309, E; VL617, N
Gloster Meteor PR.10 (Dec 1951—May 1956)
WB162, H; WB174, N; WB177, C; WB180; WH569, A; WH572
English Electric Canberra PR.7 (May 1956—   1962 & 1972—   )
WH775; WH780; WH796; WH801; WJ817; WJ825; WT508; WT519; WT530; WT538
English Electric Canberra PR.9 (1962—Oct 1976)
XH130; XH135; XH164; XH167; XH171; XH177

Commanding Officers

Maj P. L. W. Herbert	Jan 1915—Jan 1916
Maj A. C. E. Marsh	Jan 1916—Jun 1916
Maj C. W. Powell	Jun 1916—Aug 1917
Maj A. C. R. Garrod, MC	Aug 1917—Nov 1918
Maj A. P. D. Hill	Nov 1918—Jan 1919
Maj F. J. R. Roberts, MC	Jan 1919—Dec 1919
S/Ldr C. C. Durston	Apr 1924—Oct 1926
S/Ldr H. I. Hanmer, DFC	Oct 1926—Apr 1927
S/Ldr G. R. A. Deacon	Apr 1927—Oct 1927
S/Ldr H. H. McH. Fraser	Oct 1927—Nov 1929
S/Ldr J. B. Cole-Hamilton	Nov 1929—Nov 1931
S/Ldr J. Whitworth-Jones	Nov 1931—Apr 1933
S/Ldr H. L. Rough, DFC	Apr 1933—May 1934
S/Ldr P. Warburton, MBE	May 1934—Apr 1935
S/Ldr G. O. Venn	Apr 1935—Apr 1937
S/Ldr S. H. C. Gray	Apr 1937—Aug 1940
S/Ldr W. J. Crisham	Aug 1940—Apr 1941
W/Cdr R. J. Cooper	Apr 1941—Sep 1941
W/Cdr W. G. Tailyour	Sep 1941—Jul 1942
W/Cdr J. W. Deacon	Jul 1942—Oct 1942
W/Cdr W. L. Drummond	Oct 1942—Feb 1943
W/Cdr W. L. Thomas	Feb 1943—May 1943
W/Cdr J. R. Thompson, DFC	May 1943—May 1944
W/Cdr A. H. W. Ball, DSO, DFC	Sep 1946—Nov 1946
W/Cdr A. M. Brown, DFC	Nov 1946—Mar 1947
S/Ldr R. N. Hampson	Mar 1947—Dec 1948
S/Ldr J. C. T. Hewell, DSO, DFC	Dec 1948—Dec 1949
S/Ldr L. V. Bachellier, AFC	Dec 1949—Jun 1952
S/Ldr P. Wigley, DFC	Jun 1952—Sep 1954
S/Ldr P. P. Vilia	Sep 1954—Feb 1956
S/Ldr S. F. Field	Feb 1956—Mar 1958
S/Ldr C. Crichton	Mar 1958—Oct 1960
S/Ldr R. V. Tavanyar	Oct 1960—Mar 1963
S/Ldr J. H. D. Daly	Mar 1963—Apr 1965
S/Ldr R. J. Littlejohn	Apr 1965—Sep 1967
S/Ldr R. J. Jackson	Sep 1967—Mar 1969
W/Cdr J. D. V. McPherson	Mar 1969—Dec 1970
W/Cdr J. F. Woodard	Dec 1970—Apr 1973
W/Cdr J. B. Parkinson	Apr 1973—Jul 1975
W/Cdr J. Bredenkamp	Jul 1975—Jul 1977
W/Cdr H. W. Hughes	Jul 1977—Aug 1979
W/Cdr A. L. Terrett	Aug 1979—

Aircraft Insignia

From April, 1916 the B.E.s had a horizontal band painted along the fuselage from nose to tail, black on clear-doped aircraft, white on drab aircraft. This was retained on the R.E.8s as well. Between the wars the only known insignia was the carrying of the badge on the fin, as an unofficial emblem on the Audaxes (a dagger through 'XIII') and officially on a white six-pointed star on the Hectors and Lysanders. This was replaced by code letters 'AN' on the fuselage in 1939, changing to 'OO' in September, 1939. These were retained on the Lysanders and Blenheim IVs but, on moving to N. Africa in November, 1942 unit insignia were dropped. Specific squadron insignia did not re-appear until the advent of the Canberras. At first the emblem was carried on a white disc on the fin; by the late sixties some aircraft also carried the badge under the cockpit. From 1974 the fin emblem was painted on a red disc as part of the toning-down of the camouflage and this has been retained since.

(See also *Bomber Squadrons of the RAF*, pp. 30–1.)

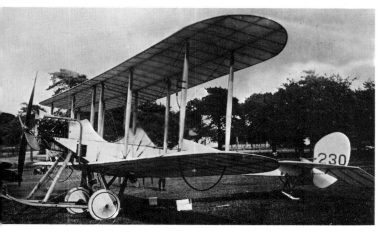

No. 2 Squadron principally flew B.E.2a's, including 230 shown here, taking them by air to Montrose and then by air to France on the outbreak of war.

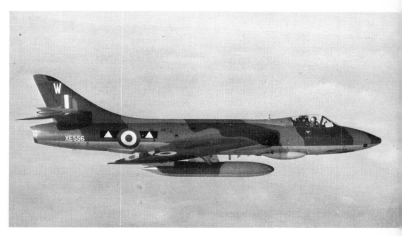

This Hunter FR.10 of No. 2 Squadron was the culmination of the fighter reconnaissance type and was used from Gütersloh in the sixties. Note the Squadron's triangle marking which has been consistently carried, except for World War II days, for most of the Squadron's existence.

Lined up at Odiham in 1939 are the Westland Lysander IIs of No. 4 Squadron, just prior to taking them to France. Note the Squadron emblem on the six-pointed star on the fin, the code letters FY and the Flight colour bands on the wheel spats.

Typical of the B.E2c's which became 'Fokker fodder' in 1916-17 is this machine, 2742, flown by No. 5 Squadron (note the black bands forward of the roundel and forward of the tail) and shot down on 28 September, 1916.

No. 5 Squadron used Bristol Fighters on the North-West Frontier for eleven years through the twenties. D8036 M is shown here with the Squadron number painted on the fin.

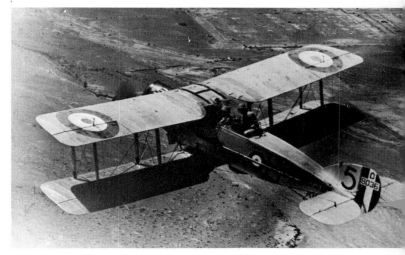

On the outbreak of World War II there were two army co-operation squadrons in Egypt ready for the Western Desert war. No. 6 Squadron was one of these and it was flying Westland Lysander Mk IIs, seen here in the Canal Zone ca February, 1940. JV : D is L6878.

No. 7 Squadron had used R.E.8s from July, 1917 on Corps tasks on the Western Front and after the Armistice settled at Bickendorff on Army of Occupation duties where this photograph was taken in December, 1918.

Tasked with the protection of the Aden Protectorate and the seas around, No. 8 Squadron served predominantly in the maritime role in World War II, its Bristol Blenheim VAs being painted in Coastal Command colours. Two of them are seen awaiting maintenance at Aden ; BA974 A is in the background.

Wellington XIIIs, of which this is one, provided most of No. 8's anti-shipping sorties out across the Indian Ocean and up the Red Sea.

Currently fulfilling the Airborne Early Warning role No. 8 Squadron now flies Avro Shackleton AEW.2s out of Lossiemouth (WR960 here) to provide a radar screen for the UK and direction for Strike Command's Lightnings and Phantoms.

No. 10 Squadron's transport service began with Douglas Dakotas, at first in India as shown here and then on the Berlin Airlift after World War II.

Since 1966 No. 10 Squadron has provided long-distance transport, covering the whole world, with the BAC VC.10s of which XV105 is named *Albert Ball, VC.*

Almost as soon as World War I ended the Bristol Fighter took over the army co-operation work from the R.E.8. F4661 B6 belonged to No. 12 Squadron at Heumar in May, 1920.

Last of the classic army co-operation biplanes to serve with the RAF was the Hawker Hector of which No. 13 Squadron at Odiham was an early exponent.

The universal photo-reconnaissance aircraft in RAF service from the late fifties to the early eighties has been the English Electric Canberra PR.7. No. 13 Squadron flew it to the last, being finally based at Wyton where WT519 is seen in September, 1981.

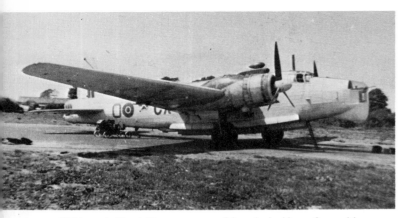

Chivenor in North Devon was one of the principal bases for maritime recce squadrons guarding the Western Approaches. On this sunny, summer dispersal in 1944 is a Wellington XIV CX : 0 of No. 14 Squadron.

Casually posed outside a Bessoneau hangar at Senlis in 1918 is D4847, an R.E.8 of No. 15 Squadron. The '15' on the fuselage is not the squadron number but the 'aircraft in squadron' number, just coincidentally having the same number as the unit.

Full of atmosphere is this morning photograph of No. 16 Squadron B.E.2c's standing outside the hangars as the pilots and observers walk out and the mechanics make the final checks or stand ready to swing the four-blade propellers. The place is almost certainly La Gorgue in 1916.

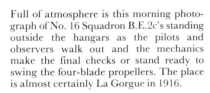

No. 16 Squadron was the first to fly the Westland Lysander, from Old Sarum in 1938. Salisbury Cathedral makes a good backdrop for this trio of the Squadron's Lysander Mk.Is.

After years of low-level army co-operation and fighter recce No. 16 Squadron added high-level photo reconnaissance to its tasks in 1944, one of its Spitfire XIs seen here high above the cloud cover.

No. 17 Squadron had the thankless task in World War I of providing army co-operation requirements for the forces in Salonika. This B.E.12, equipped as a single-seater, is taking off for a visual reconnaissance.

No. 18 Squadron pioneered the Westland Wessex in RAF service and used them from January, 1964 until 1981, most of this time being spent as a front-line squadron in RAF Germany. The Squadron's emblem is a red pegasus rampant and it can be seen on the white disc on XV725's fin in May, 1970.

The medium-lift Boeing Vertol Chinook HC.1 has now become No. 18 Squadron's mount and this, too, will be used by it in Germany.

Although the Westland Lysander was a death trap for army co-operation duties in the European fighting it was able to serve reasonably successfully in the Burma war where one of its proponents was No. 20 Squadron who used it into 1943. This particular aircraft, DG445 HN : K, is interesting in that it is one of six which were transferred to the RAF from the RCAF.

The R.E.7 was an unsuccessful design which only saw limited service on the Western Front, principally with No. 21 Squadron. No. 2194 shown here was one of this squadron's aircraft though probably, when this photograph was taken, was serving with No. 35 Reserve Squadron at Northolt.

After a successful anti-shipping career from the UK with Beauforts No. 22 Squadron moved to Ceylon in 1942 and eventually flew Beaufighters on coastal strike duties. NE478 V is seen here airborne from Ratmalana in June, 1944.

Since World War II No. 22 has been the longest-serving Search and Rescue Squadron in the UK and has achieved many notable and dangerous rescues with its Whirlwinds which it has used, in two different forms, since February, 1955 until 1981. In this practice rescue XR483 is a HAR.Mk.10.

One of the many types that No. 24 Squadron used on communications duties in the thirties was the Hawker Hart Trainer. The Squadron number was carried in black and the Squadron's unofficial red/blue chevron on the fin.

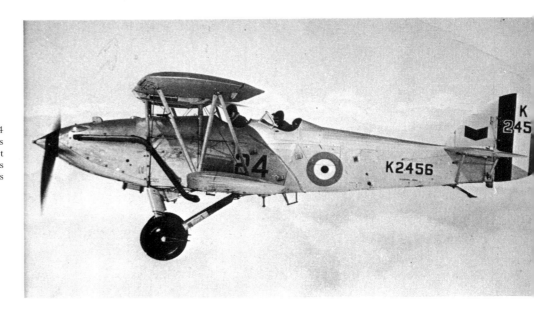

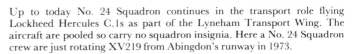

Hendon, the base of No. 24 Squadron during World War II, saw many strange types on its turf; none stranger than the Squadron's Wellington IA transports, such as N2990 NQ:D seen here in 1943. Note the mock nose turret to intimidate marauding Germans.

Up to today No. 24 Squadron continues in the transport role flying Lockheed Hercules C.1s as part of the Lyneham Transport Wing. The aircraft are pooled so carry no squadron insignia. Here a No. 24 Squadron crew are just rotating XV219 from Abingdon's runway in 1973.

After a spell in Burma with Lysanders, No. 28 Squadron made full use of the Hawker Hurricane IIC there in the fighter-recce role at low level.

The principal user of the Vickers Valetta C.1 transport in the UK was No. 30 Squadron who flew it from 1950-1957 on European flights. VW842 here takes off from Northolt, the RAF's London terminal.

The Hawker Audax served valiantly on the North-West Frontier of India with No. 28 Squadron right up until the end of 1942. This interesting photo shows one of the Squadron's aircraft in 1941, K4839, in full camouflage and carrying code letters US, which were the pre-war allocation but, presumably, still used by No. 26.

No. 26 Squadron used the North American Mustang I for most of its offensive sorties in World War II, commencing in January, 1942. At first these carried the code letters RM but in December, 1944 it began to use XC as on AG 425.

During the twenties and thirties most of the army co-operation flying took place in and around Salisbury Plain but the RAF had a base at Catterick in Yorkshire and its exponents of the art were the members of No. 26 Squadron, one of whose Armstrong Whitworth Atlas Is is seen here at Catterick in July, 1929.

No. 31 Squadron converted to the transport role in the summer of 1939, receiving Vickers Valentias relinquished by 216 Squadron and using them both in India and Iraq.

When war came to No. 31 Squadron the Valentias were hastily supplemented by any other transports available, including this Douglas DC-2 VT-APA acquired from Indian Airlines.

When No. 33 Squadron re-formed at Odiham on 14 June, 1971 it was in the helicopter close support role and was the first unit to fly the Aerospatiale/Westland Puma HC.1. It has since flown these on 'active service' in Northern Ireland and Belize. In this formation flypast the lead aircraft, XW205 CB, carried the Squadron's flag.

No. 34 Squadron flew R.E.8s for most of its operations in World War I, both on the Western Front and in Italy. The Squadron's markings consisted of two white sloping bars each side of the roundel, seen here on D4790 N.

After World War II No. 34 Squadron was used on PR duties in the Far East with Spitfire PR.19s, one of which was PM546 G.

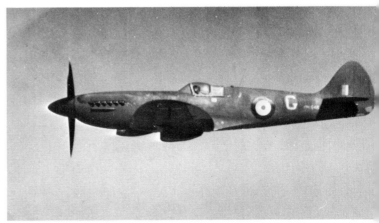

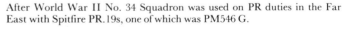

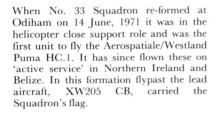

No. 14 SQUADRON

BADGE
A winged plate charged with cross throughout
and surmounted by the head and
shoulder-pieces of a suit of armour

MOTTO
'I spread my wings and keep my promise'

The St. George's Cross signifies the idea of a
crusader associated with the Squadron's
service in Palestine in World War I.

No. 14 Squadron formed in the UK (Shoreham) on 3 February, 1915 with the intention of being sent overseas. It worked up with Farman and Martinsyde biplanes until November, 1915 when it embarked for Egypt, arriving at Ismailia on 3 December where it joined with No. 17 Squadron to form the 5th Wing. Originally equipped with B.E.2c aircraft it sent detachments in various directions in 1916: those in the Western Desert waged a campaign against the Senussi tribe whilst the detachment on the Suez Canal formed part of the Canal defence force. This was No. 14's task until November, 1916 when it concentrated at Mustabig for the advance across Sinai. Its task was largely army support (recce, supply and message dropping and the occasional bombing and photographic sortie). It also sent a detachment down to Mecca to protect the Holy City from the Turks. In the summer of 1917 the Squadron was united for the Third Battle of Gaza. Its area of operation was now to be exclusively Palestine and No. 14 fought through to the end of the campaign, being one of the Squadrons which routed the Turkish 7th Army in the Wadi el Far'a in September, 1918, bombing and machine-gunning the enemy forces until they were destroyed. Because the ground advance was so rapid No. 14 also acted as a rudimentary transport squadron carrying personnel and supplies forward in addition to its Corps duties. After the war it remained in Palestine until January, 1919 when it returned to the UK (probably without aircraft) and was disbanded at Tangmere on 4 February, 1919.

On 1 February, 1920 No. 14 was re-formed in Palestine once more by re-numbering No. 111 Squadron at Ramleh. It was now equipped with Bristol Fighters for army co-operation duties and began policing flying to keep the peace between the various contesting forces. In 1924 it received some D.H.9As to supplement the Bristols and in 1926 became a bomber squadron entirely equipped with D.H.9As. In fact it remained a bomber squadron until 1951, serving in the Middle East with Fairey IIIFs and Gordons and entering World War II with Vickers Wellesleys. These it used in the East African campaign, then flew Blenheims both in the Western Desert and in various other Middle East areas before becoming the RAF's first squadron with Martin Marauders. These were used mainly for anti-shipping work in the Mediterranean until September, 1944. It then returned to the UK and flew for eight months on Coastal Command duties. For these it was based at Chivenor from 24 October, 1944 onwards, with a detachment at Portreath. It flew Vickers Wellington GR.XIVs on anti-submarine patrols and anti-shipping work in the Western Approaches and down the west coast of France and Biscay. By this time, however, the war in the west was drawing to its closing stages and soon after VE-Day the Squadron was disbanded again at Chivenor on 8 June, 1945. On the same day No. 143 Squadron at Banff was re-numbered No. 14 Squadron. It was now a Coastal Command Mosquito strike squadron and it continued to train in this role until 31 March, 1946 when the Banff Strike Wing disbanded.

The following day No. 14 re-formed yet again, this time as a bomber squadron once more by re-numbering No. 128 Squadron at Wahn in Germany. Flying Mosquito B.16s and B.35s to begin with,

it has served with RAF Germany ever since, becoming a fighter squadron again in February, 1951 with Vampires, Venoms and Hunters, reverting to the bomber role with Canberra B(I).8s in 1962 and then turning to fighter/ground attack with Phantoms and now Jaguars.

Bases etc.

Formed at Shoreham on 3 February, 1915.

Shoreham	Feb	1915—Nov 1915
en route to Egypt	Nov	1915—Dec 1915
Ismailia, det. Mersa Matruh, Sollum, Cantara, Heliopolis, Rabigh	Dec	1915—Nov 1916
Mustabig, det. Rabigh	Nov	1916—Dec 1917
Aqaba, det. Junction Station	Dec	1917—Mar 1918
Junction Staton, det. Jericho, Jerusalem	Mar	1918—Jan 1919
Tangmere	Jan	1919—Feb 1919

Disbanded at Tangmere on 4 February, 1919. Re-formed by re-numbering No. 111 Squadron at Ramleh, Palestine.

Ramleh, det. Amman	Feb	1920—mid 1926

In mid-1926 it became a bomber squadron and served in that role until October, 1944. In October, 1944 the Squadron personnel assembled in the UK and became a general recce squadron at Chivenor on 24 October, 1944.

Chivenor, det. Portreath	Oct	1944—Jun 1945

On 1 June, 1945 it was disbanded at Chivenor. It re-formed on 1 June, 1945 at Banff by re-numbering No. 143 Squadron and flew in the coastal strike role.

Banff	Jun	1945—Mar 1946

On 31 March, 1946 it was disbanded at Banff. It re-formed on 1 April, 1946 as a bomber squadron at Wahn in RAF Germany and has served there since.

Main Equipment

UK training types: – It flew Maurice Farman and Martinsyde S.1 at Shoreham from February, 1915 to November, 1915.

B.E.2c (Dec 1915—Oct 1917)
4395; 4478; 4483; 4488; 4529; 5421; 5429

B.E.2e (Sep 1916—Oct 1917)
A1801; A3065

D.H.1A (1916—   1916)
4607

B.E.12a (Oct 1917—Oct 1917)
No serials known

R.E.8 (Oct 1917—Jan 1919)
B6604

Fighter Types Bristol Scout C & D
4688; 4689; 7032

Martinsyde G.100
7474

D.H.2
A4779

Bristol F.2B (Feb 1920—   1926)
J7829

Flew in bomber role 1926 to 1944

Vickers Wellington XIV (Oct 1944—Jun 1945)
HF124; HF196; HF312; HF387; HF415; HF450; MF727; MF762; NB825; NB838; NB856; NB867; NB909; CX:K

de Havilland Mosquito FB.6 (Jun 1945—Mar 1946)
HR373; HR436; CX:J; HR604; PZ415; PZ466; RF622; RF646; RS501; RS625

Commanding Officers

Maj G. E. Todd	Feb	1915—Jan 1916
Maj R. W. Freeman	Jan	1916—Jul 1916
Maj A. J. Bannantyne	Jul	1916—May 1917
Maj A. C. Boddam-Whetham	May	1917—Oct 1917
Maj C. E. H. Medhurst	Oct	1917—Jan 1919
W/Cdr E. Donovan	Oct	1944—Apr 1945
W/Cdr G. I. Rawson	Apr	1945—Jun 1945
W/Cdr C. N. Foxley-Norris, DSO	Jun	1945—Mar 1946

Aircraft Insignia

As far as is known No. 14 Squadron's aircraft carried no distinguishing squadron marking in the Middle East in World War I. The Wellington XIVs at Chivenor carried the code letters 'CX' on the fuselage and this code combination was also used by the Mosquitoes at Banff.
(See also *Bomber Squadrons of the RAF*, pp. 31–3 and *Fighter Squadrons of the RAF*, pp. 39–41 & 562–3.)

No. 15 SQUADRON

BADGE
A hind's head affrontee erased at the neck
between wings elevated and conjoined in base
MOTTO
'Aim sure'

Based on the Squadron's own previous design,
the badge incorporated a hind's head as No. 15
was flying the Hawker Hind at the time the
badge was authorised.

The Squadron was formed at South Farnborough on 1 March, 1915, drawing on personnel from No. 1 Reserve Squadron and the Recruits Depot. A month later it moved to Hounslow and then to Dover where it was engaged in training crews for operations and working up itself. It went to France on 23 December, 1915 and joined No. 2 Wing in January, 1916 with its B.E.2c's. Its first operation, a reconnaissance of the 2nd British Army's front, was flown on 10 January. A week later No. 15 lost its first crew to a Fokker. In March it moved to the 4th Army front, the Somme, but before the month was out it became a corps squadron attached to VIII Corps. It was now mainly involved in artillery 'shoots', photography and contact patrols and that summer it took part in the Somme offensive. As light relief it would attack the German observation balloons, often shooting them down in flames. Later in the battle No. 15 was transferred to V Corps for 'air liaison' work, in other words any task the Corps commander wanted. These included ground-strafing and bombing in addition to normal corps duties. By the end of the year No. 15 had transferred to XIII Corps and continued actively on operations despite the bitter winter.

In the battle of Arras in 1917 the Squadron was heavily involved but in May, 1917 No. 15 re-equipped with R.E.8s and after a period with the General Reserve joined IV Corps. With this organisation it also engaged in bombing raids in the autumn of 1917 flying with other squadrons in mass raids over the lines. Then it was fully involved in the battle of Cambrai, and after that with the German offensive in the March of 1918. Artillery observation was always the priority and No. 15 flew many long hours over German positions recording the fall of the shells and reporting them by morse to their own batteries, being shelled themselves by anti-aircraft fire.

When the Allies took the offensive in the summer of 1918 No. 15 was very busy. A new task came its way, that of dropping ammunition supplies by parachute to the forward troops. It remained heavily involved until the Armistice in November, 1918 after which it moved wherever V Corps went. In January, 1919 it relinquished its aircraft, eventually returning to the UK and disbanding at Fowlmere on 31 December, 1919.

When the Squadron re-formed on 20 March, 1924 it was in a novel role. It became part of the Aeroplane & Armament Experimental Establishment (AAEE) at Martlesham Heath. On paper it was to be a day bomber squadron, and was given some D.H.9As for that purpose, but its main duty was to provide crews for experimental and armament testing. This involved a wide range of aircraft and a wide range of trials varying from new equipment to gunnery and bomb ballistic trials. The major part of No. 15's work was on armament trials and for some of these it flew exotic prototype aircraft which its sister squadron at Martlesham, No. 22, had found unsuitable for service use! In October, 1926 the paper D.H.9As for its bomber role were replaced by Hawker Horsleys. The Squadron continued in this Jekyll and Hyde existence until June, 1934 when it left Martlesham and formed at a regular bomber squadron Abingdon.

Thereafter No. 15 has served continuously in the bomber role, at first as a light bomber squadron with Harts, Hinds, Battles and Blenheims, then as a night bomber squadron with 3 Group and from 1940 onwards with Wellingtons, Stirlings and Lancasters. After World War II it flew Lincolns, Washingtons, Canberras and Victors before joining RAF Germany with Buccaneer S.2Bs where it serves today.

Bases etc.

Formed at S. Farnborough on 1 March, 1915.

S. Farnborough	Mar 1915	Apr 1915
Hounslow	Apr 1915	May 1915
Dover (Swingate Downs)	May 1915	Dec 1915
St. Omer	Dec 1915	Jan 1916
Droglandt	Jan 1916	Mar 1916
Vert Galand	Mar 1916	Mar 1916
Marieux	Mar 1916	Oct 1916
Lealvilliers	Oct 1916	Jun 1917
Courcelles-le-Comte	Jun 1917	Jul 1917
La Gorgue	Jul 1917	Aug 1917
Savy	Aug 1917	Aug 1917
Longavesnes	Aug 1917	Oct 1917
Lechelle	Oct 1917	Nov 1917
Bapaume	Nov 1917	Dec 1917
Lechelle	Dec 1917	Mar 1918
Lavieville	Mar 1918	Mar 1918
La Houssoye	Mar 1918	Mar 1918
Fienvillers	Mar 1918	Apr 1918
Vert Galand	Apr 1918	Sep 1918
Senlis	Sep 1918	Oct 1918
Quatre Vents Farm	Oct 1918	Oct 1918
Guillemin Farm	Oct 1918	Dec 1918
Vignacourt	Dec 1918	Feb 1919
Fowlmere	Feb 1919	Dec 1919

Disbanded at Fowlmere on 31 December, 1919. Re-form at Martlesham Heath as a bomber and experimental squadron on 20 March, 1924.

Martlesham Heath	Mar 1924	May 1934

Disbanded at Martlesham Heath 31 May, 1934. Re-formed at Abingdon on 1 June, 1934 in the bomber role.

Main Equipment

B.E.2c (Aug 1915—   1917)
2077; 2120; 2532; 2578; 2618; 2639; 2715; 2767; 4019; 4116; 4187; 4201; 4205
B.E.2d
6255; 6733
Scout Aircraft (Feb 1916—   1916)
Bristol Scout
4669; 5314
F.E.2b
5202; 6328; 6331
B.E.2e (1916—Aug 1917)
2548; 2788; 2868; 3166; 5835; 6286; 7105; 7178; 7254; A2780; A2841; A2895; A3166
R.E.8 (May 1917—Jan 1919)
A4704, 9; B742; B836, 15; B2276, 13; B3422; B5068; B5897; B6521; B6661, 8; B7887; C2489; C2881; C5065; D4733; D4847, 15; D6732; E52; E107; E1216; F6014; F6270; H7018
D.H.9A (Mar 1924—Oct 1926)
J7864
Horsley I, II (Oct 1926—May 1934)
Horsley I
J8007; J8008; J8018; J8019
Horsley II
J8606; J8608; J8610; J8611; J8612; J8613; J8619
Trials Aircraft (Mar 1924—May 1934)
N.B. Not a complete list.
Atlas J9129; **Siskin IIIA** J8627; **Aldershot I** J6853; **Antelope** J9183; **Bison** N9599; **B & P Bugle** J7260; **Fawn II** J7224; **Ferret** N192; **Fox I** J8426; **Gamecock I** J7891; **Gloster SS.18** J9125; **Handcross** J7500; **Hyderabad** J7748; **Hornbill** J7782; **Pixie II** J7323; **Chamois** J7295; **Snipe** J2498; **Venture** J7282; **Vireo** N211; **Wapiti** J8495

Commanding Officers

Maj P. B. Joubert de la Ferte	Apr 1915	Sep 1915
Maj E. R. Ludlow-Hewitt	Sep 1915	Nov 1915
Maj H. Le M. Brock, DSO	Nov 1915	Dec 1916
Maj G. I. Carmichael, DSO	Dec 1916	Feb 1917
Maj H. S. Walker	Feb 1917	Jan 1918
Maj H. V. Stammers	Jan 1918	Nov 1918
Maj C. C. Durston	Nov 1918	Dec 1919
S/Ldr P. C. Sherren, MC	Mar 1924	Nov 1927
S/Ldr C. E. H. James, MC	Nov 1927	Sep 1929
W/Cdr J. K. Wells, AFC	Sep 1929	Mar 1930
S/Ldr G. H. Martingell, AFC	Mar 1930	Mar 1933
S/Ldr E. S. Goodwin, AFC	Mar 1933	May 1933
S/Ldr R. M. Foster, DFC, AFC	May 1933	May 1934

Aircraft Insignia

In April, 1916 the Squadron was allocated an identity marking consisting of a band painted around the fuselage immediately in front of the tailplane.

No. 16 SQUADRON

BADGE
Two keys in saltire, the wards upwards and outwards

MOTTO
'Operta aperta'
('Hidden things shall be revealed')

The keys are indicative of the Army co-operation role of revealing hidden enemy positions; the keys, one black, one white, indicate round-the-clock operation.

Unlike most of the early RFC squadrons, No. 16 was formed in France, from detachments of No. 2, 5 and 6 Squadrons at St. Omer on 10 February, 1915. It was thus able to begin operations without a work-up and flew its first reconnaissance on 26 February. It was operating no fewer than seven different types of aircraft, mainly on reconnaissance, artillery co-operation, photography and bombing. No. 16 was the first squadron to employ aircraft with wireless to report back on the progress of the infantry during the battle of Abures Ridge in May, 1915 and thus was the contact patrol born. By early 1916 the Squadron was equipped with B.E.2c's and a couple of Bristol Scouts and settled down as a corps squadron in the main. Bombing was also part of the task, Don, Carvin, Menin and Avion being favourite targets, some raids taking place at night. The Squadron also flew anti-Zeppelin patrols. In April, 1917 the first R.E.8s arrived on the Squadron, and it continued to fly the varieties of operation required by the corps. It now flew its own escorts on some of the missions, helping to cut down the casualties that the B.E.s had received. In 1918 it reverted to bombing raids, by night using parachute flares, and as the year wore on the tasks became more those of attack than static fighting. After the war it returned to the UK without its aircraft and was disbanded at Fowlmere on 31 December, 1919.

No. 16 was re-formed in the army co-operation role on 1 April, 1924, equipped at first with Bristol Fighters. Its permanent base was Old Sarum from where it flew with Southern Command. The tasks involved flying around the country in many army exercises and aircraft, in their ones and twos, were detached to many temporary bases during the course of each year. In January, 1931 the first Atlas aircraft replaced the Bristols and three years later these in turn were replaced by Audaxes. In June, 1938 the Squadron received the first Westland Lysanders, working them into service, and began more warlike activities, but when war came in September, 1939 No. 16 did not immediately go to France. Many of its crews were taken for the Air Component and the Squadron also tested other types (Anson, Oxford, etc.) for suitability in the army co-op role. One of its new tasks was to practise gas spraying on infantry in case it should be needed. In April, 1940 it moved to France and when the fighting began it was heavily engaged in tactical recces in the Le Cateau and St. Quentin areas. Losses were heavy although one or two German aircraft were also claimed. After twelve days of fighting the Squadron withdrew to Lympne and from there flew Tac/Rs to Dunkirk, covering the evacuation of the BEF. In June it began dawn and dusk coastal recces with the object of detecting any possible invasion forces. These continued right through to April, 1941 by which time the Squadron's Lysanders were also operating a detached Flight for ASR work. It was not until that summer that the Squadron fully reverted to army work.

In April, 1942 No. 16 re-equipped with the Mustang I and resumed operations in October, 1942 flying convoy patrols and *Lagoons* over the Channel and the French coast. In November it lost two aircraft and in December one on such missions, and it did not resume operations until March, 1943 when *Lagoons* and *Populars*

were flown. In June *Anti-Rhubarbs* (patrols to counter the Bf109 and FW190 fighter-bomber raids) were flown, 78 operational sorties being accumulated in the month.

In September, 1943 the Squadron began to change its role to high-level photo recce and converted to Spitfire XIs for this task, working up in preparation for the invasion. During the next months it concentrated on N. France both for this task and to site all the V1 bases; as 1944 wore on the pressure increased and in May 244 sorties were flown. It now acquired Spitfire IXs as well for low-level work and moved on to French soil in September to follow the advancing armies, providing PR at high and low level. As the year closed targets were mainly in Holland and Germany and the Mk.IX Spitfires were dropped. 1945 saw the continuance of PR operations up to 7 May when three last sorties were flown. The Squadron was disbanded at Eindhoven on 19 September, 1945, briefly re-formed at Celle on the same day and then returned to England, where it was disbanded at Dunsfold on 20 October, 1945.

On 1 April, 1946 No. 16 was re-formed at Lüneburg with Tempests in the fighter role and has continued as part of RAF Germany ever since, at first in the ground attack task with Vampires and Venoms until disbanding at Celle on 15 September, 1957. It was re-formed in the strike role with Canberra B(I)8s and Buccaneer S.2Bs from 1 March, 1958 onwards.

Bases etc.

Formed at St. Omer on 10 February, 1915 from Flights of Nos. 2, 5 & 6 Squadrons.

St. Omer, det. Aire	Feb 1915—	Mar 1915
La Gorgue	Mar 1915—	Jun 1915
Chocques	Jun 1915—	Jun 1915
Merville	Jun 1915—	Dec 1915
La Gorgue	Dec 1915—	Sep 1916
Bruay	Sep 1916—	May 1917
Camplain L'Abbé	May 1917—	Oct 1918
La Brayelle	Oct 1918—	Oct 1918
Auchey	Oct 1918—	Feb 1919
Fowlmere	Feb 1919—	Dec 1919

Disbanded at Fowlmere on 31 December, 1919. Re-formed at Old Sarum on 1 April, 1924.

Old Sarum	Apr 1924—	Feb 1937
Odiham	Feb 1937—	1937
Old Sarum	1937—	Feb 1940
Hawkinge	Feb 1940—	Apr 1940
Bertangles	Apr 1940—	May 1940
Hawkinge	May 1940—	Jun 1940
Redhill	Jun 1940—	Jun 1940
Teversham	Jun 1940—	Aug 1940
Okehampton	Aug 1940—	Aug 1940
Weston Zoyland, det. Teversham, Roborough	Aug 1940—	Jan 1943
Andover	Jan 1943—	Mar 1943
Ford	Mar 1943—	Jun 1943
Middle Wallop	Jun 1943—	Jun 1943
Hartford Bridge	Jun 1943—	Apr 1944
Northolt	Apr 1944—	Sep 1944
A.12	Sep 1944—	Sep 1944
Amiens/Glisy	Sep 1944—	Sep 1944
Melsbroek	Sep 1944—	Apr 1945
Eindhoven	Apr 1945—	Sep 1945

Disbanded at Eindhoven 22 September, 1945. Meanwhile No. 268 Squadron was renumbered No. 16 Squadron at Celle on 19 September, 1945.

Celle	Sep 1945—	Oct 1945
Dunsfold	Oct 1945—	Oct 1945

Disbanded at Dunsfold 20 October, 1945. In the meantime No. 487 Squadron at Epinoy equipped with Mosquito FB.VIs had also been renumbered No. 16 Squadron on 19 September, 1945 but was disbanded there on 16 October, 1945. On 1 April, 1946 No. 56 Squadron at Lüneburg Heath was renumbered No. 16 Squadron and from then on the Squadron flew in the fighter/ground attack role.

Main Equipment

Blériot XI (Feb 1915—   1916)
1828

Vickers F.B5 'Gunbus' (Feb 1915—   1916)
1618
Voisin (Mar 1915—Sep 1915)
1877
B.E.9 (Sep 1915—   1915)
1700
Maurice Farman (May 1915—Sep 1915)
1857; 5009; 5015; 5027; 5030; 5036
B.E.2c (Feb 1915—Apr 1917)
1705; 1731; 1777; 2037; 2529; 2580; 2612; 2669; 2748; 4077; 4121; 4179;
4494; 4587
B.E.2d (June 1916—Nov 1916)
5746; 5771; 5797; 5806; 5810; 5856
Bristol Scout C & D (Aug 1915—Jun 1916)
4670, (C); 5302, (D); 5575, (D)
B.E.2e (1917—May 1917)
2565; 6754; 7171; 7206; A1820; A2778; A3154
B.E.2f (Apr 1917)
2552; 6818
B.E.2g (Apr 1917)
2553; 7164; A2761; A2942;
R.E.8 (May 1917—Feb 1919)
A3194; A3236; A3471; A3531; A3648; A3774; A3839 16; A4217; A4300;
A4426; A4596; A4688; B843; A5010, 17; B5028, 15; B5892; B6664;
C2518; C5048, 25; D4851; E22
A.W. F.K.8 (1917—1918)
B5837, B5839
Bristol F.2B (1918—1918 & Apr 1924—Mar 1931)
C968; C986 (both 1918); F4513; F4519; F4957
A. W. Atlas (Jan 1931—Jan 1934)
K1034; K1037; K1511; K1525; K1537; K1551; K1552
Hawker Audax I (Dec 1933—Jun 1938)
K2025; K3688; K3692; K3696; K3700; K3709; K3712
Westland Lysander I (Jun 1938—Apr 1939 & 1940—Sep 1940)
L4675; L4680; L4689, KJ:V; L4691; P1669; B1684, UG:A; P1687;
UG:F
Westland Lysander II (Apr 1939—Nov 1940)
L4795, KJ:M; L4806, KJ:E, later UG:E; L4813, KJ:O; L6855, KJ:Q;
N1244, UG:K; P1685, UG:P; P1720, UG:L; P9059; P9077; P9108;
P9127
Gloster Gladiator II (May 1940—Sep 1940)
N2304, UG:D
Bristol Blenheim IV (1940—1940)
N3556
de Havilland Tiger Moth II (1940—1941)
N6928; R4958
Percival Proctor I (1940—1941) P6189; P6256
Westland Lysander III (Oct 11940—Jun 1941)
P9110; R9014; R9058; R9110; T1551; T1631; T1705
Westland Lysander IIIA May 1941—Jul 1942)
V9296; V9356; V9489; V9546; V9551
North American Mustang I (Apr 1942—Oct 1943)
AG384; AG431, D; AG549; AG622; AL996; AM102, Y; AM226;
AM235; AP168; AP221; AP239

Vickers-Supermarine Spitfire PR.XI (Sep 1943—Sep 1945)
EN654; EN684; MB902; MB954, K; MB958; PA838; PA853; PA902;
PL765; PL823; PL850; PL903; PL970, E; PM125
Vickers-Supermarine Spitfire LF.IX (Jun 1944—Nov 1944)
EN387, V; MK322; MK716; MK918; ML206; ML302; ML374
Vickers-Supermarine Spitfire PR.19 (Mar 1945—Oct 1945)
PS833; PS835; PS849; PS853, C
Vickers-Supermarine Spitfire FR.14E (Sep 1945—Oct 1945)
No known serials

Commanding Officers

Maj F. V. Holt		Feb	1915—Jul	1915
Maj H. C. T. Dowding		Jul	1915—Jan	1916
Maj D. W. Powell		Jan	1916—Aug	1916
Maj P. C. Maltby		Aug	1916—Jun	1917
Maj C. F. A. Portal		Jun	1917—Jun	1918
Maj A. W. C. V. Parr		Jun	1918—	1919
Sqn Ldr J. O. Archer, CBE		Apr	1914—Sep	1925
S/Ldr W. A. Coryton, MVO, DFC		Sep	1925—Sep	1928
S/Ldr D. O. Mulholland, AFC		Sep	1928—Aug	1931
S/Ldr A. R. Churchman, DFC		Aug	1931—Oct	1933
S/Ldr J. R. I. Scrambler, AFC		Oct	1933—Jun	1934
S/Ldr R. P. Musgrave-Witham, OBE, MC		Jun	1934—Jan	1936
S/Ldr G. P. Charles		Jan	1936—Jun	1938
S/Ldr T. Humble		Jun	1938—Sep	1938
S/Ldr G. P. Charles		Sep	1938—Sep	1939
S/Ldr R. E. S. Skelton		Sep	1939—Mar	1940
W/Cdr T. Humble		Mar	1940—Jun	1940
S/Ldr R. E. S. Skelton		Jun	1940—Jun	1941
W/Cdr P. W. Stansfeld		Jun	1941—Jul	1942
W/Cdr J. R. Davenport		Jul	1942—	1943
W/Cdr R. I. M. Bowen			1943—Jun	1943
S/Ldr K. F. Mackie, DFC		Jun	1943—Sep	1943
S/Ldr E. M. Goodale, DSO		Sep	1943—Aug	1944
S/Ldr A. N. Davis, DFC		Aug	1944—Sep	1945

Aircraft Insignia

No unit insignia was carried until April, 1916 from when two bands were painted around the fuselage one each side of the roundel. These were black on clear-doped aircraft and white on khaki-drab aircraft. This was retained until the end of World War I. It is not known what the post-war Bristol Fighter carried but the Atlas and Audax both had one black band around the fuselage; on the Atlas it was aft of the roundel and on the Audax forward. In addition the Audax carried the Squadron emblem in a white six-pointed star on the fin from 1937 onwards. The Lysanders carried the code letters 'KJ' from 1938 until September 1939 when the letters were changed, possibly initially to 'EE' but by the time of moving to France they had become 'UG'. This code remained at least until 1942 after which it is believed that no squadron insignia was carried.
(See also *Fighter Squadrons of the RAF*, pp. 41–2, and *Bomber Squadrons of the RAF*, pp. 37 & 387–8)

No. 17 SQUADRON

BADGE
A gauntlet

MOTTO
'Excellere contende'
('Strive to excel')

The badge symbolises armed strength and also commemorates the type of aircraft the Squadron was flying when the badge was awarded.

No. 17 Squadron was formed at Gosport on 1 February, 1915 for service overseas and, with No. 14 Squadron, formed 5 Wing in Egypt. Here it began an existence of many detachments for its task was to serve in three separate areas. In the Western Desert based at El Hammam part of the Squadron flew daily recces to keep an eye on the Senussi, another detachment went to Suez to fight against the Turks in Sinai, whilst the rest of the Squadron fought the same enemy in Arabia, with HQ at Heliopolis. Basically it was equipped with B.E.2c's and variants, with Bristol Scouts and D.H.2s for escort duties, but other types came and went. In April, 1916 the Suez detachment went to the Sudan where it flew recces in the battle of El Fasher on 15 May.

In July, 1916 the whole Squadron was transferred to Salonika as the first RFC unit in this area, where it flew daily visual recces together with wireless and photo flights for XVI Corps. On 13 December, 1916 the presence of the scouts was justified when Lt G. W. Murlis-Green shot down a German aircraft and in February, 1917 the German raids with AEGs became more frequent; Murlis-Green scored another victory on 18 March.

In March, 1917 the Squadron flew its own bombing raids (B.E.2c's escorted by B.E.12s), and these raids became a stable feature of the Squadron's life in addition to its army work. In 1918 it was at last established on a one-type basis with A.W. F.K.8s and the following month the scouts, now S.E.5As, were hived off into No. 150 Squadron. For the rest of the war No. 17 flew mainly reconnaissance duties until the final offensive on Bulgaria when it was engaged in intensive ground-strafing sorties on the retreating Bulgars. With the war over the Squadron retired to Constantinople except for A Flight which went to Batum to fight the Bolsheviks until 14 November, 1919 when it disbanded at Constantinople.

No. 17 re-formed on 1 April, 1924 as a fighter squadron at Hawkinge and served the major part of its existence in this role, flying Hurricanes in the Battle of Britain in 1940, then transferring to Burma where it fought throughout that campaign with Hurricanes and later Spitfires, taking the latter as part of the occupation forces in Japan until February, 1948. For two years from March, 1949 it served as an AAC squadron, based at Chivenor, and was then re-formed on an operational basis at Wahn on 1 June, 1956 as a photo-recce squadron in RAF Germany. It was equipped with English Electric Canberra PR.7s and was operational on high and low-level photo reconnaissance duties from that year. It moved to its permanent base, Wildenrath, in April, 1957, remaining there on this task for twelve years. It eventually disbanded there in June, 1969.

Sixteen months later No. 17 Squadron reverted to the fighter/ground attack role when it was re-formed with Phantoms, and subsequently Jaguars, at Brüggen.

Bases etc.

Formed at Gosport on 1 February, 1915.

Gosport	Feb 1915—Nov 1915	
en route to Egypt	Nov 1915—Dec 1915	
Gabbari	Dec 1915—Dec 1915	
Heliopolis, det. El Hammam, Fayoum, Minia, Assiut, Suez, Gehel, Mikra Bay, Lahana, Avret Hisar, Orljak, Amberkoj	Dec 1915—Jul 1916	
Mikra Bay, det. Avret Hisar, Lahana, Orljak, Amberkoj	Jul 1916—Dec 1917	
Lahana, det. Avret Hisar, Orljak, Amberkoj, Marian	Dec 1917—Sep 1918	
Amberkoj, det. Stojakovo, Rabova, Phillipopolis, Mustapha Pasha	Sep 1918—Jan 1919	
Batum, det. Kars, Tiflis, San Stefano	Jan 1919—Nov 1919	

Disbanded at San Stefano on 14 November, 1919. Re-formed as a fighter squadron at Hawkinge on 1 April, 1924. Re-formed at Wahn in the photo reconnaissance role at Wahn on 1 June, 1956.

Wahn	Jun 1956—Apr 1957
Wildenrath	Apr 1957—Jun 1969

Disbanded at Wildenrath on 12 June, 1969. Reformed in the fighter/ground attack role at Brüggen on 16 October, 1970.

Main Equipment

B.E.2c (Feb 1915—1918)
2125; 2078; 4124; 4149; 4345; 4444; 4522; 4574; 5413; 5422; 5438
B.E.2e (Apr 1917—Apr 1918)
6803; 6811; A1269; A1335; A1386; A3084; A3085
D.H.1A (Dec 1916—Jan 1917)
4612

D.H.2 (Feb 1917—Nov 1917)
A2586; A4769
Bristol Scout D (Aug 1916—Nov 1916)
5321; 5324; 5599
Nieuport Scout (Aug 1916—Apr 1918)
N.1228; 3284; 3492; 3781; 4507; 5177; 5514
B.E.12 (Nov 1916—Jun 1918)
6600; 6601; 6605; 6675; A4006; A4007
B.E.12a (Jun 1917—Oct 1918)
A6327; A6330; A6334
Avro 504C (Aug 1917—1917)
1476
AW. F.K.3A (Jul 1917—Sep 1917)
5528; 6200; A1466
Bristol M.1C (Mar 1918—Apr 1918)
C4906; C4912; C4913
S.E.5A (Jan 1918—Apr 1918)
B28; B613; B690; B693; B694
A. W. F.K.8 (Mar 1918—Dec 1918)
B3331; B3337; B3353; B3385; B3596; C3600; C3696; C4811
D.H.9 (Oct 1918—Nov 1919)
C6215; C6233; C6299; C6336; C6339; D2837; D2845; D3151
Sopwith Camel (1919—Nov 1919)
C1600; D6549; D6641; E5170; E5172; F1911
English Electric Canberra PR.7 (Jun 1956—Dec 1969)
WH792; WH801, X; WH804; WJ817; WT507; WT513; WT525, R; WT533; WT538
T.Mk.4:
WT479; WT487

Commanding Officers

Maj E. N. Fuller	Feb 1915—Dec 1916
Capt F. Hudson	Dec 1916—Dec 1917
Maj J. H. Herring	Dec 1917—Apr 1918
Maj S. G. Hodges, MC	Apr 1918—Nov 1919
S/Ldr B. R. M. Wade, DFC	Jun 1956—Feb 1959
W/Cdr D. T. M. Lumsden, MBE	Feb 1959—Sep 1961
W/Cdr D. G. Walker	Sep 1961—
W/Cdr M. J. Armitage	—Dec 1969

Aircraft Insignia

It is not believed that the aircraft flown by No. 17 Squadron between February, 1915 and November, 1919 carried any squadron insignia or identity markings. The Canberras carried a white disc on the fin with a double black zigzag on it and on the nose the Squadron badge with a white rectangle each side with the double black zigzag again.
(See also *Fighter Squadrons of the RAF*, pp. 42–7 and 563)

No. 18 SQUADRON

BADGE
A Pegasus rampant

MOTTO
'Animo et fide'
('With courage and faith')

The Pegasus was chosen to commemorate the unit being the first to co-operate with the Cavalry Corps in the Somme in World War I.

On 11 May, 1915 No. 18 Squadron was formed from a nucleus of No. 4 Reserve Squadron at Northolt. At first it served in the training role with diverse types of aircraft but in November, 1915 it went to France equipped, in the main, with the Vickers F.B.5. With these it flew fighter and recce sorties from Treizennes and Auchel, re-equipping with the F.E.2B with which it broadened its activities to artillery observation and contact patrols with the Cavalry Corps on the Somme. Bombing was also undertaken and this led up to No. 18 becoming entirely a bombing squadron in June, 1917 when it re-equipped with the D.H.4. It fought on in this role until the war was over and then disbanded in September, 1919.

No. 18 re-formed as a bomber squadron at Upper Heyford with Hawker Harts and by the outbreak of war in 1939 was flying Blenheim IVs which it used in the daylight bombing of the Continent, also operating from Malta on anti-shipping work. It took part in the liberation of North Africa in November, 1942 and it was here,

flying Blenheim VAs, that the Squadron made heroic attacks and was rewarded with a posthumous VC for its CO, W/Cdr H. G. Malcolm. Soon after it converted to Bostons and flew on in support of the Sicilian, Italian and Southern France campaigns. No. 18 Squadron was disbanded at Hassani on 31 March, 1946. On 1 September, 1946 it re-formed at Ein Shemer by re-numbering No. 621 Squadron in the maritime role with Lancaster GR.3s but fourteen days later was again disbanded. On 15 March, 1947 No. 18 re-formed at Kabrit as a light bomber squadron with Mosquito FB.6s and served in the Canal Zone until 15 November, 1947 when it was re-numbered as No. 1300 (Met) Flight.

Its next existence was as a Transport squadron, being re-formed at Netheravon on 8 December, 1947 with Douglas Dakota C.4s. Hardly had it worked up with these than it became involved in the Berlin Airlift, at first detached to Germany and then being based at Fassberg from July to October, 1948. This was maintained until the airlift was over in 1949; by then the Dakota force was far greater than needed and amongst the Squadrons surplus was No. 18 which disbanded at Oakington on 20 February, 1950. The Squadron then reverted to the bomber role flying Canberras from August, 1953 to February, 1957 and Valiants from December, 1958 to April, 1963.

On 27 January, 1964 No. 18 Squadron appeared once more when the Intensive Flying Trials Unit at Odiham, which had been working the Westland Wessex HC.2 helicopter into service, was expanded into a full squadron. Its role was that of battlefield support and a year later it went to Gütersloh as support to BAOR. Whilst there it maintained a Flight in Nicosia for United Nations peace-keeping duties. In January, 1968 the Squadron returned to the UK and was attached to the army in this country until August, 1970 when it returned to Gütersloh where it has subsequently served.

It was disbanded there on 1 December, 1980. On 4 August, 1981 No. 18 re-formed at Odiham as the RAF's first squadron to operate the Boeing Vertol Chinook HC.1 medium-lift helicopter. In due course it will ply this in support role in Germany from Gütersloh.

Bases etc.

Formed at Northolt on 11 May, 1915 from No. 4 Reserve Squadron

Northolt	May 1915—Aug 1915
Norwich	Aug 1915—Nov 1915
St. Omer	Nov 1915—Nov 1915
Treizennes	Nov 1915—Feb 1916
Auchel	Feb 1916—Apr 1916
Bruay	Apr 1916—Jul 1916
Treizennes	Jul 1916—Aug 1916
Bruay	Aug 1916—Sep 1916
Lavieville	Sep 1916—Dec 1916
St. Leger-les-Authie	Dec 1916—Jan 1917
Bertangles	Jan 1917—May 1917
Baizieux	May 1917—Jun 1917

In June, 1917 it was re-organised fully in the bomber role. It served in this role until March, 1946. On 1 September, 1946 it was re-formed in the maritime reconnaissance role at Ein Shemer by re-numbering No. 621 Squadron.

Ein Shemer	Sep 1946—Sep 1946

It was again disbanded at Ein Shemer on 15 September, 1946. On 15 March, 1947 it re-formed at Kabrit.

Kabrit	Mar 1947—Mar 1947
Mingaladon	Mar 1947— 1947
Changi	1947—Nov 1947

It was disbanded at Changi, Singapore, on 15 November, 1947 by renumbering as No. 1300 (Met.) Flight. Three weeks later it re-formed in the UK in the transport role at Netheravon on 8 December, 1947.

Netheravon	Dec 1947—Dec 1947
Waterbeach, det. Wunstorf	Dec 1947—Jul 1948
Fassberg	Jul 1948—Oct 1948
Waterbeach	Oct 1948—Oct 1948
Lübeck	Oct 1948—Jan 1949
Oakington	Jan 1949—Feb 1950

Disbanded at Oakington on 20 February, 1950. It was re-formed in the bomber role again at Scampton on 1 August, 1953, eventually ending that role at Finningley on 31 March 1963. On 27 January, 1964 it re-formed in the helicopter battlefield support role at Odiham.

Odiham	Jan 1964—Jan 1965
Gütersloh, det. Nicosia	Jan 1965—Jan 1968
Abingdon	Jan 1968—Jul 1969
Odiham	Jul 1969—Aug 1970
Gütersloh, det. Wildenrath	Aug 1970—Dec 1980

Disbanded at Gütersloh on 1 December, 1980. Re-formed at Odiham on 4 August, 1981.

Odiham	Aug 1981—

Main Equipment (other than in the bomber role)

D.H.2 (Nov 1915—Apr 1916)
5916; 5919
Vickers F.B.5 (Oct 1915—Apr 1916)
No serials known
F.E.2b (Apr 1916—Jun 1917)
4898; 4967; 4984; 4995; A785; A863; A5443; A5474; A5483; A5502
Avro Lancaster GR.3 (Sep 1946—Sep 1946)
RF313, F; RF302, B; RF322, T; SW288, G; SW295, L
de Havilland Mosquito FB.6 (Mar 1947—Nov 1947)
TE879; TW110, N; (T.Mk.3)
Douglas Dakota C.4 (Dec 1947—Feb 1950)
KK131; KN217; KN446; KN499; KN506; KN553; KN566; KN607
Westland Wessex HC.2 (Jan 1964—)
XR499, A; XR504, F, later BF; XR508, K; XR518 L, later BL, later BB; XR521, BK; XS679, BP; XT603, BT; XT676, BG; XT681, Q, later BA; XV724, BQ; XV731, BZ
Boeing Vertol Chinook HC.1 (Aug 1981—)
ZA670, BS; ZA680, BW; ZA682, BY; ZA704, BU

Commanding Officers

Maj G. I. Carmichael, DSO	May 1915—Dec 1916
Maj R. S. Maxwell, MC	Dec 1916—Mar 1917
Maj G. R. M. Reid, MC	Mar 1917—Jun 1917
W/Cdr B. E. Peck	Sep 1946—Sep 1946
S/Ldr R. M. Burns	Dec 1947—May 1948
S/Ldr J. D. Kirwan, DFC	May 1948—Feb 1950
S/Ldr H. H. J. Browning	Jan 1964—Jan 1965
S/Ldr P. G. C. Wilson	Jan 1965—Oct 1966
W/Cdr P. R. Harding	Oct 1966—Oct 1969
W/Cdr P. L. Gray	Oct 1969—Dec 1971
W/Cdr I. S. C. Jones, AFC	Dec 1971—Nov 1973
W/Cdr J. E. Maitland	Nov 1973—Mar 1976
W/Cdr J. W. Canning	Mar 1976—Mar 1978
W/Cdr A. F. C. Hunter, AFC	Mar 1978—Dec 1980
W/Cdr A. J. Stables	Aug 1981—

Aircraft Insignia

In World War I no distinctive squadron insignia was carried before transferring to the bombing role. As far as is known the Lancaster, Mosquito and Dakota periods were also without such markings. However since equipped with Wessexes the Squadron has carried the Pegasus emblem in red on a disc on the fin, originally white but since the mid-1970's on a black disc. In addition it has carried two-letter codes since 1970, the 'B' denoting No. 18 Squadron and the following letter being the aircraft letter.
(See also *Bomber Squadrons of the RAF*, pp. 37—40)

No. 20 SQUADRON

BADGE
In front of a rising sun an eagle, wings elevated, perched on a sword
MOTTO
'Facta non verba'
('Deeds not words')

No. 20 Squadron was formed at Netheravon on 1 September, 1915 as one of the first entirely fighter squadrons (known as scout squadrons at the time). Equipped with F.E.2Bs it fought in France from January, 1916 until the Armistice, the F.E.s giving place to Bristol Fighters in August, 1917. After the war No. 20 sailed for India where it became an army co-operation squadron being based at Risalpur.

Here it was immediately thrown into the Third Afghan War, being sent on three detachments of four aircraft each at Tank, Bannu and Sora Rogha. Flying bombing and strafing raids against the tribesmen was a daunting task and more than one crew was lost either to sniping rifle fire or to the hazardous territory. As time went on the Squadron was hampered by lack of spares but continued to fly as much as possible. This spares situation was remedied later on in the 'twenties and the Squadron, flying from Peshawar, soldiered on with Brisfits until May, 1931 when it was re-equipped with the Westland Wapiti. These were used on the same task for four years and then replaced by Hawker Audax Is. It continued to serve in the

North-West Frontier area, in the sporadic war situation there, until February, 1941 when A and B Flights were detached to Bombay and Madras for coastal defence. It now had some Lysanders and A Flight acquired some Blenheim Is as well. At the end of the year No. 20 was completely equipped with Lysander IIs as an army co-operation squadron in Eastern Command but in May most of the Squadron retired to Peshawar to form No. 151 OTU. A small nucleus remained from which a new No. 20 was built. In July it sent a detachment to Tezpur for operations but the aircraft was no use at this altitude. However, in August it flew operationally with 22nd Division, Chinese Army, on message picking-up duties and low-level photo recce. In September, 1942 it made five abortive attempts to reach Imphal from Tezpur, whilst the main part of the Squadron was now flying internal security flights from Jamshedpur. In October the detachment moved to Feni and flew recces whilst the main body of the Squadron flew AA co-operation. On 1 November it managed to reach Imphal and flew tactical recces from there and Feni. One particularly fine sortie was flown by Sgt Carmichael in P9107 when he bombed buildings at Maungdaw and killed 28 soldiers. In January, 1943 Hurricane IIBs arrived for the main Tac/R work, the Lysanders turning to ASR duties at Feni. These double duties continued until March, 1943 when the Squadron became a fighter (ground attack) unit with Hurricane IIBs and IIDs.

It fought the war out with Hurricanes in the Burmese campaign, converting to Spitfires after the war was over. These it took to Siam, returning to India to receive Tempest F.2s but disbanding at Agra in June, 1946. No. 20 re-formed in March, 1949 as an AAC squadron at Llanbedr until 14 June, 1952 when it again disbanded. Later that year No. 20 re-formed as a fighter squadron in 2nd TAF, Germany with, successively, Vampires, Sabres and Hunters for eight years, disbanding in 1960. The next year it re-formed with Hunters in Singapore for ten years. Disbanding at Tengah on 1 February, 1970 No. 20 re-formed at Wildenrath on 1 December that year with Hawker Siddeley Harriers serving with the RAF Germany Harrier Wing until the end of 1976 when it was disbanded by being combined into Nos. 3 and 4 Squadrons. The next month No. 20 was again re-formed at Brüggen in Germany with Sepecat Jaguar GR.1s.

Bases etc.

Became an army co-operation squadron at Risalpur 19 June, 1919.
Risalpur, det. Tank, Bannu, Parachinar,

Sora Rogha	Jun 1919—Oct 1921	
Ambala	Oct 1921—Oct 1922	
Quetta	Oct 1922—Jan 1925	
Peshawar, det. Miranshah	Jan 1925—Apr 1937	
Miranshah	Apr 1937—Oct 1937	
Peshawar, det. Miranshah, Kohat	Oct 1937—Aug 1939	
Miranshah, det. Manzai	Aug 1939—Dec 1939	
Peshawar, det. Kohat, Miranshah	Dec 1939—Apr 1940	
Kohat, det. Madras	Apr 1940—Jun 1941	
Secunderabad	Jun 1941—Mar 1942	
Peshawar	Mar 1942—May 1942	
Chakulia	May 1942—Jun 1941	
Jamshedpur, det. Tezpur, Feni, Imphal	Jun 1942—Nov 1942	
Charra	Nov 1942—Mar 1943	

In March, 1942 it became a fighter squadron in which role it has served ever since.

Main Equipment (in the army co-op role)
Bristol F.2B (Jun 1919—Feb 1932)
C957; D8039; E2429; E2605; F4446; F4602; F4720; F4947; H1428; H1508; J6588; J6638; J6656; J6741; J6792; J7682

Westland Wapiti IIA (May 1931—Dec 1935)
K1126; K1277; K1294; K2296
Hawker Audax I (Dec 1935—Dec 1941)
K3117; K4838; K4843; K4847; K4851; K4859, HN:E; K4862; K5567; K5572; K5577; K5580; K5585
Westland Lysander II (May 1939—Mar 1943)
L4740; L4776, HN:A; L6886; N1217, HN:C; N1251, HN:X; N1270 HN:A; N1314; P1669; P1734, HN:B; P9067, HN:M; P9138; R1991, HN:D; R2026; DG445, HN:K
Bristol Blenheim I (Jun 1941—Dec 1941)
L8404. No other known serials
Hawker Hurricane IIB (Jan 1943—)
BN135; BN699

Commanding Officers

Maj J. C. Russell	Jun 1919—Apr 1920
S/Ldr J. H. S. Tyssen	Apr 1920—Jan 1924
S/Ldr C. B. Cooke	Jan 1924—Oct 1925
S/Ldr J. B. Cole-Hamilton	Oct 1925—Jul 1926
S/Ldr J. C. Steele	Jul 1926—May 1928
S/Ldr C. H. Nicholas	May 1928—Apr 1930
S/Ldr L. O. Brown	Apr 1930—Nov 1932
S/Ldr L. W. Hollinghurst	Nov 1932—Oct 1934
S/Ldr N. McG. Fairweather	Oct 1924—May 1936
S/Ldr L. de V. Chisman	May 1936—Oct 1937
S/Ldr R. J. Carvell	Oct 1937—Nov 1937
S/Ldr B. E. Embry	Nov 1937—Oct 1938
S/Ldr R. C. Mead	Oct 1938— 1939
S/Ldr O. H. D. Blomfield	1939— 1941
S/Ldr W. Surplice, DFC	1941—Oct 1941
S/Ldr Trall, DFC	Oct 1941—Mar 1942
S/Ldr F. F. Lambert, DFC	Apr 1942—Jun 1942
S/Ldr H. G. Fletcher, DFC	Jun 1942—Mar 1943

Aircraft Insignia

The Bristol Fighters in India carried a black band around the fuselage from at least 1924 until being re-equipped with Wapitis. It is not known what markings these latter bore but the Hawker Audaxes had a black band around the fuselage forward of the roundel at first. In 1939 the Squadron was allotted the two-letter code combination 'PM' but it is not known whether this was carried. This was changed to 'HN' in September, 1939 and this combination was carried both on the Lysanders and the Audaxes and Hurricanes.

(See also *Fighter Squadrons of the RAF*, pp. 54–7 & 564)

No. 21 SQUADRON

BADGE
A hand erased at the wrist, holding a dumb-bell

MOTTO
'Viribus vincimus'
('By strength we conquer')

The dumb-bell was used as an unofficial badge by the Squadron in 1917 and signifies strength.

The Squadron was formed on 23 July, 1915 at Netheravon and received the R.E.7 as its main equipment. This type it took to France in January, 1916, becoming operational the following month on bombing and long-range reconnaissance sorties. In the Somme offensive it was mainly bombing but the aircraft had engine troubles and many forced landings ensued. In July, 1916 B.E.12s replaced the R.E.s and a more army-orientated period of operations followed with line patrols, although many gun batteries were bombed in the Messines offensive in 1917. With the advent of R.E.8s that year No. 21 became a corps squadron entirely and flew line recces, artillery shoots, photo sorties, contact patrols and message dropping until the Armistice. It was particularly to the fore in the Messines offensive. It returned to the UK in February, 1919 and was disbanded at Fowlmere on 1 October, 1919.

When No. 21 re-formed on 3 December, 1935 at Bircham Newton it was as a light bomber squadron and it has remained as such for most of its history. By the outbreak of war it had Blenheim IVs and flew many sorties against enemy shipping as well as daylight low-level raids on the Low Countries. In 1942 it re-equipped with the Ventura and a year later with the Mosquito, carrying on the offensive with 2 Group until the war ended. It was disbanded in 1947,

after which it flew two periods as a Canberra squadron, finally relinquishing this role on 15 January, 1959.

On 1 May, 1959 No. 21 became a light transport squadron when it was re-formed at Benson with Scottish Aviation Twin Pioneer CC.1s. Four months later it took these to Kenya where it flew both communications and army support roles, with the British army, the King's African Rifles and the police. This was continued until June, 1965 when it was disbanded at Nairobi. At the same time No. 78 Squadron at Aden was re-numbered No. 21 and the Squadron continued the same roles in the Aden Protectorate with Twin Pioneers, and also Andover CC.2 and Dakota C.4 aircraft, this period lasting until September, 1967. On 3 February, 1969 No. 21 again re-formed in the communications role at Andover with Devons and Pembrokes until 31 March, 1976.

Bases etc.

Formed at Netheravon on 23 July, 1915.

Netheravon	Jul 1915—Jan 1916
Boisdinghem	Jan 1916—Apr 1916
St. André-aux-Bois	Apr 1916—Jun 1916
Fienvillers	Jun 1916—Jul 1916
Boisdinghem	Jul 1916—Aug 1916
Bertangles	Aug 1916—Feb 1917
Boisdinghem	Feb 1917—Mar 1917
Droglandt	Mar 1917—May 1917
La Lovie	May 1917—Apr 1918
St. Inglevert	Apr 1918—Apr 1918
Floringhem	Apr 1918—Oct 1918
Hesdigneul	Oct 1918—Oct 1918
Seclin	Oct 1918—Nov 1918
Froidmont	Nov 1918—Nov 1918
Sweveghem	Nov 1918—Dec 1918

Coucou   Dec 1918—Feb 1919
Fowlmere   Feb 1919—Oct 1919
Disbanded at Fowlmere on 1 October, 1919. Re-formed at Bircham Newton
on 3 December, 1935 in the bomber role in which it served until 15 January,
1959. Re-formed in the communications and army support role at Benson on
1 May, 1959.
Benson   May 1959—Sep 1959
Eastleigh (Nairobi)   Sep 1959—Jun 1965
Disbanded at Nairobi in June, 1965. At the same time re-formed at Khor-
maksar by re-numbering No. 78 Squadron.
Khormaksar   Jun 1965—Sep 1967
Disbanded at Khormaksar in September, 1967. Re-formed at Andover by
re-numbering Western Comms. Squadron on 3 February, 1969.
Andover   Feb 1969—Mar 1976
Disbanded at Andover on 31 March, 1976.

Main Equipment

R.E.7 (Jul 1915—Jul 1916)
2194; 2372; 2373; 2375; 2377; 2380
B.E.12 (Jul 1916—Feb 1917)
6573, 4; 6646
R.E.8 (Feb 1917—Feb 1919)
A115; A4351, 2; A3666; A3747; B5855; B5897; B5927; C2359; C2399;
C2478; C2736; D4815; D4932; D6745; E31; E89; E246; F5901
Twin Pioneer CC.1 (May 1959—Sep 1967)
XM283; XM286; XM291; XM939; XM957; XM960, C; XM163, B
Hawker Siddeley Andover CC.2 (Jun 1965—Sep 1967)
XS791; XS793

Douglas Dakota C.4 (Jun 1965—Sep 1967)
KJ955
de Havilland Devon C.2 (Feb 1969—Mar 1976)
VP952; VP956; VP961; VP973; VP976
Hunting Percival Pembroke C.1 (Feb 1969—Mar 1976)
WV701; WV733; WV740; WV746; XK885; XF798
Westland Whirlwind HAR.10 (—Mar 1976)
XP330

Commanding Officers

Maj F. W. Richey	Jul 1915—Apr 1916
Maj R. C. Heathcote	Apr 1916—Feb 1917
Maj P. L. Gethin	Feb 1917—Jul 1917
Maj L. T. N. Gould	Jul 1917—Sep 1918
Maj A. A. Walser	Sep 1918—Dec 1918
Capt J. R. Hopkins	Dec 1918—Oct 1919
S/Ldr W. J. Bishop, MBE	May 1959—
F/Lt E. Ginger	— 1964
F/Lt A. E. F. Pullen	1964—Jun 1965
S/Ldr P. Cornish	Feb 1969— 1970
S/Ldr N. C. Lea	1970—
S/Ldr B. Butterworth	—

Aircraft Insignia

From the inception of the B.E.12 the Squadron carried a white, horizontal
dumb-bell on its aircraft in World War I. No insignia was carried on the
comms. aircraft from 1959 onwards apart from the standard badge carried
below the pilot's cockpit from time to time on some aircraft.
(See also *Bomber Squadrons of the RAF*, pp. 40–1)

No. 22 SQUADRON

BADGE
On a torteau, a Maltese cross throughout,
overall a 'π' fimbriated.

MOTTO
'Preux et Audacieux'
('Valiant and Brave')

Whilst serving in France its aircraft often took
off over 7th Wing HQ. The equation 22/7 is
well known mathematically as 'pi', so the
Greek sign 'pi' was adopted by the Squadron
and placed on a Maltese cross as it was
serving in Malta at the time the badge was
approved.

No. 22 formed at Gosport on 1 September, 1915 and went to France
as a scout (fighter) squadron. It fought throughout World War I in
this role, re-equipping with Bristol Fighters in 1917, with which it
flew many bomber escorts. It was disbanded at Ford on 31
December, 1919. The Squadron was re-formed on 24 July, 1923 as
an adjunct to the Aeroplane and Armament Experimental Establishment (AAEE) at Martlesham Heath. However, this research role
ended in 1934 when the Squadron was disbanded and re-formed on
the same day (1 May) at Donibristle with six Vickers Vildebeest
torpedo-bombers. It immediately began torpedo training and by
September was flying in exercises with the Home Fleet to which it
was committed for much of its work. This continued until October
1935 when it moved to Malta in view of the Abyssinian crisis,
remaining there, to attack the Italian fleet if necessary, until August,
1936. On its return B Flight was expanded to squadron status and
became No. 42 Squadron but so short were aircraft that both units
shared the same machines. It returned to its preoccupation with the
Home Fleet and moved to Thorney Island in March, 1938, mobilis-
ing in September that year because of the Munich crisis.

When war broke out No. 22 was still flying Vildebeests using
them for anti-submarine patrols in the Channel although its first
Bristol Beaufort arrived in November. By April, 1940 it had worked
up on this type and began operations with mine-laying sorties. In
May it threw its weight into the action off Dunkirk bombing a
cruiser off Nordeney on 7th, followed by Dutch oil depots and
shipping. The following month it came off ops for two months to
sort out Beaufort problems and for Toraplane* training; it also

An unsuccessful experimental winged torpedo

received three Marylands for evaluation in the Coastal roles unsuccessfully. That month bombing was resumed and the first torpedo
attack by No. 22 Squadron was made in September against a convoy
at Calais. It now settled into a regular operational routine of mining,
shipping *Rovers* with mines both off the Dutch coast and in the
Western Approaches with a detachment at St. Eval.

This was continued into 1941 with the aircraft ranging further
eastwards over the North Sea. In eight sorties in March 16,500 tons
of shipping was destroyed for the loss of two aircraft, whilst the
detachment at St. Eval turned its attention to the *Scharnhorst* and
Gneisenau in the French Atlantic ports, during which F/O Kenneth
Campbell, flying N1016 OA:T, made a courageous lone attack on
the latter in Brest, putting it out of action for nine months; he and
his crew died in the attack and he was awarded a posthumous VC.
Detachments were made to various places depending where shipping was to be attacked, Squadron aircraft going as far afield as
Iceland. Many ships were damaged or sunk but this was not without
loss; in August fourteen crews were lost in operations or flying
accidents. In October the whole Squadron concentrated at St. Eval
but by the end of the year No. 22 came off operations; in 27 months
it had sunk over 100,000 tons of enemy shipping.

In January, 1942 No. 22 was posted overseas, its aircrews going
to No. 86 Squadron and the long journey began. By May it was
assembled at Ratmalana, Ceylon and began flying in co-operation
with the fleet. However, coastal strike opportunities were minimal
in the Indian Ocean and although it began anti-shipping patrols in
December and convoy and ASR duties as well no action came the
Beauforts' way. In May, 1944 it re-equipped with Beaufighters and
operations began in July initially with torpedo but later with RP
armament. It was now involved in the Burma fighting, flying strikes
against coastal and river shipping around the Irrawaddy Delta
adding day and night *Rhubarbs* to its repertoire. By March, 1945 it
had reached a tempo of 680 operational hours in the month with two
seagoing vessels destroyed and eight damaged, flying more operations than any other in the Wing. May saw it fighting in Operation
Dracula (the capture of Rangoon) but thereafter, flying tailed off
and No. 22 was disbanded at Gannavarum on 30 September, 1945.
In May, 1946 it was re-formed with Mosquito FB.6s but four
months later was again disbanded there, on 30 September, 1945.

A long pause followed but on 15 February, 1955 No. 22 re-
formed in a very different role. Equipped with Westland Whirlwind
HAR.2 and Bristol Sycamore HC.14 helicopters it established

search and rescue Flights around the south and east coasts. The Squadron was in at the beginning of what has become a major role of the RAF in peacetime in providing a force of rescue helicopters for military and civilian rescue. The Sycamores did not last long with No. 22 but over the years the Squadron has flown the Whirlwind on very many rescue tasks. Within eighteen months it had earned its first George Medal when AC2 Martin winched two unconscious survivors from a sinking yacht and the following spring (1957) F/Sgt Prim took aboard eleven crew from a trawler in the North Sea, more than the Whirlwind was designed for. This heroic pattern has been followed down the years; a training flight was established at St. Mawgan in July, 1959 as the service expanded and through the 'sixties its Whirlwinds were continually operational in this role. The Westland Wessex supplemented the Whirlwind with the Squadron in 1976. The Whirlwind was phased out on 30 November, 1981.

Bases etc.

Formed 1 September, 1915 at Gosport and served in France on fighter duties until disbanded at Ford on 31 December, 1919. Re-formed at Martlesham Heath on 24 July, 1923 for testing duties with the A&AEE, disbanded there on 1 May, 1934. Re-formed at Donibristle on 1 May, 1934 as a torpedo-bomber squadron.

Donibristle	May 1934—Oct 1935
Hal Far	Oct 1935—Sep 1936
Donibristle	Sep 1936—Mar 1938
Thorney Island, det. Detling	Mar 1938—Apr 1940
North Coates, det. Wick, Gosport, St. Eval, Iceland, Leuchars, Bircham Newton	Apr 1940—Oct 1941
St. Eval	Oct 1941—Mar 1942
en route to Ceylon	Mar 1942—May 1942
Ratmalana	May 1942—Sep 1942
Minneriya, det. Ratmalana, Vavuyina	Sep 1942—Feb 1943
Vavuyina, det. Santa Cruz	Feb 1943—Apr 1944
Ratmalana	Apr 1944—Jul 1944
Vavuyina	Jul 1944—Dec 1944
Kumbhirgram	Dec 1944—Jan 1945
Dohazari	Jan 1945—Jan 1945
Joari	Jan 1945—Apr 1945
Chiringa	Apr 1945—Jun 1945
Gannavarum	Jun 1945—Sep 1945

Disbanded at Gannavarum 30 September, 1945. Re-formed by re-numbering No. 89 Squadron at Seletar on 1 May, 1946.

Seletar	May 1946—Aug 1946

Disbanded at Seletar on 15 August, 1946. Re-formed at Thorney Island in the SAR role on 2 February, 1955.

Thorney Island, det. Martlesham Heath, Felixstowe & Valley	Feb 1955—Jun 1956
St. Mawgan, det. Chivenor, Felixstowe, Tangmere, Thorney Island, Valley, Christmas Island, Brawdy, Manston	Jun 1956—
Finningley, det. Brawdy, Valley, Coltishall, Manston	

Main Equipment

Vickers Vildebeest I (May 1934—Sep 1938)
S1708; K2810; K2812, 5; K2822

Vickers Vildebeest III (1936—Feb 1940)
K4156; K4157; K4160; K4187, OA:Y; K4588; K4591; K4596, OA:Z; K4602; K4606; K4612, OA:D; K6395; K6397

Bristol Beaufort I (Nov 1939—Jun 1944)
L4461, OA:J; L4475, OA:E; L4516 OA:W; L9792, OA:G; L9817, OA:F; L9891, OA:F; L9939, OA:L; N1082, OA:J; N1144, OA:C; N1171, OA:H; W6537, OA:F; X8934, OA: ; AW220, Q; DD947, U; DD987, Y; DW814, H; DW858, X; DW922, S; DW939, G; EK987, K; JM509, Q

Bristol Beaufighter X (Jun 1944—Sep 1945)
NE407, H; NE478, V; NE629, Q; NE716, B; RD515, Q

Westland Whirlwind HAR.2 (Feb 1955— 1963)
XD165, K; XJ432, B; XJ435; XJ727; XJXJ756; XJ763, L; XL109

Bristol Sycamore HC.14 (May 1955—Jun 1955)
No serials known

Westland Whirlwind HAR.10 (1962—Nov 1981)
XD165; XD186; XJ426; XJ765; XL112; XP347; XP351; XP354; XP361; XR457

Westland Wessex HAR.2 (Nov 1976—)
XR518; XR588; XS675

Commanding Officers

S/Ldr T. A. Warne-Browne	May 1934—Sep 1935
S/Ldr R. J. M. de St. Leger	Sep 1935—Apr 1937
S/Ldr W. G. Campbell	Apr 1937—Mar 1938
S/Ldr M. V. Ridgeway	Mar 1938—Nov 1939
W/Cdr H. M. Mellor	Nov 1939—May 1940
W/Cdr F. J. St. G. Braithwaite	Jun 1940—Aug 1941
W/Cdr J. C. Mayhew	Aug 1941—Dec 1941
W/Cdr W. A. L. Davis	Dec 1941—Jan 1942
S/Ldr J. A. Bateson	Jan 1942—Oct 1943
W/Cdr J. M. Lander, DFC	Oct 1943—Jan 1945
W/Cdr C. R. Gee, DFC	Feb 1945—Sep 1945
W/Cdr A. Pleasance, CBE, DFC	May 1946—Aug 1946
S/Ldr P. C. Bowry	Feb 1955—Jan 1957
S/Ldr J. R. Ritchie, AFC	Jan 1957—Nov 1958
S/Ldr A. P. Dunn	Nov 1958—Mar 1961
S/Ldr G. L. Verran	Mar 1961—Jun 1962
S/Ldr L. A. Barber	Jun 1962—Jul 1964
S/Ldr I. C. Annable	Jul 1964—Aug 1966
S/Ldr D. A. W. Todman, DFC	Aug 1966—Jul 1968
S/Ldr A. Salter	Jul 1968—Aug 1970
S/Ldr J. Weaver	Aug 1970—Apr 1972
S/Ldr J. W. Hoskins	Apr 1972—Nov 1974
S/Ldr C. G. Ford	Nov 1974—Nov 1976
S/Ldr A. C. Sneddon	Nov 1976—

Aircraft Insignia

It is doubtful if the Vildebeests carried any unit markings other than possibly the squadron emblem until near or at the outbreak of World War II. The Squadron was allotted the code combination 'QD' but whether this was carried prior to the war is not known. From September 1939 onwards the combination was changed to 'OA' and this was carried, in light grey, on Vildebeests and Beaufort Is up to the time of the Squadron leaving for the Far East after which no identity markings were carried. On the Whirlwinds markings have been confined to the Squadron badge on various locations and, on the Wessexes, the emblem on a white disc on the fin.
(See also *Fighter Squadrons of the RAF*, pp. 57–8)

No. 24 SQUADRON

BADGE
A black cock

MOTTO
'In omnia parati'
('Prepared for all things')

The Squadron was formed at Hounslow on 21 September, 1915 and after a period on training duties re-equipped with scouts and went to France in February, 1916. It was soon in action with its D.H.2s against the Fokker monoplanes and flew this type and later the S.E.5A with great success until the Armistice. No. 24 then returned to the UK in February, 1919 and was disbanded at Northolt on 12th of that month.

A year later, on 1 February, 1920, No. 24 Squadron was re-formed at Kenley as a communications unit charged with the responsibility of providing air transport for the government, heads of state and the leaders of the three services. To carry this out it was equipped with a variety of aircraft (Bristol F.2B, D.H.4A, D.H.9A, Avro 504K, Vickers Vimy) and these were augmented by other types as time went on. Through the 'twenties it flew only ex-wartime types and during the General Strike of 1926 its Bristols and D.H.9s were used on seven routes for carrying government despatches around the country. Towards the end of the decade new types appeared (Gipsy Moth & Fairey IIIF) and by now sufficient respectability had been acquired to carry Prime Ministers and, more enthusiastically, royalty. Some of these latter were overseas trips as, for example, flying the Duke of York to Copenhagen in October, 1928.

By now the Squadron was at Northolt where it remained until moving to Hendon in 1933. During the 'thirties the tempo greatly increased as did the number of types it flew, including D.H.89A

Rapides and the D.H.86B Express airliners. It also retained Gipsy Moths and Tomtits for use by senior officers at Air Ministry to keep their flying hands in; this was the specific task of B Flight at the time.

With the outbreak of war No. 24 began regular flights to Paris, mainly with Rapides, acquiring several requisitioned civil aircraft for this task. Also a Hendon–Harrogate service was inaugurated to carry papers and personnel to the many government departments evacuated there. During the winter Squadron aircraft were based in France for communications work within the British forces in France. When the fighting broke out in May, 1940 the Squadron was engaged in a welter of activity, eventually ending in evacuating as many people as possible and many aircraft were lost in the departure from France.

Back in the UK the Squadron re-organised itself for communication routes within the UK starting a daily service to N. Ireland in July; also that month No. 24 began ambulance flights with two Oxfords presented by the Girl Guides. In October A Flight hangar was bombed and fifteen squadron aircraft destroyed. During 1941 this type of work was continued and on into 1942. Increasingly the Squadron had been involved in delivery flights of aircraft and in that year it set up No. 1 Air Delivery Flight at Croydon as an off-shoot of the Squadron.

In April, 1942 the Squadron began regular overseas flights to Gibraltar using Hudsons and these were soon extended to Malta as the need arose; in fact on 20 May Hudson AE533 took the Island's George Medal there. Also in 1942 some of the Squadron's aircraft were allotted for use by the USAAF in this country.

In 1943 the Squadron became more involved in overseas flights, a fourth Flight being established with Dakotas; the Squadron was also initially responsible for carrying Winston Churchill in his York *Ascalon*. However, this role was modified when all the Dakotas became No. 512 Squadron in August. Flights were now going as far afield as India. By now most of the internal communications work had been taken over by No. 510 Squadron which had formed out of No. 24 Squadron and the latter concentrated on long-distance sorties throughout 1944, being little affected by the Second Front, except for some casevac (casualty evacuation) trips from Normandy bases in August and September. By the end of the year it was almost entirely equipped with Dakotas and became the short-range VIP unit in 1945, returning many important people and royalty to their liberated countries in the summer and carrying the Royal family to such places as the Channel Islands.

In October, 1945 the Squadron was busily engaged in running personnel to and from the Nuremberg trials; also that month a detachment was set up at Blackbushe to run an experimental mail and freight service to Prestwick on an all-weather basis. This set a new norm for Transport Command crews and paved the way for efficient peacetime transport duties. In February, 1946 No. 24 at last left Hendon for Bassingbourn and there concentrated on VIP flying with Dakotas, Yorks and Lancastrians. In 1947 it was re-organised on a Commonwealth basis, drawing its crews from all their Air Forces. The Berlin Airlift took up much of the Squadron's effort in 1948–49 but soon after this it was re-equipped with Hastings and for eighteen years flew this type, predominantly on the Transport Command routes around the world. In January, 1968 No. 24 moved to Lyneham and re-equipped with the Hercules, becoming part of the Lyneham Transport Wing with whom it has flown ever since. Apart from working up in tactical transport duties and flying the routes it has also taken part in many special operations such as famine relief in Nepal 1973, refugee evacuation (Cyprus 1974), and a support of the British garrison in Belize.

Bases etc.

Formed 21 September, 1915 at Hounslow and served in the scout (fighter) role in World War I. Disbanded at Northolt on 12 February, 1919. Reformed in the communications role at Kenley on 1 February, 1920.

Kenley	Feb 1920—Jan 1927
Northolt	Jan 1927—Jul 1933
Hendon, det. Le Mans, Rheims, Amiens, Gibraltar, Blackbushe	Jul 1933—Feb 1946
Bassingbourn	Feb 1946—Jun 1949
Waterbeach	Jun 1949—Feb 1950
Oakington	Feb 1950—Feb 1951
Lyneham	Feb 1951—Apr 1952
Dishforth	Apr 1952— 1953
Abingdon	1953—Jan 1957
Colerne	Jan 1957—Jan 1968
Lyneham	Jan 1968—

Main Equipment

Bristol F.2B (Feb 1920— 1928)
F4571; H1604; H1617; J6681; J8430
D.H.4A (Feb 1920—)
F5764
Vickers Vimy (Feb 1920—)
F9152
D.H.9A (Feb 1920—Jun 1927)
J7310
Avro 504N (192?— 1931)
J8758; J8759; K1989
D.H.60X Cirrus Moth (Jan 1928— 1929)
J9104; J9112; J9114; J9118
Fairey IIIF (Apr 1928—Jan 1933)
J9061; J9799; J9673; K1115; K1118; K1749
Westland Wapiti I (Apr 1928— 1930)
J9095; J9096
Hawker Tomtit (Jul 1930— 1934)
J9772; K1782
D.H.60M Moth (Dec 1930— 1934)
K1112; K1215; K1221; K1825; K1837; K1846; K1864
Avro Tutor I (Jun 1932— 1938)
K1234; K3359; K4809; K4834; K6090
Bristol Bulldog IIA (1932— 1933)
K2209
Hawker Hart (Jan 1933—Mar 1940)
K2350; K2455; K3140; K3747; K3874; K4297
D.H.82A Tiger Moth II (1933—Oct 1940)
K2568; K2576; K4277; K4284; N6747; N9444
D.H.89A Rapide/Dominie (Mar 1935—Aug 1944)
K4772; K5070; P1764; G-ACPP; G-AEAM; G-AEBW- G-AFSO; W6424; X8510; BD143
D.H.86B (Oct 1937—Apr 1942)
L7596
Miles Nighthawk (Jul 1937—Jun 1939)
L6846
Miles Magister I (Jul 1937—Jul 1942)
L5931; L8208; L8209; L8345
Miles Mentor I (May 1938—Oct 1940)
L4395; L4400; L4404; L4416; L4420
Percival Vega Gull (Nov 1938—Oct 1942)
L7272; P1749; P1754; X9391; P5993
Percival Q.6 (Jul 1939— 1941)
P5635; P5636; P5638
Lockheed Electra (Sep 1939—Jun 1942)
G-AEPN/W9105; G-AEPO/W9106; G-AFEB/W9104
D.H.95/Hertfordshire (Oct 1940—Jun 1944)
G-AFUE; T5357; R2764; X9317; AE444
Lockheed Hudson I/V (Jun 1940—Oct 1944)
N7364; AE533; AE636; AM717; FH460; FK482
Avro Anson (Jul 1940—May 1945)
K6290; N9784; MG589; NK703; NK715; NK734
Airspeed Oxford (Jul 1940—Apr 1945)
P8832; P8833 (Amb.); MP350; NM589
Vickers Wellington I (Aug 1940—Dec 1943)
L4340; N2906; N2990; T2567; T2569
Curtiss Cleveland I (1940—Oct 1940)
AS468
Airspeed Envoy (May 1937—Oct 1940)
L7270
Stinson Reliant (Mar 1942—Sep 1943)
W7978; W7981; X9596
Percival Proctor I (Jun 1940—Oct 1942)
P6129; P6319; R7495; Z7212; DX231
Lockheed 12A (1942—Jun 1944)
X9316; LA619; LA620; LA622
D.H. 87B Hornet Moth (1942— 1943)
X9321; X9391
Douglas Dakota I (Mar 1943—Aug 1943)
FD772, ZK:Y; FD782; FD797, NQ:A
Avro York I (May 1943— 1944)
LV633
Douglas Dakota III (Feb 1944— 1945)
FZ666; KG320; KG339; FL613; FZ646; FZ518; KG528; KG583; KG656; KG729
Douglas Dakota IV (1944— 1950)
KJ876; KJ932, NQ:P; KJ979; KN284, NQ:U; KN520; KN615; KN648, NQ:V; KP251, NQ:K; KP258, NQ:L; TJ170
Douglas C-54A (1945)
EW999

Avro York C.1 (Feb 1946—   1950)
MW101; MW140; MW178; MW230; MW287; MW319, U
Avro Lancastrian C.2 (Jul 1946—Oct 1949)
VL980; VM701; VM725; VM727; VM736
Handley Page Hastings C.1/C.1A (Dec 1950—Feb 1958)
TG510; TG523; TG532; TG556; TG575; TG601; TG608; TG621
Handley Page Hastings C.2 (1953—Feb 1968)
WD477; WD489; WD493; WJ327; WJ340
Handley Page Hastings C.4 (1953—   195?)
WD500; WJ324; WJ325; WJ326
Lockheed Hercules C.1 (Jan 1968—   ). Aircraft centrally serviced
by Lyneham but aircraft known to have been used by No. 24 Sqdn incl.
XV177; XV192; XV211; XV215

Commanding Officers

S/Ldr E. H. Johnstone	Feb 1920	Feb 1923
S/Ldr E. R. L. Corballis	Feb 1923	Oct 1923
S/Ldr R. S. Maxwell	Oct 1923	Aug 1925
S/Ldr W. H. L. O'Neill	Aug 1925	Aug 1927
S/Ldr S. N. Cole	Aug 1927	Apr 1929
S/Ldr D. S. Don, MVO	Apr 1929	Oct 1931
S/Ldr J. Whitford	Oct 1931	Dec 1935
W/Cdr H. K. Goode, DSO, DFC, AFC	Dec 1935	Jun 1939
W/Cdr D. F. Anderson, DFC, AFC	Jun 1939	Oct 1939
W/Cdr H. K. Goode, DSO, DFC, AFC	Oct 1939	Feb 1941
W/Cdr H. G. Lee, DFC, AFC	Feb 1941	Jun 1941
W/Cdr P. W. M. Wright, DFC	Jun 1941	Jul 1942
W/Cdr H. B. Collings, MVO, DFC	Jul 1942	Aug 1944
W/Cdr T. H. Archbell, DFC	Aug 1944	Sep 1945
W/Cdr E. L. A. Walter	Sep 1945	Sep 1946
W/Cdr C. W. K. Nicholls	Sep 1946	Mar 1948
W/Cdr P. H. Lombard	Mar 1948	Mar 1950
W/Cdr C. F. Read	Mar 1950	Dec 1950
S/Ldr H. A. Nash	Dec 1950	Oct 1951
Maj J. N. Robbs, SAAF	Oct 1951	Oct 1953
S/Ldr J. L. Kerr	Oct 1953	Sep 1955
S/Ldr R. B. Bolt, RNZAF	Sep 1955	Feb 1957
S/Ldr M. M. Mair	Feb 1957	Oct 1957
W/Cdr D. W. Hitchins, RAAF	Oct 1957	Oct 1959
W/Cdr H. D. Archer	Oct 1959	Nov 1961
W/Cdr R. B. Sillars	Nov 1961	Nov 1963
W/Cdr R. T. Saunders	Nov 1963	Jan 1966
W/Cdr G. Moss	Jan 1966	Jan 1968
W/Cdr J. F. H. Tetley	Jan 1968	Jul 1970
W/Cdr R. D. Bates	Jul 1970	Jul 1972
W/Cdr M. J. Hardy	Jul 1972	Jul 1974
W/Cdr C. E. Evans	Jul 1974	Sep 1976
W/Cdr M. C. A. Davis	Sep 1976	Aug 1978
W/Cdr K. Chapman	Aug 1978	—

Aircraft Insignia

Although a comms unit the Squadron in the mid-twenties adopted a red/blue/red chevron marking on the fins of its aircraft which was retained well into the thirties. During this latter period it became the custom for Squadron aircraft to carry the Squadron number '24' in black on the fuselage side. With the outbreak of war markings were dropped and did not re-appear generally until ca 1943. The Squadron had been allocated the code letters 'ZK' (duplicating with No. 25 Squadron) and these appeared on the occasional aircraft (eg. Proctor P5993) in April, 1940, but generally on the arrival of Dakotas. The duplication was later noticed and the code changed in 1943 to 'NQ' which appeared both on the Dakotas and Wellingtons. This continued on some, but not all, of the Dakotas post-war but no specific insignia, other than transport nose codes, was carried on Yorks and Lancastrians. The Hastings at first carried no markings but in the late fifties a blue diamond was painted at the top of the fins with the white number '24' in it. In the 1960s this was dropped in favour of the Squadron's emblem, a black cock, painted on the fin; however the Squadron aircraft were later pooled with those of No. 36 Squadron as the Colerne Wing and the Squadron marking deleted. (See also *Fighter Squadrons of the RAF*, pp. 65–6.)

No. 26 SQUADRON

BADGE
A springbok's head couped

MOTTO
'N Wagter in die Lug'
('The Watcher in the Sky')

The springbok, emblem of South Africa, commemorates the Squadron's service with Gen. Smuts' forces in German East Africa in World War I and the fact that it originally comprised South African aircrew.

The origins of No. 26 Squadron are found in a group of South African officers who learned to fly before World War I and, in November, 1914, comprised a flying unit, set up at Farnborough, to serve in the German South-West African campaign. When this was concluded in July, 1915 this unit returned to the UK and was included in No. 26 (South African) Squadron which formed at Farnborough on 7 October, 1915. Its stay in UK was short, embarking for East African service on 23 December and arriving there in February, 1916. It went into action almost as soon as its aircraft were assembled, flying recces around Sarengeti and dropping bombs on Taveta. In a campaign of this type the Squadron was closely identfied with the army units (of 2nd Division) it was supporting and in the course of the year had many detachments alongside them. The Squadron also co-operated closely with a RNAS detachment of Caudrons in the area. Most of the task was reconnaissance but during the rainy season operations ceased and all efforts were made to preserve the aircraft. The offensive was taken up again in 1917 as the successful advance went forward and No. 26 hopping to any forward landing ground that the army could reach. Despite this, by May the Squadron was so far from the front line that its contribution was minimal until moving again. By August a new bombing method had been proved – incendiaries were dropped to drive the enemy out of the bandas and then HE to kill them. That summer fighting was intensive and the Squadron heavily involved, so effectively that by November most of the enemy were either

captured or driven into Portuguese East Africa. In February, 1918 the Squadron moved up to Egypt and then on to England where it disbanded at Blandford in July.

On 11 October, 1927 No. 26 was re-formed at Catterick as an army co-operation squadron. Progress was slow originally as the personnel were required to work up the station as well as the Squadron. By the summer of 1928 it was working with Northern and Scottish Commands, beginning the detachments inevitable in this work. By 1933 Audaxes replaced the A.W.Atlas and in 1935 the Squadron was at Mildenhall for the Royal Review. By the outbreak of war it had Lysanders and went overseas with the BEF Air Component. In May, 1940 it was used extensively on contact and Tac/R patrols and became easy targets for the German fighters. On moving from France it was based at Lympne and heavily involved in supporting the British forces in Calais until its capture. It was also using Rouen for an Advanced Landing Ground until mid-June. On 18 June activities over France ceased and the Squadron began dawn and dusk anti-invasion patrols around the English coastline (Sheerness to Newhaven was No. 26's 'beat'). These tailed off at the end of the year and the Squadron flew no operations, working up for army co-operation once more and also undertaking AA calibration flying. Tomahawks arrived in March and in October the Squadron returned to operations, flying *Rhubarbs* over N. France, also doing low-level PR at the same time, 22 sorties being flown that month. In the following month these were interspersed with artillery spotting for naval guns shelling St. Inglevert airfield, and shipping PR.

In January, 1942 Mustangs arrived and the Squadron began *Populars*, which continued on a small scale through the year. At this time No. 26 was something of a trials squadron having many types for evaluation on FR duties. August was a busy month with *Populars* and Operation Jubilee (Dieppe) in which Tac/Rs were flown and the Squadron lost five pilots. A new task for the Mustang was the resumption of dawn and dusk coastal patrols, this time to intercept Bf 109 and FW 190s fighter bombers raiding the coastal towns. This mixture of operations continued until March, 1943 when No. 26 came off operations until July, which was a month of many

Rhubarbs. By November it reached a total of 62 ops in the month consisting of day and night *Rangers*, *Intruders*, *Jim Crows* and convoy patrols. After a period off ops in the north it converted to Spitfires and returned south with a new task – over D-Day and subsequently the Squadron flew gun-spotting sorties for RN and US warships shelling the beachheads and invasion targets. Its naval co-operation tasks included anti-human torpedo patrols in the Seine and Orne estuaries, E-boat attacks and further bombardment spotting which continued until the end of the year when it reverted to Mustangs. In the New Year its task was PR again, low-level sorties against the V2 sites, although in April it reverted to naval shoots once more before the war ended. It moved to the Continent in August, 1945, becoming part of BAFO with Spitfire XIVs. It disbanded on 1 April, 1946 but was re-formed on the same day at Lübeck by re-numbering No. 41 Squadron. It now flew in the fighter role with Tempests, then Vampires, Sabres and Hunters as part of the 2nd TAF in Germany until December, 1960 when it was disbanded at Gütersloh.

On 1 June, 1962 No. 26 Squadron was re-formed at Odiham as a transport helicopter unit with Bristol Belvedere HC.1s. These it took to Aden in 1963 where it was used for army support in the Radfan area and in the policing duties in that area. It remained there until November, 1965 when it moved to Singapore and was by the month's end absorbed by No. 66 Squadron.

The Squadron re-appeated again, on 3 February, 1969 in the communications role when the Northern Comms Squadron at Topcliffe, equipped with Pembrokes and Bassets, became No. 26. It flew on these duties until again disbanding at Wyton on 1 April, 1o76.

Bases etc.

Formed at Farnborough on 7 October, 1915.

Farnborough	Oct 1915	Oct 1915
Netheravon	Oct 1915	Dec 1915
en route to East Africa		
Mbuyuni, det. Sarengeti, Railhead, Taveta, Kahe	Feb 1916	May 1916
Marago Opuni	May 1916	May 1916
Old Lassiti	May 1916	Jun 1916
Kwa Lokua	Jun 1916	Jun 1916
Palms	Jun 1916	Jun 1916
Mbagui	Jun 1916	Aug 1916
Dakawa	Aug 1916	Aug 1916
Morogoro, det. Tulo, Iringa, Kilwa, Njombe, Fort Johnston, Likuju, Itigi, Tabora, Mtonia, Shinyanga, Mwembe, Songea	Aug 1916	Jul 1917
Dar-es-Salaam, det. Kilwa, Likuju, Mssindye, Nahungu, Songea, Mtua, Mtoa	Jul 1917	Feb 1918
Egypt (base unknown)	Feb 1918	Jul 1918
Blandford	Jul 1918	Jul 1918

Disbanded at Blandford in July, 1918. Re-formed in the army co-operation role at Catterick on 11 October, 1927.

Catterick	Oct 1927	Sep 1939
Le Plessiel	Oct 1939	Dec 1939
Le Tricquerie, det. Lille/Ronchin	Dec 1939	Apr 1940
Dieppe	Apr 1940	May 1940
Authie	May 1940	May 1940
Cherbourg	May 1940	May 1940
Lympne	May 1940	Jun 1940
West Malling	Jun 1940	Sep 1940
Gatwick	Sep 1940	Nov 1941
Manston	Nov 1941	Nov 1941
Gatwick, det. Weston Zoyland, West Malling	Nov 1941	Jan 1943
Detling	Jan 1943	Mar 1943
Stoney Cross	Mar 1943	Apr 1943
Gatwick	Apr 1943	Jun 1943
Detling, det. Ballyhalbert	Jun 1943	Jul 1943
Church Fenton	Jul 1943	Oct 1943
Snailwell, det. Church Fenton	Oct 1943	Dec 1943
Hutton Cranswick	Dec 1943	Mar 1944
Peterhead	Mar 1944	Apr 1944
Dundonald	Apr 1944	Apr 1944
Ayr	Apr 1944	Apr 1944
Lee-on-Solent	Apr 1944	Oct 1944
Hawkinge	Oct 1944	Oct 1944
Tangmere	Oct 1944	Dec 1944
Exeter, det. Coltishall	Dec 1944	Jan 1945
Harrowbeer	Jan 1945	Jan 1945
North Weald	Jan 1945	Apr 1945
Harrowbeer	Apr 1945	Apr 1945
Château Bernard	Apr 1945	May 1945
Harrowbeer	May 1945	May 1945
Chilbolton	May 1945	Aug 1945
Schleswig (B.164)	Aug 1945	Sep 1945
Lübeck (B.158)	Sep 1945	Apr 1946

Disbanded at Lübeck on 1 April, 1946. Re-formed on the same day by re-numbering No. 41 Squadron; now served in the fighter role until December, 1960. On 1 June, 1962 re-formed in the transport helicopter role at Odiham.

Odiham	Jun 1962	Jan 1963
en route to Aden		
Khormaksar	Mar 1963	Nov 1965
Seletar	Nov 1965	Nov 1965

On 30 November, 1965 the Squadron was disbanded by being absorbed into No. 66 Squadron. It was re-formed on 3 February, 1969 at Topcliffe by re-numbering the Northern Communications Squadron.

Topcliffe, det. Turnhouse	Feb 1969	1970
Wyton, det. Turnhouse	1970	Apr 1976

Disbanded at Wyton on 1 April, 1976.

Main Equipment

B.E.2c (Oct 1915—Nov 1917)
4318; 4344; 4357; 4410; 4497; 4591; 8425; 8428

Henri Farman (May 1916—Mar 1917)
7753; 7754; 7749

B.E.2e (Dec 1916—Nov 1917)
6306; 6764; 6783; 7134; A3074; A3076

A. W. Atlas I (Oct 1927—Sep 1933)
J8800; J9518; J9521; J9997; K1004; K1037; K1531

Hawker Audax I (Jul 1933—Sep 1937)
K3067; K3070; K3074; K3079; K3096; K3119; K7382

Hawker Hector I (Sep 1937—May 1939)
K9715; K9717; K9724; K9731; K9738

Westland Lysander II (Feb 1939—Nov 1940)
L4770; L4777; L4788, RM; L4810; L6848; L6863; N1200; N1211; N1243; N1275; N1306; P1689; P1714; P9080, RM

Westland Lysander III/IIIA (Oct 1940—Sep 1942)
T1429, RM:H; T1436; T1449; T1451, RM; V9318, RM:W; V9736

Curtiss Tomahawk I/IIA (Feb 1941—Sep 1942)
AH749; AH755; AH791; AH830, RM:E; AH839, RM:A; AH850, RM:D; AH860, RM:F; AH896; AK125

North American Mustang I (Jan 1942—Mar 1944 & Dec 1944—Jun 1945)
AG367, RM:Z; AG399; AG425, XC:F; AG497; AG500; AG522; AG564, RM:A; AG616, Q; AG651; AL966; AM110; AM148, RM:G; AM202; AP201, RM:G

Fairey Battle I (Jun 1942—May 1943)
L5051; L5460

Vickers-Supermarine Spitfire VB (Mar 1944—Jan 1945)
W3432; W3638; AD133; AD204; AD299; BL477; BL549; BL719; BM256; BM476; EN862; EP233

Vickers-Supermarine Spitfire XIV (Jun 1945—Apr 1946)
NH925, XC:B

Vickers-Supermarine Spitfire XI (Sep 1945—Apr 1946)
MB953; PA839, XC:M; PL892; PL995, XC:W

Bristol Belvedere HC.1 (Jun 1962—Nov 1965)
XG453, N; XG459, G; XG464, F; XG468, A; XG474, B

Hunting-Percival Pembroke C.1 (Feb 1969—Mar 1971)
WV735; WV739; XF797

Beagle Basset CC.1 (Feb 1969—May 1974)
XS765; XS766; XS771; XS775; XS783

de Havilland Devon C.2 (1971—Apr 1976)
VP958; VP968; VP978; WB533; WB534

Commanding Officers

Maj G. P. Wallace, DSO	Oct 1915	Nov 1917
S/Ldr R. L. Stevenson, MBE	Oct 1927	Feb 1931
S/Ldr P. B. Hunter	Feb 1931	Aug 1932
S/Ldr G. R. A. Deacon, MC	Aug 1932	Feb 1934
S/Ldr C. H. Stillwell	Feb 1934	Oct 1935
S/Ldr C. P. Brown, DFC	Oct 1935	Oct 1937
S/Ldr T. J. Arbuthnot	Oct 1937	Jan 1940
S/Ldr R. C. M. Ferrers	Jan 1940	Jun 1940
W/Cdr R. W. K. Stevens	Jun 1940	Oct 1940
W/Cdr W. D. Butler	Oct 1940	Jul 1942
W/Cdr T. W. C. Fazan	Jul 1942	Apr 1943
W/Cdr J. R. Wilson, DFC	Apr 1943	May 1943
W/Cdr P. Hadfield	May 1943	May 1943
S/Ldr A. H. Baird, DFC	May 1943	Mar 1944
S/Ldr B. J. A. Fleming	Mar 1944	Jan 1945
S/Ldr J. F. Roberts, DFC	Jan 1945	Jun 1946
S/Ldr P. H. Hart	Jun 1962	Nov 1965

Aircraft Insignia

In World War I no Squadron insignia was carried on the aircraft. It is believed this policy was continued between the wars with the exception of the standard representation of the Squadron's emblem on a white grenade on the fin of the Audaxes and Hectors from ca 1936 onwards. Before World War II the code combination 'HL' was allocated to No. 26 and it is presumed that this was carried on its Lysanders. This was changed to 'RM' on the outbreak of war and this latter combination was in evidence on Squadron aircraft up to 1942/43. Then for a while the aircraft were unmarked but by the time it was

re-equipped with Mustang Is again in 1944 it had been allocated 'XC' which was carried on these and the Spitfire XIs and XIVs. The Belvederes carried a white disc on the fin with the springbok emblem in it, flanked by a black bar outlined in green with a green lightning flash in each half.
(See also *Fighter Squadrons of the RAF*, pp. 73–5.)

No. 27 SQUADRON

BADGE
An elephant

MOTTO
'Quam celerrime ad astra'
('With all speed to the stars')

An elephant was chosen as a badge during World War I to perpetuate the memory of the Squadron's first aircraft, the Martinsyde Elephant. It is also appropriate in view of No. 27's years of service in India.

No. 27 Squadron was formed at Hounslow on 5 November, 1915 and went to France the following March equipped with Martinsyde Elephants in the scout role. In this task the type was unsuccessful so the Squadron turned to bombing and recce duties which it continued with D.H.4s and D.H.9s. After the Armistice it returned to the UK and was disbanded on 22 January, 1920. Three months later it was re-formed by re-numbering No. 99 Squadron at Mianwali in India and between the wars it served as a bomber squadron on the N. W. Frontier. By the time war broke out in the Pacific it had become a night-fighter squadron in Malaya where it was virtually wiped out by the Japanese invasion. It re-formed at Amarda Road, India on 19 September, 1942 and served throughout the war as a long-range strike squadron with Beaufighters in the Burma campaign, disbanding on 1 February, 1946.

On 24 November, 1947 No. 27 Squadron was re-formed in the transport role, a nucleus of aircrews from No. 46 Squadron at Abingdon forming the new unit. It thus started as a 'going concern' and in the last six days of that month flew 58,000 miles with its Dakota aircraft. On forming it had moved to Oakington which was to be its home base for most of its transport existence. In April, 1948 it was detached to Schleswigland for airborne support training with the British Army of Occupation; this was intended to last until June, 1948 but the Berlin crisis occurred in that month so No. 27 remained in Germany, moving to Wunstorf in July to take part in Operation Plainfare – the Berlin Airlift. For six weeks the Squadron flew three sorties a day into Berlin before returning to Oakington in September, leaving Berlin to the 4-engined transports. The Squadron reverted to route-flying and airborne supply exercises. It was not until December, 1949 that this routine was changed with a

detachment to Lagos for exercises with the West African Army which lasted until February, 1950. On its return the Squadron was re-titled No. 27 (Airborne Forces) Squadron, working closely with this army formation from then on. The Squadron took up the role, begun by TCDU, of glider-snatching, for which the Dakotas were fitted with a long-hook which would engage a wire attached to the glider's nose and thus pull it off the ground gently under the influence of a deceleration reel inside the Dakota. Successful trials resulted in the feat being performed at the 1950 RAF Display at Farnborough, one of the few public demonstrations of the technique. The Squadron continued in the airborne forces role until November when it was suddenly disbanded.

Three years later No. 27 re-formed at Scampton in the bomber role and has served there since, flying Canberras and Vulcans in the bomber and strategic recce role.

Bases, etc. (in the transport role)
24 November, 1947, re-formed at Abingdon from a nucleus of No. 46 Squadron crews.

Abingdon	Nov 1947—	Nov 1947
Oakington (det. Schleswigland Jun–Jul 1948)	Nov 1947—	Jul 1948
Wunstorf	Jul 1948—	Jul 1948
Fassberg	Jul 1948—	Sep 1948
Oakington (det. Lagos Dec 1949—Feb 1950)	Sep 1948—	Jun 1950
Netheravon	Jun 1950—	Nov 1950

Disbanded at Netheravon 10 November, 1950.

Main Equipment (in the transport role)
Douglas Dakota C.4
KJ834; KJ866; KJ907; KK129; KK141; KN213; KN223; KN274; KN330; KN388; KN415; KN512; KN641; KP238

Commanding Officers

S/Ldr E. J. Harrod	Nov 1947—	Sep 1949
S/Ldr K. Jones, DFC	Sep 1949—	Mar 1950
S/Ldr D. J. Penman, DSO, DFC	Mar 1950—	Nov 1950

Aircraft Insignia
As far as is known no distinctive squadron insignia was carried on the Squadron's aircraft during the Dakota period.
(See also *Bomber Squadrons of the RAF*, pp. 44–5 & 388–9 and *Fighter Squadrons of the RAF*, pp. 75–7.)

No. 28 SQUADRON

BADGE
In front of a demi-Pegasus, a fasces

MOTTO
'Quicquid ages age'
('Whatever you may do, do')

The demi-Pegasus represents the white horse on the Downs near Yatesbury where the Squadron first became an operational unit and the fasces denote the Squadron's operations in Italy in World War I.

No. 28 Squadron was formed at Gosport on 7 November, 1915 and remained in a training role until July, 1917 when it became a scout

(fighter) squadron. It went to France with Sopwith Camels later that year, moving on to Italy in November where it fought successfully in the Italian campaign until the war ended. It returned to the UK in February, 1919 and was disbanded at Eastleigh on 20 January, 1920.

On 1 April, 1920 No. 28 Squadron was re-formed at Ambala in Northern India by re-numbering No. 114 Squadron. It is believed that at this time it was still flying B.E.2c's but was soon re-equipped with Bristol Fighters in the army-co-operation role. No. 28 Squadron became one of those for whom the peace brought no relaxation from fighting for, from December, 1921 onwards, it was continuously involved in the operations on the North-West Frontier, co-operating with the political officers in trying to curb the raiding tribes. The country was very difficult to fly over and occasional casualties took place due to the terrain and to sniper's bullets. This type of operation continued spasmodically for twenty years until the Burmese fighting proved a greater priority. During these years No. 28 continued to fly over the mountain passes strafing and bombing the raiders' camps as required. Experimental mail runs were flown between Quetta and Simla in 1925 and in January, 1933 four Wapitis of the Squadron made a formation cross-country to Singapore and back. On several occasions the Squadron was called upon to fly escort to the Viceroy of India's Avro X and in June 1935 it flew earthquake relief sorties into stricken Quetta. 1937 brought a flare-up in Waziristan where the Squadron flew many close-support sorties to the army.

It was not until February, 1942 that No. 28 Squadron left its own little war and joined in the wider conflict. It was now flying Lysanders and began light tactical bombing sorties over the Salween river coupled with more normal army co-op duties; it suffered heavy casualties and was withdrawn for building up again. In fact it was not again in action until January, 1943, having reverted to the NW Frontier for a while. By now its operations were flown on Hurricanes flying recces and PR in the Rathedaung area. The next few months were very busy with many Tac/R sorties flown, photomosaics made of the battle area and offensive recces used to sink Japanese launches in the Mayu river. A detachment at Imphal was flying high-level PR. This type of operational activity was maintained throughout 1943 but not at the same intensity, although at least one hundred operational sorties were flown each month, even during the monsoon period. As 1944 opened the tempo increased again, by March 12 sorties a day being flown, mainly Tac/R flights ahead of the army formations; in April the Hurricanes also flew a mail run between Imphal and Dimapur. By May the Squadron's losses were increasing and with the onset of the monsoon No. 28 was withdrawn from operations in July, for five months.

In December, 1944 No. 28 moved to Tamu and resumed tactical recce duties, flying up to 20 sorties a day in the early months of 1945 reaching a peak in March when 584 operational sorties were flown in the month. Thereafter the Squadron moved down to the Rangoon area and resumed fighting there but unserviceability and weather brought the Squadron to a standstill in summer 1945. A few sorties were flown on No. 28s new Spitfires and then the war ended.

With the war over No. 28 became a part of the permanent Far East Air Force with Spitfire FR.14s and FR.18s based first in Singapore and then, from 1949, at Hong Kong. Here it transferred to a primarily fighter role which it maintained with Vampires, Venoms and Hunters until 1967, when it disbanded there on 2 January.

Just over a year later, on 1 March, 1968, No. 28 re-formed at Kai Tak as a tactical support helicopter squadron with Whirlwind HAR.10s and has continued this role with Wessexes since 1972. In effect it is a jack-of-all-trades squadron ministering to the needs of the colony itself, though primarily tasked with the Army and comes in for a full share of rescue and other sorties in addition to its tactical role.

Bases etc.

Formed at Gosport on 7 November, 1915. Served in the training and scout roles until disbanding at Eastleigh on 20 January, 1920. Re-formed as an army co-operation squadron at Ambala on 1 February, 1920 by renumbering No. 114 Squadron.

Ambala	Feb 1920—	Dec 1921
Kohat, det. Dardoni	Dec 1921—	Apr 1923
Peshawar, det. Tank	Apr 1923—	Jan 1925
Quetta	Jan 1925—	Jan 1927
Ambala	Jan 1927—	Apr 1937
Marzai	Apr 1937—	Jul 1937
Ambala, det. Miranshah	Jul 1937—	Mar 1939
Kohat, det. Miranshah, Peshawar, Arawali, Marzai, Karachi, New Delhi, Jhelum	Mar 1939—	Jan 1942
Lashio, det. Zayatkwin, Port Blair	Jan 1942—	Feb 1942
Magwe, det. Mingaladon	Feb 1942—	Mar 1942
Asanol	Mar 1942—	Mar 1942
Lahore	Mar 1942—	Apr 1942
Ranchi	Apr 1942—	Jul 1942
Kohat	Apr 1942—	Aug 1942

Ranchi, det. Maungdaw, Imphal, Cox's Bazaar	Aug 1942—	May 1943
Alipore, det. Agartala, Imphal	May 1943—	Jan 1944
Imphal, det. Ratnap	Jan 1944—	Apr 1944
Jorhat, det. Imphal, Dalbumghar	Apr 1944—	Jul 1944
Dalbumghar	Jul 1944—	Aug 1944
Ranchi	Aug 1944—	Sep 1944
Dalbumghar	Sep 1944—	Dec 1944
Tamu	Dec 1944—	Jan 1945
Kalemyo	Jan 1945—	Jan 1945
Ye-U	Jan 1945—	Feb 1945
Sadaung	Feb 1945—	Apr 1945
Meiktela	Apr 1945—	May 1945
Mingaladon, det. Meiktela	May 1945—	1945
Kuala Lumpur	1945—	1945
Penang	1945—	Feb 1947
Tengah	Feb 1947—	Jan 1948
Sembawang	Jan 1948—	1949
Kai Tak	1949—	Jan 1967

Disbanded at Kai Tak on 2 January, 1967. Re-formed there on 1 March, 1968.

Kai Tak	Mar 1968—	Jun 1978
Sek Kong	Jun 1978—	

Main Equipment

Bristol F.2B (Feb 1920—Sep 1931)
E2442; E4630; H1508; H1541; H1548; J7677
Westland Wapiti IIA (Sep 1931—Jun 1936)
J9493, F; J9718, E; K1272, S; K1299, A; K1300, J; K2296
Hawker Audax I (Jun 1936—Oct 1941)
4838, US:L; K4849; K4851, B; K4862, C; K5563, F; K5575; K5583, B
Westland Lysander II (Sep 1941—Jan 1943)
L4787; L4815; N1224, BF:E; N1273, BF:J; P1727, BF:G; P1936; P9137, BF:C; P9193, BF:D; R2026
Hawker Hurricane IIB (Dec 1942—end 1944)
AG342; AP857; BE199; BE488; BG685; BG872, R; BH134; BM912; BN166; BN952; BW928; BX117; HL717; HV775; HW265; HW656; JS242; KW699
Hawker Hurricane IIC/IV (Mar 1944—Jul 1945)
HV653; HL857; JS440; KZ353, G; LB615; LD172; LD263
Vickers-Supermarine Spitfire XI (Jul 1945—Aug 1945)
No serials known
Vickers-Supermarine Spitfire FR.14 (Aug 1945—   1947)
MV301, T; MV349, A; NH926, P; RM988, J; SM880, N; SM936, W; TZ117 E;
Westland Whirlwind HAR.10 (Mar 1968—Mar 1972)
XK968, H; XP301, A; XP328, K; XP358, S; XP393, U; XR455, J; XR482, W
Westland Wessex HC.2 (Feb 1972—   )
XR500, A; XR515, B; XR527, C; XR588, D; XT605, E; XT667, F; XT673, G

Commanding Officers

S/Ldr R. J. F. Barton, OBE	Feb 1920—	1923
W/Cdr . . Murray	1923—	Feb 1926
S/Ldr A. W. Mylne	Feb 1926—	Feb 1928
S/Ldr A. F. Broke	Feb 1928—	Nov 1931
S/Ldr F. W. Trott	Nov 1931—	Mar 1932
S/Ldr F. Fernihough, MC	Mar 1932—	Sep 1934
S/Ldr C. J. S. Dearlove	Sep 1934—	Jun 1936
S/Ldr A. F. Hutton, DFC	Jun 1936—	Jan 1938
S/Ldr E. L. S. Ward	Jan 1938—	Dec 1939
S/Ldr G. E. Jackson, DFC	Dec 1939—	Jan 1941
S/Ldr R. M. Coad, AFC	Jan 1941—	1941
S/Ldr P. N. Jennings	1941—	Mar 1942
S/Ldr O. R. W. Hammerbeck	Mar 1942—	Nov 1942
S/Ldr A. S. Mann	Nov 1942—	Mar 1943
S/Ldr T. R. Pierce	Mar 1943—	Aug 1943
S/Ldr H. G. F. Larsen	Aug 1943—	Jul 1944
F/Lt A. E. Guymer	Jul 1944—	Oct 1944
S/Ldr H. G. F. Larsen, DFC	Oct 1944—	Feb 1945
S/Ldr E. G. Pannell	Feb 1945—	Apr 1945
S/Ldr A. E. Guymer	Apr 1945—	Jul 1945
S/Ldr J. Rhind	Jun 1945—	Jul 1945
S/Ldr J. Cumming	Apr 1968—	

Aircraft Insignia

Little is known about the markings carried by the Bristol Fighters in the early twenties by No. 28 Squadron. With the Wapitis a black band was painted around the rear fuselages of the aircraft and a black aircraft letter carried and this was continued on the Audax, the Squadron emblem being painted on a white six-pointed star on the fins. With the war came the need to camouflage aircraft and the Audaxes originally carried the code letters 'US', this changing c. 1941 to 'BF'. Code letters were dropped with the arrival of the Hurricanes, and they and the Spitfires had no squadron insignia as far as is known. With the Whirlwinds and later Wessexes the Squadron badge was carried on the fin.

(See also *Fighter Squadrons of the RAF*, pp. 77–80)

No. 30 SQUADRON

BADGE
A date palm tree

MOTTO
'Ventre a terre'
('All out')

The badge is based on a design used unofficially
by the Squadron previously, denoting its
Middle East service.

In 1914 a small RFC detachment was sent to Egypt for the defence of the Suez Canal. On 24 March, 1915 this was expanded to squadron strength and numbered No. 30 Squadron at Ismailia with one Flight at Basra. Equipped with B.E.2c's and Farmans it went into action in December with recces from Ali Gharbi and by February 1916 was flying as many as 41 operational sorties in the month, including artillery shoots as well as recce flights. It was joined by an RNAS detachment on the Mesopotamian front which was welcome for No. 30 Squadron was down to four aircraft. Perhaps the most important task during this time, however, was the supply-dropping sorties which were flown to the garrison cut off at Kut and this built up during April, 32 sorties being flown in three days at the end of the month. The enemy had some Fokker fighters and several pilots were wounded during this operation. After the fall of Kut the Squadron continued to fly as aircraft permitted, mainly on tactical recce, though some bombing raids were made. Some artillery and trench registration flights were also flown, all ops taking place at 6000 ft to avoid ground fire. In the summer it was found that the great heat in the area was warping the aircraft; as the autumn came the emphasis was on photo-recce and in September bombing raids were stepped up, especially at night. In December Lt Malon managed to shoot down No. 30s first aircraft, an Albatros. In 1917 the advance began, No. 30 moving up to Baghdad, much of its work being to bomb the retreating enemy, the Squadron's Martinsydes being useful for this. Air combats still took place; and in April Lt Page in a B.E.2c rammed a Fokker and brought it down, whilst 2/Lt Maguire in a Bristol Scout shot down another. Several Squadron pilots were also shot down in the campaign which tailed off in June. Whilst this was No. 30's main campaign it had detached flights on other fronts and these, together with the main force on the Tigris, continued in desultory action until the war's end. It remained in the area until April, 1919 when it was reduced to cadre but was restored to full strength on 1 February, 1920 and served as a bomber squadron in Iraq until World War II when it moved to Egypt where it fought with Blenheim bombers in the Western Desert and Greece. In 1941 its aircraft were converted to fighters and No. 30 began a new career as a fighter squadron in the Western Desert and, from 1942 onwards, in the Burma campaign, flying Hurricanes and Thunderbolts. After the war it remained in India until disbanding at Agra on 1 April, 1947. No. 30 re-formed at Oakington on 24 November, 1947 in the transport role, equipped with Dakotas, and was immediately thrown into the Berlin Airlift using Wunstorf as an advanced base. This task continued into 1949 with the Squadron at full stretch during this period. When the blockade was over No. 30 returned to the UK and, whilst most of the other airlift squadrons were disbanded No. 30 remained as a short-range transport unit for intra-European flights from the UK. As such it was re-equipped with Vickers Valettas and with these flew throughout the UK and to Europe, including many flights into Poland at this time. It continued in this role until May, 1957, when it re-equipped with Blackburn Beverleys and became a heavy-lift tactical transport squadron at Dishforth. It served in this role to begin with in the UK but in October 1959 moved to the Middle East being based at Eastleigh (Nairobi) with a detachment in Aden. Not only did it fly on the routes but was part of the 'Fire brigade' force in the area, being heavily involved in the Kuwait reinforcements in 1961 and the famine relief food drops in Kenya. With the contraction of Britain's overseas commitments it moved to Muharraq in the Arabian Gulf in October, 1964 where it was disbanded on 6 September, 1967.

However No. 30 was re-formed once more as a transport squadron at Fairford on 1 May, 1968, equipped with the Lockheed Hercules C.1. Its role was now a dual one, of flying the Transport Command routes and of supplying tactical transport to the army, being available for paratroop dropping and heavy load carrying. In February, 1971 the Squadron moved to Lyneham with the concentration of the Hercules force there and has flown as part of the Lyneham Wing since, taking part in many of the mercy flights which have come up as additional to the scheduled work.

Bases etc.

Formed at Ismailia on 24 March, 1915.

Ismailia, det. Basrah	Apr 1915—Dec	1915
Basrah, det. Kut-el-Amara, Ali Gharbi, Musandaq Bend, Hibsh, Sheik Saad, Orah	Dec 1915—May	1916
Sheik Saad, det. Nasriyah	May 1916—Oct	1916
Arab Village	Oct 1916—Mar	1917
Sheik Saad	Mar 1917—Mar	1917
Aziziyah	Mar 1917—Mar	1917
Zeur	Mar 1917—Mar	1917
Bustan	Mar 1917—Mar	1917
Baghdad, det. Baqubah, Khasirin, Kuwar Reach, Barurah Reach	Mar 1917—Apr	1917
Barurah Reach	Apr 1917—May	1917
Baghdad, det. Sindiyeh, Khan Jedidah, Tuz Khurtmatli	May 1917—May	1918
Baquba, det. Kifri, Ramadi, Hamadan	May 1918—Oct	1918
Kifri, det. Zenjan, Hamadan	Oct 1918—Apr	1919

In April, 1919 the Squadron was reduced to a cadre at Baghdad. It was re-formed at full strength there on 1 February, 1920 and became a bomber squadron until 1941 transferring to fighter duties until disbanding at Agra on 1 April, 1947. The Squadron then re-formed at Oakington on 24 November, 1947 in the transport role.

Oakington, det. Wunstorf	Nov 1947—Nov	1950
Abingdon	Nov 1950—May	1952
Benson	May 1952—	1953
Dishforth	1953—Apr	1957
Eastleigh, det. Khormaksar	Apr 1957—Oct	1964
Muharraq	Oct 1964—Sep	1967

Disbanded at Muharraq on 6 September, 1967. Re-formed as a tactical suppot transport squadron at Fairford on 1 May, 1968.

Fairford	May 1968—Feb	1971
Lyneham	Feb 1971—	

Main Equipment

B.E.2c (Apr 1915—   1918)
4141; 4186; 4322; 4362; 4412; 4443; 4564; 4594; 5427
(B.E.2e)
A3079
Maurice Farman (Apr 1915—Nov 1916)
5008; 5909; 7346; 7347; 7348
Voisin (Apr 1916—Sep 1916)
8506; 8523
Short 184 (Apr 1916—   1916)
8043
Martinsyde Elephant (Dec 1916—   1917)
7459; 7466; 7468; 7493; A1595; A3940; A3975
Bristol Scout D (1917—   1917)
7033; 7047
R.E.8 (Apr 1918—Apr 1919)
B3447; B3448; B3449; B3450
Douglas Dakota C.4 (Nov 1947—Nov 1950)
KN360, JN:K; KN383, JN:M; KN402; KN415, JN:N; KN498, JN:J; KN441, JN:S; KN567; KN627; KN652, JN:H
Vickers Valetta C.1 (Nov 1950—May 1957)
VL277, JN:H; VL282; VW158, JN:K; VW163, JN:A; VW190; VW201; VW820, JN:B; VW838, JN:B; VW855, JN:Y; VW863, JN:G; VX494, JN:V
Vickers Valetta C.2
VX576, JN:C
Blackburn Beverley C.1 ((Apr 1957—Sep 1967)
XB263, K; XH118, A; XH119, B; XH120, C; XH122, D; XH123, F; XH124, G; XL130, H; XL131, J; XL148, U; XL149, X; XL152, A; XM103, K; XM109, R
Lockheed Hercules C.1 (May 1968—   )
XV201; XV210; XV223; XV292; XV293; XV301

Maj H. L. Reilly	Apr 1915—Nov 1915	
Maj S. D. Massy	Nov 1915—Jul 1916	
Maj J. E. Tennant	Jul 1916—Jan 1917	
Maj H. de Havilland, DSO	Jan 1917—Apr 1918	
Maj O. A. Westendarp	Apr 1918—May 1918	
Maj J. Everidge	May 1918—Apr 1919	
S/Ldr A. M. Johnstone	Nov 1947—	
S/Ldr P. L. Whitaker, DFC		
S/Ldr T. C. Waugh, DFC	Apr 1960—	
W/Cdr K. J. Parfitt	May 1968—	
W/Cdr J. R. Hardwick	Jan 1975—Jul 1977	
W/Cdr A. C. Tolhurst	Jul 1977—	

Aircraft Insignia

As far as is known no squadron markings were carried on the aircraft in the 1914–18 war. When re-equipped with Dakotas in 1947 the code letter combination 'JN' was used on the Dakotas and on the Valettas for some time before it fell into disuse in the mid-fifties. Later the Valettas carried a red diamond at the top of the fin with '30' in white on it and this was carried through to the Beverleys being used throughout their service. At times, both on the Valettas and the Beverleys, the Squadron badge, in standard format, was carried on the fuselage side, usually below the pilot's cockpit. No markings are carried on the Hercules.
(See also *Bomber Squadrons of the RAF*, pp. 46–7 and *Fighter Squadrons of the RAF*, pp. 86–8.)

No. 31 SQUADRON

BADGE
In front of a wreath of laurel, a mullet

MOTTO
'In caelum indicum primus'
('First in Indian skies')

As its motto indicates, No. 31 Squadron was formed with the specific purpose of providing the first unit of British military aviation in India. Its gestation was lengthy, A Flight forming at Farnborough in October, 1915 and embarked a month later, B Flight (drawn from No. 22 Squadron), left England in February, 1916 and C Flight left England in May, having had its origins in the Home Defence Brigade at Gosport. However, by March, 1916 A Flight was already working up artillery co-operation with the Royal Horse Artillery and Royal Field Artillery from Risalpur and in November the Squadron began operations in the Gandah Valley in the North-West Frontier region. The combination of guns and aircraft was immediately effectively in dispersing the tribesmen who initially held the aircraft in awe. In 1917 Tank became the main operating base and operations continued at pressure until November when peace was declared. By then the Squadron had grown in size having 26 B.E.2c's, 34 Henri Farmans, three B.E.2e's and one F.E.2b. However in February, 1918 fighting flared up in Baluchistan and No. 31 went into action there until peace broke out in April.

No. 31 had already set the pattern for the RAF operations in India in peacetime, a task in which it was joined by several other squadrons. It remained on the frontier, engaged in sporadic action against the dissidents. In 1921 No. 31 was reduced to near impotency by a chronic lack of spares, all its aircraft becoming unserviceable, in 1928 it flew escort to the Vickers Victorias relieving Kabul. June, 1930 found it sending out recces to find a raiding party which had abducted two officers and a lady but more seriously was involved with unrest on the Afghan border. The early thirties saw it operating out of Fort Sandeman in the Zhob area until May, 1935 when the severe earthquake at its base, Quetta, forced it to leave the NW Frontier for Karachi. The following year, however, it returned to the frontier, rotating the Flights on continuous operational readiness and this continued until the summer of 1939 when it returned to Karachi to convert to the transport role.

Equipped with No. 216 Squadron's old Vickers Valentias it used these in the bomber-transport task, providing a bigger bomb load in frontier raids and being used for transport to and from the operational area; it also flew relief flights to areas suffering from famine. In March, 1941 No. 31 flew army reinforcements into Shaibah from India and a detachment remained in the Persian Gulf flying daily flights into the beleagured base at Habbaniya. From there it also operated in the Syrian campaign, until August when it returned to Karachi. In October, now supplemented with DC-2s, it sent a detachment to Bilbais for milk runs up the Western Desert, flying casevac sorties on the return but this was discontinued in February, 1942 as No. 31 Squadron was fully occupied on India's eastern border.

Two aircraft had already moved to Mingaladon in December, 1941 and in 1942 the whole Squadron was in action maintaining communications between the scattered formations and then evacuating RAF units as the Japanese advanced. The aircraft took much punishment in this campaign and in April No. 31 Squadron retired to Lahore to overhaul them. The next month it returned to the front and flew supply dropping sorties to army units, pioneering the methods of flying into small clearings and narrow valleys to keep the army alive in dense jungle, often behind Japanese lines. What No. 31 pioneered many other squadrons followed. By now 31 Squadron had DC-3s as well and with both types it flew a mixture of hectic supply-dropping operations on the Burma front and VIP flights around India, one aircraft being at the disposal of HRH The Duke of Gloucester. The pressure was mounting during 1942 and in September 291 operational sorties were flown in Burma. That month a few Hudsons joined the operations but the DC-2s and 3s did most of the work.

By January, 1943 ops were up to 335 in the month, with 376,000 lbs of supplies dropped. Enemy aircraft were active, too, and several aircraft were shot down. In May, 1943 the Squadron implemented a mail run into Imphal in addition to the drops before the monsoon cut down the operational hours. Now Dakotas were arriving to supplement the fleet of ex-civil DC-2s and DC-3s on which No. 31 had relied for so long. In October the operational hours per month rose to over a thousand and this level was maintained until May, 1944 took them up to 2,030 hrs. By December, 1943 certain dropping sorties were escorted by Hurricanes due to enemy activity and the Squadron had begun runs into China over the 'Hump' route. In January, 1944 two aircraft were lost, one being shot down but the pace continued to increase, the main effort going into the Imphal fighting with casevacs playing a large part. At last in July, 1944 came a rest; most of its aircraft were allotted to Nos. 52 and 353 Squadrons and it retired to Calcutta, flying mail runs and experimenting with glider-towing. By November it was back in action again, flying drops into Kalemyo and Kalewa and also flying night *Nickel* sorties, dropping leaflets into Burma. 1945 brought hectic activity, 906 operational trips being flown in support of IV Corps in the Myitha valley fighting. This opened out into widespread supply-dropping in every part of Burma during the early months of 1945, until April when activity was concentrated on the advance on Rangoon. The pressure gradually relaxed until VJ-Day brought a temporary cease. But the fighting was not over for No. 31 for after peace had been declared it moved to Singapore and from there it was involved in the insurrection in the Dutch East Indies until it could be replaced by Dutch units. It was then disbanded on 30 September, 1946. A new No. 31 Dakota Squadron appeared soon after by re-numbering No. 77 Squadron at Mauripur on 1 November, 1946 and for a year it flew both routes and army support roles there until itself disbanding on 31 December, 1947.

The Squadron's next appearance was at Hendon when the Metropolitan Communications Unit was re-numbered No. 31 Squadron on 19 July, 1948. Here it was involved in providing transport flying for the Government departments and Service ministries within the UK and the Continent being mainly equipped with Ansons.

Complementary to the R.E.8 as principal army co-operation aircraft from 1917 onwards was the Armstrong Whitworth F.K.8. This type was used by No. 35 Squadron which worked up at Narborough towards the end of 1916 where B5752 is seen.

Torpedo-bombing was an increasing pre-occupation of the RAF in the thirties, one of the types used being the Hawker Horsley. No. 36 Squadron flew these at Donibristle and then took them to Singapore in 1930.

Continuing in the maritime role No. 36 Squadron flew the Lockheed Neptune MR.1 from Topcliffe in the mid-fifties. The Squadron number was painted in green on the fuselage side.

No. 37 Squadron also served in the maritime role after World War II, at first in Malta and then, from 1957 onwards, at Aden from where this Shackleton MR.2 is operating.

No. 38 Squadron had converted from bombing to maritime recce in Egypt in 1942, originally using its Wellingtons for torpedo-bombing. By the time it had re-equipped with these Mk.XIVs in January, 1945 it was based in Italy covering the Adriatic, Mediterranean and Aegean.

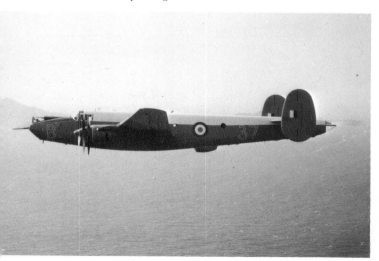

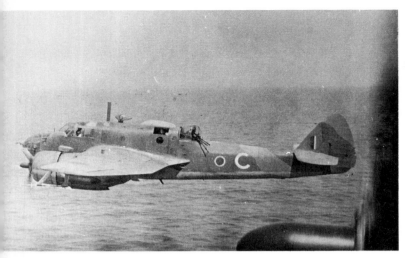

Many epic shipping strikes were made with Bristol Beauforts in the Mediterranean, principally by No. 39 Squadron from 1941 to 1943. Aircraft *Charlie* is here seen on a daylight sweep in the spring of 1943. Note the ASV aerials under the wingtip.

No. 39 remains, briefly, the last of the RAF's photo reconnaissance squadrons, flying Canberra PR.9s from Wyton and having used these from Malta and Wyton since 1962. Note the toned-down Flying Bomb emblem on the fin.

A white square was No. 42 Squadron's marking in World War I, prominently displayed by this R.E.8 just beginning to taxi for a Corps recce sortie.

Impeccably lined up at Thorney Island in early 1938 are No. 42 Squadron's Vickers Vildebeest IVs. It actually flew these old biplanes on convoy patrols in the English Channel and off the East Coast until re-equipment with Beauforts in the summer of 1940.

In 1951–52 Coastal Command expanded greatly by re-equipping with Avro Shackletons. No. 42 was one of the newly-reformed squadrons and was based at St. Eval with Mk.1As, WG511 A : A1 seen there in July, 1952.

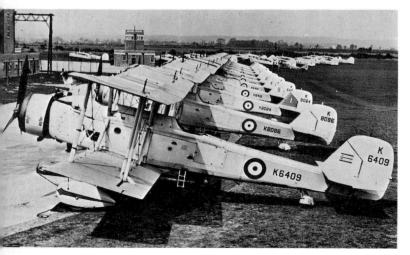

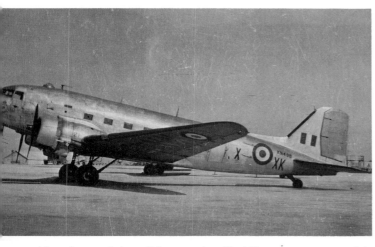

After a long period as a fighter squadron No. 46 became a transport unit in January, 1945. After the war it converted to Douglas Dakotas and used these in the Berlin Airlift as well as on the Middle East runs, KN498 XK : X seen here in sunny climes.

No. 47 Squadron was another unit which achieved success in torpedo strikes in the Mediterranean, in this case between October, 1942 and June, 1943. W6488 was one of its aircraft seen in this pleasing study.

The Handley Page Hastings will always be associated with No. 47 Squadron, which unit introduced this important type in 1948 and flew them in the Berlin Airlift. TG524 L of the Squadron is seen here in its original 1948 livery.

No. 48 Squadron had the interesting task of introducing into RAF service the first monoplane with retractable undercarriage – the Avro Anson. It was still flying the type on war service four years later, seeing service over Dunkirk in 1940 and actually shooting down a Messerschmitt Bf 109. Three of its Ansons are seen here flying off Lancashire after No. 48 had moved north to Hooton Park.

At the end of 1942 No. 48 Squadron took its Hudsons to Gibraltar to cover the sea routes for the Operation Torch, the North African landings and it remained on anti-submarine work from the Rock until February, 1944. FK747 C was a Hudson IIIA which served with No. 48 Squadron at Gibraltar until February, 1944.

One of the less publicised tasks of de Havilland's Comet airliner was on radar reconnaissance duties with No. 51 Squadron at Wyton. XK659 was one of the Comet 2Rs thus used; note the cartoon version of No. 51's goose volant on the fin.

The radar reconnaissance task of No. 51 Squadron is continued today using Hawker Siddeley Nimrod R.1s of which XW665 is one. This also carries the goose in red on the fin.

No. 52 Squadron introduced the R.E.8 into RFC service in November, 1916 but at first it suffered many casualties. Later it went on to use them successfully on the Western Front. The zigzag on the fuselage was No. 52's official marking.

For three years No. 52 Squadron flew Hawker Siddeley Andover C 1s on Far East Air Force's transport routes out of Singapore until the cutting of FEAF brought premature disbandment.

The second squadron to use the RAF's tallest aircraft, the Blackburn Beverley C.1 freighter, was No. 53 at Abingdon. XB290 W wears the Squadron's green diamond on its fins.

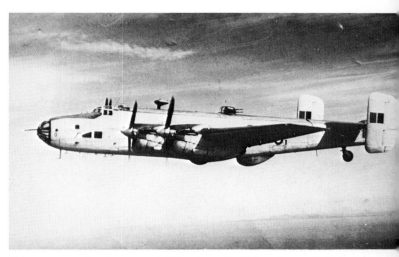

The heavy-lift tradition was maintained by No. 53 Squadron after the Beverley period, it being the only unit to fly the Short Belfast C.1, ten of which it operated out of Brize Norton from 1966 to 1976.

Flying out over the Welsh coast is HR744 0 of No. 58 Squadron, a Halifax II Srs.1A on anti-submarine patrol. The date is 1944, when the Squadron was based at St. David's.

No. 59 Squadron re-formed on army co-operation duties in 1937 for night recce tasks with Hawker Hectors. This photograph shows the immediate pre-war camouflage with PJ code letters, B Type roundels and alternate black and white underwing paint scheme.

By mid-war No. 59 had become a maritime reconnaissance squadron with Liberators. This aircraft, FL946, was a Mk.V seen here on detachment at Ballykelly.

Lined up in the desert sun at Samarra are R.E.8s and a D.H.6 of No. 63 Squadron from where it operated against the Turks in 1917–18.

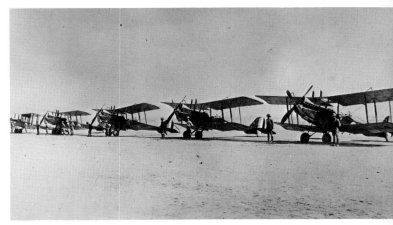

No. 66 had the distinction of being the first squadron to operate twin-engined helicopters in the RAF. These were Westland Belvedere HC.1s and are seen here demonstrating their lifting capabilities in 1961. The Squadron took them to Singapore the following year where they played an important role in the counter-insurgency operations for seven years.

With Martin Baltimores such as FA546 C from Malta in 1943–44 No. 69 Squadron flew shipping patrols in the Central Mediterranean.

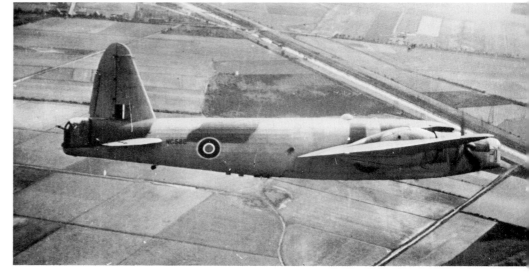

This rare photograph shows one of No. 69 Squadron's modified Wellington XIIIs, NC588, flying from its base at Eindhoven in Holland just after VE-Day.

No. 70 Squadron has long served in the transport role, principally in the Middle East. One of its least publicised periods was in the early fifties when, as part of the Middle East Transport Wing, it flew Vickers Valetta C.1s out of Fayid. The cheat line down VW195's fuselage was yellow to denote No. 70 Squadron.

No. 72 became the second squadron with Westland Belvedere HC.1s for heavy-lift helicoptering in the UK. Here XB455 B is operating from one of the Navy's aircraft carriers.

For many years since 1964, No. 72 has been the home-based army support helicopter squadron flying Wessexes from Odiham and, latterly, Benson. It has also maintained detachments in Northern Ireland during the troubles there. XR521 C is seen here hustling back to Odiham in July, 1966. Note the Squadron's Swift emblem on the fin flanked by the red/blue fighter type marking.

One of the many bomber squadrons which went over to transport duties at the end of World War II was No. 77 which served on the Berlin Airlift and on overseas routes (KJ866 is seen here at Thornhill in Southern Rhodesia) until 1949.

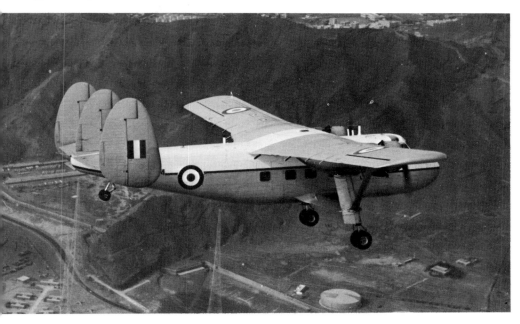

No. 78 Squadron operated Twin Pioneers from Aden (seen here) and Sharjah in the Arabian Gulf from 1965 to 1971.

Flying low over Germany on a fighter recce sortie is WL265 L, a Gloster Meteor FR.9 of No. 79 Squadron from Bückeburg. Note the red arrow along the side of the fuselage, an official use of No. 79's pre-war marking.

The Vickers-Supermarine Swift FR.5 was used by two squadrons in RAF Germany for high-speed low-level fighter recce. They were Nos. 2 and 79, the aircraft here displaying the official version of No. 79 Squadron's marking.

Here visiting Odiham from Brüggen is an English Electric Canberra PR.7 of No. 80 Squadron which flew PR duties in RAF Germany from 1955 to 1969.

Although final confirmation is lacking, it is almost certain that this photograph shows for the first time one of No. 81 Squadron's Tiger Moths, N9159, landing at Lille/Seclin early in 1940. Note the 'operational' camouflage and deletion of underwing serial numbers.

The Ace of Spades card on the nose of this Hunting Pembroke C (PR).1 reveals it belonging to No. 81 Squadron at Seletar in Singapore.

The final aircraft type flown by No. 82 Squadron was the English Electric Canberra PR.7 (WH779 shown here) up to 1956.

Here seen at Mukeiras in the Aden Protectorate is Beverley C.1 XM108 of No. 84 Squadron in 1967. Note the two-tone brown camouflage, black undersides, the Squadron's scorpion emblem on the nose and the Ace of Spades on the fin, a tradition dating back at least to the early twenties.

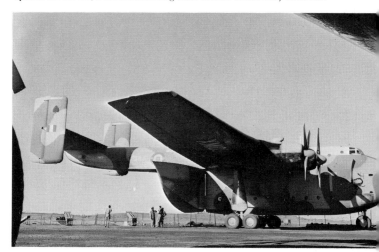

This role was fulfilled until 1955 when it again reverted to the title of Metropolitan Communications Squadron. On the same day (1 March, 1955) a new No. 31 Squadron formed at Laarbruch as a photo reconnaissance unit equipped with Canberras. As part of RAF Germany the Squadron now had a much more operational role and was active in both tactical and strategic PR duties, establishing a very high standard of professionalism. In 1963, 1965 and 1967 it won the Royal Flush competitions within NATO. It transferred to the low-level role in the 'sixties, having first flown high-level sorties. With the RAF re-adjustments in the 'seventies No. 31 Squadron was disbanded as a PR squadron at Laarbruch on 31 March, 1971. The following October it re-formed at Brüggen as a fighter ground-attack unit with Phantoms, subsequently re-equipping with Jaguars.

Bases etc.

A Flight formed Farnborough 11 October, 1915, B Flight formed at Gosport 18 January, 1916, C Flight formed Gosport 10 May, 1916.

Farnborough	Oct 1915	Dec 1915
en route to India	Dec 1915	Jan 1916
Dib Piai	Jan 1916	Feb 1916
Risalpur	Feb 1916	Jul 1916
Murree, det. Shabkadar	Jul 1916	Nov 1916
Risalpur, det. Tank, Dera, Rawalpindi, Lahore, Kohat, Bannu	Nov 1916	Mar 1920
Mhow	Mar 1920	Nov 1920
Cawnpore, det. Jhanai	Nov 1920	Oct 1921
Peshawar	Oct 1921	Mar 1922
Tank	Mar 1922	Apr 1922
Dardoni	Apr 1922	May 1922
Tank	May 1922	May 1922
Parachinar	May 1922	Apr 1923
Dardoni	Apr 1923	Mar 1924
Ambala	Mar 1924	Dec 1926
Quetta, det. Poona, Jacobabad, Delhi	Dec 1926	Feb 1931
Delhi	Feb 1931	Feb 1931
Quetta, det. Fort Sandeman	Feb 1931	May 1935
Drigh Road, det. Quetta, Fort Sandeman	May 1935	Oct 1938
Lahore, det. Fort Sandeman	Oct 1938	1939
Drigh Road	1939	Apr 1940
Peshawar	Apr 1940	Feb 1941
Lahore	Feb 1941	Mar 1941
Drigh Road, det. Shaibah, Basrah, Habbaniya	Mar 1941	Sep 1941
Lahore, det. Bilbais	Sep 1941	Dec 1941
Mingaladon, det. Bilbais	Dec 1941	Feb 1942
Akyab	Feb 1942	Feb 1942
Dum Dum, det. Dinjan	Feb 1942	Apr 1942
Lahore, det. Dinjan, Tezpur	Apr 1942	Feb 1943
Palam, det. Tezpur, Agartala	Feb 1943	Mar 1943
Dhubalia, det. Agartala	Mar 1943	May 1943
Khargpur, det. Agartala, Tezpur, Sylhet	May 1943	Jul 1944
Basal, det. Dum Dum	Jul 1944	Nov 1944
Agartala	Nov 1944	Jan 1945
Comilla	Jan 1945	Feb 1945
Hathazari	Feb 1945	May 1945
Kyaukpyu	May 1945	Aug 1945
Akyab, det. Kyaukpyu, Mingaladon, Toungoo, Tilda	Aug 1945	Sep 1945
Kallang, det. Kemajoran	Sep 1945	Jan 1946
Kemajoran	Jan 1946	Sep 1946

Disbanded at Kallang 30 September, 1946. Re-formed by re-numbering No. 77 Squadron at Mauripur on 1 November, 1946.

Mauripur	Nov 1946	Sep 1947
Palam	Sep 1947	Nov 1947
Mauripur	Nov 1947	Dec 1947

Disbanded at Mauripur on 31 December, 1947. Re-formed at Hendon on 19 July, 1948 by re-naming Metropolitan Communications Squadron.

Hendon	Jul 1948	Mar 1955

Disbanded at Hendon on 1 March, 1955 by re-naming as Metropolitan Communications Squadron. Re-formed on the same date at Laarbruch in the photo recce role.

Laarbruch	Mar 1955	Mar 1971

Disbanded at Laarbruch on 31 March, 1971. Re-formed at Brüggen in October, 1971 in the fighter ground attack role.

Main Equipment

B.E.2c (Oct 1915— 1919)
 4131, B2; 4142; 4143; 4445
Henri Farman (Jun 1917— 1918)
 445; 455
B.E.2e (1917—Feb 1920)
 B4472, C4

F.E.2b (Jun 1917— 1918) & **A.W. F.K.8** (Dec 1918— 1919)
 1 aircraft each only
 C3588
Handley Page V/1500 (Mar 1919—May 1919) 1 aircraft only
 J1936
Bristol F.2B (1919—Apr 1931)
 D7807; D8034; E2297; F4463, L; F4494, F; F4555, E; F4814, F; H1510; J6623; J6663, C; J6781
Westland Wapiti IIA (Feb 1931—mid 1939)
 J9387, F, later 2; J9388, L; J9400, D; J9724, E; J9737, B; J9744, K; K1278, A; K1282, C; K1292; K1302; K1414; K2292
Vickers Valentia I (mid 1939—Feb 1941)
 K1312; K2340, A; K2807; K3600; K3609; K3611
Douglas DC-2 (Apr 1941—Nov 1943) Impressed civil airliners
 AX755; AX767; AX769; DG468, D; DG470, R; DG476, Y; DG479, B
Douglas DC-3 (Apr 1942—Apr 1943)
 LR230, D; LR231, E; LR233, H; LR235, J; MA925, MA943
Lockheed Hudson IIIA (Sep 1942—Dec 1942)
 FH431; FK485
Douglas Dakota I (Mar 1943— 1944)
 FD780; FD783, M; FD788; FD791, W; FD801, K; FD803, A; FD810, H; FD811, V
Douglas Dakota III (May 1943— 1945)
 FD820, E; FD834; FD897; FD948, T; FL516; FL543, J; FL577, U; FL642; FZ579; FZ612; FZ684; KG554, X; KG680; KG758
Douglas Dakota IV (Feb 1945—Sep 1946 & Nov 1946—Dec 1947)
 KJ846, U; KJ918, Q; KJ960, Y; KK118, W; KK167, X; KN309, P; KN535, U; KN639, H; KN672, R; KP229, C; KP275, U
Percival Proctor C.4 (Jul 1948—Mar 1955)
 LZ571, VS:H; LZ637,VS:P; LZ677, VS:Z; LZ795, VS:S; NP387, VS:B; RM176
Avro Anson C.12 (Jul 1948—Mar 1955)
 PH530; PH546, X; PH706; PH716, CB:S; PH817, W
Avro Anson C.19 (Jul 1948—Mar 1955)
 TX186; TX196, CB:K; TX210, CB:T; TX227, CB:L; VM311, CB:Z; VM378
de Havilland Devon C.1 (Jul 1948—Mar 1955)
 VP955; VP961; VP963; VP965, CB:G; VP977
English Electric Canberra PR.7 (Mar 1955—Mar 1971)
 WH773; WH775; WH798; WJ816; WJ818; WT509; WT513; WT518; WT520; WT525; WT531; WT533; WT537

Commanding Officers

Capt G. M. MacDonald	Oct 1915	Apr 1916
Capt A. F. A. Hooper	Apr 1916	Jun 1916
Maj C. R. S. Bradley	Jun 1916	May 1917
Maj S. Hutchinson	May 1917	Dec 1918
Maj E. L. Millar, MBE	Dec 1918	Aug 1919
S/Ldr D. H. M. Carberry, MC, DFC	Aug 1919	Jan 1920
S/Ldr A. L. Neale, MC	Jan 1920	1921
S/Ldr A. T. Harris, AFC	1921	May 1922
S/Ldr A. C. Maunde, CBE, DSO	May 1922	May 1924
S/Ldr A. D. Walser, MC, DFC	May 1924	Jun 1924
S/Ldr H. S. Powell, MC	Jun 1924	Nov 1925
S/Ldr J. O. Archer, CBE	Nov 1925	Apr 1926
S/Ldr J. F. Gordon, DFC	Apr 1926	Mar 1931
S/Ldr B. Ankers, DCM	Mar 1931	Feb 1934
S/Ldr C. J. S. Dearlove	Feb 1934	Sep 1934
S/Ldr R. M. C. MacFarlane, MC	Nov 1934	Oct 1935
S/Ldr J. L. Airey, DFC	Oct 1935	Jun 1937
S/Ldr A. V. Hammond	Jun 1937	Oct 1938
S/Ldr F. F. Wicks, DFC	Oct 1938	Nov 1938
S/Ldr C. Stephenson	Nov 1938	1939
W/Cdr Reid, AFC	1939	Dec 1940
W/Cdr Nicholls	Dec 1940	Jun 1941
W/Cdr S. E. Ubee, AFC	Jun 1941	Oct 1941
W/Cdr H. P. Jenkins	Oct 1941	Jun 1942
W/Cdr W. H. Burbury, DFC, AFC	Jun 1942	May 1943
W/Cdr H. A. Oliver	May 1943	Jan 1944
W/Cdr W. H. Burbury, DFC, AFC	Jan 1944	Jan 1945
W/Cdr R. O. Altmann, DFC	Jan 1945	Sep 1945
W/Cdr B. R. MacNamara, DSO	Sep 1945	Jul 1946
W/Cdr T. W. Gillan	Jul 1946	Sep 1946
W/Cdr R. G. F. Drinkwater	Sep 1946	Sep 1946
W/Cdr J. M. Cooke, DFC, AFC	Nov 1946	Sep 1947
W/Cdr C. Fothergill	Sep 1947	Dec 1947
W/Cdr A. R. Fane de Salis	Jul 1948	Mar 1950
W/Cdr R. E. Ridgway, DSO	Mar 1950	Apr 1952
S/Ldr C. G. Jefferies	Apr 1952	Nov 1952
S/Ldr N. Williamson	Nov 1952	Nov 1954
S/Ldr R. F. V. Ellis	Nov 1954	Mar 1955
S/Ldr J. C. Stead, DFC	Mar 1955	Jul 1957
S/Ldr F. H. P. Cattle, AFC	Jul 1957	Feb 1958
W/Cdr P. A. Kennedy, DSO, DFC, AFC	Feb 1958	Jun 1960
W/Cdr C. T. Dalziel	Jun 1960	Nov 1962
W/Cdr R. H. L. Scott, AFC	Nov 1962	Apr 1965
W/Cdr R. G. Price	Apr 1965	Jun 1967

Aircraft Insignia

As far as is known no squadron insignia was carried on No. 31 Squadron's aircraft until the 'thirties when the Wapitis had a black band around the fuselage aft of the roundels, changing later to two black bands aft of the roundels. During its transport service markings again appear to have been dropped and they re-appear in the period when 31 was a communications squadron, the aircraft carrying 'CB' and 'VS' code letters. When re-formed as a PR Canberra squadron the squadron badge was carried on the nose and a yellow mullet on a green disc on the fin.
(See also *Fighter Squadrons of the RAF*, p. 566)

No. 33 SQUADRON

BADGE
A hart's head affrontee, couped at the neck

MOTTO
'*Loyalty*'

The hart's head commemorates the fact that the Squadron was the first to equip with the Hawker Hart bomber.

The Squadron was formed at Filton on 12 January, 1916 at first on training duties and then as a Home Defence unit in Yorkshire where it served until the war ended. It was disbanded on 13 June, 1919. It re-formed as a day-bomber squadron at Netheravon on 1 March, 1929 and served in the UK until October, 1935 when it moved to Egypt and transferred to the fighter role in February, 1938. As such it fought in the Western Desert and Greek campaigns until November, 1942 after which it became part of the Canal Zone defence force. In April, 1944 the Squadron returned to the UK and flew Spitfires as part of 2nd TAF until the war ended. Re-equipped with Tempests it served for four years in BAFO then moved to the Far East being based at Hong Kong from April, 1949. The following year No. 33 moved to Malaya where it used Tempests and Hornets in the fight against the terrorists, disbanding there on 1 April, 1955. On 15 October that year it re-formed at Driffield as a night-fighter squadron with Venoms, disbanding again on 3 June, 1957. On 30 September, 1957 it was again re-formed as a night-fighter squadron by re-numbering No. 264 Squadron at Leeming, flying Meteors and Javelins until again disbanding on 17 November, 1962.

On 14 June, 1971 No. 33 Squadron re-formed in the tactical helicopter role at Odiham and became the first unit to equip with the Anglo-French Aérospatiale/Westland SA.330 Puma HC.1. It was at first involved in working this type into squadron service but was soon available, as part of 38 Group, for deployment with the army wherever required. This has resulted in many exercises in Norway as well as deployments to various trouble spots, taking its turn in joining the security forces in Northern Ireland and maintaining a detachment at Belize to help keep the peace there.

Bases etc.

Re-formed at Odiham on 14 June, 1971.
Odiham   Jun 1971—

Main Equipment

Aérospatiale/Westland Puma HC.1 (Jun 1971—   )
    XW204, CA; XW206, CC; XW210, CG; XW212, CJ; XW226, CN;
    XW231, CO; XW236, CP, later CQ

Commanding Officers

W/Cdr F. D. Hoskins	Jun 1971—Aug 1973	
W/Cdr J. F. Strong, MBE	Aug 1973—Jul 1975	
W/Cdr G. F. Poyser	Jul 1975—Jun 1977	
W/Cdr K. O. Harding	Jun 1977—	

Aircraft Insignia

The Squadron emblem of a hart's head is carried on the sides of the cockpit flanked by the red and blue horizontal bars which No. 33 carried as a fighter squadron. In addition the helicopters carry two-letter identity codes of which the first letter, 'C', identifies No. 33 Squadron.
(See also *Bomber Squadrons of the RAF*, pp. 48–9 and *Fighter Squadrons of the RAF*, pp. 95–9).

No. 34 SQUADRON

BADGE
In front of a crescent moon a wolf passant

MOTTO
'*Lupus vult, lupus volat*'
('Wolf wishes, wolf flies')

The original squadron badge was a star and crescent, adopted from the badge of the 33rd Punjabis, one of whose officers was the first CO.

No. 34 Squadron was formed at Castle Bromwich on 7 January, 1916 and became the first Squadron equipped with the B.E.2E. These it took to France in July, 1916 and was immediately thrown into battle at the Somme, Lt H.M. Probyn flying the first contact patrol on 12th. Thereafter the Squadron was engaged in artillery patrols, special recces, photography, artillery observation sorties, flash recces and counter battery patrols, the latter using Klaxon horns to transmit messages to the ground. By August the Squadron was flying 40 to 50 hours per day and this in spite of a spate of engine problems. The work more and more involved bombing and strafing trenches as the battle wore on and for this two armour-plated B.E.2e's arrived. As the winter came on the operations dropped off,

the engine problems were not solved and by January, 1917 No. 34 was waiting to re-equip. R.E.8s came at the end of January, 1917 and with these it concentrated on low-level work as the Germans withdrew. Again the pressure increased until in the summer it moved north for the Battle of Ypres. Here it was very busy, on one day in July 61 hours were flown and 34 Squadron experimented with dropping grenades into the trenches at low level.

On 29 October No. 34 was withdrawn from operations and moved to the Italian Front, beginning operations there on 29 November. It was now fulfilling much more traditional corps duties although some bombing sorties were flown in addition. For the next year the Squadron flew continuously on this work as the offensive against the Austrian armies unfolded. Its last operation was on 16 November, 1918. It remained in Italy, flying training and delivery flights until April, 1919 when it returned to the UK and was disbanded at Old Sarum on 25 September, 1919.

No. 34 Squadron re-formed on 3 December, 1935 as a bomber unit at Bircham Newton and remained in this role until May, 1943. By then it had moved to the Far East, being virtually destroyed in the fall of Singapore. It was rebuilt in India and fought in the Burma campaign becoming a Hurricane fighter ground attack squadron in 1943 and finishing the war there with Thunderbolts, disbanding at

Palam on 18 October, 1945. Next there followed two short existences in differing roles. On 1 August, 1946 No. 681 Squadron at Palam was re-numbered No. 34. It was now equipped with Spitfire PR.19s and engaged in photo-reconnaissance work which at that time mainly consisted of aerial survey although some operational sorties were made in addition. However, this period only last until 31 July, 1947 when the Squadron was again disbanded. Its next existence was as a non-operational anti-aircraft co-operation squadron at Horsham St. Faith from March, 1949 to November, 1952.

However, No. 34 came to life once more as a fighter squadron in July, 1954 at Tangmere with Meteors and then Hunters flying as part of the Tangmere Wing until 10 January, 1958 when it was disbanded to provide the personnel for 208 Squadron's re-forming.

No. 34 Squadron's final existence began on 1 October, 1960 when it re-formed in the transport role. It was equipped with Blackburn Beverley C.1s and flew these around the Far East providing the heavy-lift component of the FEAF Transport Force. This involved tactical flying with the army in Malaya and Borneo as well as route-flying to Hong Kong and elsewhere, and this task continued for seven years, the Squadron disbanding at Seletar on 31 December, 1967.

Bases etc.

Formed at Castle Bromwich on 7 January, 1916.

Castle Bromwich	Jan 1916—Mar 1916	
Beverley	Mar 1916—Jun 1916	
Lilbourne	Jun 1916—Jul 1916	
Allonville	Jul 1916—Jan 1917	
Villers Brettoneux	Jan 1917—May 1917	
Nurlu	May 1917—Jun 1917	
Estree-en-Chaussee	Jun 1917—Jul 1917	
Bray Dunes	Jul 1917—Oct 1917	
Candas	Oct 1917—Nov 1917	
Milazzo	Nov 1917—Nov 1917	
Montichari	Nov 1917—Nov 1917	
Verona	Nov 1917—Nov 1917	
Grossa, det. Marcou	Nov 1917—Dec 1917	
Istrana	Dec 1917—Mar 1918	
Villaverla, det. Casoni	Mar 1918—Oct 1918	
Santa Luca	Oct 1918—Nov 1918	
Villaverla	Nov 1918—Feb 1919	
Caldiero	Feb 1919—May 1919	
Old Sarum	May 1919—Sep 1919	

Disbanded at Old Sarum 25 September, 1919. Re-formed at Bircham Newton 3 December, 1935 as a bomber squadron and served in this and fighter roles until disbanding at Palam on 18 October, 1945. Re-formed as a photo reconnaissance squadron at Palam by re-numbering No. 681 Squadron on 1 August, 1946.

Palam, det. Kallang	Aug 1946—Jul 1947

Disbanded at Palam on 31 July, 1947. Thereafter served in the AAC and fighter roles from March, 1949 to January, 1958. Re-formed at Seletar on 1 October, 1960 in the heavy transport role, from No. 48 Squadron's Beverley Flight.

Seletar	Oct 1960—Dec 1967

Disbanded at Seletar on 31 December, 1967.

Main Equipment

B.E.2e (Jun 1916—Jan 1917)
5737; 5749; 5815; 5826; 5843; 5855; 6748; 7086; 7096; 7100; 7154; 7165
B.E.2c (Jan 1916—Nov 1916)
2556; 4583 (Armour-plated)
R.E.8. (Jan 1917—May 1919)
A78; A99; A3428; A3474, 18; A3614; A3660; A4200; A4723; B2254; B5029; B5084; B6485; B6530; B8875; B8886; C5029; C5070; D4831; D4908; D6833; E131; E238; E264
Bristol Fighter F.2B (Mar 1918—Jun 1918)
Bristol Fighter Flt. Formed 139 Sqdn. 3/7/18
B1214; B1230; C4674; C4757
Vickers-Supermarine Spitfire PR.19 (Aug 1946—Jul 1947)
PM514, E; PM542, F; PM546, D; PM547, B
Blackburn Beverley C.1 (Oct 1960—Dec 1967)
XB260, U; XB262, W; XB264; XB283; XB289; XB291; XL150; XM104, P; XM112, V

Commanding Officers

Maj J. A. Chamier	Jan 1916—Apr 1917
Maj A. H. Morton	Apr 1917—Jun 1917
Maj C. H. B. Blount	Jun 1917—Apr 1918
Maj R. J. Mounsey	Apr 1918—Mar 1919
Capt W. H. Naylor	Mar 1919—May 1919
S/Ldr J. W. Adams	Oct 1960—
S/Ldr M. G. Bennett	—
W/Cdr D. J. Green	1964— 1966
S/Ldr M. G. Bennett, DFC	1966—Dec 1967

Aircraft Insignia

It is not known what markings the B.E.2e's had but the R.E.8s, whilst in Italy at least, carried two white vertical bars, one each side of the roundels, inclined inwards at the top. It is believed that the Spitfire PR.19s carried no squadron insignia at all. The Beverleys carried the Squadron badge on the fuselage sides under the cockpit and a green diamond at the top of the fin with a white '34' in it.
(See also *Bomber Squadrons of the RAF*, pp. 48–9 and *Fighter Squadrons of the RAF*, pp. 95–9).

No. 35 SQUADRON

BADGE
A horse's head winged

MOTTO
'Uno animus agimus'
('We act with one accord')

The badge commemorates co-operation with
the cavalry during World War I.

No. 35 Squadron was formed from a nucleus of No. 9 (Reserve) Squadron at Thetford on 1 February, 1916 and equipped with various training types, eg Farmans, Vickers F.B.5s, B.E.2c's, B.E.2e's and A.W. F.K.3s. Initially it too had a training role but in June it moved to Narborough and began to work up for service in France. Whilst here it re-equipped with the A.W. F.K.8 and it took this type to France on 25 January, 1917. It had been especially trained to work with the Cavalry Corps on army co-operation duties and it served with the Corps throughout World War I. This meant that its primary task was reconnaissance but it was naturally thrown into other tasks, particularly during the March, 1918 withdrawal when it was involved in low-attack work against enemy troops. No. 35 also indulged in night bombing attacks at this time and from February to July, 1918 had a Flight of Bristol Fighters. Many contact patrols were flown with the Corps during the two years of operations. With the war in France over it remained there until March, 1919 when it returned to the UK and was disbanded at Netheravon on 26 June, 1919.

No. 35 re-formed ten years later as a bomber squadron in which role it has served ever since, at first with light bombers, Fairey IIIFs, Gordons, Wellesleys and Battles, becoming an OTU (No. 17) on 8 April, 1940, and re-forming on 5 November, 1940 to pioneer the Handley Page Halifax into RAF service. Throughout World War II it flew the Halifax, at first as part of 4 Group, then transferring to No. 8 (Pathfinder) Group. Since World War II it has served in Bomber Command and Strike Command with Lancasters, Lincolns, Washingtons, Canberras and Vulcans.

Bases etc.

Formed at Thetford 1 February, 1916.

Thetford	Feb 1916—Jun 1916	
Narborough	Jun 1916—Jan 1917	
St. Omer	Jan 1917—Feb 1917	
St. André aux Bois	Feb 1917—Mar 1917	
Savy	Mar 1917—May 1917	
Villers Brettoneux	May 1917—May 1917	

Mons-en-Chaussee	May 1917—Jul 1917	
Savy	Jul 1917—Aug 1917	
La Gorgue	Aug 1917—Oct 1917	
La Lovie	Oct 1917—Oct 1917	
Bruay	Oct 1917—Nov 1917	
Estree-en-Chaussee	Nov 1917—Mar 1918	
Chipilly	Mar 1918—Mar 1918	
Poulaineville	Mar 1918—Mar 1918	
Abbeville	Mar 1918—Apr 1918	
Poulaineville	Apr 1918—May 1918	
Villers Bocage	May 1918—Sep 1918	
Suzanne	Sep 1918—Sep 1918	
Moislains	Sep 1918—Oct 1918	
Longavesnes	Oct 1918—Oct 1918	
Elincourt	Oct 1918—Nov 1918	
Flaumont	Nov 1918—Nov 1918	
Le Grand Fayt	Nov 1918—Nov 1918	
Elincourt	Nov 1918—Nov 1918	
La Bellevue	Nov 1918—Jan 1919	
St. Marie-Cappel	Jan 1919—Mar 1919	
Netheravon	Mar 1919—Jun 1919	

Disbanded at Netheravon on 26 June, 1919. Re-formed on 1 March, 1929 in the bomber role at Bircham Newton.

Main Equipment

Training types (Feb 1916—   1916)
F.E.2b
    6941
A.W. F.K.3
    A8117, A
A.W. F.K.8 (1916—Mar 1919)
    A2685; A2688; B283; B327; B3305; B3313; B5781; B5825; C3390;
    C8588; D5051; D5109; E8838; F7383; F7446
Bristol F.2B Fighter (Feb 1918—Jul 1918 & Sep 1918—Mar 1919)
    A7221; B1134; C4849; D7903

Commanding Officers

Maj B. F. Vernon-Harcourt	Feb 1916—Feb 1917
Maj A. V. Holt, DSO	Feb 1917—Apr 1918
Maj K. F. Balmain	Apr 1918—Sep 1918
Maj D. F. Stevenson, DSO, MC	Sep 1918—Jun 1919

Aircraft Insignia

Whilst a training unit at Thetford its aircraft had a variety of markings as did most training units but once it had gone to France its Armstrong-Whitworth F.K.8s carried a horizontal white bar along the side of the fuselage.

No. 36 SQUADRON

BADGE
An eagle, wings elevated, perched on a torpedo

MOTTO
'Rajawali raja langit'
('Eagle, King of the Sky')

The badge commemorates the Squadron's
niche in RAF history as the first
fully-operational torpedo-bomber squadron.

In its World War I existence No. 36 was a fighter squadron, formed at Cramlington on 1 February, 1916 and used throughout that war on Home Defence duties. It scored one Zeppelin, *L.34*, on 27 November, 1916. It was disbanded on 13 June, 1919 at Ashington.

On 1 October, 1928 the Coastal Defence Torpedo Flight, which had formed at Donibristle on 7 July that year, was numbered 36 Squadron. It was equipped with Hawker Horsley aircraft together with one Blackburn Dart for making smoke screens. Immediately it was thrown into exercises with the Home Fleet and in the next year's war games it could claim six hits out of 18 dummy torpedoes dropped. By the end of 1929 it had dropped 735 torpedoes. But its time with the Home Fleet was running out for in September, 1930 it was transferred overseas, with its eight Horsleys beginning the slow ferry flight to Singapore. It eventually set up base there on 17 December. Initially No. 36 flew survey flights around the Malayan area looking for landing grounds but by March 1931 it was into Fleet exercises once more. At the same time it was detached to Rangoon where it flew bombing sorties against rebels at Tharawaddy. Thereafter it settled down to a routine of torpedo and survey flying with ASR as a significant part of its taskings. In the next few years quite a few Horsleys were lost and in 1935 Vildebeests came as replacements. Flying was intensified with these and practice reinforcement flights to India were flown in 1936.

The outbreak of World War II had little effect on No. 36 and for the next year it was mainly involved in photography, taking mosaics of the surrounding operational areas. It still had Vildebeests when Japan attacked Malaya and although it gallantly went into action against the Japanese naval forces the Squadron was almost wiped out. The survivors fled to Java where they fought with their last remaining aircraft and were eventually captured.

On 22 October, 1942 No. 36 Squadron was re-formed on paper at Tanjor. However, it was not until December that any real organisation took place and its first Wellington VIIIs arrived. The Squadron's task was maritime reconnaissance and it flew its first operation, a shipping escort, on 13 January, 1943. By April it was up to 43 sorties per month but the Indian Ocean provided no action and in May it moved to North Africa where it concentrated on U-boat hunts. On 31 August F/O R. Keady made the Squadron's first U-boat attack but no results could be seen. At this time No. 36 was flying six different versions of the Wellington (Mk. IC, VIII, X, XI, XII & XIII), most of its operations being at night. In October it flew 135 operational sorties but opposition was forthcoming and many crews reported attacks by Ju 88s. On 3 November Sgt Gallagher straddled a U-boat with his depth-charges, whilst in January, 1944 five attacks were made. The Squadron was now established with detached bases at several points around the Mediterranean and patrols were worked out so as to fly between bases, enabling more time spent over the sea. In February came the landings at Anzio with the Squadron covering the convoy and in May No. 36 found and led the Navy to three U-boats which were then sunk. As the year wore on the Squadron diversified into supply-dropping for partisans and recces for human torpedoes until September when it moved to the UK.

In England it set up base at Chivenor flying anti-shipping box patrols off the Channel Islands and attempting to find Schnorchel U-boats. In March, 1945 it moved to the Hebrides and flew A/S patrols and convoy escorts for three months, by which time the war ended and the Squadron disbanded on 4 June, 1945.

On 1 October, 1946 No. 36 re-formed at Thorney Island by re-numbering No. 248 Squadron. For a year it flew coastal strike duties with Mosquito FB.6s until disbanding again at Thorney Island on 15 October, 1947.

When Coastal Command expanded again in the fifties No. 36 Squadron was re-formed once more. At Topcliffe on 1 July, 1953 it became a maritime recce unit with Lockheed Neptune MR.1s, its sphere of operation the Norwegian coast and beyond. This existence lasted for four years until Coastal Command standardised on Shackletons and the Neptunes were returned to the US Navy. The Squadron disbanded on 28 February, 1957. On 1 September, 1958 No. 36 re-formed in a new role, this time as a transport Squadron. The base was Colerne, No. 36 forming part of the Colerne Hastings Wing and flying Transport Command routes with them until July, 1967. It also flew in the army support role carrying out paradrops when required. This role was continued when No. 36 became the first RAF squadron to receive Lockheed Hercules in 1967 and, after working these into service, became the forerunner of the Lyneham Transport Wing, being joined by other Hercules squadrons as the years progressed. However, with the drastic defence cuts in 1975 No. 36 Squadron was disbanded on 3 November that year.

Bases etc.

Formed at Cramlington on 1 February, 1916 in the Home Defence role. Disbanded at Ashington on 13 June, 1919. Re-formed from the Coastal Defence Torpedo Flight at Donibristle on 1 October, 1928.

Donibristle	Oct 1928—Jun 1930	
Kenley	Jun 1930—Jun 1930	
Donibristle	Jun 1930—Sep 1930	
en route to Singapore	Sep 1930—Dec 1930	
Seletar	Dec 1930—Aug 1941	
Kuantan	Aug 1941—Aug 1941	
Seletar	Aug 1941—Dec 1941	
Kota Bharu	Dec 1941—Dec 1941	
Gong Khedah	Dec 1941—Jan 1942	
Kuantan	Jan 1942—Jan 1942	
Seletar	Jan 1942—Feb 1942	
Tjikampek	Feb 1942—Feb 1942	
Tjikamber	Feb 1942—Mar 1942	

On 7 March, 1942 No. 36 Squadron ceased to exist at Tjikamber. It re-formed at Tanjore on 22 October, 1942 in the maritime reconnaissance role.

Tanjore, det. Cholavarum, Vizagapatam	Oct 1942—Mar 1943	
Dhubalia	Mar 1943—Jun 1943	
Blida, det. Protville, Tafaroui, Bone, La Senia, Borizzo, Ghisoniacca, Gibraltar, Grottaglie, Monte Corvino	Jun 1943—Apr 1944	
Reghaia, det. Blida, La Senia, Bone, Grottaglie, Alghero	Apr 1944—Sep 1944	
Alghero	Sep 1944—Sep 1944	
Tarquinia	Sep 1944—Sep 1944	
Thorney Island	Sep 1944—Sep 1944	
Chivenor	Sep 1944—Mar 1945	
Benbecula	Mar 1945—Jun 1945	

Disbanded at Benbecula 1 June, 1945. Re-formed by re-numbering No. 248 Squadron at Thorney Island on 1 October, 1946 in the coastal strike role.

Thorney Island	Oct 1946—Oct 1947	

Disbanded at Thorney Island 15 October, 1947. Re-formed at Topcliffe on 1 July, 1953 in the maritime recce role.

Topcliffe	Jul 1953—Feb 1957	

Disbanded at Topcliffe 28 February, 1957. Re-formed at Colerne in the transport role in 1 September, 1958.

Colerne	Sep 1958—Jul 1967	
Lyneham	Jul 1967—Nov 1975	

Disbanded at Lyneham on 3 November, 1975.

Main Equipment

Hawker Horsley (Oct 1928—Jul 1935)
J8014; J8601; J8620; S1237, 1; S1246; S1437, U; S1439; S1440; S1443, M; S1598; S1604, P; S1610; S1613, U

Vickers Vildebeest III (Jun 1935—Mar 1942)
K2940 (Mk. II); K4166, S; K4167, M; K4169, A; K4173, W; K4175, V; K4176, B; K4182, D; K4599, VU:J; K6387; K6394, B; K6402, J

Vickers Wellington IC (Dec 1942—Oct 1943)
Z8769, A; BB470, F; DV499; DV943, G; HE120, F; HE128, L; HX429, U

Vickers Wellington VIII (Dec 1942—Oct 1943)
HF537, C; HX574, P; HX679, V; HX725, O; LB110, K; LB136, S; LB227, L

Vickers Wellington X (Jun 1943—Oct 1943)
HF533, G; HF570, Q; LN267, M

Vickers Wellington XI (Jun 1943—Nov 1943)
MP625, Y; MP651, K

Vickers Wellington XII (Jun 1943—Nov 1943)
HF119, L; HF120, K; MP650, Y

Vickers Wellington XIII (Jun 1943—Jan 1944)
HZ586, F; HZ589, V; HZ707, C; HZ883, D; MP704, A; MP748, O

Vickers Wellington XIV (Oct 1943—Jun 1945)
HF129, RW:U; HF224, T; HF272, X; HF310, RW:E; HF357, Q; MP795, V; MP807, H; MP823, N; NB824, RW:C; NB878, RW:K; NB912, RW:A; NB961, RW:F

de Havilland Mosquito FB.6 (Oct 1946—Oct 1947)
No serials known

Lockheed Neptune MR.1 (Jul 1953—Feb 1957)
WX521, T:B; WX543, E; WX546, T:D; WX550, T:A; WX553, T:F; WX556, H

Handley Page Hastings C.1A (Sep 1958—Jul 1967)
TG516; TG522; TG577; TG582

Handley Page Hastings C.2 (Sep 1958—Jul 1967)
WD477; WD491; WJ327; WJ329; WJ339; WJ343

Lockheed Hercules C.1 (Jul 1967—Nov 1975)
XV181; XV191; XV194; XV215; XV220; XV302

Commanding Officers

S/Ldr A. W. Mylne	Jul 1928—Nov 1932	
S/Ldr T. A. Langford-Sainsbury, DFC, AFC	Nov 1932—Sep 1935	
S/Ldr A. H. Paull	Sep 1935—Oct 1935	
S/Ldr E. D. H. Davies	Oct 1935—Dec 1936	
S/Ldr G. A. Beardsworth	Dec 1936—Oct 1938	
S/Ldr R. L. Wallace	Oct 1938—Dec 1939	
S/Ldr D. S. E. Vines	Dec 1939—Feb 1941	
S/Ldr R. C. Gaskell	Feb 1941—Nov 1941	
S/Ldr G. F. Witney	Nov 1941— 1942	
F/O T. S. Percival	Oct 1942—Dec 1942	
F/Ldr D. E. Hawkins, DFC	Dec 1942—Jan 1943	
W/Cdr K. J. Mellor, DFC	Jan 1943—May 1943	
W/Cdr E. K. Piercy	May 1943—Sep 1943	
W/Cdr D. P. Marvin, DFC	Sep 1943—Jun 1944	
W/Cdr D. Williams	Jun 1944—Jun 1945	
S/Ldr P. R. Godly	Jul 1953—Aug 1955	
W/Cdr D. A. Lindsay, OBE, DFC	Aug 1955—Jan 1957	
S/Ldr C. L. Roy, DSO	Jan 1957—Feb 1957	
S/Ldr D. D. Pearce	Feb 1957—Sep 1957	
W/Cdr L. W. Green, DFC	Sep 1958—Jun 1960	
W/Cdr L. F. Wolsey	Jun 1960—Dec 1962	
W/Cdr R. J. Wilson	Dec 1962—Oct 1964	
W/Cdr D. J. Dodimead	Oct 1964—	
W/Cdr J. D. Payling	— 1966	
W/Cdr G. H. Gilbert	Oct 1969—Sep 1971	
W/Cdr R. McN. Brown	Sep 1971—Aug 1973	
W/Cdr R. A. Miller	Aug 1973—Nov 1975	

Aircraft Insignia

As far as is known no squadron insignia was carried until the Squadron returned to the UK in 1944, although it is likely that some form of code lettering was carried by the Vildebeests in Singapore from 1939 to 1942, the combination 'VU' being used for the period up to September, 1939. Whilst based at Chivenor in 1944–5 the Wellington XIVs carried the code letters 'RW'; it is generally accepted that when No. 248 Squadron became No. 36 in 1946 the Squadron retained the 'DM' code letters on its Mosquitoes.

During the Neptune period the aircraft at first carried a two-letter combination of which the first letter, 'T' denoted No. 36 Squadron. This was later dropped and the Squadron number, '36' painted in its place in green, outlined in white. The Squadron badge was also carried on the fuselage sides below the pilots' cockpit. The Hastings at first carried a dark blue diamond on the fin top with '36' in it in white. This was dropped in the early sixties and replaced by the Squadron emblem but when the Colerne Wing went over to centralised servicing this was deleted. No specific squadron markings were carried on the Hercules.
(See also *Fighter Squadrons of the RAF*, p. 102.)

No. 37 SQUADRON

BADGE
A hawk hooded, belled and fessed, wings elevated and addorsed

MOTTO
'Wise without eyes'

The badge is indicative of the duties of blind flying.

Originally formed on 15 April, 1916 at Orfordness No. 37 Squadron's first existence was but a month, when it became absorbed into the experimental unit on its base. It reformed as a Home Defence fighter squadron at Woodham Mortimer on 15 September, 1916, serving as such until 1 July, 1919 when it was disbanded at Biggin Hill. When No. 37 re-formed again from a nucleus of No. 214 Squadron it was as a bomber squadron at Feltwell and it served in that role throughout World War II, mainly in the Mediterrranean area, finally disbanding at Fayid on 1 April, 1947.

No. 37 re-formed on 14 September, 1947 at Ein Shemer in the Canal Zone as a maritime reconnaissance unit with Avro Lancasters and was responsible for the Eastern Mediterranean area. In April, 1948 it moved to Malta, with a detachment at Gibraltar, and flew all over the Mediterranean on maritime surveillance duties. In August, 1953 the Lancasters were replaced by Avro Shackleton MR.2s and these were used operationally during the 1956 Suez operations. In 1957 the Squadron moved to Aden for covering the Southern Arabian and Indian Ocean areas and was also used for colonial policing, supplementing the forces already there. Consequently its Shackletons were involved in 1961 when the Kuwait crisis blew up. In March, 1966, when sanctions were imposed on Rhodesia the Squadron sent a detachment to Majunga to begin the Beira Strait patrols. Eighteen months after this British Forces withdrew from Aden so No. 37 Squadron was disbanded, in September, 1967.

Bases etc.

Re-formed in the maritime role at Ein Shemer on 14 September, 1947.

Ein Shemer	Sep	1947—Apr 1948
Luqa, det. Gibraltar, Trucial Oman, Durban	Apr	1948—Jul 1957
Khormaksar, det. Majunga	Jul	1957—Sep 1967

Disbanded at Khormaksar in September, 1967.

Main Equipment

Avro 683 Lancaster GR.3 (Sep 1947—Aug 1953)
RE167 F, later J; RE173, A; RF291 K, later G; RF308, F; SW287, C; SW336, B; SW344, B; SW372, C; TX267

Avro Shackleton MR.2 (Aug 1953—Sep 1967)
WG556, K; WL754 H, later E WL785, E; WL788, A; WL797, C; WL800, X; WR962, A

Aircraft Insignia

No markings, other than the Squadron badge in standard format under the cockpit, was carried until the Squadron moved to Aden when '37' painted red in white outline was painted on the aft fuselage.
(See also *Bomber Squadrons of the RAF*, pp. 54—7 and *Fighter Squadrons of the RAF*, p.103)

No. 38 SQUADRON

BADGE
A heron volant

MOTTO
'Ante lucem'
('Before the Dawn')

The heron was chosen as being typical of East Anglia, where the Squadron was originally formed. As the heron rarely misses its mark, becomes active as twilight descends and is a formidable fighter when attacked it was deemed suitable for a night bomber squadron.

The Squadron was originally formed at Thetford on 1 April, 1916, serving only 52 days before disbanding into No. 25 Reserve Squadron. It re-formed on 14 July, 1916 at Castle Bromwich as a Home Defence squadron for the West Midlands until May, 1918 when it took its night-fighters (F.E.2b's) to Dunkirk for night-bombing duties which it carried out until the end of October, 1918. It returned to England in February, 1919 and was disbanded at Hawkinge on 4 July, 1919.

On 16 September, 1935 No. 38 was re-formed at Mildenhall as a heavy bomber squadron and served in this role over the Continent until November, 1940 having used Heyfords, Hendons and Wellingtons. In that month it transferred to the Middle East, flying from Egyptian bases on raids throughout the Eastern Mediterranean and Italy. In January, 1942, whilst carrying out bombing raids, it was also experimenting with torpedoes, the Wellington ICs being fitted to carry two Mk.XII torpedoes (the nose turret was deleted to save weight). The idea was to increase the range of the torpedo-bombing force in Egypt. In February the Squadron transferred to No. 201 Naval Co-operation Group and now exclusively flew against maritime targets. As the year progressed No. 38 was chiefly flying mining sorties, although two attempts at torpedo attacks were abortive due to not finding the convoys to be attacked. However, at the end of May two torpedo attacks were made on convoys in which hits were achieved resulting in one ship having to beach near Benghazi. These operations were flown from ALGs in the desert and at Malta. June was a busy month with 59 sorties flown, mounting to 144 in July, including straight bombing, mining and torpedo attacks with several hits. In August it acquired its own ASV-equipped aircraft, thus building up a hunter/killer tactic which bore fruition on 26th with a tanker torpedoed and sunk.

Operations continued on this basis into 1943 although the accent changed to anti-submarine work as the year drew on. On 19 February F/O Butler, AFC found a sub whilst on convoy escort in LB177 S, directed a destroyer to it and it was sunk, typical of the more successful of No. 38 Squadron's work. Torpedoes were still carried at times but most of the Squadron's work now comprised normal convoy escorts and A/S hunts. On 13 June F/Sgt Taylor bombed two ships and blew one out of the water, one of the more satisfying opportunities as more offensive shipping strikes came up on the programme. In the last month of the year No. 38 flew a record number of sorties (210) of which 128 were on A/S patrols, 64 on offensive strikes in the Aegean and 18 were mining sorties.

These operations were not without loss, usually about two aircraft per month being lost. The pattern through 1944 was much the same, the Squadron being actively involved in the liberation of Greece and being stationed there for a short while at the end of the year. Torpedo operations were now a thing of the past, the Squadron having become a normal maritime Wellington unit. In November, 1944 control of the Squadron was transferred to the Balkan Air Force and No. 38 was involved in supply-dropping and leaflet dropping in Greece and the Aegean Islands. In 1945 it transferred its attention to the Adriatic Sea as the land forces advanced up Italy. In April it concentrated in attacking midget submarines, scoring one confirmed and two probables. As the war ended the Squadron flew more ASR sorties and was also involved in minespotting.

In July, 1945 No. 38 moved to Malta and became an ASR Squadron, re-equipping with Warwicks for this purpose. This became its peacetime role until October, 1946 when it re-equipped with Lancasters with which it flew both ASR and maritime reconnaissance sorties. Primarily it was based at Malta although it flew spells from Egypt and Gibraltar. At the end of 1954 the Shackleton MR.2 replaced the Lancasters and this type was used for thirteen years during which time it was increasingly involved in tracing the movement of Soviet submarines and surface vessels. No. 38 also became involved in various 'fire brigade' activities such as Suez and Kuwait and for the last year of its operations it had a detachment in Madagascar flying sanction patrols in the Mozambique Channel. On 31 March, 1967 the Squadron was disbanded at Hal Far, Malta.

Bases etc

In January, 1942 the Squadron transferred to the maritime role at Shallufa.

Shallufa, det. LG.05, Luqa, St. Jean, LG. 226	Jan	1942—Nov 1942
Gambut, det. Berca	Nov	1942—Feb 1943
Shallufa, det. Berca III, Misurata, LG. 91	Feb	1943—Nov 1944
Kalamaki	Nov	1944—Eec 1944
Grottaglie	Dec	1944—Feb 1945
Foggia, det. Hal Far, Rosignano	Feb	1945—Apr 1945
Falconara	Apr	1945—Jul 1945
Luqa, det. Elmas, Benina	Jul	1945—Dec 1946
Ein Shemer	Dec	1946—Nov 1947
Luqa, det. Ramat David	Nov	1947— 1950
Gibraltar	1950— 1950
Luqa, det. Majunga	1950—Sep 1965
Hal Far	Sep	1965—Mar 1967

Disbanded at Hal Far on 31 March, 1967

Main Equipment
(in the maritime role)

Vickers Wellington IC (Jan 1942—Feb 1943)
N2740, Y; T2570, P; T2825, Q; W5624, J; W5648, S; X3168, T; X9693, Z; X9735, H; X9947, U; Z8762, K; Z8908, H; A593, Q; DV542, A; HD965, Z; HF896, F; HX591, J

Vickers Wellington VIII (Mar 1942—Aug 1943)
T2825, Y; T2831, F; HX366, Y; HX397, M; HX442, Q; HX470, W; HX627, D; HX633, E; HX685, C; HX727, B; LB111, P; LB146, D; LB177, S; LB197, D; LB233, C;

Vickers Wellington XI (Jul 1943—Apr 1944)
HZ308, A; HZ315, U; HZ394, V; MP582, J; MP616, O; MP633, Q; MP643, M;

Vickers Wellington XIII (1943—Jan 1945)
HZ598, P; HZ602, X; HZ706, K; HX881, F; HZ970, Y; JA108, H; JA141, K; JA359, D; JA566, Z; ME930, E; ME944, D; MF153, S; MF206, D; MF259, X; MP742, D; MP757, Y
Vickers Wellington XIV (Jan 1945—Jun 1946)
HF384, C; MP797, N; NB885, V; NB925, Z; NB966, B; NC511, Y; NC674, K; NC771, O,
Vickers Warwick I (Jul 1945—Nov 1946)
BV284, U; BV342; BV387; BV436, X; BV437, Y; HG414
Avro Lancaster ASR.3 (Nov 1946—   1949)
PB305; RE123 RL:R, RF269; RF300 RL:N, RF310, RL:O, later Y SW288 RL:P TX269, RL:N
Avro Lancaster GR.3 (1948—Dec 1954)
RF273, T; SW288, P; SW295, Q; SW325, P; SW374, Z; TX272, S
Avro Shackleton MR. 2 (Dec 1954—Mar 1967)
WG533, W; WL740, Y, later U; WL756, T, later V; WL787, S; WL789, V; WL791, Q; WL794, Y; WL798, X; WL801, T, later Z; WR954, Z; WR961, S; WR964, V; WR967, Z; WR969, S

Commanding Officers

W/Cdr Gosnell		1942—Jun 1942
W/Cdr J. H. Chaplin, DSO	Jun 1942	—Jul 1942
W/Cdr C. V. J. Pratt	Jul 1942	—Dec 1942
W/Cdr B. G. Meharg, AFC	Dec 1942	—Jun 1943
W/Cdr F. R. Worthington	Jun 1943	—Aug 1943
W/Cdr W. T. Ritchie, AFC	Aug 1943	—Jan 1944
W/Cdr W. Appleby-Brown, DFC	Jan 1944	—Jan 1945
W/Cdr R. R. Banker, DSO, DFC	Jan 1945	—May 1945
W/Cdr J. H. Simpson, DFC	May 1945—	
S/Ldr E. D. T. Norman		(1952)
W/Cdr A. W. Harding, MBE	Nov 1960—	
W/Cdr I. Thomas, OBE		
W/Cdr M. O. Bergh		—Mar 1967

Aircraft Insignia

No specific Squadron markings were carried until the arrival of the Lancaster ASR.3s in 1946. These came from No. 279 Squadron, which disbanded, and the code letters RL were retained by 38 Squadron for some time. Later the Squadron badge was carried on the fuselage side beneath the cockpit. This was continued with the Shackleton MR 2s until the late fifties when the Squadron number was painted on the aft fuselage sides in red outlined in white. At the same time the Squadron's heron emblem was carried in a white disc on the fin top.

(See also *Bomber Squadrons of the RAF*, pp. 57–8 and *Fighter Squadrons of the RAF*, p. 104)

No. 39 SQUADRON

BADGE
A winged bomb

MOTTO
'Die Noctuque'
('By day and night')

The badge, which is self-explanatory, is based on the squadron's original unofficial badge.

No. 39 Squadron's first role was Home Defence and for this it was formed at Sutton's Farm and Hainault Farm on 15 April, 1916. Its task was to defend NE London. In September, 1916 it out-scored all other Home Defence units by destroying four Zeppelins in one month. Thereafter action was desultory and just before the end of the war it transferred to France but the Armistice came before it found any action. It was disbanded at Bavichove on 16 November, 1918.

However it re-formed from No. 37 Home Defence Squadron at Biggin Hill on 1 July, 1919 and became a day-bomber squadron two years later serving in the UK until the end of 1928 and then moving to the NW Frontier of India. On the outbreak of war it moved to Singapore but in April, 1940 it was transferred west to reinforce Aden from where it flew bombing raids in the Eritrean campaign. Then it moved up to Egypt for the Western Desert battles. Here, in January, 1941 it turned its attention to maritime reconnaissance, flying Blenheim Is and Marylands. However, in August No. 39 began to re-equip with Beaufort torpedo-bombers, acquiring crews from No. 86 Squadron and henceforward its role was to be coastal strike. In September the Marylands went to No. 12 SAAF Squadron and it concentrated on its new role. Operation Plug began in October in which No. 39 was engaged in armed recces of the sea around Greece and Crete to attack all enemy shipping. First action was by Sgt Harvey who attacked a U-boat without result. In November 70 sea recces were flown, one crew failed to return but on 24th the Squadron found an enemy convoy, led the Navy to it and it was destroyed.

The New Year saw one Flight on torpedo training. The first torpedo attack was on 23 January, the target being a 20,000-ton liner which was hit but not sunk. Ops continued with recces predominating; however on 9 March eight aircraft attacked a Tripoli convoy, sank a destroyer and damaged other ships, shooting down an escorting Ju 88. The Squadron was now heavily involved in attacks, using Malta as an advanced base. Losses, too, were heavy, seventeen aircrew perishing in April. By mid-May the Squadron was temporarily off operations, with a shortage of aircraft, but resumed early in June. On 15th twelve aircraft attacked the Italian battlefleet; only five got through, having torpedoed a battleship and

destroyer. By July the Squadron was flying day and night operations and was increasingly operating from Malta, more and more ships being hit and disabled. By the end of September virtually all the Squadron was in Malta and what was left in Egypt became No. 47 Squadron. The intensive operations lasted until 22 September and in October the Squadron returned to the Canal Zone. From here a detachment resumed attacks on Tobruk shipping. In November it returned to Malta and flew operations in both easterly and westerly directions, minelaying in the North African harbours to support the Allied landings. By the end of the year operations had turned more to conventional A/S patrols from Malta. 1943 saw No. 39 Squadron building up again with many new crews in Egypt, with a detachment in Malta flying operations. By February it was back flying all its operations from Malta with the ground crews at Shallufa with nothing to do. That month 100 offensive sorties were flown, eight attacks being made and at least two ships sunk. Operations continued at this rate until March but from April most sorties were at night, led by an ASV Wellington as target-finder.

In June, 1943 No. 39 moved to Protville where it began converting to the Beaufighter. Operations began in July as part of 328 Wing with Nos. 47 and 144 Squadrons. In that month four aircraft were lost but two ships were sunk and two damaged. This pace continued until the end of September when it came off operations for a month. When it resumed it was flying from Sicily on convoy patrols, *Stopper* patrols (intercepting enemy shipping recce aircraft) and at the same time converting to RP-equipped aircraft. In February, 1944 it moved to Sardinia from where it attacked shipping in Southern France, using RP for the first time in March. As the year wore on operations in this area dropped and, with a detachment in Italy, sorties were flown as far east as Salonika. In July the Squadron moved to Italy and concentrated on the Adriatic area and Yugoslavia. In October civil war broke out in Greece and this became the Squadron's next target area, flying RP strikes on road transport and being based in Athens in December.

In this month the main Squadron began converting to Marauders and resuming the pure bombing role whilst the Greek detachment continued operations against the ELAS guerillas until the 18 January, 1945 when it returned to Biferno.

As a bomber squadron No. 39 flew its Marauders until the war in Italy ended then it moved by stages to Khartoum and re-equipped with Mosquitoes. On 8 September, 1946 it disbanded there.

On 1 March, 1949 No. 39 re-formed as a fighter squadron and served in this role in the Middle East until June, 1958, flying Mosquito NF.36s and Meteor NF.13s, becoming operational again, from Cyprus, during the Suez troubles. It disbanded once more on 30 June, 1958.

The following day, 1 July, 1958 No. 69 Squadron at Luqa was re-numbered 39 Squadron and it now flew in the photo reconnaissance role. Equipped with Canberras it covered the Mediterranean and also flew survey work in Aden and East Africa. Re-equipping with the PR.9 version of the Canberra in 1962 it now operated detachments for survey work in many places, Africa, Germany, Italy, Greece, Turkey and the Far East all being visited. In addition, the Squadron changed over to the low-level recce role as part of the southern flank of NATO. In October, 1970 the Squadron returned to the UK, after 42 years absence, and became a low-level tactical recce unit in NATO, in addition having a shipping recce commitment as well as some survey work.

Bases etc.

In January, 1941 the Squadron transferred to the shipping recce and strike role at Helwan.

Helwan	Jan	1941—Jan	1941
Heliopolis	Jan	1941—Mar	1941
Shandur	Mar	1941—May	1941
Wadi Natrun, det. Burg-el-Arab, Edku	May	1941—Oct	1941
Mariut, det. Maaten Bagush, Edku	Oct	1941—Dec	1941
Aboukir, det. Sidi Barrani, Bu Amud, Luqa	Dec	1941—May	1942
Shallufa, det. Luqa	May	1942—May	1942
LG. 86, det. Sidi Barrani	May	1942—Jun	1942
Shandur, det. Sidi Barrani, Luqa	Jun	1942—Sep	1942
Luqa	Sep	1942—Oct	1942
Shallufa, det. Gianaclis	Oct	1942—Nov	1942
Luqa	Nov	1942—Dec	1942
Shallufa, det. Luqa, Berca, Gambut	Dec	1942—Jun	1943
Protville	Jun	1943—Oct	1943
Sidi Amor, det. Grottaglie	Oct	1943—Nov	1943
Reghaia, det. Grottaglie	Nov	1943—Feb	1944
Alghero, det. Grottaglie	Feb	1944—Jul	1944
Biferno, det. Reghaia, Hassani	Jul	1944—Jan	1945

In January, 1945 the Squadron reverted to the bomber role and was eventually disbanded in this role at Khartoum on 8 September, 1946. It was reformed as a fighter squadron there on 1 April, 1948 and disbanded in this role on 30 June, 1958. On 1 July, 1958 the Squadron was re-formed, by re-numbering No. 69 Squadron at Luqa, in the photo reconnaissance role.

Luqa	Jul	1958—Oct	1970
Wyton	Oct	1970—

Main Equipment

Bristol Blenheim I (Jan 1941—Jan 1941)
L1498; L8387; L8402, X; L8543; L8612
Martin Maryland I (Jan 1941—Jan 1942)
AH227; AH284; AH297; AH359; AH425; AR749; AR776; AX689

Bristol Beaufort I (Aug 1941—Dec 1942)
L4502; L9824; L9875; L9894; N1033; N1091; N1153; N1165; W6495; W6505; W6518; X8924; AW219; DD952, V; DE116, O; DE122, D; DW802, P; DW835, Z; DE880, X
Bristol Beaufort II (Jul 1942—Jun 1943)
AW280R; AW300, B; AW349, R; AW362, E; DD878, W; DD898, I; DD902, D; DD927, F; DD934, N; DD942, V
Bristol Beaufighter X (Jun 1943—Jan 1945)
JM316, X; JM387, N; JM408, Y; JM417, R; LX785, A; LX810, J; LX867, S; LX882, T; LX907, W; LX999, S; LZ142, Y; LZ338, H; LZ460; NE248, Z; NE362, J; NE412, F; NE466, A; NE549, G; NT998, F; NV250, O; NV597, P
English Electric Canberra PR.3 (Jul 1958—Oct 1962)
WE135; WE137, A; WE144, D; WE173, S; WF926; WH861, (T.4);
English Electric Canberra PR.9 (Oct 1962—   )
XH131; XH133; XH137; XH167; XH169; XH170, E; XH174; XH177

Commanding Officers

S/Ldr A. M. J. Bouman, DFC and Bar	Apr	1931—Sep 1941
W/Cdr R. B. Cox	Sep	1941—Dec 1941
W/Cdr A. J. Mason, DFC	Dec	1941—Sep 1942
W/Cdr R. P. M. Gibbs, DSO, DFC and Bar	Sep	1942—Sep 1942
W/Cdr M. L. Gaine, AFC	Sep	1942—Jun 1943
W/Cdr N. B. Harvey	Jun	1943—Jun 1944
W/Cdr A. R. de L. Inniss	Jun	1944—Jan 1945
W/Cdr V. C. Woodward, DFC	Jul	1958—Aug 1959
W/Cdr R. L. Wade, DFC	Aug	1959—Dec 1960
W/Cdr W. L. McD.Scott	Dec	1960—Dec1962
W/Cdr F. G. Agnew, AFC	Dec	1962—Jun 1965
W/Cdr H. A. Callard	Jun	1965—Mar 1967
W/Cdr T. P. O'Brien	Mar	1967—Jun 1967
W/Cdr A. McI.Cobban	Jun	1967—Jun 1969
W/Cdr C. H. Foale	Jun	1969—Apr 1971
W/Cdr T. P. O'Brien	Apr	1971—Apr 1973
W/Cdr F. Allen	Apr	1973—Jun 1975
W/Cdr B. Higgs	Jun	1975—Dec 1977
W/Cdr L. S. Frame	Dec	1977—

Aircraft Insignia

During the wartime period under review no specific squadron markings were carried. Upon re-equipping with Canberras the aircraft at first carried rectangles on the tip tanks with black and yellow interlocking triangles and the Squadron badge was carried on the nose sides. Later, this marking was changed to a stylised black and yellow flash on the tip tanks with the number '39' in the middle (see illustrations). With the coming of the Canberra PR.9s yet another change took place, the Squadron now carrying the emblem from the badge on a white fin disc. Since the toning-down of aircraft markings this has changed to the emblem on the fin in its own colour.
(See also *Bomber Squadrons* pp. 59–60 and *Fighter Squadrons of the RAF*, pp. 104–5.)

No. 40 SQUADRON

BADGE
A broom

MOTTO
'Hostem a caelo Expellere'
('To drive the enemy from the sky')

The broom immortalises the expression used by a famous World War I member of the Squadron, Major Mannock VC – 'Sweep the . . . Huns from the air'.

The Squadron formed at Gosport on 26 February, 1916 and flew gloriously in World War I as a scout (fighter) squadron with F.E.8s, Nieuports and S.E.5As. It remained in service until 4 July, 1919 when it was disbanded.

The Squadron re-formed on 1 April, 1931 in the bomber role and served as such in World War II with Blenheims, Wellingtons and Liberators from the UK until June, 1942 and then in the Middle East and Italy. After World War II it remained in the Canal Zone until 1 April, 1947 when it was disbanded at Shallufa.

On 1 December, 1947 No. 40 re-formed as a transport squadron at Abingdon and was equipped with Avro York C.1s. When the Berlin blockade began the Squadron was detached to Wunstorf and flew consistently on the Berlin Airlift until 1949 when the blockade was lifted. The Squadron was then based at Bassingbourn where it again disbanded on 15 March, 1950.

Its final existence was as a bomber squadron once more from 28 October, 1953 until 15 December, 1956, flying Canberras from Coningsby, Wittering and Upwood.

Bases, etc. (in the transport role)

Abingdon, det. Wunstorf	Dec	1947—Jun 1949
Bassingbourn	Jun	1949—Mar 1950

Main Equipment

Avro York C. 1 (Dec. 1947—Mar 1950)
MW142; MW193; MW195; MW206; MW244; PE101

Aircraft Insignia

As far as is known the Yorks of No. 40 Squadron carried no distinguishing insignia apart from the Transport Command call-sign code of MOWA on the nose.
(See also *Bomber Squadrons of the RAF*, pp. 60–2 and *Fighter Squadrons of the RAF*, pp. 105–6.)

No. 42 SQUADRON

BADGE
On a terrestrial globe the figure of Perseus

MOTTO
'Fortiter in re'
('Bravely in action')

No. 42 Squadron was the first to use the Bristol Perseus engine and this accounts for the presence of Perseus in the badge; he was known always to achieve his object and destroy his enemies and he stands in front of a globe to signify his activities over many lands and seas.

No. 42 Squadron, RFC formed as a corps reconnaissance squadron at Filton on 1 April, 1916. It worked up with the B.E.2d and went to France in August fully equipped with B.E.2e's. There it flew corps duties on the Somme with the 2nd Brigade, most of this consisting of recce patrols and artillery co-operation, interspersed with the occasional tactical bombing raid.

Early in 1917 the Squadron re-equipped with the R.E.8 and transferred to the 7th Brigade fighting in the Battle of Arras more effectively with its new equipment although in June it acquired some more B.E.2e's temporarily when its establishment was increased to 24 aircraft for the Battle of Messines and then Menin Ridge in September. These battles involved the Squadron in a high level of army co-operation work, inevitably bringing casualties as well and in December No. 42 was pulled out of the line and sent to the Italian Front. Here activity was much more peaceful but when the German offensive on the Western Front opened in March, 1918 the Squadron returned as reinforcement. Its task now was as a low-level bomber squadron attacking the positions behind the German lines and in this task the R.E.8 was not the most suitable aircraft. When the offensive had been turned back No. 42 resumed more traditional recce and artillery co-operation duties, taking part in the fight right through to the Armistice. It returned to England in February, 1919 and was disbanded at Netheravon on 26 June, 1919.

On 14 December, 1936 B Flight of No. 22 Squadron was expanded into a new No. 42 Squadron. Its new role was that of torpedo-bomber but until February, 1937 it had to share aircraft with No. 22 Squadron; in fact, there were only three Vickers Vildebeest IIIs between the two squadrons. No. 42s own Mk. I Vildebeests came then and were soon replaced by Mk. IIIs during the year. By March the Squadron was ready for exercises with the Battle Fleet and in that month it also took over the first Mk. IV Vildebeests with Perseus sleeve-valve engines. The year was a busy one, with attendance at the final RAF Display at Hendon, Armament Practice Camp and further Fleet exercises, typical peacetime activities which continued after a move to Thorney Island in 1938. As war drew closer in 1939 the Squadron also flew 'Trade Protection' sorties and its pilots went on twin conversion in anticipation of re-equipment. However, when war came it began East Coast convoy patrols from its war station in the same old biplanes. This activity continued until the summer of 1940 when No. 42 at last began converting go Beauforts. At first these were used for convoy and escort work but in June, 1940 the Squadron was detached northwards for operations against the German Navy, dive-bombing the *Scharnhorst* on 21st and losing three aircraft in the attack. This was followed by a grounding due to engine problems and it was not until August that operations resumed, with mining sorties.

The first ship sunk by No. 42 was on 26 October, a naval transport in Asfofjord, when one Messerschmitt Bf 109 was also shot down and two Beauforts lost. The Squadron was operating both off Norway and in the English Channel at this time, more and more of its sorties being at night. The Squadron was now flying about 90 sorties a month on shipping recce, mining and bombing attacks. February, 1941 was a busy month with more torpedo attacks recorded, two destroyers being damaged as well as merchant shipping. Norway remained the principal operational area. In June

No. 42 hit the *Lützow* (ex-*Deutschland*) successfully and during the summer night and day *Rovers* were flown with many successful attacks. This was not without cost, however, and casualties mounted, in fact the *Daily Mirror* referred to No. 42 as 'The Death Squadron'. In October the Squadron's attacks were now escorted by Beaufighters which cut down the casualties and the attacks were augmented by ASV-fitted Beauforts. On 23 February, 1942 S/Ldr W. H. Cliff, in L9965, led a 6-aircraft attack on *Tirpitz* but did not find it.

On the return trip his aircraft caught fire and he ditched in the North Sea. In the dinghy the crew had a carrier pigeon with them so, strapping a message to its leg, they sent the pigeon off. A pigeon from the crashed aircraft arrived near Broughty Ferry and was found with oil on it which led to the theory that it had landed on a tanker on route. A position was plotted for a tanker in the North Sea and eventually a searching Hudson found the dinghy and the crew were picked up.

The tempo increased reaching a climax on 17 May, 1942 when twelve aircraft attacked the *Prinz Eugen*, scoring two torpedo hits. Ten days later operations ceased and No. 42 prepared for overseas. In June it moved to Malta where its aircraft were taken over by Nos. 39 and 47 Squadrons. For a while No. 42s aircrew flew with No. 47 Squadron attacking shipping in the Eastern Mediterranean until the Squadron was reconstituted in the Canal Zone in October and moved on to the Far East.

Here No. 42 began life as a bomber unit with Blenheims flying on the Burma Front until re-equipping with Hurricanes in the fighter ground attack role in 1943. It fought on until the Burma campaign was ended and then disbanded at Meiktela on 31 December, 1945.

The Squadron re-formed as a torpedo-bomber unit for the last time on 1 October, 1946 when No. 254 Squadron was re-numbered at Thorney Island. It was now flying Beaufighters, the last home-based torpedo-bomber squadron in the RAF. This was short-lived, however, and the Squadron disbanded there on 15 October, 1947.

However, on 28 June, 1952 No. 42 Squadron was again re-formed, this time as a long-range maritime recce squadron equipped with the new Avro Shackleton MR.1s. After a work up on this type the Squadron settled into a routine of exercises and overseas trips, flying a goodwill visit to South Africa that year, and regular navigation exercises to Gibraltar. ASR became a secondary role of the Squadron but this was of no avail when two Squadron aircraft were lost off Fastnet Rock early in 1955.

Later that year a further secondary role was assumed, that of troop transport and this was flown in earnest in 1956 with the EOKA terrorist troubles in Cyprus requiring reinforcements. An even bigger lift was carried out for the Suez crisis. 1957 saw the Squadron involved in yet another task, that of colonial policing. A detachment went to Aden where, for two years, No. 42 carried out work in conjunction with the political officers, aerial photography, coastal patrols and freight carrying, as well as leaflet dropping.

After this the Squadron concentrated once more on the maritime role except for two aircraft in the Arabian Gulf. It still was involved in troop lifts, however, and at the same time accustomed itself to the new equipment in its up-dated Shackleton Mk. 2C aircraft. Such was the nature of anti-submarine warfare that new devices had to be continually incorporated in the aircraft to cope with more sophisticated submarine tactics and so the Squadron was always learning new equipment and new methods. In 1959 a goodwill tour of the Caribbean took place.

In 1965 NATO exercises were intensified and the Squadron's routine had settled into a pattern which was maintained until 1967 when the Squadron again became a dispersed one with detachments in Singapore, Aden and Majunga and this was continued the following year, No. 42 at one time providing A/S cover of the Mediterranean from Malta. By now the Shackleton was becoming old for its role and in 1970 the first of No. 42 crews began conversion to the Nimrod, the Squadron becoming a Nimrod unit in April, 1971 and its final Shackleton leaving in September. Since then the Squadron has flown in the pure ASW role over the Western Approaches with ASR as a secondary duty and has modified its tactics to cope with new developments in submarine deployment and operation.

Bases etc.

Formed at Filton on 1 April, 1916.

Filton	Apr	1916—Aug	1916
St. Omer	Aug	1916—Aug	1916
La Gorgue	Aug	1916—Sep	1916
Bailleul, det. Abeele	Sep	1916—Nov	1917
Fienvilliers	Nov	1917—Dec	1917
Santa Pelagio	Dec	1917—Dec	1917
Istrana	Dec	1917—Dec	1917
Grossa, det. Limbraga	Dec	1917—Feb	1918
San Luca	Feb	1918—Mar	1918
Poggia Renatico	Mar	1918—Mar	1918
Fienvilliers	Mar	1918—Mar	1918
Chocques	Mar	1918—Apr	1918
Treizennes	Apr	1918—Apr	1918
Rely	Apr	1918—Oct	1918
Chocques	Oct	1918—Oct	1918
Ascq	Oct	1918—Nov	1918
Marquain	Nov	1918—Nov	1918
Aulnoy	Nov	1918—Dec	1918
Saultain	Dec	1918—Dec	1918
Abscon	Dec	1918—Feb	1919
Netheravon	Feb	1919—Jun	1919

Disbanded at Netheravon on 26 Jun, 1919. Re-formed in the torpedo-bombing role out of B Flight, No. 22 Squadron at Donibristle on 14 December, 1936.

Donibristle, det. Andover, Gosport, Eastleigh	Dec	1936—Mar	1938
Thorney Island, det. Thornaby	Mar	1938—Aug	1939
Bircham Newton	Aug	1939—Apr	1940
Thorney Island, det. Sumburgh, St. Eval, Bircham Newton	Apr	1940—Jun	1940
Wick, det. Thorney Island	Jun	1940—Mar	1941
Leuchars, det. North Coates, Wick, Sumburgh	Mar	1941—Jun	1942
en route to Middle and Far East	Jun	1942—Oct	1942

In October, 1942 re-equipped with Blenheim VA's and changed to the bomber role. Disbanded at Meiktela as a ground-attack squadron on 31 December, 1945. Re-formed in the torpedo-bomber role at Thorney Island by renumbering No. 254 Squadron.

Thorney Island	Oct	1946—Oct	1947

Disbanded at Thorney Island on 15 October, 1947. Re-formed in the maritime reconnaissance role at St. Eval on 28 June, 1952.

St. Eval, det. Khormaksar, Masirah,	Jun	1952—Oct	1958
St. Mawgan, det. Gibraltar, Aldergrove, Belize, Khormaksar, Masirah, Tengah Majunga, Luqa	Oct	1958—	

Main Equipment

B.E.2d (Apr 1916—Aug 1916)
  5772; 5856
B.E.2e (1916—Apr 1917)
  6260; 6264; 6279; 6751; 7062; 7067; 7070; 7073; 7089
R.E.8 (Apr 1917—Feb 1919)
  A3235; A4213; B783, F; B2256; B7739; C2300; C2409; C2515; C2557; C2689; C2707; C2822; D4698; D4889; D6740; E27; E109; F3015
Vickers Vildebeest I (Jan 1937—Mar 1937)
  K2810; K2812; K2817; K2822
Vickers Vildebeest III (Dec 1936—   1940)
  K4588; K4590; K4595; K4598; K4603; K4607; K4612
Vickers Vildebeest IV (Mar 1937—Apr 1940)
  K6409; K6411 AW:D; K6413; K6414; K8078; K8080; K8085
Bristol Beaufort I (Apr 1940—Jan 1942)
  L4484 AW:E- L4491, AW:R; L4502, AW:P; L9825, AW:N; L9939, AW:W; L9965, AW:M; N1001, AW:E; N1042, AW:G; N1148, AW:D; W6472, AW:H; W6532, AW:D; X8929, AW:P; AW212, AW:V; AW243, AW:O

Bristol Beaufort II (Jan 1942—Jun 1942)
  AW274, AW:T; AW286, AW:M; AW307, AW:K; AW359, AW:O; AW384, AW:S
Bristol Beaufighter TF.10 (Oct 1946—Oct 1947)
  RD578, QM:D; RD579, QM:F; RD690, QM:B; SR914, QM:Y
Avro Shackleton MR.1/MR.1A 1(Jun 1952—Jul 1954)
  VP293, A:F; WG511, A:A1; WG525, A:B; WG527, A:D; WG529, A:H
Avro Shackleton MR.2 (Jan 1953—Jan 1966)
  WG531, A:H; WG558, 42:B; WL737, 42:B; WL743, A:F; WL757, 42:B; WL788, 42:F; WR951, A:J; WR955, 42:C; WR959, A:G
Avro Shackleton MR.3 (Jan 1966—Sep 1971)
  WR773, 42:B; WR984, 42:C; WR988, 42:E; XF701, 42:B; XF706, 42:D; XF711, 42:G
Hawker Siddeley Nimrod MR.1 (Apr 1971—   ) These aircraft are on the strength of St. Mawgan, used jointly by No. 42 Squadron & No. 236 OCU.
  XV230; XV235; XV242; XV255; XZ285

Commanding Officers

Maj J. K. Kinnear	Apr	1916—Nov	1917
Maj K. T. Dowding	Nov	1917—Jan	1918
Maj R. G. Gould	Jan	1918—Apr	1918
Maj H. J. F. Hunter	Apr	1918—Nov	1918
Capt W. Ledlie	Nov	1918—Dec	1918
Maj G. H. B. McCall	Dec	1918—Feb	1919
F/Lt W. G. Campbell	Dec	1936—Apr	1937
S/Ldr G. C. Bladon	Apr	1937—Dec	1938
S/Ldr H. Waring	Dec	1938—Dec	1940
S/Ldr R. Faville	Dec	1940—Oct	1941
W/Cdr Gibson	Oct	1941—Jan	1942
W/Cdr M. F. D. Williams	Jan	1942—Apr	1942
S/Ldr W. H. Cliff, DSO	Apr	1942—May	1942
W/Cdr M. McLoughlin	May	1942—Nov	1942
S/Ldr D. T. M. Lumsden	Oct	1946—Feb	1947
W/Cdr A. Gadd, DFC	Feb	1947—Sep	1947
S/Ldr R. S. Hyland, DFC, AFC	Sep	1947—Oct	1947
S/Ldr D. H. Sutton	Jun	1952—Jul	1954
S/Ldr N. H. Wilson	Jul	1954—Jun	1955
W/Cdr E. Donovan, DFC	Jun	1955—Aug	1957
W/Cdr T. P. Seymour	Aug	1957—Oct	1957
W/Cdr B. W. Parsons, DFC, AFC	Oct	1957—Nov	1959
W/Cdr J. R. Ramsden, AFC	Nov	1959—Nov	1961
W/Cdr H. Mansell	Nov	1961—Feb	1964
W/Cdr R. A. Carson, MC, AFC	Feb	1964—Nov	1965
W/Cdr D. O. Parry Davies	Nov	1965—Nov	1967
W/Cdr J. A. Ryan	Nov	1967—Dec	1969
W/Cdr B. W. Lofthouse	Dec	1969—Aug	1972
W/Cdr D. W. Hann	Aug	1972—Sep	1974
W/Cdr T. H. Watson	Sep	1974—Jul	1976
W/Cdr A. G. Hicks	Jul	1976—Jan	1978
W/Cdr D. R. Green	Jan	1978—	
W/Cdr D. L. Bough	Jan	1982—	

Aircraft Insignia

Whilst in France in World War I the Squadron's aircraft carried a white square on the fuselage sides aft of the roundel. The Vildebeests simply carried the flashes on the wheel spats, coloured according to the Flights. However, when they were later camouflaged the Squadron was allotted the code letters 'QD' which were almost certainly applied. These were changed to 'AW' on the outbreak of war in September, 1939 and these letters were used also on the Beauforts. When No. 42 Squadron was re-formed from No. 254 Squadron in October, 1946 it retained that squadron's letters 'QM'. The Shackletons at first carried a single identity letter 'A' on the rear fuselage but in the late fifties this was changed to the number '42' in red, outlined white, on the rear fuselage and the squadron emblem was carried on a white disc on the fin. Towards the end of the sixties the aircraft at St. Mawgan were pooled and squadron markings were deleted. This applies also to the Nimrods although for special occasions individual aircraft have carried the squadron badge on the nose or the emblem on the fin or both.
(See also *Bomber Squadrons of the RAF*, p. 63 and *Fighter Squadrons of the RAF*, pp.114—115)

No. 46 SQUADRON

BADGE
Two arrowheads, surmounted by a third, all in bend

MOTTO
'We rise to conquer'

The arrows in the badge signify speed in getting into action and their position and number signify three aircraft flying.

No. 46 has predominantly been a fighter squadron. In World War I it was formed at Wyton on 19 April, 1916 and went to France in October as a scout squadron with Nieuports, replaced by Sopwith Pups the following spring and Camels later that year. It fought on the Western Front continually until the war's end and was disbanded at Rendcombe on 31 December, 1919. No. 46 re-formed again in the fighter role at Kenley on 3 September, 1936 with Gauntlets and fought with Hurricanes in the Norwegian campaign and then in the Battle of Britain in defence of London. Early in 1941 it went to the Middle East, the ground crews to Egypt and the pilots and aircraft to Malta where they formed 126 Squadron. On 7 April, 1942 a new No. 46 Squadron formed at Edku in the night-fighter role with Beaufighters and served there until December, 1944.

It then forsook the fighter role and returned to the UK to become a transport squadron. No. 46 reconstituted itself at Stoney Cross as part of 47 Group, Transport Command and was equipped with Short Stirling Vs. After work-up it began operations in April, 1945 flying freight schedules to India and Ceylon (Dum Dum, St. Thomas Mount and Ratmalana being its terminals). This was added to in July by establishing a shuttle service between Cairo West and Mauripur. However the following month the Squadron changed its sphere of operation to the Middle East, its new schedules feeding Malta, North Africa and the Persian Gulf.

No. 46 remained on these tasks until May, 1946 when it was re-equipped with Dakotas and with these its operations were more varied. In 1948 it became involved in the Berlin Airlift, flying on this until its completion. Soon after it was disbanded, at Oakington, on 20 February, 1950.

On 15 August, 1954 it re-formed at Odiham, now in the night-fighter role once more, and served with Meteors and Javelins until 30 June, 1961 when it again disbanded, at Waterbeach.

No. 46 again entered the transport role on 1 December, 1966 when it re-formed at Abingdon, equipped with Hawker Siddeley Andover C.1s. The Squadron became the home-based short-range tactical transport squadron with this type and was involved with army units in many tactical exercises, the aircraft's short-landing and take-off abilities coming to the fore. It also flew regular commitments within NATO, one of these being regular casevac flight from Germany to the UK with members of the British Forces there. In addition, the Squadron was committed to the ACE Mobile Force and as such was sent to various parts of the world as required. An example of this was its detachment to Anguilla in July, 1969 when the crisis arose in Antigua, the Squadron supplying all the transport needs. No. 46 remained on this task until 31 August, 1975 when it was disbanded at Thorney Island in one of the sweeping Defence cuts of the period.

Bases, etc. (in the transport role)

Returned to the UK in December, 1944 for the transport role. Based at Stoney Cross.

Stoney Cross	Jan 1945—Oct 1946
Manston	Oct 1946—Dec 1946
Abingdon, det. Wunstorf, Fassberg, Lübeck	Dec 1946—Aug 1949
Oakington	Aug 1949—Feb 1950

Disbanded at Oakington on 20 February, 1950. Re-formed as a short-range tactical transport squadron at Abingdon on 1 December, 1966.

Abingdon	Dec 1966—Sep 1970
Thorney Island	Sep 1970—Aug 1975

Disbanded at Thorney Island 31 August, 1975.

Main Equipment

Short Stirling V (Jan 1945—May 1946)
PJ903, XK:Y; PJ936, XK:X; PJ988, XK:Bw; PK129, XK:G; PK139, XK:M; PK157, XK:K
Douglas Dakota C.4 (May 1946—Feb 1950)
KJ801, XK:Y; KJ837, XK:P; KJ910, XK:H; KK197, XK:O; KK213, XK:G; KN241, XK:K; KN274, XK:X; KN402, XK:V; KN498, XK:R; KN518, XK:L; KP279, XK:U
Hawker Siddeley Andover C.1 (Dec 1966—Aug 1975)
XS594; XS597; NS601, XS603; XS608; XS609, XS610, XS613; XS638; XS645

Commanding Officers

W/Cdr B. A. Coventry	Jan 1945—	Dec 1945
W/Cdr S. G. Baggott	Dec 1945—	Mar 1946
W/Cdr R. G. Dutton, DSO, DFC	Mar 1946—	Jul 1946
W/Cdr G. Burges, OBE, DFC	Jul 1946—	Oct 1947
S/Ldr E. Moody	Oct 1947—	Mar 1948
S/Ldr A. G. Salter	Mar 1948—	Feb 1960
S/Ldr M. J. Rayson	Dec 1966—	1969
S/Ldr J. B. Gratton	1969—	1970
S/Ldr D. Crwys-Williams	1970—	
W/Cdr J. A. Scambler	Apr 1973—	Apr 1975
W/Cdr S. Hitchen	Apr 1975—	Aug 1975

Aircraft Insignia

During the Stirling and Dakota periods the Squadron used the code letter combination 'XK' and the Andovers in the sixties and seventies carried the three red arrows emblem on a white disc on the fin.
(See also *Fighter Squadrons of the RAF*, pp.126–129)

No. 47 SQUADRON

BADGE
In front of a fountain a demoiselle crane's head erased

MOTTO
'Nili nomen roboris omen'
('The name of the Nile is an omen of our strength')

The Squadron served in Russia and the Sudan and the crane is found in both areas. The fountain commemorates the squadron's amphibious role.

No. 47 Squadron was formed at Beverley on 1 March, 1916 equipped with B.E.12 aircraft, intended for Home Defence. This, however, was short-lived for in September 1916 it went overseas with B.E.2c's, Avros and A.W. F.K.3s to Salonika, moving to its operational area the following month. Here it was dispersed at landing grounds along the front and engaged in recce and artillery co-operation work in the main with a considerable photographic commitment as well. In 1917 it added bombing to its tasks and even became a fighter squadron, countering hostile bombing raids, for which it used B.E.12s and D.H.2s. In January, 1918 it co-operated with the Navy by bombing the German-Turkish cruiser *Goeben* aground in the Dardanelles. The fighting continued throughout that year, the Squadron's fighter flight becoming 150 Squadron in April, enabling No. 47 to concentrate on Corps duties. With the arrival of D.H.9s it now embarked on long-distance recces and bombing raids, and these were instrumental in the final campaign in Macedonia.

After the Armistice No. 47 moved on, early in 1919 to South Russia where it became 'A' Squadron, RAF Mission, in October, fighting against the Bolsheviks. It was re-formed as a day-bomber squadron on 1 February, 1920 by renumbering 206 Squadron at Helwan in Egypt and served in the Sudan until May, 1941 as a bomber unit. Then it entered the Eritrean campaign for the rest of that year.

In January, 1942 No. 47 moved north to Egypt where it was absorbed by 201 Group for general reconnaissance duties. It was flying Vickers Wellesleys and moved around various bases on local recce tasks until September, 1942 when it was joined by a detachment from No. 42 Squadron and re-equipped with Bristol Beauforts. It now worked up for torpedo duties and began operations in October. Its first strikes, on shipping at Tobruk, were costly and ineffectual and the Squadron thereafter concentrated on convoy escorts and A/S patrols, with some mining in addition. In June, 1943 it received Beaufighters, moving to Protville and resumed torpedo work, blowing up a 3,000 ton motor vessel on 21 June, and a tanker on 23rd. Its main task had become *Armed Rovers* and operations escalated; in July thirteen squadron strikes were flown. In August four ships were destroyed for the loss of five aircraft. September brought sorties against Junkers Ju 52 transports flying between Corsica and Italy, and some ASR duties. 1944 brought a transfer of attention to the Aegean Sea where *Armed Rovers* were the normal operation. This continued until March when the Squadron came off operations and moved to the Far East theatre.

For some time it maintained a strike force at readiness but no operations were forthcoming, and in July it resumed torpedo training. By October the only operations which had come the Squadron's way were a few ASR searches so it moved base and re-equipped with Mosquito VIs. The following month these were grounded so it re-acquired Beaufighters and joined 908 Wing in January, 1945.

It was now in the thick of operations over Burma, attacking oil dumps, flying *Rhubarbs* and beginning night operations, intruding over enemy airfields. During the army's crossing of the Irrawaddy in February No. 47 flew *Cloak* operations, dummy attacks with Verey cartridges to simulate ground fighting. That month it began to re-equip with Mosquitoes once again. It was now flying round the clock with night *Rhubarbs* and daytime attacks on Irrawaddy traffic and railways. 963 operational hours were flown in March, mostly on army support sorties and this prevailed in April also, but in May the aircraft were beginning to suffer from the climate once more and it was not until July that a number of operations could be flown again, only to be overtaken by the war's end in August. However, in November the Squadron was sent to the Netherland's East Indies where insurrection had taken place and flew sorties against the Indonesians in Java. This campaign continued desultorily until March, 1946 when the Squadron was disbanded.

On 1 September, 1946 No. 47 Squadron was re-formed by re-numbering 644 Squadron at Qastina in Palestine. It was now a transport unit equipped with Halifaxes which it immediately brought back to the UK. It flew in the airborne role, with paratroops and with a glider-towing capability. In 1948 it received the first Handley Page Hastings in the RAF and used them initially on the Berlin Airlift on which it made over 3,000 flights carrying upwards of 22,000 tons of supplies mainly coal. On its return to the UK in 1949 the Squadron began flying the Transport Command trunk routes to Japan, Singapore, New Zealand, Australia and Canada. It also flew some 'specials', one of these being the dropping of supplies to the British North Greenland expedition on the ice cap in October, 1952. One aircraft was lost on this task, force-landing on the ice in a 'white-out' situation, the crew being rescued after nine days.

In May, 1956 No. 47 worked another transport aircraft into RAF front-line service, the Blackburn Beverley. It continued and extended the Hastings task with this aircraft, flying world-wide trooping flights, maintaining the paratroop support role and developing the dropping by parachute of heavy loads. It also took part in several crisis situations such as Kuwait and the East African relief sorties. The Beverley period lasted eleven years, No. 47 disbanding at Abingdon on 31 October, 1967.

It returned to transport work in February, 1968 when a new No. 47 Squadron re-formed at Fairford. The role was the same, this time with Lockheed Hercules C.1s flying transport support for the army as well as the route-flying for the British Services. In 1971 it joined the Lyneham Transport Wing with which it has since served.

Bases etc.

Formed at Beverley 1 March, 1916.

Beverley	Mar 1916—Apr 1916	
Bramham Moor	Apr 1916—Sep 1916	
en route to Salonika	Sep 1916—Oct 1916	
Janes, det. Kubus, Mikras Bay, Mudros	Oct 1916—Apr 1918	
Marian	Apr 1918—Sep 1918	
Yanesh, det. Hajdarli	Sep 1918—Oct 1918	
Drama	Oct 1918—Jun 1919	
Novorossisk, det. Gnildaksar Iskaya	Jun 1919—Jun 1919	
Ekateri Nodar, det. Beketovka	Jun 1919—Oct 1919	

Redesignated 'A' Squadron, RAF Mission, S. Russia October, 1919. Re-formed as a bomber squadron for coastal reconnaissance duties at Burgh-el-Arab in January, 1942.

Burgh-el-Arab	Jan 1942—Apr 1942	
Kasfareet, det. Burgh-el-Mair, Shandur, St. Jean, LG.89	Apr 1942—Sep 1942	
Shandur, det. St. Jean, Gianaclis, LG.227, LG.08	Sep 1942—Jan 1943	
Gianaclis, det. LG.07, St. Jean	Jan 1943—Mar 1943	
Misurata West	Mar 1943—Jun 1943	
Protville	Jun 1943—Oct 1943	
Sidi Amor	Oct 1943—Nov 1943	
Gambut III	Nov 1943—Mar 1944	
Amriya South	Mar 1944—Mar 1944	

en route to Far East	Mar 1944—Oct 1944	
Cholavarum, det. Vavuyina	Mar 1944—Oct 1944	
Yelahanka	Oct 1944—Nov 1944	
Ranchi	Nov 1944—Jan 1945	
Kumbhirgram	Jan 1945—Apr 1945	
Kinmagon	Apr 1945—Aug 1945	
Hmawbi	Aug 1945—Nov 1945	
Kemajoran	Nov 1945—Jan 1946	
Butterworth, det. Kemajoran	Jan 1946—Mar 1946	

Disbanded at Butterworth 21 January, 1946. Re-formed at Qastina on 1 September, 1946 by re-numbering No. 644 Squadron.

Qastina	Sep 1946—Sep 1946	
Fairford	Sep 1946—Sep 1948	
Dishforth	Sep 1948—Nov 1948	
Schleswigland	Nov 1948—May 1949	
Topcliffe	May 1949—Nov 1953	
Abingdon, det. Khormaksar	Nov 1953—Oct 1967	

Disbanded at Abingdon on 31 October, 1967. Re-formed at Fairford in February, 1968.

Fairford	Feb 1968—Feb 1971	
Lyneham	Feb 1971—	

Main Equipment

B.E.2c (Apr 1916—Sep 1916)
2661; 2720
Avro 504 (Apr 1916—Sep 1916)
7730; 7731; 7732; 7736; 7737; 7738
A.W. F.K.3 (Apr 1916—Mar 1918)
5511; 5516; 5539; 5547; 5614; 6187; 6212; 6221; 6226; A1463; A1468; A1477
Bristol Scout (Oct 1916—   1917)
5325; 5599; 5603
B.E.12 (Dec 1916—Mar 1918)
6557; 6602; 6676; A4008; A4022; A4046
D.H.2 (May 1917—Dec 1917)
A2584; A2630; A4766; A4772; A4784
Vickers F.B.19. Mk. II (Aug 1917—Mar 1918)
A5225; A5226; A5228
B.E.2e (Nov 1917—Mar 1918)
A3081; A8688; A8689; A8690; A8691
S.E.5A (Jan 1918—Apr 1918) to No. 150 Squadron
B30; B688; B692; B695
Bristol M1C (1918—Apr 1918) to No. 150 Squadron
C4904; C4909; C4911; C4926; C4963
A.W. F.K.8 (Mar 1918—Nov 1918)
B3335; B3347; B3391; C3555; C3590; C8403; C8409
D.H.9 (Aug 1918—Oct 1919)
C6214; C6216; C6235; C6236; D2840; D2846; D2942; F1164; F1202
D.H.9A (Aug 1919—Oct 1919)
F1086
Vickers Wellesley I (Jan 1942—Mar 1943)
K7769; K8528; K8531; L2645; L2667; L2712; L2715
Bristol Beaufort I (Sep 1942—Jun 1943)
DD978, X; DE111, V; DE112, R; DE119, P; DW811, P; DW829, M;
Bristol Beaufighter X (Jun 1943—Oct 1944 & Dec 1944—Apr 1945)
LX863, A; LX997, M; LZ384, P; LZ457, V; KW324, X; KW382, N;
KW414, W; NE301, O; NE368, E; NE411, D; NE459, F; NE502, R;
NT898, Z; NV551, V; NV608, Q; RD577, Q
de Havilland Mosquito VI (Oct 1944—Dec 1944 & Feb 1945—Mar 1946)
HR301, O; HR334, Z; HR486, G; HR523, Z; HX943; RF649, J;
RF649, J; RF695, Y; RF713, L; RF780, P; RF818, K; RF891, W;
RF942, H; TE650, KU:Y
Handley Page Halifax A.9 (Sep 1946—Oct 1948)
RT762, G; RT795, F; RT826, K; RT849, C; RT873, C; RT890, X;
RT901, G; RT923, H
Handley Page Hastings C.1 (Oct 1948—Mar 1956)
TG505, K; TG511, V; TG524, L; TG553; TG563, Z; TG582; TG601
Handley Page Hastings C.2 (Feb 1953—Mar 1956)
WD475, G; WD479, K; WD485, W; WD486, Y; WD492, U; WD495;
WJ342, U
Blackburn Beverley C.1 (Mar 1956—Oct 1967)
XB263, A; XB265, A; XB268, D; XB283, G; XB285, J; XB290, X;
XH123, N; XL131, L; XM105, P; XM111, D
Lockheed Hercules C.1 (Feb 1968—   ). Aircraft belong to Lyneham Wing
XV182; XV201; XV292; XV294; XV300

Commanding Officers

Maj F. G. Small	Mar 1916—Aug 1916	
Maj C. C. Wigram	Aug 1916—Jan 1917	
Maj F. F. Minshin	Jan 1917—Mar 1918	
Maj C. D. Gardner	Mar 1918—Jun 1918	
Capt B. E. Berrington	Jun 1918—Aug 1918	
Maj F. A. Bates	Aug 1918—Jan 1919	
Capt F. W. Hudson	Jan 1919—Jun 1919	
Maj R. Collishaw, DSO	Jun 1919—Oct 1919	
S/Ldr E. B. Grace	Nov 1941—Sep 1942	

S/Ldr R. L. B. Carr	Sep 1942—Oct 1942
W/Cdr R. A. Sprague, DFC	Oct 1942—Dec 1942
W/Cdr D. E. Bennett	Dec 1942—May 1943
W/Cdr A. M. Taylor, DFC	May 1943—Jul 1943
W/Cdr J. A. Lee-Evans, DFC	Jul 1943—Nov 1943
W/Cdr W. D. L. Filson-Young, DFC	Nov 1943—May 1945
F/Lt J. H. Etherington, DFC	May 1945—Jun 1945
W/Cdr V. S. H. Ductor	Jun 1945—Oct 1945
W/Cdr G. H. Melville-Jackson, DFC	Oct 1945—Mar 1946
W/Cdr W. H. Ingle, DFC	Sep 1946—Jun 1947
S/Ldr W. P. Peters, DFC, AFC	Jun 1947—Oct 1948
S/Ldr P. J. S. Finlayson, AFC	Oct 1948—Nov 1949
S/Ldr W. J. McLean, DSO, DFC, AFC	Nov 1949—Mar 1951
S/Ldr R. C. Wood	Mar 1951—Oct 1952
S/Ldr E. W. Merrington, MBE, DFM	Oct 1952—Oct 1954
S/Ldr D. P. Boulnois	Oct 1954—Aug 1956
S/Ldr A. St. J. Price	Aug 1956—Sep 1957
S/Ldr G. S. Taylor	Sep 1957—Jul 1959
W/Cdr V. H. Hemming, MBE	Jul 1959—Aug 1961
W/Cdr J. J. Barr	Aug 1961—Jul 1963
W/Cdr E. W. Cropper	Jul 1963—Oct 1964

W/Cdr D. H. Chandler, OBE	Oct 1954—Oct 1967
	Feb 1968—May 1970
W/Cdr J. E. Hannah	May 1970—Nov 1974
W/Cdr J. Hardstaff	Nov 1974—Apr 1978
W/Cdr R. L. Fitzpatrick	Apr 1978—

Aircraft Insignia

As far as is known no unit insignia was carried by the Squadron in World War I. When it became a coastal recce squadron in 1942 its Wellesleys had been using the code combination 'KU' on its aircraft but it is believed that this was dropped by this time. No markings were subsequently carried until the Mosquito period when, at some stage, probably towards the end of the war, the letters 'KU' came into use again.

In the transport role no unit markings were carried until the arrival of the Beverleys. These at first had a green diamond on the fin with '47' therein in white. This later gave way to the Squadron emblem on the fin. The Hercules carry no markings as they are Wing aircraft, the exception being XV294 which carried 47s emblem on its nose for the Royal Review at Finningley in July, 1977.

(See also *Bomber Squadrons of the RAF*, pp. 69–72)

No. 48 SQUADRON

BADGE
On an equilateral triangle, a petrel's head
erased

MOTTO
'Forte et fidele'
('By strength and faithfulness')

No. 48 Squadron was formed on 15 April, 1916 as a scout squadron and became the first unit to use the Bristol Fighter in action. It went to France in March, 1917 and fought there until the Armistice after which it went to India in June, 1919 and was re-numbered No. 5 Squadron on 1 April, 1920.

On 25 November, 1935 it re-formed at Bicester from C Flight of No. 101 Squadron. This unit was a bomber squadron, but the new No. 48 Squadron was intended for general reconnaissance duties and moved to Manston in December where it became the first squadron to receive the Avro Anson. This brought other 'firsts' with it – the first squadron to be fully equipped with monoplanes, breaking the Air Ministry's long prejudice against this configuration (apart from the Bristol Monoplane of World War I) the first squadron to use retractable undercarriages in the RAF was another of No. 48s claims to fame. In January, 1936 it also assimilated B Flight of the Training Squadron at Calshot with Saro Cloud amphibians but six months later this Flight left the Squadron to return to Calshot after some early attempts at ASR on the Goodwins. The first Anson arrived on 6 March and soon No. 48 was working up in its GR role and, by night, co-operating with the ADEE at Biggin Hill by flying simulated bomber sorties over Southern England. 1937 saw it more fully in the maritime role co-operating in all the Fleet exercises, it also flew several VIP communication flights and was still in demand, as the most modern type in the RAF, to provide simulated enemy bomber raids. In 1938 it forsook the largely training role for 16 Group where it fully participated in coastal activities, in March, 1939 searching for the German Fleet in the North Sea and taking photographs of it.

With the outbreak of war the Squadron was at Thorney Island with detachments at Detling and Guernsey, flying Channel patrols and sweeps, and escorting convoys to and from France. An interesting sidelight came with night flights over Thanet to check up on the efficiency of the blackout restrictions. In March, 1940 it transferred to the East Coast where it concentrated on convoy work, and, during the evacuation from Dunkirk, Dutch coast patrols. This was a busy time for the Squadron. On 19 May nine enemy minesweepers were attacked and on 29th three Ansons were attacked by nine Bf 109s of which one was shot down. 16 June was its busiest day with thirteen convoy patrols, sixteen French coast search patrols and three night searches.

At the end of June, 1940 No. 48 received Beauforts and ceased operations in July for conversion. However, the Beaufort training never came to much and No. 48 soldiered on with convoy escorts, the Beauforts eventually going to No. 217 Squadron in October. By now the Squadron was at Hooton Park and its task was to shepherd the convoys in and out of Liverpool and the Clyde and cover the northern Irish Sea, for which Ansons were still deemed suitable. In the summer of 1941 crews began converting to Hudsons at other bases and the first operational Hudson flight took place on 19 September when AM546 OY:G attacked a U-boat on the surface. Hudsons now soon took over, the last operational Anson flight being on 13 October.

In 1942 No. 48 Squadron moved north to operate over the North Sea and fly attacks on shipping on the Norwegian coast. The routine now was convoy and A/S patrols and *Armed Rovers*. On 24 April a 2,000-ton motor vessel was set on fire and three days later an oil depot was bombed and fired. May saw more shipping attacked and a U-boat damaged on 23rd whilst on 13 June four U-boats were attacked, one being damaged. At the end of the autumn the Squadron moved south and, on 23 December, transferred to Gibraltar from where it began its new task of escorting convoys to and from the forces in North Africa and generally bottling up the western end of the Mediterranean.

This was a busy time for the Squadron, each month produced at least one U-boat attack and in February 235 operational sorties were flown. By June the Hudsons were using UPs (Unguided Projectiles, ie rockets) in their attacks on U-boats and surface vessels, the Hudsons were also having combats with FW 200 Condors on the Atlantic side of their duties at this time. As the North African campaign drew to its close and the Allies moved into Sicily so the level of operations reduced, although there were occasional U-boat attacks even in early 1944. However, in February, 1944 the Squadron left Gibraltar for the UK and new tasks.

On 26 February the Squadron assembled at Down Ampney to convert to the transport role. It re-trained with Douglas Dakotas for paratroop operations and whilst working up flew *Nickel* raids (leaflets) over N. France by night, from April onwards. Also in April it began glider-towing training; May saw intensive training. Then came June and the invasion of France. By now the Squadron was a large one and over the night of 5–6 June thirty of the Squadron's aircraft took 517 paratroops across the Channel. Each aircraft carried twelve 20 lb bombs to keep the enemy gunners' heads down whilst the troops jumped; 514 of the troops were dropped and all the aircraft returned safely. Then on the evening of D-Day twenty-two aircraft towed Horsa gliders to the beachhead, one aircraft crash-landing in the Caen canal. For the next few days the Squadron was busy on re-supply missions, dropping parachute supplies to the forward troops; then it began flying 2nd TAF Wings into the Continental airstrips. In July No. 48 was flying regular daily trips to France bringing casualties back to the UK; it also had a Flight at Northolt for VIP flights to the Continent.

September brought the next big airborne operations, Market. On 17 September twenty-three Squadron aircraft set off towing Horsas to Arnhem; one cast off at Abingdon, two into the Channel and one on the Dutch isle of Schouwen but the rest arrived safely. A second lift took another twenty-six there without incident. Two days later sixteen of the Squadron flew re-supply missions, into intense Flak and with no fighter escort; many aircraft were hit and two failed to return. Re-supply missions continued over the next four days, the Squadron losing six more aircraft and many damaged. Then No. 48 returned to the shuttle flying to Continental bases. This continued at high intensity for the next six months. On 24 March twelve Dakotas of No. 48 Squadron towed Horsas for the Rhine crossing, losing two cast-offs en route. As the war drew to a close the Continental runs became more structured and after VE-Day scheduled services were set up. In August the Squadron transferred to the Far East and threw itself into the end of the Burma campaign, flying freight and food into Burma and East Bengal and returning with passengers and casualties. With the war over there, too, activity lessened and on 16 January, 1946 the Squadron was disbanded at Patenga.

A month later No. 215 Squadron at Seletar was re-numbered 48 Squadron. It was now involved in flying routes for the Far East Air Force throughout that area as well as maintaining a detachment in Java flying tactical sorties with the army against the insurgents. Dakotas were flown for the next five years from various Burmese and Malayan bases, the Squadron playing a leading role in supply missions and drops in the Malayan emergency. Valettas replaced the Dakotas in 1951 and carried on with the same task; these gave way to Hastings in 1957. The four-engined Hastings enabled the Squadron to operate further afield as well as flying the tactical sorties. The arrival of Beverleys in 1959 gave the Squadron a heavy lift capability, but the Beverley Flight became No. 34 Squadron in October, 1960. In December, 1962 came the revolt in Brunei and No. 48 became heavily committed in the British operations there. In 1963 the Squadron was involved in evacuating British civilians from Djakarta during the troubles in Indonesia. By the time the Borneo confrontation ended the Squadron had flown more than 2,000 sorties by December, 1966. Soon after it was disbanded at Changi on 31 March, 1967.

However, a new No. 48 Squadron was formed at Colerne on 2 October, 1967 with Lockheed Hercules C.1 and these it flew out to Changi the following month. Here it took up the role of Far East transport squadron once more until Defence cuts resulted in the withdrawal of the British presence from the Far East. The Squadron then moved to Lyneham and became part of the Transport Wing there in September, 1971 surviving until further Defence cuts brought about its disbandment in January, 1976.

Bases etc.

Served as a scout Squadron from 15 April, 1916 to 1 April, 1920 when it was re-numbered No. 5 Squadron at Quetta. Re-formed at Bicester from C Flight, 101 Squadron on 25 November, 1935.

Bicester	Nov 1935—	Dec 1935
Manston, det. Eastleigh	Dec 1935—	Sep 1938
Eastchurch, det. Eastleigh, Evanton, Manston, Detling	Sep 1938—	Aug 1939
Thorney Island, det. Detling, Guernsey, Bircham Newton, St. Eval, Carew Cheriton	Aug 1939—	Jul 1940
Hooton Park, det. Aldergrove, Port Ellen, Stornoway	Jul 1940—	Jul 1941
Stornoway	Jul 1941—	Oct 1941
Skitten	Oct 1941—	Jan 1942
Wick	Jan 1942—	Sep 1942
Sumburgh	Sep 1942—	Nov 1942
Gosport	Nov 1942—	Dec 1942
Gibraltar, det. Agadir	Dec 1942—	Feb 1944
Bircham Newton	Feb 1944—	Feb 1944
Down Ampney, det. Netheravon, Northolt, Bircham	Feb 1944—	Aug 1945
Patenga	Aug 1945—	Jan 1946

Disbanded at Patenga on 15 January, 1946. Re-formed at Seletar on 15 February, 1946 by re-numbering No. 215 Squadron.

Seletar, det. Kemajoran	Feb 1946—	1946
Changi	1946—Mar	1947
Mingaladon	Mar 1947—	May 1947
Changi	May 1947—	1948
Chittagong	1948—	1948
Changi	1948—Mar	1950
Kuala Lumpur	Mar 1950—	May 1951
Changi	May 1951—Mar	1967

Disbanded at Changi 31 Mar, 1967. Re-formed at Colerne on 2 October, 1967.

Colerne	Oct 1967—	Nov 1967
Changi	Nov 1967—	Sep 1971
Lyneham	Sep 1971—	Jan 1976

Disbanded at Lyneham on 7 January, 1976.

Main Equipment

Avro Anson I (Mar 1936—Oct 1941)
K6156, C; K6162, M; K6173, G; K6175, OY:K; K6224, OY:S; K6234, OY:X; K6279; K8706, OY:L; K8770, L; K8775, OY:P; K8823, OY:T; L7047; L7058, OY:J; L9151; N5106; N5373; N9896; N9908; R3305; R3318, OY:A; R3331; R3369, OY:J; R9629; W1652; W1769; W1887
Bristol Beaufort I (Jun 1940—Oct 1940)
L9821; L9861; L9862; L9867; L9868
Lockheed Hudson III, V (Sep 1941—Nov 1942)
V9105, OY:Y; AE645, OY:N; AM546, OY:G; AM659, OY:G; AM713, OY:E; AM730, OY:U; AM809, OY:W; AM824, OY:B; AM858, OY:D; AM871, OY:R; AM899, OY:Q; AM908, OY:P;
Lockheed Hudson VI (Nov 1942—Feb 1944)
EW891 A; EW910, F; EW916, H; EW929, S; FK398, P; FK410, Y; FK458, U; FK462, V; FK502, J; FK513, C; FK531, L
Douglas Dakota III (Feb 1944—Feb 1946)
FD844; FD898; FL537; FZ592, I2:UZ; FZ624, I2:UO; FZ671, I2:UN; KG346, 12:AY; KG394, 12:AM; KG423, 12:AZ; KG486, 12:WF; KG563, 12:AM; KG645, 12:WX
Douglas Dakota IV (Apr 1945—Jan 1946 & Feb 1946—May 1951)
KJ843, K; KJ987; KK176, C; KK210, X; KN310, P; KN413, I2:WH; KN511, I2:MR; KN599, T; KN622, O; KN684, Z; KP211
Vickers Valetta C.1 (June 1950—Dec 1957)
VX485, J; VX500; VX509; VX528, Z; VX546, W; VX555; WD158; WD169; WJ497
Handley Page Hastings C.1 (Aug 1957—Mar 1967)
TG516, GPL; TG526; TG531, GPX; TG536; TG579, GPS; TG610, GPH; TG620
Handley Page Hastings C.2 (Aug 1957—Mar 1967)
WD481, GPA; WD488, GPC; WD499; WJ333; WJ337
Blackburn Beverley C.1 (Feb 1959—Oct 1960)
XB260, U; XB262, W; XM104; XM112, V
Lockheed Hercules C.1 (Oct 1967—Nov 1975)
XV194; XV199; XV201; XV204; XV211; XV219; XV222

Commanding Officers

F/Lt A. H. Love	Nov 1935—	Jan 1936
S/Ldr T. A. Langford-Sainsbury, DFC, AFC	Jan 1936—	1938
W/Cdr J. L. Findlay	1938—	Nov 1940
S/Ldr R. H. Harris	Nov 1940—	May 1941
W/Cdr C. Broughton	May 1941—	Mar 1942
W/Cdr A. de V. Leach	Mar 1942—	Jul 1942
W/Cdr D. J. Devitt	Jul 1942—	Sep 1943
W/Cdr T. F. U. Lang, AFC	Sep 1943—	Jul 1944
W/Cdr J. A. Sproule	Jul 1944—	Sep 1944
W/Cdr M. Hallam, DFC	Sep 1944—	Feb 1945
W/Cdr P. D. Squires, DFC	Feb 1945—	Jan 1946
W/Cdr T. M. Buchanan	Feb 1946—	Oct 1947
S/Ldr T. R. N. Wheatley-Smith	Oct 1947—	Feb 1948
S/Ldr R. C. Wood	Feb 1948—	Feb 1949
S/Ldr J. R. St. John, DSO, DFC	Feb 1949—	Feb 1950
S/Ldr T. H. T. Forshaw	Feb 1950—	Apr 1953
S/Ldr B. V. Kerwin	Apr 1953—	Sep 1955
S/Ldr L. Hague	Sep 1955—	Feb 1958
S/Ldr K. H. Miles, AFC	Feb 1958—	Sep 1960
S/Ldr J. L. Gilbert, DFC	Sep 1960—	Oct 1962
S/Ldr W. J. P. Straker, AFC	Oct 1962—	Jun 1965
S/Ldr J. M. Crowley, AFC	Jun 1965—	Mar 1967
W/Cdr F. M. N. Taplin	Oct 1967—	

Aircraft Insignia

The Ansons are not believed to have carried any specific squadron markings until code letters were introduced late in 1938. At first No. 48 was allocated 'ZW' but these were changed on the outbreak of war to 'OY' which were retained until the move to Gibraltar, when code letters were dropped. When the Dakotas arrived the letters 'I2' were used and each Flight had a third letter to distinguish it, at first 'A' and 'U', then, from May 1945, 'M' and 'W'. In the Far East only the Hastings carried markings, a red fin triangle with '48' in white (subsequently a diamond), and the call sign 'GP' and a letter on the fuselage.

(See also *Fighter Squadrons of the RAF*, pp. 129–30)

No. 51 SQUADRON

BADGE
A goose volant

MOTTO
'Swift and sure'

When the Squadron was awarded a badge, it was equipped with Anson aircraft and the goose was chosen as a play on the words 'Anson/Anser', the latter meaning a goose. As the goose is a fast day and night flyer and one of the heavier wildfowl it was deemed appropriate for a heavy bomber squadron.

In World War I No. 51 Squadron served on Home Defence duties with a variety of aircraft, being formed at Thetford on 15 May, 1916 and disbanded at Sutton's Farm on 13 June, 1919.

It re-formed from B Flight of No. 58 Squadron as a heavy-bomber squadron at Driffield on 15 March, 1937 and was part of 4 Group, Bomber Command throughout World War II, flying operationally with Whitley and Halifax bombers. For two periods it had a detachment on loan to Coastal Command, in November/December, 1939 when its aircraft moved to Kinloss for operations over the North Sea, and from May to October, 1942 when it concentrated on flying anti-submarine patrols over the Bay of Biscay from Chivenor.

With the war in Europe over No. 51 Squadron transferred from Bomber to Transport Command on 7 May, 1945 and was re-equipped with Stirling C.5s. With these aircraft it flew on the routes to India with freight but the aircraft was not generally suitable for this work and in January, 1946 the Squadron converted to Avro Yorks. These it flew on the routes through to the Far East until the beginning of the Berlin blockade in 1948 then it divided its attention between the routes and flying on the Berlin Airlift. Soon after this ended the size of Transport Command was cut down and No. 51 Squadron was disbanded at Bassingbourn on 30 October, 1950.

On 21 August, 1958 No. 192 Squadron at Watton was re-numbered 51 Squadron. Its new task was radar reconnaissance and

it was equipped with Avro Lincolns and English Electric Canberras. In March, 1963 it moved to Wyton by which time the Lincolns had been replaced by Comets and these have since given way to Hawker Siddeley Nimrods.

Bases etc.

Transferred to Transport Command on 7 May, 1945.

Stradishall	May 1945—Jan 1946
Waterbeach	Jan 1946—Jul 1948
Abingdon	Jul 1948—Jun 1949
Bassingbourn	Jun 1949—Oct 1950

Disbanded at Bassingbourn on 30 October, 1950. Re-formed by re-numbering No. 192 Squadron at Watton on 21 August, 1958.

Watton	Aug 1958—Mar 1963
Wyton	Mar 1963—

Main Equipment

Short Stirling C.5 (Jun 1945—Jan 1946)
PJ940, TB:B; PJ952. TB:F; PJ956, TB:D; PK115, TB:X; PK125, TB:P; PK148, TB:Yw; PK179, TB:N

Avro York C.1 (Jan 1946—Oct 1950)
MW115, TB:G; MW132, MH:C; MW148, TB:D; MW164, TB:D; MW196, TB:F; MW206, TB:V; MW318, MH:K; MW331, MH:H

Avro Lincoln B.2 (Aug 1958— 1963)
RA685, M; SX942, L; WD148, P

English Electric Canberra B.2 B.6 (Aug 1958—)
WH711; WJ567; WJ640; WJ973

de Haviland Comet 2R (1963—1974)
XK655; XK659; XK663; XK695

Hawker Siddeley Nimrod R.1 (Jul 1971—)
XW664; XW665; XW666

Aircraft Insignia

Upon transferring to Transport Command No. 51 Squadron was given the code letters 'TB' which it carried on the Stirlings and Yorks. During the period with Yorks, however, these were changed to the wartime combination 'MH'. In its radar reconnaissance role the Squadron generally has not carried squadron insignia although in the late 1950s the Canberra B.2s did at one stage carry the goose emblem on the aircrafts' fins, and this is now carried on the Nimrods.
(See also *Bomber Squadrons of the RAF*, pp. 78–80 and *Fighter Squadrons of the RAF*, p. 131.)

No. 52 SQUADRON

BADGE
A lion rampant guardant holding in the fore-paws a flash of lightning

MOTTO
'Sudore quam sanguine'
('By sweat and blood')

The lion comes from the arms of Heston and Isleworth where the Squadron was formed and the flash of lightning is the insignia carried by the Squadron's aircraft in World War I.

Formed as a corps reconnaissance squadron, at Hounslow on 15 May, 1916, it was intended to send it to France as the first R.E.8 squadron. It settled in at Bertangles in November, 1916 but suffered so many casualties due to the aircraft's flying deficiencies that the R.E.8s were withdrawn in February, 1917 and replaced by B.E.2e's. Only when other squadrons had proved the R.E.8s more amenable and the Squadron's morale recovered did No. 52 again fly R.E.8s. These it took to the Belgian coast for the Second Battle of Ypres and for the rest of the year fought heavily, flying army co-operation duties.

After a rest it moved back to the 5th Army Front in 1918 where it became heavily involved in night bombing before the German offensive of March, 1918. In this No. 52 suffered heavy casualties whilst fighting at ground level against the advancing troops. Despite this some air victories also ensued; for example Lt Taylor & 2/Lt Lane shot down two Fokker Triplanes that attacked them on 10

April. In the summer it joined the IX Corps and French 6th Army, again involved in a retreat during which it flew exclusively photo work and formation bombing. It then moved back to the British front for the final advance. By February, 1919 No. 52 returned to England without aircraft and reduced to a cadre which itself was disbanded on 23 October, 1919 at Lopcombe Corner. On 18 January, 1937 No. 52 was re-formed at Abingdon with Hawker Harts as a day-bomber squadron, converting to Fairey Battles. On the outbreak of war it remained as a training squadron and was disbanded into 12 OTU at Benson on 8 April, 1940.

On 1 July, 1941 it was re-formed at Habbaniya, Iraq as a Maintenance Unit but it had Hawker Audaxes on charge and these were occasionally flown on recce work by pilots of other units based there. In November the Audaxes went and the Squadron was without aircraft until October, 1942, having moved to Mosul two months before. No. 52 now received Blenheims and Baltimores for general purposes in Iraq but moved to the Canal Zone in February, 1943 where it received Baltimores once more. Working up on these it became operational in June from Tunisian bases flying shipping searches and ASR duties. These formed the Squadron's routine into 1944 with detachments at Malta and elsewhere. It managed to find and shoot down some Junkers Ju 52s whilst on these tasks. In February, 1944 it moved to Gibraltar and from there flew anti-submarine patrols until 31 March, 1944 when it again disbanded.

On 1 July, 1944 C & D Flights of No. 353 Squadron were combined to form a new No. 52 Squadron at Dum Dum and it was immediately operational flying mail into China over the 'Hump' route with Dakotas. It opened up other mail routes to Bombay, Colombo and Ranchi, being in effect a flying postal service for 221 and 224 Groups. In December one aircraft was kept permanently at Kunming, China for possible evacuation of Britons and that same month the Squadron received Liberators with extra tanks for the 'Hump' route. The following month the establishment was increased to fifty crews and the Squadron began a weekly evacuation service to Chungking. As the year wore on new flights were made into Burma, by April the Squadron had 26 Dakotas, one Harvard, two Expeditors and four Tiger Moth Ambulances. However, a growing shortage of crews and aircraft caused the cancellation of more and more services (twenty in July, thirty in August when 50% of the aircraft were unserviceable).

With the war over serviceability improved and the mail routes were extended through to Hong Kong; the Squadron also took on jungle rescue duties.

In 1947 No. 52 Squadron moved to Singapore and became almost wholly involved in supply-dropping sorties with Dakotas to the forces engaged in the anti-guerilla battle in Malaya. Some of its aircraft were fitted with loudspeakers for relaying messages to the terrorists. In 1951 Valettas replaced most of the Dakotas and these continued to serve in this role until 25 April, 1966 when the Squadron was disbanded again at Changi.

However, on 1 December, 1966 No. 52 Squadron was re-formed at Abingdon with Hawker Siddeley Andover C.1s and these it took to Singapore three weeks' later where it flew in the transport support role until the 31 December, 1969 when it was again disbanded.

Bases etc.

Formed at Hounslow on 15 May, 1916.

Hounslow	May	1916—Nov 1916
Bertangles	Nov	1916—Dec 1916
Chipilly	Dec	1916—Jan 1917
Citadel	Jan	1917—Mar 1917
Longavesnes	Mar	1917—Jun 1917
Bray Dunes	Jun	1917—Dec 1917
Le Hameau	Dec	1917—Jan 1918
La Houssoye	Jan	1918—Jan 1918
Matigny	Jan	1918—Jan 1918
Bonneuil	Jan	1918—Mar 1918
Catigny	Mar	1918—Mar 1918
La Houssoye	Mar	1918—Mar 1918
Poulainville	Mar	1918—Mar 1918
Abbeville	Mar	1918—May 1918
Serches	May	1918—May 1918
Fismes	May	1918—May 1918
Cramaille	May	1918—May 1918
La Ferte	May	1918—May 1918
Trecon	May	1918—Jun 1918
Aix-le-Chateau	Jun	1918—Aug 1918
Le Hameau	Aug	1918—Aug 1918
Savy	Aug	1918—Oct 1918
Bourlon	Oct	1918—Oct 1918
Avesnes-le-Sec	Oct	1918—Nov 1918
Aulnoy	Nov	1918—Nov 1918
Linselles	Nov	1918—Nov 1918
Aulnoy	Nov	1918—Feb 1919
Netheravon	Nov	1919—Aug 1919
Lopcombe Corner	Aug	1919—Oct 1919

Disbanded at Lopcombe Corner on 23 October, 1919. Re-formed in the day-bomber role at Abingdon on 18 January, 1937. Disbanded into No. 12 OTU at Benson on 8 April, 1940. Re-formed as a Maintenance Unit at Habbaniya on 1 July, 1941.

Habbaniya	Jul	1941—Aug 1941
Mosul	Aug	1942—Feb 1943
Kasfareet	Feb	1943—Feb 1943
LG.43	Feb	1943—Jun 1943
Protville	Jun	1943—Nov 1943
Bo Rizzo, det. Luqa	Nov	1943—Feb 1944
Gibraltar	Feb	1944—Mar 1944

Disbanded at Gibraltar on 31 March, 1944. Re-formed at Dum Dum on 1 July, 1944 out of C & D Flights, No. 353 Squadron, as a transport squadron.

Dum Dum, det. Alipore	Jul	1944—Oct 1946
Mingaladon	Oct	1946—Jul 1947

Changi	Jul	1947—Nov 1948
Kuala Lumpur	Nov	1948—Jun 1949
Changi	Jun	1949—Nov 1949
Kuala Lumpur	Nov	1949—Jul 1951
Changi, det. Kuala Lumpur	Jul	1951—Sep 1959
Kuala Lumpur	Sep	1959—Sep 1960
Butterworth	Sep	1960—Apr 1966

Disbanded at Butterworth 25 April, 1966. Re-formed at Abingdon 1 December, 1966.

Abingdon	Dec	1966—Dec 1966
Seletar	Dec	1966— 1969
Changi		1969—Dec 1969

Disbanded at Changi 31 December, 1969

Main Equipment

R.E.8 (Nov 1916—Feb 1917 & Jun 1917—Feb 1919)
A3409; A3434; A3537; A3642; A4417, 15; B792; B6524; B6571; C5052; C5057

B.E.2e (Feb 1917—Jun 1917)
2838; 5823; 7209; 7241

Hawker Audax I (Aug 1941—Nov 1941)
K3107; K3124; K7503; K7514; K7526; K7530

Bristol Blenheim IV (Oct 1942—Feb 1943)
B3701; Z5945, U; Z7784; Z7982; Z9420; Z9544, X; Z9615

Martin Baltimore IIIA (Jan 1943—Mar 1944)
FA108; FA186; FA288; FA322; FA367; FA378

Martin Baltimore IV/V (Sep 1943—Mar 1944)
FA453; FA489; FA504; FA571; FA634; FA668; FW348

Douglas Dakota III (Jul 1944— 1945)
FD819; FD862; FD916; FD954; FL555; FL643; FZ608; FZ684; KG463; KG561; KG679; KG722; KG764

Douglas Dakota IV (Sep 1944— 1951)
KJ813; KJ842; KJ904; KJ947, Y; KK190, X; KN203; KN240, S; KN303, C; KN467, A; KN534; KN547, P; KN620, G; KN633

Consolidated Liberator VI (Dec 1944—Dec 1945)
KH117; KH169; KH309; KH745

Vickers Valetta C.1 (Jul 1951—Apr 1966)
VW148; VW808; VW830; VW849; VX512; VX521; VX529; WD167

Hawker Siddeley Andover C.1 (Dec 1966—Dec 1969)
XS606; XS607; XS608; XS612

Commanding Officers

Maj R. A. Bradley	May	1916—Nov 1916
Maj L. Parker	Nov	1916—Dec 1916
Maj A. A. Walser	Jan	1917—Nov 1917
Maj A. M. Morison	Nov	1917—Feb 1919
P/O F. Kerr	Jul	1941—Sep 1941
F/Lt P. Geary	Sep	1941—Nov 1941
F/Lt R. B. Whittington	Nov	1941—Dec 1941
S/Ldr F. L. Newall	Dec	1941—Sep 1942
S/Ldr K. H. O. Young, DFC	Sep	1942—Feb 1943
W/Cdr C. D. R. McDonald	Feb	1943—Feb 1944
W/Cdr H. S. Grimsey	Feb	1944—Mar 1944
W/Cdr R. E. La F. Wyatt	Jul	1944—Feb 1945
W/Cdr W. H. Barbery, DFC, AFC	Feb	1945—Mar 1945
W/Cdr J. T. S. Horsfall	Mar	1945—Sep 1945
W/Cdr K. R. Slater, AFC	Sep	1945—Jan 1947
W/Cdr A. R. L. Griffiths	Jan	1947—Sep 1947
W/Cdr P. D. Squires	Sep	1947—Mar 1948
W/Cdr B. Smith, DFC	Mar	1948—Feb 1949
W/Cdr V. C. Owens-Jones	Feb	1949—Jun 1950
W/Cdr E. Baldwin, DSO, DFC, DFM	Jun	1950—Oct 1952
W/Cdr S. J. Rawlins, DFC	Oct	1952—Apr 1955
W/Cdr H. D. Archer, DFC	Apr	1955—Sep 1955
W/Cdr E. W. Forwell, DFC	Sep	1955—Feb 1957
W/Cdr D. G. F. Palmer	Feb	1957—Jul 1959
W/Cdr S. R. Dixon	Jul	1959—Mar 1960
W/Cdr G. Moss, AFC	Mar	1960—Jul 1962
W/Cdr J. H. Elliott	Jul	1962—Apr 1965
W/Cdr D. S. White	Apr	1965—Dec 1966
W/Cdr B. C. Northwood	Dec	1966—Jan 1969
W/Cdr D. M. Higgs	Jan	1969—Dec 1969

Aircraft Insignia

In World War I the R.E.8s and B.E.2e's carried a white zigzag marking on the aft fuselage sides. As far as is known no markings were carried during the Middle East Wartime period and it was not until after World War II that the aircraft carried the squadron badge on the side of the nose.
(See also *Bomber Squadrons of the RAF*, p. 81)

No. 53 SQUADRON

BADGE
In front of a saltire a thistle slipped and leaved
MOTTO
'United in effort'

On 15 May, 1916 No. 53 Squadron, RFC, was formed at Catterick for corps reconnaissance duties. After work up there it moved to Farnborough at the end of the year and re-equipped with B.E.2e's moving on to France two weeks later. As part of the IX Corps it flew army co-operation sorties with the B.E.s but re-equipped in April with R.E.8s in time for the Battle of Messines in which it played a prominent part and received congratulations from the Army commander. When the German advance came in early 1918 the Squadron was heavily engaged in the St. Quentin area tactical bombing being one of its foremost roles at this time, at which it suffered heavy casualties and was withdrawn. It returned to operations in April at Ypres where it eventually served the French cavalry corps, flying continuous patrols round-the-clock and taking many recce photographs. From 10 July the Squadron was transferred to the X Corps for whom it flew until the Armistice. It returned to the UK in April, 1919 and was disbanded at Old Sarum on 25 October, 1919.

No. 53 was re-formed, again with an army co-operation role, at Farnborough on 28 June, 1937. With Hawker Hectors it worked up as a specialist night reconnaissance unit, also carrying out day tactical recce. In 1938 it added survey work to its repertoire and in April, 1938 received Vickers Valentia K2344 with which it spent four months' experimental use for troop-carrying. Early in 1939 Blenheims replaced the Hectors but the role remained the same and in September the Squadron joined the Air Component of the BEF in France flying survey work of the BEF area by day and recces of Germany (Hannover, Minden, Hamm, Bremen, Osnabrück and Münster) by night. When the German offensive opened in May, 1940 No. 53 was immediately thrown into the battle for both tactical and strategic recces. Losses ran at about two aircraft per day. Operations were soon hampered by the need to retreat and No. 53 had six bases within the month, returning to the UK on 31 May. For a fortnight it maintained an Advanced LG in France and continued to operate over the British forces then in July the Squadron was transferred to Coastal Command.

Now it turned its attention to the Continental harbours, flying day and night anti-invasion recces and attacking shipping where seen. In July 282 operational sorties were flown. August was similar but losses were heavier, den Helder airfield being bombed on 13th and five Blenheims lost. This offensive action was strenuously pursued right through to the end of November with intruder sorties, convoy attacks, strikes on naval guns at Cap Gris Nez in addition to the usual recces. In the New Year (1941) it began to visit Brest and this harbour more than any other saw No. 53s Blenheims in action that year with moderately heavy losses. In July it moved to East Anglia and converted to Hudsons returning to operations on the 3 August flying ASR and shipping searches. It soon moved to Limavady with a detachment at St. Eval and these flew A/S patrols and U-boat searches. On 21 September PZ-T and PZ-X attacked the Squadron's first U-boat; in November another three were attacked. The Squadron was also having combats over Biscay with He 115s and FW 200s.

In 1942 it returned to the East Coast, flying shipping *Rovers* over the North Sea until May when it once more operated over Biscay, on 11 June PZ-O probably destroying a U-boat. That month its aircraft were painted all white, fitted with *Yagi* aerials and the Squadron flew off to the USA. It began operating from American soil and then moved to Trinidad from where, in August it had a hectic time attacking the U-boats feeding on the US coastal shipping routes, making no fewer than seven attacks in the month, explosions, oil patches and debris being seen after four of them. Three more attacks were made in September and 1,064 operational hours flown.

Thereafter the threat receded and at the end of the year the Squadron returned to the UK.

No. 53 now re-equipped with Whitleys as an interim measure and began operations in April. However, the following month the first Liberators began to arrive and operations did not resume until June when the Squadron began flying *Musketry* patrols over Biscay. In July three U-boat attacks took place and twice aircraft were shot at by packs of Junkers Ju 88s; on 1st F/O Merrifield's crew managed to shoot down two of the four Ju 88s attacking them. This became the pattern for the next few months with approximately 50 sorties being flown a month. In October the Squadron took time off operations to convert its aircraft and crews to Leigh Light operation. Most of the sorties were now flown at night and aircraft would set off for Biscay, fly a long patrol and land at Gibraltar at the end of it, returning on a similar operation another day. Two promising U-boat attacks were made in December, one resulting in floating bodies seen afterwards.

In 1944 the area changed, the Squadron now being set to provide 24 hour cover of the Western Approaches, with only a few Biscay patrols. Three U-boat attacks were made in January and seven in February. This rate was maintained and in May F/Lt Forbes obtained a hat-trick by making three successive U-boat attacks on three successive sorties. June saw the Squadron flying continuous Box patrols to prevent U-boats entering the Channel. On the night of 6–7 June F/Lt Carmichael in BZ944 L made two U-boat attacks, sinking one, F/Lt Bruton made one attack, and one Liberator was lost. On 30 July the Squadron shared in the first aerial sonobuoy sinking of a U-boat. In September No. 53 moved to Iceland, shifting its operational area to mid-Atlantic and the northern waters. Convoy patrols and anti-submarine patrols were the routine now with relatively little action. In March, 1945 the Leigh Lights were removed and the Squadron returned to daylight operations; meteorological sorties were also flown on behalf of No. 251 Squadron. April brought 107 operational sorties with two U-boat attacks after which it was mainly looking for surrendered U-boats in May and Greenland weather recces.

The following month the Squadron returned to the UK and transferred to Transport Command and in October began trooping flights to and from India. These were continued until June, 1946 when, on 15th, the Squadron was disbanded at Upwood.

On 1 November, 1946 No. 53 was re-formed at Netheravon by re-numbering No. 187 Squadron. It was now part of the 46 Group Dakota transport force specialising in transport support duties with the army, undertaking glider-towing duties. In 1947 it transferred to Continental route-flying and then in 1948 moved to Germany for Operation Plainfare flying supplies into Berlin. In July, 1949 it was disbanded, being merged into other Dakota squadrons operating on the Berlin Airlift but on 1 August, 1949 a new No. 53 Squadron formed at Topcliffe with Handley Page Hastings. With these it flew the main Transport Command routes to the Middle and Far East and in addition some special sorties as well. In October, 1951 it was involved in evacuating British civilians from the Canal Zone and in 1956 its aircraft dropped paratroops on Port Said in the Suez operations.

In January, 1957 No. 53 re-equipped with Beverleys for both trooping and heavy-lift duties, and that August it was used to fly troops in support of the Sultan of Oman. Another emergency in the Arabian Gulf sent the Squadron to Kuwait in 1962, but the following year the Squadron disbanded on 28 June by being merged with No. 47 Squadron.

In November, 1965 No. 53 re-formed at Brize Norton and became the RAF's heavy-lift squadron operating the Short Belfast C.1. It had ten of these huge aircraft and flew worldwide transporting heavy and bulky loads on behalf of the three Services and the Government. In this it was a unique unit and when, due to Defence cuts, it was disbanded at Brize Norton on 14 September, 1976 the RAF lost the services of its only heavy-lift unit.

Bases etc.

Formed at Catterick on 15 May, 1916.

Catterick	May	1916—Dec	1916
Farnborough	Dec	1916—Dec	1916
St. Omer	Dec	1916—Jan	1917
Bailleul	Jan	1917—Feb	1918
Abeele	Feb	1918—Feb	1918
Villesneux	Feb	1918—Mar	1918
Allonville	Mar	1918—Mar	1918
Fienvilliers	Mar	1918—Mar	1918
Boisdinghem	Mar	1918—Apr	1918
Abeele	Apr	1918—Apr	1918
Clairmarais	Apr	1918—Sep	1918
Abeele East	Sep	1918—Oct	1918
Coucou	Oct	1918—Nov	1918
Sweveghem	Nov	1918—Nov	1918
Seclin	Nov	1918—Nov	1918
Reumont	Nov	1918—Nov	1918
Raneffe	Nov	1918—Apr	1919
Old Sarum	Apr	1919—Oct	1919

Disbanded at Old Sarum 25 October, 1919. Re-formed at Farnborough 28 June, 1937.

Farnborough	Jun	1937—Apr	1938
Odiham	Apr	1938—Sep	1939
Plivot	Sep	1939—Oct	1939
Poix	Oct	1939—May	1940
Crecy	May	1940—May	1940
Lympne	May	1940—May	1940
Andover	May	1940—May	1940
Eastchurch	May	1940—Jun	1940
Gatwick	Jun	1940—Jun	1940
Detling	Jun	1940—Nov	1940
Thorney Island, det. Bircham Newton	Nov	1940—Feb	1941
St. Eval	Feb	1941—Jul	1941
Bircham Newton, det. Limavady, St. Eval	Jul	1941—Oct	1941
St. Eval	Oct	1941—Dec	1941
Limavady	Dec	1941—Feb	1942
North Coates	Feb	1942—May	1942
St. Eval	May	1942—Jul	1942
Quonset Point	Jul	1942—Aug	1942
Waller Field, Trinidad	Aug	1942—Aug	1942
Edinburgh Field, Trinidad, det. Zandery	Aug	1942—Nov	1942
Norfolk, Va.	Nov	1942—Dec	1942
en route to UK	Dec	1942—Feb	1943
Davidstow Moor	Feb	1943—Feb	1943
Docking	Feb	1943—Mar	1943
Bircham Newton	Mar	1943—Apr	1943
Thorney Island, det. St. Eval	Apr	1943—Sep	1943
Beaulieu, det. St. Eval	Sep	1943—Jan	1944
St. Eval, det. Ballykelly	Jan	1944—Sep	1944
Reykjavik	Sep	1944—Jun	1945
St. David's	Jun	1945—Sep	1945
Merryfield	Sep	1945—Dec	1945
Gransden Lodge	Dec	1945—Feb	1946
Upwood	Feb	1946—Jun	1946

Disbanded at Upwood 15 Jun, 1946. Re-formed in the transport role at Netheravon on 1 November, 1946 by re-numbering No. 187 Squadron.

Netheravon	Nov	1946—Nov	1948
Waterbeach	Nov	1948—Jul	1949

Disbanded into other Dakota squadrons in July, 1949. Re-formed at Topcliffe 1 August, 1949.

Topcliffe, det. Schleswigland, Wunstorf	Aug	1949—Mar	1951
Lyneham	Feb	1951—Feb	1957
Abingdon	Feb	1957—Jun	1963

Disbanded at Abingdon by merging into No. 47 Squadron, 28 Jun, 1963. Re-formed at Brize Norton on 1 November, 1965.

Brize Norton	Jan	1966—Sep	1976

Disbanded at Brize Norton on 14 September, 1976

Main Equipment

Avro 504K/A.W. F.K.3 (May 1916—Dec 1916)
No serials known
B.E.2e (Dec 1916—Apr 1917)
6311; 6323; 7250; 7257; A3162
R.E.8 (Apr 1917—Apr 1919)
A3243; A3619; A3847; A3938; A4236; A4308; A4438; A4632; B2251; B3931; B5887; B6464; B6596; C5026; C5061; C6453; D4699; D4834
Hawker Hector I (Jun 1937—Jan 1939)
K8139; K8147; K8150; K9687; K9696; K9703; K9711; K9712
Bristol Blenheim IV (Jan 1939—Jul 1941)
L4837, TE:G; L4847, PZ:D: L4860, PZ:E; L8789, PZ:E; L8863, PZ:O; L9329, TE:L; L9466, PZ:B; N3551, PZ:E; N3630, PZ:N; N6195, PZ:Z; R2773, PZ:V; R3679, PZ:P; R3735, PZ:C;T2043, PZ:M;

T2222, PZ:D; T2332, PZ:U; T2398, PZ:E; V5420, PZ:H; Z5765, PZ:A, Z5879, PZ:L
Lockheed Hudson III/V (Jul 1941—Dec 1941)
T9461, PZ:O; V9096, PZ:P; V9105, PZ:K; V9197, PZ:B; V9253, PZ:L; AE509, PZ:Z; AE639, PZ:Y;AM727, PZ:D; AM797, PZ:W; AM826, PZ:Q; AM885, PZ:G; FH271, PZ:F; FH356, PZ:U; FH433, PZ:C
Armstrong Whitworth Whitley VII (Feb 1943—May 1943)
No serial numbers known
Consolidated Liberator V (May 1943—Jul 1944)
BZ716, B; BZ720, N; BZ749, P; BZ793, H; BZ802, G; BZ816, N; BZ870, Q; BZ945, O
Consolidated Liberator VI (Jul 1944—Jun 1946)
EV877, C; EV899, W; EV953, FH:F; EW291, FH:Z, EW302, FH:G; KH198, FH:V; KH200, FH:K; KH279, FH:B; KH388, FH:B; KH419, FH:CW; KL622, FH:H, KL642, FH:O; KN706, FH:M; KN748, FH:J; TT343, FH:D
Consolidated Liberator VIII (Jan 1945—Jun 1946)
KH180, FH:Q; KH222, FH:H; KH337, FH:E; KH347, FH:P; KH413, FH:U
Douglas Dakota IV (Nov 1946—Jul 1949)
KJ911, PU:X; KK193, PU:F; KN286, PU:A; KN328, PU:Q; KN383, PU:V; KN418, PU:R; KN496, PU:S; KN517, PU:Y; KN655, PU:H; KN701, PU:N; KP233, PU:F
Handley Page Hastings C.1 (Aug 1949—Feb 1957)
TG517; TG536, GAU; TG569; TG577, GAM; TG605, W; TG610, P
Handley Page Hastings C.2 (1950—Feb 1957)
WD481; WD488; WD491, GAF; WD497; WD499; WJ329; WJ332; WJ333
Blackburn Beverley C.1 (Jan 1957—Jun 1963)
XB286, S; XB289, V; XB291, X; XH116, Y; XH121 Z
Short Belfast C.1 (Jan 1966—Sep 1976)
XR362, *Samson*; XR364, *Pallas*; XR367, *Heracles*; XR369, *Spartacus*; XR371, *Encelades*

Commanding Officers

Capt A. Claud Wright	Jun	1916—Oct	1916
Maj C. S. Wynne-Eyton	Oct	1916—Nov	1917
Maj G. Henderson	Nov	1917—Jan	1919
Capt G. B. A. Baker	Jan	1919—Feb	1919
Capt F. H. Davies	Feb	1919—Feb	1919
Maj G. B. H. McCall	Feb	1919—Mar	1919
Capt J. L. Vachell	Mar	1919—Apr	1919
S/Ldr A. P. C. Hannay, MC	Jun	1937—Apr	1939
S/Ldr W. B. Murray	Apr	1939—Jun	1940
W/Cdr E. C. T. Edwards	Jun	1940—Sep	1940
W/Cdr W. B. Murray, DFC	Sep	1940—Mar	1941
W/Cdr G. W. P. Grant	Mar	1941—Feb	1942
W/Cdr J. R. Leggate	Feb	1942—Feb	1943
W/Cdr H. R. A. Edwards, AFC	Feb	1943—Nov	1943
W/Cdr R. T. F. Gates, AFC	Nov	1943—Aug	1944
W/Cdr N. B. Littlejohn, OBE	Aug	1944—Nov	1944
W/Cdr A. R. Holmes	Nov	1944—Nov	1945
W/Cdr D. McKenzie	Jun	1945—Dec	1945
W/Cdr A. Frame	Dec	1945—Jun	1946
W/Cdr P. Fleming	Dec	1946—Jun	1947
W/Cdr G. H. Gatheral	Jul	1947—Dec	1947
S/Ldr M. B. Cooper	Dec	1947—Jun	1948
S/Ldr P. C. Lemon, DSO, DFC	Jun	1948—Aug	1949
S/Ldr J. P. Trant	Aug	1949—May	1952
S/Ldr H. H. Worts	May	1952—Jun	1954
S/Ldr A. B. J. Pearson, AFC	Jun	1954—Jul	1956
S/Ldr A. Brown, DFC	Jul	1956—Mar	1958
S/Ldr B. W. Taylor	Mar	1958—Aug	1960
W/Cdr A. A. J. Sanders	Aug	1960—Aug	1962
W/Cdr E. W. Cropper	Aug	1962—Jun	1963
W/Cdr A. D. A. Honley, AFC	Nov	1965—Jan	1968
W/Cdr J. D. Spottiswood	Jan	1968—Jun	1970
W/Cdr N. A. D. Nugent	Jun	1970—Apr	1971
W/Cdr C. A. Herbert	Apr	1971—Sep	1974
W/Cdr C. A. Simpson	Sep	1974—Sep	1976

Aircraft Insignia

In World War I the Squadron's aircraft carried a crescent moon in white on the sides of the rear fuselage. No markings were carried by the Hectors but with the Blenheims the code letters 'TE' were carried to September, 1939 and 'PZ' thereafter until the end of 1942. At first the Liberators carried no markings then in 1944 the code combination 'FH' was introduced on the Liberators. When No. 53 Squadron was re-formed in 1946 the code combination used by No. 187 Squadron PU, was retained. The Hastings eventually carried a white diamond at the top of the fin with '53' on it in black and this was also used on the Beverleys. On the Belfasts the squadron badge, in standard form, was carried on the nose.

No. 58 SQUADRON

BADGE
On a branch an owl
MOTTO
'Alis nocturnis'
('On the wings of the night')

The owl, a night-flying bird of prey, is
symbolic of the Squadron's night-bombing
role.

No. 58 Squadron was formed at Cramlington on 10 January, 1916 in a training role, becoming a night-bombing squadron in December, 1917, when it went to France in the following month and began operations. It formed part of the Independent Air Force serving through World War I and moving to Suez in July, 1919 where it was re-numbered 70 Squadron on 1 February, 1920.

A new squadron was formed as No. 58 at Worthy Down on 1 April, 1924 again in the night-bombing role, flying a succession of biplane bombers until 1937 when it received Armstrong-Whitworth Whitleys. These it flew on operations with 4 Group on the offensive over Germany until April, 1942.

In that month No. 58 transferred to Coastal Command for operations over the Bay of Biscay, setting up base at St. Eval. These began on 19th with Exercise Constance the following day the first Whitley was lost on Coastal duties. In May 60 operations were flown, almost all anti-shipping patrols and one U-boat was attacked by F/Sgt Strutt's crew and probably destroyed. The operations remained much the same through the summer, one U-boat attack taking place in June with three aircraft failing to return whilst in July three such attacks were made and a detachment sent to Wick for patrols in northern waters. At the end of the year the Squadron moved to Holmesley South and began conversion to Halifaxes.

From here the Squadron resumed Biscay patrols, returning to St. Eval in March. Its duties were A/S patrols and convoy escorts and activity was brisk, not only with U-boat attacks but also with Ju 88 combats. In May eleven U-boats were attacked of which two were destroyed and two seriously damaged. By the end of the summer the enemy interceptions were intensified resulting in several losses. In October the Squadron went over to night ops, using flares for attacks. In the first fortnight of 1944 four attacks were made; No. 58 was now averaging 70 sorties a month. As the year wore on more surface vessels became targets. In June the Squadron concentrated on the Brest peninsula to keep U-boats out of the Channel during the Normandy landings and made three U-boat attacks. The following month this work continued and armed recces were also flown in the Channel. By now some U-boats were fighting back and two Halifaxes were shot down during attacks. At the end of August No. 58 moved to the Hebrides and returned to anti-U-boat patrols up to Iceland and across to the Norwegian coast. This resulted in no less than twelve attacks in October and again in November and 21 anti-shipping attacks in December, all by night.

In the early months of 1945 anti-shipping work off the Norwegian coast increased heavily with 55 attacks in March and 44 in April. In that month Hercules-engined Halifaxes arrived but the following month all operations ceased and on 25 May, 1945 the Squadron was disbanded at Stornoway.

On 1 October, 1946 No. 58 re-formed at Benson in the photo recce role with Mosquito PR.34s and Anson C.19s. It was principally involved in ordnance survey flying, originally covering Great Britain on this task and moving to Wyton in 1953 where it re-equipped with Canberras. With these it also flew operational reconnaissance duties until 30 September, 1970 when it again disbanded.

On 1 August, 1973 No. 58 was re-formed at Wittering in the strike fighter role providing a reserve of trained strike pilots.

Bases etc.

Transferred to Coastal Command at St. Eval on 5 April, 1942.

St. Eval, det. Wick	Apr 1942—Aug 1942
Stornoway	Aug 1942—Dec 1942
Holmesley South, det. St. Eval	Dec 1942—Mar 1943
St. Eval	Mar 1943—Jul 1943
Holmesley South	Jul 1943—Dec 1943
St. David's	Dec 1943—Aug 1944
Stornoway	Aug 1944—May 1945

Disbanded at Stornoway on 25 May, 1945. Re-formed in the photo recce role at Benson on 1 October, 1946.

Benson	Oct 1946—Jan 1953
Wyton	Jan 1953—Sep 1970

Disbanded at Wyton on 30 September, 1970. Re-formed in the fighter ground attack role at Wittering on 1 August, 1973.

Main Equipment

Armstrong Whitworth Whitley V (Apr 1942—Aug 1942)
Z9142, GE:S; Z9200, GE:D; Z9291, GE:P; Z9317, GE:B; Z9426, GE:H; Z9442, GE:G; AD711, GE:Z

Armstrong Whitworth Whitley VII (May 1942—Jan 1943)
Z9135, GE:C; Z9374, GE:E; Z9528, GE:K; BD426, GE:Q; BD431, GE:A; BD434, GE:D; BD562, GE:H; BD623, GE:K; BD693, GE:D; EB327, GE:V; EB333, GE:E

Handley Page Halifax II (Jan 1943—Mar 1944)
BB256, A; BB262, C; BB268, D; BB276, F; DT636, J; DT642, E; DT665, K

Handley Page Halifax II Series IA (Apr 1943—Apr 1945)
HR741, H; HR744, O; HR774, R; HR792, A; HR983, R; HX152, M; HX177, F; HX223, E; HX225, L; JD176, W; JD178, V; JP165, BY:D; JP173, BY:H; HP255, BY:T; JP298, BY:V, JP300, BY:K; JP333, BY:O; JP339, BY:H

Handley Page Halifax III (Apr 1945—May 1945)
NA226, BY:D; NA235, BY:F; PN183, BY:V; PN202, BY:02; PN399, BY:S2; RG363, BY:L; RG395, BY:K

de Havilland Mosquito PR.34 (Oct 1946—   1953)
PF602, OT:T; PF671; PF678; RG193, OT:D; RG198; RG231; RG259; VL619

Avro Anson C.19/2 (Oct 1946—   1953)
TX2090, T:M; VL353, T:W; VL357, OT:P; VM352, Y; M368, OT:Q; VP514, A

de Havilland Mosquito PR.35 (1952—   1953)
RG700; TJ124; TK656; VR803

English Electric Canberra PR.3 (1953—   )
WE148; WE151; WE175

English Electric Canberra PR.7 (**1953—Sep 1970**)
WH773; WH794; WH802; WJ815; WJ819; WJ824; WJ825; WT504; WT512; WT532

English Electric Canberra PR. 9 (1960—   )
XH136; XH165; XH168; XH173

Commanding Officers

W/Cdr R. B. Harvey	Mar 1942—May 1942
W/Cdr R. W. M. Clark, OBE, DFC	May 1942—Aug 1942
W/Cdr A. G. F. Stewart	Aug 1942—Mar 1943
W/Cdr W. E. Oulton, DFC	Mar 1943—Sep 1943
W/Cdr J. M. D. Ker	Sep 1943—Apr 1944
W/Cdr J. B. Grant	Apr 1944—Mar 1945
W/Cdr W. H. Ingle	Mar 1945—May 1945
W/Cdr A. D. Panton	Oct 1946—Sep 1947
W/Cdr A. Gadd	Sep 1947—Nov 1947
S/Ldr J. M. Rumsey	Nov 1947—Feb 1949
S/Ldr M. M. Mair	Feb 1949—May 1951
S/Ldr A. D. Maclaren	May 1951—Jun 1951
S/Ldr J. G. Bishop	Jun 1951—Apr 1952
S/Ldr R. A. Hosking	Apr 1952—Jun 1954
S/Ldr E. J. Holloway	Jun 1954—Jul 1957
W/Cdr C. M. Fell	Jul 1957—Oct 1959
W/Cdr N. C. Thorne	Oct 1959—Nov 1962
W/Cdr P. D. Thompson	Nov 1962—Mar 1964
W/Cdr R. H. D. Dixon	Mar 1964—Oct 1967
W/Cdr R. L. Easterbrook	Oct 1967—

Aircraft Insignia

After transferring to Coastal Command the Squadron continued to use the code letters 'GE' allocated in Bomber Command. These were discontinued when the Whitleys left and for some while no identification was carried. However, in 1944 the Halifaxes were painted with 'BY' letters which were retained until after World War II ended. After the war the codes 'OT' were used until the early 1950's. However, when re-equipped with Canberras the Squadron now carried a black fin patch with a white disc thereon and the owl emblem in the middle of this

See also *Bomber Squadrons of the RAF*, pp. 89–91 & *Fighter Squadrons of the RAF*, p. 570)

No. 59 SQUADRON

BADGE
A broken wheel

MOTTO
'Ab uno disce omnes'
('From one learn all')

The badge refers to an action on the Western Front in September, 1918 when Capt D. H. N. Carbery and his observer in a No. 59 Squadron aircraft bombed an enemy gun limber. It was taken over by the British infantry and subsequently presented to the RAF.

No. 59 Squadron, RFC was formed at Narborough on 1 August, 1916 and flew a variety of aircraft on training duties for the rest of that year. In February, 1917 it re-equipped with the R.E.8 and went to France, flying its first line patrols on 1 March. These became regular duties together with artillery patrols, shoots and recce flights but No. 59 Squadron became most prominent in photographic work, acquiring a great reputation for its photographs of the lines and enemy positions, its photos being in great demand. Unlike many squadrons No. 59 stayed on the same front (Arras to St. Quentin) throughout the war. Losses were initially heavy, partly due to the aircraft's characteristics but these were soon mastered. The work remained much the same throughout 1917 and 1918, at times bombing raids were undertaken with 25 lb bombs, the Squadron concentrating its fighting against enemy artillery. After the Armistice the Squadron flew aerial post duties as part of the Army of Occupation leaving on 4 August, 1919 for disbandment.

No. 59 re-formed in a similar role on 28 June, 1937 at Old Sarum as a night reconnaissance unit for the II Corps. The Hawker Hector was its equipment and with these it had many detachments to army units throughout the country. At the end of 1938 crews were attached to No. 90 Squadron to convert to Blenheims and No. 59s own Blenheims arrived in May, 1939. By the outbreak of war about half the Squadron was operationally converted; the following month it moved to France and kept two crews at stand-by, still in its night recce role. The first such operation was on 30 April, 1940 when F/Lt Hallmark went to Köln and Düsseldorf. With the German attack in May the Squadron was thrown into hectic action, flying PR and recce sorties over the advancing German forces and their transport and supply routes. Losses mounted and the Squadron retired to Crecy and then to the UK on 20th. From there it maintained a limited task over what was left of the fighting, flying one or two Tac/Rs per day. The task changed to anti-invasion channel sweeps and the Squadron was transferred to Coastal Command, flying shipping attacks as well as raids on Northern French targets. During the summer and autumn the Squadron became heavily involved in day and night raids on the Channel ports, particularly where invasion barges were massed.

As the threat of invasion receded the Squadron began concentrating more on recce and raids on the Britanny ports. This was intensified in the spring of 1941 then came a transfer to the East Coast with convoy patrols and shipping attacks off Holland. April 1941 was a busy month with five raids on Havre, two on Caen-Carpiquet airfield and several shipping attacks including a destroyer, in addition to the normal convoy duties. This type of work continued until July when a start was made in converting to Hudsons.

With Hudsons the first task was to fly dusk and dawn patrols along the lines Cherbourg to Ostend, bombing and attacking any enemy shipping seen. At the end of the year a detachment was sent to Wick and in the New Year No. 59 was virtually non-operational sending its crews to the Far East. It was back fully operational in March, escorting the commando raid on St. Nazaire amongst other tasks. By April it had reached 74 sorties in the month, mainly *Rovers* and night recces. Five aircraft were lost in May but three ships had been set on fire, and by June No. 59 had ventured as far east as Bremen; by now nearly all its sorties were at night. In August it

came off operations to convert to Liberators and did not resume activity until October when it commenced *Keeper* operations (anti-submarine convoy escorts) from St. Eval. November was a busy month with three submarines attacked (one sunk) and five surface vessels attacked. Then No. 59 was again withdrawn to convert to Fortresses. With these operations began in January, 1943, anti-shipping patrols in the Western Approaches. In February and March three U-boats were attacked and one sunk and two combats with FW 200s took place, two Fortresses being lost. Then the Squadron converted back to Liberators once more.

The Squadron was now wholly involved in the Atlantic battle flying long anti-submarine escort duties to the convoys coming into the Liverpool and Clyde areas. A total of 53 sorties were flown in June (807 hours), mainly down to the Outer Biscay area, and four U-boat attacks were made. This pattern remained the same throughout 1943 and into early 1944 with U-boat activity stepping up. May, 1944 was a busy month with five attacks. In June the Squadron was switched to 19 Group for French coast patrol during the Normandy landings, 98 sorties being flown in the month. July was notable for a detachment operating off the Norwegian coast and the fitting of the aircraft with sonobuoys. And so the rest of the year passed, mainly on anti-submarine patrols and convoy duties. The sonobuoys came into their own and in January the Squadron homed surface vessels on to U-boats on four occasions. The number of sorties went up (118 in April, 1945 being the highest) but attacks were now few. Soon after VE-Day the Squadron transferred to Transport Command and began trooping flights to India in October. In November alone 1,460 hours were flown on this task as No. 59 settled into its new routine. The Squadron disbanded at Waterbeach on 15 June, 1946 but re-formed at Abingdon on 1 December, 1947 with Yorks in the transport role once more. It was heavily involved in the Berlin Airlift but also spent some time on the Commonwealth routes until 31 October, 1950 when it again disbanded.

A new No. 59 Squadron re-formed in the bomber/intruder role at Gütersloh on 20 August, 1956 with Canberra B(I)8s becoming No. 3 Squadron on 4 January, 1961.

Bases etc.

Formed at Narborough on 1 August, 1916.

Narborough	Aug 1916	Feb 1917
St. Omer	Feb 1917	Feb 1917
La Bellevue	Feb 1917	Jun 1917
Le Hameau	Jun 1917	Jun 1917
Longavesnes	Jun 1917	Jul 1917
Mons-en-Chausseé	Jul 1917	Oct 1917
Longavesnes	Oct 1917	Nov 1917
Estrees-en-Chaussee	Nov 1917	Dec 1917
Courcelles-le-Comte	Dec 1917	Mar 1918
Lealvilliers	Mar 1918	Mar 1918
Fienvilliers	Mar 1918	Apr 1918
Vert Galand	Apr 1918	Sep 1918
Beugnatre	Sep 1918	Oct 1918
Caudry	Oct 1918	Nov 1918
Gerpinnes	Nov 1918	Mar 1919
Bickendorff	Mar 1919	May 1919
Düren	May 1919	Aug 1919

Disbanded on 4 August, 1919, possibly at Düren. Re-formed on 28 June, 1937 at Old Sarum.

Old Sarum	Jun 1937	May 1939
Andover	May 1939	Oct 1939
Poix	Oct 1939	May 1940
Crecy	May 1940	May 1940
Andover	May 1940	May 1940
Eastchurch	May 1940	Jun 1940
Odiham	Jun 1940	Jul 1940
Thorney Island, det. Manston, St. Eval, Bircham Newton, Detling	Jul 1940	Jun 1941
Detling	Jun 1941	Aug 1941
Thorney Island, det. Detling, Bircham Newton	Aug 1941	Jan 1942
North Coates	Jan 1942	Aug 1942
Thorney Island, det. St. Eval, Chivenor	Aug 1942	Feb 1943
Chivenor	Feb 1943	Mar 1943
Thorney Island	Mar 1943	May 1943
Aldergrove, det. St. Eval, Gibraltar, Reykjavik	May 1943	Sep 1943

Ballykelly, det. Reykjavik   Sep 1943—Jun 1945
Waterbeach   Jun 1945—Jun 1946
Disbanded at Waterbeach on 15 June, 1946. Re-formed at Abingdon on 1 December, 1947.
Abingdon   Dec 1947—Jun 1949
Bassingbourn   Jun 1949—Oct 1950
Disbanded at Bassingbourn on 31 October, 1950. Re-formed in the bomber intruder role at Gütersloh on 20 August, 1956. Disbanded by re-numbering as No. 3 Squadron at Geilenkirchen on 4 January, 1961.

Main Equipment

R.E.8 (Feb 1917—Aug 1918)
     A109; A112; A3199; A3210; A3418; A3433; A4189; A4230; A4665; B6514; B6547; C2270; C2899; C2982; D2910; D6838; E1163; E2819; F1689; F6279; H2326; H7029

Bristol Fighter (Apr 1918—Aug 1919)
     A7129; C9897; D2660; E2015

Hawker Hector (Jun 1937—Sep 1939)
     K9689; K9691, PJ:M; K9694; K9700, W; K9705; K9710, X; K9714, U; K9739

Bristol Blenheim IV (May 1939—Sep 1941)
     L4855; L4857; L4881; L8790, TR:B; L8793, TR:M; L9473, TR:Z; N3535, TR:A; N3537, TR:J; N6169, TR:M; N6179, TR:D; R2815, TR:P; R3586, TR:E; R3610, TR:O; R3668, TR:D; T1991, TR:H; T2397, TR:G

Lockheed Hudson IIIA, V, VI (Aug 1941—Sep 1942)
     AM524,TR:V; AM568, TR:T; AM623, TR:D; AM694, TR:F; AM727, TR:E; AM789, TR:C; AM826, TR:D; EW904, TR:S; EW919, TR:K; FH260, TR:X; FH350, TR:U; FH426, TR:B

Consolidated Liberator III (Sep 1942—Dec 1942)
     FK232, F; FK237, R; FK238, C; FL913, A; FL925, J; FL930, E; FL933, S;

Boeing Fortress II, IIA (Dec 1942—Apr 1943)
     FA698, V; FA703, T; FA704, R; FK198, M; FK202, B; FK209, J; FL462, C

Consolidated Liberator V (Apr 1943—Mar 1945)
     BZ712, 1:D; BZ764, 1:J; BZ781, WE:A; BZ821, WE:Q; BZ912, WE:Z; FL946, 1:M; FL951, 1:J; FL976, WE:N; FL981, 1:B; FL988, WE:R

Consolidated Liberator VIII (Mar 1945—Jun 1946)
     KG987; KH125; KH130; KH414, WE:B; KK289, WE:D;

KK294, WE:H; KK322, WE:N; KK331, WE:U; KK368, WE:M; KN835, BY:A

Consolidated Liberator VI (Jun 1945—Jun 1946)
     EV862, EV997; KG936, BY:J; KG989; KL576; KL628; KN707

Avro York C.1 (Dec 1947—Oct 1950)
     MW143, BY:B; MW164, BY:V; MW193, BY:Y; MW227, BY:F; MW297, BY:G; MW309, BY:I; PE108, BY:A

Commanding Officers

Capt A. C. Horsbrugh	Aug 1916—Aug 1916
Maj R. Egerton	Aug 1916—Dec 1917
Maj C. J. Mackay	Dec 1917—Dec 1918
Maj A. P. D. Hill	Dec 1918—Jan 1919
Maj C. C. Durston	Jan 1919—Aug 1919
S/Ldr J. Warburton	Jun 1937—Dec 1937
S/Ldr J. B. Fyfe, DFC	Dec 1937—Jun 1940
S/Ldr R. G. S. Morgan Weld-Smith	Jun 1940—Aug 1940
W/Cdr J. A. C. Stratton	Aug 1940—Sep 1941
W/Cdr C. M. M. Grece, DFC	Sep 1941—Apr 1942
W/Cdr R. H. Niven, DFC	Apr 1942—May 1942
W/Cdr G. C. C. Bartlett	Jun 1942—Jul 1943
W/Cdr P. A. Gilchrist, DFC	Jul 1943—Jul 1944
W/Cdr A. A. de Gruyther, DFC	Jul 1944—Mar 1945
W/Cdr N. B. Littlejohn, CBE	Mar 1945—Jun 1945
W/Cdr S. R. Hinks, AFC	Jun 1945—Jun 1946
S/Ldr E. V. Best, AFC	Dec 1947—Oct 1949
S/Ldr A. H. Middleton, DSO, AFC	Oct 1949—Oct 1950

Aircraft Insignia

In World War I the R.E.8s carried an identity marking of two white vertical bands round the fuselage aft of the roundels. No markings were initially carried on the Hectors but, after camouflaging in September, 1938 the code letters 'PJ' were used by Hectors and Blenheims up to September, 1939. Thereafter the combination 'TR' was used until late 1942 on Blenheims and Hudsons, and possibly on the Liberator IIIs. The Fortresses carried no markings as far as is known but the Liberator Vs originally carried the numeral '1' on the side. This was changed to the code combination 'WE' in 1944 and, when transferred to Transport Command in 1945, to 'BY' which was also used by the Yorks.
(See also *Bomber Squadrons of the RAF*, p. 91)

No. 62 SQUADRON

BADGE
A meteor

MOTTO
'Insperato'
('Unexpectedly')

The meteor symbolises speed and striking power.

No. 62 Squadron was formed on 8 August, 1916 but did not become a fighting unit until May, 1917 when it began to equip with Bristol Fighters. This came to nought and it was not until January, 1918 that it eventually re-equipped with Bristols and fought on the 5th Army Front for the rest of World War I, being disbanded in Germany on 3 July, 1919. No. 62 re-formed as a bomber squadron on 12 April, 1937, going overseas in August, 1939 to Singapore. It fought in the disastrous Far East campaign being very severely mauled and eventually becoming part of No. 1 Squadron, RAAF at Semplak (Java) on 18 February, 1942.

On 30 April, 1942 No. 139 Squadron at Calcutta was re-numbered as 62 Squadron. The unit was now a general reconnaissance unit with Lockheed Hudsons flying offensive recces with bombs, of the Chindwin river, coastal patrols and anti-submarine patrols off the Burma coast. In August it added anti-invasion patrols to these tasks. Most of the time the patrols found nothing although on 18 August P/O P. Smith chanced upon a Japanese flying-boat bombing a merchant ship and drove it off. So passed the year. In January, 1943 No. 62 was withdrawn from the maritime field and transferred to bombing duties for which it worked up but when it again became operational this consisted of offensive recces down the Arakan coast and shipping attacks. However, in February it began a night offensive flying between thirty and fifty sorties per month until May.

Then No. 62 transferred to the transport role, its Hudsons having the ventral guns moved and the doors altered for parachuting purposes. Before it became operational however it was re-equipped with Dakotas and after working up with these began supply-dropping operations in January, 1944. It was now flying intensively, in February 488 sorties were flown in the month and to these it added two special re-inforcing operations, Op Thursday in March, re-supplying 'Broadway' and 'Whitehall' in April reinforcing 'Aberdeen' strip. The pressure continued and by June it was flying over a thousand sorties a month as well as training crews for No. 215 Squadron. From then on activity dropped off and on 7 August ceased. After a rest period the operations resumed on 5 November. Again it was mainly supply-dropping, interspersed with *Nickel* raids and train straffing. As 1945 came in the accent was less on drops and more on supplying forward airfields in Imphal. By May the presure was up to 1,000 sorties once more with the Squadron working out of Akyab. Despite the monsoon the flying carried on supplying bases in Central Burma until the end of July. In August a move was made south and No. 62 began flying occupation troops into Singapore and bringing back POWs, followed by services into Bangkok and Saigon. These two types of schedule were continued through until 15 March, 1946 when the Squadron disbanded at Mingaladon.

It was re-formed on 1 September, 1946 by remembering No. 76 Squadron at Mingaladon. Again it was a Dakota transport unit but did not become more than a cadre until June, 1947 after moving to India. However, it was disbanded at Mauripur on 10 August, 1947.

The Squadron was again re-formed as a Dakota unit but this time at Manston in December, 1947, taking part in the Berlin Airlift as well as flying transport routes. It served from the UK and in Germany until 1 June, 1949 when it again disbanded, at Oakington.

Bases etc.

Served as a fighter squadron in the UK and France/Germany from 8 August, 1916 to 31 July, 1919 and as a bomber squadron in the UK and Far East from 12 April, 1937 to 18 February, 1942. Re-formed by re-numbering No. 139 Squadron at Dum Dum on 30 April, 1942.

Dum Dum	Apr 1942—Jun 1942	
Cuttack, det. Vizagapatam, Asansol	Jun 1942—Jan 1943	
Dhubalia	Jan 1943—Feb 1943	
Jessore	Feb 1943—May 1943	
Chaklala, det. Basal	May 1943—Jan 1944	
Comilla	Jan 1944—Apr 1944	
Chandina, det. Kangla, Agartala	Apr 1944—Jul 1944	
Agartala, det. Basal	Jul 1944—Dec 1944	
Comilla, det. Imphal, Kangla, Hathazari	Dec 1944—Mar 1945	
Mawnubyin	Mar 1945—May 1945	
Akyab Main	May 1945—Aug 1945	
Mingaladon	Aug 1945—Mar 1946	

Disbanded at Mingaladon 15 March, 1946. Re-formed at Mingaladon on 1 September, 1946 by re-numbering No. 76 Squadron.

Mingaladon	Sep 1946—Mar 1947	
Palam	Mar 1947—Mar 1947	
Mauripur, det. Chaklala	Mar 1947—Aug 1947	

Disbanded at Mauripur on 10 August, 1947. Re-formed at Manston in December, 1947.

Manston	Dec 1947—	
Waterbeach		

Oakington
Disbanded at Oakington on 1 June, 1949.

Main Equipment

Lockheed Hudson III (Apr 1942—Aug 1943)
V9124, G; V9176, J; V9178, W; V9193, N; AE486; AE518, Y; AE540, E; AE593, H; AM941; FH234, T; FH290, P; FH342, B; FH383, L; FH443, P

Douglas Dakota III (Jul 1943—Nov 1945)
FD846, A; FD915, L; FD946, P; FD952, N; FL503, X; FL52? FL569, X; FL600, S; FL602, X; KG447; KG551

Douglas Dakota IV (Nov 1945—Mar 1946 & Sep 1946—Aug 1947 & Dec 1947—Jun 1949)
KK185; KN276, K; KN293; KN385; KN450; KN476; KN508; KN608; KN625; KN660; KP257, Y

Commanding Officers

W/Cdr D. Halliday, DFC	Apr 1942—Aug 1943
W/Cdr E. B. Fielden	Aug 1943—Feb 1944
W/Cdr M. L. Wells, DFC	Feb 1944—Oct 1944
W/Cdr R. W. Davy, DFC	Oct 1944—Sep 1945
S/Ldr P. G. Bell, DFC	Sep 1945—Dec 1945
W/Cdr Peveler, DSO, DFC	Dec 1945—Mar 1946

Aircraft Insignia

As far as is known No. 62 Squadron carried no unit insignia during its period as a general reconnaissance and transport Squadron.
(See also *Bomber Squadrons of the RAF*, pp. 96–7 & *Fighter Squadrons of the RAF*, pp. 151–2)

No. 63 SQUADRON

BADGE
A dexter arm in bend couped below the elbow grasping in the hand a battle axe

MOTTO
'Pone nos ad hostem'
('Follow us to find the enemy')

The battle axe, held by a strong arm signified both the type of aircraft the Squadron flew when the badge was approved and was also indicative of leading into battle.

The Squadron was formed at Stirling on 5 July, 1916, the intention being that it should go to France as a light bomber unit. However, after a protracted period, it eventually left the UK in June, 1917 and arrived in Basra in August, 1917 where it equipped with R.E.8s. No. 63 took some time to become operational due to disease amongst the personnel and gales damaging the aircraft. It was not until October that it began serious operations and then lost two aircraft in quick succession. It eventually became settled with two flights of R.E.8s and a fighter flight with Spads, Bristol Scouts and Martinsydes. The Squadron took over the Tigris Front from No. 30 Squadron. It discovered 2,000 Turkish troops north of Samarra enabling the 7th Division to engage, the Squadron providing recce and spotting facilities during the subsequent advance. In December C Flight moved to Akab to work with the cavalry. At this time the Squadron took part in a succession of bombing raids on German aerodromes principally Humr and also strafed a supply convoy mounted on 160 camels with great success.

Early in 1918 the Squadron was busy on reconnaissance in the north to check on German and Turkish troop movements towards Persia, once the Russians had returned to deal with their own revolution. In March the Turks started retreating on the Euphrates Front so No. 63 went in with bombs and thereafter the Squadron was involved every time the British troops advanced, particularly in the final October advance, when the Squadron was able to catch enemy columns in the Fat-ha Gorge and bomb and gun them to good effect.

With the war over No. 63 remained in Mesopotamia flying recce, photographic and policing duties against dissident Arab tribes while the detachment in Persia flew in co-operation with British troops in

the campaign against the Jungalis. Eventually the Squadron was disbanded at Baghdad on 29 February, 1920.

No. 63 re-formed on 15 February, 1937 as a light bomber squadron being the first to receive Fairey Battles and serving in 6 Group until 8 April, 1940 when it was disbanded into No. 12 OTU at Benson.

It was not until 15 June, 1942 that No. 63 was again re-formed, out of an element of No. 239 Squadron at Gatwick. It was equipped with Mustang Is for Tac/R duties and flew its first operations, PR of the French coast, on 11 January, 1943. The following month it began *Rhubarbs* and during the month two pilots were lost on ops. However it concentrated on convoy patrols from its Scottish bases. Moving south in November the Squadron came up to full operational pitch in December on *Lagoons* and *Populars*, flying 83 sorties. In addition it carried out photo recce of *Crossbow* targets. In February, 1944 it began practising combined operations under control of a HQ ship; this was for its role at D-Day. Before then it had two quick changes of equipment and when the invasion came it flew 76 sorties on spotting for the naval bombardment in Spitfires.

This task was continued, on a diminishing scale, through June and again in September when the Navy attacked Le Havre. After this it went over to escort duties, escorting supply aircraft and bombing raids. In October it escorted the Lancasters dropping supplies to the Dutch at Walcheren and then spotting for the naval bombardment of Walcheren in November. At the end of January it was disbanded at North Weald on 30th. The Squadron re-formed at Middle Wallop on 1 September, 1946 by re-numbering No. 164 Squadron and served as a fighter squadron until 24 October, 1958 when it disbanded at Waterbeach.

Bases etc.

Formed at Stirling on 5 July, 1916.

Stirling	Jul 1916—Oct 1916	
Cramlington	Oct 1916—Jun 1917	
en route to Persian Gulf	Jun 1917—Aug 1917	
Basra, det. Akab	Aug 1917—Sep 1917	
Samarra, det. Tikrit	Sep 1917—Nov 1918	
Samarra, det. Mosul, Ramadi	Nov 1918—Feb 1919	
Baghdad, det. Kasvin, Bushire	Feb 1919—Feb 1920	

Disbanded at Baghdad on 29 February, 1920. Re-formed as a bomber squadron at Andover on 15 February, 1937. Disbanded into No. 12 OTU at Benson on 8 April, 1940. Re-formed in the Tac/R role at Gatwick on 15 June, 1942.

Gatwick	Jun 1942—Jul 1942
Catterick	Jul 1942—Dec 1942
Macmerry, det. Odiham, Dundonald, Dalcross, Turnhouse	Dec 1942—Jul 1943
Turnhouse	Jul 1943—Nov 1943
Thruxton	Nov 1943—Nov 1943
Sawbridgeworth	Nov 1943—Nov 1943
North Weald, det. Benson	Nov 1943—Jan 1944
Turnhouse, det. Peterhead, Tealing, Dundonald, Ballyhalbert	Jan 1944—Apr 1944
Woodvale, det. Dundonald	Apr 1944—May 1944
Lee-on-Solent	May 1944—Jul 1944
Woodvale, det. Ballyhalbert	Jul 1944—Aug 1944
Lee-on-Solent, det. Ballyhalbert	Aug 1944—Sep 1944
North Weald	Sep 1944—Nov 1944
Manston	Nov 1944—Nov 1944
North Weald	Nov 1944—Jan 1945

Disbanded at North Weald on 30 January, 1945. Re-formed at Middle Wallop on 1 September, 1946 by re-numbering No. 164 Squadron as a fighter squadron. Disbanded at Waterbeach on 24 October, 1958.

Training Types (Jul 1916—Aug 1917)
including B.E.2c, 2846; B.E.2e, 6246
R.E.8 (Aug 1917—Feb 1920)
A4346; B6542
North American Mustang I (Jun 1942—Nov 1943)
AG460, T; AG498, P; AG539; AG575; AG596; AG613; AL965, E; AM156, Y; AM157, C; AM205, C; AP177; AP196, B
North American Mustang IA (Nov 1943—May 1944)
FD445; FD495; FD528; FD540; FD561

Hawker Hurricane IIC (Mar 1944—May 1944 & Sep 1944—Dec 1944)
BH201; HL732
Vickers-Supermarine Spitfire VB (May 1944—Jan 1945)
P8799; W3443, H; W3713; AA848; AA929; AB138; AB167; AR604; BL688; BL753, N; BL826; BL990; BM195; BM201; BM577, V; BM588, Q; EE626; EN837; EP504

Commanding Officers

Maj A. C. Boddam-Whetham	Aug 1916—Apr 1917
Maj J. C. Quinnell	Apr 1917—Nov 1917
Maj R. A. Bradley	Nov 1917—Apr 1918
Maj F. L. Robinson	Apr 1918—Feb 1920
S/Ldr R. Gray	Jun 1942—Jul 1942
W/Cdr T. K. Lacey	Jul 1942—Jul 1943
W/Cdr W. Cooper	Jul 1943—Aug 1943
S/Ldr R. J. Hardiman, DFC	Sep 1943—Oct 1943
S/Ldr A. S. Mann	Oct 1943—Dec 1943
S/Ldr M. Savage	Jan 1944—Sep 1944
S/Ldr R. W. Campbell	Sep 1944—Oct 1944
S/Ldr M. Savage	Oct 1944—Jan 1945

Aircraft Insignia

As far as is known no unit insignia was carried on the Squadron's aircraft during World War I. In World War II it is unlikely that any markings were carried on the Mustangs and it is not known what, if any, was used by the Hurricanes and Spitfires.
(See also *Bomber Squadrons of the RAF*, pp. 97–8 & *Fighter Squadrons of the RAF*, pp. 152–3)

No. 66 SQUADRON

BADGE
A rattlesnake

MOTTO
'Cavete praemonui'
('Beware, I have warned')

The rattlesnake typifies aggressive spirit and striking power.

For almost all its career No. 66 Squadron has been a fighter squadron. It formed at Filton on 30 June, 1916 and went to France the following year with Sopwith Pups re-equipping with Camels and moving on to the Italian Front in 1917 also. Here it fought until the war's end, disbanding at Leighterton on 25 October, 1919. It re-formed at Duxford on 20 July, 1936 and flew Spitfires in the Battle of Britain and throughout World War II, disbanding again at Twente on 30 April, 1945. After the war No. 66 re-formed at Duxford by re-numbering No. 165 Squadron and flew Meteors, Sabres and Hunters until 30 September, 1960 when it disbanded at Acklington.

On 15 September, 1961 the Squadron re-formed at Odiham to fly the RAFs largest helicopter, the Bristol Belvedere. It absorbed the Belvedere Trials Unit and for a year was the principal unit involved in working up the operational role. In June, 1962 it handed its aircraft over to No. 72 Squadron and moved to the Far East where it received a new batch of aircraft. It flew heavy-lift sorties and trooping, jungle and SAR duties in this area, Malaya, Borneo etc. for some years, receiving additional aircraft from the other Belvedere squadrons until March, 1969 when it was finally disbanded.

Bases etc.

Re-formed at Odiham on 15 September, 1961.

Odiham	Sep 1961—Jun 1962
Seletar, det. Kuching	Jul 1962—Mar 1969

Disbanded at Seletar in March, 1969.

Main Equipment

Westland/Bristol Belvedere HC.1 (Sep 1961—Mar 1969)
XG448, A; XG451, E, later C; XG456, H, later F; XG458, E; XG459, G, later H; XG464, K; XG466, K, later L; XG468, N; XG474, O; XG476, F, later P

Commanding Officers

S/Ldr J. R. Dowling, MBE, DFC, AFC	Sep 1961—Jun 1962
S/Ldr P. Sawyer	Jun 1962— 1964
S/Ldr P. D. A. Austin	1964—Jun 1966
S/Ldr P. L. Gray	Jun 1966—Mar 1969

Aircraft Insignia

The only markings carried by the Squadron's Belvederes was the Squadron badge on the fuselage sides at various periods during its Far East service.

No. 69 SQUADRON

BADGE
In front of an anchor a telescope

MOTTO
'With vigilance we serve'

The combination of the anchor and telescope symbolises the Squadron's World War II role as eyes of the Mediterranean Fleet.

No. 69 Squadron was formed at South Carlton on 28 December, 1916 out of Australians who had come over from Egypt as a corps reconnaissance unit. It spent nine months there working up and then went to France with R.E.8s where it flew its entire operations in support of the I ANZAC, later Australian, Corps. For them it flew artillery spotting, reconnaissance, photography sorties, line patrols, bombing raids and infantry liaison duties. On 19 January, 1918 it was redesignated No. 3 Squadron, Australian Flying Corps and served under this title until disbanded at Charleroi in February, 1919.

On 10 January, 1941 No. 69 re-formed out of No. 431 Flight at Luqa, Malta equipped with Martin Marylands which it used for long-range reconnaissance over the Mediterranean area, principally of naval targets and harbours with additional sorties to keep up-to-date information on enemy airfields. These sorties were being flown whilst Malta was under siege so the Squadron was not without losses, either operationally or at its own base. During the year the Squadron grew, adding other types such as Hurricanes, Beauforts and Blenheims as it could acquire them and in June it flew 160 sorties (3 bombing trips, the rest recces). This pace was maintained month by month with losses averaging one a month. In January, 1942 No. 69 acquired Beaufighters and Mosquitoes (two of each) and became more and more involved in air combat with consequent increased losses. This, combined with low serviceability, reduced the Squadron's activity in March, 1942 and now it began flying Spitfires; by May all its operations being flown on this type. By mid-summer the position was regularised – A Flight used Baltimores for co-operation with Beaufort shipping strikes, B Flight flew Spitfire IVs on high-altitude PR and C Flight used Marylands and Special Duty Flight Wellingtons which were used for night shipping strikes and special signals' tasks. This diverse collection of tasks continued with losses mounting (five crews in January, 1943) until February, 1943 when the Wellingtons were transferred to No. 458 Squadron, the Spitfire Flight formed No. 683 Squadron and No. 69 was left with Baltimores.

It was thus back to shipping searches and patrols, flying about 50 sorties per month. As the enemy were more and more driven back up Italy the work became less intense and consisted largely of convoy patrols by the end of the year. In February, 1944 it moved to Italy but was not long there, ceasing operations on 2 April and sailing to the UK.

Here it was built up at Northolt in 34 Wing for night recce duties with Wellington XIIIs. First operations came on 5 June, just prior to D-Day with recce flights of the roads around Beauvais. That month 35 sorties were flown for the loss of two aircraft. In July 162 sorties took place, mainly road and river recces by night with some flare-dropping for 2 Group thrown in; one aircraft was lost but one enemy aircraft was shot down and two damaged. The Squadron was now very busy, both target illuminating and flying photo and visual night recces, making many experimental photo sorties. In September it moved to France itself and by October was operating over Germany, sortie rate being about 70 per month.

Eleven aircraft were destroyed at Melsbroek in the Luftwaffe's New Year's Day attacks despite which the Squadron pressed on. Its aircraft now carried bombs whilst on night recce to drop on any suitable targets seen. By March all the flying was on visual recce, the aircraft now carried equipment to detect the German infra-red searchlights. By April targets were getting scarce so the Squadron began daylight searches off the coast for one-man submarines and explosive motor boats. This continued until 7 May when flying ceased. In July No. 69 went to Denmark to carry out Norwegian and Danish survey work and a month later, on 7 August, it was disbanded at its base at Eindhoven.

There followed two periods as a light bomber squadron. On 8 August, 1945 No. 69 was re-formed by re-numbering No. 613 Squadron at Cambrai/Epinoy with Mosquito FB.6s disbanding there on 28 March, 1946, re-forming from No. 180 Squadron at Wahn on 1 April, 1946 and disbanding there on 6 November, 1947.

On 5 May, 1954 the Squadron was re-formed as a photo reconnaissance unit at Laarbruch as part of RAF Germany, equipped with Canberra PR.3s. Its task combined strategical with tactical reconnaissance. From August, 1955 it maintained a detachment at Luqa for reconnaissance over the Central Mediterranean. As time went on the Mediterranean task predominated and the Squadron moved to Malta where it was re-numbered as No. 39 Squadron on 1 July, 1958.

Bases etc.

Formed at South Carlton on 28 December, 1916.

South Carlton	Dec	1916—Sep 1917
Savy	Sep	1917—Nov 1917
Bailleul	Nov	1917—Aug 1918
Villers Bocage	Aug	1918—Sep 1918
Proyart	Sep	1918—Sep 1918
Bouvincourt	Sep	1918—Oct 1918
Bernes	Oct	1918—Oct 1918
Premont	Oct	1918—Dec 1918
Charleroi	Dec	1918—Feb 1919

Disbanded at Charleroi in February, 1919, having been re-designated No. 3 Squadron, Australian Flying Corps on 19 January, 1918. Re-formed by re-numbering and expanding No. 431 Flight at Luqa on 10 January, 1941.

Luqa	Jan	1914—Oct 1941
Ta Kali	Oct	1941—Nov 1941
Luqa	Nov	1941—Feb 1944
Montecorvino	Feb	1944—Apr 1944
Northolt	May	1944—Sep 1944
Amiens/Glisy	Sep	1944—Sep 1944
Melsbroek	Sep	1944—Apr 1945
Eindhoven, det. Aalborg West	Apr	1945—Aug 1945

Disbanded at Eindhoven on 7 August, 1945. Re-formed as a light bomber squadron on 8 August 1945 at Cambrai/Epinoy, disbanded there on 28 March, 1946. Re-formed at Wahn on 1 April, 1946 also in the same role, disbanded there on 6 November, 1947. Re-formed as a PR squadron at Laarbruch on 5 May, 1954.

Laarbruch, det. Luqa, Idris, El Adem	May 1954—	
Luqa	—Jul	1958

Disbanded at Luqa on 1 July, 1958 by re-numbering as No. 39 Squadron.

Main Equipment

R.E.8 (Sep 1917—Feb 1919)
A3662; A3755; A3815; A4439; A4759; B3420; B2253; B5018; B5097; B5890; B6491; C2309; D6817; E180; F6016; H7042, J

Bristol Fighter (Sep 1918—Feb 1919)
C917; C995; E2529

Martin Maryland I/II (Jan 1941—Sep 1942)
AR705; AR711; AR724; AR733; AR741; BJ427; BS766; 1624 (SAAF)

Hawker Hurricane I/II (Apr 1941—   1941)
V7101; Z2332; Z3053; Z3173

Bristol Beaufort I (Aug 1941—Sep 1941)
L9875; W6518

Bristol Blenheim IV (Sep 1941—Oct 1941)
V5821; V6183; Z7627, N

de Havilland Mosquito I (Jan 1942—Mar 1943)
W4062; W4063

Bristol Beaufighter IC (Jan 1942—   1943)
T3301; T4705; V8222, N

Vickers-Supermarine Spitfire IV (Mar 1942—Feb 1943)
AB300; BP885; BP911; BR358; BR364; BR423; BR496; BR662; BS367; BS500

Vickers-Wellington VIII (Aug 1942—Feb 1943)
HX376, Z; HX441, S; HX509, V; HX537, P; HX582, R; HX605, L; HX728, D

Martin Baltimore I/II (Jun 1942—May 1943)
AG709, Q; AG734, D; AG779, M; AG801, A; AG831, L

Martin Baltimore III/IV (Apr 1943—Apr 1944)
AG937, X; AH125; AH152, P; FA122; FA147; FA160; FA209; FA355, B; FA396, H; FA413, A; FA465, B; FA509, L; FA661, C

Martin Baltimore V (Jan 1944—Apr 1944)
FW286, X; FW319, O; FW334, P; FW363, K; FW374, L; FW396, E

Vickers Wellington XIII (May 1944—Aug 1945)
HZ761; HZ796; HZ862; JA147; JA381; JA425; JA584; JA628; ME397; ME902; ME950; MF130; MF235; MF397; NC509; NC555

English Electric Canberra PR.3 (May 1954—Jul 1958)
WE138; WE142; WE144; WE168; WE174; WF924; WF927

English Electric Canberra PR.7
WT509

Commanding Officers

Maj D. Blake	Dec	1916—Jan 1918
S/Ldr E. A. Whiteley	Jan	1941—Jun 1941
S/Ldr R. D. Welland	Jun	1941—Jul 1941
S/Ldr E. Tennant	Jul	1941—Sep 1941
W/Cdr J. N. Dowland, GC	Sep	1941—Jan 1942
W/Cdr E. Tennant	Jan	1942—Jun 1942
P/O Foster	Jun	1942—Aug 1942
W/Cdr A. Warburton, DSO, DFC	Aug	1942—Mar 1943
W/Cdr R. C. Mackay, DFC	Mar	1943—May 1943
W/Cdr T. M. Channon, DSO	May	1943—Jul 1944
W/Cdr F. O. S. Dobell	Jul	1944—Sep 1944
W/Cdr M. J. A. Shaw, DSO	Sep	1944—Aug 1945
S/Ldr N. A. J. Mackie, DSO, DFC	1955—	1956

Aircraft Insignia

During World War I the Squadron was identified by a white disc painted on the sides of the fuselage, aft of the roundels. It is not believed that any distinguishing insignia was carried by the Squadron during World War II. No regular markings appear to have been used on the Canberras although one or two individual aircraft markings have been noted.
(See also *Bomber Squadrons of the RAF*, p. 98.)

Four of No. 86 Squadron's Bristol Beaufort Is climb away over AW239 on a shipping strike in 1941.

Sitting on the hard standing at Kai Tak airport Hong Kong in 1947 is Short Sunderland GR.5 SZ570 of No. 88 Squadron.

Short Sunderland III JM671 of No. 95 Squadron rests temporarily immobile in Mid-Atlantic after being forced down by engine trouble.

No. 99 Squadron flew Handley Page Hastings on Transport Command's routes for ten years from 1949. WJ338 is one of the Squadron's C.Mk2s, the letters GAC being part of the aircraft's call sign and no form of squadron identity.

A typical transport scene at Akrotiri in 1970. In the background is a Hercules C.1 from the Lyneham Transport Wing whilst in the foreground, awaiting its passengers for Lyneham, is Bristol Britannia C.1 XM518 of No. 99 Squadron.

The second torpedo-bomber squadron based at Singapore up to the outbreak of World War II was No. 100 with Vickers Vildebeest IIIs. K4176 B is seen here over the waterfront with a practice torpedo slung.

No. 103 Squadron flew Bristol Sycamore HC.14s on Search and Rescue and supply sorties during the Cyprus troubles from 1959 to 1963. This aircraft is seen over St. Hilarion Castle near Khyrenia.

No. 110 Squadron was based at Singapore and there flew both army support and SAR duties with Whirlwind HAR.10 until February, 1971.

One of the squadrons in the Middle East Transport Wing in the fifties was No. 114, flying Vickers Valetta C.1s from Kabrit. Their aircraft, of which VW844 was one, were distinguished by green propellers and cheat line.

In May, 1959 No. 114 re-formed as a Hastings squadron at Colerne, TG524 shown here at Blackbushe, being one of their C. Mk.1s, displaying the blue fin diamond.

Very few RAF squadrons operated aircraft styled *Pan American Airways System* but No. 117 Squadron acquired this DC-3 N16094, hastily painted with the American star in 1942 and allocated to the Squadron for its use from Bilbeis, Egypt where it is seen.

No. 118 Squadron's short spell in the helicopter world lasted but two years, from 1960 to 1962. Its Sycamores were emblazoned with the fighter markings previously carried on its Hunters, as seen here on XG502 at Upavon.

The Fairey Swordfish served with few RAF squadrons. No. 119 was one such unit, using Mk. IIIs for night attacks on midget submarines in 1945. These are believed to be part of the detachment at Knocke in Belgium.

No. 120 Squadron was re-formed on 1 June, 1941 to use the Consolidated Liberator I to close the mid-Atlantic gap in the fight against the U-boats. AM918 OH: L was one of its first aircraft, equipped with the early ASV aerials and an underbelly tray of four 20mm cannon.

No. 120 Squadron has remained in the anti-shipping business continuously since the war. This is one of its Shackleton MR. 3s in operational pose in the sixties. The white propeller spinners probably denoted the Squadron.

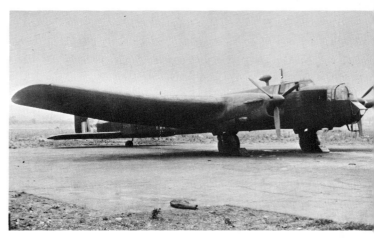

In 1941 the Special Duties Flights, which had begun flying spies into Europe, were formed into No. 138 Squadron. This interesting photograph shows what happened to Squadron Leader Nesbit-Dufort's Lysander, T1508, after trying to fly back to Tangmere with two agents through a cold front on Operation Beryl II. After icing up he landed in France and he and the agents escaped. The Squadron says the date was 28 February, 1942, Nesbit-Dufort's book 'late January, 1942'.

The principal aircraft used by 138 Squadron to drop supplies to resistance movements all over Europe was the Armstrong Whitworth Whitley V. Here is Z9428 NF:F on its dispersal at Stradishall late in 1942.

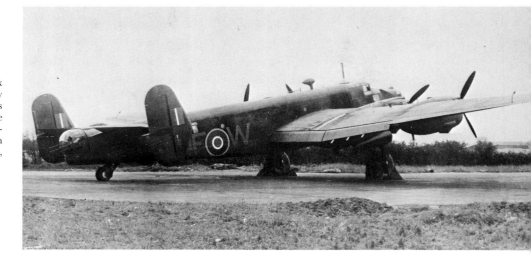

The Whitley was replaced by the Halifax in 138 Squadron, enabling greater flexibility due to its increased performance. This very early Mk.II L9618 was one of the Squadron's first aircraft, serving throughout 1942, until going missing between Malta and Gibraltar on 10 December, 1942.

Reconnaissance Spitfire IA R7139 of No. 140 Squadron about to start up at Benson for a sortie over Northern France in September/October, 1941. Note the modified hood, no aerial mast and camera bulge under the roundel.

This Bristol Blenheim IVF was the initial equipment of No. 143 Squadron and was used for convoy and AA patrols until replaced by Beaufighters in 1942.

No. 144 Squadron had served in 5 Group as a bomber unit with Handley Page Hampdens until April, 1942 when it moved to Leuchars and transferred to Coastal, using its Hampdens for bombing attacks on Norway. AE436 is seen flying from Leuchars shortly after the transfer.

Seen from the roof of Croydon Airport's control tower is this Dakota of No. 147 Squadron, KG783, with a Dutch Air Force Dakota in the background. The date is 1946. Note the patch of paint in front of the roundel where the route marking has been painted out and the white circle on the extreme nose which contained the code FM.

No. 148 was the Italy-based spy-dropping and agent supplying squadron using Lysanders and Halifaxes such as this Mk.V M seen at dispersal at Brindisi in 1944.

Following the success of the Royal Navy's Whirlwinds in Malaya in the early fifties No. 155 Squadron was formed in the RAF to use the HAR.4 version for army support and anti-terrorist duties. Aircraft T XJ421 is seen over typical terrain.

Setting out on one of its maritime patrols is this Liberator VI of No. 160 Squadron.

Sitting at its Tempsford dispersal is Lysander IIIA V9367 MA:B of No. 161 Squadron, awaiting the nightfall for its agent-running activities.

No. 162 was the Middle East's electronics squadron during World War II using mainly Wellingtons and Blenheims, Mk.IV R3864 seen starting up for a calibration sortie, probably at Shallufa, in 1942.

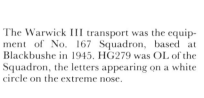

The Warwick III transport was the equipment of No. 167 Squadron, based at Blackbushe in 1945. HG279 was OL of the Squadron, the letters appearing on a white circle on the extreme nose.

No. 172 Squadron was formed at Chivenor in 1942 to operate the first Wellington VIIIs equipped with Leigh Lights against submarines. HX379 WN:A was one of these and is seen here over the Atlantic on 28 October, 1942.

The Warwick V was the anti-submarine version of this aircraft and only one unit flew it operationally from the UK – No. 179 Squadron at St. Eval. Two of the Squadron's aircraft fly over typical sea fret off the Cornish coast. OZ:R is PN807.

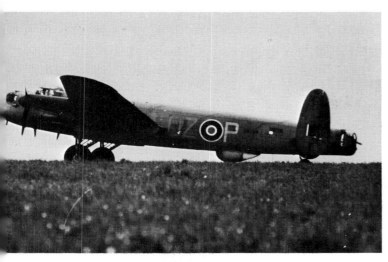

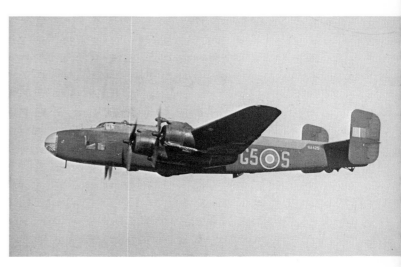

No. 179 Squadron replaced its Warwicks by Avro Lancaster ASR.3s in February, 1946 at St. Eval, only to be re-numbered No. 210 Squadron four months later.

The Handley Page Halifax bomber was also effective as a glider-tug and paratroop dropper and for transport duties and used as such by several units. One of No. 190 Squadron's Halifax A.7s is shown here flying from Great Dunmow in August, 1945.

One of the transport units to achieve a great reputation in the Burma campaign was No. 194 Squadron, which was dubbed 'The Friendly Firm'. It began its operations there in 1943 with Lockheed Hudson VIs.

Most of No. 194 Squadron's activities were flown by Douglas Dakotas. Here is Mk.IV KK122 X.

Another bomber which was turned into a transport was the Short Stirling and No. 196 Squadron was one unit which flew both versions, the Mk.IV and the Mk.V, the latter shown here, the aircraft being PK144 ZO:F.

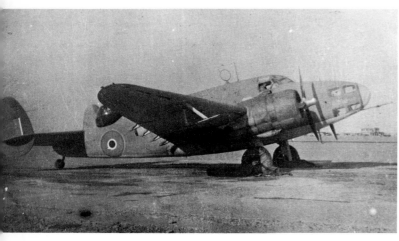

In 1941 there was a great need for maritime reconnaissance over the South Atlantic as convoys were going to Egypt and the Far East around the Cape. No. 200 Squadron was based in West Africa with Lockheed Hudsons to supplement the Sunderland squadrons and one of its Hudson VIs, FK591 is seen here on a transport trip to the Middle East.

No. 200 Squadron moved itself by air from West Africa (Yundum) to its new operational base of St. Thomas Mount in March, 1944. Mk. III FL926 J is seen at Fayid en route.

An overcast October day in 1929 at Calshot reveals two of No. 201 Squadron's Supermarine Southampton IIs (S1229 the nearest) taxying in after landing.

Saro Londons joined No. 201 Squadron at Calshot and served with it right into the beginnings of World War II, being used on convoy patrols until April, 1940. K5259 W, K5261 U and K5262 Z practise formation flying over Southampton Water ca 1936.

Food supplies are being unloaded from Sunderland GR.5 VB889 of No. 201 Squadron on Lake Havel at Berlin in 1949 during the Berlin Airlift.

No. 70 SQUADRON

BADGE
A demi-winged lion erased

MOTTO
'*Usquam*'
('Anywhere')

The lion was No. 70s badge from early days,
probably commemorating the Napier Lion
engines used by the Squadron's aircraft.

The first RFC Squadron with the Sopwith 1½ Strutter, No. 70 was
formed at Farnborough on 22 April, 1916 and served in France from
July, mainly on scout duties (fighter). After the war it returned to
UK and was disbanded on 22 January, 1920 at Spitalgate. It re-
formed by re-numbering No. 58 Squadron at Heliopolis on 1 February, 1920 as a bomber squadron, moving to Iraq in 1921 and
increasingly taking on transport duties. These were assisted by
re-equipping with Vickers Vernons in 1922. They were regularly
used on the mail route across the desert. In addition No. 70 flew
what would now be called logistic support flights to the operations in
Northern Iraq and also took part in bombing operations, being
officially designated a bomber-transport squadron. It remained in
this role in Iraq until August, 1939 when it moved to Egypt and,
with the outbreak of World War II, became a routine bomber
squadron once more. It was finally disbanded in this role at Shallufa
on 1 April, 1947.

On 1 May, 1948 No. 215 Squadron at Kabrit was re-numbered
No. 70 Squadron and so it returned to the transport role. Equipped
with Dakotas it flew the Middle East routes and any special trips
that were required. Valettas replaced the Dakotas in 1950 and
served six years with the Squadron, being involved in extra trooping
flights in connection with the unrest in Cyprus and the Mau Mau
terrorists in Kenya. In 1956 No. 70 having moved out many
civilians from Egypt, moved itself to Cyprus and was based there for
nearly twenty years. Hastings replaced the Valettas in 1956; being
based in Cyprus the Squadron was involved in regular paratroop
training sorties as well as flying the CENTO routes. After eleven
years with the Hastings the Squadron received turbo-prop equipment in the shape of the Argosy and this aircraft remained as the sole
four-engined transport squadron in the Middle East until the RAF
were pulled out of Cyprus in 1975. By the 1970s Argosies had been
augmented by Hercules and the Squadron moved to the UK, for the
first time since 1919, to become part of the Hercules Wing at
Lyneham with which it has served ever since.

Bases etc.

Formed 22 April, 1916 at Farnborough in the Scout (fighter) role. Disbanded at Spitalgate on 22 January, 1920. Re-formed in the bomber, and

bomber-transport roles, at Heliopolis on 1 February, 1920 by re-numbering
No. 58 Squadron. Disbanded at Shallufa on 1 April, 1947. Re-formed in the
transport role at Kabrit on 1 May, 1948 by re-numbering No. 215 Squadron.

Kabrit	May 1948—	1949
Fayid	1949—Feb	1956
Nicosia	Feb 1956—Jul	1966
Akrotiri	Jul 1966—Jan	1975
Lyneham	Jan 1975—	

Main Equipment

Douglas Dakota C.4 (May 1948—   1950)
KP226; KP263
Vickers Valetta C.1 (1950—Feb 1956)
VW148; VW154; VW181; VW186; VW195; VW803; VW810; VW829;
VW833; VW841; VW859; VX572
Handley Page Hastings C.1/C.2 (Jan 1956—Jul 1968)
TG509; TG513; TG524; TG530; TG535; TG551; TG563; TG575;
TG614; WD475; WD483; WJ324; WJ328; WJ337
Handley Page C.4
WD500
Armstrong-Whitworth Argosy C.1 (Nov 1967—Feb 1972)
XN818; XN820; XN848; XN858; XP410; XP445; XP450; XR107
Lockheed Hercules C.1 (1970—   )
Aircraft belong to Lyneham but the following are known to have been
used by No. 70 Squadron: XV188; XV192; XV294; XV305

Commanding Officers

S/Ldr R. M. Burns	May 1948—Jul	1949
S/Ldr P. O. V. Green, AFC	Jul 1949—Apr	1951
S/Ldr L. Reavell-Carter, MBE	Apr 1951—Dec	1952
S/Ldr J. C. Ward	Dec 1952—Apr	1955
S/Ldr T. N. Staples, DFM	Apr 1955—Jan	1956
S/Ldr W. K. Greer, AFC	Jan 1956—Sep	1958
S/Ldr P. Ainley, DFC	Sep 1958—Apr	1961
W/Cdr L. G. Holmes, OBE, DFC, AFC	Apr 1961—Sep	1962
S/Ldr L. E. Moran, DFC	Sep 1962—Feb	1963
S/Ldr J. H. W. Grobler	Feb 1963—Sep	1965
S/Ldr R. M. Gammon	Sep 1965—Oct	1967
S/Ldr R. M. Sparkes	Oct 1967—Nov	1968
S/Ldr M. A. Fish	Nov 1968—Feb	1971
S/Ldr D. L. Bates	Feb 1971—Feb	1972
W/Cdr A. C. Curry	Feb 1972—Mar	1974
W/Cdr R. M. Sparkes	Mar 1974—Nov	1975
W/Cdr P. Henley	Nov 1975—Sep	1977
W/Cdr P. S. E. Tootal	Sep 1977—Jul	1979
W/Cdr N. J. G. Hodnett	Jul 1979—	

Aircraft Insignia

It is not known if any insignia was carried by the Dakotas; with the Valettas
the Squadron badge was carried below the pilots' cockpit and its aircraft had
white spinners. The Hastings had a black diamond at the top of the fin with
'LXX' in white on it. The Argosies and Hercules carried the Squadron
emblem on the fin although this was deleted on No. 70's return to the UK.
(See also *Bomber Squadrons of the RAF*, pp. 98–101.)

No. 72 SQUADRON

BADGE
A swift volant

MOTTO
'*Swift*'

The swift in the Squadron's badge is symbolic of
speed.

For most of its existence No. 72 Squadron has been a fighter squadron. It originally formed at Upavon on 2 July, 1917 from part of the
Central Flying School and moved to Mesopotamia at the end of that
year. Here it served until disbanding at Baghdad on 22 September,
1919. It re-formed at Tangmere on 22 March, 1937 from a Flight of
No. 1 Squadron, receiving the first Gloster Gladiators in RAF
service. It fought throughout World War II with Spitfires, in the
Battle of Britain, and in the offensive over France, moving to North

Africa in 1942 and on into Sicily and the Italian campaign. It was
disbanded at Zeltweg, Austria on 30 December, 1946. On 31 January, 1947 No. 72 was again re-formed by re-numbering No.130
Squadron at Odiham and it remained as part of Fighter Command
until disbanding at Leconfield on 15 June, 1961.

On 15 November, 1961 No. 72 was re-formed, again at Odiham,
in a new role, that of a heavy-lift helicopter squadron with
Westland/Bristol Belvedere HC.1s. This type provided the army
with the ability to lift guns and heavy pieces of equipment. This
scope was widened to lift other helicopters and the Squadron
entered the national limelight when the CO, on 28 April, 1962,
successfully lowered into place the spire of the new Coventry
cathedral. The Squadron also became fully operational for landing
aboard Fleet carriers to increase its mobility. During 1964 it re-
equipped with Westland Wessex HC.2s and this enabled it to
concentrate on its task as a 38 Group mobile support helicopter

unit, operating in the field in support of the army. As such it has sent detachments to many places where the Army has been exercising or operating, including Northern Ireland.

Bases etc.

Re-formed as a helicopter squadron at Odiham on 15 November, 1961.
Odiham   Nov 1961—Nov 1980
Benson   Nov 1981—

Main Equipment

Westland/Bristol Belvedere HC.1 (Nov 1961—Sep 1965)
XG453, N; XG455, B; XG458, E; XG460, L; XG464, F; XG466, K; XG467, C
Westland Wessex HC.2 (Aug 1964—   )
XR498, M, later AM; XR502, D; XR506, AV; XR511, AL; XR520, B, later AB; XR522, D, later AY; XR527, J; XS678, K, later AK; XT668, S, later AS; XT675, Z, later AZ; XV719, A, later AA; XV723, AQ; XV729, AF

Commanding Officers

S/Ldr J. R. Dowling, MBE, DFC, AFC	Nov 1961—Nov 1962
S/Ldr A. T. Shaw	Nov 1962—Oct 1964
S/Ldr F. Braybrook	Oct 1964—May 1965
S/Ldr B. H. Smith	May 1965—Nov 1966
W/Cdr P. D. M. Moore	Jun 1967—Nov 1970
W/Cdr J. W. Price	Nov 1970— 1972
W/Cdr C. Reineck	1972— 1974
W/Cdr A. Salter	Dec 1976—Nov 1978
W/Cdr A. E. Ryle	Nov 1978—

Aircraft Markings

Both the Belvederes and the Wessexes have carried the old fighter squadron insignia on the tail fins comprising the swift emblem on a white disc flanked by a blue rectangle edged in red. In addition, since 1970 it has carried two-letter codes on its Wessexes, the first letter, 'A', denoting No. 72 Squadron.
(See also *Fighter Squadrons of the RAF*, pp. 176–81.)

No. 76 SQUADRON

BADGE
In front of a rose, a lion passant, guardant
MOTTO
'*Resolute*'

The white rose is introduced in the badge to commemorate the squadron's association with Yorkshire where it was formed. The lion is indicative of its readiness to attack or defend at all times.

In World War I No. 77 Squadron was a Home Defence squadron forming at Ripon on 15 September, 1916 and disbanding at Tadcaster on 13 June, 1919. It re-formed as a bomber unit at Finningley on 12 April, 1937 as the first squadron with Vickers Wellesleys but by the outbreak of war had re-equipped and became part of 16 Operational Training Unit at Upper Heyford on 12 April, 1940. After an abortive re-start later that month it re-formed as a Halifax bomber squadron in May, 1941 and served with 4 Group until 7 May, 1945 when it transferred to Transport Command.

Its task at first in Transport Command was on the Indian routes but by the end of August No. 76 had re-equipped with Dakotas and in September it moved out to India where it served on Army support for a year, being re-numbered as No. 62 Squadron on 1 September, 1946 at Mauripur. It again served in the bomber role from 1953 to 1960.

Bases etc.

Transferred to Transport Command on 7 May, 1945 at Holme-on-Spalding Moor.

Holme-on-Spalding Moor, det. Pocklington	May 1945—Sep 1945
Portreath	Sep 1945—Sep 1945
Tilda	Sep 1945—Nov 1945
Poona	Nov 1945—May 1946
Palam	May 1946— 1946
Mauripur	1946—Sep 1946

Disbanded at Mauripur on 1 September, 1946 by re-numbering as No. 62 Squadron. Re-formed as a bomber squadron at Wittering on 9 December, 1953.

Main Equipment

Douglas Dakota C.4 (Sep 1945—Sep 1946)
KJ969; KK177; KN550; KN559, MP:S; KP243; KP256; KP262, MP:Z

Commanding Officers

W/Cdr L. G. A. Whyte	Jan 1945—Jun 1945
W/Cdr R. K. Cassels, AFC	Jun 1945—Jul 1945
W/Cdr P. A. Nicholas, DFC	Jul 1945—Sep 1946

Aircraft Insignia

The Squadron continued to use the two-letter code 'MP' which had been used on the Halifaxes during the war.
(See also *Bomber Squadrons of the RAF*, pp. 104–6 & *Fighter Squadrons of the RAF*, p. 192)

No. 77 SQUADRON

BADGE
A thistle
MOTTO
'*Esse potius quam videre*'
('To be rather than to seem')

The thistle commemorates the Squadron's first forming in Scotland.

In World War I No. 77 Squadron was a Home Defence squadron forming at Turnhouse on 1 October, 1916 and disbanding at Penston on 13 June, 1919. It re-formed in the bomber role on 14 June, 1937 at Finningley with Vickers Wellesleys, re-equipping with Whitleys a year later and serving throughout World War II with these and Halifaxes as part of 4 Group although flying on detachment at Chivenor on anti-submarine patrols over the Bay of Biscay between May and October, 1942 with Whitleys.

On 7 May, 1945 the Squadron transferred to Transport Command at Full Sutton slowly re-equipping with Dakotas. These it took to India in September where it served mainly on trooping duties until 1 November, 1946 when it was re-numbered No. 31 Squadron at Mauripur. A month later, on 1 December, 1946, No. 271 Squadron at Broadwell was re-numbered No. 77 Squadron. It was now a Dakota squadron in 46 Group and was involved in flying army support duties as well as European route-flying. In 1948 it was caught up in Operation Plainfare and flew many sorties into Berlin with supplies. With the end of this, Transport Command was reduced in size and No. 77 Squadron was disbanded at Waterbeach on 1 June, 1949. From 1958 to 1963 it served as a Thor ICBM unit.

Bases etc.

Transferred to Transport Command 7 May, 1945 at Full Sutton.

Full Sutton	May 1945— 1945
Broadwell	1945—Sep 1945

Khargi Road | Sep 1945— 1945
Palam | 1945— 1945
Mauripur | 1945—Nov 1946

Disbanded at Mauripur 1 November, 1946 by re-numbering as No. 31 Squadron. Re-formed at Broadwell on 1 December, 1946 by re-numbering No. 271 Squadron.

Broadwell | Dec 1946—Sep 1947
Manston | Sep 1947—Nov 1948
Waterbeach | Nov 1948—Jun 1949

Disbanded at Waterbeach on 1 June, 1949.

Main Equipment

Douglas Dakota III, IV (May 1945—Nov 1946 & Dec 1946—Jun 1949)
KG436, KN:T; KJ836, KN:Y; KJ998, KN:C; KK150, KN:C;
KN296, KN:T; KN658, KN:Q; KP272, KN:S; KJ881, YS:K;
KJ907, YS:S; KK128, YS:U; KN553, YS:O; KN696, YS:H

Commanding Officers

W/Cdr J. K. M. Cooke, DSO, DFC | Jul 1945—

Aircraft Insignia

For the period 1945 to 1946 the Squadron used the code letters previously carried on its Halifaxes, namely 'KN'. When re-formed from No. 271 Squadron in December 1946 it continued to use its letters, viz. 'YS'.
(See also *Bomber Squadrons of the RAF*, pp. 107–9 & *Fighting Squadrons of the RAF*, p. 193)

No. 78 SQUADRON

BADGE
An heraldic tiger, rampant and double queued

MOTTO
'Nemo non paratus'
('Nobody unprepared')

The double queued tiger has reference to the aircraft used by the Squadron at the time the badge was issued, the Whitley with two Tiger engines and twin fins and rudders.

No. 78 Squadron served in World War I on Home Defence duties, being formed at Harrietsham on 1 November, 1916 and disbanded at Sutton's Farm on 31 December, 1919. It re-formed in the bomber role at Boscombe Down on 1 November, 1936 and became part of 4 Group, serving in the bomber offensive over Germany with Whitleys and Halifaxes throughout World War II.

It transferred to Transport Command at Breighton on 7 May, 1945 and after re-equipping with Dakotas, moved to Egypt where it formed part of the Middle East Transport Wing, flying the routes around the Mediterranean, Northern Africa and Arabia as well as providing tactical support flying for the army units. In 1950 it re-equipped with Valettas which continued in this role until 30 September, 1954 when it disbanded at Fayid.

The Squadron again re-formed as a short-range transport unit at Aden in 1956, equipped with Pioneers and later Twin Pioneers and flew in support of the army units policing the Protectorate. In 1965 the Twin Pioneers were replaced by Wessex helicopters which were used in the same role, transferring to the Persian Gulf in 1967. Here it included SAR in its tasks until disbanding in December, 1971.

Bases etc.

Transferred to Transport Command at Breighton on 7 May, 1945.

Breighton | May 1945—Sep 1945
Almaza, det. Maison Blanche | Sep 1945— 1946
Kabrit | 1946—Feb 1951
Fayid | Feb 1951—Sep 1954

Disbanded at Fayid on 30 September, 1954. Re-formed at Khormaksar on 24 April, 1956.

Khormaksar | Apr 1956—Jun 1965

Disbanded at Khormaksar by re-numbering as No. 21 Squadron. Re-formed there at the same time in the helicopter role.

Khormaksar | Jun 1965— 1967
Sharjah | 1967—Dec 1971

Disbanded at Sharjah in December, 1971.

Main Equipment

Douglas Dakota C.4 (Jul 1945— 1950)
KJ870, EY:H; KJ877, EY:Z; KN354, EY:S; KN650, EY:L;
KN694, EY:V; KP218, EY:J
Vickers Valetta C.1 (1950—Sep 1954)
VW146; VW148; VW155; VW161; VW206; VW808; VW813; VW846
S.A. Pioneer CC.1 (Apr 1956—Nov 1958)
XL517; XL519; XL520; XL553; XL554; XL665; XL706
S.A. Twin Pioneer CC.1 (Nov 1958—Jan 1965)
XL991, W; XL993, Y; XL994, Z; XM284, A; XM287, C; XM289, E;
XM957, D; XM963, K;
Westland Wessex HC.2 (1967—Dec 1971)
XR518, C; XR527, E; XR529, H; XS675, J; XT602, Y; XT680, G;
XV729, D; XV731, U;

Commanding Officers

S/Ldr F. J. Fenton | Oct 1945—May 1948
S/Ldr W. H. E. Trewin | May 1948—Nov 1949
S/Ldr H. B. Kirk | Nov 1949—Jan 1951
S/Ldr A. H. Piper, DFC | Jan 1951—Dec 1952
S/Ldr V. Nedved, MBE, DFC | Dec 1952—Nov 1953
S/Ldr T. N. Staples, DFM | Nov 1953—Sep 1954
S/Ldr R. A. McKay | May 1956—Jan 1957
S/Ldr L. L. Doveton, AFC | Jan 1957—Jun 1958
S/Ldr W. G. Hester | Jun 1958—May 1960
S/Ldr J. N. Phillips | May 1960—May 1962
S/Ldr F. Rimmer | May 1962—Apr 1964
S/Ldr B. M. Burley | Apr 1964—Jun 1965
S/Ldr F. Braybrook | Jun 1965—May 1967
S/Ldr T. J. C. Hooper | May 1967—Jun 1968
S/Ldr C. H. Reineck | Jun 1969—Jul 1970
S/Ldr P. D. Cliff | Jul 1970—Jun 1971
F/Lt M. D. Timbers | Jun 1971—Aug 1971
S/Ldr E. H. Roberts | Aug 1971—

Aircraft Markings

The Dakotas continued to use the two-letter code carried on the Squadron's Halifaxes, namely 'EY'. Whilst in the Middle East Transport Wing the Valettas of the Squadron were distinguished by red propellor spinners. It is not believed that any squadron markings were carried whilst at Aden or in the Gulf.
(See also *Bomber Squadrons of the RAF*, pp. 109–11 & *Fighting Squadrons of the RAF*, pp. 193)

No. 79 SQUADRON

BADGE
A salamander salient

MOTTO
'Nil nobis obstare potest'
('Nothing can withstand us')

The salamander was always ready to face any danger.

No. 79 Squadron was formed at Gosport on 8 August, 1917 and after a period as a training unit became a ground-attack squadron going to France in February, 1918. It fought there until the Armistice and was disbanded at Bickendorff on 15 July, 1919. It re-formed as a fighter squadron by re-numbering B Flight of 32 Squadron at Biggin Hill on 22 March, 1937. It fought with Hurricanes throughout the Battle of Britain, thereafter going to India in 1942 and fighting in the Burma campaign with Hurricanes and Thunderbolts, eventually disbanding at Meiktela on 30 December, 1945.

On 15 November, 1951 No. 79 was re-formed at Bückeburg in Germany as a fighter-reconnaissance squadron in 2nd TAF equipped with Gloster Meteor FR.9s. These it flew in the low-level tactical reconnaissance role for five years when they were replaced by Vickers-Supermarine Swift FR.5s. These continued flying this task in RAF Germany until 1 January, 1961 when the Squadron was disbanded at Gütersloh by being absorbed into No. 4 Squadron.

Bases etc.

Re-formed at Bückeburg on 15 November, 1951.

Bückeburg	Nov 1951—Nov	1951
Gütersloh	Nov 1951—Jul	1954
Bückeburg	Jul 1954—	1954
Laarbruch	1954—	1956
Gütersloh	1956—Jan	1961

Disbanded 1 January, 1961 into No. 4 Squadron.

Main Equipment

Gloster Meteor FR.9 (Nov 1951—   1956)
VZ586, T:E; VZ590, T:U; VZ609, T:U; WB113, T:B; WB121, T:H; WB135, T:N; WB141, T:C; WH534, T:D; WH557, T:R; WL255, T:T; WL260, T:B; WX972, T:F;

Vickers-Supermarine Swift FR.5 (1956—Jan 1961)
WK281, S; WK296, J; WK301, F; WK315, P; XD905, O; XD921, G; XD957, U; XD976, B

Commanding Officers

S/Ldr H. M. Chinnery, AFC	Nov 1951—Jul	1954
S/Ldr N. K. McCallum, DFC, AFC	Jul 1954—Feb	1957
S/Ldr H. Harrison, AFC	Feb 1957—Jun	1959
S/Ldr R. J. T. Buchanan, AFC	Jun 1959—Jan	1961

Aircraft Insignia

At first the aircraft were distinguished by the single-letter code 'T' but later this was replaced by a red arrow. On the Swifts this was normalised into a white rectangle each side of the roundel with a forward-pointing red arrow on it. Some of the aircraft also carried the Squadron's red salamander emblem on the port engine intake.
(See also *Fighter Squadrons of the RAF*, pp. 193–6)

No. 80 SQUADRON

BADGE
A bell

MOTTO
'Strike true'

The badge is in commemoration of one of No. 80s early commanders, Major V. D. Bell.

Almost the entire history of No. 80 Squadron is of fighter operations in two World Wars and after. It was first formed as a Camel squadron at Montrose on 10 August, 1917 and served in France from January, 1918 onwards, moving out to Egypt in 1919 where it was re-numbered No. 56 Squadron at Aboukir on 1 February, 1920.

No. 80 re-formed at Kenley on 8 March, 1937, moving to Egypt once more in 1938 and fought with Gladiators and Hurricanes in the Western Desert, Greece, Sicily and Italy, later receiving Spitfires. In 1944 it returned to the UK and, with Spitfires and then Tempests, flew with 2nd TAF in the liberation of Northern Europe, remaining in BAFO until 1949 when it took its Spitfires out to Hong Kong where it remained as the garrison squadron until 1 May, 1955 when it disbanded at Kai Tak. On 20 June, 1955 No. 80 re-formed in the photo-reconnaissance role at Laarbruch with English Electric Canberra PR.7s. It now provided a high and low-level strategic and tactical recce capability to 2nd TAF for fourteen years. It was finally disbanded at Brüggen on 28 September, 1969.

Bases etc.

Re-formed in the photo-recce role at Laarbruch on 20 June, 1955.

Laarbruch	Jun 1955—Jul	1957
Brüggen	Jul 1957—	1963
Laarbruch	1963—	1963
Brüggen	1963—Sep	1969

Disbanded at Brüggen on 28 September, 1969.

Main Equipment

English Electric Canberra PR.7 (Jun 1955—Sep 1969)
WH798; WT516; WT518; WT522; WT524; WT538

Commanding Officers

S/Ldr E. F. Brown, DFC	Jul 1955—Feb	1958
W/Cdr E. F. Brown, DFC	Feb 1958—Dec	1958
W/Cdr J. Hurry, DSO, DFC	Dec 1958—Jul	1961
W/Cdr K. R. Richardson, DFC	Jul 1961—Jan	1964
W/Cdr R. C. Simpson	Jan 1964—Dec	1965
W/Cdr B. Stansfield	Dec 1965—Aug	1966
W/Cdr R. E. W. Nettley	Aug 1966—	
W/Cdr R. J. Offord	—Sep	1969

Aircraft Insignia

The Canberras carried a blue diamond at the top of the fin with the bell emblem in yellow.
(See also *Fighter Squadrons of the RAF*, pp. 196–200)

No. 81 SQUADRON

BADGE
In front of a mullet, a dagger erect

MOTTO
'Non solum nobis'
('Not only by us')

The Red Star signifies the Squadron's Russian activities and the dagger its association with the First Army.

The Squadron was originally formed at Upper Heyford on 20 November, 1918 consisting entirely of Canadian personnel and was also designated No. 1 Squadron, CAF. It flew several fighter types until disbanding at Shoreham on 28 January, 1920.

On 25 August, 1939 No. 81 re-formed at Andover as a short-range communications unit equipped with de Havilland Tiger Moths and moved to France in September as part of the Field Component of the British Expeditionary Force. Here it flew courier duties with Tiger Moths, Magisters and Hawker Harts. Part of the Squadron's task was to fly mail runs between units and generally make itself useful to the commanders in the field. For two months it flew the second of the Cierva C.40 autogiros to evaluate it for army co-operation duties, including Corps battery work. Another task which fell to the Squadron during the 'phoney war' was camouflage examination from the air. When fighting broke out in earnest the Squadron was found far too vulnerable and withdrew to Boulogne and came home by ship, the personnel being dispersed to other units although the Squadron was not officially disbanded until 15 June, 1940.

On 29 July, 1941 No. 81 was re-formed as a fighter squadron at Debden from A Flight of 504 Squadron and served in the fighter role first of all as part of the RAF Fighter Wing in the Soviet Union and then in North Africa, Sicily, Italy and the Far East where it ended its fighter days at Kemajoran on 28 June, 1946.

On 1 September, 1946 it was re-formed at Seletar by re-numbering No. 684 Squadron. Its new duty was that of photo-reconnaissance for which it was equipped with de Havilland Mosquito PR.34s. Its first task was to complete a survey of the area comprising Malaya, Java and the Lesser Sundas, followed by a similar task over Western Thailand. The Squadron also acquired a Flight of Spitfire FR.18 which were used for a survey of Singapore and the Malayan airfields.

The Squadron had now acquired a reputation for survey work in the Far East so it went on, in 1947, to cover Sarawak and British North Borneo and in the years ahead Hong Kong, Thailand and Burma were also visited for this purpose. When the Malayan emergency blew up in 1948 the Squadron concentrated its flying sorties for Operation Firedog. This continued for some years and it fell to No. 81s lot to fly the last operational sortie with a Spitfire, on 1 April, 1954 and similarly with a Mosquito on 15 December, 1955. These types had been replaced by Gloster Meteor PR.10s and, in 1960, by Canberras. By then the emergency was virtually over with only occasional sorties against terrorists. The Squadron then returned to survey work but this was interrupted by the insurrection in Brunei with 81 keeping cover of the area and of Indonesia during early 1963. The whole of British Borneo was kept covered by the Squadron. Thereafter it was back in the main to survey work until January, 1970 when the Squadron was disbanded with the run-down in Far East Air Force.

Bases etc.

Re-formed in the communications role at Andover on 25 August, 1939.

Andover	Aug 1939—Sep 1939
Laval	Sep 1939—Oct 1939
Mont Jois, det. Rosieres	Oct 1939—May 1940
en route to UK	May 1940—Jun 1940

Disbanded *in vacuo* 15 June, 1940. Re-formed as a fighter squadron at Debden, 29 July, 1941. Disbanded as a fighter squadron at Kemajoran on 30 June, 1946. Re-formed in the PR role at Seletar on 1 September, 1946 by re-numbering No. 684 Squadron.

Seletar, det. Java, Mingaladon, Labuan	Sep 1946—Oct 1947
Changi, det. Mingaladon, Butterworth, Kai Tak	Oct 1947—Feb 1948
Tengah, det. Labuan, Kai Tak, Kaula Lumpur, Saigon	Feb 1948—Mar 1950
Seletar, det. Butterworth, Kai Tak, Labuan	Mar 1950—Apr 1958
Tengah, det. Labuan	Apr 1958—Jan 1970

Disbanded at Tengah in January, 1970.

Main Equipment

de Havilland Tiger Moth II (Sep 1939—May 1940)
N6747; N6799; N6802; N6847; N6933; N9154; N9157; N9206
Miles Magister I (Sep 1939—   1939)
L8232; L8233; N3708; N3911
Hawker Hart (Aug 1939—Sep 1939)
K3038; K3961
Cierva C.40 (Oct 1939—Dec 1939)
L7590
de Havilland Mosquito PR.34 (Sep 1946—Dec 1955)
PF620; PF622; PF652; PF668; PF677; RG177; RG189; RG205; RG211; RG235; RG254; RG262; RG308; RG314; VL614; VL622
Vickers-Supermarine Spitfire FR.18E (1946—   1947)
TP208; TP223; TP275; TP407
Vickers-Supermarine Spitfire PR.19 (Jam 1949—Apr 1954)
PM574; PS836; PS852; PS888; PS890
Gloster Meteor PR.10 (Nov 1955—Jul 1961)
VS971; VS987; VW377; WB159; WB163; WB166
Hunting Percival Pembroke C(PR).1 (Aug 1956—Jul 1960)
WV751; WV755; XF796; XF797; XF798; XF799
English Electric Canberra PR.7 (Jan 1960—Jan 1970)
WH777; WH778; WH780; WH791; WH795; WH797; WJ822

Commanding Officers

S/Ldr G. R. Ashton, AFC	Sep 1939—Mar 1940
S/Ldr J. H. Hill	Mar 1940—Jun 1940
W/Cdr J. R. H. Merrifield, DFC	Sep 1946—Jun 1947
S/Ldr B. A. Fairhurst, DFC	Jun 1947—Jan 1949
S/Ldr P. D. Thompson, DFC, DFM	Jan 1949—Sep 1951
S/Ldr J. Morgan, DSO	Sep 1951—Feb 1953
S/Ldr W. P. Swaby	Feb 1953—Aug 1955
S/Ldr S. McCreith, AFC	Aug 1955—Dec 1957
S/Ldr R. J. Linford	Dec 1957—Feb 1961
S/Ldr S. J. West	Feb 1961—Aug 1963
S/Ldr G. M. Gilbert	Aug 1963—
S/Ldr J. B. Fitzpatrick	

Aircraft Insignia

It is believed that no insignia was carried on the Squadron's aircraft during the communications period in 1939—1940. Likewise, no specific insignia was carried on the Mosquitoes and Spitfires. However, with the arrival of the Meteors the Squadron revived the 'Ace of Spades' playing card marking used on the Thunderbolts during the war and this was also carried on the Pembrokes, and the Canberras, in addition to the Squadron badge.
(See also *Fighter Squadrons of the RAF*, pp. 200–2)

No. 82 SQUADRON

BADGE
In front of a sun in splendour, a weathercock

MOTTO
'*Super omnia ubique*'
('Over all things everywhere')

The sun in splendour is taken from the Squadron's unofficial World War I badge and the weathercock signifies everywhere.

The Squadron formed at Doncaster on 7 February, 1917 and eventually worked up and went to France in November. It was not fully operational until January, 1918 when it began work with XIII Corps flying artillery patrols and escorts but principally photographic work on which it specialised. In March it was forced into flying contact patrols by the serious German advance, having to retreat through four different bases in six days. At this time, too, it was answering more artillery calls to provide targetting than other squadrons in the Wing. With the crisis over, the Squadron now turned its attention mostly to bombing, flying one or two raids every day through May, and establishing a bridge record for a bombing squadron. By mid-summer the accent changed once more with a transfer to the French army front where it largely flew infantry co-operation and ground-strafing. After a month of this the Squadron resumed bombing with II Corps and also flew ammunition and supply dropping sorties to forward troops, many pilots flying up to eight sorties a day in support of the Belgian troops. This, in essence, continued No. 82s work until the war ended. It returned to the UK in February, 1919 and was disbanded at Tangmere on 30 June, 1919.

When the Squadron was re-formed on 14 June, 1937 it was as a bomber unit with Hinds and then Blenheims. In 1942 it went to India, converted to Vengeances, and fought in the Burma campaign, ending up on Mosquitoes. It disbanded after the war at St. Thomas Mount on 15 March, 1946.

On 1 October, 1946 No. 82 Squadron was re-formed from a Flight of No. 541 Squadron at Benson. Its task was to survey Africa and it served in West Africa and Kenya, using Lancasters and Spitfires to accomplish this duty. It was not until October, 1952 that the task was completed and it returned to Benson. The following year it moved to Wyton and re-equipped with Canberras for survey work in the UK. This continued for three years, the Squadron disbanding at Wyton on 1 September, 1956.

Bases etc.

Formed at Doncaster on 7 February, 1917.

Doncaster	Feb	1917—Feb	1917
Beverley	Feb	1917—Mar	1917
Waddington	Mar	1917—Nov	1917
St. Omer	Nov	1917—Nov	1917
Savy	Nov	1917—Jan	1918
Bonneuil	Jan	1918—Mar	1918
Catigny	Mar	1918—Mar	1918
Allonville	Mar	1918—Mar	1918
Bertangles	Mar	1918—Mar	1918
Argenvilliers	Mar	1918—Jun	1918
Quevauvillers	Jun	1918—Jul	1918
Haussimont	Jul	1918—Aug	1918
Quelmes	Aug	1918—Sep	1918
Droglandt	Sep	1918—Sep	1918
Proven	Sep	1918—Oct	1918
Bisseghem	Oct	1918—Nov	1918
Coucou	Nov	1918—Nov	1918
Bertangles	Nov	1918—Feb	1919
Shoreham	Feb	1919—May	1919
Tangmere	May	1919—June	1919

Disbanded at Tangmere on 30 June, 1919. Served in the bomber role from 14 June, 1937 to 15 March, 1946. Re-formed as a photo reconnaissance unit at Benson from a Flight of No. 541 Squadron on 1 October, 1946.

Benson, det. Accra, Eastleigh, Takoradi	Oct	1946—Oct	1952
Benson	Oct	1952—Mar	1953
Wyton	Mar	1953—Sep	1956

Disbanded at Wyton on 1 September, 1956.

Main Equipment

B.E.2c (Feb 1917—Apr 1917)
2617; 2774; 2775; 4546; 5430
Avro 504K (Feb 1917—   1917)
6227; A5936; A5937; A8523; A8524; B392
B.E.2e (Feb 1917—Nov 1917)
A1263; A1844; A1845; A1846; A2871

R.E.7 (Mar 1917—   1917)
2194; 2227; 2329; 2401; A5156
R.E.8 (Aug 1917—Nov 1917)
A3641; B3439
A.W. F.K.8 (Nov 1917—Feb 1919)
B3375; B3381; B5764; B5783; B5817; B5836; B5844; C3525; C3639; C3647; C3662; C8448; C8460; C8527; C8601; C8647; D5006; D5024; D5072; D5114; D5179; F3471; F7411; H4463
Avro Lancaster PR.1 (Oct 1946—Mar 1953)
PA427, M; PA439, D; PA475, H; SW302, G; TW658, J; TW868, A; TW884, B; TW904, E
English Electric Canberra PR.3 (Mar 1953—? 1954)
WE169; WE173; WF922; WF924; WF926; WF772
English Electric Canberra PR.7 (1954—Sep 1956)
WH773; WH779; WH796; WH800; WJ818; WJ820

Commanding Officers

Maj J. A. Cunningham	Feb	1917—Jul	1917
Maj A. H. Jackson	Jul	1917—Apr	1918
Maj J. B. Solomon, MC	Apr	1918—Feb	1919
W/Cdr R. J. S. Edwards	Oct	1946—Mar	1947
W/Cdr R. J. Abrahams, OBE	Mar	1947—Jun	1949
W/Cdr D. C. Torrens, OBE	Jun	1949—Jun	1951
W/Cdr S. G. Wise, CBE, DFC	Jun	1951—Nov	1952
S/Ldr H. Grant	Nov	1952—Dec	1952
F/Lt D. E. Thompson, DFC	Dec	1952—Feb	1953
S/Ldr K. Richley	Feb	1953—Jan	1955
S/Ldr J. A. Bush, DFC	Jan	1955—Jan	1956
S/Ldr D. G. Bailey	Jan	1956—Apr	1956
S/Ldr D. A. Hammatt, AFC, DFM	Apr	1956—Sep	1956

Aircraft Insignia

The A.W.F.K.8s of the Squadron were identified by two white vertical bars aft of the fuselage roundels. The Lancasters only carried the Squadron badge beneath the pilot's cockpit. This was also carried on the Canberras and in addition these had red/green nosewheel doors, divided diagonally.

No. 84 SQUADRON

BADGE
A scorpion

MOTTO
'*Scorpiones pungunt*'
('Scorpions sting')

The scorpion was used by No. 84 as its badge long before the official badge was authorised. As much of the Squadron's service has been in areas where scorpions abound and as at one time the Squadron was equipped with Jupiter-engined aircraft the allegorical relationship between a scorpion and Jupiter are both of significance

The Squadron was formed as a fighter unit at Beaulieu in January, 1917 and served in this role on the Western Front for the rest of World War I, eventually disbanding at Kenley on 30 January, 1920. On 13 August, 1920 it was re-formed at Baghdad and served in Iraq in the light bomber/general purpose role until 1941 when, equipped with Blenheims, it fought in the Greek campaign. It then served again in Iraq and in the Western Desert until the beginning of 1942 when it transferred to the Far East, arriving there after the fall of Singapore and attempting to operate from Sumatra. The situation was too bad, however, and the Squadron re-embarked for India. From here No. 84 eventually fought in the Burma campaign with Vultee Vengeances and Mosquitoes, moving into Singapore after the war ended and then taking part in the Indonesian campaign. After this it returned to Singapore and fought in the Malayan terrorist campaign until disbanding at Tengah on 20 February, 1945.

On the same day No. 204 Squadron was re-numbered 84 Squadron. This was at Fayid in the Canal Zone and the Squadron now took on a transport role equipped with Vickers Valettas. At first it served on the Middle East transport routes but in January, 1957 it moved to Aden to supplement the Aden Communications Flight's Valettas in providing air transport in the Arabian Peninsula and particularly in the many needs within the Aden Protectorate. In June, 1958 these were supplemented by Blackburn Beverleys which could get into the small desert strips with heavy loads and in 1960 these became the Squadron's only type, it now concentrated on tactical support of the ground forces in the area. In August, 1967 it moved to Bahrein and re-equipped with Hawker Siddeley Andovers to provide Air Forces Gulf with air transport. Tactically it supported the army units in the Trucial States and Muscat and Oman as well as flying local routes within the Gulf and keeping one aircraft ready for medical evacuation duties. The Squadron remained in the area until the withdrawal of British Forces, being disbanded at Muharraq in September, 1971.

In January, 1972 No. 84 was re-formed once more, this time at Akrotiri in Cyprus from No. 1563 Flight. Its task was to provide search and rescue facilities at this base and within the Cyprus area and it was equipped with Whirlwind HAR.10 helicopters for this purpose. It also took over from No. 230 Squadron the detachment of Whirlwind 10s at Nicosia which provide a helicopter component for the United Nations forces on the island, flying supplies in and out of the small mountain posts on the Khyrenia range, and any other task needed.

Bases etc.

Re-formed in the transport role at Fayid on 20 February, 1953 by re-numbering No. 204 Squadron.

Fayid	Feb	1953—Jan	1957
Khormaksar, det. Bahrein	Jan	1957—Aug	1967
Sharjah	Aug	1967—Dec	1970
Muharraq	Dec	1970—Sep	1971

Disbanded at Muharraq September, 1971. Re-formed from No. 1563 Flight at Akrotiri in the SAR role in January, 1972.
Akrotiri, det. Nicosia .... Jan 1972—

Main Equipment

Vickers Valetta C.1 (Feb 1953—Sep 1960)
VW140; VW154; VW162; VW192; VW196; VW202; VW803; VW817; VW826; VW837; VW860; VX506; WD157; WD161
Blackburgh Beverley C.1 (Jun 1958—Aug 1967)
XB266, V; XB284; XH120; XH122; XL130, Y; XL151, L; XM111, W
Hawker Siddeley Andover C.1 (Aug 1967—Sep 1971)
XS595, A; XS611; XS641; XS643, D; XS645, E; XS646, F
Westland Whirlwind HAR.10 (Jan 1972—)
XK970, P; XK986, U; XP329, V; XP346; XP398; XR454

Commanding Officers

S/Ldr H. H. Jenkins	Feb 1953	Oct 1954
S/Ldr J. H. Dunn	Oct 1954	Sep 1956
S/Ldr F. L. Spencer	Sep 1956	Dec 1956
S/Ldr K. R. Bowhill, OBE	Dec 1956	Apr 1957
S/Ldr E. W. Talbot, DFC	Apr 1957	Jun 1958
S/Ldr H. W. Guile	Jun 1958	Sep 1960
S/Ldr K. H. Perry, DSO, AFC	Sep 1960	Sep 1962
S/Ldr K. J. Parfit	Sep 1962	Oct 1964
S/Ldr R. J. Barnden	Oct 1964	Oct 1966
S/Ldr S. Hitchen	Oct 1966	Aug 1967
S/Ldr A. E. Radnor	Aug 1967	Sep 1968
S/Ldr D. S. Gates	Sep 1968	Oct 1969
S/Ldr I. G. C. Chalmers	Oct 1969	Nov 1970
S/Ldr A. B. Stephens	Nov 1970	Dec 1970
S/Ldr D. R. Ikin	Dec 1970	Jan 1972
S/Ldr G. S. Puddy, AFC	Jan 1972	Apr 1974
S/Ldr L. Banham, MBE	Apr 1974	Dec 1976
S/Ldr S. M. St. C. Collins, MBE	Dec 1976	Jan 1979
S/Ldr M. P. W. Chapple	Jan 1979	—

Aircraft Insignia

On the Valettas the Squadron badge was carried on each side of the nose and card suits on the fin. Beverleys carried the scorpion emblem on the nose and one of the card suits on the fin – a pre-war tradition of the Squadron. The Andovers carried the scorpion on a white disc on the fin and yellow spinners, whilst the Whirlwinds carry the card suits on the fin.
(See also *Bomber Squadrons of the RAF*, pp. 115–18, & *Fighter Squadrons of the RAF*, p. 203)

No. 86 SQUADRON

BADGE
A gull volant, carrying in the beak a flash of lightning

MOTTO
'Ad libertatem volamus'
('We fly for liberty')

The gull signifies flying over the ocean and the flash of lightning the ability to strike.

The Squadron had two brief existences in World War I, neither of which came to anything. It first formed at Wye in September, 1917 but, before becoming operational, was disbanded on 4 July, 1918. On 30 October, 1918 a new No. 86 Squadron began to form at Brockworth but this was suspended when the Armistice took place on 11 November, 1918.

No. 86 Squadron formed for the third time on 6 December, 1940 at Gosport with Blenheim IVs for service with Coastal Command. It became operational on 28 March, 1941 after two moves of base, flying convoy escorts from Wattisham. This type of task was its only duty for some months. In June it added ASR searches to its task and began to re-equip with Beauforts which it first flew on mining operations. It now flew armed recces and made its first ship attack (with bombs) in November. With a detachment at St. Eval it began anti-shipping patrols in 1942, using torpedoes and claimed two ships sunk in February. In March it transferred to patrols off Norway with little result. In the summer it moved south and sent detachments into the Mediterranean, being reduced to cadre in August and its crews posted to Middle East squadrons.

For the rest of 1942 No. 86 trained crews on Liberators and it was not until February, 1943 that it resumed ops as a Liberator squadron. It was now flying out over the Atlantic on anti-submarine escort duties; on 4 May P/O J. C. Green scored the Squadron's first U-boat sunk and from now on a number of attacks were made each month. In August encounters were made with FW 200s and Ju 88s. Two more U-boats were sunk in October. 1944 was a busy year (681 operational hours were flown in May) but few sightings were made until June and July when action again became fierce and in September 841 hours were flown. The Squadron had been operating in Iceland from March to July but saw the war out at Tain finding the occasional submarine until June, 1945 when No. 86 transferred to Transport Command (301 Wing) and moved to Oakington in August. In October it began trooping flights to India which were continued until disbandment on 16 April, 1946.

Bases etc.

Formed at Gosport on 6 December, 1940.

Gosport	Dec 1940	Feb 1941
Leuchars	Feb 1941	Mar 1941
Wattisham, det. Ipswich & North Coates	Mar 1941	May 1941
North Coates, det. St. Eval 12/41—1/42)	May 1941	Jan 1942
St. Eval, det. North Coates (2/42—3/42)	Jan 1942	Mar 1942
Skitten	Mar 1942	Jul 1942
Thorney Island (aircrews to Middle East)	Jul 1942	Mar 1943
Aldergrove	Mar 1943	Sep 1943
Ballykelly	Sep 1943	Mar 1944
Reykjavik, det. Tain (6/44—7/44)	Mar 1944	Jul 1944
Tain	Jul 1944	Aug 1945
Oakington	Aug 1945	Apr 1946

Disbanded at Oakington on 16 April, 1945.

Main Equipment

Bristol Blenheim IV (Dec 1940—Jun 1941)
L4899, BX:A; T2432, BX:X; V5393, BX:D; V5626, BX:J; V5850, BX:Q; V6083, BX:Y; V6173, BX:R; Z5882, BX:L
Bristol Beaufort I (Jun 1941—Feb 1942)
L4471, BX:B; L9854, BX:K; N1019, BX:L; W6533, BX:B; W6542, BX:D; X8927, BX:R; AW192, BX:T; AW210, BX:P
Bristol Beaufort II (Jan 1942—Aug 1942)
AW284, BX:V; AW296, BX:B; AW308, BX:H; AW361, BX:T; AW381, BX:W; DD872, BX:V
Consolidated Liberator IIIA (Feb 1943—Aug 1944)
FK223, U; FK226, G; FK231, K; FK241, Y; FL907, F; FL916, N; FL922, Z; FL943, L
Consolidated Liberator V (Apr 1943—Dec 1943 & Jul 1944—Mar 1945)
BZ724, E; BZ788, W; BZ870, S; BZ877, B; BZ919, T; BZ943, N; FL944, Y; FL954, Z
Consolidated Liberator VIII (Mar 1945—Apr 1946)
KH225, XQ:M; KH266, XQ:Z; KH347, XQ:G; KH411, XQ:L
Consolidated Liberator C.VI (Aug 1945—Apr 1946)
KH420, XQ:L; KK251, XQ:S; KN704, XQ:O; TS539, XQ:U

Commanding Officers

W/Cdr C. J. P. Flood	Dec 1940	Apr 1942
W/Cdr R. C. Gaskell	Apr 1942	Jul 1942
W/Cdr V. C. Darling	Jul 1942	Sep 1942
W/Cdr R. D. Williams	Sep 1942	Nov 1943
W/Cdr C. E. Drapper	Nov 1943	Aug 1944
W/Cdr J. J. K. Fleetwood	Aug 1944	Aug 1945
S/Ldr J. G. Wilkinson	Aug 1945	Apr 1946

Aircraft Insignia

The two-letter identity combination 'BX' was carried on the sides of the Blenheims and Beauforts between December 1940 and August 1942. As far as is known no squadron identity markings were carried on the Liberators until 1945 when the letters 'XQ' were used up to the disbandment in April, 1946

No. 88 SQUADRON

MOTTO
'En Garde'
('Be on your guard')

The snake is based on the WWI badge of
Escadrille SPA.88 of the French Air Service
with which this Squadron was associated.

No. 88 Squadron originally formed at Gosport on 24 July, 1917
with Bristol Fighters serving on the Western Front with them from
April, 1918. It was disbanded in Belgium on 10 August, 1919
without returning to the UK.

When No. 88 re-formed it was as a bomber squadron at Wad-
dington on 7 June, 1937. It fought throughout World War II with
Fairey Battles, Bristol Blenheims and Douglas Bostons as part of 2
Group, first with Bomber Command then in 2nd TAF.

At the end of the war it was quickly disbanded, at Vitry, on 6
April, 1945.

On 1 September, 1946 No. 1430 Flight at Hong Kong was re-
numbered 88 Squadron and it was now a flying-boat unit equipped
with Sunderland Vs. These were used for shipping and anti-piracy
patrols as well as transport duties until the outbreak of the Korean
war when it began patrols along the Korean coastline from Japan
which were maintained until the ceasefire brought a return to its

more peaceful tasks once more. No. 88 was eventually disbanded at
Seletar in October, 1954 but not before having flown 165 sorties
against the Malayan terrorists.

The Squadron re-formed once more in the bombing role in
Wildenrath on 15 January, 1956 with Canberra B(I)8s amd served
there until 17 December, 1962 when it was re-numbered 14 Squadron.

Bases etc.

Formed from No. 1430 Flight at Kai Tak, 1 September, 1946.

Kai Tak	Sep 1946—May 1948
Koggala	May 1948—
Seletar	—Apr 1950
Kai Tak	Apr 1950—Jul 1950
Iwakuni	Jul 1950—Jun 1951
Seletar	Jun 1951—Oct 1954

Disbanded at Seletar 1 October, 1954.

Main Equipment

Short Sunderland GR.5 (Sep 1946—Oct 1954)
EJ155, U; ML745, B; ML772; ML882; NJ272; PP114; PP148;
RN282, C; RN302, C; SZ570, D; SZ578, L; VB883, B

Aircraft Markings
Only the Squadron badge, carried at times, distinguished the Squadron's
Sunderlands.
(See also *Bomber Squadrons of the RAF*, pp. 118–20 & *Fighter Squadrons of
the RAF*, p. 214.)

No. 95 SQUADRON

BADGE
On a mount of waves in the sea in front of a
palm tree a crowned crane displayed

MOTTO
'Trans mare exivi'
('I went out over the sea')

The badge combines the elements of a large
flying bird, indigenous to West Africa, also
signified by the palm tree, flying over the
ocean.

Little is known about No. 95 Squadron's World War I service. It
was originally formed in September, 1917 but never became operational, being disbanded on 4 July, 1918. A new No. 95 Squadron
formed at Kenley on 1 October, 1918 but lasted little more than a
month before again disbanding. Information on its equipment is not
available.

On 15 January, 1941 the Squadron was re-born out of a Flight of
No. 210 Squadron at Oban. The following day it moved to Pembroke Dock and two weeks later began its journey to its operational
base in West Africa via Mount Batten and Gibraltar, losing one
aircraft which forced landed in Portugal. The aircraft arrived at
Freetown during March and began convoy escorts on 24 March.
These became the main regular duty for the Squadron's Sunderlands, flying ten hour sorties out over the South Atlantic. It also flew
anti-shipping searches, looking for German surface raiders and
U-boats, and hunts for survivors from torpedoed ships, three such
ships being found in April alone. That month No. 95 established a
detachment at Bathurst and was involved from then on in keeping
an eye on French West Africa and the Vichy French ships sailing
from there. In September it began night sorties, using the moon and
its ASV to track down enemy vessels, but without success. On 20
October No. 95's first sub sighting was made but no attack was
possible. As the west coast of Africa was the main route for sea
transport to the Middle and Far East the Squadron's vital function
was escorting this traffic which involved long, dull flying. Over the
months occasional aircraft were lost, one at Malta in February 1942,

one failed to return from patrol in June, 1942, another was blown to
pieces at its moorings by mines. The Squadron flew an average of 40
sorties per month until the end of 1942 when operations tailed off,
picking up again in 1943 when a move to Bathurst took place. On 5
April, 1943 F/Sgt Wharton and crew found a U-boat and attacked it
causing damage, the only attack in the Squadron's history. Port
Etienne was now being used as a base and was busier than Bathurst.

In 1944 work increased with up to 50 sorties a month; amongst
these were flights to the Cape Verde Islands with yellow fever
serum. With the opening of the Mediterranean to convoys in 1944
the convoy work died down and most activity was anti-submarine
flying. This tailed off in 1945 and flying ceased on 25 May, 1945.
Serviceable aircraft were ferried back to the UK and the Squadron
disbanded on 30 June, 1945.

Bases etc.

Formed at Oban on 15 January, 1941 from a Flight of 210 Squadron.

Oban	Jan 1941—Jan 1941
Pembroke Dock	Jan 1941—Feb 1941
Freetown	Feb 1941—Apr 1941
Freetown, det. Bathurst	Apr 1941—Feb 1942
Freetown, det. Bathurst & Gibraltar	Feb 1942—Apr 1942
Jui	Apr 1942—May 1942
Jui, det. Bathurst	May 1942—Mar 1943
Bathurst	Mar 1943—Apr 1943
Bathurst, det. Port Etienne	Apr 1943—Apr 1944
Bathurst, det. Jui & Port Etienne	Apr 1944—Jun 1945

30 June, 1945 disbanded at Bathurst.

Main Equipment

Short Sunderland I (Jan 1941—Nov 1942)
L2163, G; L5802, SE:F; L5805, SE:B; N9050, SE:D; P9623, SE:E;
T9046, SE:J; T9078, SE:A

Short Sunderland III (Aug 1942—Jun 1945)
W6015, M; W6076, D; DV956, L; DV973, P; DW107, R; DP186, J;
EJ144, A; EJ163, K; EK587, F; JM670, M; JM677, S; ML873, G

Commanding Officers

W/Cdr F. J. Fressanges	Jan 1941—Mar 1941
W/Cdr F. A. Pearce	Mar 1941—Nov 1941

Aircraft Insignia

The Squadron was allotted the code letters 'SE' on its formation and these were carried on the first aircraft used by the Squadron in West Africa. It is believed that replacement aircraft dropped the letters and by the time the Mk III Sunderlands came into service no squadron insignia was being carried.

No. 99 SQUADRON

BADGE
A puma salient

MOTTO
'Quisque tenax'
('Each tenacious')

Not only does the puma associate with the Squadron's first aircraft – the D.H.9. with Puma engines, but it also signifies independence and tenacity of purpose.

The Squadron was first formed at Yatesbury on 15 August, 1917 as a bomber unit and served with the Independent Air Force towards the end of World War I. After the Armistice it flew air mail duties within Germany until May 1919 when it moved to India and was re-numbered No. 27 Squadron on 1 April, 1920. No. 99 re-formed once more in the UK as a bomber squadron on 1 April, 1924 at Netheravon, becoming a heavy-bomber squadron in the inter-war years and entering World War II with Wellingtons as part of 3 Group. It flew in the night offensive against Germany until January, 1942 when it set out for the Far East and thereafter was occupied in long-range bombing against the Japanese until disbanding on the Cocos Island on the 15 November, 1945.

On 17 November, 1947 No. 99 again re-formed, this time in the transport role, at Lyneham and was equipped with Avro Yorks. These were originally used on the routes to the various commonwealth countries but in 1948 the Squadron was pulled into the Berlin Airlift and, flying from Wunstorf, was heavily involved. In August, 1949 it finished this task and re-equipped with Handley Page Hastings, turning its attention once more to the routes through the Middle East to India and the Far East. It also had a tactical support role and this was exercised in 1956 when the Squadron dropped paratroops on Gamil airfield during the fighting for the Suez Canal.

Three years later the Squadron received the first Bristol Britannias in RAF service and flew these on the Transport Command trunk routes across the world as well as being available for special flights, many of which included evacuating civilians from the world's troublespots, such as Leopoldville in the Congo in 1960, Kuwait in 1961 and Belize in 1961. In 1965/66 No. 99 was busy ferrying oil to Zambia and in November, 1967 it was evacuating the British troops from Aden. It was eventually disbanded in January, 1976 at Brize Norton when the Britannia force was sold.

Bases etc.

Re-formed in the transport role at Lyneham on 17 November, 1947.

Lyneham, det. Wunstorf	Nov 1947—Jun 1970
Brize Norton	Jun 1970—Jan 1976

Disbanded at Brize Norton in January, 1976.

Main Equipment

Avro York C.1 (Nov 1947/Aug 1949)
MW136, AT; MW179, AH; MW237, AZ; MW263, AG; MW294, AF; MW305, AW; PE103, AO

Handley Page Hastings C.1 (Aug 1949—Jun 1959)
TG524, JAQ; TG537, F; TG551, GAN; TG563, GAT; TG603, B; TG613, P

Handley Page Hastings C.2 (1950—Jan 1959)
WD475, GAQ; WD485, GAG; WD488, JAM; WD499, JAV; WJ330; WJ332, JAA; WJ337, GAF

Bristol Britannia C.1/C.2 (Jan 1959—Jan 1976)
XL636; XL638; XL640; XL657; XL660; XM498; XM517

Bristol Britannia C.2
XN404

Commanding Officers

W/Cdr B. C. Barnett, AFC	1950—	1952
S/Ldr K. B. Orr	Sep 1952—Jul	1954
S/Ldr R. F. B. Powell	Jul 1954—Apr	1965
S/Ldr D. R. Ware, DFC, AFC	Apr 1956—May	1957
S/Ldr T. M. Stafford	May 1957—Jan	1959
W/Cdr J. O. Barnard, OBE	Jan 1959—Oct	1959
W/Cdr W. E. F. Gray, AFC	Oct 1959—Sep	1961
W/Cdr P. Barber, DFC	Sep 1961—Nov	1963
W/Cdr R. M. Jenkins, AFC	Nov 1963—Dec	1965
W/Cdr T. L. Kennedy, AFC	Dec 1965—Aug	1967
W/Cdr F. B. Yetman	Aug 1967—Jun	1969
W/Cdr W. C. Milne	Jun 1969—Jun	1971
W/Cdr F. Appleyard	Jun 1971—Sep	1973
W/Cdr C. E. Bowles	Sep 1973—	

Aircraft Insignia

The only identity markings on the Yorks were the last two letters of the Squadron's Transport Command code ('A' and an aircraft letter). The Hastings not infrequently carried the aircraft's call sign on the fuselage, usually a three-letter sequence commencing 'GA' or 'JA' and in addition carried a black diamond on the top if the fin with '99' in white thereon. The Britannias carried no squadron identity as these aircraft were pooled with No. 511 Squadron.

(See also *Bomber Squadrons of the RAF*, pp. 127–30).

No. 103 SQUADRON

BADGE
A swan, wings elevated and addorsed

MOTTO
'Noli me tangere'
('Touch me not')

The swan, being strong on the wing and able to defend itself was, chosen as fitting by the Squadron.

No. 103 Squadron has predominantly been a bomber unit. It was formed at Beaulieu on 1 September, 1917 and went to France with D.H.9s in May, 1918 serving in the bombing and reconnaissance roles. It returned to the UK after the war and was disbanded at Shotwick on 1 October, 1919. It re-formed on 10 August, 1936 as a bomber squadron once more, serving in France in 1939–40, the remnants returning to the UK and, re-equipped as a heavy bomber squadron, took part in the aerial offensive against Germany until the war's end. It was disbanded on 26 November, 1945 by re-numbering as 57 Squadron. A further period of service took place between November, 1954 and July, 1956 when No. 10 was a Canberra squadron in 2nd TAF.

On 1 August, 1959 the Squadron re-appeared in a different role when No. 284 Squadron was re-numbered. It was now a search and rescue helicopter unit in Cyprus with Bristol Sycamore HR.14s, and from 1960 onwards took responsibility for a detached Flight at El Adem. Because of the emergency in Cyprus itself the Squadron maintained a standby for the local Army Commander to move troops to ambush positions or to set up road blocks, so performing a dual role. No. 103 made many successful calls to accidents, aircraft crashes and sea rescues in the area, particularly impressive being the grounding of the Yugoslav freighter *Snjeznik* in Famagusta harbour on 6 February, 1960. Not only was one helicopter lost during this rescue but thirteen seamen and the crew of the crashed helicopter were all safely rescued. This period of the Squadron's life ended on 31 July, 1963 when the Cyprus-based unit became No. 1563 Flight and the Flight in El Adem No. 1564 Flight.

The following month B Flight of No. 110 Squadron at Seletar was expanded to Squadron status and numbered 103 Squadron. After a quick work-up on Whirlwind HAR.10 helicopters it sent a detachment to Kuching in Borneo to provide support to the army's heavy fighting against the insurrection. Troop lifts, re-supply missions and casevac became the daily routine, flying into small and difficult jungle clearings in most instances. Back in Singapore the HQ of the Squadron was engaged against Indonesians infiltrating Western Malaysia as well as providing a SAR standby for the Singapore area. More than sixty calls were made on the squadron in 1966. Late in 1972 the Whirlwinds gave way to Wessex HC.2s to continue the army close-support role in the Far East. These flew on until 31 July, 1975 when the Squadron disbanded at Tengah.

Bases etc.

Re-formed in the SAR role at Nicosia by re-numbering No. 284 Squadron on 1 August, 1959.

Nicosia, det. El Adem	Aug 1959—Jul 1963

Disbanded by re-numbering No. 1563 Flight Nicosia and No. 1564 Flight El Adem on 31 July, 1963. Re-formed at Seletar by re-numbering and increasing B Flight of 110 Squadron, in August, 1963. It now flew in the tactical support role.

Seletar, det. Kuching, Labuan	Aug 1963— 1969
Tengah	1969—Jul 1975

Disbanded at Tengah on 31 July, 1975.

Main Equipment

Bristol Sycamore HR.14 (Aug 1959—Jul 1963)
XE307; XF269; XG508; XG517; XJ384; XL820; XL824
Westland Whirlwind HAR.10 (Aug 1963—Nov 1972)
XJ762, P; XK988, D; XP362, R; XP393, U; XP401, R; XR455, A; XR484, Y
Westland Wessex HC.2 (Nov 1972—Jul 1975)
XR497, M; XR508, D; XS675, C; XT603, A; XT680, E; XV729, O; XV730, B

Commanding Officers

S/Ldr J. L. Price	Aug 1959—Aug 1961
S/Ldr L. A. Wilson	Aug 1961—Aug 1963
S/Ldr P. L. Davis, MC, DFC	Aug 1963—Aug 1965
S/Ldr F. D. Hoskins	Aug 1965—Feb 1968
S/Ldr I. Horrocks	Feb 1968—
S/Ldr P. R. Bond	

Aircraft Markings

On the Whirlwinds and Wessexes the Squadron emblem was carried in a white disc on the fin.
(See also *Bomber Squadrons of the RAF*, pp. 142–3)

No. 105 SQUADRON

BADGE
A battle axe

MOTTO
'Fortis in proeliis'
('Valiant in battles')

The battle axe commemorates the fact that the Squadron was at one time equipped with Fairey Battle aircraft. Further, the squadron's service in Ireland is shown by the emerald green axe handle.

No. 105 Squadron was first formed at Andover on 14 September, 1917 and served there for six months in a training role, at the same time working up in the corps recce and artillery observation roles. However, at the same time as the RAF became merged into the RAF No. 105 Squadron was re-equipped throughout with R.E.8s and the following month moved to Ireland where it was based at Omagh with Flights detached to Oranmore and Castlebar. The Squadron now performed two distinct roles, flying army support as had been planned and trained for but also flying anti-submarine patrols around the coast, many submarines using the southern Irish coast as cover. This continued until the Armistice when it simply reverted to army co-operation duties. For these it re-equipped with Bristol Fighters at the turn of the year; it remained thus employed throughout 1919, disbanding on 1 February, 1920.

No. 105 re-formed as a bomber squadron on 26 April, 1937 with Hawker Audaxes, but soon re-equipped with Fairey Battles which it took to France, and war, in 1939. Returning to England after the French collapse in 1940 it re-equipped with Blenheims, then in 1942 Mosquitoes, pioneering the low-level attacks for which the Mosquito became famous. After World War II it was disbanded at Upwood on 1 February, 1946.

When No. 105 eventually re-formed it was in the transport role; the place was Benson, the date 21 February, 1962. The new No. 105

Squadron became the second unit to equip with the new Hawker Siddeley Argosy C.1 and spent four months working up on this aircraft at Benson. In June the Squadron moved out to Aden where it set up permanent base. Here it flew route-proving flights around the Middle East and carried out tropical trials on two Argosies. In October it received its full complement of aircraft and commenced route flying in earnest, covering the Middle East, east to Pakistan and India and south to Kenya and Rhodesia. In addition it had a tactical role in the Aden Protectorate itself, carrying out para-dropping to the ground forces. By 1964 these practices were flown 'for real' when the Radfan troubles began. In 1965 the Squadron had to detach to Changi in the Far East to supplement the Argosy squadron there due to the groundings of all Hastings, and this brought operations with the forces in Borneo.

Another aircraft, supporting the RAF Himalayan expedition was caught at Peshawar when the India/Pakistan war broke out and was retained for possible evacuation duties. The Rhodesian crisis brought extra duties, particularly the regular supply of the base at Majunga on Malagasy. In 1966 terrorist activities intensified and No. 105 was engaged in more air-dropping in Aden itself. It also took on search and rescue duties to supplement the Shackletons. In 1967 the routes for No. 105 were reduced enabling it to concentrate more on anti-terrorist flying but the end of the Aden Protectorate had been planned and the Squadron moved to Muharraq on the island of Bahrein from which to cover the final withdrawal. This accomplished No. 105 disbanded at Bahrein on 20 January, 1968.

Bases etc.

Formed at Andover on 14 September, 1917.

Andover	Sep 1917—May 1918
Omagh, det. Oranmore, Castlebar)	May 1918—Feb 1920

Disbanded at Omagh on 1 February, 1920. Re-formed in the bomber role at Harwell on 26 April, 1937. Disbanded at Upwood on 1 February, 1946. Re-formed, in the transport role, at Benson on 21 February, 1962.

Benson	Feb 1962—Jun 1962
Khormaksar	Jun 1962—Aug 1967

Muharraq
Disbanded at Muharraq 20 January, 1968. Aug 1967—Jan 1968

Main Equipment

Training Types (Sep. 1917—Apr 1918)
D.H.6: B.E.2b: B.E.2d: D.H.9
No known serial numbers
R.E.8 (Apr 1918—Jan 1919)
No known serial numbers
Bristol F.2B (Dec 1918—Feb 1920)
No known serial numbers
Hawker Siddeley Argocy C.1 (Feb 1962—Jan 1968)
XN813; XN820; XN852; XP408; XP412; XP439; XR109

Commanding Officers

Capt H. G. Bowen	Sep 1917—Mar 1918
Maj D. G. Joy	Mar 1918—Jan 1919
Maj H. J. F. Hunter	Jan 1919—Feb 1920
W/Cdr W. I. Harris, AFC	Feb 1962—Aug 1964
W/Cdr J. E. W. Teager, AFC	Aug 1964—Jun 1966
W/Cdr E. C. Rigg	Jun 1966—Jan 1968

Aircraft Insignia

It is not believed that No. 105 carried any specific squadron insignia on its aircraft during the above periods.
(See also *Bomber Squadrons of the RAF*, pp. 146–8)

No. 110 SQUADRON

BADGE
Issuant from an astral crown a demi-tiger
MOTTO
'*Nec timeo nec sperno*'
('I neither fear nor despise')

The demi-tiger was the crest of the Nizam of
Hyderabad who presented the squadron with
its original D.H.9A aircraft in 1918.

In both World Wars No. 110 Squadron has served as a bomber squadron with distinction, changing to the transport role after World War II. It was originally formed at Rendcombe on 1 November, 1917 and flew with D.H.9As as part of the Independent Air Force from August, 1918 until the Armistice. It was disbanded in France on the 27 August, 1919 and re-formed, again as a bomber squadron on 18 May, 1937 at Waddington. It fought in World War II at first with 2 Group as a Blenheim bomber squadron and then from 1942 onwards in India and Burma with Vultee Vengeances, ending up in Borneo where it was disbanded on 15 April, 1946.

No. 110 was re-formed in the transport role on 15 June, 1946 by re-numbering No. 96 Squadron. This unit was based at Kai Tak airfield, Hong Kong and was equipped with Dakotas. It had three tasks whilst there, carrying out route-flying over specific routes stretching from Calcutta to Iwakuni (Japan), to make special flights for VIPs, and to stand-by for typhoon evacuation flying. In addition it found itself supply-dropping to natives in the Burmese highlands who had run out of food. The Squadron's existence was short-lived for, with the rationalisation of forces in FEAF the schedules out of Hong Kong were taken over by No. 48 Squadron into which a reduced 110 was disbanded in July, 1947. However, a new No. 110 Squadron was re-formed at Changi on 15 September, 1947, again with Dakotas but this time to serve in the Transport Support role. It was now a medium range squadron with some weekly schedules but also army support duties, principally in Malaya. It worked up in the supply dropping role which it soon used in earnest to the troops fighting in the emergency in Malaya. A subsidiary task was the establishment of re-supply squadrons at Hong Kong, No. 110 flying the transport necessary to take fighter or other units there and this was practised when No. 28 Squadron moved up early in 1948. Its main task was still the Malayan jungle and it was not without casualties, two fatal crashes taking place in 1948. The Squadron continued in this vital role, flying both scheduled routes and supply drops whilst at Changi and only supply drops whilst at Kuala Lumpur. In addition, it established an ASR detachment at Negombo, Ceylon in 1950 to guide rescue craft to ships in trouble and a detachment at Kai Tak for certain routes. In 1951 the first Valettas began to supplement the Dakotas and in 1952 some of the latter were used for 'Sky-Shouting'. Eventually No. 110 became an all-Valetta squadron and its tasks continued until 31 December, 1957 when it disbanded.

However, the Squadron re-appeared at Kuala Lumpur on 3 June, 1959, being the amalgamation of Nos. 155 and 194 Squadrons. It was now a helicopter unit equipped with Whirlwind HAR.4s and Bristol Sycamore HR.14s. These it used in intimate support of the

anti-terrorist forces operating near the Thai border. Its two main operational tasks were the re-supply of forward positions, fresh troops being flown in, and the evacuation of sick and wounded being brought out from the army positions. This involved flying over miles of jungle which meant a crash in the trees on engine-failure and landing and taking-off from small clearings in the jungle.

Although the official end of the emergency came in August, 1960 sporadic attacks continued so No. 110 was still engaged in anti-terrorist tasks but on not such a hectic scale. This remained the pattern until January, 1963 when trouble broke out in Borneo and No. 110 moved there in support. It was now flying the turbine-engined Whirlwind HAR.10 and these it used principally for communications flying at first then re-supply duties. As a result of this long stretch from Butterworth to Borneo the Squadron HQ was later moved to Singapore. In 1964 operations had quietened enough to enable the Squadron to assist in survey work, airlifting the surveyors to inaccessible spots. When Indonesia invaded Malaya later that year No. 110 was back in the re-supply work in Malaya.

These incursions occurred on a regular basis over the months ahead. Borneo continued to take up most of the Squadron's time until confrontation ended in August, 1966 when No. 110 left a small detachment there until October, 1967. Thereafter it maintained a detachment at Hong Kong for a year but by now the clouds were gathering over FEAF and eventually the Squadron was disbanded on the British withdrawal from South-East Asia.

Bases etc.

Re-formed at Kai Tak on 15 June, 1946 by re-numbering No. 96 Squadron.

Kai Tak	Jun 1946—Jul 1947

Absorbed into 48 Squadron in July, 1947. Re-formed at Changi on 15 September, 1947.

Changi	Sep 1947—Jun 1948
Kuala Lumpur	Jun 1948—Nov 1948
Changi	Nov 1948—Dec 1949
Kuala Lumpur, det. Changi May–Jul 1950	Dec 1949—Jul 1950
Changi	Jul 1950—Jul 1951
Kuala Lumpur	Jul 1951—Oct 1951
Changi	Oct 1951—Dec 1957

Disbanded at Changi on 31 December, 1957. Re-formed at Kuala Lumpur on 3 June, 1959 by the amalgamation of Nos. 155 and 194 Squadrons.

Kuala Lumpur	Jun 1959—Sep 1959
Butterworth, det. Brunei, Kuching	Sep 1959—Jan 1964
Seletar	Jan 1964—Sep 1965
Kuching	Sep 1965—May 1966
Simanggang	May 1966—Nov 1967
Seletar	Nov 1967—Mar 1969
Changi	Mar 1969—Feb 1971

Disbanded at Changi on 15 February, 1971.

Main Equipment (in the transport role)

Douglas Dakota C.4 (Jun 1946— 1952)
KJ843, J; KJ887; KK114, R; KK152, Y; KN221, P; KN301, L; KN352, GW; KN400, DW; KN414, C) KN534, N; KN579, Z; KN611, L; KN633, P; KP254
Vickers Valetta C.1 (Oct 1951—Dec 1957)
VW153; VW815; VX484; VX495; VX513; VX523; VX537; WD170; WJ493; WJ495
Westland Whirlwind HAR.4 (Jun 1959— 1963)
XD182; XJ410; XJ411; XJ414; XJ426; XJ428; XJ723

Bristol Sycamore HR.14 (Jun 1959— 1963)
    XE310, E; XE311, B; XF266; XG519; XG538; XJ382; XJ918;
    XL822, V; XL835
Westland Whirlwind HAR.10 (Apr 1963—Feb 1971)
    XD183, F; XJ407, E; XJ432; XJ760; XK988, D; XL109, H;
    XN126, G; XP328, R; XP358, K; XP363; XP401; XR455, J;
    XR479, A; XR484

Commanding Officers

W/Cdr T. M. Buchnan	Jun 1946—Aug 1946
S/Ldr D. W. Barber	Aug 1946—Oct 1946
S/Ldr C. J. McKenzie, DFC, AFC	Oct 1946—Jul 1947
S/Ldr M. W. Ramsey, DFC	Aug 1947—Sep 1947
S/Ldr R. Lloyd, DFC, AFC	Sep 1947—Dec 1947
S/Ldr J. S. Higgins, DFC, AFC	Dec 1947—Mar 1948
S/Ldr D. K. Hayes	Mar 1948—Nov 1948
S/Ldr P. O. V. Green, AFC	Nov 1948—Sep 1949
S/Ldr J. H. Johnson, DFC	Sep 1949—Feb 1950

S/Ldr C. F. Craven	Feb 1950—Feb 1952
S/Ldr J. E. D. Taylor	Feb 1952—Mar 1952
S/Ldr A. F. Peers	Mar 1952—Jun 1953
S/Ldr B. A. Q. Wynward-Wright	Jun 1953—Nov 1953
S/Ldr J. R. Lake	Nov 1953—Dec 1957
S/Ldr F. Barnes	Jun 1959—Aug 1960
S/Ldr C. A. E. Symons	Aug 1960—Dec 1962
S/Ldr D. L. Eley	Dec 1962—Nov 1964
S/Ldr J. W. Price	Nov 1964—Jul 1966
S/Ldr R. H. J. Hadlow	Jul 1966—Dec 1968
S/Ldr T. M. Jeffrey	Dec 1968—Feb 1971

Aircraft Insignia

It is not believed that No. 110 Squadron carried any unit insignia during its transport roles. However, latterly, on the Whirlwind HAR.10s the Squadron emblem was carried as a white disc on the fins of these helicopters. (See also *Bomber Squadrons of the RAF*, 155–6)

No. 114 SQUADRON

BADGE
A cobra's head

MOTTO
'With speed I strike'

The cobra's head associates the badge with
India where the Squadron first served.

The Squadron was formed at Lahore in India from a nucleus of No. 31 Squadron in September, 1917. Its task was patrol duty, keeping an eye open for incursions of the frontier and generally policing its area of the frontier. This was a hazardous task in the primitive types used (Farman and B.E.2c). It moved to Quetta in September, 1918 and from there sent a detachment to Aden for policing duties. After the war it was re-equipped with more modern types but on 31 January, 1920 was re-numbered 28 Squadron.

When No. 114 re-formed at Wyton on 1 December, 1936 it was as a light bomber squadron and became the first unit to fly the Blenheim bomber. It used this type operationally from France in 1939–40 and then in 2 Group raids until the end of 1942 when it went to North Africa, fighting in that, the Sicilian and Italian campaigns having converted to Bostons in 1943. After the war it moved to Aden where it disbanded on 1 September, 1946 by re-numbering as No. 8 Squadron.

No. 114 re-formed eleven months later at Kabrit on 1 August, 1947. It was now a transport squadron in the Middle East Transport Wing flying Dakotas on the Middle East routes and providing a tactical transport force for the army in Egypt and Cyprus. It flew Dakotas for three years, re-equipping with Valettas. It moved to Cyprus in March, 1956, being busily involved in the evacuation of British personnel from Egypt that year. It was also part of the transport force involved in the Suez operations leading the airborne assault. On 31 December, 1957 it disbanded at Nicosia. On 20 November, 1958 No. 114 re-formed at Hullavington in an unique role as an anti-terrorist unit, moving to Cyprus the following month and flying anti-EOKA patrols within the island for four months before disbanding once more on 14 March, 1959.

Two months later No. 114 became a transport squadron once more on 5 May, 1959 at Colerne, flying as part of the Hastings Wing there on tactical support and route-flying. This lasted for two years, the Squadron disbanding there on 30 September, 1961. The next day it re-formed at Benson; it now had an important task, to bring the Hawker Siddeley Argosy C.1 into squadron service. These came to the Squadron in February, 1962. Its main task was now to be the Tactical Transport Force for 38 Group. As well as providing para-dropping and landing facilities for the airborne forces it was also busily involved in airlifts to deploy troops within the European and Mediterranean areas. The Squadron also provided support aircraft for the Red Arrows and Falcons display teams. From 1967 the Squadron also maintained a detachment at Bahrein for Air Forces Gulf.

In one of the many Defence cuts of the sixties and seventies the Argosy was prematurely retired from RAF service and No. 114 was not only the first but also the last squadron to operate the type in the transport role, being disbanded at Benson on 8 October, 1971.

Bases etc.

Formed at Lahore September, 1917 from a nucleus of No. 31 Squadron.

Lahore	Sep 1917—Sep 1918
Quetta, det. Khormaksar, Lahore	Sep 1918—Jan 1920

Disbanded at Lahore on 31 January, 1920 by re-numbering as No. 28 Squadron. Re-formed at Wyton on 1 December, 1936 at Wyton as a light bomber squadron. Disbanded in this role at Aden on 1 September, 1946.

Re-formed as a transport squadron at Kabrit on 1 August, 1947.

Kabrit	Aug 1947—Mar 1956
Nicosia	Mar 1956—Dec 1957

Disbanded at Nicosia on 31 December, 1957. Re-formed at Hullavington on 20 November, 1958 in the security reconnaissance role.

Hullavington	Nov 1958—Dec 1958
Nicosia	Dec 1958—Mar 1959

Disbanded at Nicosia on 14 March, 1959. Re-formed as a transport squadron at Colerne on 5 May, 1959.

Colerne	May 1959—Sep 1961

Disbanded at Colerne on 30 September, 1961. Re-formed at Benson on 1 October, 1961.

Benson, det. Bahrein	Oct 1961—Oct 1971

Disbanded at Benson on 8 October, 1971.

Main Equipment

B.E.2c (Sep 1917— 1918)
    4143
B.E.2e (Sep 1917—Jan 1920)
    No serials known
Farman (Sep 1917— 1918)
    No serials known
Bristol F.2B (1919—Jan 1920)
    E2248; F4634; F4640; H1499; H1509; H1514; H1541
Douglas Dakota C.4 (Aug 1947— 1950)
    KN331; KP263
Vickers Valetta C.1 (Oct 1949—Dec 1957)
    VL276; VW141; VW154; VW157, A; VW162; VW189; VW803, B;
    VW817; VW829; VW844; VX492; VX507; WD157
D.H. Canada Chipmunk T.10 (Nov 1958—Mar 1959)
    WG471, A; WG486, G; WK586, E; WP897, F; WZ884, D
Handley Page Hastings C.1A (May 1959—Sep 1961)
    TG524; TG527; TG557; TG605; TG606; TG616
Handley Page Hastings C.2 (May 1959—Sep 1961)
    WD475; WD481; WD485; WD495; WJ330; WJ337
Hawker Siddeley Argosy C.1 (Feb 1962—Oct 1971)
    XN815; XN820; XN847; XN851; XN857; XP408; XP443; XR135

Commanding Officers

Maj S. Hutcheson	Sep 1917—Jan 1920
S/Ldr F. A. Drury, DFC	Aug 1947—Mar 1948
S/Ldr F. J. Fenton	Mar 1948—Dec 1948
S/Ldr G. H. Everitt, DSO, DFC	Dec 1948—Sep 1950
S/Ldr K. V. Gilling, AFC	Sep 1950—Dec 1952
S/Ldr R. J. Dempsey, DFC	Dec 1952—Apr 1954
S/Ldr D. B. Delany, AFC	Apr 1954—Jan 1957
S/Ldr F. L. Spencer	Jan 1957—Dec 1957

S/Ldr J. L. Bayley	Dec 1958—Mar 1959
S/Ldr E. K. Adair	Mar 1959—Aug 1959
W/Cdr L. V. Craxton	Aug 1959—Sep 1961
W/Cdr W. I. Harris, AFC	Oct 1961—Jul 1962
W/Cdr L. B. Foskett, AFC	Jul 1962—Aug 1964
W/Cdr C. R. Evans	Aug 1964—Aug 1966
W/Cdr J. A. Steff-Langston, MBE	Aug 1966—Jul 1968
W/Cdr J. L. Price, AFC	Jul 1968—Jun 1970
W/Cdr S. A. Price	Jun 1970—Oct 1971

Aircraft Insignia

No information is available about markings carried in World War I. After World War II the Valettas were distinguished by having green propeller spinners and, possibly, green cheat line along the fuselage. The Chipmunks carried no distinguishing markings. The Hastings were distinguished by a navy blue fin diamond with '114' in white thereon whilst the Argosies carried the Squadron's cobra emblem on a white disc at the top of the fin. (See also *Bomber Squadrons of the RAF*, pp. 158–60.)

No. 117 SQUADRON

BADGE
A terrestrial globe
MOTTO
'It shall be done'

The Squadron had two beginnings in World War I but in neither case did it work up to operational status; it was originally formed at Beaulieu on 1 January, 1918, disbanding in June that year, re-forming at Norwich in September but again disbanding before the Armistice on 6 October, 1918.

C Flight of No. 216 Squadron at Khartoum became No. 117 Squadron on 30 April, 1941 and the task was to fly the reinforcement route to and from Takoradi. For this it began with six Bristol Bombays but added Wellesleys, a Caproni Ca148, and some ex-Yugoslav Savoia-Marchetti SM79Ks. It also embraced the Gladiators of the Met Flight at Khartoum. This task lasted until November when it moved north and began flying routes supplying the army and RAF forward posts in the Western Desert. Its fleet was now regularised to Douglas DC-2s and de Havilland DH.86Bs. Within a couple of months these had changed to DC-3s and Lodestars, Hudsons coming in July, 1942. During 1942 the Squadron worked up to a great intensity, flying routes to West Africa and Malta as well as along the North African coastline. This was not all without opposition and several aircraft were attacked by German fighters, there being some losses. At the end of the year most activity centred around flying supplies and ammunition to the forces rolling Rommel back from El Alamein, and bringing casevacs back.

1943 saw the Squadron entirely Hudson-equipped and following the 8th Army fortunes with its supply flights. This continued until October when No. 117 was withdrawn and moved to India.

It took with it the Dakotas which it had begun to receive and with these No. 117 began supply-dropping in February, 1944, soon being involved in supporting the Wingate forces at Broadway. In seven flights in March 1323 troops, 221 mules and 47 horses were flown in. The presure continued until November both on this and on the shuttle into Imphal, no fewer than 2,681 operational hours being flown in July, three aircraft being lost in the month. In November and December the Squadron was non-operational, training on glider-towing, then in 1945 moved to the Arakan front, flying drops and casevacs for the occupation of Akyab. It now also flew L-5 Sentinels as well as the Dakotas and in February totalled 3,868 hours on operations. But now the character of the work changed from individual drops to small units amongst the hills to being part of a large fleet putting the maximum amount of supplies across in the shortest possible time. In June its area was the Sittang valley, as well as flying regular mail runs to Rangoon; in July the Squadron flew 871 sorties. By then the war was almost over and the task changed to route-flying to Bangkok, Saigon, Butterworth and into China itself. These continued until 17 December, 1945 when No. 117 Squadron was disbanded at Hmawbi.

Bases etc.

Formed at Khartoum on 30 April, 1941 from C Flight, 216 Squadron.

Khartoum	Apr 1941—Nov 1941
Bilbeis	Nov 1941—Nov 1942
El Adem (det. Marble Arch)	Nov 1942—Jan 1943
Marble Arch	Jan 1943—Mar 1943
Castel Benito	Mar 1943—Apr 1943
Gabes	Apr 1943—Apr 1943
El-Djem	Apr 1943—May 1943
Castel Benito (det. Fez)	May 1943—Jun 1943
Bilbeis	Jun 1943—Jul 1943
Castel Benito (det. Cassibile)	Jul 1943—Sep 1943
Catania	Sep 1943—Oct 1943
Bari	Oct 1943—Oct 1943
Cairo	Oct 1943—Oct 1943
Dhamial (det. Gwalior)	Oct 1943—Feb 1944
Lalmai (det. Tulihall)	Feb 1944—Mar 1944
Sylhet	Mar 1944—Jun 1944
Agartala (det. Sylhet)	Jun 1944—Nov 1944
Risalpur	Nov 1944—Nov 1944
Bikram	Nov 1944—Dec 1944
Hathazari (det. Ramree Island)	Dec 1944—May 1945
Kyaukpyu (Ramree)	May 1945—Jun 1945
Petanga	Jun 1945—Aug 1945
Hmawbi	Aug 1945—Dec 1945

Disbanded at Hmawbi on 17 December, 1945.

Main Equipment

Bristol Bombay I (Apr 1941—Nov 1941)
L5811; L5828; L5833; L5840; L5856
Vickers Wellesley I (Apr 1941—Sep 1941)
K7767; L2645; L2657; L2710; L2713
Savoia-Marchetti S.M.79K (May 1941—ca Oct 1941)
AX702; AX705
Percial Proctor I (Apr 1941—Nov 1941)
P6127
Douglas D.C.2 (Oct 1941—Apr 1942 & Mar 1943—Jun 1943)
AX767; AX768; AX769; HK821; HK837; HK847
de Havilland D.H.86B (Mar 1942—May 1942)
AX762; HK829; HK843; HK844
Lockheed Lodestar II (May 1942—Oct 1942)
EW987; EW990; EW991; EW993; EW997
Douglas DC-3 (May 1942—Sep 1942)
N33653 (US civil reg.); FJ709; FJ710; FJ711
Lockheed Hudson VI (Jul 1942—Jul 1943)
EW877; EW947, LD:N; EW955; EW970, LD:Q; FK381;
FK385, LD:D; FK473; FK492; FK505, LD:S; FK527, LD:B;
FK615, LD:G
Douglas Dakota III (Jul 1943—Dec 1945)
FD847, G; FD875; FD896; FD926, K; FL552, T; FL620, Y;
FZ590, C; FZ612, S; KG636, L; KG698, M; KG755, H
Douglas Dakota IV (Nov 1944—Dec 1945)
KJ993, O; KK120, C; KK163, X; KK211, 'H2'; KN257, O;
KN326, F; KN569, B2; KN682, D
Stinson L-5 Sentinel (Jan 1945—   1945)
No recorded serials

Commanding Officers

W/Cdr W. E. Rankin	Apr 1941—Jul 1942
W/Cdr R. G. Yaxley, DSO, MC, DFC	Jul 1942—Feb 1943
W/Cdr J. Goodhead	Feb 1943—May 1943
W/Cdr W. E. Coles, AMDFC, AFC	May 1943—Jun 1944
W/Cdr W. J. McLean, DFC, AFC	Jun 1944—May 1945
W/Cdr A. J. Samson, DFC	May 1945—Sep 1945
W/Cdr L. T. Bryant-Fenn, DFC	Oct 1945—Dec 1945

Aircraft Insignia

As far as is known, the only squadron identity markings carried by No. 117 Squadron was during the Hudson period in 1942—1943 when the code letters 'LD' were used.

No. 118 SQUADRON

BADGE
On waves of the sea an ancient ship in full
flames
MOTTO
'Occido redioque'
('I kill and return')

The badge acknowledges the Squadron's
prowess in sinking shipping.

No. 118 Squadron was first formed at Catterick on 1 January, 1918 as a heavy bomber squadron and began equipping with Handley Page 0/400s. It never became operational and was disbanded at Bicester in November, 1918.

It re-formed at Filton on 20 February, 1941 as a Spitfire squadron and flew throughout the rest of World War II in this role with Spitfires and Mustangs, disbanding on 10 March, 1946. It re-formed in the same role but in RAF Germany on 15 May, 1951 and served there with Vampires, Venoms and Hunters until disbanding at Jever on 31 July, 1957.

On 12 May, 1960 a new No. 118 was re-formed from the Sycamore Flight of No. 228 Squadron at Aldergrove. It now became part of Transport Command and used its Sycamore helicopters in various liaison and communications roles. It also experimented in helicopter traffic control duties and flew such a task at the RAF Fifty Years Display at Upavon in June, 1962. Soon after, on 31 August, 1962 the Squadron was disbanded at Aldergrove.

Bases etc.

Re-formed at Aldergrove on 12 May, 1960 from the Sycamore Flight of No. 228 Squadron.
Aldergrove   May 1960—Aug 1962
Disbanded at Aldergrove on 31 August, 1962.

Main Equipment

Bristol Sycamore HR.14 (May 1960—Aug 1962)
  XE317; XG502; XG506; XG544

Aircraft Insignia

The Sycamores carried the fighter-style insignia of three white and two black wavy lines each side of the fuselage roundel. This had previously been carried on the Squadron's Hunters in Germany.
(See also *Fighter Squadrons of the RAF*, pp. 249–52)

No. 119 SQUADRON

BADGE
A sword, the point downwards, and an anchor
in saltire
MOTTO
'By night and by day'

The Squadron was first formed at Andover on 1 January, 1918 and worked up to become a bomber unit with DH.4s and DH.9s but never became operational, disbanding in November, 1918 after the Armistice.

No. 119 re-formed on 13 March, 1941 at Bowmore, Anglesey, from G flight which had formed six months earlier to operate the three G-Class flying boats in an anti-submarine role. Because of the unsatisfactory maintenance state of these boats the Squadron also used a couple of C-boats and Sunderlands from other units. In June the G-boats left; No. 119 also had a Catalina but this went to No. 413 Squadron. The Squadron was now non-operational until April, 1942 when it received Catalinas and began flying from Iceland on ops but soon reverted to a non-operational role ferrying Catalinas from the US. In November, 1942 it converted to Sunderlands and began regular anti-shipping patrols, convoy escorts, ASRs and recces. In December it flew 33 operations and maintained this level until April, 1942 when it was disbanded.

No. 119 was re-formed on 19 July, 1944 from the Albacore Flight of 415 Squadron at Manston and flew anti-shipping patrols in the southern North Sea and off the Dutch coast. In August it flew 152 sorties, destroying one U-boat and probably damaging another U-boat. All these sorties were flown at night as armed recces. This work continued in the New Year, from Belgian bases and with Swordfishes, midget submarines becoming the principal targets; in March four such were sunk. With the end of the European war the Squadron was disbanded at Bircham Newton on 25 May, 1945.

Bases etc.

Formed at Bowmore on 13 March, 1941 from G Flight.
Bowmore   Mar 1941—Aug 1941
Pembroke Dock   Aug 1941—Apr 1942
Lough Erne, det. Reykjavik   Apr 1942—Aug 1942
Pembroke Dock   Aug 1942—Apr 1943
Disbanded at Pembroke Dock on 17 April, 1943. Re-formed from the Albacore Flight of No. 415 Squadron at Manston on 19 July, 1944.
Manston   July 1944—Aug 1944
Swingfield   Aug 1944—Oct 1944
Bircham Newton, det. St. Croix, Maldeghem,
  Knokke and Manston   Oct 1944—May 1945
Disbanded at Bircham Newton on 25 May, 1945.

Main Equipment

Short S.26 'G' Class (Mar 1941—Jun 1941 & Sep 1941—Nov 1941)
  X8273, *Golden Horn*; X8274, *Golden Fleece*; X8275, *Golden Hind*
Short S.23 'C' Class (Apr 1941—Aug 1941)
  AX659, *Clio*; AX660, *Cordelia*
Consolidated Catalina I (Jun 1941—Jul 1941)
  W8419, U; AH545; AH561
Consolidated Catalina IIIA (Jun 1942—Nov 1942)
  FP528; FP529; FP533
Short Sunderland III (Nov 1942—Apr 1943)
  W4028, O; W4030, C; W6002, R, (**Mk. II**); DP176, D; DP179, V;
  DV971, A; EJ133, F; EJ142, B; JM676, H
Fairey Albacore I (Jul 1944—Feb 1945)
  L7123, NH:C1; N4380; T9150; X9222, NH:A1; X9271, NH:J1;
  X9281, NH:K; BF588, NH:M; BF600, NH:P1
Fairey Swordfish III (Jan 1945—May 1945)
  NF272; NF304; NF342; NF374, NH:M; NF401; NF410, NH:F

Commanding Officers

W/Cdr A. G. F. Stewart   Mar 1941—Apr 1942
W/Cdr D. McC. Gordon, AFC   Apr 1942—Apr 1943
S/Ldr D. T. J. Davis, DFC   Jul 1944—Sep 1944
S/Ldr N. Williamson   Sep 1944—May 1945

Aircraft Insignia

It is not believed that the 'G' and 'C' Boats carried any unit identity markings; whether the Catalinas or Sunderlands did is still unknown. With the Albacores and Swordfish the code letter combination 'NH' which had been carried by No. 415 Squadron was retained.

No. 120 SQUADRON

BADGE
Standing on a demi-terrestrial globe, a falcon
close

MOTTO
'Endurance'

The falcon, an Icelandic falcon,
commemorates the Squadron's stay there and
also indicates the squadron's predatory
instinct.

No. 120 Squadron formed at Lympne on 1 January, 1918 with the intention of it becoming a bomber unit. In due course it was equipped with D.H.9As but before it was operational the war ended. A new role was envisaged for the Squadron, that of mail-flying and on 1 March, 1919 the first schedule began, the unit being responsible for all mail-carrying between Hawkinge and Maison-celle in France. From there other units distributed it around the British Army of Occupation. By May it had extended its range by flying direct to Cologne and it then operated a D.H.10 on a trial night flight for this purpose. The mail flying continued with D.H.9As for five months, No. 120 flying its last service on 24 August, 1919. It disbanded at Hawkinge on 21 October, 1919.

The Squadron was re-formed on 1 June, 1941 at Nutt's Corner in Northern Ireland with a specific purpose. This was to use the long range of the Consolidated Liberator bomber to close the gap of air cover in the mid-Atlantic where U-boats were causing unacceptable shipping losses. It began training on Liberator Is and made its first U-boat sighting before becoming operational, reporting it back to 16 Group HQ. On 20 September the CO flew the first operation in AM924 D and from then on 8-hour sweeps over the Atlantic were the daily round. The aircraft at this time had a non-standard 4-cannon fitting under the nose and on 4 October F/O Llewellyn fired 184 cannon shells in a combat with a FW 200. Eighteen days later F/Lt Bulloch (known as 'The Bull') made the first U-boat attack. By December the tasks were varied, not simply anti-submarine patrols but convoy escorts, Met flights, shipping recces (including a search for *Prinz Eugen*) and two strikes in the Biscay area in which four ships were attacked. On 11 January, 1942 F/O Crudy found a U-boat and tanker side by side, depth-charged them both then had combats with two Heinkel He 115s and set them both on fire. Two other U-boats were attacked that month. Mostly, however, the patrols brought nothing but sea in sight and it was not until May that the next U-boat was attacked. By July the Squadron was operating three different versions of the Liberator; four U-boats were attacked in August, two Liberators being lost in the process.

In order to extend No. 120s range a detachment was maintained in Iceland from September, 1942 onwards at regular intervals, and in October two aircraft were also sent to the Middle East. It was in that month that S/Ldr Bulloch scored the Squadron's first U-boat kill when he sent *U-597* to the bottom. He continued his successes, in November attacking two with one probably destroyed and in December no fewer than eight of which one was destroyed.

That month (December) the Squadron attacked no fewer than twenty submarines. There was no let up in 1943 and in April the whole Squadron moved to Iceland, having made nineteen U-boat attacks in March. During the summer the pace dropped off but October was a record month with twenty attacks and three definitely destroyed. In January, 1944 the first Leigh Lights were introduced on Liberator Vs necessitating a new technique of attack. The Squadron now turned primarily to night attacks. It returned to Ireland in March; that month F/Lt Kerrigan attacked a U-boat, was hit and No. 4 engine set on fire and a crew member killed. Despite this, he attacked two more U-boats when two more crew members were mortally wounded and another engine went out, but he returned to Skitten where he belly-landed.

In May, 1944 the Squadron changed its sphere of operations to the Norwegian coast under 18 Group except for the period around D-Day when it was flying night sorties over the Western Approaches, during which it attacked two U-boats and scored one probable. From then on it settled into a regular pattern of 70–90 anti-submarine sorties a month with very few sightings or attacks and this continued virtually until the war ended. With the end of the war came disbandment at Ballykelly on 4 June, 1945. It was then Coastal Command's top-scoring squadron with 16 confirmed U-boat victories to its credit.

On 1 October, 1946 No. 160 Squadron, just returned from the Far East, was re-numbered No. 120 Squadron at St. Eval. Very quickly it re-equipped with Avro Lancasters and moved to Leuchars for maritime recce duties once more. It also had a SAR role and made the first successful drop of an airborne liferaft in May, 1947. Later that year it sent a detachment to Palestine to search for illegal immigrants into Israel. Two years later the Squadron made a successful goodwill tour of Canada and a similar trip to Pakistan in 1950.

In 1951 the Squadron became the first with Avro Shackletons and had the task of intensively working them into service life. It was now involved in the hectic round of NATO anti-submarine exercises which have continued over the years. In 1956 it also took on an auxiliary trooping role, flying troops out to Cyprus for the emergency there. Two years later another good willtour took place, to Canada and the USA. In addition to its normal shadowing tasks the Squadron was busy in 1962 keeping an eye on the Soviet ships taking missiles to Cuba. Soon after this the Squadron developed a new system whereby a high-level recce aircraft (at this time a Valiant) passed radar contacts to the Squadron's Shackletons to investigate at low-level. 1966 saw No. 120 deployed to Changi on detachment to FEAF and two crews flew on to New Zealand. A similar detachment took place in Sharjah in 1968. Two years later the first Nimrods arrived on the Squadron and with these regular deployments were also flown to FEAF until 1975. In 1973 the Squadron became involved on patrols in the 'Cod War' and this was followed in 1977 by Operation Tapestry, the patrolling of the 200 mile fishing limits of the UK. This was extended also to give surveillance of the North Sea oil installations.

Bases etc.

Formed at Lympne on 1 January, 1918

Lympne	Jan 1918—	1919
Hawkinge	1919—Oct	1919

Disbanded at Hawkinge on 21 October, 1919. Re-formed at Nutt's Corner on 1 June, 1941.

Nutt's Corner	Jun 1941—Jul	1942
Ballykelly, det. Reykjavik, Aldergrove	Jul 1942—Apr	1943
Reykjavik	Apr 1943—Mar	1944
Ballykelly, det. Tain	Mar 1944—Jun	1945

Disbanded at Ballykelly on 4 June, 1945. Re-formed by re-numbering No. 160 Squadron at St. Eval on 1 October, 1946.

St. Eval	Oct 1946—Oct	1946
Leuchars	Oct 1946—Jan	1950
Kinloss	Jan 1950—Apr	1952
Aldergrove, det. Sola	Apr 1952—Apr	1959
Kinloss	Apr 1959—	

Main Equipment

D.H.9A (1918—Oct 1919)
No serials known
Consolidated Liberator I (Jun 1941—Dec 1943)
AM910, OH:M; AM916, OH:L; AM919, OH:P; AM921, OH:B; AM924, OH:D; AM928, OH:A
Consolidated Liberator II (Nov 1941—Oct 1942)
AL513, OH:K; AL520, OH:N; AL542, OH:O; AL552, OH:H; AL558, OH:V; AL560, OH:Y
Consolidated Liberator III (Jul 1942—Feb 1944)
FK214, B; FK220, K; FK233, J; FL928, R; FL943, N; LV340, X; LV345, G
Consolidated Liberator V (Jan 1944—Jan 1945)
BZ714; BZ771, K; BZ787, H; BZ820, G; BZ874; BZ910, F; BZ941, E
Consolidated Liberator VI/VIII (Dec 1944—Jun 1945 & Oct 1946—Oct 1946)
KG980; KG985; KG988; KH128; KH177, OH:D; KH202; KH265, OH:X; KH302; KL489, BS:F; KL533, BS:G; KN777, BS:A

Avro Lancaster GR.3 (Oct 1946—May 1951)
HK655, BS:F; ME325, BS:P; PB641, BS:C; RE158, BS:B; RE207, BS:D; RF302, BS:G; SW284, BS:A;
Avro Shackleton MR.1 (Mar 1951—Mar 1953)
VP258, A:C; VP262, A:D; VP267, A:H; WB844, A:F; WB854, A:H; WG511, A:J
Avro Shackleton MR.2 (Mar 1953—Nov 1958)
WG530, H; WG558, K; WL745, B; WL750, J; WR956, A; WR968, D
Avro Shackleton MR.3 (Nov 1958—Dec 1970)
WR971, E; WR979, D; WR987, G; WR990, F, later N; XF700, A; XF709, D
Hawker Siddeley Nimrod MR.1 (Oct 1970—　　　　)
XV242; XV254; XZ280 (These aircraft are pooled in the Kinloss Wing but the foregoing have been used by 120 Squadron crew)

Commanding Officers

Maj A. R. Stanley Clarke, MC	Jan	1918—May	1919
W/Cdr W. N. Cumming, DFC	May	1941—Aug	1941
W/Cdr V. H. A. McBratney, AFC	Aug	1941—Jul	1942
W/Cdr S. J. Harrison, DFC	Jul	1942—Feb	1943
W/Cdr P. A. Gilchrist	Feb	1943—Apr	1943
W/Cdr R. M. Longmore, OBE	Apr	1943—Oct	1943
W/Cdr J. R. Bland	Oct	1943—Jul	1944
W/Cdr J. Avent, DFC	Jul	1944—Jun	1945
W/Cdr R. D. Williams	Oct	1946—Aug	1948
S/Ldr V. F. Cave	Aug	1948—Feb	1949
S/Ldr F. A. Pentycross	Feb	1949—Jan	1951
S/Ldr P. G. D. Farr, OBE, DFC	Jan	1951—Jan	1952
S/Ldr A. W. Harding	Jan	1952—May	1952

S/Ldr H. M. Simmonds, DFC	May	1952—Jul	1953
S/Ldr R. G. Ravenscroft	Jul	1953—Apr	1955
W/Cdr P. R. Casement, DSO, DFC, AFC	Apr	1955—Oct	1956
W/Cdr G. Buckle	Oct	1956—Nov	1958
W/Cdr L. G. A. Reed, MVO, DFC	Nov	1958—Jan	1961
W/Cdr H. M. Carson	Jan	1961—Jan	1963
W/Cdr R. Courtnage, OBE, AFC	Jan	1963—Dec	1964
W/Cdr N. G. Ashcroft	Dec	1964—Nov	1966
W/Cdr P. J. Wells	Nov	1966—Apr	1969
W/Cdr A. R. Amos	Apr	1969—Dec	1971
W/Cdr C. J. Phillips	Dec	1971—Jan	1974
W/Cdr R. Kidney, AFC	Jan	1974—Dec	1975
W/Cdr T. C. Flanagan	Dec	1975—Oct	1977
W/Cdr C. J. Sturt	Oct	1977—Nov	1979
W/Cdr M. G. Peakes	Nov	1979—	

Aircraft Insignia

In World War I and thereafter no distinctive squadron markings were carried. The Liberators used the code letters 'OH' from 1941 to 1943 and 1944 to 1945 and, briefly, in 1946 the letters 'BS' which had been acquired from No. 160 Squadron. These letters were perpetuated on the Lancasters; in addition the Squadron badge was carried on the nose and the spinners were red, white and blue. The Shackletons had the single identity letter 'A' until the late fifties when the number '120' replaced it and remained on the Squadron aircraft until these were pooled late in the sixties. The Squadron badge was also carried on the nose in a white rectangle. No markings are generally carried on the Nimrods as they are pooled in the Kinloss Wing but for occasional prestige trips the emblem is painted on the fin of an aircraft temporarily allocated to the Squadron.

No. 138 SQUADRON

BADGE
A sword in bend, the point uppermost severing a reef knot

MOTTO
'For Freedom'

The badge signified the Squadron's primary role in World War II of freeing those in bondage.

The Squadron was first formed on 1 May, 1918 to work up as a fighter unit but the Squadron was suspended and disbanded on 4 July, 1918. A nucleus formed a new No. 138 Squadron at Chingford on 30 September, 1918 where it remained until disbanding on 1 February, 1919.

On 25 August, 1941 No. 138 Squadron again re-formed, this time by re-numbering and expanding No. 1419 (Special Duties) Flight at Newmarket. Its task was to co-operate with the Special Operations Executive (SOE), which was engaged in running agents to and from the occupied countries, supporting them with arms and equipment. This involved actual landings in enemy territory (to pick up important people or articles) and this hazardous task was flown by specially equipped Lysanders. The more numerous type of operation was more simply to drop agents and supplies, largely arms, at pre-arranged dropping zones and for this the Whitley was used, coming down to 500 ft and, with its large wing area, being able to fly slowly and stably. Most of the operations were to the near Continent but some sorties went farther afield, for two weeks on October/November 1941 two Whitleys were based in Malta for drops in Yugoslavia. By the end of 1941 the Squadron had received a Halifax and during 1942 this type gradually replaced the Whitley. In 1941 an average of thirteen drops a month was maintained, usually one Lysander sortie a month. However with the expansion, and use of the Halifax, this total rose in 1942 to thirty per month. The task was hazardous and not many months went by without one aircraft failing to return. October was the heaviest month with 53 operations to Holland, Estonia, Denmark, Norway, France, Belgium and Czechoslovakia. By this time the Squadron had been split into 138 and 161 Squadrons, the Lysanders going to the latter.

In 1943 the Squadron flew solidly with Halifaxes building up the

intensity of its supply-dropping activities. In March aircraft were detached to Canrobert for work in Corsica and Tunisia and that month four aircraft were lost. By the summer the Squadron was concentrating on France and flew 121 sorties in August. In September eight aircraft were lost. 1944 saw a similar level of intensity, July being the record month with 160 sorties, all to France. But with the successful advance of the Allied armies across Europe and up through Italy the need for many supply drops tailed off and after December, 1944 the Squadron was withdrawn from special duties and transferred to 3 Group Bomber Command, becoming a Lancaster squadron and serving until September, 1950 with them and subsequently Lincolns. No. 138 was disbanded in September, 1950 and re-formed as the first V-bomber squadron, with Valiants, in January, 1955, serving thus until disbanding finally in April, 1962.

Bases, etc. (in the SD role)

Re-formed at Newmarket on 25 August, 1941 by re-numbering No. 1419 Flight.

Newmarket (det. Luqa)	Aug 1941—Dec 1941
Stradishall	Dec 1941—Mar 1942
Tempsford (det. Canrobert)	Mar 1942—Mar 1945

Transferred to the bomber role in March, 1945 on transferring to Tuddenham.

Main Equipment

Westland Lysander III (Aug 1941—Mar 1942)
R2626; T1508; T1770; T1771
Armstrong Whitworth Whitley V (Aug 1941—Nov 1942)
T4166, NF:B; Z6763, NF:L; Z9146, NF:P; Z9159, NF:D; Z9230, NF:N; Z9283, NF:K; Z9428, NF:F
Handley Page Halifax II (Dec 1941—　　1944)
L9613, NF:V; L9618, NF:W; W1007, NF:U; W1229, NF:A; BB313, NF:M; BB378, NF:D; DT726, NF:H; DT727, NF:K
Handley Page Halifax II Series IA (Feb 1943—ca Sep 1944)
HR666, NF:E; JD171, NF:P; JD269, NF:Q; LW280, NF:K; LW284, NF:T
Handley Page Halifax V (　　1944—　　1944)
DG252, NF:B; DG253, NF:F; LK743, NF:J; LL279
Short S.29 Stirling IV (Apr 1944—　　1944)
LJ913, NF:N; LJ932; LJ990

Commanding Officers

W/Cdr E. V. Knowles, DFC	Aug 1941—Nov 1941
W/Cdr W. K. Farley, DFC	Nov 1941—Apr 1942

W/Cdr R. C. Hockey	Apr	1942— 1943
W/Cdr Batchelor		1943—Jun 1943
W/Cdr R. D. Speare, DFC	Jun	1943—May 1944
W/Cdr W. J. Burnett, DFC	May	1944—Dec 1944
W/Cdr T. B. C. Murray	Dec	1944—Mar 1945

Aircraft Insignia

During its operations as a Special Duties squadron No. 138 carried the code letter combination 'NF' on its aircraft, although it is not believed to have been carried on the Lysanders.

(See also *Bomber Squadrons of the RAF*, pp. 164–5.)

No. 140 SQUADRON

BADGE
An eyed hawk moth
MOTTO
'Foresight'

No. 140 Squadron was formed on 1 May, 1918 at Biggin Hill and equipped with Bristol Fighters for Home Defence duties over London. However, before becoming operational it was disbanded on 4 July, 1918 to provide reinforcement for other units. It re-formed on 17 September, 1941 at Benson by re-numbering No. 1416 Flight and now flew in the photo recce role equipped with Spitfires and Blenheims. At first all the sorties were flown by the Spitfires, the target area being Northern France. The Blenheims became operational in November, flying night sorties with flares. The Squadron built up its operations until in April, 1942 it was flying over 100 sorties a month, of which only four were on Blenheims. Most of the targets were still in Northern France but some included the Belgian and Dutch coast. Later that year a detachment from St. Eval flew sorties over the French Atlantic coast. In 1943 the Squadron became part of 34 Wing, 2nd TAF; its commitment was now PR for the forthcoming invasion. In June No. 140 flew a few night operations with Venturas in place of Blenheims and also tried Mitchells but still the bulk of the work was flown by Spitfires until this was shared with Mosquitoes at the end of the year. The Squadron was now busily involved in mapping the area for the forthcoming invasion and revising its coverage to note changes in enemy displacements. The Mosquitoes were using *Gee* and later *Rebecca H* for their blind night photography. The pace increased and the Mosquito gradually replaced the Spitfires so that by D-Day they had all gone; 177 sorties were flown by the Mosquitoes that month. In August this increased to 231 of which 67 were by night. In September the Squadron moved to France to keep close to the action and continued providing photo coverage through that winter.

In March, 1945 the Squadron experimented with night sorties guided by a mobile radar control post but the range was limited.

In April, 1945, with the war nearly over, the Squadron changed to visual recce of shipping off the North German and Danish coasts, leading to successful Coastal Command strikes. On 7 May the Squadron had the privilege of flying 2nd TAF's last operational sortie when F/Lt Woan flew a Skaggerak shipping recce in NS578.

No. 140 returned to the UK in July and was disbanded at Fersfield on 10 November, 1945.

Bases etc.

Formed at Biggin Hill on 1 May, 1918.

Biggin Hill	May 1918—Jul 1918	

Disbanded at Biggin Hill on 4 July, 1918. Re-formed at Benson on 17 September, 1941 by re-numbering No. 1416 Flight.

Benson, det. Weston Zoyland,		
Mount Farm, St. Eval	Sep 1941—Mar 1943	
Hartford Bridge	Mar 1943—Apr 1944	
Northolt	Apr 1944—Sep 1944	
Balleroy (A.12)	Sep 1944—Sep 1944	
Amiens/Glisy (B.48)	Sep 1944—Sep 1944	
Melsbroek	Sep 1944—Apr 1945	
Eindhoven (B.78)	Apr 1945—Jul 1945	
Acklington	Jul 1945—Sep 1945	
Fersfield	Sep 1945—Nov 1945	

Disbanded at Fersfield 10 November, 1945.

Main Equipment

Bristol Blenheim IV (Sep 1941—Aug 1942)
L9244; R3825, ZW:L; V6033; Z5805; Z5986
Vickers-Supermarine Spitfire IA (Sep 1941—May 1942)
L1000; K9969; R6910; R7028; R7139, ZW:C
Vickers-Supermarine Spitfire Type C (Sep 1941—Aug 1942)
P9328; X4492; X4784; X4907
Vickers-Supermarine Spitfire IV (Feb 1942—Jul 1943)
P9505; X4499; X4502; AB130; AB426; AR258; BP919; BR648
Vickers-Supermarine Spitfire XI (Sep 1943—Apr 1944)
EN681; MB941; MB942; MB944; MB947
Lockheed Ventura I (Feb 1943—Sep 1943)
AE682; AE714; AE750; AE779; AE806
de Havilland Mosquito IX (Oct 1943—Sep 1944)
LR479; MM243; MM249; MM250; MM251
de Havilland Mosquito XVI (Feb 1944—Jul 1945)
MM274; MM280; MM294; MM301; MM307; MM395; NS507; NS517; NS522; NS563; NS575; NS580; NS777; NS798; RF993

Commanding Officers

W/Cdr E. C. Le Mesurier, DSO, DFC	Sep	1941—Jun 1943
W/Cdr R. I. M. Bowen	Jun	1943—Sep 1945
W/Cdr C. F. M. Chapman	Sep	1944—Sep 1944
W/Cdr F. O. S. Dobell	Oct	1944—Apr 1945
W/Cdr D. R. M. Frostick	Apr	1945—Nov 1945

Aircraft Insignia

At first the Blenheims and Spitfires carried the letters 'ZW' but with the special PR finishes on the aircraft these were dropped and it is believed that no further insignia was carried.

No. 142 SQUADRON

BADGE
A winged sphinx
MOTTO
'Determination'

The sphinx was chosen to represent No. 142's sphere of activity in World War I.

The Squadron was formed at Ismailia on 2 February, 1918 for Corps reconnaissance duties with the 40 Wing of the Palestine Brigade. In

June it transferred to the 5 Wing and co-operated with the Desert Mounted Corps in the Jordan Valley operations, which opened up in September. It co-operated particularly well with the cavalry in this area and also bombed the Turks in the famous Wadi el Far'a massacre. After the Armistice it moved to Suez Canal defence duties and was disbanded at Suez on 1 April, 1919 by re-numbering as No. 55 Squadron.

No. 142 re-formed on 1 June, 1934 at Netheravon as a light bomber squadron and served in that role and as a medium bomber squadron in Tunisia and Malta until disbanding at Reghaia on 5 October, 1944. Later that month it re-formed as a Mosquito

Pathfinder squadron in the UK serving until 28 September, 1945. It also had a short span as a fighter ground attack squadron in Kenya from 1 February to 1 April, 1959.

Bases etc.

Formed at Ismailia on 2 February, 1918.

Ismailia	Feb 1918—Feb 1918	
Julis	Feb 1918—Apr 1918	
Ramleh, det. Jerusalem	Apr 1918—Sep 1918	
Sarona	Sep 1918—Sep 1918	
Afuleh	Sep 1918—Nov 1918	
Haifa	Nov 1918—Nov 1918	
Ramleh, det. Damascus	Nov 1918—Nov 1918	
Kantara	Nov 1918—Feb 1919	
Suez	Feb 1919—Apr 1919	

Disbanded at Suez on 1 April, 1919 by re-numbering as No. 55 Squadron. Re-formed as a bomber squadron at Netheravon on 1 June, 1934.

Main Equipment

B.E.12a (Feb 1918—Jun 1918)
A575; A6323; A6328; A6329
Martinsyde Elephant (Mar 1918—Jun 1918)
A3945; A3955; A3998; A4000
R.E.8 (Apr 1918—Apr 1919)
A3807; A4410; B5050; B5056; B6610; B6683; B7709
Armstrong Whitworth F.K.8 (May 1918—Feb 1919)
C3606
B.E.2d/e (Jun 1918—Feb 1919)
A3066
D.H.9 (Jan 1919—Apr 1919)
B7633; C6302; D567; D652; D2935; E8999; F1143

Aircraft Insignia

As far as is known no Squadron insignia was carried in World War I. (See also *Bomber Squadrons of the RAF*, pp. 169–70 & *Fighter Squadrons of the RAF*, p. 571.)

No. 143 SQUADRON

BADGE
A gamecock attacking

MOTTO
'Vincere est Vivere'
('To conquer is to live')

The gamecock symbolises the fighting spirit of the unit.

No. 143 Squadron was formed on 8 February, 1918 as a Home Defence unit at Throwley and served on these duties until disbandment on 31 October, 1919.

It re-formed on 15 June, 1941 at Aldergrove as a coastal strike squadron, being formed from the personnel left in the UK after No. 252 Squadron had gone overseas. It was equipped with Blenheim IVs and Beaufighters flying convoy escort and AA patrols but in July became virtually an OTU training crews for overseas. However No. 143 was fully operational by October from the Shetlands, flying 156 sorties in the month on convoy escorts, fighter patrols and Faeroes patrols. On 19th two of the Squadron's aircraft probably destroyed a Ju 88, the unit's first score. However in December all the Beaufighters were handed over to No. 235 Squadron and No. 143 soldiered on with Blenheims for a while. By February the Squadron had been reduced to a small cadre with no aircraft but in May it received five Beaufighters and began to build up again, becoming operational at Docking in August with intruder diversion patrols at night off the Dutch coast. These were of a minor nature but in November No. 143 began daylight *Rovers* off the Dutch Coast and in December flew 68 such sorties.

1943 saw the Squadron flying mainly offensive shipping recces. It was now part of the North Coates Wing and during the summer took part in many of the Wing's shipping attacks, No. 143 usually flying the fighter role. In June it began using RPs on its aircraft and had the satisfaction in August of seeing two ships sunk with these missiles. As the Squadron was usually flying the escort role on these strikes it had more than its fair share of Ju 88s shot into the sea and when it engaged in Biscay patrols in December, 1943 its score of enemy aircraft began to mount.

After re-joining the North Coates Wing in February, 1944 it became once more the fighter support squadron in the Wing. In the summer it switched to anti-E-boat patrols in the Channel and up the Dutch coast to keep the sea clear for the invasion fleets and the subsequent heavy sea traffic. For these bombs were carried and many attacks were made; on 7 June six attacks with one boat destroyed on 13th seventeen attacks left E-boats damaged and on fire; in all 276 sorties were flown that month.

Refinements to this task came when co-operating with Swordfish of No. 819 Squadron at night and then *Swingate* patrols with No. 524 Squadron's Wellingtons providing the targets. These had all taken place from Manston; in September No. 143 moved back to the North Coates Wing once more, the targets being off Holland. These strikes, successful though they were, were not without loss and cost the Squadron seven crews in the month.

In October, 1944 the Squadron transferred to the Banff Wing and converted to Mosquitoes. Now its operational area was the Norwegian coast, flying RP-equipped armed recces. These produced many ship targets and, when striking targets on land, No. 143 usually concentrated on putting out the Flak positions whilst the other squadrons hit the target. As the war drew to a close the Squadron shared in the destruction of four U-boats in the Skagerrak and Kattegat and, on 21 April, found eighteen enemy aircraft in flight, attacked and destroyed five Ju 88s and four Ju 188s. The Squadron's last strike was on Kiel on 3 May, 1945. Thereafter it flew ASR patrols until 25 May when it was disbanded by being re-numbered No. 14 Squadron at Banff.

Bases etc.

Re-formed at Aldergrove in the coastal strike role, 15 June, 1941.

Aldergrove	Jun 1941—Jul 1941	
Thornaby	Jul 1941—Jul 1941	
Dyce	Jul 1941—Sep 1941	
Sumburgh	Sep 1941—Dec 1941	
Dyce	Dec 1941—Dec 1941	
Aldergrove	Dec 1941—Apr 1942	
Limavady	Apr 1942—Jun 1942	
Thorney Island	Jun 1942—Jul 1942	
Docking	Jul 1942—Aug 1942	
North Coates, det. Dyce, Castletown	Aug 1942—Aug 1943	
St. Eval	Aug 1943—Sep 1943	
Portreath	Sep 1943—Feb 1944	
North Coates, det. Tain, Wick, Thorney Island, Manston	Feb 1944—May 1944	
Manston	May 1944—Sep 1944	
North Coates	Sep 1944—Oct 1944	
Banff	Oct 1944—May 1945	

Disbanded at Banff on 25 May, 1945 by re-numbering as No. 14 Squadron.

Main Equipment

Bristol Blenheim IV (Jun 1941—Apr 1942)
N3531, HO:E; N3603, HO:B; R3695, HO:A; T2131, HO:C;
V5735, HO:J; Z5754, HO:W; Z6034, HO:U
Bristol Beaufighter IC (Jun 1941—Dec 1941)
T3248; T3350, HO:N; T4725; T4731; T4757, HO:R; T4773
Bristol Beaufighter IIF (Sep 1942—Mar 1943)
T3088, HO:D; T3417, HO:F; T3436, HO:K; V8159, HO:H;
V8199, HO:W; V8204, HO:Z; V8207, HO:E

Bristol Beaufighter XIC (Mar 1943—Apr 1944)
    JL877, D; JL822, J; JL893, R; JL943, Q; JM113, F; JM172, J;
    JM288, M
Bristol Beaufighter X (Feb 1944—Oct 1944)
    LX808, NE:K; LX848, NE:A; LX943, NE:U; NE223, NE:F;
    NE666, NE:Z; NE758, NE:L; NV185, NE:Z
de Havilland Mosquito VI (Oct 1944—May 1945)
    HR373, NE:N; HR414, NE:L; PZ379, NE:R; PZ413, NE:Y;
    PZ466, NE:Q; RF622, NE:K; RS625, NE:D

Commanding Officers

S/Ldr G. G. Stockdale	Jun 1941—Jul 1941	
S/Ldr G. V. Carey	Jul 1941—Jan 1942	
S/Ldr J. R. Holgate	Jan 1942—Feb 1942	

F/Lt Stewart Johnson	Feb 1942—Apr 1942	
W/Cdr E. W. Thornewill	Apr 1942—Nov 1942	
W/Cdr W. D. V. Bennett, DFC, AFC	Dec 1942—Jun 1943	
W/Cdr R. N. Lambert, DFC	Jun 1943—Nov 1943	
W/Cdr E. H. McHardy, DSO, DFC and Bar	Nov 1943—Dec 1944	
W/Cdr J. M. Maurice, DSO, DFC	Dec 1944—Feb 1945	
W/Cdr C. N. Foxley-Norris, DSO	Feb 1945—May 1945	

Aircraft Insignia

The Squadron's aircraft carried 'HO' code letters from June, 1941 until August, 1943, no markings from then until July, 1944 and 'NE' code letters from July, 1944 to May, 1945.
(See also *Fighter Squadrons of the RAF*, p. 282.)

No. 144 SQUADRON

BADGE
In front of a decrescent a boar's head erased

MOTTO
'Who shall stop us'

The boar's head in front of a waning moon commemorates the Squadron's part in defeating the Turkish armies in 1918, the boar being a fine fighter.

The Squadron was originally formed at Port Said on 20 March, 1918 and served as a bomber squadron with the Palestine Brigade until the end of World War I. It then moved to Greece for two months and returned to the UK where it disbanded at Ford Junction on 4 February, 1919.

No. 144 re-formed, again as a bomber squadron, on 11 January, 1937 at Bicester and entered World War II with Hampdens as part of 5 Group. Its first operation was an armed shipping recce over the North Sea on 26 September, 1939. It subsequently flew in the night offensive over the Low Countries and Germany up to early 1942.

On 21 April, 1942 No. 144 moved to Leuchars in Scotland and joined 18 Group, Coastal Command. Its first operation was to bomb Lister airfield Norway on 4 May but then it began converting to the torpedo-bombing role. On 27 July it flew its first operation in this role, a night attack against enemy destroyers, only two of the twelve aircraft dropping their torpedoes. In September a detachment went to North Russia for operations, five of the aircraft being destroyed *en route*. The task was to attack the enemy shipping which would attack the convoys to North Russia and on 14 September the Squadron made one attack on Alten Fjord. They then returned to the UK, leaving the aircraft for the Russians. For the rest of the year the Squadron flew anti-submarine patrols and the occasional bombing raid.

In January, 1943 the Squadron started converting to Beaufighters and began torpedo operations with these in March. The first real victory came on 4 April when attacking a convoy, in which a 3,000-ton motor vessel was blown up. However, in May the operations ceased once more as No. 144 prepared for overseas, moving to Algeria in June. Here it flew *Torpedo Rovers* over the Western Mediterranean, getting into its stride in July, sinking three motor vessels and damaging another and a destroyer. Three enemy aircraft were also shot down, for the loss of two Beaufighters. At the end of the month the Squadron prepared to return to the UK. For the rest of the year *Armed Rovers* were flown over the North Sea with little result. January, 1944 provided more targets and five ships were hit, in February 79 sorties were flown. This remained the pattern until May when the Squadron moved to Cornwall and began offensive sweeps off the French coastline. Here the Squadron found convoys escorted by destroyers and four destroyers were significantly damaged by the end of June.

A move in July brought the Squadron in co-operation with No. 415 Squadron's Wellingtons, with them it flew *Gilbeys*, night sorties in which the Wellington would direct the Squadron's Beaufighters on to suitable targets, usually E-boats off the Dutch coast. A total of 186 sorties were flown that month resulting in seven motor vessels torpedoed, four minesweepers set on fire, one escort vessel blown up, four on fire and a tanker set on fire; the Squadron lost two crews. This type of work continued until September when No. 144 joined the Banff Wing for operations off the Norwegian coast by day and night. As the year wore on so targets and victories diminished to the level of three vessels sunk in December. However, operations continued through 1945 until VE/Day, the Squadron's last sortie being a search for motor gunboats on 15 May. Ten days later it was disbanded at Dallachy.

Bases etc.

Transferred to Coastal Command on 21 April, 1942 at Leuchars.
Leuchars, det. Wick, Sumburgh, Afrikanda,

Vaenga I	Apr 1942—Apr 1943	
Tain, det. Wick	Apr 1943—Jun 1943	
Blida	Jun 1943—Jun 1943	
Protville 2	Jun 1943—Jul 1943	
Tain	Aug 1943—Oct 1943	
Wick	Oct 1943—May 1944	
Davidstow Moor	May 1944—Jul 1944	
Strubby	Jul 1944—Sep 1944	
Banff	Sep 1944—Oct 1944	
Dallachy	Oct 1944—May 1945	

Disbanded at Dallachy on 25 May, 1945.

Main Equipment

Handley Page Hampden I (Apr 1942—Jan 1943)
    L4037, T; P1150, P; P1207, T; P2080, M; P4415; P5335; X2976;
    X3053; AD987, P; AE158; AE231; AE371, J; AN160, A; AT179, F;
    AT195, Q
Bristol Beaufighter VIC (Jan 1943—Jul 1943)
    JL593, L; JL610, B; JL654, H; JL716, Q; JL722, N; JL832, A
Bristol Beaufighter X (Jun 1943—May 1945)
    JM353, R; JM380, J; JM403, G; LX899, O; LZ134, L; LZ182, A;
    LZ219, D; LZ225, O; LZ315, S; LZ438, J; LZ542, V; NE214, K;
    NE227, M; NE430, PL:W; NE538, PL:E; NE578, PL:K;
    NE7r3, PL:Y; NE831, PL:O; NT929, PL:Z; NT955, PL:N;
    NV138, PL:R; NV182, PL:E; RD393, PL:A; RD436, PL:X

Commanding Officers

W/Cdr J. J. Bennett	Apr 1942—Jul 1942	
W/Cdr J. McLaughlin	Jul 1942—Aug 1943	
W/Cdr D. O. F. Lumsden, DFC	Aug 1943—Aug 1944	
W/Cdr A. Gadd, DFC	Aug 1944—May 1945	

Aircraft Insignia

It is not known what identity markings, if any, were carried by the Hampdens and early Beaufighters. They may have originally continued to use the code letters 'PL' on the Hampdens. These letters were used again from the summer of 1944 until the end of the Squadron's existence.
(See also *Bomber Squadrons of the RAF*, pp. 170–2)

No. 147 SQUADRON

BADGE
In front of a staff a shuttle
MOTTO
'Assidue portamus'
('We carry with regularity')

The shuttle signifies the regularity with which
the Squadron flew its routes.

No. 147 Squadron never became operational in World War I, having been formed in Egypt in May, 1918. It eventually disbanded there in May, 1919.

It re-formed at St. Jean in Palestine in January, 1942, the intention being to be part of a Wing of Liberator heavy bombers. Again the Squadron was unfortunate and, due to the shortage of aircraft, never received any and was disbanded again in February, 1943.

On 5 September, 1944 No. 147 re-formed at Croydon as a transport squadron with Douglas Dakotas and a few Ansons and Oxfords. Its task was to provide regular transport services between the UK and the cities of Europe as they became liberated and in the month of its formation it began regular schedules to Paris and Brussels. In October it included one to Marseilles and extended this to Naples and in November a run to Bordeaux was instituted, carrying on to Gibraltar in the New Year.

In February, 1945 a detachment of four Ansons was set up at Melsbroek to run a shuttle between Paris and Brussels, whilst the Dakotas extended to Greece. By April it was flying twenty plus schedules a day and gradually included the Allied bases in Germany itself. With the end of the war Czechoslovakia and Norway and then other places became part of No. 147s airline and these European lines were flown until the growth of national airlines in 1946 enabled the Squadron to disband at Croydon on 13 September that year.

On 1 February, 1953 No. 147 re-formed at Abingdon from No. 1 Long Range Ferry Unit. Its task was now to ferry aircraft to and from the RAF squadrons world-wide, having no equipment of its own. It moved to Benson in April, 1953 and served there until disbanding on 15 September, 1958.

Bases etc.

Re-formed as a transport squadron at Croydon on 5 September, 1944.
Croydon, det. Melsbroek   Sep 1944—Sep 1946
Disbanded at Croydon on 13 September, 1946.

Main Equipment

Douglas Dakota C.4 (Sep 1944—Sep 1946)
  KG569; KG723; KG734; KG748, 177; KG750; KG771, 185; KG808; KG865, 129
Douglas Dakota C.4 (Sep 1944—Sep 1946)
  KJ803, 183; KJ838, 137; KJ865; KK136; KK212; KN268; KN438
Avro Anson I (Sep 1944—   1945)
  MG594; NK658; NK661; NK674
Avro Anson C.12 (1945—Sep 1946)
  PH668; PH669, D; PH767; PH809; PH811

Commanding Officers

W/Cdr C. E. F. Riley, AFC   Sep 1944—Sep 1946

Aircraft Insignia

The aircraft carried no regular insignia. At a post-war period some of the Dakotas carried a white circle on the front of the nose with the last two letters of the call-sign on, the first always being 'F'. The aircraft also carried letters and numbers on the side denoting the routes to which they were assigned. For example KG748 at one stage carried 'CMV-177'; presumably denoting Route Number 117 and the letters, possibly, Croydon–Munich–Vienna.

No. 148 SQUADRON

BADGE
Two battleaxes in saltire
MOTTO
'Trusty'

The battle axes symbolise well-tried and
formidable weapons.

No. 148 Squadron has been largely a bomber unit during its various periods of existence. From 10 February, 1918, when it formed at Andover, until 30 June, 1919 when it disbanded at Shoreham it flew as a night-bomber squadron in France with F.E.2b's. It was re-formed on 7 June, 1937 at Scampton again in the bomber role but did not immediately take part in operations in World War II, disbanding into 15 OTU at Harwell on 4 April, 1940. Twenty-six days later it did re-form in 3 Group once more but only served until 23 May, 1940, again disbanding. A more definitive No. 148 Squadron re-formed at Luqa, Malta on 14 December, 1940 with Wellingtons and this unit fought within the Mediterranean area for exactly two years before disbanding once more.

On 14 March, 1943 the Special Liberator Flight at Gambut was re-numbered 148 Squadron; it now operated in the Special Duties role with Liberator IIs and Halifax IIs. By April it was operating forty sorties a month dropping agents and supplies to organisations in Greece, Crete, Serbia and Yugoslavia. A typical load would be one agent, 15 containers, 21 packages and the aircraft would make five runs over the target, the first being a dummy. The ORB contains this quote: 'The captain emphasises that the first area should not be approached below 4,500 ft true. He considers that 10 ft clearance of mountains at night is hardly sufficient.' The Squadron built up its activities to quite a pitch with 90 sorties in May and 137 in June and July. In August Dakota FD919 was attached for a one-off landing in Greece to pick up some saboteurs and take them to Cairo. Otherwise, it was all paradropping tasks.

By 1944 most of the targets were in Albania and Greece but it soon moved further afield reaching North Italy and Poland. In February a Lysander Flight was formed using at first aircraft which had been doing target towing at Gibraltar. March brought a Wellington for *Rebecca* training and in April the Squadron was experimenting with the M.E. Delayed Parachute Opening Device. May was significant for the sorties topped the 200 figure and the Lysanders began operating into Greece, Corsica and the South of France. No. 148's aircraft were now being fitted with *Gee* as well as *Rebecca*. In July the Squadron lost five aircraft, out of a total of 263 sorties. In August seven crews and twelve aircraft were lost, four on one night, which left the Squadron with only one officer pilot. Operations were now reduced until these losses could be made up. In October the Halifaxes were switched to daylight sorties using cloud cover, concentrating mainly on the Balkans and North Italy to support partisans harassing the retreating Germans. By the end of the year the aircraft were homing on to targets using *Rebecca* and then making contact with 'S' Phones★. As 1945 wore on the operations changed in nature. By March supply-dropping was a minor task, most of the work involving personnel infiltration into Central Czechoslovakia and Southern Austria. Even Jeeps were being dropped successfully until the war's close brought an abrupt end to such activities.

No. 148 Squadron immediately began flying out POWs and converting to Liberator VIs to resume a standard bomber role once more and this was continued until 15 January, 1946 when it was disbanded at Gianaclis.

Two further periods were spent in the bomber role, between November, 1946 and July, 1955 with Lancasters and Lincolns and between July, 1956 and April, 1965 with Valiants.

★ *Limited range R/T supplied to agents*

Re-formed at Gambut Main in 14 March, 1943 by re-naming the Special Liberator Flight.

Gambut Main	Mar 1943—Apr 1943
Derna	Apr 1943—Aug 1943
Tocra, det. Protville	Aug 1943—Jan 1944
Brindisi	Jan 1944—May 1945

Transferred to bomber role at Foggia in June, 1945.

Main Equipment

Consolidated Liberator II (Mar 1943—Feb 1944)
AL506, X; AL509, Y; AL510, W; AL530, Z; AL555, O; AL630, T
Handley Page Halifax II Series I (Mar 1943—Sep 1944)
BB302, FS:H; BB318, FS:F; BB338, FS:M; BB381, FS:O;
BB421, FS:R; BB441, 3, later FS:Q
Handley Page Halifax II Series IA (Mar 1943—May 1945)
HR660, FS:U; HR674, FS:E; JD180, FS:G; JD319, FS:G;
JN888, FS:P; JN896, FS:L; JN926, FS:O; JN956, FS:E;
JP161, FS:G; JP186, FS:Y; JP229, FS:B; JP278, FS:Y; LW272, FS:K
Handley Page Halifax V (Jul 1944—May 1945)
EB147, FS:K; EB196, FS:E; LK742, FS:L; LL250, FS:V;
LL290, FS:N; LL354, FS:F; LL521, FS:T
Westland Lysander IIIA (Feb 1944—May 1945)
T1458; T1642, FS:B; T1750, FS:B; R9009, FS:A; V9670;
V9821, FS:D

Commanding Officers

W/Cdr J. Blackburn, DSO, DFC and Bar	Mar 1943—Dec 1943
W/Cdr D. L. Pitt, DSO, AFC	Dec 1943—Aug 1944
W/Cdr D. C. Hayward, DSO	Aug 1944—May 1945

Aircraft Insignia

The code letters 'FS' were carried fairly consistently by the Halifaxes and spasmodically by the Squadron's other types.
(See also *Bomber Squadrons of the RAF*, pp. 172–4)

No. 155 SQUADRON

BADGE
A sword enfiled by a serpent biting its tail

MOTTO
'Eternal Vigilance'

Predominantly a fighter squadron No. 155 had a short existence from September to December, 1918 as a night-fighter unit at Feltham without becoming operational. It re-formed at Peshawar in India on 1 April, 1942 and fought in the Burma campaign with Mohawks and Spitfires and in the post-war flare-up in the Dutch East Indies finally disbanding at Medan on 31 August, 1946.

On 1 September, 1954 No. 155 was re-formed as a tactical support helicopter squadron at Seletar and, equipped with Westland Whirlwind HAR.4s, flew in support of the security forces operating against the Malaysian communist guerillas. This involved landing troops and supplies in small jungle clearings in many different parts of Malaya and flying casevac sorties out of the jungle. It served in this exacting role until June, 1959 when, together with No. 194

Squadron, it was merged into No. 110 Squadron. During its service it had an average yearly airlift of 16,000 troops and 225,000 lbs of supplies. In addition it had pioneered the dropping of paratroops into the jungle by helicopter in 1956.

Bases etc.

Seletar, det. Kuala Lumpur	Sep 1954—Jun 1959

Disbanded by re-numbering as No. 110 Squadron at Seletar on 3 June, 1959.

Main Equipment

Westland Whirlwind HAR.4 (Sep 1954—Jun 1959)
XD188, J; XJ410; XJ421, T

Commanding Officers

S/Ldr L. L. Harland, DFC

Aircraft Insignia

As far as is known no insignia was carried by No. 155 Squadron's Whirlwinds.
(See also *Fighter Squadrons of the RAF*, pp. 296–7)

No. 160 SQUADRON

BADGE
A Sinhalese lion rampant holding a Sinhalese sword

MOTTO
'Api soya paragas mu'
('We seek and strike')

The badge indicates the Squadron's associations with Ceylon

No. 160 Squadron had no significant existence in World War I being formed in June, 1918 and disbanded a few weeks later in July. It re-formed at Thurleigh on 16 January, 1942 with Liberator IIs and moved in May to Nutt's Corner where for a short while it operated with No. 120 Squadron on convoy escorts and A/S searches over the Atlantic until 8 June when it ceased operations and moved overseas. The ground crew had already moved to Quetta in India but the aircrew and aircraft established a new identity in Palestine and operated as a bomber squadron for the rest of the year. This continued until 15 January, 1943 when the Middle East part of No. 160 Squadron was posted into No. 178 Squadron.

The remainder of the Squadron arrived at Ratmalana, Ceylon in February, 1943 and a new No. 160 Squadron received Liberator

IIIs to operate in the maritime reconnaissance role. Operations commenced over the Indian Ocean on 6 February flying 9½ hour sorties on convoy escorts, A/S patrols and detector patrols.

Operations temporarily ceased in April whilst Sigiriya was examined as a possible new base; also experiments were carried out on Liberator FL945 by painting it in Sky finish to determine better ground to air invisibility.

In May No. 160 Squadron resumed ops flying fifteen hour sorties, mainly on coastal photo recce work and ASR. Met flights also became part of the Squadron's stock-in-trade. In September a detachment went to Cuttack for PR of Car Nicobar Islands and here W/Cdr Cohen's crew, flying FL939 M was attacked by Zeros. They shot one down but were then shot down by another. Further fights with Zeros ensued and another Liberator was lost in October. On 8 November the Squadron found its first enemy submarine which was attacked by P/Os Hill and Hall unsuccessfully.

In May 1944 it also began flying Special duties dropping supplies behind Japanese lines. March, 1944 saw its busiest month with 66 sorties including night PR, diversionary strikes, special duties as well as the normal maritime tasks. In May F/O Jackson, flying a PR sortie, found an unknown Japanese airfield on Sumatra. Liberator VIs arrived in June but these were unsuitable for night-flying and Mk. Vs were retained for this purpose.

In October, 1944 there was an alert for Japanese submarines dropping agents in India and the Squadron inaugurated four-aircraft sweeps; F/Lt Netherton's crew in BZ711 A found one on 28 October, attacked it before it could submerge and sank it. February, 1945 brought a new task; the Liberators went mine-laying around the Dutch East Indies to stop the flow of oil from there to Japan, in March this was extended to cover the approaches, involving 22-hour sorties.

Mining was now the Squadron's biggest task, 56 such sorties flown in April with only four other operational trips. This changed to special operations again in June, preparing the partisans in Burma and Malaya for the final offensive, and there were 62 such sorties in July. At this time, too, there was a high rate of change of aircrew in the Squadron involving much re-training. Even after the end of the fighting 'Special' drops were still being made to forces in the jungle but this was replaced in November by providing a ferry service to and from Cocos Island, a task extended all over India and Ceylon in March, 1946. In June No. 160 began flying to the UK and settled in at Leuchars in July where it began to re-equip with Lancasters for maritime reconnaissance and ASR. In September it flew two ASR sorties but was then disbanded by re-numbering as No. 120 Squadron on 30 September, 1946.

Bases etc.

Squadron re-constituted at Ratmalana on 3 February, 1943.

Ratmalana, det. Sigiriya	Feb 1943—Aug 1943
Sigiriya, det. Cuttack, Gan, Vavuyina, Ratmalana	Aug 1943—Aug 1944
Kankesanturai	Aug 1944—Feb 1945
Minneriya, det. Ramree Is.	Feb 1945—Jun 1946
Leuchars	Jun 1946—Sep 1946

Disbanded by re-numbering as No. 120 Squadron at Leuchars on 30 September, 1945.

Main Equipment

Consolidated Liberator III, IIIA (Feb 1943—Jun 1945)
FK227; FK239, B; FL911, K; FL926, J; FL929, W; FL936, V; FL940, P; FL945, H
Consolidated Liberator V (June 1943—Oct 1945)
BZ711, A; BZ752, N; BZ825, L; BZ864, B; BZ889, Y; BZ900, BS:C; BZ939, Y; FL986, BS:B; FL991, BS:F
Consolidated Liberator VI (Jun 1944—Nov 1944)
EV821, G; EV823, T; EV889, H; EV893, O; EW314, X
Consolidated Liberator VIII (Oct 1945—Aug 1946)
KL380, BS:V; KL480, BS:F; KL497, BS:D; KL520, BS:K; KL561, BS:A; KN777, BS:A
Avro Lancaster ASR.3 & GR.3 (Aug 1946—Sep 1946)
No serials confirmed

Commanding Officers

W/Cdr C. A. Butler	Mar 1943—Jan 1944
W/Cdr G. R. Brady	Jan 1944—Nov 1944
W/Cdr J. N. Stacey, DSO, DFC	Nov 1944—May 1945
W/Cdr G. McKenzie	May 1945—Sep 1945
W/Cdr R. D. Williams	Sep 1945—Sep 1946

Aircraft Insignia

It is believed that no squadron markings were carried until *ca* December, 1944 after which the code letters 'BS' were used.
(See also *Bomber Squadrons of the RAF*, pp. 182–3)

No. 161 SQUADRON

BADGE
An open fetterlock

MOTTO
'Liberate'

The badge symbolises the Squadron's role in liberating Europe

No. 161 Squadron's first existence developed no further than a small nucleus in June, 1918 which dissipated the following month.

It re-formed at Newmarket on 14 February, 1942 from a nucleus supplied by the King's Flight under W/Cdr E. H. Fielden, MVO, AFC. A Flight was equipped with Lysanders and B Flight with Whitleys and its task was to support the resistance movements in Europe and the landing and picking-up of agents. First operation took place on 27 February when S/Ldr A. M. Murphy in Lysander V9428 took one agent to St. Saens and brought two back. Two more Lysander trips took place in March and the Whitleys began operating in April on supply-dropping. In June bombing and *Nickel* sorties were added and in September Whitleys were detached to Gibraltar for work in North Africa. In October 24 special operations were flown; the Squadron acquired two Havocs which were used for contacting ships operating off the French Atlantic coast monitoring German shipping movements out of the Brest/Lorient area, These operated from St. Eval together with a couple of Albermarles.

December, 1942 was a busy month for the Squadron for it began converting to Halifaxes and operations were flown from Malta, Gibraltar and LG.224 in the Western Desert. Meanwhile the Lysanders were flying from Tangmere. On one of these latter sorties, on 17 December, S/Ldr Lockhart had a hazardous return flight from France, his tailwheel having jammed his elevator and rudder controls. His stick was immovable fore and aft so he took off in the dark and flew back across the Channel on trimmer alone,

throttling back and stalling the aircraft every two or three minutes to allow the nose to fall below the horizon. In this condition he made a night landing without aids at Tangmere!

In 1943 Hudsons joined the Squadron and were also used for landing in France. The Havocs and Albemarles were soon abandoned as their operations were unsuccessful. By the spring the Halifaxes were operating as far afield as Poland and out of Algiers into Southern France. By the summer as many as 86 sorties a month were flown, many of these to more than one dropping or pick-up zone. Experiments were flown with Stirlings in September, these were operated by 3 Group crews and aircraft under No. 161 Squadron's aegis and continued for some months. In October F/O Bell flew a Halifax on a 2,000 mile round trip to drop an agent at Narvik in N. Norway. Hudsons were now beginning to fly *Ascension* operations (an extension of the Havoc sorties) whereby the aircrew were actually able to talk to the agents with air-to-ground communications equipment. The century was achieved in April, 1944 when 107 sorties were flown in the month by Lysanders, Halifaxes and Hudsons, only one aircraft, a Hudson, failing to return but landing in Sweden. The Squadron now began staging to Blida in North Africa, doing drops in France on the way out and a second series on the way back.

As the invasion moved across Europe much of No. 161's work was eliminated and by September 1944 the Squadron was reduced to operating over Norway and Denmark. It therefore came in for some transport duties to the Continent, carrying special passengers over and above the normal transport squadrons. By the end of the year the Lysander Flight had been disbanded and the Halifaxes had been replaced by Stirlings. 1945 brought an increasing number of transport runs, also a night of tragedy on 20/21 March when three Hudsons were lost over Germany; three Stirlings were also lost that month. With the end of the war in Europe No. 161's task was over and it was disbanded at Tempsford on 5 June, 1945.

Bases etc.

Re-formed at Newmarket from a nucleus of the King's Flight on 14 February, 1942.

Newmarket	Feb 1942—Mar 1942
Graveley	Mar 1942—Aug 1942
Tempsford, det. Tangmere, Gibraltar, Kinloss, Winkleigh, St. Eval	Aug 1942—Jun 1945

Disbanded at Tempsford on 5 June, 1945.

Main Equipment

Westland Lysander IIIA (Feb 1942—Nov 1944)
R9106, MA:K; T1445; T1770, JR:A; V9353, MA:G; V9428, MA:C;
V9595, MA:F; V9674, MA:K; V9723, MA:D, later JR:H;
V9822, MA:E
Armstrong Whitworth Whitley V (Feb 1942—Dec 1942)
Z6653, MA:O; Z6747, MA:N; Z6828, MA:R; Z9160, MA:U;
Z9224, MA:P; Z9438, MA:S; BD276, MA:T
Handley Page Halifax II Series IA/V (Dec 1942—Sep 1944)
DG283, MA:V; DG286, MA:X; DG406, MA:V; DJ996, MA:X;
DK119, MA:U; LK738, MA:T; LL120, MA:W
Douglas Havoc I (Oct 1942—Nov 1943)
AW399, MA:Z, later MA:S; BJ477, MA:V, later MA:R

Armstrong Whitworth Albemarle I (Oct 1942—Mar 1943)
P1378, MA:K, later MA:M; P1390, MA:L
Lockheed Hudson I/III (Jan 1943—Jun 1945)
N7221, MA:P; T9445, MA:O; T9463, MA:L; V90345, MA:K;
V9155, MA:Q; AE595, MA:L; FK803, MA:N
Short Stirling IV (Sep 1944—Jun 1945)
LK119, MA:Y; LK207, LK312, MA:W

Commanding Officers

W/Cdr E. H. Fielden, MVO, AFC	Feb 1942—Oct 1942	
W/Cdr P. C. Pickard, DSO, DFC	Oct 1942—May 1943	
W/Cdr L. M. Hodges, DSO, DFC	May 1943—Jan 1945	
W/Cdr G. Watson, DFM	Jan 1945—Feb 1945	
W/Cdr M. A. Brogan, DFC	Feb 1945—Feb 1945	
W/Cdr L. F. Ratcliff, DSO, DFC, AFC	Mar 1945—Jun 1945	

Aircraft Insignia

The code letters 'MA' were used by No. 161 Squadron from its inception until at least April, 1944. Then the Lysander Flight changed to 'JR' but it is believed that the rest of the Squadron retained 'MA'. There is also reference in Squadron records to a Halifax 'VK:D' in June, 1943 but no satisfactory explanation of this coding is given nor is there any additional substantiating evidence.

No. 162 SQUADRON

BADGE
In front of a meteor, a bat's head erased

MOTTO
'One time, one purpose'

The bat, which uses echo-sounding for its direction-finding, is associated with the Squadron's jamming activities.

No. 162 Squadron's World War I existence grew no further than a small nucleus which formed in June, 1918 and disbanded on 4 July, 1918. It re-formed from a detachment of No. 109 Squadron at Shallufa on 4 January, 1942. Its purpose was two-fold: to provide calibration facilities for Allied radio and radar installations and, operationally, to investigate, and jam, enemy signals. It was equipped with Blenheims for the former and Wellingtons for the latter purposes.

Its main area of investigations was in Crete and Greece where the Wellingtons flew by night to determine the nature of the enemy defences. The Squadron also began a programme of development aimed at jamming enemy tank radios in the Western Desert. The Squadron's first loss took place on 6 March when Sgt Knowles and crew failed to return from the Dodecanese in Wellington Z8905 O.

More attention was paid to the radar installations at Benghazi and Derna during the year. However, in June that Squadron was called upon to augment the Western Desert bombing force on straight bombing raids. Meanwhile the Blenheims moved to detachments all around the Middle East, calibrating the extending British facilities.

By August the Squadron returned to the radio signals investigations work but carried bombs as well on such sorties, seeking targets of opportunity. A detachment at Malta in September made a complete radar survey of Taranto, Sardinia and Tripoli, and in October the Squadron concentrated on jamming activities over the land tank battles in the Desert.

In November the Wellington Flight was posted to No. 40 Squadron but the few aircraft on detachment continued their investigation work and this remained a squadron task though on a smaller scale. In early 1943 the Wellingtons were covering radio signals investigations over Crete, Sardinia, Sicily, North Africa, Italy, Greece and the Greek Islands.

Slowly the Squadron built up its Wellington force again and even resumed bombing and *Nickel* raids in April. As the year wore on, however, the frequency of operational flights tailed off and in 1944

not more than one operation a month was flown until finally No. 162 Squadron was disbanded in Idku on 25 September, 1944.

It re-formed in the bomber role as part of No. 8 (Pathfinder) Group in the UK at Bourn on 17 December, 1944 and flew Mosquitoes in this role until 14 July, 1946.

Bases etc.

Re-formed in the Signals role from a detachment of No. 109 Squadron at Shallufa on 4 January, 1942

Shallufa, det. Aqir	Jan 1942—Apr 1942
Bilbeis, det. Nicosia, Maaten Bagush, Shallufa, Habbaniya, Shaibah, Lydda, Luqa, Rayak, LG.86, Gambut Main	Apr 1942—Apr 1943
Benina, det. Luqa, Gambut	Apr 1943—Aug 1943
LG.91, det. Luqa, Gambut, LG.107, Gambut II	Aug 1943—Apr 1944
Idku	Apr 1944—Sep 1944

Disbanded at Idku 25 September, 1944, B Flight becoming No. 26 AACU.

Main Equipment

Vickers Wellington IC (Jan 1942—Mar 1944)
T2878, A; W5679, R; X9986, X; Z1165, M; Z8905, O; Z8948, W;
Z9034, D; AD589, A; AD630, T; AD643, Q; BB463, O; BB516, F;
DV489, A; DV647, D; DV931, V; HD957, T; HD972, U, later H;
HX633, F; HX673, J
Bristol Blenheim IV (Mar 1942—Jul 1942)
R3844; V5508; V6015; Z7712
Bristol Blenheim VA (Jul 1942—Dec 1943)
BA232; BA323; BA389; BA491; BA538; BA665; BA859; BA919; BA984;
BB146; EH327
Vickers Wellington III (Aug 1943—May 1944)
HF677; HF733, L; HF750; HZ123
Martin Baltimore III (Oct 1943—Sep 1944)
AG696; AG853, F; AG931; AH100, Z; AH161; FW624; FW726
de Havilland Mosquito VI (Oct 1943—Jul 1944)
HJ671
Vickers Wellington X (May 1944—Sep 1944)
LN856; LN960; LP205; LP238; MF239

Commanding Officers

W/Cdr D. H. S. Rusher, DSO	Jan 1942—Mar 1943	
W/Cdr G. F. L. Scott	Mar 1943—Dec 1943	
W/Cdr Appleby-Brown	Dec 1943—Jan 1944	
S/Ldr H. A. Lax	Jan 1944—Sep 1944	

Aircraft Insignia

There is no evidence to hand that the Squadron ever carried any unit insignia.
(See also *Bomber Squadrons of the RAF*, pp. 183–4.)

No. 167 SQUADRON

BADGE
A woodcock volant

MOTTO
'Ubique sine mora'
('Everywhere without delay')

No. 167 Squadron has had several short existences in different roles. In World War I it was formed at Bircham Newton in November, 1918 as the war ended as a heavy bomber unit, disbanding again on 21 May, 1919. It re-formed at Scorton on 6 April, 1942 as a fighter squadron and served with Spitfires in the UK until 12 June, 1943 when it was made an all-Dutch unit and re-numbered No. 322 Squadron.

On 21 October, 1944 No. 167 was again re-formed, this time in the transport role at Holmesley South as part of 110 Wing, Transport Command. It was equipped with Vickers Warwicks but due to serviceability problems it was not until December that its first aircraft was available for operations. It was intended that it should fly the longer range transport routes within Europe and the Mediterranean but it was not until January, 1945 that it took over responsibility for one route, flying 31 sorties that month. By March the total had risen to 76 sorties and the Squadron added the Rome/Athens service to its tasking. Then came Paris/Naples. However, in June two Warwicks crashed and all were grounded.

The crews at first flew with No. 147 Squadron at Croydon then acquired Dakotas as a temporary measure until the end of August when the Warwicks resumed operations. However, in September the Warwicks were withdrawn again due to engine troubles and Dakotas and Ansons flew the routes. By 1946 the national airlines were again becoming operational and on 3 February, 1946 the Squadron was disbanded at Blackbushe.

On 1 February, 1953 it was re-formed by re-numbering No. 3 (Long Range) Ferry Unit at Abingdon; it soon moved to Benson where it was used for overseas ferrying until combining with No. 147 Squadron to form the Ferry Squadron there on 15 September, 1958. It flew a few Vickers Valettas for crew positioning purposes.

Bases etc.

Re-formed in the transport role at Holmesley South on 21 October, 1944.

Holmesley South	Oct 1944	Mar 1945
Blackbushe	Mar 1945	Feb 1946

Disbanded at Blackbushe on 3 February, 1946.

Main Equipment

Vickers Warwick I (Nov 1944—May 1945)
BV243; BV244; BV246; BV250; BV253; BV255
Vickers Warwick III (Nov 1944—Feb 1946)
HG219; HG223; HG227, C; HG231; HG237; HG278; HG280, X; HG284; HG291; HG302, N; HG320, O; HG325
Avro Anson XII (Apr 1945—Feb 1946)
PH668; PH669; PH671; PH693
Douglas Dakota III (Jul 1945—Feb 1946)
FZ696; KG444; KG569; KG730; KG776; KG810
Douglas Dakota IV (Jul 1945—Feb 1946)
KJ806; KJ880; KK136; KK212; KN438; KN494
Vickers Valetta C.1 (Feb 1953—Sep 1958)
VL281; VX484, QO:E; WD166, QO:H; WD168, QO:P; WD170, QO:Q

Commanding Officers

W/Cdr H. R. Collins, AFC	Oct 1944	Feb 1946

Aircraft Insignia

As far as is known no insignia was carried during the 1944–6 period. During its ferry period it carried the code letters 'QO' and these were also used on Harvards and Meteors of the Conversion Training Flight on the Squadron. (See also *Bomber Squadrons of the RAF*, p. 185 and *Fighter Squadrons of the RAF*, p. 301.)

No. 168 SQUADRON

BADGE
In front of a scroll, a flaming arrow pointing downwards

MOTTO
'Rerum cognoscere causas'
('To know the cause of things')

The arrow symbolises attack and the scroll information gained by reconnaissance.

The Squadron first formed at Snailwell on 15 June, 1942 from a nucleus provided from No. 268 Squadron. It was equipped with Curtiss Tomahawks for fighter reconnaissance duties, but re-equipped with Mustangs before becoming operational.

Its first operation was from Odiham on 7 December, 1942 when F/Lt Mason flew a *Rhubarb* sortie over Northern France. Four days later the CO flew a *Popular* operation successfully. (*Populars* were photo recces of the French Coast). These became the pattern for limited operations in 1943; in May night flying in the moonlight period allowed *Rangers* to be flown on railway targets and the following month the Squadron was employed on standing patrols from Beachy Head to St. Catherine's Point to intercept German fighter-bombers raiding coastal towns. On 5 September a pair of Mustangs found four Messerschmitt Bf 109s and a He 111 over Arras, attacked and damaged two of the 109's. Forty-four sorties were flown in that month.

Towards the end of the year activity increased and 56 sorties were flown in December. Concentration in the New Year centred around *Noball* targets, photographing their locations for subsequent attack. Many moves took place, accustoming the unit to its likely role when the invasion started. With the spring the intensity grew with 114 sorties in May, mainly *Noballs*, *Populars* and tactical recce of the invasion area. In June, the month of the invasion, No. 168 Squadron flew 325 sorties, 36 on D-Day itself and it moved across to a beachhead airstrip three weeks after. From here it put in very intensive Tac/R effort with the 2nd Army at Caen and Argentan flying 499 sorties in July and then 550 in August, combining PR around Falaise with artillery shoots and Tac/R at Argentan. This was continued until 20 September when No. 168 was re-equipped with Typhoons and went over to the fighter-bomber role using bombs or rockets to attack enemy targets.

This activity was maintained until 20 February, 1945 when the Squadron was disbanded at Eindhoven.

Bases etc.

Formed at Snailwell on 15 June, 1942.

Snailwell	Jun 1942	Jul 1942
Bottisham	Jul 1942	Nov 1942
Odiham, det. Weston Zoyland, Tangmere	Nov 1942	Sep 1943
Hutton Cranswick	Sep 1943	Oct 1943
Thruxton	Oct 1943	Nov 1943
Sawbridgeworth	Nov 1943	Nov 1943
North Weald	Nov 1943	Jan 1944
Llanbedr	Jan 1944	Feb 1944
North Weald, det. Benson	Feb 1944	Feb 1944
Odiham, det. Bircham Newton	Feb 1944	Mar 1944
Gatwick	Mar 1944	Mar 1944
Odiham	Mar 1944	Jun 1944

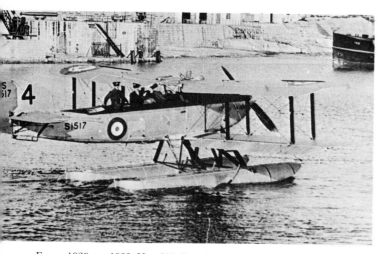

From 1929 to 1935 No. 202 Squadron was a seaplane unit based at Kalafrana, Malta. Here Fairey IIIF S1517 taxies out into the harbour at Malta prior to taking off.

No. 202 Squadron was re-formed from No. 518 Squadron in October, 1946 and served on meteorological reconnaissance duties until July, 1964. Most of this period, from October, 1950 onwards it flew Handley Page Hastings Met.1 aircraft from Aldergrove in N. Ireland and TG567 is here seen lined up for take-off there in February, 1951.

At present No. 202 Squadron is the second RAF Search and Rescue Squadron in the UK and flies the long-distance Westland SeaKing HAR.3s from four different bases around the coast. These two squadron aircraft (XZ593 the nearest) are approaching Lossiemouth from across the Moray Firth.

For eleven years No. 203 Squadron served as the resident flying-boat unit in the Persian Gulf and in the early thirties flew the Short Rangoon boats from Basra, one of which is seen here.

No. 203 was still using flying-boats early in World War II, Short Singapore IIIs, of which K6912 was one. Note the camouflage and the code letters NT:D.

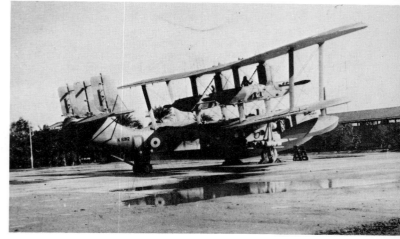

No. 204 Squadron in peacetime was the Alexandria-based RAF flying-boat unit and in the mid-thirties flew Supermarine Scapas, K4191 seen here in Alexandria Harbour. The coloured rectangle on the fin was a unit insignia.

In the Far East the resident boat squadron was No. 205, based at Seletar, Singapore and flying Short Singapore IIIs from 1935 to 1941. K3594 shown here was one which carried a card suit as identity.

After the fall of Singapore No. 205 Squadron was re-formed in Ceylon and for the rest of World War II flew Consolidated Catalinas on long-range patrols over the Indian Ocean. JX431 A, shown here is a Mk. IVB flown in 1944–45.

No. 205 Squadron continued to provide maritime reconnaissance in the Far East in the fifties and sixties, using Avro Shackleton MR.1s and 2s. Sorties were flown to Gan, the staging post in the middle of the Indian Ocean, on a routine basis where MR.1A VP288 is here seen in 1962.

Throughout World War II No. 206 Squadron served on maritime reconnaissance over the Atlantic and North Sea, flying Hudsons, Fortresses and, here, Liberator VIs and VIIIs. This Mk.VIII is KK335, flown by the Squadron in 1945.

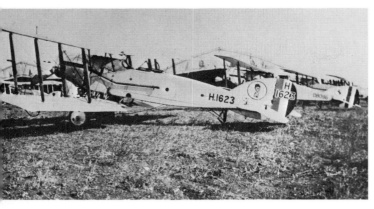

Operations in Turkey in 1922/23 were a feature of No. 208 Squadron's service after World War I. It flew Bristol Fighters embellished with cartoon characters on the fin shown in this line-up at Killia.

A few Hawker Hurricane IIs were modified for photo recce work in Egypt in the early forties and used by No. 208 Squadron amongst other units.

Four Gloster Meteor FR.9s of No. 208 Squadron carry out a formation loop over the Suez Canal from their base at Abu Sueir in 1952.

From 1930 to 1936 N. 209 Squadron operated the big Blackburn flying-boats from Mount Batten, Plymouth. S1263 was an Iris III and was named *Leda*. It carried No. 209's unofficial badge on the nose.

No. 209 Squadron was chosen to pioneer the Saro Lerwick flying-boat into service and began this task in December, 1939 at Oban. The aircraft was unsuccessful, however, and only lasted with 209 Squadron until May, 1941. WQ:Q, seen here taxying past the Isle of Kerrera, was L7265 in April, 1941.

In the spring of 1942 No. 209 Squadron took its Catalinas to East Africa for Indian Ocean patrol duty. FP265 Z is here seen taking off at Kipevu in 1944.

No. 209 finally served at Seletar in Singapore in the sixties as a short range comms. and army support squadron with Scottish Aviation Pioneers (XL706 shown) and Twin Pioneers.

The first practical torpedo-bomber was the Sopwith Cuckoo of 1920. No. 210 was the only squadron to operate this type, flying from Gosport between February, 1920 and April, 1923 and carrying out much developmental and training drops on the Stokes Bay range, as is N8011 here.

In the mid-fifties No. 210 was one of four squadrons to operate the American Lockheed P2V-6 Neptune MR.1 maritime recce patrol aircraft. WX516 of the Squadron is here at Thorney Island in September, 1954.

In its World War I existence No. 212 Squadron operated, amongst other aircraft, this Sopwith 2F.1 Camel in 1918.

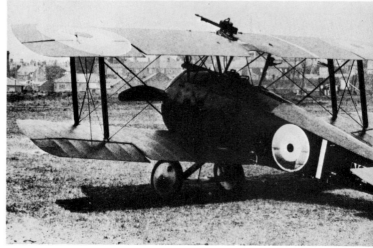

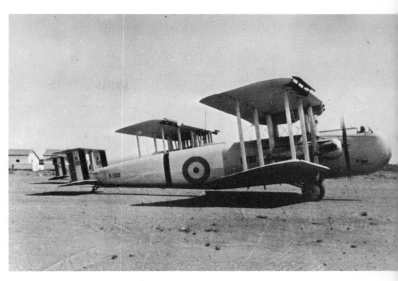

Medium-range transport duties in the Far East from 1963 to 1968 were carried out by No. 215 Squadron, using Hawker Siddeley Argosy C.1s based at Changi, including XP447.

No. 216 was one of the two bomber transport squadrons serving in the Middle East in the thirties using, in this case, a Vickers Victoria V, K1315.

The Bristol Bombay I served almost exclusively in the Middle East on transport and bombing duties and No. 216 Squadron was its original and principal user. L5832 of the Squadron is seen here at Habbaniya during the 1941 troubles there.

In May, 1956 No. 216 Squadron was chosen to bring the de Havilland Comet into RAF service following the disastrous crashes in BOAC service. At first with C.MK.2s it flew the Comet on its Transport Command routes until disbandment in June, 1975, latterly flying C.Mk.4s as XR396 here.

Beaufort Is of No. 217 Squadron dispersed, probably at Manston, in March, 1942 after operations. MW:P is X8935.

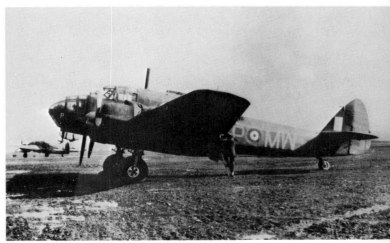

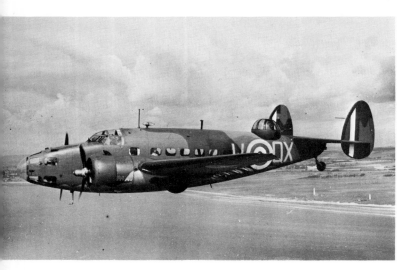

No. 220 Squadron received Lockheed Hudsons a month after World-War II broke out and began operating them on 5 October. T9277 is seen here flying from Thornaby out over the North Sea.

From October, 1943 until the war in Europe ended No. 220 Squadron provided a vital role flying anti-submarine patrols over the Atlantic from Lagens in the Azores. It used Boeing Fortress IIs and IIAs, FK200 2:B & FL459 2:J seen here at Lagens.

No. 221 Squadron was formed to operate the Vickers Wellington equipped with ASV radar against shipping, principally submarines. In this form the Wellington was designated Mk. VIII. W5674 DF:D was one of the Squadron's early Mk.VIIIs.

Another of Coastal Command's squadrons which operated throughout the war on maritime patrols, principally over the Atlantic, was No. 224 which subsequently flew Consolidated Liberator VIs & VIIIs, KN753/G being one of the latter.

No. 225, after World War II, became the first RAF squadron in the UK to develop the tactics of army support and liaison. It was equipped with Bristol Sycamore HR.14s and Westland Whirlwind HAR.4s (seen here) and operated in the main within the UK though seen here on deployment to El Adem.

Having taxied out of the line of moored Supermarine Stranraers at Felixstowe, K7297 X of No. 228 Squadron opens up to full throttle for take-off.

The RNAS Station at Felixstowe was foremost in developing the tactics of anti-submarine warfare in World War I and had a fine operational record. When it became part of the Royal Air Force on 1 April, 1918 its Flights were amalgamated into Squadrons. Thus was No. 230 Squadron born, one of its aircraft being this Curtiss H.12, 8677, seen on the slipway at Felixstowe.

No. 230 again became a flying-boat squadron in 1934 and in due course was established at Seletar, Singapore, as the second general reconnaissance unit there. It was the first to equip with Short Sunderland Is and here L2160 is moored at Port Swettenham in October, 1938, being named *Selangor* by the Sultan.

No. 230 Squadron became a helicopter unit in 1962, flying Westland Whirlwind HAR.10s in 38 Group, committed to army support. However, it maintained a detachment attached to the United Nations for many years, being based at Nicosia, Cyprus, and flying support and policing sorties in co-operation with the UN Forces at their outposts in the Khyrenia mountains of North Cyprus. XL110 is seen landing at one in the foothills in March, 1970.

The long-range transport services across the Atlantic were the commitment of No. 231 Squadron from September, 1944 until 1946 and to do this it used Coronado flying-boats, Consolidated Liberators, Dakotas and Avro Lancastrians. Amongst its fleet was *Commando* (AL504), a specially-modified Liberator II which was used for the long-distance flights of Winston Churchill.

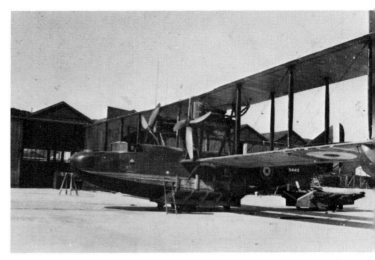

After serving with Coastal Command in the first part of World War II, No. 233 Squadron was re-formed as a transport unit in February, 1944 using Douglas Dakota IIIs, including FZ692 UK, to tow Horsas and drop paratroops in Normandy on D-Day.

Most westerly of the RAF's coastal defence squadrons in 1918 was No. 234, based at Tresco in the Scillies and operating flying-boats out over the Western Approaches. Here Felixstowe F.3 N4415 is beached for maintenance at Tresco.

The green sward of Bircham Newton in 1940 houses the Bristol Blenheim IVFs of No. 235 Squadron, engaged in shipping recces and attacks along the Dutch coast.

No. 236 was one of the successful coastal strike squadrons whose Beaufighters created such havoc with the German convoys along the Continental and Norwegian coasts. One exploit outside the line of this task was on 12 June 1942 when Flt Lt Gatward and Sgt Fern flew Beaufighter VIC T4800 ND:C at low-level over Paris, dropped a tricolor on the Arc de Triomphe and shot up the German Marine HQ.

Both Nos. 237 and 238 were coastal patrol seaplane squadrons in World War I, based at Cattewater, Plymouth and equipped with Short 184s. Here is a line-up on the breakwater there in 1918 with the seaplanes waiting to be hoist into the water by the steam crane running along the railway track.

Sommervieu (B.8)   Jun   1944—Aug 1944
S. Honorine de Ducy (B.21)   Aug   1944—Sep 1944
Avrilly (B.34)   Sep   1944—Sep 1944
Blankenburg (B.66)   Sep   1944—Oct 1944
Transferred to fighter role at Eindhoven (B.78) on 3 October, 1944.

Main Equipment

Curtiss Tomahawk IIB (Jun 1942—Nov 1942)
  AH900; AK118, EK:A, later OE:A; BK853, OE:P
North American Mustang I (Nov 1942—Jul 1943 & Feb 1944—Sep 1944)
  AG346; AG427; AG497; AG507; AG553; AG654; AL979; AM114;
  AM173; AM216; AM244; AP167; AP195; AP230
North American Mustang IA (Jul 1943—Feb 1944)
  FD439; FD444; FD478; FD502; FD531; FD565

Commanding Officers

W/Cdr G. F. Watson Smyth   Jun   1942—Jun 1943
S/Ldr P. W. Mason, DFC   Jun   1943—Jun 1944
S/Ldr D. W. Barlow, DFC   Jun   1944—Aug 1944
S/Ldr D. A. D. L. Nichols   Aug   1944—Oct 1944

Aircraft Insignia

The Squadron originally carried 'EK' code letters but within weeks this was changed to 'OE'. This latter combination was retained until identity letters were dropped by Army co-operation squadrons in the early summer of 1943. Thereafter no markings were carried.
(See also *Fighter Squadrons of the RAF*, p. 302.)

No. 169 SQUADRON

BADGE
In front of a hurt a hunting horn in bend

MOTTO
'Hunt and destroy'

The hurt signifies the night and the horn represents the intruder role.

The Squadron first formed at Twinwoods Farm on 15 June, 1942 in the fighter reconnaissance role out of B Flight of No. 613 Squadron and equipped with North American Mustangs. Its task was to work with the 42nd Armoured Division. This involved much working-up, delayed by unserviceability and aircraft modification programmes. In November crews were attached to No. 26 Squadron at Gatwick for operational experience and in December the Squadron itself became operational flying North Sea patrols and then *Lagoons* (shipping recces).

In January, 1943 it became more offensive, flying *Rhubarbs* over Holland and escort duty to Mitchells bombing Ghent. This continued until March when operations ceased once more but in April they resumed, 20 sorties being flown that month (*Lagoons*, *Populars* and *Rhubarbs*). With the increasing day raids by German fighter-bombers No. 169 Squadron began standing patrols on a Needles–Portland Bill patrol line and in July put up 78 sorties. This type of pattern continued until the end of September; the Squadron was disbanded at Middle Wallop on 1 October, 1943.

No. 169 re-formed in the night intruder role at Ayr on the same

day with Mosquito VIs and served with 100 Group in this role until disbanding at Great Massingham on 10 August, 1945.

Bases etc.

Formed at Twinwoods Farm on 15 June, 1942.
Twinwoods Farm   Jun   1942—Jul 1942
Doncaster, det. Driffield,
  Kirton-in-Lindsey   Jul   1942—Nov 1942
York   Nov   1942—Dec 1942
Duxford   Dec   1942—Mar 1943
Barford St. John   Mar   1943—Mar 1943
Gransden Lodge   Mar   1943—Mar 1943
Bottisham   Mar   1943—Mar 1943
Duxford   Mar   1943—Mar 1943
Andover, det. Oatlands Hill   Mar   1943—Jun 1943
Middle Wallop   Jun   1943—Oct 1943
Disbanded at Middle Wallop on 1 October, 1943.

Main Equipment

North American Mustang I (Jun 1942—Oct 1943)
  AG476; AG649; AL973; AL987; AL999; AM101; AM132; AM169;
  AM231; AP189; AP214; AP252

Commanding Officers

W/Cdr E. G. Campbell-Voullaire, DFC   Jun   1942—Jun 1943
S/Ldr R. Plumtree, DFC   Jun   1943—Oct 1943

Aircraft Insignia

It is not known whether the Mustangs carried any squadron identity markings.
(See also *Fighter Squadrons of the RAF*, p. 302).

No. 170 SQUADRON

BADGE
Issuant from a helmet affrontee, the vizor closed, a plume of three ostrich feathers

MOTTO
'Videre non videri'
('To see and not to be seen')

The helmet with vizor closed suggest seeing without being seen and its facing position suggest 'always ready to face the enemy'. The plume of feathers in the Guards' colours signifies the Squadron's role in co-operating with the Guards' Division.

The Squadron was formed on 15 June, 1942 at Weston Zoyland in the fighter reconnaissance role. Equipped principally with Mustangs it worked up for co-operation with the 3rd Division.

In January, 1943 No. 170 began *Lagoon* operations and *Rhubarbs* on rail targets, in February damaging seven goods trains, destroying one and damaging three locomotives. For the next two months it was off operations but in May it returned to *Lagoons* and anti-recce

patrols, by June flying 54 sorties. For its *Anti-Rhubarb* patrols it took up the patrol line Selsey to St. Catherine's Point but made no enemy contacts. Fifty sorties were flown in September and provided the pattern for the rest of the year. However on 15 January, 1944 it was disbanded at Sawbridgeworth. No. 170 re-formed as a bomber squadron at Kelstern on 15 October, 1944 and served on the bomber offensive over Germany until finally disbanding on 14 November, 1945.

Bases etc.

Formed at Weston Zoyland on 15 June, 1942.
Weston Zoyland   Jun   1942—Jun 1942
Hurn   Jun   1942—Oct 1942
Thruxton   Oct   1942—Oct 1942
Andover, det. Ibsley   Oct   1942—Feb 1943
Ford   Feb   1943—Mar 1943
Andover   Mar   1943—Mar 1943
Snailwell, det. Tangmere   Mar   1943—Sep 1943
Hutton Cranswick   Sep   1943—Oct 1943
Thruxton, det. Benson   Oct   1943—Nov 1943
Sawbridgeworth   Nov   1943—Jan 1944
Disbanded at Sawbridgeworth on 15 January, 1944.

Main Equipment

North American Mustang I (Jun 1942—Sep 1943)
 AG417; AG494; AG653; AL968; AL991; AM133; AM212; AP225
North American Mustang IA (Aug 1943—Jan 1944)
 FD480; FD494; FD509; FD543; FD559; FD566

Commanding Officers

S/Ldr G. B. Walford   Jun 1942—Aug 1942

W/Cdr J. A. C. Fuller	Aug 1942—Jun 1943
S/Ldr G. P. Wildish	Jun 1943—Jan 1944

Aircraft Insignia

The code letter combination 'BN' was carried by the Squadron aircraft from June, 1942 until the beginning of 1943 when the markings were deleted and no other form of identity carried.
(See also *Bomber Squadrons of the RAF*, pp. 185–6.)

No. 171 SQUADRON

BADGE
In front of an eagle displayed a portcullis

MOTTO
'Per dolum defendimus'
('We defend by confusion')

No. 171 Squadron was formed at Gatwick with Curtiss Tomahawks on 15 June, 1942. After three months it was re-equipped with Mustangs and in October began operations. These consisted of anti-*Rhubarb* sorties along the South Coast to pick up German fighter-bomber raids. It was also busy teaching Belgian pilots to fly the Tomahawk. The anti-*Rhubarbs* became a settled pattern, the Squadron flying the Shoreham–Beachy Head patrol line. However, the Squadron's existence was short-lived for on 31 December, 1942 it was disbanded at Hartford Bridge.

No. 171 re-formed at North Creake on 8 September, 1944 from C Flight, No. 199 Squadron. Its task was now as a RCM squadron within 100 Group, Bomber Command. As such it flew Stirlings and later Halifaxes over the North Sea and Germany principally dropping *Window* to jam the enemy radars and operating the *Mandrel* screen. It continued these duties until VE-Day and was disbanded at North Creake on 27 July, 1945.

Bases etc.

Formed at Gatwick on 15 June, 1942.

Gatwick	Jun 1942—Jul 1942	
Odiham	Jul 1942—Aug 1942	
Gatwick, det. Weston Zoyland	Aug 1942—Dec 1942	
Hartford Bridge	Dec 1943—Dec 1943	

Disbanded at Hartford Bridge 31 December, 1942. Re-formed in the RCM role at North Creake on 8 September, 1944 by re-numbering and expanding C Flight of 199 Squadron.

North Creake	Sep 1944—Jul 1945

Disbanded at North Creake 27 July, 1945.

Main Equipment

Curtiss Tomahawk II (Jun 1942—Oct 1942)
 AH781; AH831; AH863; AH930; AH946; AK181
North American Mustang I (Sep 1942—Dec 1942)
 AG374; AG441; AG538; AG545; AG579; AM110; AM184
Short Stirling III (Sep 1944— 1944)
 LJ541, 6Y:N; LJ559, 6Y:R; LJ567, 6Y:S; LJ617, 6Y:K; LJ659, 6Y:F; PW259, 6Y:A
Handley Page Halifax IIIA (1944—Jul 1945)
 LK875, 6Y:C; LW471, 6Y:H; MZ491, 6Y:V; MZ971, 6Y:E; NA109, 6Y:S; NA674, 6Y:Q; NA690,6Y:Q; PN192, 6Y:Q; PN372, 6Y:K

Commanding Officers

W/Cdr P. Hadfield	Jun 1942—Dec 1942
W/Cdr M. W. Renault	Sep 1944—Jul 1945

Aircraft Insignia

No information is available as to the markings carried by No. 171 Squadron in the Army co-operation role from June to December, 1942. Whilst flying with 100 Group from North Creake its Stirlings and Halifaxes carried the code letter combination '6Y'.

No. 172 SQUADRON

BADGE
A gannet volant in front of a tower

MOTTO
'Insidiantibus insidiamur'
('We ambush the ambushers')

On 18 March, 1942 No. 1417 Flight formed at Chivenor, to operate the Leigh Light against submarines, and it was expanded to squadron strength and re-numbered No. 172 Squadron of 4 April, 1942. It was equipped with Wellington VIIIs and began operations on 2 June flying night anti-submarine patrols. On its first night S/Ldr Greswell in ES986 F homed on one U-boat with the Leigh Light and straddled it with four depth-charges and then went on to machine-gun two others. Before the month was out two more attacks had been made. In July 55 operational sorties were flown in which three U-boats were attacked and P/O Dixon's crew had a running fight with two Arado Ar 196s – one was shot down in flames but two of the Wellington's crew were mortally wounded.

This was the pattern of operations for 1942; a detachment was sent to Wick for duty in northern waters and in September this detachment became No. 179 Squadron. Sortie level was about 50 per month and attacks averaged about two a month. By the end of the year the rate had increased to 90 sorties and the Squadron was using its depth-charges to attack surface vessels as well; in November four destroyers, nine motor vessels and two U-boats were targets for No. 172's attacks.

The better-equipped Wellington XII came in February, 1943 and the following month 119 sorties were flown resulting in seven attacks on U-boats with definite results in three attacks. Four aircraft went to Malta in April to fly similar sorties there and it was a busy month with twelve attacks, the one by P/O Stembridge's crew being confirmed as sunk. Enemy night-fighter activity was also increasing and two Wellingtons failed to return. The U-boats, too, were fighting back: on 24 July F/O Jennings' crew in H/172 attacked a U-boat which fired back causing the aircraft to blow up, the rear gunner alone escaping. Mk. XIV Wellingtons came in August and for a while losses increased. In October a detachment went to Gibraltar for operations there; sorties continued around the 100 mark each month and losses about two crews a month.

A detachment was also flying from the Azores from December until April, 1944. Around this time and onwards the Squadron was also operating against E-boats as the priority was to bottle the Channel to enemy shipping for the invasion fleets. For this task the Squadron also flew *Armed Rovers*, looking for any enemy shipping. As the Allied forces moved eastwards across Europe the Squadron's task turned again to the Atlantic U-boats but sightings dropped off and in early 1945 only about one every other month came up. The last attack on a U-boat took place as late as 11 May, 1945 but by them most of the Squadron's patrols were to round up surrendering submarines. With the war in Europe over No. 172 Squadron was quickly disbanded at Limavady on 4 June, 1945.

Bases etc.
Formed at Chivenor on 4 April, 1942 by re-numbering No. 1417 Flight.

Chivenor, det. Wick, Luqa,	
Gibraltar, Lagens	Apr 1942—Sep 1944
Limavady	Sep 1944—Jun 1945
Disbanded at Limavady on 4 June, 1945.	

Main Equipment
Vickers Wellington VIII (Apr 1942—Feb 1943)
W5733, A; BB503, D; ES986, F; HF828, C; HX396, J; HX599, J; HX653, L; LA998, F; LB114, K; LB216, W

Vickers Wellington XII (Feb 1943—Sep 1943)
MP505, B; MP515, N; MP538, H; MP590, Z; MP624, R; MP630, H

Vickers Wellington XIV (Aug 1943—Jun 1945)
HF135, 1:N; HF183, 1:D; HF197, 1:D; HF276, 1:O; HF285, 1:R; HF363, 1:Q; HF422, 1:U, later OG:U; MP791, 1:Q; MP813, 1:K; MF451, OG:J; NB800, OG:Z; NB804, OG:M; NB837, OG:V; NB870, OG:L; NC611, OG:N

Commanding Officers

W/Cdr J. B. Russell	Apr 1942—Oct 1942
W/Cdr J. B. Brolly	Oct 1942—Mar 1943
W/Cdr R. G. Musson	Mar 1943—Aug 1943
W/Cdr E. G. Palmer	Aug 1943—May 1944
W/Cdr K. Petrie	May 1944—Jun 1944
W/Cdr S. R. Ramsay Smith	Jun 1944—Apr 1945
W/Cdr C. E. Payne	Apr 1945—Jun 1954

Aircraft Insignia
No. 172 Squadron's Wellingtons originally carried the code letters 'WN' 1942–43. From 1943 to 1944 the numeral '1' denoted the Squadron but in the summer of 1944 this was replaced by the code combination 'OG'.

No. 179 SQUADRON

BADGE
In front of a harpoon, a lantern
MOTTO
'Delentem deleo'
('I destroy the destroyer')

The Squadron was formed at Wick on 1 September, 1942 from a detached flight of No. 172 Squadron equipped with Wellington VIIIs. It was immediately operational on anti-submarine patrols in northern waters. In October two U-boat attacks were made and in November the Squadron ceased operations on 16th to move to Gibraltar but not before one crew had ditched and another been shot down by a trawler.

At Gibraltar it flew intensive A/S sweeps, attempting to bottle the western end of the Mediterranean to submarines. In December it added daylight operations to its night Leigh Light patrols and flew 106 sorties. In that month No. 179 made fourteen U-boat attacks (one confirmed damaged) for the loss of four aircraft and three crews.

This intensity was continued in 1943 for there were many U-boats seeking the convoys supporting the North African landings. Slowly the pattern changed to convoy escorts along the North African coast and into the Atlantic and by the spring there were few sightings. In May the Squadron began A/S patrols to and from Chivenor, covering the Bay of Biscay, and in July the Squadron's first U-boat confirmed destroyed went to F/O E. J. Fisher's crew.

August saw Wellington XIVs in service and sightings increased dramatically, with ten attacks made in September for the loss of two crews. Intensity increased also with 129 sorties flown in October resulting in six attacks in which one U-boat was confirmed sunk. The next month the Squadron extended its range with a detachment in the Azores, continuing the same tasks into 1944.

In April, 1944 the Squadron returned to the UK and concentrated on Biscay patrols; then, in June, flew 110 *Rover* patrols in the Western Channel. They maintained 'Box' patrols in certain areas and attacked every ship in the box; other aircraft flew opportunity *Rovers* – five U-boats were sighted, three attacked and three aircraft lost. This work was continued in July with less action, but in August four attacks were made out of 100 patrols. After this the Squadron moved once more and returned to Atlantic anti-submarine patrols with little action. In November, 1944 the Squadron became the first unit to re-equip with the Warwick for anti-submarine work, cutting down on the intensity of operations. The first Warwick attack took place on 24 February when F/Lt Brownsill's crew achieved a prob-

ably destroyed U-boat. No further action came No. 179's way and after the war it flew permanent *Navex* patrols and experimented with the RN on new tactics for A/S warfare. It also flew some freight sorties for the Navy to Malta and Iceland in November. A rare opportunity came to F/Lt Potter's crew in December when, flying on Operation Deadlight he was able to drop live depth-charges on a U-boat and sink it.

In 1946 the Squadron was divided into Nos. 179X and 179Y Squadrons, the former converting to Lancaster ASR.3s. The two units continued until June when No. 179Y was re-numbered 210 Squadron. No. 179X continued until 30 September, 1946 when it, too, was disbanded into No. 210 Squadron at St. Eval.

Bases etc.
Formed from a detached Flight of 172 Squadron at Wick on 1 September, 1942.

Wick	Sep 1942—Nov 1942
Gibraltar, det. Agadir, Lagens	Nov 1942—Apr 1944
Predannack	Apr 1944—Sep 1944
Chivenor	Sep 1944—Sep 1944
Benbecula	Sep 1944—Oct 1944
Chivenor	Oct 1944—Nov 1944
St. Eval, det. Thorney Island	Nov 1944—Sep 1946
Disbanded at St. Eval 30 September, 1946 by re-numbering as No. 210 Squadron.	

Main Equipment
Vickers Wellington VIII (Sep 1942—Aug 1943)
ES986, F; HX379, A; HX444, K; HX504, N; HX531, A; HX629, Q; HX776, B; LA976, R; LB145; XLB190, K

Vickers Wellington XIV (Aug 1943—Nov 1944)
HF132, A; HF140, X; MP720; MP739

Vickers Warwick V (Nov 1944—Apr 1946)
LM780, OZ:N; LM791; LM818; PN708; PN722, OZ:N; PN746; PN800; PN811, OZ:V

Avro Lancaster ASR.3 (Feb 1946—Jun 1946)
RE115, OZ:T; RF292, OZ:Y; RF307, OZ:W

Commanding Officers

W/Cdr A. N. Combe, AFC	Sep 1942—Jun 1943
W/Cdr J. H. Gresswell, DSO, DFC	Jul 1943—Mar 1944
W/Cdr R. R. Russell	Mar 1944—Jan 1945
W/Cdr P. H. Alington, DFC	Jan 1945—Dec 1945
W/Cdr L. M. Moore	Dec 1945—Feb 1946
179X: S/Ldr A. W. Hornby	Feb 1946—Sep 1946
179Y: S/Ldr A. E. Henderson	Feb 1946—Jun 1946

Aircraft Insignia
It is not known what, if any, markings were carried by No. 179 Squadron from September, 1942 to mid-1944. From that time onwards the Squadron used the code letters 'OZ'.

No. 187 SQUADRON

BADGE
A buzzard volant carrying in its claws a propeller

MOTTO
'Versatile'

The first No. 187 Squadron flew only in a training role in World War I, forming on 1 April, 1918 at East Retford and disbanding by the end of the year. No. 187 re-formed at Merryfield on 1 February, 1945 from Transport Command's Halifax Development Flight but within a month had re-equipped with Dakotas.

Its task with these was to fly trooping flights to India, the schedule requiring 45 trips per month. These began on 26 April when six Dakotas were despatched to Poona. By June the target was reached, 986 troops being flown out and 916 back. When hostilities ceased the pressure was even greater with POWs coming home and troops for demobilisation. On 1 February, 1946 the Squadron suffered its first fatality when F/Lt Knowles crashed at Le Mans. The following month the Squadron was also given a Continental route (Base–Bückeburg–Evere–Base) on which 53 sorties were flown in the month. By May all its flying was to Continental Europe but in July it was detached to Italy to fly Balkan routes for a while. However, in November it was disbanded by re-numbering as No. 53 Squadron at Netheravon on the 1st.

On 1 February, 1953 No. 187 re-appeared, being re-formed from No. 2 Home Ferry Unit at Aston Down. Its task was now to ferry aircraft around the UK and Germany and it had a small fleet of Ansons, Varsity and Valettas to carry trooping crews. It was disbanded again on 2 September, 1957.

Bases etc.

Re-formed as a transport squadron at Merryfield on 1 February, 1945.

Merryfield, det. Almaza	Feb 1945—Sep 1945
Membury, det. Almaza, Bari, Schwechat	Sep 1945—Oct 1946
Netheravon	Oct 1946—Nov 1946

Disbanded at Netheravon on 1 November, 1946 by re-numbering as No. 53 Squadron. Re-formed at Aston Down on 1 February, 1953 by re-naming No. 2 Home Ferry Unit.

Aston Down	Feb 1953—Sep 1957

Disbanded at Aston Down on 2 September, 1957.

Main Equipment

Handley Page Halifax III (Feb 1945—Apr 1945)
No serial numbers known
Douglas Dakota IV (Mar 1945—Nov 1946)
KJ906; KJ966; KJ971; KK193, PU:F; KN286, PU:A; KN292, PU:H; KN381, PU:G; KN395, PU:J; KN423, PU:K; KN499, PU:A; KN506, PU:L; KN517, PU:Y; KN701, PU:N
Avro Anson C.19 Srs. 2 (Feb 1953—Sep 1957)
VM388
Vickers Valetta C.1 (Feb 1953—Sep 1957)
VW202, C; VW829
Vickers Varsity T.1 (Feb 1953—Sep 1957)
WL682

Commanding Officers

W/Cdr R. I. Alexander, DFC	Feb 1945—Sep 1945
W/Cdr V. G. Daw, DFC, AFC	Sep 1945—Mar 1946
W/Cdr P. Fleming	Mar 1946—Nov 1946

Aircraft Insignia

The Dakotas carried the code letters 'PU' from 1945 to 1946. As far as is known no markings were carried during the 1953/1957 ferry period.

No. 190 SQUADRON

BADGE
A cloak charged with a double-headed eagle displayed

MOTTO
'Ex tenebris'
('Through darkness')

In World War I the Squadron served as a night-flying training unit at Rochfield from 24 October, 1917 until disbanding at Newmarket in January 1919.

No. 190 re-formed as part of Coastal Command at Sullom Voe, Shetlands, on 1 March, 1943 using surplus Catalinas of No. 210 Squadron. It immediately began operations and before the month was out had sunk its first U-boat when P/O J. Fish's crew in FP125 M made two attacks and sank a submarine despite being damaged by AA fire. The following month it became fully operational, flying 49 sorties, including ice recces and Russian convoy escorts; four U-boats were attacked and one aircraft landed and picked up eight survivors of a No. 206 Squadron crew. Most of the time was spent on Operation Locomotive (trips to Grasnaya to cover Russian convoys) but No. 190 Squadron also operated to Iceland and flew cover to Operation Gearbox, the Spitzbergen raid. This continued until the end of 1943 when the Squadron was again disbanded on 31 December.

On 5 January, 1944 it re-formed in 38 Group Transport Command at Leicester East. It was equipped with Stirling IVs and worked up in the glider-towing and paratroop roles. In April it began operational flying with twenty sorties dropping supplies to the SOE in France. Its main role, however, was for the invasion of France and so on the night of the 5 June twenty-three of the Squadron aircraft carried 426 paratroops to Caen. Only one aircraft missed the DZ and brought its load home. The next evening eight-een aircraft towed Horsas to a DZ in France. After this it returned to airborne supply drops, both to the troops and to the SOE once more.

This became the pattern for July and August with over 100 sorties a month, August's total being 199. These flights continued in September, being interrupted by Operation Market, the fateful Arnhem drop. On 17th twenty-one aircraft towed Horsas there, three being lost en route. On 19th re-supply drops were begun amidst fierce Flak, ten aircraft being destroyed in four days after which the Squadron reverted to SOE sorties.

In October No. 190 Squadron was occupied in towing Horsas out to Italy but for the next few months it was all SOE operations interspersed with tactical bombing on Gee. March, 1945 saw the next big airborne operation, the crossing of the Rhine. The Squadron's contribution was thirty aircraft towing Horsas without loss. The following month No. 190 took part in Operation Amherst (dropping paratroops into Holland to disorganise German traffic); it was also flying ASR sorties at this time by day. As the war drew to a close it re-equipped with Halifaxes and then flew Stirlings for the last time on Operation Doomsday (1st Airborne Division to Oslo). It remained in Transport Command on freighting schedules within Europe for the rest of 1945, disbanding at Great Dunmow on 28 December, 1945.

Bases etc.

Re-formed at Sullom Voe 1 March, 1943.

Sullom Voe	Mar 1943—Dec 1943

Disbanded at Sullom Voe 31 December, 1943. Re-formed in the transport role at Leicester East on 5 January, 1944.

Leicester East	Jan 1944—Mar 1944
Fairford	Mar 1944—Oct 1944
Great Dunmow	Oct 1944—Dec 1945

Disbanded at Great Dunmow on 28 December, 1945.

Main Equipment

Consolidated Catalina IB (Jan 1943—Dec 1943)
FP102, L; FP115, Z; FP125, M; FP182, R; FP222, P; FP280, U; FP308, Y; FP311, T
Consolidated Catalina IV (Oct 1943—Dec 1943)
JX210, U; JX222, W
Short Stirling IV (Jan 1944—May 1945)
EE962, D; EF244, S; EF316, L; LJ818, X; LJ898, M; LJ936, N; LJ997, T; LK196, B; LK276, Y; LK298, A1; LK433, E; LK566, G; PW257, Z; TS265, O
Handley Page Halifax III (May 1945—Dec 1945)
LW385, L9:H; MZ558, G5:Y; MZ650, L9:M; MZ976, V; NA135, G5:T; NA139, L9:J
Handley Page Halifax VII (May 1945—Dec 1945)
NA343, L9:B; NA400, L9:K; NA461, L9:O; NA517, L9:E; NE628, L9:L; NA696, G5:P; PN233, G5:X; PN286, L9:D; PP341, L9:B

Commanding Officers

W/Cdr P. H. Alington, DFC	Mar 1943	—Dec 1943
W/Cdr G. E. Harrison	Jan 1944	—Sep 1944
W/Cdr R. H. Bunker, DSO, DFC and Bar	Oct 1944	—Apr 1945
W/Cdr G. H. Briggs, DFC	Apr 1945	—Jul 1945
W/Cdr L. C. Bartram	Jul 1945	—Dec 1945

Aircraft Insignia

It is almost certain that no squadron identity insignia was carried on the Catalinas. On the Stirlings and Halifaxes two sets of code letters were used, 'G5' and 'L9'; on the Stirlings listed above it is not known which were 'G5' and which 'L9' so only the aircraft letters have been quoted.

No. 191 SQUADRON

BADGE
A dolphin

MOTTO
'Vidi, vici'
('I saw, I conquered')

In World War I No. 191 Squadron served as a non-operational night training unit at Marham, Upwood and Bury St. Edmunds between 6 November, 1917 and January, 1919. No. 191 re-formed as a flying-boat squadron at Korangi Creek on 13 May, 1943 equipped with Catalinas. Eight days later it flew its first operation, a convoy escort and this began a monotonous existence flying over the Indian Ocean with very little action.

In two years of maritime reconnaissance its highest monthly sortie total was 38, in March, 1944 and it never located any submarines although one ship was torpedoed in a convoy the squadron was escorting in December, 1943. As well as the usual A/S sweeps and convoy escorts it also flew Met flights and ASR sorties and on one of these in April, 1945 it found some Liberator survivors, landed and picked them up. It was disbanded at Koggala on 15 June, 1945.

Bases etc.

Re-formed at Korangi Creek 13 May, 1943		
Korangi Creek, det. Cochin, Redhills	May 1943	—Nov 1944
Redhills, det. Korangi, Chittagong	Nov 1944	—Apr 1945
Koggala	Apr 1945	—Jun 1945
Disbanded at Koggala on 15 June, 1945.		

Main Equipment

Consolidated Catalina IB (May 1943—Jun 1945)
FP109, V; FP117, U; FP230, T; FP298, Z; FP307, V; FP320, X
Consolidated Catalina IVB (May 1944—Jun 1945)
JX270, Q; JX296, X; JX310, V; JX330, U; JX355, T; JX374, Z

Commanding Officers

W/Cdr K. E. Cornabe	May 1943	—Oct 1944
W/Cdr R. A. Phillips	Oct 1944	—Apr 1945
W/Cdr A. F. Johnson, DFC	Apr 1945	—Jun 1945

Aircraft Insignia

As far as is known no squadron insignia was carried on the Catalinas.

No. 192 SQUADRON

BADGE
In front of a flash of lightning an owl's head affrontee

MOTTO
'Dare to discover'

The Squadron was first formed at Gainsborough on 5 September, 1917 to serve in a night training role from Newmarket where it remained until disbandment in December, 1918.

No. 192 re-formed at Gransden Lodge on 4 January, 1943 from No. 1474 Flight with Wellingtons and Mosquitoes. At first it was non-operational to re-equip with Halifaxes but on 26 January resumed operations. These consisted of exploratory flights over enemy territory to identify enemy radars and establish the wavelengths used. In February a detachment went to the Mediterranean for similar duties. By March the aircraft were flying along the Norwegian, French, Spanish, Dutch and Danish coasts and inland as far as Berlin. In May a detachment went to work with Coastal Command, operating over Biscay and the Western Approaches. By mid-summer over 50 sorties a month were being flown of which three aircraft were lost (all over Biscay).

In 1944 the Squadron began flying its sorties in co-operation with bomber raids over Germany but the main task was still to keep a check on advances in enemy radar so that the other 100 Group squadrons could use the information in their jamming sorties. In May, 1944 a detachment went to Ford and flew special sorties along the line of the North Downs during the nights of the invasion of France; sortie rate reached its peak in July, 1944 with 153 trips. In September two USAAF P-38 Lightnings were attached and flew twenty-one of the 196 sorties flown; in October the work was concentrated on locating signals for enemy missiles investigating *Egon* during actual bombing raids, and *Knickebein* and *Benito* radio guidance systems. The last Wellington operation was flown on 7 January but the intensity of operations continued until the end of April, 1945 when the collapse of the Reich brought 192 Squadron's work to an end. It was disbanded at Foulsham on 22 August, 1945, being the basis of the newly-formed Central Signals Establishment.

On 15 July, 1951 it was re-formed as part of that Establishment at Watton for operational signals research and equipped with Lincolns, Canberras and Washingtons. It served actively in this role until 1958, being re-numbered 51 Squadron on 21 August.

Bases etc.

Formed from No. 1474 Flight at Gransden Lodge on 4 January, 1943.

Gransden Lodge	Jan 1943—Apr 1943
Feltwell, det. Chivenor, Lossiemouth, Davidstow Moor	Apr 1943—Nov 1943
Foulsham, det. Ford, Lossiemouth	Nov 1943—Aug 1945

Disbanded at Foulsham on 22 August, 1945. Re-formed at Watton on 15 July, 1951.

Watton	Jul 1951—Aug 1958

Disbanded by re-numbering as No. 51 Squadron at Watton on 21 August, 1958.

Main Equipment

Vickers Wellington IC (Jan 1943—Feb 1943)
N2772, DT:E; R1797; Z1162; AD590; AD600; HF837
Vickers Wellington III (Jan 1943— 1943)
X3566
Vickers Wellington X (Jan 1943—Jan 1945)
HE243, DT:K; HE380, DT:J; HE472, DT:P; HE826, DT:D;
HE857, DT:F; HZ415, DT:A2; LN172, DT:J; LN398, DT:A;
LN789, DT:C; LP156, DT:D; LP345, DT:G; NC704, DT:A
de Havilland Mosquito IV (Jan 1943—Aug 1945)
DZ376, DT:M; DZ410, DT:K; DZ491, DT:N; DZ590, DT:I;
DZ617, DT:O
Handley Page Halifax II (Jan 1943—Jul 1943)
DT735; DT737

Handley Page Halifax V (Jul 1943—Feb 1944)
DK244, DT:Q; DK246, DT:R; LL132, DT:Q
Handley Page Halifax III (Feb 1944—Aug 1945)
LK780, DT:X; LW613, DT:W; LW626, DT:V; MZ358, DT:F;
MZ449, DT:Y; MZ564, DT:X; MZ717, DT:O; MZ806, DT:R;
MZ929, DT:X; NA242, DT:D; NP970, DT:T; NR187, DT:U
Lockheed P-38L Lightning (Sep 1944—Mar 1945)
44-23156
de Havilland Mosquito XVI (Mar 1945—Aug 1945)
NS776, DT:I; NS797, DT:N; NS816, DT:O; RF974, DT:J
Avro Lincoln B.2 (1952—Aug 1958)
SS715, 53; SX980, 54; WD130, 61
Boeing Washington B.1 (1952— 1954)
WZ966, 55; WZ967, 56; WZ968, 57
English Electric Canberra B.2 (1952—Aug 1958)

Commanding Officers

W/Cdr C. D. V. Willis, DFC	Jan 1943—Mar 1944
W/Cdr E. P. M. Fernbank, DFC	Mar 1944—Jun 1944
W/Cdr D. W. Donaldson, DSO, DFC	Jun 1944—Aug 1945

Aircraft Insignia

During World War II the Squadron's aircraft carried the code letter combination 'DT' on its aircraft. During the fifties the Squadron's aircraft carried no specific insignia.

No. 194 SQUADRON

BADGE
A Malayan kris with dragonfly superimposed

MOTTO
'Surrigere colligere'
('To arise and to pick up')

The badge and motto signify the Squadron's being the first tactical helicopter unit in action with the RAF (with Dragonfly helicopters) and the kris relates to the Squadron's Far Eastern service.

The Squadron formed at Lahore on 13 October, 1942 to fly Hudsons on internal communications in India, most of the personnel coming from No. 31 Squadron. The initial schedule flight was made on 26 November when FR411 flew to Colombo in Ceylon and back. The following month runs to Cairo and Chittagong were begun. However in February, 1943 a detachment was sent to Tezpur for more active service which entailed supply-dropping in the Dinjan-Tiddim area. The Hudsons were not the best of aircraft for this duty and in June the Squadron concentrated on the routes previously flown by Indian National Airlines; this task was flown for three months.

However, the supply of Dakotas was now improving in India and so No. 194 re-equipped in June. By September it had been re-classified as an Airborne Forces Squadron and practised the role assiduously, going up to the front line in Burma in January 1944. Here at first it flew freight into Agartala but when the Japanese offensive opened up in February it began night supply drops into the Arakan flying 291 sorties that month. This was small compared with the next two months – in March, 1944 the Squadron flew 436 sorties dropping two brigades two hundred miles behind the Japanese lines and then moved 123 Brigade into beleagured Imphal. This record was beaten in April with the Squadron's Dakotas supply-dropping intensively during the Siege of Imphal, moving whole fighter squadrons in, flying casualty evacuation sorties and losing only three aircraft in 452 sorties. In May the crews began rotational rests, being augmented by crews from the Wellington squadrons to maintain intensive sorties into Imphal. Most of these sorties were short-range trips and so the Squadron mounted the total of 941

sorties in June, 1944 replenishing Imphal in particular and the Burmese forces generally. This was maintained until the end of August when 'The Friendly Firm', as 194 had become known, were taken off operations for three months rest.

At the turn of the year the Squadron was back to the same operational area, flying about 40 sorties a day to dropping zones in the hills. In January, 1945 it flew 3,393 operational hours, carrying 8,036,844 lbs of supplies and evacuated 529 casualties. This was all around Imphal but as the year wore on it turned its activities more to Meiktela and supporting the break-out there and by May it was fully involved in supporting Operation Dracula (the attack on Rangoon). In this area records were again broken, sorties going up to 1,396 in July, although now there was not the fear of enemy opposition. During 1945 it had also been equipped with a Flight of Stinson Sentinels for flying in and out of small jungle strips. By mid-August operations ceased and the Squadron turned its attention to flying routes again, principally in and out of Bangkok, and flying POWs on their way home. There were many transport tasks required in the Far East with the war over and No. 194 was busily occupied until February, 1946 when it was disbanded, on 15th, at Mingaladon.

It re-formed on 1 February, 1953 by expanding the Far East Casualty Evacuation Flight. This had been formed earlier with Westland Dragonfly helicopters and had operated these into and out of jungle clearings for quick removal of wounded men. This unit was now combined with a Fleet Air Arm Squadron, No. 848 to form the first operational helicopter Wing, No. 303, which moved up to Kuala Lumpur in May. The operational role now expanded; not simply was it a casevac unit, it now developed tactical troop movement and Tac/R operations and rescue missions where necessary. As the Malayan emergency was on at the time the Squadron was very much involved with the forces tackling the Communists. One of the tasks evolved was an elementary form of defoliation, spraying trioxene and dieselene on the enemy crops.

The Dragonfly was a very basic helicopter and in 1954 it began to be replaced by the Bristol Sycamore which was an improvement. The task continued at high pressure and by November, 1954 the Squadron had carried 4,213 passengers of which 675 were casevacs and carried or dropped 84,524 lbs of freight. But increasingly unserviceability and lack of spares was hampering the operations.

The emergency slowly ran down and No. 194 now began providing a flying doctor service in its operational area. More and more the Squadron was flying for the Police Field Force flying in and out of their jungle forts, a task more akin to the original design of the Sycamore. By October, 1958 serviceability meant there were only one or two Sycamores available each day. The type had already suffered problems and in February, 1959 194 had two fatal accidents in two months; on 27 April there was yet another Sycamore crash and they were all grounded. As a result the Squadron was disbanded into the remnant of 155 Squadron on 3 June to form 110 Squadron.

Bases etc.

Formed at Lahore on 13 October, 1942.

Lahore, det. Dum Dum, Tezpur	Oct 1942—Feb 1943	
Palam	Feb 1943—Sep 1943	
Basal, det. Chalala	Sep 1943—Feb 1944	
Agartala, det. Tulihal, Dergaon, Imphal	Feb 1944—Aug 1944	
Imphal	Aug 1944—Sep 1944	
Basal	Sep 1944—Dec 1944	
Agartala	Dec 1944—Dec 1944	
Imphal, det. Kangla	Dec 1944—Mar 1945	
Akyab, det. Wangjin, Mawnvbyin, Meiktela	Mar 1945—Aug 1945	
Mingaladon	Aug 1945—Feb 1946	

Disbanded at Mingaladon on 15 February, 1946. Re-formed from the Far East Casualty Evacuation Flight at Sembawang on 1 February, 1953.

Sembawang	Feb 1953—Mar 1953	
Kuala Lumpur	Mar 1953—Jun 1959	

Disbanded 3 June, 1953 by merging with 155 Squadron to form No. 110 Squadron.

Main Equipment

Lockheed Hudson VI (Oct 1942—Aug 1943)
EW946; EW972; FK411; FK457; FK493; FK504; FK549; FK584, W; FK605; FK642
Douglas Dakota I/III (May 1943—Feb 1946)
FD812, K; FD821, M; FD894, F; FD911, C; FL644, D; FL673, L; FZ582, C; FZ612, S; KG465, O; KG520, C; KG572, S; KG679, AA; KG702, T; KG764, AO
Douglas Dakota IV (Dec 1944—Feb 1946)
KJ854, M; KJ888, H; KJ916, Y; KJ950, B; KK114, F; KK175, Y; KN177, G; KN306, V; KN466, K; KN574, Q; KN601, P; KN627, Y; KN764, AB
Vultee-Stinson L-5 Sentinel (Jan 1945—   1945)
KJ373; KJ398; KJ405; KJ454; KJ457
Westland Dragonfly HC.2 (Feb 1953—   1955)
WF308; WF311; WF315
Bristol Sycamore HR.14 (1955—Jun 1959)
XE311, B; XE313; XE322; XF267; XJ381, P; XJ382

Commanding Officers

W/Cdr A. C. Pearson	Oct 1942—Jun 1944
W/Cdr R. T. Chisholm	Jun 1944—Dec 1944
W/Cdr R. C. Crawford	Dec 1944—Jun 1945
S/Ldr P. M. Bristow	Jun 1945—Aug 1945
W/Cdr D. Penman, DSO, DFC	Aug 1945—Feb 1946
S/Ldr G. R. G. Henderson, AFC	Feb 1953— 1955
S/Ldr C. R. Turner	1955— 1957
S/Ldr F. Barnes	1957—Jun 1959

Aircraft Insignia

As far as is known no squadron identity insignia was carried by any of No. 194 Squadron's aircraft.

No. 196 SQUADRON

BADGE
A mailed fist holding a dagger, hilt downwards
MOTTO
'Sic fidem servamus'
('Thus we keep faith')

No. 196 Squadron was formed at Driffield on 7 November, 1942 as a bomber unit. It became operational in February, 1943 flying raids at night against enemy territory on the Continent, converting to Stirlings in August and continuing thus until November, 1943.

No. 196 then moved to Leicester East to work up for transport duties. Changing to Stirling IVs it flew supply-dropping sorties to the SOE in France from February, 1944 onwards until June when it took part in Operation Overlord by sending twenty-three aircraft to Dropping Zone N in Normandy on 5 June with paratroops and containers; one aircraft failed to return. Within twenty-four hours seventeen squadron aircraft towed Horsas to Landing Zone W. Thereafter the Squadron flew re-supply drops to the troops in France for the rest of the month. For the next two months it stepped up its SOE supply-drops flying as many as 154 sorties in August. In September it was heavily involved in the Arnhem operation, dropping men of the 1st Airborne Division on 17th, then towing twenty-two Horsas there on the next day. This was followed by several days on re-supply flights through intense opposition losing one aircraft on 19th, five on 20th, two on 21st and thereafter one each day until 24th. In October it moved to East Anglia and resumed SOE sorties; it also flew ASR searches and began tactical bombing at night in the New Year. On 24 March thirty Squadron aircraft towed Horsas across the Rhine and then returned to supplying agents once more.

From April, 1945 onwards No. 196 began repatriating POWs for the next few months, also being involved in freighting to Denmark and Norway and later trooping on behalf of the RCAF. From September, 1945 onwards it began flying the Transport Command routes to India and on down to Burma and Singapore but by the end of the year it had changed its area of operation, now flying Continental mail runs every other day. This continued until 24 March, 1946 when the Squadron was disbanded at Shepherd's Grove.

Bases etc.

Formed at Driffield on 7 November, 1942 in the bomber role; transferred to Airborne duties at Leicester East on 1 December, 1943.

Leicester East	Dec 1943—Jan 1944
Tarrant Rushton	Jan 1944—Mar 1944
Keevil	Mar 1944—Oct 1944
Wethersfield	Oct 1944—Jan 1945
Shepherd's Grove	Jan 1945—Mar 1946

Disbanded at Shepherd's Grove 24 March, 1946.

Main Equipment

Short Stirling IV (Mar 1944—Mar 1946)
EF275, 7T:H; EF292, ZO:C; EF429, 7T:P; EF488, ZO:W; LJ643, 7T:J; LJ842, ZO:S; LJ926, ZO:K; LJ998; LK117, 7T:I; LK363, 7T:T; LK428, ZO:B; LK643, 7T:J; PW410, 7T:F; PW469, 7T:K
Short Stirling V (Jan 1946—Mar 1946)
PJ878, ZO:L; PJ939, 7T:C; PJ986, 7T:A; PK128, ZO:A; PK144, ZO:F

Commanding Officers

W/Cdr N. Alexander	Dec 1943—Aug 1944
W/Cdr M. W. L. Baker	Aug 1944—Feb 1945
W/Cdr R. T. F. Turner, DFC, MC	Feb 1945—Jan 1946
W/Cdr J. Blackburn, DSO, DFC	Jan 1946—Mar 1946

Aircraft Insignia

The Squadron's aircraft were distinguished by the code letter combinations 'ZO' and '7T'.
(See also *Bomber Squadrons of the RAF*, p. 190)

No. 200 SQUADRON

BADGE
In front of a fountain, a Pegasus

MOTTO
'*In loco parentis*'
('We act as guardians')

The original No. 200 Squadron was a night training unit at East Retford from 1 July, 1917 until disbandment towards the end of 1918.

It re-formed at Bircham Newton on 25 May, 1941 from personnel ex-No. 206 Squadron, received Hudsons, and on 12 June flew to Gibraltar from where it escorted 48 Hurricanes to Malta. Then it flew on to Gambia from where it began its intended role of anti-submarine and convoy cover in the South Atlantic. This task it faithfully carried out month by month seeing no sign of enemy shipping or submarines. With more aircraft in 1942 it built up the amount of flying, peaking at 172 sorties in September of that year. The Hudsons flew on for another year and were replaced by Liberators in July, 1943, giving a much greater range and endurance to the Squadron's operations. At last, in August, 1943, activity came the Squadron's way and its Liberators and Hudsons found and attacked three U-boats within the space of eight days. The first of these attacks, on 11th, was by P/O L. A. Trigg's crew in Liberator V BZ832 D; he made a particularly zealous attack and destroyed the U-boat but his aircraft was set on fire by the submarine and crashed into the sea fatally. He was awarded the VC for his gallant attack.

After this flurry of activity patrols returned to normal though at the turn of the year No. 200 Squadron was busily searching for a blockade runner without success. In March, 1944 operations ceased and the Squadron made one of the longest squadron moves by air during the war.

It set out from Yundum on 16 March and arrived at St. Thomas Mount, Ceylon thirteen days later. After a month settling in No. 200 became operational over the Indian Ocean, flying convoy escorts and anti-shipping patrols. Increasingly it added ASR sorties

and meteorological recce flights to its tasks and in December F/O R. A. Hobbs was fortunate to find a surfaced submarine which he depth-charged and damaged. The next month No. 200 ceased operations to train with the Leigh Light. This was of little significance for when it returned to operations it was to Met Flights, mine-ferrying sorties and special duties dropping supply containers to agents behind Japanese lines. On 1 May, 1945 it was disbanded by being re-numbered No. 8 Squadron at Jessore.

Bases etc.

Formed at Bircham Newton on 25 May, 1941

Bircham Newton	May 1941	Jun 1941
Gibraltar	Jun 1941	Jun 1941
Jeswang, det. Freetown, Takoradi, Port Etienne	Jun 1941	Mar 1943
Yundum, det. Rufisque	Mar 1943	Mar 1944
St. Thomas Mount, det. Cuttack, Siguriya	Mar 1944	Apr 1945
Jessore	Apr 1945	May 1945

Disbanded by re-numbering as No. 8 Squadron, Jessore, 1 May, 1945.

Main Equipment

Lockheed Hudson III/IV/VI (May 1941—Aug 1943)
V9157, N; V9179, G; V9220, O; AE568, V; AE575, H; AE615, X; AE630, D; AM953, Q; FH236, E; FH280, D; FH376, H; FH400, A; FK580, L1; FK639, H1
Consolidated Liberator V (Jul 1943—Sep 1944)
BZ823, E; BZ829, A; BZ831, C; BZ867, V; BZ884, N; BZ991, O
Consolidated Liberator VI (Feb 1944—May 1945)
EV818, P; EV863, U; EW317, P; EW321, M; KG847, M; KG854, L; KG912, G; KG990, Y; KH141, C; KH220, W

Commanding Officers

W/Cdr C. D. Candy	May 1941	Jul 1941
W/Cdr B. O. Dias	Jun 1941	Sep 1942
W/Cdr W. H. Ingle	Sep 1942	Sep 1943
W/Cdr J. B. P. Thomas	Sep 1943	Nov 1944
W/Cdr G. McKenzie	Nov 1944	May 1945

Aircraft Insignia

It is not known whether the Hudsons carried any identity markings to denote the Squadron; the Liberators, at least during their Ceylon period, did not.

No. 201 SQUADRON

BADGE
A seagull, wings elevated and addorsed

MOTTO
'*Hic et ubique*'
('Here and everywhere')

The badge had been used unofficially for a long time prior to the issue of an official one.

No. 201 Squadron originated in No. 1 Squadron, RNAS and was formed at Gosport in October, 1914, moving to Dunkirk in February, 1915. Initially flying in a recce role it soon became a fighter squadron and, operating with Vickers Gunbus, Moranes, Sopwith Triplanes and Camels, fought valiantly during World War I. During this period Sub Lt R. A. J. Warneford won the first aerial VC by shooting down Zeppelin *LZ.37.* on 6 June, 1915. After the war the Squadron returned to the UK and was disbanded at Lake Down on 31 December, 1919.

On 1 January, 1929 it re-formed by expanding No. 480 Flight at Calshot. This Flight was a GR flying-boat unit equipped with Supermarine Southamptons. It was attached to the Home Fleet and

exercised with them but also, once a year, went on a summer cruise, either around the UK or to the Baltic or Med. In 1936 Saro Londons replaced the Southampton, the routine remaining the same. These aircraft were still the backbone of the Squadron when it moved to its war station a month before war broke out in September, 1939, although No. 201 received three Stranraers for a month in September and also the first of its Sunderlands.

It was stationed in the Shetlands and flew patrols over the North Sea as far as Norway, searching for German surface-raiders and submarines. The Londons soldiered on until April, 1940 by which time two had been lost (one to enemy action). That month saw the Squadron off ops completing its conversion to Sunderlands. Now, flying from Invergordon, the Squadron ranged out over the North Atlantic on anti-sub work. In addition, the Sunderlands became involved in the Norwegian campaign, principally to reconnoitre the Far North, beyond the range of other aircraft, involving fourteen hour flights. The Squadron's first definite action came in January, 1941 when F/Lt Lindsey's crew in ZM:Y had a combat with a FW 200 Condor which subsequently ditched. At this time it was hampered by serviceability problems, having only one or two boats available each day. On 28 March F/Lt Alexander found a FW 200 attacking a motor ship and drove it off successfully. The following month 201 added Iceland ferry trips to its tasks. On 28 May F/Lt Vaughan in ZM:Z found a naval battle in progress in the Denmark Straights, seeing the battlecruiser HMS *Hood* blow up and then shadowing the *Bismarck* and *Prinz Eugen* until he had to return for lack of fuel. The following month two U-boats were found and attacked. In August F/Lt Fletcher in ZM:O was set on by Ju 88s and three days later F/O Evill's crew, in W3983, failed to return from a patrol.

In September the Squadron moved to N. Ireland but continued the same type of operation, cut down severely during the bad winter weather. This also was responsible for three fatal accidents. The work continued monotonously with little action seen although in April F/O Powell attacked a U-boat and in July F/O J. R. Traill's crew eas shot down by the convoy it was escorting; another crew was lost the next day.

Three U-boat attacks took place in March, 1943 then on 31 May F/Lt Hall and crew in ZM:R attacked and sank *U-440*, the Squadron's first confirmed U-boat. The end of the year was crowned by F/Lt Baveystock and crew finding the German raider *Alsterufer*, attacking it, then shadowing it whilst homing other aircraft on to it, one of which sank it. 1944 saw a move to Wales in March and pre-occupation with bottling up the Channel to protect the invasion fleets. Two U-boat attacks were made in June, one successful one by F/Lt Baveystock and one which caused the loss of S/Ldr Ruth and crew whilst in July F/Lt Walters' crew destroyed another U-boat and Baveystock scored his third on 18 August. After this there were no more attacks until November by which time the Squadron was back in Ireland. Thereafter action came fitfully up to the end of the war in Europe, the last submarine attack being on 6 May, 1945. It fell to the Squadron's lot to fly the last of Coastal Command's operational patrols in World War II on 3 June.

With the war over No. 201 returned to its pre-war Calshot base and training was the routine until July, 1948 when the Squadron was pressed into service on the Berlin Airlift, flying from Finkenwerder in Hamburg to Lake Havel in Berlin. Return loads comprised either manufactured goods or refugees. This lasted until December by which time sufficient transport aircraft were on the scene to enable 201 to return to its maritime duties. Cruises again became the peacetime drill and the Squadron went to the West Indies in 1951. Also that year the Squadron supported the British Greenland Expedition flying within 700 miles of the North Pole. For another six years the Squadron soldiered on with Sunderlands until on 28 February, 1957 it was disbanded at Pembroke Dock for the last time as a boat Squadron. Twenty months passed before the Squadron appeared again. Now it was a land-based maritime squadron, re-forming at St. Mawgan on 1 October, 1958 by re-numbering 220 Squadron equipped with Avro Shackleton MR.3 aircraft, this version being tricycle-undercarriage equipped. These provided a great endurance, graphically emphasised by No. 201 Squadron at the 1960 SBAC Display at Farnborough when an aircraft would take off at the beginning of each day's display and land at the beginning of the following day's display.

The Shackleton remained in service for twelve years, being continuously up-dated with new anti-submarine equipment, the Squadron joining the Kinloss Wing in 1965. Here it changed over, in 1970, to the Hawker Siddeley Nimrod MR.1 with which it has since been equipped and maintained its maritime recce role, principally checking on the Soviet ships moving in and out of the Atlantic.

Bases etc.

Re-formed at Calshot on 1 January, 1929 by re-numbering No. 480 Flight.

Calshot	Jan 1929—Sep 1938	
Invergordon	Sep 1938—Oct 1938	
Calshot	Oct 1938—Aug 1939	
Sullom Voe & Garths, Voe, det.Invergordon	Aug 1939—Sep 1941	
Lough Erne	Sep 1941—Mar 1944	
Pembroke Dock	Mar 1944—Nov 1944	
Castle Archdale	Nov 1944—Aug 1945	
Pembroke Dock	Aug 1945—Mar 1946	
Calshot	Mar 1946—Jan 1949	
Pembroke Dock	Jan 1949—Feb 1957	

Disbanded at Pembroke Dock 28 February, 1957. Re-formed at St. Mawgan on 1 October, 1958 by re-numbering No. 220 Squadron.

St. Mawgan	Oct 1958—Mar 1965	
Kinloss	Mar 1965—	

Main Equipment

Supermarine Southampton II (Jan 1929—Dec 1936)
N9900; S1038; S1039; S1043; S1058; S1122; S1125; S1129; S1151; S1160; S1228; S1233; S1249; S1301; S1464; S1643; S1649; K2965

Saro London I (Apr 1936—Jun 1938)
K5257, Y; K5259, W; K5260, X; K5261, U; K5262, Z; K5909, R

Saro London II (Jan 1938—Apr 1940)
K5260; K5261, U; K5911, G; K5912; L7038; L7040; L7043

Supermarine Stranraer (Sep 1939—Oct 1939)
K7289; K7294; K7302

Short Sunderland I (Apr 1940—Jan 1942)
L2168, ZM:Z; L5798, ZM:Z; L5800, ZM:S; L5805, ZM:Y; N6138, ZM:V; P9606, ZM:R; P9622, ZM:W; T9049, ZM:O; T9083, ZM:Q;

Short Sunderland II (May 1941—Mar 1944)
T9087, ZM:O; W3977, ZM:Q; W3981, ZM:V; W3997, ZM:S; W4002, ZM:U; W4018, ZM:Z

Short Sunderland III (Jan 1942—Jun 1945)
W6010, ZM:V; W6014, ZM:S; W6055, ZM:R; DD829, ZM:Z, later A; DD860, O; DP916, K; EJ137, ZM:T; EJ150 W, later NS:W; EK590, Y; JM666, ZM:Q; ML742, Q, later NS:Q; ML768 B, later NS:B; ML772, NS:S; ML813, NS:U; ML824, NS:Z; ML876, NS:O; ML882, NS:Y

Short Sunderland V (Feb 1945—Feb 1957)
ML824, NS:Z; NJ193, NS:L; NJ267, NS:P, later A:B; PP115, NS:C, later A:C; PP117 A:W, later 201:W; RN284, NS:C, later A:F, later 201:F; RN304, NS:L; SZ567, NS:B, later A:B; SZ577, NS:P; VB889, NS:C, later A:D

Avro Shackleton MR.3 (Oct 1958—Sep 1970)
WR977, 201:L, later O; WR979, 201N, later 201N:M; WR980, 201:0, later L; XF700, M; XF708, 201:0, later O; XF711, 201:L

Hawker Siddeley Nimrod MR.1 (Oct 1970—   )
(Operated as Wing aircraft)
XV238; XV240; XV246; XV250; XZ280; XZ282

Commanding Officers

S/Ldr D. G. Donald	Jan 1929—Nov 1929	
S/Ldr E. F. Turner	Jan 1930—Aug 1933	
S/Ldr C. G. Wigglesworth, AFC	Aug 1933—Apr 1935	
S/Ldr J. D. Breakey, DFC	Apr 1935—Sep 1937	
W/Cdr J. H. O. Jones	Sep 1937—Feb 1939	
W/Cdr C. H. Cahill, DFC, AFC	Feb 1939—Aug 1940	
W/Cdr C. S. Riccard	Aug 1940—Apr 1941	
W/Cdr W. G. Abrams	Apr 1941—Dec 1941	
W/Cdr J. L. Crosbie	Dec 1941—Aug 1942	
W/Cdr J. B. Burnett	Aug 1942—May 1943	
W/Cdr R. E. C. Van der Kiste, DSO	May 1943—Jul 1944	
W/Cdr K. R. Coates	Jul 1944—Feb 1945	
W/Cdr J. Barrett, DFC	Feb 1945—Aug 1945	
W/Cdr J. W. Louw	Aug 1945—Mar 1946	
W/Cdr W. H. Tremear	Mar 1946—May 1947	
W/Cdr J. L. Crosbie	May 1947—Sep 1947	
S/Ldr D. H. F. Horner	Sep 1947—Jan 1949	
S/Ldr R. C. L. Parkhouse	Jan 1949—Feb 1950	
S/Ldr H. A. S. Disney	Feb 1950—Dec 1950	
S/Ldr P. A. S. Rumbold	Dec 1950—Nov 1952	
S/Ldr R. A. N. McCready	Nov 1952—Jan 1955	
S/Ldr D. W. Bedford	Jan 1955—Feb 1957	
W/Cdr J. G. Roberts	Oct 1958—Aug 1959	
W/Cdr A. C. Davies	Aug 1959—Sep 1961	
W/Cdr R. B. Roache	Sep 1961—Jul 1963	
W/Cdr P. G. South	Jul 1963—Apr 1965	
W/Cdr W. S. Northcott	Mar 1965—Nov 1966	
W/Cdr N. Jones	Nov 1966—Aug 1968	
W/Cdr G. A. Chesworth	Aug 1968—Mar 1971	
W/Cdr J. B. Duxbury	Mar 1971—Oct 1971	
W/Cdr J. M. Alcock	Oct 1971—	
W/Cdr J. Morris	Aug 1975—Aug 1977	
W/Cdr P. M. Stean	Aug 1977—	

Aircraft Insignia

No Squadron identity insignia is believed to have been carried before 1938 when the code letters 'VQ' were allotted. These were changed to 'ZM' in September, 1939, dropped altogether in August, 1943; new letters NS were used from July, 1944 to 1951 when the single letter 'A' replaced them. This was retained until the late fifties when the Squadron number replaced it. This was carried on the Shackletons until they became Kinloss Wing aircraft late in the sixties. The Squadron badge was carried on the side of the Sunderlands' noses from 1946 onwards and the emblem on a shield on the fins of Shackletons. It has occasionally been reported on the Nimrods for specific occasions.

No. 202 SQUADRON

BADGE
A mallard alighting
MOTTO
'Semper vigilate'
('Be always vigilant')

The Squadron first formed, as No. 2 Squadron RNAS, on 17 October, 1914 at Eastchurch and served for two years on Home and Coastal Defence. In 1916 it became a bomber squadron in the Navy's complex at Dunkirk and flew bombing sorties on behalf of the Navy against coastal targets, eventually disbanding at Alquines on 22 January 1920.

After a short spell at Alexandria from 9 April, 1920 to 16 May, 1921 as a Fleet co-operation unit, No. 202 Squadron re-formed in an operational role once more on 1 January, 1929 when No. 481 Flight at Kalafrana, Malta, was re-numbered 202 Squadron. This Flight was equipped with Fairey IIID seaplanes. Its task was coastal reconnaissance which in effect meant sea search over the whole area around Malta. In 1930 Fairey IIIFs arrived enabling a greater range to be used and in 1931 the Squadron set out on its first cruise, to the Eastern Mediterranean. This was followed by a more ambitious expedition in 1932 as far as Khartoum. The Squadron also took part in ASR duties in the area, frequently for the Dornier Wal flying-boats of SANA airline. It had been intended from the outset that No. 202 should be a flying-boat squadron and this took place in 1935 when Supermarines Scapas replaced the IIIFs. These were immediately put on to operational patrols looking for Italian submarines as the Italian attack on Ethiopia had brought a state of tension in the Med. This had relaxed sufficiently by the end of 1936 to enable the Squadron to cruise down the West Coast of Africa looking for suitable flying-boat bases.

The second half of 1937 saw Saro Londons replacing the Scapas. With these the Squadron again flew operational patrols, this time armed with bombs, as the Spanish Civil War created tension in the Western Med. But there were now signs of the bigger conflict to come and No. 202 began commuting between Malta and Egypt, taking intelligence photos of Italian bases *en route*. In May, 1939 one Sunderland was received then sent to another Squadron; Londons had to suffice for a while. A week after war broke out in September the Squadron moved to Gibraltar and began convoy patrols, anti-sub searches and patrols to locate enemy shipping in neutral ports, using French ports as advanced landing bases. On 24 October Sgt Easton in K9683 landed to pick up survivors from a torpedoed ship but was then unable to take-off in the swell and had to be towed home by HMS *Douglas*; 65 sorties were flown that month.

All through 1940 the Squadron continued to maintain the security of the Straits of Gibraltar. This became a more difficult task with Italy entering the war and then France falling for now the southern shores of the Straits were no longer friendly territory. Several attacks were made on suspected U-boats without effect. In October Swordfishes were added to the Squadron's strength for the short-range Straits patrols enabling the Londons to range farther away. This was assisted early in 1941 by the re-equipment with Catalinas. By enabling longer patrols, these aircraft brought an immediate upsurge in action; in June three U-boats were attacked, one being subsequently destroyed by a destroyer the Catalina brought to the scene. One or two attacks now became the routine for the Squadron, which continued on into 1942. In May, 1942 F/Lt Bradley in AJ158 had a brush with Vichy French Dewoitine D.520 fighters and was brought down in the sea, the crew being rescued by a destroyer. Sunderlands joined the Squadron for two months in June and the Squadron was supplemented by aircraft and crews attached from UK Catalina squadrons with the build-up for the North African landings. This broke into intense activity in November, covering the huge incoming convoys and providing anti-shipping cover for the invasion beaches at Algiers. Three Catalinas were lost, one being shot down by a friendly convoy; altogether 80 sorties were flown by No. 202 that month.

There was a sudden flurry of U-boat activity in February, 1943, 202 making no fewer than six attacks in the month, one definite 'kill' going to F/Lt Sheardown in FP114. After this the Squadron entered a year of monotonous patrolling, 60 or 70 sorties a month with little or no enemy activity discernible. However in January, 1944 F/Lt Finch found a submarine and attacked it; then on 24 February he again found a U-boat and, with a US Navy Catalina, blew it up. Next target came in August when W/O Longden depth-charged another U-boat; the month after the Squadron left Gibraltar for the UK. Here it trained in use of the Leigh Light and began night patrols around the coasts (it was based in Ireland) looking for Schnorchel-equippped U-boats. It was not until April, 1945 that the Squadron made any attacks and then VE-Day brought the war to its end and the Squadron's disbandment which took place at Castle Archdale on 27 June, 1945.

In the next few months there began a wholesale re-numbering of RAF units to bring to life again the most famous units. So, on 1 October, 1946, No. 518 Squadron which was flying meteorological recce duties from Aldergrove in N. Ireland was re-numbered 202 Squadron. It was using Handley Page Halifaxes for this uninteresting and often uncomfortable task of flying out over the Atlantic in all weather making temperature, pressure and humidity recordings on a set pattern and at varying heights. Known as *Bismuth* flights, being their wartime code name, these were No. 202s staple duty from 1946 until 1964. In 1950 a specially equipped version of the Hastings came into service, the last Halifaxes departing in May, 1951 and the Hastings soldiered on with the task until the Squadron's duty was taken over by the Met satellites. It was disbanded at Aldergrove on 31 July, 1964.

Just over a month later the Squadron re-formed by re-numbering No. 228 Squadron on 1 September, 1964. This unit based at Leconfield, was equipped with Westland Whirlwind HAR.10s for SAR duties, with detached Flights at Acklington, Leuchars and Coltishall. Whilst primarily to rescue service airmen over the North Sea in fact it performed far more rescues of merchant shipping crews, holidaymakers and on occasion mountaineers and even farmers and shepherds during bad winter weather. At such times the Whirlwinds also flew food supplies to isolated farms and flocks. It was found though that many of the service airmen to be rescued were outside the limited range of the Whirlwind and from May, 1978, by which time the Squadron HQ had moved to Finningley, the Flights were progressively re-equipped with the Westland Sea King HAR.3. At the same time there was some shuffling of flights between 202 and 22 Squadron to maintain commonality of equipment and when finally fully equipped with Sea Kings No. 202 had Flights at Boulmer, Brawdy (in Wales), Coltishall and Lossiemouth.

Bases etc.

Re-formed at Kalafrana on 1 January, 1929, by re-numbering No. 481 Flight.

Kalafrana	Jan	1929—Sep 1938
Ras-el-Tin	Sep	1938—Oct 1938
Kalafrana	Oct	1938—Sep 1939
Gibraltar	Sep	1939—Sep 1944
Castle Archdale, det. Sullom Voe	Sep	1944—Jun 1945

Disbanded at Castle Archdale on 27 June, 1945. Re-formed at Aldergrove on 1 October, 1946 by re-numbering No. 518 Squadron.

Aldergrove	Oct	1946—Jul 1964

Disbanded at Aldergrove on 31 July, 1964. Re-formed at Leconfield on 1 September, 1964 by re-numbering No. 288 Squadron.

Leconfield, det. Acklington, Boulmer, Leuchars, Coltishall, Lossiemouth	Sep	1964—
Finningley, det. Boulmer, Brawdy, Coltishall, Lossiemouth		

Main Equipment

Fairey IIID (Jan 1929—Sep 1930)
N9571; N9730; N9777, 3; S1078
Fairey IIIF (Jul 1930—Aug 1935)
S1373, 2; S1381, 3; S1384, 2; S1386, 5; S1517, 4; S1804, 5; S1865

Vickers-Supermarine Scapa (May 1935—Dec 1937)
  K4191; K4193; K4196, 6; K4198; K4200; K7304
Saro London II (Sep 1937—Jun 1941)
  K5257; K7564, TQ:L; K5908; K5913; K6930; K6932, TQ:B;
  K9682, C; K9685; L7039; L7043
Fairey Swordfish I (Oct 1940—Jan 1942)
  K8354, TQ:D; L2807; L2808; L9769; L9770
Short Sunderland I, II, III (Jun 1942—Sep 1942)
  N9050; N6133, TQ:S; W6002, TQ:R; W4024, TQ:N; W4028, TQ:B;
  DV962, TQ:Q
Consolidated Catalina I, II (May 1941—Nov 1942)
  W8402, TQ:D; W8410, TQ:A; W8415, TQ:G; W8424, TQ:B;
  AH538, TQ:A; AH542, TQ:N; AH558, TQ:R; AH567, TQ:J;
  Z2147, TQ:L; AJ161, TQ:G
Consolidated Catalina IB (Sep 1942—Sep 1944)
  FP111, B; FP122, C; FP172, D; FP181, A; FP213, V; FP237, O;
  FP272, D
Consolidated Catalina IV (Oct 1943—Jun 1945)
  JX208, M; JX225, TJ:M; JX258, D; JX287, N; JX583, R; JX585, O
Handley Page Halifax Met. 6 (Oct 1946—May 1951)
  RG778, Y3:B; RG830, Y3:C; RG833, Y3:U; RG843, Y3:O;
  RG873, Y3:P; ST809, Y3:V, later A:V; ST818, Y3:A
Handley Page Hastings Met. 1 (Oct 1950—Jul 1964)
  TG504, C; TG512, Y3:G, later C; TG572; TG604;
  TG616; TG621, A:B; TG623, Y3:D, later A:D, later B; TG624, A
Westland Whirlwind HAR.10 (Sep 1964—Nov 1979)
  XD165; XD182; XJ414; XJ430; XJ437; XJ723; XJ729; XK969; XK990;
  XP299; XP344; XP347; XP352; XP395; XP404; XR483
Westland Sea King HAR.3 (May 1978—   )
  XZ586; XZ588; XZ593; XZ594; XZ599

Commanding Officers

S/Ldr C. Boumphrey, DFC	Jan 1929—	Jan 1930
S/Ldr R. H. Kershaw	Jan 1930—	Jul 1931
S/Ldr H. W. Evans	Jul 1931—	Sep 1932
S/Ldr A. H. Wann	Sep 1932—	May 1934
W/Cdr J. H. O. Jones	May 1934—	Dec 1935
W/Cdr E. F. Turner, AFC	Dec 1935—	Mar 1938
W/Cdr G. W. Bentley, DFC	Mar 1938—	Mar 1939
W/Cdr E. A. Blake, MM	Mar 1939—	Mar 1940
W/Cdr A. D. Rogers, AFC	Mar 1940—	Aug 1940
S/Ldr T. O. Horner	Aug 1940—	Mar 1941
W/Cdr L. F. Brown	Mar 1941—	Feb 1942
W/Cdr A. A. Case	Feb 1942—	Jan 1943
W/Cdr B. E. Dobb	Jan 1943—	Dec 1943
W/Cdr G. P. Harger, DFC	Dec 1943—	Nov 1944
W/Cdr D. S. Lindsay, DFC	Nov 1944—	Jun 1945
W/Cdr L. Coulson	Oct 1946—	Apr 1947
W/Cdr J. R. Armistead, DFC	Apr 1947—	Mar 1948
S/Ldr E. W. Deacon, DSO, DFC	Mar 1948—	Nov 1949
S/Ldr T. A. Cox, DSO, DFC	Nov 1949—	Jan 1951
S/Ldr F. Ellison, AFC	Jan 1951—	Mar 1953
S/Ldr G. T. Thain, DFC	Mar 1953—	Mar 1955
S/Ldr R. Wood, DFC	Mar 1955—	Mar 1957
S/Ldr C. A. Sullings, AFC	Mar 1957—	Mar 1959
S/Ldr K. J. Barrett	Mar 1959—	Mar 1961
S/Ldr M. J. Davis	Mar 1961—	Mar 1962
S/Ldr C. J. Petheram	Mar 1962—	Mar 1964
S/Ldr B. A. Spry	Mar 1964—	Jul 1964
S/Ldr G. Stafford	Sep 1964—	Oct 1965
S/Ldr D. E. Brett	Oct 1965—	May 1967
S/Ldr W. A. Gayer	May 1967—	Jul 1967
S/Ldr K. Henry	Jul 1967—	Jul 1969
S/Ldr P. T. Taylor, AFC	Jul 1969—	Aug 1971
S/Ldr R. G. Reekie	Aug 1971—	Jul 1973
S/Ldr I. H. R. Robins	Jul 1973—	Nov 1976
S/Ldr G. R. Spate	Nov 1976—	

Aircraft Insignia

On the Fairey IIIFs the Squadron's badge (unofficial) was carried on the sides of the engine cowlings at times. After this no markings were carried until the allotment of official code letters in 1938. The Squadron was given 'JU' but it is not known whether this was carried. On the outbreak of war this was changed to 'TQ' which was used until *ca* 1943. With the arrival of the Catalinas the code combination 'AX' was also carried and seemed to run concurrently with 'TQ'. In 1943 identity letters were dropped and not resumed until the Squadron was at Castle Archdale late in 1944 when the combination 'TJ' was used until disbandment. Upon re-formation the new No. 202 Squadron retained No. 518s code letters 'Y3' until 1951 when such letters were dropped from operational units. It then carried the single letter 'A' and later this too was dropped. In the mid-fifties the Squadron number was carried on a white disc at the top of the fin and in 1963 this was changed to carrying the Squadron's emblem on this position and the number in red, edged white, on the rear fuselage. With the Whirlwinds the badge was carried for a while on the fuselage side below the cockpit then in the seventies the mallard emblem was carried on a white disc on the tail rotor fin. This same emblem on a white disc is now carried on the fuselage sides of the Sea Kings just behind the pilots' cockpit.
(See also *Bomber Squadrons of the RAF*, p. 394)

No. 203 SQUADRON

BADGE
A winged sea-horse

MOTTO
'Occidens oriensque'
('East and West')

The sea-horse is prevalent in the Arabian Gulf where the Squadron was stationed for some years.

The origins of this Squadron go back to the first four Naval aviators trained to fly and established at the base at Eastchurch; the definitive No. 3 Squadron, RNAS, however formed at Dunkirk in June, 1916 as a fighter unit and served thus during World War I, being re-numbered No. 203 Squadron, RAF on 1 April, 1918. It was eventually disbanded at Scopwick on 21 January, 1920.

It re-formed at Leuchars in April, 1920, still with Sopwith Camels, and went to Constantinople on HMS *Argus* in August, 1922, equipped with Nieuport Nightjars but was disbanded on its return to Leuchars on 1 April, 1923.

On 1 January, 1929 No. 482 (General Reconnaissance) Flight at Cattewater, Plymouth, was re-numbered 203 Squadron. It was equipped with Supermarine Southampton IIs and on 28 February set out for its permanent overseas base, arriving at Basra on 14 March. Its task was principally to 'show the flag' to all the various sheikdoms in the Gulf area and to keep a good reconnaissance on all that was taking place. It also provided transport flights for some of the oil exploration teams in the area at the time. In October, 1929

the Squadron flew a cruise to Karachi and Hyderabad in India and repeated this five months later. In 1931 Short Rangoons replaced the Southamptons and on 29 June one of these, S1435, was on a bombing practice at 4,000 ft when all three engines failed. The pilot put it down on a lake in 15 inches of water, the aircraft sticking to the mud. The nearest anyone could get to it was 1½ miles as it was surrounded by bog so eventually the petrol was taken out in rubber dinghies and, when the wind was right, the Rangoon was flown out. This same aircraft moved to Lake Tiberias in October in case of need for the troubles in Cyprus. One of the tasks in 1932 was to look for suitable marine landing sites for the impending Imperial Airways mail flights. There was much engine trouble at the time and several of the long-distance flights were curtailed due to this.

However this did not stop three aircraft going to Melbourne in September, 1934 for the Centenary celebrations. The following year Singapore IIIs took over and 203 moved to Aden in September, 1935 due to the Ethiopian invasion by Mussolini. Here they flew submarine co-operation sorties and also transported mail. The return to Basra came in July, 1936 and for the next two years an annual cruise was flown to Singapore. In August, 1939 the Squadron moved to its war station at Aden and began anti-shipping patrols and escort work. Its time as a flying-boat squadron was now limited for in December its crews began converting to Blenheims and by February, 1940 it was flying its anti-shipping patrols with these. Its tasks were basically as maritime fighters but a bit of everything was carried out with fighter patrols, anti-submarine work and photo reconnaissance over East Africa and Abyssinia.

With Italy in the war the Squadron became very busy with convoy protection duties being stepped up and fighter patrols required over suitable ports. It also provided fighter escort for Nos. 8 and 39 Squadrons' bombing raids and managed to start a score of Italian aircraft destroyed or damaged. In September the Squadron was divided into A Flight fighter Blenheims and B Flight bombers; by the end of the year it flew 115 sorties in one month, principally on convoy patrols but also on recces.

With the New Year the accent on bombing raids increased, many Eritrean targets being attacked. The predominant sortie now was the armed recce, roaming over the land and sea attacking anything Italian. This was interrupted in April, 1941 when the Squadron was rushed to Crete where, for a week, it endeavoured to safeguard the convoys out of Greece. Then it retired to Egypt itself, with only six aircraft left. The next month it moved to Palestine with detachments along the pipeline for work with the armoured cars of the Jordan Frontier Force. It was also drawn into the Iraq campaign. This was followed by the war in Syria where it engaged in strafing enemy airfields. At Habbaniya the Squadron maintained fighter patrols and strafed enemy road transport. It continued to fight there until 29 May when it was moved back to the Canal Zone.

It now returned to its old maritime role, flying shipping recces between Crete and Libya. By July it was fully involved with a detachment in Cyprus covering the Aegean. Three U-boats and a motor vessel were bombed that month. Despite much engine trouble operations continued with several attacks on ships each month, culminating in P/O Van der Water sinking a U-boat with 250 lb bombs on 15 October. This continued until February, 1942, the Squadron being very pre-occupied with shadowing the Italian Battle Fleet in January.

In February, 1942 it was rested to form No. 459 Squadron and train it up. By the end of the month it was back in action using Hudsons and Marylands as well as the Blenheims. That summer one of its tasks was to escort formations of Hurricanes going to Malta for reinforcement, in addition to many shipping attacks; in the last ten days of May eight U-boats being bombed. By the end of the year operations had died down a little and the Squadron had concentrated on Martin Baltimores. For most of 1943 it maintained a constant stream of anti-shipping patrols, convoy escorts and ASR and PR sorties with very little action for the fighting had moved away from No. 203's area. In November, 1943 it came off operations and moved to India where it re-equipped with Wellington XIIIs and began anti-shipping work in the Indian Ocean. By March, 1944 it had worked up to 100 sorties a month but this was soon reduced as the submarine threat diminished until July when a ship was sunk and a submarine traced in the area. Eventually on 12th F/O McKay found the submarine and straddled it with depth-charges; no further sign of it was found.

By the end of 1944 the Squadron had converted to Liberators, flying patrols up the East Coast shipping lanes. In February, 1945 it moved to start shipping strikes in the Bay of Bengal and night anti-shipping sweeps became regular operations with various results, including one Liberator lost. Supply-dropping sorties were also flown but the main task was anti-shipping and two or three ships were destroyed each month until August. With the end of the war in the Far East the Squadron began a ferrying task, principally in and out of the Cocos Islands base which continued on a regular basis until May, 1946 when the Squadron returned to the UK for the first time since February, 1929.

In the UK No. 203 joined Coastal Command and re-equipped, becoming part of the St. Eval Lancaster Wing. For the next seven years it flew maritime recce duties over the Western Approaches until it moved to Yorkshire for re-equipment. Its new aircraft was the Neptune and with these it patrolled the North Sea and the Norwegian coastal area. The Neptune was replaced in 1956 and the Squadron again moved, becoming part of the Ballykelly Wing flying Shackletons for thirteen years from this base. Although the task was primarily out over the North Atlantic it was also called in to provide troop transport duties during the various overseas crises of the fifties and sixties. In January, 1969 the Squadron moved out to Malta where it became the maritime unit to cover the whole Mediterra-

nean. There it was principally involved in checking up on the growing movements of Soviet warships and submarines in and out of the Black Sea. This task was continued with Nimrods from 1971 onwards until the continual Defence cuts of the seventies meant the withdrawal of the British presence in Malta. No. 203 Squadron was disbanded there on 31 December, 1977.

Bases etc.

Re-formed by re-numbering No. 482 Flight at Cattewater (Mount Batten) on 1 January, 1929.

Mount Batten	Jan 1929—Feb 1929	
Basra	Feb 1929—Sep 1935	
Isthmus (Aden)	Sep 1935—Jul 1936	
Basra	Jul 1936—Aug 1939	
Isthmus, det. Kamaran	Aug 1939—Dec 1939	
Sheikh Othman, det. Kamaran	Dec 1939—May 1940	
Khormaksar	May 1940—Apr 1941	
Kabrit	Apr 1941—Apr 1941	
Heraklion	Apr 1941—Apr 1941	
Kabrit	Apr 1941—May 1941	
Lydda, det. Habbaniya, H.4	May 1941—May 1941	
Kabrit	May 1941—Jun 1941	
Gambut (LG.101)	Jun 1941—Dec 1941	
LG.05	Dec 1941—Jan 1942	
Buka	Jan 1942—Jan 1942	
El Gubbi	Jan 1942—Feb 1942	
Sidi Barrani (LG.39)	Feb 1942—Jun 1942	
Abu Sueir	Jun 1942—Sep 1942	
Gianaclis	Sep 1942—Mar 1943	
Berka No. 3	Mar 1943—Oct 1943	
LG.91	Oct 1943—Nov 1943	
Santa Cruz, det. Cochin, St. Thomas Mount Ratmalana	Nov 1943—Nov 1944	
Madura	Nov 1944—Feb 1945	
Kankesanturai, det. Akyab, Cocos Island	Feb 1945—May 1946	
Leuchars	May 1946—Jan 1947	
St. Eval	Jan 1947—Aug 1952	
Topcliffe	Aug 1952—Sep 1956	

Disbanded at Topcliffe on 1 September, 1956. Re-formed at Ballykelly on 1 November, 1958 by re-numbering No. 240 Squadron.

Ballykelly	Nov 1958—Jan 1969	
Luqa	Jan 1969—Dec 1977	

Disbanded at Luqa on 31 December, 1977.

Main Equipment

Supermarine Southampton II (Jan 1929—Apr 1931)
S1038; S1229, A; S1298, B; S1299, A; S1300, C; S1421; S1423
Short Rangoon I (Apr 1931—Sep 1935)
S1433; S1434; S1435; K2134; K2809; K3678
Short Singapore III (Sep 1935—Feb 1940)
K4577; K4582; K4584; K6907; K6912, NT:D; K6913; K8859
Bristol Blenheim IV (May 1940—Nov 1942)
L9044, F; L9218, R; L9332; T1821, K; T1988, Y; T2429, M; V5738, A; V6014, S; V6331, N; V6423, L; Z6367, C; Z6542, Y; Z7581, E; Z9665, T
Lockheed Hudson II/III (Feb 1942—Mar 1942)
T9397; AM939; AM950
Martin Maryland II (Feb 1942—Nov 1942)
AH280, Y; AH336, S; AH342, K; AH391, C; AH402, A; 1629, Z, later J; 1634, B
Martin Baltimore I, II, III (Aug 1942—Aug 1943)
AG687, S; AG696, N; AG707, R; AG721, F; AG749, A; AG779, M; AG801, A; AG833, Y; AG861, O; AG884, D; AG917, G; AG949, R; AH170, F
Martin Baltimore IIIA, V (May 1943—Oct 1943)
FA107, P; FA209, G; FA353, K; FA406, K; FA507, R; FA552, C; FA584, B; FA600, G
Vickers Wellington XIII (Nov 1943—Oct 1944)
HZ589; HZ972; JA106; JA411, D; JA444, B; JA516, O; MF210, P; MF256, C; MF338, G; MF489, O; MP740, H
Consolidated Liberator VI (Nov 1944—Mar 1946)
KG849, A; KG909, J; KH123, M; KH195, H; KH219, N; KH267, C; KH392, K; KH409, K
Consolidated Liberator VIII (Feb 1945—Oct 1946)
KG980, F; KH289, B; KH307, C; KL553, CJ:M; KL565, CJ:B
Avro Lancaster GR.3 (Aug 1946—Mar 1953)
RE169, CJ:J, later B:J; RE206, B:B; RF210, CJ:D; RF311, CJ:G, later B:G; SW294, CJ:E, later B:G; SW324, B:C; SW337, CJ:A; SW365, B:O; SW377, CJ:B
Lockheed Neptune MR.1 (Feb 1953—Sep 1956)
WX518, B:J, later 203:J; WX521, B:L; WX520, B:M, later 203:M; WX524, B:P; WX525, B:Q, later 203:Q
Avro Shackleton MR.1A (Nov 1958—Sep 1959)
WB856; WB859; WB860; WG507; WG509

Avro Shackleton MR.3 (Dec 1958—Jul 1962 & 1966—Jul 1971)
WR974, 203:F, later H; WR977, 203:B, later B; WR982, 203:G;
WR987, 203:D, later D; XF700, F; XF703, 203:L; XF706, 203:G;
XF708, C

Avro Shackleton MR.2 (May 1962— 1966)
WG558, 203:G; WL742, 203:H; WL753, 203:G; WL800, 203:E;
WR957, 203:J; WR949, 203:K

Hawker Siddeley Nimrod MR.1 (Jul 1971—Dec 1977)
XV228; XV232; XV240; XV249; XV257; XV260; XV263

Commanding Officers

G/Capt H. R. Busteed, OBE, DFC	Jan 1929—Feb 1929
W/Cdr T. E. B. Howe, DFC	Feb 1929—Apr 1931
G/Capt W. L. Welsh, DSC, AFC	Apr 1931—Oct 1933
G/Capt R. E. Saul	Oct 1933—Apr 1936
G/Capt W. B. Callaway, AFC	Apr 1936—Nov 1937
G/Capt R. H. Kershaw	Nov 1937—Aug 1939
S/Ldr M. Q. Chandler	Aug 1939—Oct 1939
S/Ldr J. R. Scarlett-Streatfield	Oct 1939—Aug 1940
S/Ldr A. L. H. Solarno	Aug 1940—Feb 1941
W/Cdr D. C. Smith	Feb 1941—May 1941
W/Cdr J. R. Scarlett-Streatfield	May 1941—Aug 1941
W/Cdr A. F. Johnson, DFC	Aug 1941—Jul 1942
W/Cdr E. B. Grace	Jul 1942—Mar 1943
W/Cdr E. Tennant, DFC	Mar 1943—Oct 1943
W/Cdr C. A. Masterman, OBE, DFC	Oct 1943—Jul 1944
W/Cdr L. Fox, DSO, DFC	Jul 1944—Jun 1945
W/Cdr G. R. Brady, OBE	Jul 1945— 1945
W/Cdr J. K. Fleetwood, DSO	1945—Sep 1946
S/Ldr P. H. Stembridge, DFC, AFC	Sep 1946—Nov 1947
S/Ldr P. H. Cribb, DSO, DFC	Nov 1947—Mar 1949
S/Ldr J. F. Carrick	Mar 1949—Jan 1950
S/Ldr C. S. Johnson, DFC	Jan 1950—Dec 1950
S/Ldr A. P. Dent, DSO, DFC	Dec 1950—Dec 1952
S/Ldr T. W. Horton, DSO, DFC	Dec 1952—Jan 1955
S/Ldr A. W. Barwood, DFC	Jan 1955—Sep 1956
W/Cdr H. R. Kerr, MBE	Nov 1958—Apr 1960
W/Cdr W. E. Hamilton, DFC	Apr 1960—Jul 1962
W/Cdr D. C. S. Saunders, OBE, AFC	Jul 1962—Aug 1964
W/Cdr K. J. Barratt	Aug 1964—Jun 1966
S/Ldr W. L. Smyth	Jun 1966—Sep 1966
W/Cdr J. Fennell, MBE, AFC	Sep 1966—Nov 1968
W/Cdr R. G. Bowyer	Nov 1968—Nov 1971
W/Cdr A. J. Freeborn	Nov 1971—
W/Cdr G. A. King	May 1974—Jan 1975
W/Cdr G. K. Peasley	Jan 1975—Sep 1976
W/Cdr J. H. Carter	Sep 1976—Dec 1977

Aircraft Insignia

No specific unit insignia until World War II, when code letters were adopted, the Singapores carrying the letters 'NT' from September, 1939 to April, 1940. Thereafter markings were dropped until the Liberator period at the end of the war when the combination used was 'CJ'. This was perpetuated until 1951 when the single letter 'B' was adopted instead and retained until 1956 when the Squadron number itself replaced it. This was carried also on the Shackletons whilst in the UK. The Nimrods carried the Seahorse emblem at the base of the fin.
(See also *Fighter Squadrons of the RAF*, pp. 318–19)

No. 204 SQUADRON

BADGE
On water barry wavy, a mooring buoy, thereon
a cormorant displayed

MOTTO
'Praedam mare quaro'
('I seek my prey in the sea')

The badge is based on a photograph taken by
Aircraftman Shaw (*Lawrence of Arabia*).

In World War I No. 204 served as a fighter squadron at Dunkirk, forming on 31 December, 1916 from A Squadron, 5 Wing. Originally it was a bombing squadron with Sopwith 1½ Strutters then it received Pups and later Camels with which it fought throughout the war. It was disbanded at Waddington on 31 December, 1919. No. 204 was re-formed on 1 February, 1929 at Cattewater (Mount Batten) in Plymouth as a general reconnaissance flying-boat squadron. It was equipped with Supermarine Southamptons and pursued the normal peacetime routine with one annual cruise. In 1932 this was to the Mediterranean and the following year to the Baltic. The Squadron re-equipped with Scapas in 1935 and immediately moved overseas to Egypt because of the Abyssinian crisis, flying patrols to check on Italian shipping. In August, 1936 204 returned to Plymouth and re-equipped once more, this time with Saro Londons, completing by February, 1937. Initially they had problems, two Londons catching fire on start-up but by August the Squadron was ready for exercises in the Mediterranean and in December five of the Squadron's aircraft began a six-month cruise to Australia and back, the length of time being due to two incidents with propellers and the need to wait for replacements.

Sterner things appeared with the Munich crisis of 1938 and the Squadron began patrols to find the 'pocket battleship' *Deutschland*. In June, 1939 the Squadron began re-equipping with Sunderlands and was operational by the time war broke out, flying its first convoy escort on 4 September, with F/Lt Hyde bombing two submarines on the 8th. On 9th two more U-boat attacks were made. The 18th was an epic day: F/Lt Harrison and crew bombed a U-boat and claimed a probable whilst F/Lt Barrett found the crew of the sunken *Kensington Court*, landed and picked them up. Two more U-boats were bombed that month before the submarine captains became wiser and stayed out of sight. In October two Sunderlands were lost, one with fatal results but operations continued on A/S patrols and convoy escorts.

In April, 1940 the Squadron changed its area of operations by moving to the Shetlands for patrols over the Norwegian coast. This resulted in several attacks by Ju 88s; in one F/Lt Phillips was attacked by six and the crew destroyed two of them; F/Lt Harrison in L5799, however, failed to return. This remained the Squadron's task into June; on 21st two of the Squadron were shadowing the *Scharnhorst* when N9028 KG:A was attacked by four Bf 109s and severely damaged, but the crew managed to shoot down one of them. That month, too, it put a detachment in Iceland, the whole Squadron patrolling the gap between it and the Denmark Straits to keep a lookout for U-boats and surface raiders. In April, 1941 the whole Squadron moved to Iceland where, in addition to Atlantic patrolling, it flew a survey of the country for landmarks and alighting areas.

The Squadron's stay there was only three months for in July it began moving in stages to Gibraltar, where it kept up convoy escorts and then on to Bathurst in Gambia where it established regular patrols over the South Atlantic to deter U-boats looking for pickings amongst the many convoys going round Africa. Convoy escorts were the main task, the aircraft flying up to Gibraltar, refuelling there and then back. Between October and December, 1942 activity intensified with the invasion of N. Africa. This made things easier for the Squadron as the opposition from the Vichy French forces in French West Africa was eliminated and their ports could be used. On 5 April, 1934 H/204 found a U-boat and damaged it with depth-charges, the first attack in West Africa by the Squadron. Another attack followed in July. The Squadron kept up regular patrols right through until the war in Europe ended although no further U-boats were found. The Squadron's presence, however, thwarted enemy activity to a considerable degree. Towards the end of the war No. 204 also flew meteorological recce flights. It was disbanded at Jui on 30 June, 1945.

When the Squadron re-formed it was in a different role. It took place at Kabrit, in the Suez Canal Zone on 1 August, 1947; No. 204 was now flying as a transport squadron in the Middle East Dakota Wing. This Wing flew regular schedules to the many RAF bases throughout the Near and Middle East and into Africa as well as special VIP trips and was also responsible for the airborne trooping of army units including paratrooping. In May, 1949 it received the first of the Vickers Valettas to enter Middle East service and these soon took over from the Dakota. This aircraft was very successful in No. 204s service, there being no serious accident in four years of operation, during which time it was involved in the reinforcing of the Canal Zone garrison and the evacuating of families in addition to its scheduled flying. On 20 February, 1953 it was disbanded by re-numbering as No. 84 Squadron.

However, eleven months later the Squadron re-appeared when it re-formed, once more, in Coastal Command, at Ballykelly with Avro Shackletons for maritime reconnaissance. Once again the North Atlantic was its 'patch'. In addition it would go on overseas cruises once more, one of these being to South Africa to convince them of the need to buy Shackletons, a successful outcome taking place. In 1956 No. 204 returned to its Middle East haunts in the transport role; the Suez crisis forced the Coastal squadrons into supplying backup transport duties and many troops moved out in 204s Shackletons. In 1957 it sent a detachment to Western Australia in connection with Met recce duties for the nuclear tests.

As the years went by the Shackletons were progressively updated with more modern search and ECM equipment in the ASW war of invention. Most other maritime squadrons re-equipped with Nimrods as the seventies came in but No. 204 soldiered on, moving to Suffolk in March, 1971 from where it flew air-sea rescue and shipping recce duties and, being the last maritime Shackleton squadron, sent detachments to the Far East to take over No. 205 Squadron's duties and to Majunga for the futile Beira blockade patrols. All good things come to an end and the Squadron eventually disbanded at Honington on 28 April, 1972.

Bases etc.

Re-formed at Cattewater on 1 February, 1929.

Cattewater (Mount Batten)	Feb 1929—Sep 1935	
Aboukir	Sep 1935—Oct 1935	
Alexandria	Oct 1935—Aug 1936	
Mount Batten	Aug 1936—Apr 1940	
Sullom Voe, det. Reykjavik	Apr 1940—Apr 1941	
Reykjavik	Apr 1941—Jul 1941	
Gibraltar	Jul 1941—Aug 1941	
Bathurst, det. Half Die, Freetown, Jui, Port Etienne	Aug 1941—Jan 1944	
Jui, det. Bathurst	Jan 1944—Jun 1945	

Disbanded at Jui on 30 June, 1945. Re-formed at Kabrit on 1 August, 1947 in the transport role.

Kabrit	Aug 1947—Feb 1951
Fayid	Feb 1951—Feb 1953

Disbanded at Fayid on 20 February, 1953. Re-formed in the maritime reconnaissance role at Ballykelly on 1 January, 1954.

Ballykelly	Jan 1954—Apr 1971
Honington, det. Seletar, Majunga	Apr 1971—Apr 1972

Disbanded at Honington on 28 April, 1972.

Main Equipment

Supermarine Southampton II (Feb 1929—Oct 1935)
N9900, 3; N9901, 4; S1037; S1041; S1123; S1232; S1302; S1647; K2964; K2965, 1
Supermarine Scapa (Aug 1935—Feb 1937)
S1648; K4191; K4192; K4197; K4198; K4199; K4200; K4565
Saro London II (Oct 1936—Aug 1939)
K5263; K5908; K5911, RF:G; K6927; K6930; K9686
Short Sunderland I (Jun 1939—Oct 1943)
L2158, KG:M; L5798, KG:B; L5802, RF:F, later KG:E; N9021, KG:C, later KG:G; N9028, KG:A; N9030, KG:B;

N9036, KG:J; N9044, KG:C; P9620, KG:K; P9041, KG:A T9070, KG:E; T9074, KG:L
Short Sunderland II (Jun 1941—Mar 1943)
W3978; W3980; W3981; W6063
Short Sunderland III (Sep 1942—Jun 1945)
W6012, E; W6079, C; DD833, M; DP188, C; DV959, F; DV974, G; DV991, G; DW104, K; EK580, B; EK587, J; JM627, E; JM682, H; JM710, X; ML854, M
Short Sunderland V (Apr 1945—Jun 1945)
EJ145, P; ML862; ML872, B
Douglas Dakota C.4 (Aug 1947—Jul 1949)
KJ914; KJ934; KN654
Vickers Valetta C.1 (May 1949—Feb 1953)
VW165, D; VW820; VW838; VW855; VX562; WD157
Avro Shackleton MR.2 (Jan 1954—Apr 1972)
WB833, T; WG555, 204:N, later K; WG558, 204:P; WL738, T:R, later Y; WL748, T:S, later R; WL754, H; WL793, T:O, later 204:O; WL801 204:B; WR951, 204:Q; WR956, T:Q, later Q; WR961, U; WR966, 204:O
Avro Shackleton MR.1A (Apr 1958—Feb 1960)
VP266; VP284; WB826; WB851, 204:C; WB860, 204:L

Commanding Officers

S/Ldr F. H. Laurence, MC	Feb 1929—Dec 1930	
S/Ldr K. N. Lloyd, AFC	Dec 1930—Jan 1934	
S/Ldr A. W. Fletcher, DFC, AFC, OBE	Jan 1934—Oct 1936	
S/Ldr V. P. Feather	Oct 1936—Oct 1937	
W/Cdr K. B. Lloyd, AFC	Oct 1937—Mar 1940	
W/Cdr E. S. C. Davis, AFC	Mar 1940—Aug 1940	
W/Cdr K. F. T. Pickles	Aug 1940—May 1941	
W/Cdr D. I. Coote	May 1941—Feb 1943	
W/Cdr P. R. Hatfield	Feb 1943—Mar 1943	
W/Cdr C. E. V. Evison	Mar 1943—Sep 1943	
W/Cdr H. J. L. Hawkins	Sep 1943—Aug 1944	
W/Cdr A. Frame	Aug 1944—Jan 1945	
W/Cdr D. Michell	Jan 1945—Jun 1945	
S/Ldr H. S. Hartley	Aug 1947—Jan 1948	
S/Ldr R. A. Pegler	Jan 1948—May 1950	
S/Ldr L. W. Davies	May 1950—Oct 1952	
S/Ldr H. H. Jenkins	Oct 1952—Feb 1953	
S/Ldr G. Young	Jan 1954—Jul 1955	
W/Cdr W. Beringer	Jul 1955—Jun 1957	
W/Cdr A. D. Dart, DSO, DFC	Jun 1957—Jul 1958	
W/Cdr J. C. W. Weller, DFC	Jul 1958—Jun 1960	
W/Cdr R. D. Roe, AFC	Jun 1960—Jun 1962	
W/Cdr C. K. N. Lloyd, AFC	Jun 1962—May 1964	
W/Cdr J. J. Duncombe, AFC	May 1964—Mar 1966	
W/Cdr P. Kent, MBE	Mar 1966—Jun 1968	
W/Cdr O. G. Williams	Jun 1968—Apr 1969	
W/Cdr E. P. Wild	Apr 1969—Apr 1971	
S/Ldr D. E. Leppard	Apr 1971—Apr 1972	

Aircraft Insignia

The Southamptons carried a black or dark blue line horizontally along the hull. This was replaced on the Scapas and later the Londons by a coloured rectangle on the outside of the fins (colour unknown.) In September, 1938 the Londons were painted with 'RF' code letters which were changed to 'KG' in September, 1939 on the Sunderlands. These were dropped ca 1943 and no insignia carried until the war ended. What the Dakotas carried, if anything, is not known but the Valettas had a blue fuselage flash and blue propeller spinners. The Shackletons at first carried the single identity letter 'T' which was replaced by the Squadron number '204' in red ca 1957. At the same time the Squadron emblem was carried on a white shield on the fin and the aircraft had red spinners. Late in the sixties the squadron number was dropped from the aircraft but the other markings remained.
(See also *Fighter Squadrons of the RAF*, p. 320)

No. 205 SQUADRON

BADGE
A kris and a trident in saltire

MOTTO
'Pertama di-Malaya'
('First in Malaya')

The badge indicates two aspects of the Squadron's history, the trident referring to its naval origins and the kris to its Malayan associations.

The Squadron was formed as No. 5 Squadron, RNAS, at Coudekirke on 31 December, 1916 as a day bomber squadron primarily responsible for attacking enemy naval installations along the Belgian and Dutch coasts. This it performed with Sopwith 1½ Strutters and later D.H.4s, serving on the Western Front from February, 1918 onwards. Towards the end of the war it flew photographic recce duties as well and returned to the UK early in 1919, disbanding at Hucknall on 22 January, 1920. On 8 January, 1929 No. 205 was re-formed as a flying-boat squadron at Seletar, Singapore by expanding the Far East Flight. This latter had formed in May, 1927 at Felixstowe and, with four Supermarine Southamptons, had left the UK in September, 1927 and flown together to India, Singapore, Australia, back to Singapore and around the East Indies on a combined flag-showing and marine base exploration tour which exceeded anything previously done. From September, 1928 the Flight was permanently based in Singapore, becoming No. 205 Squadron in 1929.

Much of its early work as a squadron continued to be liaison cruises in the Far East. It also flew ASR sorties for other aircraft missing in the dangerous seas and in 1931 flew one of its aircraft up the Irrawaddy to frighten the rebel tribesmen there. The same year the Squadron provided escort to No. 36 Squadron flying its Hawker Horsleys from India to take up residence at Seletar. Much of 1932 was taken up with survey flying of the Andaman and Nicobar Islands. This continued the routine for No. 204 until April, 1935 when the Southamptons were finally replaced by Short Singapore IIIs. With these the Far East cruises were continued and exercises with the Singapore-based fleet increased as the years drew on to World War II although its only immediate effect on the Squadron was to camouflage its aircraft. However, by the end of 1940 it began searching for German surface raiders believed in the area.

In March, 1941 the Squadron cruised eastwards to Manila where it picked up its replacement aircraft – Catalinas. With these it set up a detachment at Koggala and spent much of its time commuting between the two and selecting alighting bases in between. The Singapores finally left in September, 1941. On 6 December war suddenly came to No. 205 as it set out to search for a Japanese convoy in the Gulf of Siam and Catalina FV-Y was shot down by a Zero. Four days later another of the Squadron found the only remains of the battleship HMS *Repulse*, her Walrus amphibian in the water. Shipping searches were now being carried on all the time and several Catalinas had combats, one being shot down. As the situation worsened the Squadron also took on a bombing role. By the New Year No. 205 was down to five aircraft and the base was under regular air attack. The Squadron flew both recce and bombing sorties against the advancing Japanese and the situation became so bad by the middle of January that the aircraft could not be landed direct but had to alight at waiting areas and called in between air raids. By the end of the month only four aircraft remained and these evacuated to Sumatra and then on to Java where they continued to fly Sunda Strait and West Borneo patrols until 3 March when the last two aircraft escaped to Australia.

It was not until 23 July, 1942 that the Squadron was revived again. The base was Koggala and it was built up from one remaining No. 205 aircraft, two from No. 202 and four from No. 240 Squadrons. It immediately began anti-shipping patrols, interspersing them with anti-invasion patrols and ASR sorties. On 26th one of the latter located three liferafts full of survivors. In September it added PR to its tasks and the following month provided its own transport flying to set up a detachment at Addu Atoll. A submarine was sighted in October but no attack could be made; however the aircraft found the survivors from one of its victims and brought rescue ships to them. On 20 December three aircraft flew a round trip operation of over 2,000 miles when they attacked Sabang harbour with bombs.

The routine operational tasks were continued in 1943 and in addition the Squadron began special Signals operations. In July, too, it started a mail run to Australia involving 3,000 mile flights. It was November, 1943 before No. 205s first submarine attack took place and the result was inconclusive. At this time the Squadron was limited by unserviceability but on 3 March, 1944 S/Ldr Melville found a surfaced submarine in the moonlight and depth-charged it. The following month one of the Squadron's aircraft found a raft containing survivors who had been afloat for fifty days.

Most of the flying from then until the war ended was on anti-submarine sorties but ASR work continued and Met flights also took place. In June, 1945 conversion to Sunderlands took place. The Squadron remained at Koggala until 1949 when it at last returned to its old base at Seletar, Singapore. From here it sent a detachment to Japan in 1951 to fly patrols over the seas around Korea during the last stages of the fighting there. Much of the Squadron's duties again involved showing the flag around the East Indies countries now becoming independent. In March, 1953 the Squadron flew mercy flights to Tawau when a serious fire destroyed half the town. The Squadron maintained its task with Sunderlands

until May, 1959, having the honour of being the last operational flying-boat squadron in the RAF.

The Sunderlands were replaced by Shackletons and these continued to provide able maritime recce facilities in the Far East for another twelve years as well as maintaining SAR facilities and being responsible for many rescues. Eventually the RAF withdrew from the Far East and No. 205 Squadron was disbanded at Changi on 31 October, 1971.

Bases etc.

Re-formed at Seletar on 8 January, 1929, from Far East Flight.

Seletar, det. Koggala	Jan 1929—Jan 1942
Oosthaven	Jan 1942—Feb 1942
Tjilatjap	Feb 1942—Mar 1943

3 March, 1943 last two aircraft escaped to Australia where the Squadron effectively ceased to exist. Re-formed at Koggala on 23 July, 1942.

Koggala, det. Addu Atoll, China Bay	Jul 1942—Sep 1949
Seletar, det. Iwakuni	Sep 1949—May 1958
Changi, det. Seletar, Gan	May 1958—Oct 1971

Disbanded at Changi on 31 October, 1971.

Main Equipment

Supermarine Southampton II, III (Jan 1929—Apr 1935)
S1043; S1123; S1151; S1153; S1162; S1249; S1420
Short Singapore III (Apr 1935—Oct 1941)
K3592; K3594; K4581; K6911, FV:G; K6918, FV:L; K8859, H
Consolidated Catalina I (Apr 1941—Dec 1944)
W8406, T; W8412, P; W8417, FV:Y; W8426, FV:U; W8429, FV:P; Z2144, FV:R; Z2151, FV:Y; AH540; AH546, M; AJ154; AJ161, O
Consolidated Catalina IB (Jul 1942—Jun 1945)
FP109, A; FP131, L; FP223, R; FP229, N; FP241, K; FP255, U; FP276, S; FP304, P
Consolidated Catalina IVB (May 1944—Jul 1945)
JX285, J; JX316, X; JX330, N; JX352, Q; JX431, A; JX437, F; JX586, Q; JX594, M
Short Sunderland GR.5 (Jun 1945—May 1959)
DP198, O; JM667, Q; ML724; NJ193, P; NJ270, K; PP123, M; PP154, N; RN269, P; RN288, S; RN301, D; SZ571, B; SZ599, Y; VB888, Z
Avro Shackleton MR.1A (May 1958—Nov 1962)
VP254, 205:B; VP267, 205:L; VP294, 205:N; WB818, 205:A; WB825, 205:H; WG525, 205:E
Avro Shackleton MR.2 (Feb 1962—Oct 1971)
WG530, 205:G; WG553, 205:D; WL745, 205:A; WL759, 205:B, later N; WL795, 205:G; WR954, 205:F, later C; WR969, 205:A

Commanding Officers

G/Cdr H. M. Cave-Brown-Cave, DFC, AFC	Jan 1929—Jan 1930
S/Ldr G. E. Lovick, DFC, AFC	Jan 1930—Feb 1931
W/Cdr A. C. Wright, AFC	Feb 1931—Dec 1932
S/Ldr B. McEntegart	Dec 1932—Feb 1933
W/Cdr E. J. P. Barling, DSC, DFC, AFC	Feb 1933—Dec 1933
S/Ldr B. McEntegart	Dec 1933—Dec 1933
S/Ldr K. B. Lloyd, AFC	Feb 1934—Apr 1934
W/Cdr C. L. Scott, DSC	Apr 1934—Mar 1936
S/Ldr K. B. Lloyd, AFC	Mar 1936—Nov 1936
S/Ldr A. C. Stevens	Nov 1936—Dec 1936
S/Ldr A. W. Bates	Jan 1937—Mar 1937
W/Cdr P. E. Maitland, MVO	Mar 1937—Feb 1939
W/Cdr A. F. Lang, MBE, AFC	Feb 1939—Aug 1939
S/Ldr R. B. Connall	Aug 1939—Oct 1939
W/Cdr A. F. Lang, MBE, AFC	Oct 1939—Dec 1939
W/Cdr R. B. Connall	Dec 1939—Mar 1941
W/Cdr L. W. Burgess	Mar 1941—Oct 1941
W/Cdr R. B. Connall	Oct 1941—Mar 1942
W/Cdr M. D. Thunder	Jul 1942—Aug 1943
W/Cdr N. McLelland, OBE	Aug 1943—Feb 1945
W/Cdr R. J. Freeman, DFC	Feb 1945—Dec 1945
W/Cdr R. C. O. Lovelock, DFC	Dec 1945—Mar 1946
W/Cdr H. J. A. Thewles, OBE	Mar 1946—May 1946
S/Ldr J. H. Dunn	May 1946—Aug 1947
W/Cdr A. J. Mason, DFC	Aug 1947—Feb 1948
S/Ldr C. M. Owen	Feb 1948—Feb 1950
S/Ldr J. E. Proctor, DFC	Feb 1950—Feb 1952
S/Ldr J. T. Ormston, DFC	Feb 1952—Dec 1953
S/Ldr D. J. G. Norton	Dec 1953—Jul 1955
W/Cdr A. F. Fegen	Jul 1955—Feb 1958
W/Cdr R. A. N. McReady, OBE	Feb 1958—Apr 1960
W/Cdr B. A. Templeman-Rooke, DSO, DFC, AFC	Apr 1960—Oct 1961
W/Cdr A. E. Harkness, AFC	Oct 1961—
W/Cdr R. A. Pendry, AFC	—Oct 1971

No regular insignia was carried by No. 205 Squadron, as far as is known, until 1938 when it was allotted the code letters 'KM' although whether these were used or not is not known. It is known, however, that on the outbreak of war the letters 'FV' were carried until March, 1942. After that no identity marks were carried until the end of the war when the Squadron badge was carried below the cockpit. With the advent of the Shackleton the Squadron number was carried on the rear fuselage and in the 'sixties the Squadron emblem was carried on a white disc on the fin.

(See also *Bomber Squadrons of the RAF*, pp. 192–3)

No. 206 SQUADRON

BADGE
An octopus

MOTTO
'Nihil nos effugit'
('Nought escapes us')

The octopus is a very active creature and is reputed to 'jump' as it swims, thus covering a considerable distance quickly. It is indicative of the squadron's activities in many branches of the service's work.

No. 206 Squadron began life as No. 6 Squadron, RNAS at Dover on 1 November, 1916 in the fighter role, going to Dunkirk soon after to fight for nine months in this role with the Navy. Disbanding in August, 1917 it re-formed as a bomber squadron at Dover on 1 January, 1918, moving again to Dunkirk for operations with D.H.9s. It fought on bombing and photographic duties until the end of the war, moving to Egypt in June, 1919 where it was re-numbered No. 47 Squadron on 1 February, 1920.

On 15 June, 1936 C Flight of No. 48 Squadron at Manston was expanded to Squadron strength and numbered No. 206 Squadron. It soon moved to Bircham Newton. At first it served simply as a conversion unit for the large number of pilots needed to be converted to modern monoplanes but after a year it became operational and began exercises with the Home Fleet. By the time war broke out the Squadron was well-versed in its tasks but the Anson was also becoming obsolescent. On 1 September, 1939 it began shipping searches over the North Sea; four days later F/Lt Pike failed to return and four days later P/O Kean ditched in the Channel. By October it was fully into its routine, flying 123 operational sorties in the month, with detachments in Carew Cheriton and Hooton Park for convoy work. On 8 November P/O Featherstone was attacked by a He 115 seaplane but his gunner shot it into the sea. On 7 December P/O Harper in K6184 bombed a U-boat, hitting it at the base of the conning tower, and claimed it as sunk.

By March, 1940 No. 206 was beginning to re-equip with Hudsons and with these it roamed along the North German coast attacking shipping. Two months later attention was directed to the coast around Dunkirk where the Squadron flew Dutch coast and Belgian coast patrols with Hudsons and the North Sea convoys with the Ansons. Battle Flights were maintained over Dunkirk and several battles took place with Bf 109s the Hudsons scoring several victories. With the Continental fighting over the Squadron began anti-invasion patrols around UK shores but there was still time for offensive duties as on 21 June when nine aircraft attacked Den Helder and sank the Dutch coastal defence ship *Vliereede*. So the Squadron's duties were divided between convoy escorts and offensive *Rovers* along the Dutch coast. That winter the Squadron also embarked on intruder patrols over French airfields before this task was more fully taken over by Fighter Command.

1941 was a busy year for the Hudsons of No. 206 Squadron. Detachments went to Aldergrove in April to join in the anti-submarine war and St. Eval for the continual battle against the French Atlantic coast ports around Brest. This latter detachment became the principal operational part of the squadron by the summer, a probable U-boat sinking by P/O Wills taking place on 4 July and a minesweeper destroyed on 11th. In August the whole Squadron moved to Ireland to concentrate on the U-boat war in the Atlantic, and in the approaches to Liverpool and the Clyde. Each month brought a U-boat attack as the winter drew on and the Squadron ended the year with detachments as far apart as Wick and Chivenor. The early months of 1942 brought action with three U-boats attacked in two months; operations were running at over 100 sorties a month. The pressure remained on until July when the Squadron moved to the Hebrides and began converting to Fortresses. First operations with these took place on 19 September; the range at which the Squadron could now fly was greater and this gave greater coverage enabling more action. In October six U-boats were sighted and four attacked and three more in December. The Fortresses were continuously in action in 1943. Four attacks were made in May/June including one definitely sunk. In October No. 206 Squadron moved to the Azores to cover the South Atlantic gap which was becoming a U-boat focus spot and found some targets early in 1944. The patrols, however, had the effect of keeping the U-boats submerged.

In April, 1944 the Squadron returned to the UK to re-equip with Liberators. It was soon taking part in the round-the-clock Channel watch during the invasion of Normandy; on 10 June a U-boat was sunk whilst on this task. The following month (July) the Squadron moved to Scotland from where it operated off the Norwegian Coast for the rest of the war. Two U-boat attacks were made that month, another was sunk in September but the patrols were being met by Bf 110s which began to score a toll of Liberators. In November Leigh Light aircraft arrived and most of the Squadron's operations now took place at night. In January, 1945 the Squadron had much action; four U-boats, one coaster and a destroyer were illuminated and attacked. It was fighting right up to the end of hostilities, attacking five more U-boats in the last month of the war.

The Squadron transferred to 301 Wing, Transport Command in June, 1945 and began training flights to India, becoming operational in October, flying the schedules which took freight and administrators out and brought troops and POWs home. This continued until 25 April, 1946 when it was disbanded.

No. 206 re-formed again in the transport role on 17 November, 1947 at Lyneham, equipped with Avro Yorks. Almost all its activities with the York were involved on the Berlin Airlift for which it was detached to Wunstorf. This took place through 1948 and into 1949 when the Squadron transferred to the overseas schedules until 20 February, 1950 when it was again disbanded. However, No. 206 Squadron was primarily a maritime squadron and fittingly it re-formed in that role at St. Eval on 27 September, 1952 as one of the Squadrons to receive the new Avro Shackleton. It took on MR.1s and flew these consistently on maritime recce and SAR duties over the Western Approaches as well as making long-distance sorties for various reasons. For example in 1954 it flew a goodwill tour to New Zealand and Fiji and in 1956–57 provided recce and SAR facilities for the nuclear tests at Christmas Island. 1958 saw the Squadron move to St. Mawgan and receive MR.3s, these being taken to South America and South Africa on tours in subsequent years. The Squadron moved base to Scotland in 1965 to be nearer the transit routes of Soviet shipping and has remained there ever since maintaining an operational stance on this surveillance role. It re-equipped with Nimrods in November, 1970 enabling it to play a more significant role in the anti-submarine task which is its primary role.

Bases etc.

Re-formed at Manston from C Flight, 48 Squadron on 15 June, 1936.

Manston	Jun 1936—Jul 1936
Bircham Newton, det. Carew Cheriton, Hooton Park, Aldergrove, St. Eval	Jul 1936—Jul 1941

St. Eval | Jul 1941—Aug 1941
Aldergrove, det. Wick, St. Eval, Chivenor, Stornoway, Donna Nook | Aug 1941—Jul 1942
Benbecula, det. St. Eval, Thorney Island | Jul 1942—Oct 1943
Thorney Island | Oct 1943—Oct 1943
Lagens (Azores) | Oct 1943—Apr 1944
St. Eval, det. Tain | Apr 1944—Jul 1944
Leuchars, det. Tain | Jul 1944—Jul 1945
Oakington | Jul 1945—Apr 1946
Disbanded at Oakington 25 April, 1946. Re-formed at Lyneham on 17 November, 1947.
Lyneham, det. Wunstorf | Nov 1947—Feb 1950
Disbanded at Lyneham on 20 February, 1950. Re-formed at St. Eval on 27 September, 1952.
St. Eval | Sep 1952—Jan 1958
St. Mawgan | Jan 1958—Jul 1965
Kinloss | Jul 1965—

Main Equipment

Avro Anson I (Jun 1936—Jun 1940)
K6167, 206:C, later WD:C, later VX:C; K6179, 206:A, later WD:A, later VX:A; K6191, VX:B; K6288, VX:D; K8756, VX:U; K8814, VX:N; K8837, VX:F; L7974; L9157, VX:R; N9897; R3312

Lockheed Hudson I (Mar 1940—Aug 1942)
N7275, VX:R; N7311, VX:G; N7367, VX:E; N7402; P5120, VX:C; P5143, VX:M; P5178, VX:V; R4059, VX:R; T9288, VX:L; T9303, VX:V; T9350, VX:J

Lockheed Hudson II (Apr 1941—   1941)
T9383, VX:Q

Lockheed Hudson III (Apr 1941—Aug 1942)
T9392, VX:R; T9454, VX:G; T9463, VX:Q

Lockheed Hudson IV (Apr 1941—   1941)
AE612, VX:O; AE620, VX:F; AE623, VX:P; AE629, VX:T

Lockheed Hudson V (Jun 1941—Aug 1942)
AE648, VX:N; AM570, VX:P; AM587, VX:D; AM605, VX:K; AM622, VX:L; AM689, VX:P; AM711, VX:U; AM734, VX:O; AM788, VX:A; AM805, VX:W

Boeing Fortress II/IIA (Jul 1942—Apr 1944)
FA695, 1:V; FA700, 1:R; FA711, 1:E; FK195, L; FK208, B; FK213, 1:C; FL451, D; FL457, F; FL460, 1:H

Consolidated Liberator VI (Apr 1944—Apr 1946)
BZ972, PQ:B; BZ986, PQ:C; EV828, PQ:G; EV872, PQ:M; EV887, PQ:H; EV952, PQ:A; EV988, PQ:O; EW311, PQ:E; KG859, PQ:B; KH380, PQ:B; KH410, PQ:N; KK256, PQ:J; KK375, PQ:L; KL351, PQ:S; KL494, PQ:M; KL623, PQ:T; KL665, PQ:U; KL669, PQ:P

Consolidated Liberator VIII (Mar 1945—Apr 1946)
KG959, PQ:Z; KG979, PQ:N; KH380; KH410, PQ:N; KK250, PQ:T; KK292, PQ:P; KK335, PQ:L

Avro York C.1 (Nov 1947—Feb 1950)
MW136; MW262; MW286; MW303; MW305

Avro Shackleton MR.1A (Sep 1952—May 1958)
VP263, B:U, later 206:G; VP293, B:A, later 206:A; WB821, 206:D; WB832, B:W, later B:G; WG508, B:X, later B:E; WG526, B:C, later 206:C; WG529, B:F, later 206:F

Avro Shackleton MR.2 (Feb 1953—Jun 1954)
WG557, B:Z; WG558, B:Y; WL742, B:Z1; WR952, B:Z

Avro Shackleton MR.3 (Jan 1958—Oct 1970)
WR977, 206:B; WR979, 206:B; WR981, 206:A; WR984, 206:D; WR985, 206:E, later T; XF700, U; XF701, 206:E, later T; XF703, 206:D, later R; XF730, 206:C

Hawker Siddeley Nimrod MR.1 (Nov 1970—   ) (Kinloss Wing Aircraft)
XV238; XV250; XV259; XV262

Commanding Officers

S/Ldr A. H. Love | Jun 1936—Jul 1936
W/Cdr F. J. Vincent, DFC | Jul 1936—Oct 1936
W/Cdr H. O. Long, DSO | Oct 1936—May 1938
S/Ldr H. H. Martin | May 1938—Jan 1939
W/Cdr N. H. d'Aeth | Jan 1939—Jun 1940
W/Cdr J. Constable-Roberts | Jun 1940—Feb 1941
W/Cdr C. D. Candy | Feb 1941—Aug 1941
W/Cdr A. F. Hards | Aug 1941—Jun 1942
W/Cdr J. R. S. Romanes, DFC | Jun 1942—May 1943
W/Cdr R. B. Thompson, DSO | May 1943—Mar 1944
W/Cdr A. de V. Leach, DFC | Mar 1944—Jan 1945
W/Cdr J. P. Selby | Jan 1945—Jul 1945
W/Cdr T. W. T. McCombe, OBE | Jul 1945—Apr 1946
S/Ldr F. C. Blackmore | Nov 1947—Mar 1948
S/Ldr J. C. Blair | Mar 1948—Jul 1948
S/Ldr E. Moody | Jul 1948—Nov 1949
S/Ldr E. A. Rockliffe | Nov 1949—Feb 1950
S/Ldr J. D. Beresford | Feb 1950—Dec 1954
S/Ldr E. K. Paine | Dec 1954—Apr 1956
W/Cdr J. E. Preston | Apr 1956—Apr 1958
W/Cdr R. T. Billett | Apr 1958—Jul 1960
W/Cdr J. E. Bazalgette, DFC | Jul 1960—Jun 1962
W/Cdr E. R. Locke, OBE | Jun 1962—Oct 1964
W/Cdr H. R. Williams | Oct 1964—Aug 1966
W/Cdr S. G. Nunn, OBE, DFC | Aug 1966—Oct 1968
W/Cdr D. R. Dewar | Oct 1968—May 1970
W/Cdr J. Wild | May 1970—
W/Cdr M. J. W. Pierson, MBE |
W/Cdr J. Wild | —   1972
W/Cdr R. C. McKinlay | Apr 1979—

Aircraft Insignia

From 1937 onwards the Ansons carried the Squadron number on the side until the allocation of code letters late in 1938. Until the outbreak of war these were 'WD', changing then to 'VX' which was carried until the arrival of the Fortresses. At first no markings were carried then the numeral '1' denoted No. 206 Squadron. This was changed to 'PQ' letters with the Liberators. It is believed that the Yorks carried no markings; the Shackletons at first carried the letter 'B' then the number '206' which was supplemented by the emblem on a white shield on the fin. Nimrods carry the Squadron emblem on an occasional basis, being Wing aircraft.
(See also *Bomber Squadrons of the RAF*, pp. 193–4 and *Fighter Squadrons of the RAF*, p. 321)

No. 208 SQUADRON

BADGE
A sphinx affrontee

MOTTO
'Vigilant'

The Gizah sphinx signifies the Squadron's motto as well as representing the Squadron's association with Egypt from 1920 onwards.

No. 208 Squadron started its existence on 25 October, 1916 as No. 8 Squadron, RNAS, and earned itself a great reputation as a fighter unit on the Western Front in World War I becoming known as 'Naval Eight'. It was disbanded at Netheravon on 7 November, 1919.

When No. 208 re-formed again it was an army co-operation unit in Egypt when No. 113 Squadron at Ismailia was re-numbered 208 on 1 February, 1920. It was first equipped with R.E.8s but within eight months these had gone and Bristol Fighters took their place. Two years later the Squadron embarked for operations in Turkey during the Turkish/Greek troubles there. In Turkey its principal task was photo reconnaissance, backed up by visual recce to give the British troops, and particularly the cavalry patrols, up-to-date information as to the whereabouts of the Turkish troops. It would speed up this process by dropping messages to the troops in the field. In April, 1923 it was also involved in experiments with the Navy, trying to drop bombs on a running torpedo – an optimistic feat which appeared to have gone off satisfactorily. It is interesting to note that one of the Bristols used by No. 208 at this time was D8096, the only genuine Bristol F.2B still flying, now in the hands of the Shuttleworth Trust. Hostilities ended in August, 1923 and the Squadron was back at Ismailia the following month.

A long period of peace now enabled the Squadron to develop all the facets of army co-operation work such as tactical bombing, message picking-up, artillery co-operation, smoke-screen laying and so on. In September, 1929 a Flight of the Squadron returned to operations, being despatched to Palestine for daily recce flights to cover the disturbances between Jews and Arabs and strafing any terrorists attacking villages. This, however, only lasted for a month. The following year the tired Bristol Fighters were replaced by Armstrong Whitworth Atlas aircraft. With these the Squadron moved further afield, making trips to Baghdad and Khartoum. In 1932 it became the only army co-operation squadron in the Command and increased its hours to cope with all such demands. To do this it acquired additional ground transport to make it a fully mobile unit. In the mid-thirties Audaxes took the place of the Atlas, with a fourth, Demon, Flight formed in 1935. This was brought about by the threat posed by Mussolini's excursions in Ethiopia and for this the Squadron sent a forward detachment to Mersa Matruh, in case of trouble from the direction of Libya.

In 1936 it moved from possible operations in the Western Desert to actual fighting in Palestine, searching for armed bands around Bethlehem, ground strafing one such group in October. The Squadron returned to Egypt in December.

This activity was maintained throughout the years of peace, re-equipping with Lysander Is in January, 1939. When war broke out No. 208 was stationed in the Western Desert ready for action. This came with the entry of Italy into the war in June, 1940, whereupon No. 208 began daily recce flights along the frontier and artillery shoots carried out on Bardia. It was soon found that No. 208 could only operate with fighter escort as its aircraft were easy targets for the Italian fighters. As the British advance went on the Squadron also indulged in ground strafing, with bombs where necessary. When the German advance into Egypt took place the Squadron's reconnaissances were essential to keep track of the armies in the desert; most trips now being unescorted and casualties rose. To deal with this problem one Flight was re-equipped with Hurricanes in November for visual recce. These were vital in the December advance, the Lysanders being relegated to the southern area. During this period the Hurricanes were fitted with cameras to enable PR to be carried out. The Hurricanes were also more suitable for ground strafing with their eight machine guns and could look after themselves when intercepted.

With the advance in 1941 the Lysanders came back into the action as fighter support could be provided and gave valuable service in the attack on Bardia, with artillery shoots. This was followed up with the taking of Tobruk, the Squadron moving up all the time to keep near the fighting. This went on with the advance until at the end of February the Squadron retired to Egypt for a rest. First transferred to Palestine and largely Lysander-equipped, it was soon moved on to take part in the Greek fighting, arriving at the end of March. The Lysanders soon succumbed to the German Messerschmitts operating there. Left with just two Hurricanes and, eventually, three Lysanders, No. 208 could only carry out limited local recce around the retreating and evacuating troops. A move to Crete resulted in all the aircraft being destroyed there by bombing and No. 208 personnel were evacuated to Egypt.

From there it moved back to Palestine to re-equip. At this time the Syrian campaign had opened up and No. 208 had to provide fighter cover in lieu of recce work. It also had a detachment at Habbaniya which took part in the fighting there as required. By mid-summer the invasion of Syria took place and 208 became very involved, flying its true fighter-recce role and playing an important part in the capture of Damascus. In October, 1941 the Squadron moved back to the Western Desert. Here it was tasked with locating and tracking the enemy forces as the British began their advance. As this misfired and the situation became confused the Squadron's role was vital in quickly establishing where the opposing forces were. As the advance proceeded, once again 208 moved westwards to keep up with the advancing troops. At this time the Squadron was involved in many air combats, with some success. No. 208 fought on until the end of March when it retired for a rest.

It returned to the desert fighting at the end of May with Tomahawks and aged Hurricane Is. Its task was now to cover a retreating army and information of enemy positions was vital; No. 208 fought on regardless of heavy casualties. At the end of June it was forced back into Egypt from where it flew recces along the Alamein line which set up a high casualty rate. This was kept up until just before the breakthrough, No. 208 being withdrawn from ops in November, 1942.

Early in 1943 it moved to Iraq, flying training sorties throughout the whole year from there and Palestine. At the end of the year it re-equipped with Spitfires and moved to Italy in March, 1944. Tactical recce was now the main task, flown at 6–8,000 feet and warmly welcomed by enemy AA fire. However, in May, 1944 it began continuous artillery co-op during the advance for Rome, flying 20 sorties a day. The advance meant the Squadron being on the move at frequent intervals as the Germans retreated on the Gothic Line. At the same time Tac/R again became a feature of operations. Its next hectic period of operation was September when it flew 462 sorties, mainly on Tac/R sorties before the muddy winter brought a slow down to the fighting. As spring came in 1945 the Squadron was back to artillery shoots as the army set about the strongly fortified defence on the River Senio. VE-Day brought an end to Italy for the Squadron and it moved to Palestine in June.

Here No. 208 became involved in the Jewish rioting and sabotage, flying policing and recce sorties and being hampered by demobilisation removing most of its personnel. In 1947 it flew away to East Africa for a while, carrying out a 'showing the flag' tour highly successfully. In 1948 it moved to Cyprus, flying photo recce over Palestine with a detachment. This detachment, on 22 May, kept up a standing patrol over Ramat David, its base which had been strafed by a lone Spitfire. Further Egyptian Spitfires came to bomb and the Squadron shot down two of them in the first attack and two in the second. Soon after the Squadron returned to Egypt and here it was again involved with the Jews as it was sent to reconnoitre Jewish advances into Egypt. Whilst doing so it lost four aircraft on 7 January, 1949, being bounced by Jewish Spitfires, one pilot being killed, two captured by Jews and the third escaping.

In 1951 No. 208 re-equipped with Meteors for the fighter-recce task which became vital when Egypt started its non-co-operation policy. In April it sent a detachment to the Arabian Gulf to police the Oman coast for infiltration. In 1954 a visit to the Union of South Africa was flown in addition to normal commitments. Early in 1956 it left Egypt for Malta where it also maintained an interceptor role for a while with a detachment in Aden for border recce. When the Suez campaign began No. 208 took no part as it was running down prior to disbanding and a new No. 208 forming in the fighter/ground attack role. This took place at Tangmere on 5 January, 1958 since when it has served in this role in Cyprus, East Africa, Aden and the Persian Gulf until finally disbanding with Hunters at Muharraq on 10 September, 1971.

No. 208 re-formed at Honington on 1 July, 1974 as a strike bomber squadron with Hawker Siddeley Buccaneers and has served in this role ever since.

Bases etc.

Re-formed at Ismailia in the army co-operation role by re-numbering No. 113 Squadron on 1 February, 1920.

Ismailia	Feb	1920—Sep 1922
San Stephano	Sep	1922—Sep 1923
Ismailia	Sep	1923—Oct 1927
Heliopolis, det. Mersa Metruh, Amriya	Oct	1927—Jan 1936
Mersa Matruh	Jan	1936—Apr 1936
Heliopolis, det. Ramleh, Fayid, Mersa Matruh	Apr	1936—Sep 1938
Mersa Matruh	Sep	1938—Aug 1939
Qasaba	Aug	1939—Nov 1939
Heliopolis	Nov	1939—Jun 1940
Qasaba, det. Sidi Barrani	Jun	1940—Jan 1941
Gambut	Jan	1941—Feb 1941
Barce	Feb	1941—Mar 1941
Heliopolis	Mar	1941—Mar 1941
Kazaklar	Mar	1941—Apr 1941
Pharsala	Apr	1941—Apr 1941
Elevsis	Apr	1941—Apr 1941
Argos	Apr	1941—May 1941
Gaza	May	1941—Jun 1941
Ramleh	Jun	1941—Sep 1941
Aqir	Sep	1941—Oct 1941
Gerawla	Oct	1941—Dec 1941
Bir el Gubi	Dec	1941—Dec 1941
Tmimi	Dec	1941—Feb 1942
Acroma	Feb	1942—Feb 1942
Sidi Azeiz	Feb	1942—Mar 1942
Moascar	Mar	1942—May 1942
Sidi Azeiz	May	1942—Jun 1942
LG 103	Jun	1942—Jun 1942
LG 100	Jun	1942—Jul 1942
Heliopolis	Jul	1942—Jul 1942

LG 100, det. LG 202	Jul	1942—Nov	1942
Burg el Arab	Nov	1942—Jan	1943
Aqsu	Jan	1943—Feb	1943
LG K1	Feb	1943—Jul	1943
Rayak	Jul	1943—Nov	1943
El Bassa	Nov	1943—Jan	1944
Megiddo	Jan	1944—Mar	1944
Trigno	Mar	1944—May	1944
St. Angelo	May	1944—Jun	1944
Venafro	Jun	1944—Jun	1944
Aquino	Jun	1944—Jun	1944
Osa	Jun	1944—Jun	1944
Falerium North	Jun	1944—Jun	1944
Orvieto Main	Jun	1944—Jul	1944
Castiglione	Jul	1944—Aug	1944
Malignano	Aug	1944—Oct	1944
Florence	Oct	1944—Apr	1945
Bologna	Apr	1945—Apr	1945
Villa France	Apr	1945—Jun	1945
Bari	Jun	1945—Jul	1945
Ramat David	Jul	1945—Aug	1945
Petah Tiqva	Aug	1945—Mar	1946
Aqir	Mar	1946—Jun	1946
Ein Shemer	Jun	1946—Mar	1948
Nicosia, det. Ramat David	Mar	1948—Nov	1948
Fayid	Nov	1948—May	1950
Khartoum	May	1950—Aug	1950
Fayid	Aug	1950—Oct	1951
Abu Sueir	Oct	1951—Jan	1956
Hal Far	Jan	1956—Mar	1956
Akrotiri	Mar	1956—Aug	1956
Ta Kali, det. Khormaksar	Aug	1956—Mar	1958
Nicosia, det. Khormaksar	Mar	1958—Dec	1958

Squadron run down and finally disbanded in December, 1958. A new 208 Squadron was formed at Tangmere on 5 December, 1958 in the fighter/ground attack role.

Main Equipment

R.E.8 (Feb 1920—Oct 1920)
No serial numbers known
Bristol Fighter (Oct 1920—Apr 1930)
C4651; D7839; D8096; E2299; FR4582; FR4589; F4791; F4950; H1454; H1490; H1623; H1670; JR6767; J6794; J6798; J7640
Armstrong Whitworth Atlas I (Apr 1930—Aug 1935)
J9958; J9966; JR9975; K1013; K1561; K1569; KR1572; K1575
Hawker Audax I (Aug 1935—Apr 1939)
K3088; K3105; K3111; K3118; K3125; K3714; K7506; K7549
Westland Lysander I (Jan 1939—end 1941)
L4675; L4680; L4689; L4707; L4711, GA:B; L4717; L4720; L4728, B; L4734
Westland Lysander Mk. II
L4783; P9124; P9182
Hawker Hurricane I (Nov 1940— 1942)
N2611; N2626; P2638; P3270; P3826; P5173; T9536; V7295; V7431; V7670; V7830; W9328; Z4063; Z4252; Z4539; Z4775
Hawker Hurricane IIA, IIB, IIC (May 1942—Dec 1943)
Z4954; BD793; BE709; BG691; BG998; BN127; BP604; DG622; DG638; HL566; HL591; HL678; HL739; HL830, L; HL875

Vickers-Supermarine Spitfire IXC (Apr 1944—May 1947)
BS467, RG:C; JL230; MA481; MA515; MA630; MH423; MH656; MH772, RG:R; MJ179; MJ778; MK229; ML355; NH256; PT403, RG:D; PT705; PV119, RG:Q; RK837, RG:V; RR210; SM443, RG:P; TA857
Vickers-Supermarine Spitfire Mk. VC
ER963
Vickers-Supermarine Spitfire FR.18E (Aug 1946—Mar 1951)
TP278, RG:A; TP317, RG:D; TP345, RG:B; TP391, RG:N; TP443, RG:V; TP453, Y; TZ203, W, later J; TZ216, RG:W; TZ240, RG:A
Gloster Meteor FR.9 (Jan 1951—Jan 1958)
VW363, O; VW370, A; VZ578, R; VZ583, N; VZ594, G; WB121; WH544; WX962, Q

Commanding Officers

S/Ldr W. J. Guilfoyle, OBE, MC	Feb	1920—Feb 1922
S/Ldr A. ap Ellis	Feb	1922—Nov 1923
W/Cdr A. C. Winter	Nov	1923—Mar 1924
S/Ldr H. M. Probyn	Mar	1924—Dec 1925
S/Ldr A. S. C. MacLaren, OBE, MC, DFC, AFC	Dec	1925—Mar 1927
S/Ldr V. S. E. Lindop	Mar	1927—Apr 1930
S/Ldr M. Moore, OBE	Apr	1930—Apr 1933
S/Ldr J. Whitworth Jones	Apr	1933—Nov 1934
S/Ldr A. H. Flower	Nov	1934—Dec 1936
S/Ldr W. A. D. Brook	Dec	1936—Dec 1938
S/Ldr G. N. J. Stanley-Turner	Dec	1938—Apr 1940
S/KLdr R. A. Sprague	Apr	1940—Dec 1940
S/Ldr J. R. Wilson	Dec	1940—Oct 1941
S/Ldr L. G. Burnand, DFC	Oct	1941—Jun 1942
W/Cdr J. K. Rogers	Jun	1942—Sep 1942
W/Cdr M. A. Johnson, DFC	Sep	1942—Sep 1943
W/Cdr E. P. H. Wheeler	Sep	1943—Jan 1944
Lt Col J. P. D. Blaauw, DFC	Jan	1944—Mar 1945
W/Cdr J. B. A. Fleming, OBE	Mar	1945—Oct 1945
S/Ldr J. F. Norton, DFC	Oct	1945—Feb 1946
S/Ldr R. T. Llewellyn, DFM	Feb	1946—Jun 1946
S/Ldr F. J. Roder	Jun	1946—May 1947
S/Ldr C. F. Ambrose, DFC	May	1947—Jul 1948
S/Ldr J. M. Morgan, DFC	Jul	1948—Nov 1950
S/Ldr F. V. Morello	Nov	1950—May 1953
S/Ldr T. F. Neil	May	1953—Nov 1955
S/Ldr J. N. Thorne	Nov	1955—Jan 1958

Aircraft Insignia

The Bristol Fighters carried a white disc on the fin with, originally, cartoon characters on it. These were replaced by card suits later, repeated under lower wings. The Atlas carried the flying eye motif across the rudders. The Lysanders carried 'GA' code letters before the war. From September, 1939 these were changed to 'RG' but this was rarely carried on the Squadron aircraft until 1945. In the 1941–42 period the Hurricanes carried an unofficial white lightning flash each side of the fuselage roundel. 'RG' was carried consistently on the Spitfire IXs and 18s and on the latter the badge appeared on the cowlings. The Meteors carried this on the nacelle sides and a rectangle each side of the roundel containing blue/yellow/blue horizontal bands. (See also *Bomber Squadrons of the RAF*, p. 394 and *Fighter Squadrons of the RAF*, pp. 321–4)

No. 209 SQUADRON

BADGE
An eagle volant recursant descendant in pale, wings overture

MOTTO
'Might and main'

The eagle falling symbolises the destruction of Baron von Richthofen who, in World War I, fell to the guns of 209 Squadron

The Squadron was formed as No. 9 Squadron, RNAS at St. Pol on 1 February, 1917 and served throughout World War I as a fighter unit. As commemorated in the badge Capt Roy Brown shot down Germany's leading ace, Manfred von Richthofen in April, 1918. It was disbanded after the war at Scopwick on 24 June, 1919.

No. 209 re-formed as a flying-boat squadron at Mount Batten on 15 January, 1930. The Squadron was intended to be using Black-burn flying-boats and received its first Iris III in February, 1930. By June two more had arrived and during the subsequent years, due to unserviceability and mishap it maintained but two aircraft on its strength. These were later converted to Mk. V configuration in 1932–3. The following year they were replaced by three Blackburn Perths which the Squadron used over the Western Approaches and English Channel. However, these were grounded between October, 1934 and July, 1935 and 209 was forced to use the Saro London, Supermarine Scapa and Short Knuckleduster prototypes from Felixstowe during the interim. The Perths returned in July, 1935 and served successfully until the following year by which time Short Singapore IIIs were in sufficient supply to enable the re-equipment of the Squadron. In 1937 the Squadron flew a cruise to Malta; it also co-operated with radio and radar experiments with RAF Bawdsey. Later that year it moved to Malta for anti-piracy and anti-submarine patrols, only returning from the Med at the end of the year. 1938 was interrupted by its crew delivering Sunderlands to the Far East but in September it moved to its war station during the Munich crisis. At the end of the year No. 209 re-equipped once more and with the Stranraer it began its war operations on 3 September, flying North Sea patrols and searches off the Norwegian Coast for the German Battle Fleet. The original Consolidated PBY-4 (Catalina) was attached for experiments and was used for courier flights.

In December, 1939, however, it was chosen as the first squadron to receive the Saro Lerwick, beginning operations with it on Christmas Day. The Lerwicks were found to be very unserviceable operationally and both types were operated early in 1940 until the Lerwicks were grounded in February as the throttles would snap. At the end of the month operations were resumed and in March the last Stranraer op was flown and 376 operational hours had been amassed. After many mods the Lerwick was now greatly improved but engines were still troublesome; however 75 sorties were flown in June and a suspect submarine bombed on 20th. Next month a move was made to Wales but in August the aircraft were again grounded and only four sorties flown when operations were resumed in October. The following month the Squadron began converting to Catalinas as well as resuming tentative operations from Stranraer with Lerwicks. Twenty-six sorties were flown in December, including a sub strike on an oil streak. 1941 saw regular operations flown (convoy escorts, shipping searches and anti-submarine patrols). One Lerwick suffered a fatal accident in January and the CO failed to return from patrol in February. The Lerwicks were finally removed in May and the Squadron now increased its tempo; on 15th F/Lt Spotswood depth-charged a U-boat and scored a probable. On 26th P/O Briggs found the *Bismark* and shadowed it for 4½ hours.

In August, 1941 the Squadron moved to Iceland to cover the Atlantic Gap and before the month was out two U-boat attacks had been made, F/O Jewiss's on the 25th being definitely sunk. Two more attacks took place before the Squadron returned to the UK in October. The patrols continued, some being flown from Gibraltar at the end of the year, up to the first quarter of 1942. In March operations ceased as the Squadron set off for East Africa, establishing base at Kipevu in June and beginning operations over the Indian Ocean on 2 July. No. 209 now established bases on the various islands and up and down the coast and flew A/S patrols in transit to these bases, thus giving greater range. The operational pressure was less in this part of the world and little action came the Squadron's way. It was not until 1 June, 1943 that the Squadron dropped depth charges in anger on an oil streak which was never confirmed. Towards the end of the year it was largely occupied as a Flying-Boat Conversion Unit for the new Catalina squadrons forming in the area and little operational activity happened in 1944. Early in 1945 No. 209 re-equipped with Sunderlands and moved across to Ceylon where it began attacks on Japanese shipping off Burma, Thailand and Malya from an advanced base at Rangoon. With the war over it moved, by stages, to take up residence at Hong Kong.

A year later it transferred to Singapore and was involved from 1948 onwards in the Korean War, flying anti-shipping patrols as well as supplying a transport route between Singapore and Borneo from 1946 to 1949. With the rundown of flying-boat operations in the fifties No. 209 was eventually disbanded into No. 205 at Seletar on 1 January, 1955.

The Squadron re-formed on 1 November, 1958 at Kuala Lumpur by re-numbering No. 267 Squadron. It was now a short-range unit equipped with Scottish Aviation Pioneers and its task was Army support in the jungles of Malaya, flying into and out of small clearings with troops, supplies and also flying casualty evacuation. It also, for the first year, had a Flight of Dakotas which were used for longer-range trips but principally for 'voice-shouting', equipped with loudspeakers under the fuselage, these aircraft were used to shout messages to the insurgents in the jungle. In 1959 Twin Pioneers augmented the Pioneers and for the next nine years the Squadron continued on these essential support duties. The Squadron eventually disbanded at Seletar on 31 December, 1968, having maintained a detachment in Borneo during the troubles there during the mid-sixties.

Bases etc.

Re-formed at Mount Batten 15 January, 1930.

Mount Batten	Jan 1930	May 1935
Felixstowe	May 1935	Sep 1937
Kalafrana	Sep 1937	Sep 1937
Arzew	Sep 1937	Dec 1937
Felixstowe	Dec 1937	Sep 1938
Invergordon	Sep 1938	Oct 1938
Felixstowe	Oct 1938	Aug 1939
Invergordon, det. Sullom Voe, Falmouth	Aug 1939	Oct 1939
Oban	Oct 1939	Jul 1940
Pembroke Dock, det. Stranraer	Jul 1940	Dec 1940
Stranraer	Dec 1940	Mar 1941
Lough Erne	Mar 1941	Jul 1941
Reykjavik	Aug 1941	Oct 1941
Pembroke Dock	Oct 1941	Mar 1942
en route to East Africa	Mar 1942	Jun 1942
Kipevu, det. Kisumu, Aden, Masirah, Congella, Kilindini, Seychelles, Diego Suarez	Jun 1942	Jul 1945
Koggala, det. Rangoon, Kai Tak	Jul 1945	Oct 1945
Kai Tak	Oct 1945	Sep 1946
Seletar, det. Iwakuni	Sep 1946	Jan 1955

1 January, 1955 disbanded by merging into No. 205 Squadron. Re-formed at Kuala Lumpur on 1 November, 1958 by re-numbering No. 267 Squadron.

Kuala Lumpur, det. Penang	Nov 1958	Oct 1959
Seletar, det. Labuan	Oct 1959	Dec 1968

Disbanded at Seletar on 31 December, 1968.

Main Equipment

Blackburn Iris III, V (Jan 1930—Apr 1934)
Mk. III
N238; S1263; S1264; S1593
Mk. V
S1263; S1593
Blackburn Perth (Jan 1934—May 1936)
K3580; K3581; K3582
Interim Aircraft (Dec 1934—Aug 1935)
Supermarine Scapa S1648; Saro London K3560; Short R.24/31 K3574
Short Singapore III (Feb 1936—Dec 1938)
K4580; K6909; K6914, C; K6919, Y; K6921, Z; K8565; K8567, M; K8857
Vickers-Supermarine Stranraer (Nov 1938—Apr 1940)
K7289, WQ:C; K7290, WQ:N; K7292, WQ:X; K7296; K7299, WQ:D; K7302, WQ:B
Saro Lerwick I (Dec 1939—May 1941)
L7250, WQ:B; L7252; L7254, WQ:M; L7258, WQ:G; L7261, WQ:L; L7265, WQ:Q
Consolidated Catalina I (Apr 1941—Apr 1945)
W8145, J; W8428, K; Z2142, Q, later T; Z2149; AH530, WQ:T; AH545, WQ:Z; AH553, WQ:J; AH565; AH569; AJ160; FP107, S; FP227, X; FP273, L; FP281, Y; FP302, R; FP318, W
Consolidated Catalina Mk. IIA
VA703, WQ:M; VA715, N; VA727, P
Short Sunderland GR.5 (Feb 1945—Feb 1955)
DP198; ML881; NJ177, V; NJ267, WQ:S; PP103, U; PP116, WQ:L; PP151, N; RN264; RN298, WQ:R; RN303, X; SZ565, WQ:S; SZ571, Y; SZ599; VB884, WQ:X; VB888
Scottish Aviation Pioneer CC.1 (Nov 1958—Dec 1968)
XE515; XG558; XJ465; XL558, W; XL666; XL700, Z; XL706
Douglas Dakota C.4 (Nov 1958—Nov 1959)
KJ810; KJ955; KP277
Scottish Aviation Twin Pioneer CC.1, CC.2 (Oct 1959—Nov 1968)
XL970, C; XL997, H; XM939; XM957; XM963; XN318; XN321; XP294

Commanding Officers

S/Ldr J. H. O. Jones	Feb 1930	Aug 1930
W/Cdr C. G. Tucker	Aug 1930	Feb 1931
W/Cdr E. J. P. Burling, DSC, DFC, AFC	Apr 1931	Oct 1931
S/Ldr J. H. O. Hones	Oct 1931	Sep 1932
S/Ldr H. M. Massey, MC	Sep 1932	May 1934
W/Cdr G. E. Livock, DFC, AFC	May 1934	Jan 1936
W/Cdr C. R. Cox, OBE, AFC	Jan 1936	Oct 1936
W/Cdr G. W. Bentley, DFC	Oct 1936	Jan 1938
W/Cdr C. L. Scott, DSC	Jan 1938	Nov 1938
S/Ldr W. G. Abrams	Nov 1938	Jan 1939
W/Cdr C. G. Wigglesworth, AFC	Jan 1939	Jun 1940
W/Cdr J. E. M. Bainbridge	Jun 1940	Feb 1941
W/Cdr T. J. MacDermot	Feb 1941	Nov 1941
W/Cdr F. R. Drew	Nov 1941	Dec 1942
W/Cdr J. Barraclough, DFC, AFC	Dec 1942	May 1943
W/Cdr G. E. Wallace	May 1943	May 1943
W/Cdr J. T. D. Rivell	Aug 1943	Apr 1944
W/Cdr D. B. Fitzpatrick	Apr 1944	Sep 1944
W/Cdr P. R. Woodward, DFC	Sep 1944	May 1945
Lt Col H. J. T. Sheldon (SAAF)	May 1945	Nov 1946

W/Cdr L. M. Lawes   1946—   1947
S/Ldr P. R. Hatfield, DFC   1947—
S/Ldr J. Cartwright, MBE   1960—

Aircraft Insignia

The Squadron's unofficial emblem was carried on the cockpit side of the Iris

and Perth. The Stranraers carried 'WQ' code letters from September, 1939 onwards and perhaps 'FK' before the war. 'WQ' was also carried until the Squadron moved to East Africa and was resumed from 1945–51 on the Sunderlands. On the Pioneers and Twin Pioneers the Squadron's emblem was carried on a white disc on the fin.
(See also *Fighter Squadrons of the RAF*, pp. 324–5)

No. 210 SQUADRON

BADGE
A griffin segreant

MOTTO
'*Yn y nwyfre yn hedfan*'
('Hovering in the heavens')

The griffin associated the Squadron with
Wales where it was long stationed.

No. 210 Squadron was first formed at St. Pol on 12 February, 1917 and was then No. 10 Squadron, RNAS, becoming 210 again on 1 April, 1918 with the formation of the RAF. During World War I it served as a fighter unit equipped with Sopwith Triplanes and Camels. After the war it returned to the UK in February, 1919 and was disbanded at Scopwick on 24 June, 1919.

On 1 February, 1920 No. 210 re-formed at Gosport to bring into service the RAFs new torpedo-bomber, the Sopwith Cuckoo. For three years it was almost the sole landplane proponent of this art, developing techniques by using the ranges in Stokes Bay but on 1 April, 1923 it was disbanded again at Gosport.

On 1 March, 1931 No. 210 was again re-formed, as a flying-boat squadron, at Felixstowe and received its first aircraft, a Southampton in May, moving to Pembroke Dock to establish the new base there. By the autumn of 1932 it had worked up sufficiently for its first cruise which was to Denmark, Norway and Sweden. Peacetime training continued and in 1934 much time was spent preparing to re-equip with Short Singapore IIIs, the first of which arrived in November, 1934. Its first task, however, was to deliver Singapores to No. 205 Squadron in Singapore; *en route* one crew was killed by hitting a mountain near Messina. It was not until 1936 that the Squadron was really a going concern for it next had to give its Singapores to No. 203 at Basra, temporarily using their Short Rangoons until more Singapores were available. Even in 1936 it had to surrender its better aircraft to No. 230 Squadron and repair others to remain in business. However, in 1937 the Squadron finally became operational and was busily occupied with the Home Fleet in exercises and going on a Mediterranean cruise. The Squadron received a filip when F/Lt Canavan won the Sassoon Photography Trophy, the first time it had been won by a flying-boat Squadron. At the end of the year it was sent to Arzew in Algeria to fly anti-piracy patrols in conjunction with the French.

The Squadron came into the limelight in 1938 when it became the first unit to re-equip with the Short Sunderland; June was the month when the first two arrived. Not only was it busy working up the new type itself but crews were also used to ferry aircraft to Singapore for No. 230 Squadron. One of the early Sunderlands was lost in a landing accident on 20 September but in spite of all this when the Munich crisis arose at the end of the month the Squadron took six aircraft to its war station at Newport on the Tay. This was a false alarm but during the next year No. 210 worked up for the real thing a year later. When war came it immediately began patrols over the Western Approaches and also had aircraft detached in the Shetlands and at Woodhaven. In that first month of war the Squadron made five attacks on U-boats but with no confirmation of kills. In October the convoy system had been established and this took up most of No. 210s tasking, having detachments at Sullom Voe and Invergordon to help out the Squadrons there. Sorties averaged about twenty per month, mostly seeing no action but keeping the convoys covered. By mid-summer the sortie rate had gone up to

over 50 per month, both the Atlantic and the Norwegian coast being visited. The Squadron moved up to Oban in July, 1940 to concentrate on anti-submarine and convoy patrols. On 16 August F/O Baker found a surfaced U-boat and made three attacks with ample evidence of severe damage to the vessel. Two weeks later he attacked another U-boat which the convoy estimated as sunk. The work continued month by month; more attacks were made as the winter drew on and all this activity was not without loss, three crews dying during the year.

January, 1941 gave the Squadron its first definite kill of the war when F/Lt Baker depth-charged the Italian submarine *Marcella* which sank. It also brought the Squadron's first combat with a FW 200 which resulted in both aircraft being damaged. April, 1941 saw the Squadron re-equipping, this time with the long-range Catalina which, in various forms, was to serve it until the war's end. First Catalina sorties were made on 19 April when two aircraft left on patrol, one failing to return. The following month saw the Squadron busy in the hunt for the *Bismark*; just before midnight on 26 May F/Lt Hatfield found it and began shadowing, giving its position to the surface ships closing in until he had to return to base at 0300 hrs, by which time battle had been engaged. In June, 1941 the Squadron began basing aircraft in Iceland to extend its Atlantic coverage. This brought a new influx of submarine sightings but none of the subsequent attacks proved to be entirely successful.

Early in 1942 the Squadron transferred to the Shetlands, moving its operational area up to the Arctic Circle and making barrier patrols to intercept U-boats in transit. This was followed by escort duty to the Russian convoys during which many U-boats were found and attacked, the attack by F/Sgt Simmons on 21 September, whilst protecting convoy QP.14, resulted in the destruction of *U-253*. But operational needs changed and the following month No. 210 returned to Pembroke Dock and sent a large detachment to Gibraltar to provide convoy cover for the large fleets moving in for the North African landings. This task was continued until August, 1943, one crew being lost in this time. At Pembroke Dock the Squadron experimented with Leigh Lights fitted to Catalinas and on 10 March, 1943 F/Lt Martin made the first such illumination although the subsequent attack failed. That same month the Squadron began concentrating on the Bay of Biscay and this work continued when it moved its base to Dorset. Seven U-boats were sighted and two attacked and severely damaged, with one crew lost and one fatal crash. However, December, 1943 saw the Squadron running down and it eventually disbanded, the aircraft and crews being dispersed amongst other Squadrons.

It was not out of the war for long for on 1 January, 1944 No. 190 Squadron at Sullom Voe was re-numbered 210 Squadron. It was now back to Atlantic convoy patrols and anti-submarine patrols off Norwegian waters and its equipment was again the Catalina. On 25 February, 1944 S/Ldr French set out to escort a convoy. The convoy could not be found but a radar contact produced *U-601* which French attacked accurately and destroyed, survivors being seen in the water. It was also involved in Russian convoys once more until May, 1944 when the last convoy was safely escorted. Thereafter it concentrated on the U-boat war. That same month four attacks had been made and two more kills obtained, by F/O Bastable and Capt Maxwell. Two or three attacks were coming up each month during the summer of 1944 and in July No. 210 scored its 6th and 7th kills, the attack by F/O Cruickshank on 17th being a particularly brave effort. On the first run the depth charges would not release but on the second attack, in heavy AA fire the U-boat was straddled although the navigator was killed and the Captain severely wounded. He maintained command of the aircraft for the 5½ hr flight back, though lapsing into unconsciousness and insisting in helping his inexperienced co-pilot with the landing and mooring. On reaching hospital he was seen to have 72 wounds. For his gallantry he received the VC, and the good news that he had destroyed *U-347*. The other kill was *U-742*, destroyed by F/O Vaughan on 18 July.

The battle went on but the next confirmed victim was not until 7 May, 1945 when F/Lt Murray, using non-directional sonobuoys (code-name *High Tea*) detected and destroyed *U-320*. By then the war was virtually over. For the next month the Squadron flew a mail run to Norwegian ports but was disbanded at Sullom Voe on 4 June, 1945.

It re-formed in the peacetime RAF by the re-numbering of one of the Flights of 179 Squadron at St. Eval on 1 June, 1946. Thus it returned to the maritime reconnaissance role but with landplanes, its equipment being six Avro Lancasters. It was back to co-operating with the Home Fleet in exercises and was also involved in met flights for a while. Peacetime training was the norm once more although in January, 1948 a detachment went to Ein Shemer in Palestine to help No. 38 Squadron fly anti-immigrant patrols to locate ships carrying illegal Jewish immigrants. The following year a detachment went to Gibraltar for fleet exercises. At the end of November, 1949 the whole Squadron set out on a tour to Singapore where they flew on an anti-submarine exercise, returning to St. Eval on 12 December.

As time went on the number of exercises, both within Coastal Command and for NATO increased year in year out. No. 210 left St. Eval in September, 1952, its new permanent base being Top-cliffe where, in February, 1953 it re-equipped with Lockheed Neptunes. It was some time before 210 became operational because the aircraft lacked much of their search equipment but eventually it was flying in all the exercises again. In December, 1954 it took part in Christmas mail drops to the ocean weather ships in the Atlantic. Another unusual task came its way in the summer of 1955 when the Neptunes dropped dry ice on to clouds in Cumberland to try and cause rain to alleviate the drought. In 1956 a detachment went hurriedly to Malta to try and trace and track a Soviet submarine thought to be on its way to Egypt. In doing so it found other Soviet submarines whose presence had been unknown. Now that Shackletons were coming into service in sufficient numbers the need for Neptunes was dwindling and on 10 January, 1957 No. 210 Squadron was again disbanded, at Topcliffe.

Just under two years later No. 210 Squadron re-formed at Ballykelly on 1 December, 1958 with Avro Shackleton MR.2s, by re-numbering No. 269 Squadron. It continued the maritime role of that Squadron and took part in the continual round of exercises and overseas trips involved in the day-to-day life of Coastal squadrons in the sixties. Majunga saw its aircraft as it took its turn in the Beira patrols, concerned with blockading Rhodesia and as defence cuts reduced more and more overseas squadrons its aircraft went on detachment to fill the gaps, notably in the Persian Gulf area. On 31 October 1970 it became the subject of a defence cut itself and was disbanded at Ballykelly. However, the next day the Shackleton detachment at Sharjah was re-formed into No. 210 Squadron and it served as a component part of Air Forces Arabian Gulf for a year before again disbanding, at Sharjah, on 15 November, 1971.

Bases etc.

Re-formed at Gosport on 1 February, 1920.

Gosport	Feb 1920—Apr 1923	

Disbanded at Gosport on 1 April, 1923. Re-formed at Felixstowe on 1 March, 1931.

Felixstowe	Mar 1931—Jun 1931	
Pembroke Dock	Jun 1931—Jul 1931	
Felixstowe	Jul 1931—Oct 1931	
Pembroke Dock	Oct 1931—Sep 1935	
Gibraltar	Sep 1935—Aug 1936	
Pembroke Dock	Aug 1936—Sep 1937	
Arzew	Sep 1937—Dec 1937	
Pembroke Dock	Dec 1937—Sep 1938	
Newport	Sep 1938—Oct 1938	
Pembroke Dock, det. Woodhaven, Sullom Voe, Invergordon, Stranraer, Oban	Oct 1938—Jul 1940	
Oban, det. Reykjavik, Sullom Voe, Stranraer	Jul 1940—Feb 1942	
Sullom Voe	Feb 1942—Oct 1942	
Pembroke Dock, det. Gibraltar	Oct 1942—Apr 1943	
Hamworthy Junction, det. Gibraltar	Apr 1943—Dec 1943	

Disbanded at Hamworthy Junction in December, 1943. Re-formed by re-numbering No. 190 Squadron at Sullom Voe on 1 January, 1944.

Sullom Voe, det. Pembroke Dock	Jan 1944—Jun 1945

Disbanded at Sullom Voe on 4 June, 1945. Re-formed from a Flight of 179 Squadron at St. Eval on 1 June, 1946.

St. Eval, det. Ein Shemer, Gibraltar, Luqa	Jun 1946—Sep 1952
Ballykelly	Sep 1952—Sep 1952
Topcliffe	Sep 1952—Jan 1957

Disbanded at Topcliffe on 31 January, 1957. Re-formed by re-numbering No. 269 Squadron at Ballykelly on 1 December, 1958.

Ballykelly, det. Majunga, Sharjah	Dec 1958—Oct 1970

Disbanded at Ballykelly on 31 October, 1970. Re-formed 1 November, 1970 at Sharjah.

Sharjah	Nov 1970—Nov 1971

Disbanded at Sharjah on 15 November, 1971.

Main Equipment

Sopwith Cuckoo (Feb 1920—Apr 1923)
N8011
Supermarine Southampton II (May 1931—Jul 1935)
S1038; S1041; S1042; S1043; S1421; S1464
Service Trials Types (1932— 1935)
Short Singapore II N246; Saro London I K3560; Supermarine Stranraer K3973
Short Rangoon I (Aug 1935—Jul 1936)
S1433; S1434; S1435; K2134; K2809; K3678
Short Singapore III (Nov 1934—Nov 1938)
K3592, 2; K3594; K4578; K4582; K4584; K6916; K6920; K8565; K8566; K8568; K8856, D; K8859
Short Sunderland I (Jun 1938—Apr 1941)
L2162, G; L2163, DA:G; L2165, B, later DA:B; L5798, A, later DA:A; L5802; L5806; N6135; N9022; N9027, DA:J; N9048; N9050; N9600; P9624, DA:H; T9041, DA:A; T9044; T9073; T9076
Consolidated Catalina I (Apr 1941— 1943)
W8406, F; W8416, DA:E; W8424; Z2145, DA:B; AH531, DA:A; AH539, DA:K; AH545; AH550, DA:L; AH562
Consolidated Catalina IB (1942— 1945)
FP102; FP121; FP131, G; FP154; FP185, K; FP213, E; FP222; FP237, O; FP242; FP252, M; FP259, L; FP262, A; FP277; FP287; FP308; FP311
Consolidated Catalina IIA, III (1942— 1943)
Mk. IIA
VA722; VA725; VA728; VA729
Mk. III
FP536
Consolidated Catalina IVA, IVB (Jan 1944— 1945)
JV928; JV931; JX202; JX222; JX247; JX255; JX264;
IVB
JX574; JX583; JX604
Avro Lancaster GR.3 (Jun 1946—Feb 1953)
ME525, L:S; PA982; PB641, OZ:T, later L:T; RE115, OZ:T, later L:T; RE175, OZ:Z; RF272; RF307, OZ:W, later L:W; RF314; RF325; SW283, OZ:U; SW319, OZ:X; SW320, OZ:V, later L:V; SW367, OZ:Y, later L:Y; SW377, L:W
Lockheed Neptune MR.1 (Dec 1952—Jan 1957)
WX507, L:S; WX514, L:R, later 210:R; WX516, L:T, later :T; WX519, 210:U; WX525, 210:Y; WX528, L:Y; WX529, L:V, later 210:V; WX548; WX556, 210:Z
Avro Shackleton MR.2 (Dec 1958—Nov 1971)
WB833, 210:T; WG554, 210:V; WG558, 210:Y; WL737, 210:Z; WL748, 210:X; WL757, 210:W; WL787, 210:T; WL793, 210:S; WR954, 210:T; WR961, 210:U; WR968, 210:Z

Commanding Officers

S/Ldr J. A. G. de Courcy	Feb 1920—Apr 1920	
S/Ldr C. W. H. Pulford	Apr 1920—Sep 1920	
W/Cdr N. J. Gill	Sep 1920—Apr 1923	
W/Cdr R. Leckie, DSO, DSC, DFC	Mar 1931—Mar 1933	
W/Cdr A. T. Harris	Mar 1933—Jul 1933	
W/Cdr R. H. Kershaw	Jul 1933—May 1934	
S/Ldr A. F. Lang	May 1934—Oct 1935	
W/Cdr W. N. Plenderleith	Oct 1935—Dec 1938	
S/Ldr G. A. Bolland	Dec 1938—Jan 1939	
W/Cdr W. J. Daddo-Langlois	Jan 1939—Jan 1940	
W/Cdr W. J. Fressanges	Jan 1940—Jan 1941	
W/Cdr G. G. Barrett	Jan 1941—Nov 1941	
W/Cdr W. H. Hutton	Nov 1941—Jun 1942	

W/Cdr H. B. Johnson	Jun 1942—Jan 1943
W/Cdr C. H. Brandon	Jan 1943—Nov 1943
W/Cdr S. R. Gibbs, DFC	Nov 1943—Dec 1943
W/Cdr P. H. Allington	Jan 1944—Mar 1944
W/Cdr L. W. Burgess	Mar 1944—Oct 1944
W/Cdr R. W. Whittome	Oct 1944—Jun 1945
S/Ldr A. Henderson, AFC	Jun 1946—Jan 1947
S/Ldr F. G. Paisley, DFC	Jan 1947—Oct 1947
S/Ldr W. D. Hodgkinson, DFC, AFC	Oct 1947—Apr 1949
S/Ldr P. R. Casement, DSO, DFC	Apr 1949—Jun 1951
S/Ldr P. J. Cundy	Jun 1951—Nov 1951
S/Ldr E. F. J. Odoire, DFC, AFC	Nov 1951—Aug 1952
S/Ldr H. H. Eccles	Aug 1952—Jan 1954
S/Ldr H. R. Kerr, MBE	Jan 1954—Dec 1955
W/Cdr J. L. Nunn, DFC	Dec 1955—Jan 1957
W/Cdr J. F. Halton	Dec 1958—
W/Cdr J. W. King	
W/Cdr D. G. F. Fulton	
S/Ldr G. Moule	—Oct 1970
S/Ldr G. Moule	Nov 1970—Nov 1971

Aircraft Insignia

As far as is known, no Squadron insignia was carried until the arrival of the Sunderlands which originally carried the badge by the cockpit. The Squadron was allocated the pre-war code letters 'VG' then carried the wartime letters 'DA' until *ca* 1943 after which no identity was carried until the Lancasters used No. 179 Squadron's code letters 'OZ'. This was changed to the single letter 'L' in 1951 and the Squadron number *ca* 1956. The Squadron badge was carried on the Lancasters, Neptunes and Shackletons below the cockpit and the Squadron emblem on a white disc on the Shackleton fins *ca* 1960. The Lancasters were originally identified by white spinners and the Shackletons by green spinners.
(See also *Fighter Squadrons of the RAF*, p. 325)

No. 211 SQUADRON

BADGE
A lion disjointed, ducally crowned

MOTTO
'Toujours a propos'
(Always at the right moment')

The lion is taken from the arms of Bruges and is disjointed to show the main task of the Squadron in World War I, the bombing of Bruges Docks.

No. 11 Squadron RNAS originally formed as a fighter unit at Dunkirk on 8 March, 1917 but never materialised and was disbanded at the end of August. It re-formed in March, 1918, becoming No. 211 Squadron on 1 April, with the formation of the RAF. Its task was naval bombing which it performed with D.H.9s for the rest of World War I, returning to Wyton in March, 1919 and disbanding there on 24 June that year. It re-formed in the bomber role at Mildenhall on 14 June, 1937 moving to Egypt in May, 1938 where, with Blenheims it fought in the Western Desert, Greece and Syria. With the Japanese attack in the Far East the Squadron was hastily sent there, arriving after the fall of Singapore and fighting briefly from Sumatra and then Java before amalgamating with 84 Squadron in February, 1942.

In April, 1943 No. 211 re-formed at Phaphamau in India for long-range coastal fighter strike duties and was equipped with Blenheim Vs and Beaufighters. By the beginning of 1944 it had moved to Silchar from where it began operations with Beaufighters on 8 January. It was intended to use 60 lb rockets against bridge, shipping and rail targets but although it flew 50 sorties that month the results were disappointing as the targets were not suitable for RPs. The next month, however, it transferred its attention to Moulmein and Mandalay and was much more successful, and in March it concentrated on the airfields around Rangoon flying 107 sorties, but losing six Beaus. April and May were similar, but in June No. 211 changed its main role to attacking shipping targets in a successful series of strikes although three crews were lost. By August it had transferred to Northern Burma where it found difficult targets once more and it was a relief in September to get back to shipping; on 10th six aircraft made a memorable strike destroying or damaging thirteen vessels. The following month it began night sorties but found few targets.

As 1945 came in the Squadron was dividing its attention between rail targets and shipping on the Irrawaddy with upwards of 100 sorties a month. In April it contributed 97 sorties to Operation Dracula, the attack on Rangoon where it concentrated on communications targets. However, on 10 May it came off operations and moved back to Yelahanka to convert to Mosquitoes. During the conversion it had two fatal accidents and was not operational before the war ended. In November No. 211 moved to Bangkok and here one of its aircraft broke up in the air resulting in the grounding of the Mosquitoes in January, 1946. The aircraft had spar checks but before the Squadron could get going again it was disbanded at Don Muang at the end of February, 1946.

Bases etc.

Re-formed at Phaphamau in Aug, 1943.

Phaphamau	Aug	1943—Nov	1943
Ranchi	Nov	1943—	1943
Silchar		1943—Jan	1944
Bhatpara	Jan	1944—May	1944
Feni	May	1944—Jul	1944
Chiringa, det. Ranchi	Jul	1944—May	1945
Yelahanka	May	1945—Jun	1945
St. Thomas Mount	Jun	1945—Sep	1945
Cholavarum	Sep	1945—Nov	1945
Akyab	Nov	1945—Nov	1945
Don Muang (Bangkok)	Nov	1945—Feb	1946

Disbanded at Don Muang Airport end February, 1946.

Main Equipment

Bristol Beaufighter X (Aug 1943—May 1945)
LX938, B; LX996, G; LZ114, P; LZ157, M; LZ216, H; LZ270, L; LZ343, J; LZ372, E; LZ401, K; LZ479, O; LZ515, X; LZ527, Y; NE292, D; NW317, X; NE366, T; NE4401, K; NE539, Z; NE603, O; NE713, Z; NE814, B; NT994, G; NV114, M; NV202, P; RD387, A
de Havilland Mosquito VI (May 1945—Feb 1946)
RF779

Commanding Officers

W/Cdr P. E. Meagher, DFC	Oct	1943—Aug 1944
S/Ldr J. S. R. Muller-Rowland, DFC	Aug	1944—Oct 1944
S/Ldr H. E. Martineau	Oct	1944—Jan 1945
W/Cdr R. S. O. Lovelock, DFC	Jan	1945—Aug 1945
W/Cdr D. L. Harvey	Aug	1945—Feb 1946

Aircraft Insignia

No information is to hand regarding any insignia carried by this Squadron on its Beaufighters and Mosquitoes.
(See also *Bomber Squadrons of the RAF*, pp. 199–200)

No. 212 SQUADRON

BADGE
Rising from water barry wavy, a flying fish
MOTTO
'Amari ad astra'
('From the sea to the stars')

The flying fish is symbolic of the Squadron's
maritime flying-boat operations and is
numerous in the ocean over which the
Squadron flew.

The Number 212 Squadron was given to one of the Flights at the Great Yarmouth naval air station in August, 1918 in World War I which continued North Sea patrols. Whether the number was actually used is doubtful as another coastal unit at Dover also assumed the number 212. The unit was disbanded on 1 February, 1920.

On 10 February, 1940 No. 212 became the first squadron re-formed to fly operational photo reconnaissance work as a result of Cotton's photographic development flying at Heston. This was No. 212s base and it was equipped with Blenheim IVs, Hudsons and modified Spitfire Is. It sent a detachment to France which put in brief service during the hectic campaign of May/June, 1940, returning to Heston on 14 June. Two days later the Squadron was disbanded, being absorbed into the Photographic Reconnaissance Unit.

No. 212 Squadron re-formed once more, this time as a maritime reconnaissance unit at Korangi on 22 October, 1942, receiving its first aircraft, Catalinas, in October and beginning operations on 20 December with a convoy escort.

Through 1943 it flew about 30 sorties a month, mainly long boring convoy escorts or anti-submarine patrols. It had many detachments around the coast of the Indian sub-continent. Early in 1944 activity increased with the known presence of submarines in the area and on 17 March F/Lt Gallagher and crew found one on the surface but it had submerged before he could attack. Twelve days later F/O Chaple dropped depth charges on a doubtful contact with no result seen. Thereafter the excitement subsided once more and routine flying continued. In 1945 No. 212 added ASR sorties to its

tasks supporting the 20th US Bomb Group's raids on Singapore. It had several successes in this role in February and March. It also flew the occasional Special Duty flight, laying down supplies for insurgents in enemy-held territories. Before the war ended in the East it had been disbanded by re-numbering as No. 240 Squadron on 1 July, 1945.

Bases etc.

Formed out of a Flight at Great Yarmouth RNAS in August, 1918.
Great Yarmouth   Aug 1918—Feb 1920
Disbanded at Great Yarmouth 1 February, 1920. Re-formed at Heston on 10 February, 1940.
Heston, det. France   Feb 1940—Jun 1940
Disbanded into the PRU at Heston 10 June, 1940. Re-formed at Korangi Creek 11 December, 1942.
Korangi Creek, det. Keamari, Jiwani,
 Red Hills Lake, Trombay, Bally Dec 1942—Apr 1945
Red Hills Lake   Apr 1945—Jul 1945
Disbanded by re-numbering as No. 240 Squadron at Red Hills Lake 1 July, 1945.

Main Equipment

Sopwith F1 Camel
 B3882; B3897; B5666; B6369
Bristol Blenheim IV & Lockheed Hudson (Feb 1940—Jun 1940)
 No serials known
Vickers-Supermarine Spitfire I (Feb 1940—Jun 1940)
 N3116; P9331; P9392; P9394; P9396; P9453
Consolidated Catalina IB (Dec 1942—Jul 1945)
 FP152, C; FP165, H; FP175, B; FP202, D; FP231, K; FP246, A; FP284, B
Consolidated Catalina IVB (Sep 1944—Jul 1945)
 JX271, F; JX308, A, later G; JX324, B; JX341, H; JX366, C, later A; JX597, F

Commanding Officers

W/Cdr R. T. Gething, AFC   Dec 1942—Oct 1943
W/Cdr H. A. B. Porteous   Oct 1943—Jul 1945

Aircraft Insignia

No information is to hand as to any Squadron markings carried by this unit during its various existences.

No. 215 SQUADRON

BADGE
A porcupine
MOTTO
'Surgite nox adest'
('Arise, night is at hand')

The porcupine is part of the arms of
Coudekirke where the Squadron was formed
originally.

For most of its existence No. 215 Squadron was a bomber squadron, flying in World War I as one of the Handley Page heavy bombers from March, 1918 to October, 1919. It re-formed at Worthy Down on 1 October, 1935 and entered World War II with Wellingtons but did not become operational and was disbanded into 11 OTU at Bassingbourn in April, 1940. On 8 April it immediately re-formed at Honington as a Wellington squadron but this No. 215 Squadron was also absorbed into 11 OTU in May, 1940. A further No. 215 Wellington Squadron was formed at Newmarket on 9 December, 1941 and immediately sailed for India where it joined No. 99 Squadron to form a heavy bomber Wing, converting to Liberators in August, 1944. Eight months later it changed its role to that of a transport unit at Dhubalia in April and began conversion to Douglas Dakotas.

No. 215 Squadron began operations from Tulihal on 7 May, its main task being to supply the airstrips in Central Burma and provide transport for 36th Division. In June it paused to embark on

some glider towing training, then moved to support the Chittagong area dropping stores, both free drops and parachute drops, and landing stores and personnel where airstrips were available. In this final flush of fighting the Squadron was flying intensively, 376 sorties in August, 1945. Then came the war's end.

Now the Squadron was involved with Siam (Thailand), flying regular supply flights taking in occupation forces and bringing out POWs. In October it moved to Singapore where its routes were up into Malaya and across to Indonesia, together with POW lifting. Soon it had to fly supply drops once more as British troops became involved in the fighting in Java. By the end of the year the Squadron had six daily schedules with a detachment at Hong Kong for flights into China. This continued until 15 February, 1946 when it was disbanded, being re-numbered No. 48 Squadron.

A new No. 215 Squadron was re-formed at Kabrit in the Suez Canal Zone, equipped with Dakotas and attached to the Middle East Transport Wing. It flew the Middle East routes until 1 May, 1948 when it was re-numbered 70 Squadron.

On 30 April, 1956 No. 215 re-formed once more in a different role. It was now at Dishforth, Yorkshire and equipped with Scottish Aviation Pioneer CC.1s which it used for short-range army support duties. These STOL aircraft could land and take-off in small fields and formed a useful unit operating with the army until helicopters took over. On 1 September, 1958 this unit was re-numbered 230 Squadron. Five years later No. 215 Squadron re-appeared at Benson on 1 May, 1963. It was now a transport squadron once more, equipped with Argosies and after a short work-up it moved to its permanent base of Changi at Singapore, providing a medium-range transport and tactical support squadron for the Far East Air Force. It flew the main routes in the FEATO area and also provided parachute support for the army in Malaya for five years before defence cuts eliminated the Squadron once more, it being disbanded at Changi on 31 December, 1968.

Bases etc.

Transferred to the transport role at Dhubalia in April, 1945.

Dhubalia	Apr 1945—May 1945
Tulihal	May 1945—Jun 1945
Basal	Jun 1945—Jul 1945
Patenga	Jul 1945—Aug 1945
Hmawbi	Aug 1945—Oct 1945
Kallang, det. Kai Tak	Oct 1945—Feb 1946

Disbanded at Kallang on 15 February, 1946 by re-numbering as 48 Squadron. Re-formed at Kabrit on 1 August, 1947.

Kabrit	Aug 1947—May 1948

Disbanded at Kabrit on 1 May, 1948 by re-numbering as 70 Squadron. Re-formed at Dishforth on 30 April, 1956 in the army support role.

Dishforth	Apr 1956—Sep 1958

Disbanded at Dishforth on 1 September, 1958 by re-numbering as 230 Squadron. Re-formed at Benson on 1 May, 1963.

Benson	May 1963—Aug 1963
Changi	Aug 1963—Dec 1968

Disbanded at Changi on 31 December, 1968.

Main Equipment

Douglas Dakota III (Apr 1945—Feb 1946)
FD837, N; FD894, B; FD954, H; FZ589, Z; FZ619, N; KG391, F; KG795, T
Douglas Dakota IV (Apr 1945—Feb 1946 & Aug 1947—May 1948)
KJ824, L; KJ895, HW; KJ918, Q; KJ978, Q; KJ992, R; KK127, X; KK176, C; KK211, C; KN242, J; KN310, P; KN391, D; KN421, L; KN579, U; KN622, O; KN684, Z
Scottish Aviation Pioneer CC.1 (Apr 1956—Sep 1958)
XK367; XK369; XK370; XL555; XL557; XL558; XL702; XL703
Hawker Siddeley Argosy C.1 (May 1963—Dec 1968)
XN818; XN851; XP445; XP447; XP448; XP450; XR106; XR108

Commanding Officers

W/Cdr T. M. Buchanan	May 1945—Feb 1946
S/Ldr E. Bell, AFC	Aug 1947—Feb 1948
S/Ldr R. M. Burns	Feb 1948—May 1948
S/Ldr J. J. Woods, DFC	May 1956—Sep 1956
S/Ldr G. F. Turner, DFC	Sep 1956—Jul 1958
S/Ldr W. J. Simpson, DFC	Jul 1958—Sep 1958
W/Cdr A. Talbot-Williams	May 1963—
W/Cdr D. Gray	—Dec 1968

Aircraft Insignia

As far as is known, the only aircraft to carry squadron insignia since April, 1945 have been the Argosies, which had the porcupine emblem on the fins. (See also *Bomber Squadrons of the RAF*, pp. 206–8)

No. 216 SQUADRON

BADGE
An eagle, wings elevated, holding in the claws a bomb
MOTTO
'*CCXVI dona ferens*'
('216 bearing gifts')

The badge is one which had been in use for many years before the issue of official badges.

No. 216 Squadron's origins are involved. It originally existed as a detached flight of No. 7 Squadron, RNAS, operating from Redcar in Yorkshire with Handley Page O/100s on anti-submarine patrols over the North Sea. Despite great success (in one month it found eleven submarines and bombed seven of them), the use of this type for maritime work was discontinued and in October, 1917 it became the nucleus of A Squadron, the first unit destined for the Independent Bombing Force, and as such began long-range bombing operations in March, 1918. It was by then re-numbered No. 16 Squadron, RNAS from January, 1918 and became No. 216 Squadron RAF on 1 April, 1918, serving in this role until the war's end.

In May, 1919 it transferred to Egypt with O/400s and, although officially a bomber squadron, flew more in the role of a transport squadron than a bomber unit, a fact officially recognised in 1931 when it was re-designated as a Bomber-Transport squadron. The O/400s began a rudimentary passenger and mail service within the RAFs Middle East bases, flying regularly from Egypt to Palestine and Iraq. A regular Baghdad Air Mail was flown by the Squadron with D.H.10s but these had acquired an unfortunate reputation and were replaced by Vimys in 1922. The latter were used until Victorias arrived in 1926 at the same time as the mail route was taken over by Imperial Airways. With Victorias No. 216 now turned its attention to pioneering another route, south through Khartoum and then west to the coast at Bathurst. This route was later taken over commercially in 1936. The Squadron also flew on troop reinforcement duties, taking the South Wales Borderers to Palestine in 1929 to quell riots there, and in 1930 supported the Transjordan Frontier Force. A similar task on a larger scale took place in 1931 when the 1st King's Regiment was hastily lifted from Palestine to Cyprus to deal with the first 'Enosis' riots.

This continued to be No. 216s activity through the 'thirties and on the outbreak of war it was flying Valentias, soon after partially re-equipping with Bristol Bombays. With the latter the dual role came more into prominence, the tasks including reconnaissance missions and, after Italy entered the war in June, 1940, bombing raids along the North African coast. But still the transport routes were flown with both types, the West African route being taken over again to forge it into the air supply route that saved the day when the Mediterranean became closed. With the opening up of the war in Eritrea the Squadron became involved there, also both with support flying and bombing raids. At the end of 1940 it took over 70 Squadron's aircraft at Habbaniya and operated in Iraq as well. Much of its time was involved in support flying up and down the Western Desert as well as bombing at night, flying round the clock and inevitably building up a casevac capability. This intensified with the disastrous Greek and Crete campaigns and the Squadron was heavily involved in these evacuations. In May it was fighting in the Crete campaign, gun-running to Iraq and dropping troops into Syria to blow up bridges behind enemy lines. Not until September, 1941 did the Squadron relinquish its Valentias and become completely a Bombay unit. Soon after it worked up in the paradropping role and on 16 November five aircraft made the first airborne drop in the Middle East at Tmimi. At the end of the year the Squadron added four ex-civil D.H.86s for air ambulance work in the desert, but these only lasted a month. For the first half of 1942 the Western Desert fighting took up most of No. 216s energies; in July it began to re-equip with Hudsons and Lodestars. That month the Bombays flew an audacious sortie to a landing ground 200 miles behind the enemy lines to support a Fleet Air Arm Albacore squadron making a surprise raid on a convoy off Tobruk. This paved the way for Operation Chocolate in which, in November, a Hurricane Wing was placed and sustained for several days behind enemy lines in order to harass the retreating German transport in their back areas. A Bombay first flew into the desert landing ground (LG.125) to check its suitability then No. 216's Hudsons, together with some from No. 117 and 267 Squadrons, flew in escorting the Hurricanes. For three days the Hurricanes were supported, enabling them to create havoc on the enemy's supply routes then the whole lot was evacuated successfully once more. The Squadron also flew various Operation Diversion's, dropping self-destroying dummy paratroops behind enemy lines.

In 1943 the work became much more that of routine trips, including some VIP flights with royalty to Tehran and long sorties to Durban. Dakotas arrived in March and by May had ousted the Bombays and Hudsons. The Squadron was now flying schedules west to Casablanca and east to Shaibah, and south and west to Khartoum and Kano. After some refresher training paratroops were dropped once more, this time on Samos Island and this was followed up by supply drops through the autumn there and on Leros and Seriphos, flying 40 such sorties in five days in November. At the end of the year it became involved in VIP runs to the Teheran conference and then on to Moscow. The Squadron sent a large detachment from the Middle East in April, 1944, joining the Dakota force in the Far East. Here it immediately began supply-dropping and the evacuations from 'Aberdeen' and 'Broadway' (Operation Holiday). With this complete the Squadron flew regular daylight supply-drops into Burma until June when it retired from India to fly the routes, now including a detachment in Italy. Here it set up schedules on behalf of the army in Italy and in August began flying to Paris and the UK. As the war progressed No. 216 was responsible for opening up new air transport routes within the Med and Southern Europe so that by the end of the year it had services to Bucharest, Sofia, Athens and Belgrade and was maintaining an Athens/Crete shuttle. It still found time to fly some 'Specials' including taking secret equipment to the Soviet Union and support for the forces coping with the troubles in Greece.

Early in 1945 the detachment from Italy returned and No. 216 concentrated on the routes out of Egypt; it was now a big squadron having fifty aircraft on strength, and detachments in Aden, the Sudan and Kenya, as well as keeping one aircraft for the AOCs personal use.

With the war over the Squadron remained in Egypt, as part of the Middle East Transport Wing for ten years, replacing its Dakotas by Valettas, and flying the peacetime routes. It also maintained a paratrooping capability.

In November, 1955 the Squadron left Egypt for the UK. Here it had a completely new task. After a series of catastrophic disasters the de Havilland Comet jet airliner had been re-built on a safe basis and needed to be operated intensively to prove its viability for the airlines. At the same time the RAF needed to move into jet transports for the worldwide carriage of VIPs and No. 216 Squadron was chosen to fill this task. The first two aircraft, designated T.Mk. 2s, joined the Squadron in June, 1956 and intensive crew training followed. The first operational flight also took place that month, taking the Secretary of State for Air to Tushino Airport, Moscow. The Suez crisis in November enabled No. 216 to show its prowess, carrying VIPs back and fro to the bases in Cyprus. As more aircraft became available so No. 216 was able to establish regular schedules, both to America and to Australia, the latter becoming a five day round trip. In addition, the Squadron was continually flying 'Specials' including VIPs (the Queen made her first Comet flight in 1957) and trooping and casevac flights to points of emergency, for example in June, 1958 almost all the Squadron's activity was directed to the emergency in Cyprus. The Squadron's complement of Comet C.2s was ten and in February, 1962 these were supplemented by five Comet C.4s which eventually took over, the last C.2 flight being at the end of March, 1967. From then on the five Comets maintained a vital service for the RAF in their world-wide sorties but the contraction of the British Forces overseas made ample excuse for further transport cuts and on 27 June, 1975 No. 216 Squadron was disbanded at Lyneham and its Comets sold.

The Squadron re-formed in January, 1979 in the strike bomber role at Honington with Buccaneer S.2Bs.

Bases etc.

Moved to Kantara in Egypt in July, 1919 and began transport work as ancillary to its primary bombing role.

Kantara	Jul 1919—Apr 1925
Heliopolis, det. Eastleigh, Habbaniya, Khartoum, Lydda	Apr 1925—Oct 1941
Khanka (Cairo West), det. LG.224, El Adem, Marble Arch, Castel Benito, Khartoum, Gabes El Djem, Nicosia, Ramat David, Mauripur, Agartala, Bevinco, Bari, Tatoi, Habbaniya,	
Khormaksar, Eastleigh	Oct 1941—Mar 1946
Almaza	Mar 1946— 1946
Kabrit, det. Aqir	1946—Sep 1946
Fayid	Sep 1946—Feb 1947
Kabrit	Feb 1947—Nov 1955
Lyneham	Nov 1955—Jun 1975

Disbanded at Lyneham on 27 June, 1975. Re-formed at Honington in the strike bomber role in January, 1979.

Main Equipment

D.H.10 (Oct 1921—Jun 1922)
E7847; E7854; E9060; E9066; E9090; F1868; F1871
Vickers Vimy (Jun 1922—Aug 1926)
H653; HR5089; J7443; J7451; J7494
Vickers Victoria III (Jan 1926— 1929)
J7928; J7930; JR7931; JR8062; J8230; J8231; JR8920
Vickers Victoria V (1929—Sep 1935)
J9764, E; JR8063, H; J9766; K1313; K1315; K2341; K2343, 3; K2798
Vickers Valentia I (Feb 1935—Sep 1941)
JR9760, A; J9762; J9764; K1312; K1314; K2342, D; K2345; K2793; K2798; K2808; K3163; K3169, W; K3600; K3604, W; K3607; K3612, VT:D; K4632; K4633, C, later A; K8848
Bristol Bombay I (Nov 1939—May 1943)
L5810, SH:C; L5814; L5828; L5832, R; L5845, D; L5851, SH:G; L5857, SH:C
de Havilland D.H.86A (Dec 1941—Jan 1942)
AX672; HK829; HK830; HK831
Lockheed Lodestar (Jul 1942—Sep 1942)
AX686
Lockheed Hudson VI (Jul 1942—May 1943)
EW876; EW900; EW968; FK367; FK384, Q; FK503; FK600
Douglas Dakota I (Mar 1943—Jun 1944)
FD768; FD779; FD785; FD790; FD804; FD808; FD814; FD817
Douglas Dakota III (May 1943—Feb 1947)
FD833; FD886; FD898; FD923; FL510; FL552; FL605; FZ573; FZ689; KG510; KG549; KG633; KG712; KG753
Douglas Dakota IV (1944—Feb 1951)
KJ831; KJ906, HX; KJ938; KK207, HM; KN228; KN334, HY; KN475, HU; KN522, HP; KN653, HD; KN689, HA; KP265, HC
Vickers Valetta C.1 (Feb 1951—May 1956)
VL279; VW149; VW155; VW163; VW181; VW189; VW195; VW205; VW811; VW823; VW832; VX544; VX556; VX564; WD157
de Havilland Comet T.2 and C.2 (May 1956—Apr 1967)
XK669, *Taurus*; XK670, *Corvus*; XK671, *Aquila*; XK695, *Perseus*; XK696, *Orion*; XK697, *Cygnus*; XK698, *Pegasus*; XK699, *Sagittarius*; XK715, *Columba*; XK716, *Cepheus*
de Havilland Comet C.4 (Feb 1962—Jun 1975)
XR395; XR396; XR397; XR398; XR399

Commanding Officers

Maj W. R. Read	Jul 1919—Jan 1920	
Maj M. Henderson, DSO	1921— 1922	
S/Ldr C. O. F. Modin	1922—Oct 1924	
W/Cdr L. D. D. Gardnier, DSO, DFC	Oct 1924—Nov 1929	
W/Cdr E. A. B. Rice	Nov 1929—Apr 1933	
W/Cdr C. W. MacKey	Apr 1933—Jan 1937	
W/Cdr G. C. Gardiner, DSO, DFC	Jan 1937—May 1940	
W/Cdr S. D. Chichester	May 1940—Oct 1940	
W/Cdr F. J. Laine	Oct 1940—Aug 1941	
W/Cdr G. R. Howie	Aug 1941—Jul 1942	
W/Cdr P. Ruston	Jul 1942—Dec 1942	
W/Cdr E. M. Morris	Dec 1942—Jun 1944	
W/Cdr A. L. T. Naish	Jun 1944—Nov 1944	
W/Cdr J. H. Williams, AFC	Nov 1944—Jul 1945	
W/Cdr J. E. S. Morton, DFC	Jul 1945—Aug 1946	
W/Cdr G. R. Howie, DSO	Aug 1946—May 1947	
S/Ldr R. T. Mason	Jun 1947—Sep 1948	
S/Ldr F. Welburn	Sep 1948—Mar 1951	
S/Ldr E. A. Rockliffe	Mar 1951—Nov 1951	
S/Ldr C. M. Fell	Nov 1951—Sep 1953	
S/Ldr W. J. Swift	Sep 1953—Mar 1956	
W/Cdr B. D. Schlick, DSO, DFC	Jun 1956—Sep 1958	
W/Cdr R. G. Churcher, DSO, MVO, DFC	—Oct 1960	
W/Cdr N. E. Hoad, AFC	Oct 1960—	
W/Cdr D. Wright, AFC		
W/Cdr P. Walker	May 1972—Apr 1974	
W/Cdr A. R. King	Apr 1974—Jun 1975	

Aircraft Insignia

The D.H.10s carried card suit emblems on the nose and coloured horizontal bands at the top of the fin. Vimys, Victorias and Valentias in the twenties and thirties generally carried no distinctive markings, although the Victorias at one stage had a black band around the rear fuselage. In 1938 the code letters 'VT' were carried, changing to 'SH' on the outbreak of war, which was retained until *ca* 1942. Since then no markings have been carried to denote the Squadron although the Comet C.2s were each named (see above). (See also *Bomber Squadrons of the RAF*, pp. 208–11)

No. 217 SQUADRON

BADGE
A demi-shark erased
MOTTO
'Woe to the unwary'

The original No. 217 Squadron was formed on 1 April, 1918 from No. 17 Squadron RNAS, a D.H.4 bomber unit at Dunkirk. It fought in this role until the war ended then, after a period of transport duties, returned to the UK and was disbanded at Driffield on 19 October, 1919.

No. 217 Squadron was re-formed at Boscombe Down on 15 March, 1937 as a general reconniassance unit receiving Avro Ansons for this task. Three months later its Ansons took part in the massed formation flypast at the final Hendon Display and in 1938 flew as escort to the King and Queen as they sailed to France. From September, 1938 the Squadron acted in a quasi-operational role checking on all submarine movements in the English Channel and photographing suspect ones. It moved to Warmwell as its war station on the outbreak of war and then on down to St. Eval where it flew convoy escorts and anti-submarine patrols; by December it was flying as many as 94 sorties a month. On 2 April F/O Fenton, in Anson N9894, found a submarine and bombed it, claiming a probable kill. The following month the first Bristol Beauforts for the Squadron arrived and it began conversion. This was a lengthy process and before becoming operational the aircraft were given to 22 Squadron. In the meantime F/Sgt Welsh had attacked an enemy seaplane on 11 July and shot it down and Sgt Mott had bombed four E-boats, whilst F/Sgt Webb bombed and machine-gunned a U-boat in August.

In September the Ansons ventured as far as Brest where they bombed enemy shipping and two days later they were joined by Beauforts – No. 217's first sortie with this type. These operations were all at night, the Ansons visiting French ports also to bomb barge concentrations to scotch any invasion plans. By November the Squadron was operating in the ratio of 83 Anson sorties to five Beaufort ones, but by the end of the year the Anson was withdrawn and Beauforts were doing it all. These activities consisted in the main of raids on Brest, Lorient and the other Atlantic Coast ports. For these attacks they were using mainly IMPS (Impact Magnesium Percussion Mines) and TIMS (Time Impact Mines).

January, 1941 was a busy month with such attacks, then on 20th the Squadron began Biscay patrols as well. On 1 February the Squadron tried a day attack on *Hipper* in drydock at Brest but two of the six Beauforts failed to return. This type of work continued until the beginning of March when No. 217 was withdrawn from these bombing raids. It now returned to convoy escort and also to flying escort to the civil DC-3s flying the Chivenor/Lisbon service. In April it returned to the Biscay and Atlantic coast operations and these were intensively flown through the summer, losing about three crews a month whilst so occupied. A peak was reached in October with 86 sorties on these duties then the Squadron began torpedo at Abbotsinch. It now moved to the Channel for its operating area, working up to the Hook of Holland. It was rewarded by a very successful attack on a motor vessel on 27 November, using Manston as an advanced landing ground. From here it made a fruitless attack on the battleships *Scharnhorst* and *Gneisenau* in the Channel on 12 February, losing one crew. It now suffered from personnel shortage, many of its crews being taken for overseas and two months later the Squadron itself ceased operations to go overseas.

In August, 1942 No. 217 reached Minneriya in Ceylon. Here, two months later it received Lockheed Hudsons and began A/S patrols in November. In April, 1943 it received Beauforts once more and in August it ceased its convoy and A/S patrols to work up on torpedo attacks again, resuming operations in October. It continued flying Beauforts on these operations until July, 1944 without finding any enemy shipping or submarines to attack. In July it re-equipped with Beaufighters. In October No. 217 worked up in the RP role

and flew fighter affiliation training but in January, 1945 it reverted to the long-range torpedo role. From February to April the Squadron was non-operational waiting for a move (it became known as Ceylon's Home Guard). In July it moved at last only to find that it had to transfer to the RP and cannon role once more and the war ended before it became operational. No. 217 Squadron was disbanded at Gannavarum on 30 September, 1945.

It re-formed at St. Eval on 14 January, 1952 in the maritime reconnaissance role where it worked up the Lockheed Neptune into RAF service and established itself operationally at Kinloss, flying the Neptunes on search patrols over the northern North Sea for five years before disbanding again on 31 March, 1957.

No. 217 briefly re-formed as a SAR unit at St. Mawgan on 1 February, 1959 by re-numbering No. 1360 Flight and served in this role at Christmas Island for the nuclear tests there returning to this country to disband again on 13 November, 1959.

Bases etc.

Re-formed at Boscombe Down on 15 March, 1937.

Boscombe Down	Mar 1937	Jun 1937
Tangmere, det. Warmwell, Carew Cheriton	Jun 1937	Aug 1939
Warmwell, det. Carew Cheriton	Aug 1939	Oct 1939
St. Eval, det. Carew Cheriton, Limavady	Oct 1939	Oct 1941
Thorney Island, det. Manston	Oct 1941	Mar 1942
Leuchars, det. Thorney Island, Bircham Newton	Mar 1942	Apr 1942
en route to Ceylon	Apr 1942	Jul 1942
Minneriya, det. Ratmalana	Jul 1942	Feb 1943
Vavuyina, det. Ratmalana, Addu Atoll, Cochin, Santa Cruz	Feb 1943	Apr 1944
Ratmalana	Apr 1944	Sep 1944
Vavuyina	Sep 1944	Jun 1945
Gannavarum	Jun 1945	Sep 1945

Disbanded at Gannavarum 30 September, 1945. Re-formed at St. Eval on 14 January, 1952 in the maritime recce role.

St. Eval	Jan 1952	Jul 1952
Kinloss	Jul 1952	Mar 1957

Disbanded at Kinloss on 31 March, 1957. Re-formed at St. Mawgan on 1 February, 1958 in the SAR role, by re-numbering No. 1360 Flight.

St. Mawgan	Feb 1958	1958
Christmas Island	1958	1959
UK (? St. Mawgan)	1959	Nov 1959

Disbanded in the UK on 13 November, 1959.

Main Equipment

Avro Anson I (Mar 1937—Dec 1940)
K6167, K6285, MW:F; K6310, YQ:A; K6311, MW:P; K8714, MW:J; K8743, 217:O; K8745, YQ:Q; K8769, YQ:J; K8784, 217:N; K8787, MW:N; K8813, MW:V; L7994, MW:U; L9150, MW:K; N9889, MW:R; N9894, MW:F; R3346, MW:B; R9599, MW:B

Bristol Beaufort I (May 1940—Apr 1942 & Apr 1943—Aug 1944)
L9794, MW:R; L9835, MW:W; L9878, MW:R; L4471, MW:A; L4487, MW:E; L9972, MW:F; N1012, MW:S; N1039, MW:O; N1173, MW:E; W6501, MW:P; W6537, MW:N; X8935, MW:P; AW190, MW:K; AW242, MW:B; DE108; DW888, C; DW920, H; DW994, G; DX121, W; EK999, G; JM508

Bristol Beaufort II (Nov 1941—Apr 1942)
AW247, MW:W; AW250, MW:Z; AW274, MW:L; AW278, MW:F; AW312, MW:D

Lockheed Hudson IIIA/VI (Oct 1942—Jun 1943)
V9106, V; AE555, K; EW902, G; FH274, N; FH349, S; FH417, B; FH430, R; FK441, D

Bristol Beaufighter X (Jul 1944—Sep 1945)
NE618; NE659; NE818; NV319; NV382; RD522

Lockheed Neptune MR.1 (Jan 1952—Mar 1957)
WX495, A:F; WX496, A:D; WX504, A:H; WX509, A:C; WX511, 217:F; WX528, 217:D; WX548, 217:H; WX554, A:A

Westland Whirlwind HAR.2 (Feb 1958—Nov 1959)
No serials known

Commanding Officers

S/Ldr D. D'H. Humphries	Mar 1937	May 1939
W/Cdr A. P. Revington	May 1939	Jun 1940
W/Cdr L. H. Anderson	Jun 1940	Jul 1940
S/Ldr L. B. B. King	Jul 1940	Jul 1940
W/Cdr C. A. Bolland	Jul 1940	Mar 1941
W/Cdr L. W. C. Bower	Mar 1941	Jan 1942
W/Cdr Larkin	Jan 1942	Feb 1942
S/Ldr Taylor, DFC, AFC	Feb 1942	Feb 1942

W/Cdr S. M. Boal, DFC	Feb 1942—Apr 1942		
S/Ldr Taylor, DFC, AFC	Apr 1942—Apr 1942		
W/Cdr W. A. L. Davis	Apr 1942—Aug 1942		
F/O C. Buckley	Aug 1942—Oct 1942		
F/O W. E. M. Price	Oct 1942—Nov 1942		
W/Cdr A. D. W. Miller	Nov 1942—Mar 1943		
W/Cdr R. J. Walker	Mar 1943—Mar 1944		
W/Cdr J. Child	Mar 1944—Aug 1944		
W/Cdr J. G. Lingard, DFC	Aug 1944—Aug 1945		
W/Cdr A. F. Binks, DFC	Aug 1945—Sep 1945		
S/Ldr M. A. Ensor, DSO, DFC	Jan 1952—Mar 1954		

S/Ldr P. H. Stembridge, DFC, AFC   Mar 1954—

Aircraft Insignia

The Ansons originally carried the Squadron number in flight colours on the rear fuselage and the emblem on a six-pointed white star on the fin. When the aircraft were camouflaged this latter was retained but the letters 'YQ' were substituted for the number. These letters were changed to 'MW' in September, 1939 which was retained until moving to Ceylon. It is doubtful if any insignia was carried during 1942–45 in Ceylon. The Neptunes at first carried the single identity letters 'A' but this was later changed to the Squadron number once more.

No. 219 SQUADRON

BADGE
A death's head hawk moth

MOTTO
'From dusk until dawn'

The badge symbolises the Squadron's
night-fighter role

No. 219 Squadron was formed in August, 1918 by combining the Coastal Flights at Manston and Westgate as one unit. It flew coastal patrols until the end of the war and remained in being until 7 February, 1920 when it disbanded.

No. 219 re-formed in World War II as a night-fighter unit, on 4 October, 1939 and served in this role until disbanding on 1 September, 1946 having become part of 2nd TAF in 1944 after a spell in North Africa. Since World War II it has had two brief existences, both as a night-fighter squadron, from March, 1951 to September,

1954 in the Suez Canal Zone and from September, 1955 to July, 1957 in the UK.

Bases etc.

Formed at Manston in August, 1918
Manston, det. Westgate   Aug 1918—Feb 1920
Disbanded at Manston on 7 February, 1920.

Main Equipment

Sopwith/Hamble Baby (Aug 1918—Feb 1920)
   N1019; N1962
Short 184 (Aug 1918—Feb 1920)
   N1229; N1264; N1782; N2636; N2807; N2938; N2995; N9058
Airco D.H.9 (Aug 1918—Feb 1920)
   No serials known
Fairey IIIB (1918—Feb 1920)
   N2232; N2234; N2245

Commanding Officers

Not known.
(See also *Fighter Squadrons of the RAF*, pp. 328–30.)

No. 220 SQUADRON

BADGE
On a pellet, between two eight-pointed stars, a
torch enflamed

MOTTO
'Kathoraemen aichtoi'
('We observe unseen')

The unit was formed at Imbros, an island
associated with the Cabiri which were
mythological divinities believed to be the
guardians of mariners. A pine-burning torch
was one of their symbols and, as some writers
identify the Cabiri with Castor and Pollux two
stars have been introduced into the badge.

No. 220 Squadron did not officially happen until September, 1918 when C Squadron, RNAS at Imbros in the Gallipoli area used the number given to it on 1 April, 1918 when it became part of the RAF. It was a general purpose naval unit, having been formed at Mudros early in 1916, most of its operations, as No. 220, being bombing raids, although it also flew reconnaissance patrols widely and had a fighter elements. To all intents and purposes it had ended its flying at the end of 1918 although it was not officially disbanded until August, 1919.

The Squadron re-formed in a general reconnaissance role at Bircham Newton as one of the expanding Coastal Command force of

Avro Ansons. It remained there until 21 August, 1939 when it moved to its war station at Thornaby and began anti-submarine patrols over the North Sea on 4 September. That same month it began to convert to Lockheed Hudsons, flying its first operation with this type on 5 October. By November it was tangling with Luftwaffe seaplanes and flying boats, having four combats during the month and destroying two Do 18s for no loss. That month, too, the last Anson sorties were flown. Before the year was out the Squadron was attacking enemy surface vessels, scoring one patrol boat damaged.

On 1 January the Squadron lost its first aircraft to enemy action when Hudsons NR:T and L attacked two He 111s shooting one into the sea but losing T in the fight. On 16 February the Squadron was instrumental in finding the *Altmark*, the auxiliary and prison ship escorting the *Admiral Graf Spee*, and directing naval vessels to it. The Squadron's operating areas were the Norwegian coast and the North Sea down to the Dutch coast, and it spent much time bombing enemy shipping in the spring of 1940. The Norwegian campaign involved intense activity and in May 182 sorties were flown in this area. No. 220 then turned its attention to Holland bombing oil storage at Rotterdam to prevent the Germans using it. It was in on the Dunkirk beach patrols in June, on one occasion the Battle Flight attacked forty Ju 87s and claimed five shot down. It still had time to operate to Norway and on 22nd sank a 6,000 ton ship in

Kristiansund, ending June with 249 operational sorties in the month. In July it transferred its operational area to the Danish and North German coasts and kept up a succession of shipping attacks, including several on surfaced U-boats. Considering the task casualties were light. As the winter came on No. 220 settled into a routine of armed recces over this area and also sent a detachment to St. Eval for similar work off Northern France. More and more operations took place from this detachment; they were mostly night sorties, taking advantage of full moon illumination.

The tempo reduced in 1941. In April the Squadron moved to Wick to operate to Norway once more during which attacks were made on the heavy cruiser *Hipper* and several U-boats.

These were in addition to the routine convoy escorts and anti-submarine searches which took place month by month. Throughout the year this continued to be the Squadron's life, the highlight of the year being on 29 October when nine aircraft made a highly successful strike on Halesund leaving behind seven ships sunk. The Hudson days were now numbered for it was deemed that No. 220 should convert to Fortresses.

This came about in an odd way. No. 90 Squadron, a bomber unit with Fortress Is had found this version useless over Europe and has sent a detachment to Egypt. In December this detachment was renumbered 220 Squadron whilst the original No. 220 was still flying Hudsons. This latter became non-operational and moved to Polebrook on 1 January, 1942 where No. 90 Squadron was based, to convert to the Fortress I, took over No. 90's aircraft and moved to N. Ireland for coastal operations, the Middle East detachment joining them in February.

In April, 1942 it resumed anti-submarine operations with Hudsons and two Fortress Is, the latter flying 308 operational hours in May. By July the Squadron was standardising on Fortress IIAs and in that month flew 19 convoy escorts, one A/S patrol and four ASR sorties with them. Slowly it built up its N. Atlantic operations, sending a detachment to St. Eval to fly met flights in November. That same month F/Lt Wright depth-charged a U-boat for No. 220's first attack with Fortresses, and the Squadron roamed far and wide using Benbecula and Reykjavik as advanced landing grounds.

The Squadron's activity increased in 1943 with two U-boat attacks in February, one being severely damaged. For the next few months No. 220 logged three attacks a month with some results. In September, however, the Squadron began a move overseas, settling in at Lagens in the Azores in October and immediately covering the mid-Atlantic convoy routes. S/Ldr Webster's crew were lost on 25th but a fortnight later F/Lt Drummond made up for this by attacking a U-boat and sinking it.

A stable pattern now emerged for the Squadron with approx 50 sorties a month, building up to 100 in the summer. Occasional U-boat attacks were made but it was largely monotonous patrolling. The next definite kill was on 26 September by F/Lt Wallace and crew. The following month crews were detached to St. Davids to convert to Leigh Light Liberators and brought aircraft back with them to re-equip, the first Liberator operation being on 4 December. Gradually this type took over from the Fortresses in 1945, the pattern of sorties changing so that by April the Squadron was flying mostly ASR operations. With the European war over No. 220 returned to the UK in June and transferred to Transport Command that month, moving base in September.

At the end of that month the Squadron began flying the transport routes to India carrying freight and troops in both directions. This continued until the post-war re-adjustment of forces had taken place and the transport force was cut down, No. 220 disbanding at Waterbeach on 25 May, 1946.

On 24 September, 1951 No. 220 Squadron was re-formed in the maritime reconnaissance role at Kinloss and equipped with Avro Shackletons. It soon moved to St. Eval where it became part of the coastal force there, flying out over the Western Approaches, taking part in overseas goodwill trips and occasional trooping sorties when crises arose around the world. It progressed through the various Shackleton variants until 1958 when, shortly after receiving Mk.3s, it was renumbered 201 Squadron at St. Mawgan on 10 October.

From 1959 to 1963 another No. 220 Squadron existed at North Pickenham as a Thor Inter-Continental Ballistic Missile unit within Bomber Command.

Bases etc.
Re-formed at Bircham Newton on 17 August, 1936.

Bircham Newton	Aug 1936—Aug 1939
Thornaby, det. Wick, St. Eval	Aug 1939—Apr 1941
Wick, det. Shallufa	Apr 1941—Feb 1942
Nutt's Corner	Feb 1942—Jun 1942
Ballykelly, det. St. Eval	Jun 1942—Feb 1943
Aldergrove	Feb 1943—Mar 1943
Benbecula, det. St. Eval	Mar 1943—Sep 1943
Thorney Island	Sep 1943—Oct 1943
Lagens	Oct 1943—Jun 1945
St. David's	Jun 1945—Sep 1945
Waterbeach	Sep 1945—May 1946

Disbanded at Waterbeach on 25 May, 1946. Re-formed at Kinloss on 24 September, 1951.

Kinloss	Sep 1951—Nov 1951
St. Eval	Nov 1951—Sep 1957
St. Mawgan	Sep 1957—Oct 1958

Disbanded 10 October, 1958 by re-numbering as 201 Squadron.

Main Equipment
Avro Anson I (Aug 1936—Nov 1939)
K6188, 220:H, later NR:X; K6207, 220:M, later HU:M, later NR:M; K6224, HU:T, K6228, NR:G; K8750, NR:H; K8755, 220:P; K8818, HU:W, later NR:W; K8825, NR:Z
Lockheed Hudson I, III (Sep 1939—Apr 1942)
N7221; N7232, NR:T; N7261; N7283, NR:Z; N7289, NR:L; N7291, NR:K; N7295, NR:F; N7316, NR:Y; P5116; P5124, NR:F; P5151, NR:B; AM815, NR:D
Boeing Fortress I (Dec 1941—Jul 1942)
AN518, MB:B; AN527, NR:A; AN530; AN531; AN532; AN537
Boeing Fortress II/IIA (Jul 1942—Jan 1945)
FA697, 2:R; FA707, 2:Z; FA710, 2:M; FK186, S; FK189, 2:X; FK191, 2:P; FK200, B, later 2:B; FK206, K; FK212, V; FL450, U; FL456, 2:N; FL458, A, later Q; FL459, 2:J; FL462, W
Boeing Fortress III (Jul 1944—Feb 1945)
HB786; HB791; HB792, U
Consolidated Liberator V, VI, VIII (Dec 1944—May 1946)
BZ743, ZZ:C; BZ984, ZZ:C; EV995, ZZ:I; KG904, ZZ:E; KG990, ZZ:Y; KH133, ZZ:Q; KH222, ZZ:J; KH337, ZZ:W; KH411, ZZ:S; KK255, 8D:B; KK322, ZZ:Z; KK340, 8D:J; KL548, ZZ:T; KL620, ZZ:AW; KN703, ZZ:K
Avro Shackleton MR.1A (Sep 1951—Oct 1958)
VP257, T:P, later T:K; VP294, 220:P; WB821, T:L, later 220:L; WB828, T:K, later 220:K; WB837, T:S, later T:B; WG508, T:L; WG525, T:P
Avro Shackleton MR.2 (Mar 1953—Jul 1954)
WG557, T:L; WL737, T:K; WL743, T:P; WL745, T:O; WR966; WR969
Avro Shackleton MR.3 (Aug 1957—Oct 1958)
WR975, 220:P; WR977, 220:L; WR979, 220:N; WR980, 220:O; WR987, 220:R

Commanding Officers
S/Ldr W. M. M. Hurley	Aug 1936—Dec 1936
S/Ldr F. P. Smythies	Dec 1936—Jan 1939
W/Cdr A. H. Paul, AFC	Jan 1939—May 1940
W/Cdr T. H. Carr, DFC, AFC	May 1940—Jul 1941
W/Cdr C. F. C. Wright, DFC	Jul 1941—Feb 1942
W/Cdr R. T. F. Gates	Feb 1942—Sep 1942
W/Cdr P. E. Hadow	Sep 1942—Jan 1944
W/Cdr J. M. N. Pike, DSO, DFC	Jan 1944—Sep 1944
S/Ldr R. G. English	Sep 1944—Nov 1944
W/Cdr B. O. Dias, DFC	Nov 1944—
S/Ldr A. E. W. Laband	Sep 1951—Oct 1953
S/Ldr C. W. Cornish	Oct 1953—Nov 1954
S/Ldr C. B. Brown	Nov 1954—Mar 1956
W/Cdr R. E. Glover	Mar 1956—Oct 1958

Aircraft Insignia
From 1936 to 1938 the aircraft carried the Squadron number. This was replaced by the code letters 'HU' in the autumn, changing to 'NR' on the outbreak of war. These letters were retained until mid-1943 when letters were dropped until Nos. 206 and 220 Squadron were using Fortresses at the same station in 1943 when No. 220 adopted the number '2' on their aircraft. This continued until some time in 1944 when code letters 'ZZ' were adopted, possibly coincident with the arrival of Liberators. After transferring to Transport Command the letters '8D' were used as well. The Shackletons used the single letter 'T' at first, changing to the Squadron number ca. 1956. (See also *Bomber Squadrons of the RAF*, pp. 214–15.)

No. 221 SQUADRON

BADGE
A flying fish
MOTTO
'From sea to sea'

The badge and motto indicate the Squadron's
maritime reconnaissance role.

The Squadron began as D Squadron, RNAS, one of the units flown by the Navy at Mudros in the Gallipoli campaign. It became No. 221 Squadron on 1 April, 1918 on the formation of the RAF. In July its tasks were more clearly defined as a bombing unit on a mobile basis. As such, after World War I was over it was sent to South Russia where it served on policing duties with its D.H.9s. It disbanded at Petrovsk on 1 September, 1919.

The Squadron was re-formed at Bircham Newton on 21 November, 1940. With the coming of ASV radar Coastal Command were anxious to use this equipment in a large landplane and 221 was formed to employ the Wellington for this purpose. It worked up on Wellington ICs, ASV being first fitted on T2919 in January, 1941 and eventually the equipment went into operational trials when the Squadron began flying EMRO patrols. These involved flying the entire length of the Dutch coast just before dawn to trace enemy shipping movements and were first flown on 2 March. These sorties attracted the attention of German Bf 110s, and one aircraft was followed back to Norfolk and shot down in the circuit at Langham (by a Ju 88) on 10 April. The Squadron had also sent B Flight to N. Ireland to use its ASV on A/S patrols over the Atlantic. In April it also put its equipment to use searching for the *Scharnhorst* unsuccessfully. In May it moved to Limavady to concentrate on the North-Western Approaches. After flying 95 sorties in May the Squadron's first U-boat came up on 18 June when P/O Ramsay and crew made a depth-charge attack. July was a busy month with 92 sorties, four U-boat attacks (2 in one day), two air combats in which two Wellingtons were lost. The pressure increased through the next few months and in September five attacks were made on U-boats picked up by the ASV. At the end of the month No. 221 moved to Iceland to get nearer to the submarines' hunting ground and made five attacks in October, claiming one U-boat damaged. From there it also flew ice patrols until the year's end when it returned to its original base to prepare for moving to the Middle East.

In January, 1942 it began A/S sweeps from LG.87 and on 26 April F/Sgt Nixon found and attacked an enemy convoy. By June it had established itself on a new routine whereby its ASV-equipped Wellington VIIIs (known as 'Goofingtons') operated as search aircraft for torpedo Wellingtons of No. 38 and subsequent squadrons (known as 'Fishingtons'), enabling night strikes to be made on enemy supply convoys. These were interspersed with the normal general recce duties involving convoy and A/S patrols and on one of these on 21 August, 1942 Sgt Clark found a U-boat and sank it. As the year wore on No. 221s work became more intensive as it moved bases to keep pace where the action was.

In 1943 it began using its own 'Fishingtons' and on 24th was able to record that a motor vessel it had attacked was burnt out. More and more it was operating from Malta and in February it was very successful, sinking two ships, blowing a tanker in two and setting two other ships on fire for the loss of three crews. The offensive continued through the year; in addition in May No. 221 joined the land offensive, taking part in bombing raids on Marsala and dropping *Nickels* (leaflets). In July it started 'Taranto Block' patrols at night to keep enemy shipping out of the way.

The pressure continued building up to 100 sorties a month right through the winter. In 1944 the Squadron became primarily involved in operations in the Aegean. In March it moved base to Italy and flew offensive shipping recces in the main with occasional bursts of U-boat hunting. In October it moved to Greece to fly mine-spotting and anti-E-boat patrols and also bombed roads and bridges, in the anti-ELAS campaign. In fact, for a while it ceased from maritime operations altogether until the ELAS rebels surrendered in January, 1945. By now there was little maritime interest in the Mediterranean and No. 221 flew leaflet, transport and the occasional bombing sortie, interspersed with Red Cross supply runs. In April it moved back to Egypt and flew sea and desert ASR duties with detachments in Libya and Palestine. On 25 August, 1945 it was disbanded at Edku.

Bases etc.

Re-formed at Bircham Newton on 21 November, 1940.

Bircham Newton, det. Limavady, St. Eval	Nov 1940	May 1941
Limavady, det. St. Eval	May 1941	Sep 1941
Reykjavik	Sep 1941	Dec 1941
Bircham Newton	Dec 1941	Jan 1942
LG.87	Jan 1942	Mar 1942
LG.89	Mar 1942	Jun 1942
Shandur, det. St. Jean	Jun 1942	Aug 1942
Shallufa	Aug 1942	Nov 1942
Gambut	Nov 1942	Dec 1942
Berka 2, det. Luqa	Dec 1942	Mar 1944
Grottaglie, det. Foggia, Gambut	Mar 1944	Oct 1944
Kalamaki, det. El Adem	Oct 1944	Apr 1945
Edku, det. El Adem, Aqir, Benina	Apr 1945	Aug 1945

Disbanded at Edku on 25 August, 1945.

Main Equipment

Vickers Wellington IC (Nov 1940—Jul 1941)
L7861, DF:E; L7898; N2736; P9223; R1152; R1276; T2555; T2840; T2896; T2915, DF:M; T2998, DF:K; W5651, DF:N; W5732; X3161

Vickers Wellington VIII (Mar 1941—Jun 1943)
T2919; T2979, DF:L; T2988, DF:H; W5615, DF:C; W5631, DF:T; W5655, DF:F; W5671; W5676, DF:G; Z8705; Z8719; BB431; BB466, B; BB656, L; HF869; HF889; HF901; HX487, Y; HX534, J; HX686; HX738, B; LB153, E; LB173, C

Vickers Wellington XI/XII (Jun 1943—Sep 1943)
HF114; HF119; HF804; HZ116; HZ395, M; HZ417; MP537; MP598, B; MP619; MP646; MP701

Vickers Wellington XIII (Sep 1943—Aug 1945)
HZ593, Q; HZ604; HZ707, D; HZ780; HZ865, J; HZ974, E; JA145, Z; JA179, P; JA206, Z; JA272, W; JA318, A; JA412, S, later J; JA568, N; ME895, H; MF263, F; MF356, B; NF465, G; NF592, U

Commanding Officers

W/Cdr T. R. Vickers	Nov 1940	Sep 1941
W/Cdr A. M. Murdoch	Sep 1941	May 1942
W/Cdr J. D. T. Revell	May 1942	Sep 1942
W/Cdr R. A. Sprague, DFC	Sep 1942	Oct 1942
W/Cdr E. P. W. Hutton, AFC	Oct 1942	Jun 1943
W/Cdr M. J. A. Shaw	Jun 1943	Oct 1943
W/Cdr J. H. Hoskins, DFC	Oct 1943	Jul 1944
W/Cdr J. H. Simpson, DFC	Jul 1944	Dec 1944
W/Cdr R. H. Prior, DFC	Dec 1944	Jun 1945
W/Cdr G. Taylor, DFC, AFC	Jun 1945	Jul 1945
W/Cdr W. H. Hankin	Jul 1945	Aug 1945

Aircraft Insignia

Upon re-forming the Squadron was allocated the code letters 'DF' which it carried forthwith, although they were dropped soon after proceeding to the Middle East.

(See also *Bomber Squadrons of the RAF*, p. 215)

No. 224 SQUADRON

BADGE
On a rock, a tower entwined by a serpent
drinking from a lamp therein

MOTTO
'Fedel all'amico'
('Faithful to a friend')

The badge is based on the arms of Otranto
where the Squadron was formed and the motto
refers to the unit's aid to Italy in World War I.

No. 224 Squadron was formed on 1 April, 1918 out of the bombing flights of No. 66 Wing, RNAS at Otranto. Flying D.H.4s and D.H.9s it fought on that front, being disbanded in May, 1919.

It re-formed at Manston on 1 February, 1937 from No. 48 Squadron personnel as a general reconnaissance unit in Coastal Command and was equipped with Ansons, after moving to Boscombe Down that month. It had the honour of leading the massed formation of 250 aircraft at the 1937 Hendon Display. In 1938 No. 224 specialised in night shipping recce work and in May, 1939 became the first squadron to re-equip with the Lockheed Hudson. These it took on operations the day war broke out, now operating from Leuchars over the North Sea. In the first month of the war it flew 113 sorties and had four combats with German flying-boats, losing one crew. In October three of the Squadron managed to down a Do 18 on 7th. A detachment was set up at Abbotsinch with Tiger Moths for coastal patrol work in the Clyde area but this became an independent unit in December. The main Squadron continued its work over the North Sea, making its first U-boat attack, with bombs, on 5 December (P/O Dewar and crew). In January, 1940 the Battle Flight made an attack on three enemy destroyers and the pattern remained unchanged until Germany's invasion of Norway caused No. 224 to concentrate heavily on this campaign, bombing harbours and attacking shipping. Even after resistance was over the Squadron mainly operated in this area, bombing enemy convoys and making strikes as far south as Heligoland.

Losses were not light, one or two crews failing to return each month and the sortie rate going up to 163 in September. With the onset of winter the Squadron settled into convoy escorts and Stand patrols along the Norwegian coast, losing three crews in December on this work. In 1941 the Squadron worked away in this area, seeking to deny German shipping the shelter of the Norwegian coast until April. It then moved to N. Ireland and settled into covering the mass of convoys moving into and out of Liverpool and the Clyde, seeking to protect them in the North Western Approaches. Occasionally U-boat sightings and attacks took place but mostly it was monotonous convoy escort work.

At the end of the year No. 224 moved to Cornwall to fly *Stopper* patrols, to do the same along the NW French coast as it had along the Norwegian coast previously. It made several ship attacks on this and then reverted to the NW Approach work in February, 1942. In March two U-boats were found and depth-charged but no results were observed. In July replacements at last arrived for the Hudsons in the shape of Liberators. Operations continued whilst the Squadron converted but in September 224 moved to Hampshire to complete the conversion, resuming operations from there in October. On 20th of that month F/O Sleep, in Liberator FL910, found a U-boat and attacked, destroying it, but in the explosion of the depth-charges the aircraft's elevators were destroyed and it became almost uncontrollable, the control columns having to be tied forward. All loose articles were jettisoned and the aircraft eventually made a crash landing at Predannack. In November two attacks were made on enemy motor vessels and in 1943 the Squadron moved to St. Eval from where most of its recent operations had been flown. On 4 April another U-boat was attacked. The Squadron was now largely flying anti-submarine patrols and searches and in May this produced seven attacks, one of which obviously damaged the submarine severely. This pace was maintained during the summer,

with a definite kill recorded to S/Ldr Candy on 3 July. The Squadron was now meeting fighter opposition and on 2 September two of the Squadron's aircraft were brought down. In October the first attack by the Squadron using RPs against a U-boat took place and these were used for the next few months. At the end of the year intensive Leigh Light training took place.

In January, 1944 five more U-boats were attacked, four in the first week. The Squadron was concentrating on attempting to cut the transit routes in and out of the French Atlantic ports and June was a heavy month with seven attacks producing at least one kill but two Liberators were lost with crews. A move of area took place in September when the Squadron turned its attention to the Norwegian coast as the French Atlantic ports had been flushed out. Four U-boats were immediately attacked and one definitely sunk and motor vessels set about with depth-charges. There was no let-up as 1945 came in the Squadron now entirely concerned with anti-submarine patrols and four more attacks came in March and April. Even though VE-Day came the Squadron remained operational until 2 June when F/Lt Pretlove, in XB:N, flew No. 224s last operational sortie. Its final score was 11 U-boats destroyed and three others shared.

The war over the Squadron set up permanent base at St. Mawgan where it re-equipped with Lancasters in 1946, taking on ASR as another facet of its maritime role. Here No. 224 was disbanded on 10 November, 1947. It re-formed on 1 May, 1948 in N. Ireland at Aldergrove with Halifaxes. These it flew on met reconnaissance duties and set up a detachment at Gibraltar. Three years later the whole squadron moved there forming the maritime unit for the Rock and including general reconnaissance of shipping in the area. This role was expanded as it re-equipped with Shackletons and maintained a particular watch on naval shipping moving through the Straits. In addition it flew a goodwill tour of South America and the Caribbean in 1957 and in 1959 sent a detachment to Masirah for colonial policing duties in the Arabian Gulf. In 1960 it threw its energies into taking supplies into Agadir and evacuating casualties after the severe earthquake. In 1961 it again toured the Caribbean in addition to its tasks at Gibraltar. However, the sixties brought successive reductions in RAF strength and No. 224 Squadron was disbanded at Gibraltar on 31 October, 1966.

Bases etc.

Re-formed 1 February, 1937 at Manston.

Manston	Feb 1937	Feb 1937
Boscombe Down	Feb 1937	Jul 1937
Thornaby, det. Eastleigh	Jul 1937	Sep 1939
Leuchars, det. Thornaby, Abbotsinch, Aldergrove	Sep 1939	Apr 1941
Limavady	Apr 1941	Dec 1941
St. Eval	Dec 1941	Feb 1942
Limavady, det. Stornoway	Feb 1942	Apr 1942
Tiree, det. North Coates	Apr 1942	Sep 1942
Beaulieu, det. St. Eval	Sep 1942	Apr 1943
St. Eval	Apr 1943	Sep 1944
Milltown	Sep 1944	Jul 1945
St. Eval	Jul 1945	Nov 1947

Disbanded at St. Eval on 10 November, 1947. Re-formed at Aldergrove on 1 May, 1948.

Aldergrove, det. Gibraltar	May 1948	Aug 1951
Gibraltar, det. Masirah	Aug 1951	Oct 1966

Disbanded at Gibraltar on 31 October, 1966.

Main Equipment

Avro Anson I (Feb 1937—May 1939)
K6172; K6249; K6282; K6289, 224:F; K8742; K8747; K8786, 224:P; K8787, 224:S; K8813; K8818, 224:W; K8820; K8825; N4953

Lockheed Hudson I (May 1939—May 1941)
N7212, QX:H; N7222, QX:N; N7247, QX:G; N7307, QX:E; N7358, QX:H; N7392, QX:S; P5122, QX:S; P5136, QX:M; P5161, QX:D; T9251, QX:X; T9337, QX:F; T9344, QX:P

Lockheed Hudson III (Dec 1941—Sep 1942)
V9068, QX:N; V9090, QX:O; V9091, QX:B; V9092, QX:A

Lockheed Hudson V (May 1941—Sep 1942)
AE639, QX:Q; AE643, QX:W; AE651, QX:Z; AM530, QX:Q; AM565, QX:W; AM623, QX:F; AM694, QX:T; AM714, QX:X; AM757, QX:K; AM781, QX:G; AM827, QX:D; AM882, QX:M

Consolidated Liberator IIIA (Sep 1942—Apr 1943)
FK230, J; FK225, G; FK242, K; FK244, E; FL906, O; FL910, H
Mk. II
AL507, Z
Consolidated Liberator V (Mar 1943—   1944)
FL228, XB:Y; FL925, G; FL937, H; FL948, M; FL959, P;
FL964, XB:O
Consolidated Liberator VI/VIII (1944—Oct 1946)
KG964, XB:G; KH189, XB:S; KH414, XB:V; KH751, XB:G;
KK300, XB:B; KK323, XB:F; KK344, XB:K; KK363, XB:P;
KK381, XB:L; KN722, XB:B; KN753, XB:L
Avro Lancaster GR.3 (Oct 1946—Nov 1947)
RE164, XB:Q; RE175, XB:P; PB529, XB:F; RF292, XB:O;
RF314, XB:Q; SW294, XB:P
Handley Page Halifax GR.6 (May 1948—Mar 1952)
RG778, XB:D; RG836, XB:J; RG851, B:O; RG873, XB: ;
ST804, B:K
Avro Shackleton MR.1A (Aug 1951—Oct 1954)
VP256, B:A; VP287, B:B; VP291, B:C; WB819, B:H; WB832, B:K;
WB844, B:M; WB854, B:S
Avro Shackleton MR.2 (May 1953—Oct 1966)
WG532, 224:S; WG554, 224:M; WG558, B:R; WL750, 224:W;
WL753, B:Q; WL789, 224:W, later A; WL800, 224:B;
WR951, 224:W; WR955, B:P; WR957, 224:R; WR961, 224:L;
WR968, B:R, later R

Commanding Officers

S/Ldr R. N. Waite	Mar 1937	Jan 1939
W/Cdr E. A. Hodgson	Jan 1939	Dec 1940
W/Cdr R. N. Clark	Dec 1940	Mar 1941
W/Cdr T. C. Curnow	Mar 1941	Mar 1942
W/Cdr W. H. Kearney	Mar 1942	Apr 1943
W/Cdr A. E. Clouston, DFC, AFC	Apr 1943	Feb 1944
W/Cdr W. T. McComb, OBE	Feb 1944	Jan 1945
W/Cdr M. A. Ensor, DSO and Bar, DFC and Bar, AFC	Jan 1945	1946
S/Ldr H. M. S. Green	1946	Nov 1947
S/Ldr G. Davison	May 1948	Aug 1948
S/Ldr A. H. Dart, DSO, DFC	Aug 1948	Oct 1948
S/Ldr F. A. B. Tarns	Oct 1948	Nov 1949
S/Ldr G. F. Morley-Mower, DFC	Nov 1949	Feb 1952
S/Ldr G. L. Mattey	Feb 1952	Oct 1953
S/Ldr J. G. Roberts, DFC, DFM	Oct 1953	Apr 1955
W/Cdr J. D. E. Hughes, DFC	Apr 1955	Jan 1957
W/Cdr G. E. Willis, DFC, AFC	Jan 1957	Jan 1959
W/Cdr A. S. Baker, OBE, DFC	Jan 1959	Feb 1959
W/Cdr B. Lewin, DFC	Dec 1959	Oct 1960
W/Cdr J. G. Duncan, MBE	Oct 1960	Dec 1962
W/Cdr E. J. A. Patterson	Dec 1962	1964
W/Cdr G. Bates	1964	Oct 1966

Aircraft Insignia

From 1937 to late 1938 the Ansons carried the Squadron number on the side. In 1938 it was allocated the code letters 'PW' but no confirmation of their use has come to hand. From September, 1939 the Hudsons did use 'QX' and this was also used on the Liberator IIIs. Then code letters were dropped in 1943 and not used again until 1944 when the combination 'XB' was used until 1951, on Liberators, Lancasters and Halifaxes. This was replaced by the single letter 'B' which was used on Halifaxes and Shackletons until *ca* 1956 when the Squadron reverted to using its number and the Squadron emblem also appeared on a white shield on the nose.
(See also *Bomber Squadron of the RAF*, p. 218)

No. 225 SQUADRON

BADGE
In front of an anchor, two swords in saltire, points uppermost
MOTTO
'We guide the sword'

The combination of an anchor with cross swords associated the Squadron with its RNAS beginnings and its Army co-operation activities in World War II.

No precise date is known for the Squadron's original formation. It was some time after 1 April, 1918 when the RAF was formed and No. 225 consisted of a uniting of several RNAS units at Aliminni in Italy as part of 66 Wing. It is reported to have flown Sopwith 1½ Strutters, D.H.9s, D.H.9As and Sopwith Camels on raids against Albania. It was disbanded at Otranto in December, 1918.

On 3 October, 1939 No. 225 was re-formed at Odiham from B Flight, No. 614 Squadron, being known as No. 614A Squadron for the first week. Equipped with Lysanders, its first task was to ferry other Lysanders to the operational squadrons in France. It then began a leisurely work-up. It missed the action in France in 1940, beginning operations in June, flying dawn and dusk coastal anti-invasion recces on the line Selsey Bill to St. Alban's Head. These patrols were extended from Bognor Regis to the Lizard from July onwards, using St. Eval as an ALG. This was all in addition to working up with its Army components and beginning occasional photo recce survey work in the UK. By the summer of 1941 the coastal recces had ceased but now a detachment was set up at Pembrey for ASR duties, the first sortie being on 6 May. This detachment was transferred to Fighter Command's use at the end of

the month. More and more the Squadron was involved in army exercises, being detached to many small landing fields for this purpose.

Early in 1942 No. 225 converted to Hurricanes and added Mustangs to work up the fighter-recce task and in August became operational flying convoy and anti-intruder coastal patrols. At the end of the month, however, it moved to Scotland and prepared for moving overseas. It became part of the RAF's contribution to the North African landings, flying its Hurricanes into Maison Blanche airfield, Algiers on 13 November. Four days later it began Tac/R operations and by the end of the month had lost four pilots in action. December was a hectic month with 76 Tac/R sorties and in addition airfield strafes and pathfinder sorties to Blenheim V raids filled the days. In the New Year it joined 324 Wing using its Hurricanes for tactical bombing and borrowing Spitfires from No. 93 and 111 Squadrons for high-level Tac/R sorties. In February it received its own Spitfires and could now step up its activities, flying 181 sorties in the month, many in bombing enemy motor transport in the Kasserine Pass, using its Hurribombers as well. It was now mainly flying tactical bombing sorties on tanks and motor transport, building up to 255 sorties in March and 381 in April, by which time it was almost entirely Tac/R again. In that month it also began shipping recces off the coast but the pace began to slow from then on. On 12 May the campaign ended, No. 225 having flown 806 Tac/Rs, 22 artillery recces, 82 shipping recces, 92 PRs, 44 battery recces, 4 contact patrols, 2 message drops and 211 tactical bombing sorties, losing thirty aircraft but only nine pilots.

Now the Squadron moved forward and took part in Operation Corkscrew, the attacks on Pantellaria and Lampedusa. Next operations were against Sicily at the end of August and the pace was once again at a high level as the armies taking over Sicily needed close support from No. 225. From here the Squadron flew support to Operation Avalanche, the Salerno landings, and based itself in the Salerno bridgehead on 15 September, although it had to move out later and just maintain a detachment there due to enemy air raids. The Squadron was continuously engaged on the West Coast battle flying 408 sorties in October, predominantly Tac/R duties but with some sorties trying to locate 500 escaped British POWs. Many base moves took place in Italy as the Squadron kept up with the troops and then at the end of the year transferred to the east coast and began, on 19 December, operations over Yugoslavia. These were largely PR missions on which the Spitfires were escorted by other Spitfire squadrons. Early in January, 1944 the Squadron returned to the west to support the X Corps Front in the advance to Rome. In February the concentration shifted to artillery recces for the NZ Corps at Cassino, followed by the Anzio bridgehead in March which involved a hectic period for No. 225. During April half the Squadron was stood down in turn for a rest from operations but in May a record number of sorties (499) was flown, mainly artillery recces and Tac/Rs. As the Army broke out of the bridgehead in June the Squadron made three moves in a fortnight to keep up with the troops.

Towards the end of July No. 225 Squadron moved to Corsica from where it supported Operation Dragoon, the Southern France landings, flying spotting duties for the naval guns and Tac/Rs for the troops ashore. It followed them ashore on 20 August but in less than a month the army had moved so fast that the Squadron was out of range of operations and returned to Italy, where it flew artillery recces for the II and XIII Corps.

By the end of the year it was flying a daily rail recce to check on movements in the Bologna area.

The pressure was maintained at a high level during the first months of 1945 as the final battles in Italy opened up. By April, when 431 sorties were flown, it was flying *Pineapples*, operations in which 225 itself called-up fighter-bombers to suitable targets. Suddenly the war ended although No. 225 remained busy for a while flying policing operations over Trieste. In October it moved into Austria from where it patrolled the Yugoslav frontier and began PR sorties to map Austria. In June, 1946 it moved back to Italy where it was eventually disbanded at Campoformido on 21 January, 1947.

On 1 January, 1960 the Squadron was re-formed by expanding the Joint Experimental Helicopter Unit at Andover into an operational squadron. It was equipped with Sycamore and Whirlwind helicopters and its role was army support. This role was worked up over the next few years and in 1964 it moved to Borneo where it played a vital role in the operations, flying both rescue and casevac sorties together with army support operations. With this over it returned to the UK and was disbanded in November, 1965.

Bases etc.

Re-formed at Odiham on 3 October, 1939 from B Flight, 614 Squadron.

Odiham, det. Weston Zoyland, Roborough	Oct 1939	Jun 1940
Old Sarum	Jun 1940	Jun 1940
Tilshead, det. Hatfield, Oakhampton, Pembrey, Worthy Down, Andover, Samlesbury, Shrewton	Jun 1940	Jul 1941
Thruxton, det. Weston Zoyland, Docking, Warmwell, Abbotsinch, Dumfries	Jul 1941	Aug 1942
Macmerry	Aug 1942	Nov 1942
Maison Blanche	Nov 1942	Nov 1942
Bone	Nov 1942	Dec 1942
Souk-el-Arba	Dec 1942	Dec 1942
Souk-el-Khemis	Dec 1942	Dec 1942
Constantine	Dec 1942	Jan 1943
Souk-el-Khemis	Jan 1943	Apr 1943
Marylebone	Apr 1943	May 1943
Ariana, det. Korba (N), Setif	May 1943	Aug 1943
Francesco	Aug 1943	Sep 1943
Milazzo	Sep 1943	Sep 1943
Salerno, det. Isola No. 2	Sep 1943	Sep 1943
Scanzano, det. Salerno	Sep 1943	Sep 1943
Gioia del Monte	Sep 1943	Oct 1943
Isola, det. Scanzano, Serretelle, Pallazzo, Foggia	Oct 1943	Oct 1943
Capodochino	Oct 1943	Jan 1944
Lago	Jan 1944	Jun 1944
Tre Cancelli	Jun 1944	Jun 1944
Galoria	Jun 1944	Jun 1944
Voltone	Jun 1944	Jul 1944
Follonica	Jul 1944	Jul 1944
Calvi	Jul 1944	Aug 1944
Ramatuelle	Aug 1944	Aug 1944
Sisteron	Aug 1944	Sep 1944
Satolas	Sep 1944	Sep 1944
Las Jasse	Sep 1944	Sep 1944
Peretola	Sep 1944	Apr 1945
Bologna	Apr 1945	Apr 1945
Villa Franca	Apr 1945	May 1945
Tissano	May 1945	Aug 1945
Klagenfurt, det. Udine	Aug 1945	Jun 1946
Tissano	Jun 1946	Jul 1946
Campoformido	Jul 1946	Jan 1947

Disbanded at Campoformido on 21 January, 1947. Re-formed from the JEHU (Joint Experimental Helicopter Unit) at Andover on 1 January, 1960.

Andover, det. El Adem	Jan 1960	Jun 1960
Odiham	Jun 1960	1962
Kuching	1962	1965
Odiham	1965	Nov 1965

Disbanded at Odiham on 1 November, 1965.

Main Equipment

Westland Lysander II (Oct 1939—Mar 1941)
L4753, LX:L; L4787, LX:U; L6865, LX:E; L6868, LX:Y; N1224, LX:B; N1256, LX:L; N1293, LX:H; P1738, LX:W; P9121; P9133, LX:R; R1998, LX:X, R2007, LX:U; R9122, LX:L; R9125, LX:N

Westland Lysander III/IIIA (Oct 1940—Jun 1942)
T1529; T1700; V9310; V1361; V9444; V9457; V9497; V9570; V9595, WU:F

Hawker Hurricane I (Jan 1942—Jun 1942)
P2001; P3112, J; V6603, A; V6740, O; V6774, N; V6842, B; AF959, K; AF995, H

Hawker Hurricane IIB/IIC (Feb 1942—Apr 1943)
BG967; BN360; BN372; BP654; HL800; HL877; HL953; HL985; HM140; HV139; HV664; HV889; HW184; HW645

North American Mustang I (May 1942—Oct 1942)
AG470, O; AG566, R; AL964; AM117; AM169

North American P-51-NA (Apr 1943—Jul 1943)
41-137361; 41-137366; 41-137424; 41-137428

Vickers-Supermarine Spitfire VC (Feb 1943—Mar 1945)
EF605, WU:T; EF715, WU:Q; EF733, WU:E; EP666; EP701; ER136; ER270, WU:R; ER338; ER531, WU:B; ER725, WU:S; ER808, WU:X; ES144, WU:O; ES246; JK112, WU:A; JG890, WU:X; JK673; JK814; JL184, WU:U; JL213; MA680

Vickers-Supermarine Spitfire IX (May 1944—Jan 1947)
EN199; EN390; MA243; MA452; MA680; MH545; MH789; MH983; MJ424; MJ621; MJ823; MJ996; MK367; NH182; NH253; PL340; PL458; PT379; PT420; PT677; PV191; RK850; SM441; TB983

Bristol Sycamore HR.14 (Jan 1960— 1962)
XG500, Z, later D; XG515, W; XG523, L; XJ364, M; XJ919, F

Westland Whirlwind HAR.2/HAR.4 (Jan 1960— 1962)
XD165, K; XJ411, F; XJ724, B; XJ764, A; XK970,E; XK988, G; XK991, J

Westland Whirlwind HAR.10 (1962—   )
XP327, A; XP329, C; XP330, D; XP339, G; XP357, J; XP360, M; XP362, U

Commanding Officers

S/Ldr P. L. Donkin	Oct 1939	Jun 1940
W/Cdr G. H. Stilwell	Jun 1940	Feb 1941
W/Cdr A. A. N. Malan	Feb 1941	Oct 1941
W/Cdr R. J. Burrough	Oct 1941	Apr 1942
W/Cdr H. V. Alloway	Apr 1942	Oct 1942
W/Cdr E. G. L. Millington, DFC	Oct 1942	Sep 1943
S/Ldr A. W. McCandlish, DFC	Sep 1943	Dec 1943
Lt Col R. H. Rogers, DFC	Dec 1943	May 1944
W/Cdr J. W. C. Goldthorp	May 1944	Sep 1944
Maj W. G. Andrew	Sep 1944	Oct 1944
W/Cdr A. W. McCandlish, DFC	Oct 1944	Oct 1945
W/Cdr W. A. Laurie, DFC	Oct 1945	Jan 1946
S/Ldr G. Henderson, DFC	Jan 1946	Oct 1946
F/Lt Stonier	Oct 1946	Jan 1947
S/Ldr A. Twigg	Jan 1960	Apr 1962
S/Ldr H. T. Price	Apr 1962	Nov 1964
S/Ldr P. J. Bulford	Nov 1964	Nov 1965

Aircraft Insignia

From October, 1939 until 1942 the aircraft carried 'LX' code letters. These were changed to 'WU' in 1942. It is doubtful if this code was carried during the North African landings but was probably re-instated for the invasion of Sicily and continued until January, 1947. The helicopters carried a yellow fin diamond with '225' on it from 1960 to 1962, otherwise no insignia.

153

No. 227 SQUADRON

(Neither badge nor motto have been authorised)

The original No. 227 Squadron was formed at Taranto on 18 April, 1918 out of the RNAS Caproni Squadron there. It was re-equipped with D.H.4s and D.H.9s but did not become operational as a bomber squadron before the war ended and disbanded there on 9 December, 1918.

Another No. 227 Squadron formed in UK to serve in the Middle East but when it arrived its aircrew were absorbed into No. 272 Squadron and the ground crew used to service the aircraft of 10 Squadron's detachment in Palestine. However, in August, 1942 there was a detachment of No. 235 Squadron at Luqa, Malta and on 20th this was re-designated No. 227 Squadron, thus becoming an independent unit. It was immediately operational as a shipping strike unit and on the day of its formation put up twelve aircraft to escort 39 Squadron on a convoy attack in which one ship was sunk, a destroyer damaged and an Italian Cant Z.501 floatplane shot down, but two of No. 227's Beaus were lost. This continued to be No. 227's role and after ten days two more aircraft had been destroyed, one probable and two damaged. However, serviceability and losses brought the Squadron down to three operational aircraft at October's end. In November the Squadron began patrolling on its own account and on 13th destroyed six SM.82s and a Do 24. The next day the Squadron strafed Bizerta airfield destroying three aircraft but losing two to Messerschmitts. By the end of the month night intruders were also part of the routine as were road strafing in Tripolitania, behind the German lines. The tempo built up with 85 sorties in December resulting in eight aircraft destroyed, three probables and nine damaged, three ships set on fire and three Beaufighters lost. This pressure continued in January, 1943 but in February it came off operations, the crews being posted away.

However, on 3 March a new No. 227 Squadron was constituted at Idku from personnel of No. 252 and 272 Squadrons. On 15 April one aircraft took Air Chief Marshal Tedder from El Adem to Malta and on 21st operations began once more. It was now flying shipping recces in the Aegean Sea, together with the occasional shipping strike. These were mainly on caiques and the Squadron sank them with regularity. In July the Squadron took part in several strikes on Crete as well as the shipping recces and in August it moved to Cyprus to cover the Aegean more effectively. The pressure now built up in this area and an increasing number of ships were sunk or left on fire or listing.

This was not without loss, at least one crew failing to return each month. In October no fewer than 206 sorties were flown, many of them giving fighter protection to convoys. This became the main task in December, together with attempting to provide a fighter defence for the garrisons on Kos and Leros. In 1944 the Squadron continued this type of work, mainly in the Aegean where offensive sweeps kept up with targets such as caiques, tankers, R-boats and motor vessels with Ju 52s and Ju 88s providing aerial targets. In April a detachment was sent all the way to Algiers for similar work there. However in July the Squadron came off operations to join the new Balkan Air Force, the RAF aircrew were posted out and SAAF men posted in and, on 12 August 1944 it was re-numbered No. 19 Squadron SAAF at Biferno.

On 7 October, 1944 a new No. 227 Squadron was formed at Bardney with Avro Lancasters and flew on the Bomber Command offensive against Germany until the war ended. It was disbanded at Graveley on 5 September, 1945.

Bases etc.

Re-formed at Luqa on 20 August, 1942 from a detachment of 235 Squadron.

Luqa	Aug 1942—Nov 1942
Ta Kali	Nov 1942—Feb 1943

Crews posted away February, 1943. New Squadron constituted at Idku from 252 and 272 Squadron personnel, 3 March, 1943.

Idku	Mar 1943—May 1943
Derna	May 1943—Jun 1943
Magrun N.	Jun 1943—Jul 1943
Gardabia West	Jul 1943—Jul 1943
Derna	Jul 1943—Aug 1943
Limassol	Aug 1943—Sep 1943
Nicosia	Sep 1943—Dec 1943
Berka No. 3, det. Reghaia	Dec 1943—Aug 1944
Biferno	Aug 1944—Aug 1944

Re-numbered No. 19 Squadron, SAAF on 12 August, 1944.

Main Equipment

Bristol Beaufighter IC/VIC (Aug 1942—Aug 1944)
    T4666, Y; T4897, P; T5135, W; T5175, R; V8333, N; X7633, Z; X8032, K; X8074, Y; X8137, W; X8165, G; EL232, J; EL397, V; EL466, F; EL525, K; EL648, N; EL735, W; JL514, R; JL619, X; JL644, F; JL733, J; KV916, H
Bristol Beaufighter X/XIC (Sep 1943—Aug 1944)
    JM233, W; JM274, T; LX864, O; LZ331, R

Commanding Officers

W/Cdr D. R. Shore, DFC	Aug 1942—Oct 1942
W/Cdr C. A. Masterman, OBE	Oct 1942—Jan 1943
W/Cdr A. Watson	Jan 1943—Feb 1943
W/Cdr R. M. Mackenzie, DFC, AFC	Apr 1943—Oct 1943
W/Cdr J. K. Buchanan	Oct 1943—Feb 1944
S/Ldr D. B. Bennett, DFC	Feb 1944—Mar 1944
W/Cdr J. R. Blackburn	Mar 1944—Aug 1944

Aircraft Insignia

It is not known whether No. 227 Squadron carried any unit insignia whilst flying Beaufighters.

(See also *Bomber Squadrons of the RAF*, p. 221.)

No. 228 SQUADRON

BADGE
A winged helmet
MOTTO
'Auxilium a caelo'
('Help from the heavens')

On 20 August, 1918 the flying-boat Flights at RNAS Great Yarmouth were combined into one unit which was numbered 228 Squadron RAF. It was equipped with Felixstowe F.2As and these were used principally for anti-submarine patrols over the North Sea to the Dutch and North German coasts. In addition, the Squadron would fly in co-operation with the Harwich Motor Torpedo Boat Force attacking German minesweepers, sending a flight of three flying-boats out on an operation, locating the minesweepers and directing the force on to them. The Squadron's final operation was on 24 October, 1918. In January, 1919 the Squadron moved to North Killingholme and was disbanded there on 30 June, 1919.

On 15 December, 1936 it was re-formed as a flying-boat squadron intended for the new Supermarine Stranraer at Pembroke Dock but until they were ready it flew any spare boats available including a London, Scapa and Singapore IIIs. The Stranraers began arriving in April, 1937. The usual peacetime flying-boat routine was adopted with Home Fleet exercises taking priority. In 1938 the Squadron flew several exercises with the radar station at Bawdsey. By now No. 228 was fully operational and took part in its first cruise, in September, to Lisbon, Gibraltar, Malta and Bizerta. But before that it had suffered two fatal accidents. At the end of the year its crews participated in delivering Sunderlands to the Far East and to Malta. In May, 1939 it moved to Malta with Sunderlands, with a detachment in Egypt, and flew all around the Mediterranean seeking suitable bases in case of war. However, a week after war broke out the whole Squadron returned to Pembroke Dock. From here it began A/S patrols in the Atlantic and convoy escorts. A month later, on 21 October, F/Lt Brooks made the Squadron's first U-boat attack. The monthly routine involved about 35 sorties, mostly convoy escorts but anti-shipping strikes and patrols brought the occasional action; the CO attacked a submarine in December and F/Lt Brooks another one in January. In March, 1940 the Squadron began patrol off the Norwegian coast from its detachment at Invergordon. During the campaign there the Squadron flew several important VIP trips into and out of Norway, being bombed and machine-gunned in the process, as well as normal anti-shipping operations. In June it moved to Alexandria to reinforce the Med Fleet with Italy's entry into the war, flying endless 'chain' patrols between Mersa Matruh and Crete. Two submarines were bombed before the month was out. A detachment went to Gibraltar to help No. 202 Squadron with the Western Med patrols. On 9 July F/Lt McKinley found the Italian battle fleet and shadowed it for nine hours handing over to S/Ldr Menzies who continued with it. On 12th S/Ldr Menzies bombed a submarine and destroyed it and on 6 August he bombed a tanker. Again in September the Squadron shadowed the enemy fleet. November was busy for the Squadron, in addition to its normal duties it flew moonlight recces for the FAA attack on Taranto, escorted Hurricanes into Malta and led the British forces, on 27 November, to the Italian fleet and observed the action.

In 1941 the Squadron began dropping agents at various points. More Hurricane escorts took place and one Sunderland was bombed and destroyed whilst in Malta. In April much of the Squadron's activity was involved with the fighting in Greece and Crete, many VIP transport flights being made, followed by evacuation duties. That month two more Sunderlands were lost at Malta. In June No. 228 began a detachment at Bathurst, the Squadron moving there in August and then coming off operations in September. It now returned to the UK by ship and assembled at Stranraer to re-form. Its first task after work up was to fly ferry trips of Sunderlands out to Egypt and it was not until February, 1942 that it began operations, flying convoy patrols out over the Atlantic. In March F/O Maynard found and depth-charged a U-boat. About thirty operations was the average monthly sortie rate but the Squadron had a run of casualties, four fatal accidents between May and September including the one in August which killed the CO and the Duke of Kent.

The Squadron continued with its NW Approaches operations in a lower key into 1943, moving to N. Ireland for them. On 19 March F/Lt Church found a U-boat and attacked it but otherwise little action was seen. On 4 May, 1943 the Squadron moved to S. Wales, the ground crew moving in a novel way: they boarded Horsa gliders at St. Angelo and were towed to Talbenny by Albemarles, escorted by the Squadron Sunderlands. The sortie rate went up and before the month was up F/Lt Church and crew and another crew had failed to return but F/O French had attacked and destroyed a U-boat, counting 30–40 bodies in the water. June provided two U-boat attacks in Biscay, which was now 228s area, and one loss and in July another crew was lost but F/O Hanbury destroyed another U-boat. Two attacks followed in August and F/O Hanbury shared a kill with No. 461 Squadron. The work went on, by December the Squadron was up to 64 sorties a month, mainly on A/S patrols.

January, 1944 followed in this pattern but three crews were lost. Fewer contacts were being made now and it was not until June, when the Squadron joined in bottling up the Western end of the Channel, that the next attack came, followed quickly by three more. By August the Squadron was patrolling just off the French Atlantic U-boat bases and this produced three attacks with two of the U-boats damaged. This was the last of the action for seven months although the Squadron was regularly on patrol throughout. Two more attacks were made on Schnorchel contacts and in the second the Sunderland crashed fatally during the attack. Then the war was over and soon after No. 228 was disbanded at Lough Erne on 4 June, 1945.

On 1 June, 1946 No. 228 re-formed from part of No. 224 Squad-

ron at St. Eval with Liberators and flew transport services to Coastal bases in Iceland, Gibraltar, the Azores and Morocco. It also flew ASR and met recce duties but this was soon over when the Squadron again disbanded on 30 September, 1946.

It re-formed once more in the maritime role at St. Eval on 1 July, 1954 and was equipped with Avro Shackletons. The following year No. 228 took part in an extended goodwill visit around South America in addition to its regular maritime patrol training. In 1956 it was called in to provide trooping flights to the Middle East crises of that year. By April, 1958 it again turned its attention westwards, flying to the Caribbean to support HRH Princess Margaret's tour, but soon after was back trooping to the Middle East once more. Later that year it established a detachment at Sharjah to police the Gulf but at the end of the year this was withdrawn and five months later, on 6 May, 1959, the Squadron was disbanded at St. Mawgan.

On 1 September that year, however, No. 275 Squadron at Leconfield was re-numbered 228 Squadron. It was now flying SAR duties with Sycamore and Whirlwind helicopters at various bases on the East Coast. The Squadron soon standardised on the Whirlwind HAR.10 version and many rescues were flown with this type until, on 1 September, 1964, it was re-numbered No. 202 Squadron.

Bases etc.

Formed at Great Yarmouth on 20 August, 1918 from the flying-boat Flights there.

Great Yarmouth	Aug 1918—Jan 1919
North Killingholme	Jan 1919—Jun 1919

Disbanded at North Killingholme on 30 June, 1919. Re-formed at Pembroke Dock on 15 December, 1936.

Pembroke Dock, det. Calshot, Oban	Dec 1936—Sep 1939
Invergordon	Sep 1938—Oct 1938
Pembroke Dock	Oct 1938—May 1939
Kalafrana, det. Aboukir	May 1939—Sep 1939
Pembroke Dock, det. Invergordon	Sep 1939—Jun 1940
Alexandria, det. Gibraltar	Jun 1940—Jul 1940
Aboukir	Jul 1940—Sep 1940
Kalafrana	Sep 1940—Mar 1941
Aboukir, det. Bathurst	Mar 1941—Aug 1941
Bathurst	Aug 1941—Sep 1941
Stranraer, det. Lough Erne	Oct 1941—Mar 1942
Oban	Mar 1942—Dec 1942
Lough Erne	Dec 1942—May 1943
Pembroke Dock	May 1943—Jun 1945

Disbanded at Pembroke Dock on 4 June, 1945. Re-formed from 224Y Squadron at St. Eval on 1 June, 1946.

St. Eval	Jun 1946—Sep 1946

Disbanded at St. Eval on 30 September, 1946. Re-formed at St. Eval on 1 July, 1954.

St. Eval	Jul 1954— 1958
St. Mawgan, det. Sharajah	1958—May 1969

Disbanded at St. Mawgan on 6 May, 1959. Re-formed at Leconfield on 1 September, 1959 by re-numbering No. 275 Squadron.

Leconfield, det. Acklington, Leuchars, Coltishall	Sep 1959—Aug 1964

Disbanded on 31 August, 1964 by re-numbering as 202 Squadron.

Main Equipment

Curtiss H.12 (Aug 1918— 1918)
8660; 8662; 8666; 8692
Felixstowe F.2A (Aug 1918—Jun 1919)
N4283; N4289; N4295; N4298; N4303; N4305; N4511; N4512; N4549; N4550
Interim Aircraft (Dec 1936—Aug 1938)
Supermarine Scapa K7306, Z; Saro London K5258;
Short Singapore III K4579; K6913
Supermarine Stranraer I (Apr 1937—Nov 1938)
K7287; K7288; K7289; K7290; K7292; K7293, S; K7296; K7297, X
Short Sunderland I (Nov 1938—Sep 1941)
L2160, DQ:T; L2163; L2168; L5803, DQ:T; L5806, DQ:Q;
L5807, later DQ:F; N9020, DQ:W; N9025; P9600, DQ:T;
P9622; T9048, DQ:N
Short Sunderland II (Nov 1941—Dec 1942)
T9084, DQ:M; T9089, DQ:O; T9112, DQ:N; W3989, DQ:L;
WW3991, DQ:M; W3995, DQ:P; W6004, DQ:U
Short Sunderland III (May 1942—Feb 1945)
W4017, DQ:T; W4026, DQ:M; DD834, S; DD838, X; DD864, K;
DV970, Z; DV977, J; DW111; EK572, V; JM679; JM708, N;
ML763, UE:J; ML770, UE:P; ML815; ML879, UE:M; NJ171, UE:A;
NJ192; PP136
Short Sunderland V (Feb 1945—Jun 1945)
PP112; PP118; PP163; RN277; RN283, UE:F; RN285

Consolidated Liberator VI (Jun 1946—Sep 1946)
  No serial numbers known
Avro Shackleton MR.2 (Jul 1954—May 1959)
  WG557, L:L; WL744; WR951, L:K; WR956, 1; WR958, 228:O;
  WR960, L:P, later 228:X; WR961, L:Q, later 228:Y; WR966, 228:U;
  WR969, 228:T
Bristol Sycamore HR.14 (Sep 1959—   1961)
  XJ364; XJ380; XJ915; XJ919; XL823
Westland Whirlwind HAR.2/HAR.4 (1961—Aug 1964)
  XD165; XJ409; XJ761; XL110; XL113
Westland Whirlwind HAR.10 (1961—Aug 1964)
  XD182; XD186; XJ729; XK969; XP403; XP405

Commanding Officers

Maj R. Leckie	Aug 1918—	1919
S/Ldr J. E. Gray-Hill Thomas, DFC	Feb 1937—Mar 1939	
W/Cdr L. K. Barnes	Mar 1939—Nov 1939	
W/Cdr G. E. Nicholetts, DFC	Nov 1939—May 1941	
W/Cdr E. J. Brooks, DFC	May 1941—May 1942	
W/Cdr Moseley	May 1942—Aug 1942	
W/Cdr N. F. Eagleton, DFC	Sep 1942—Aug 1943	
W/Cdr P. A. Lombard	Sep 1943—Oct 1944	
W/Cdr A. M. G. Lywood, DFC	Oct 1944—Jun 1945	
S/Ldr K. M. Murray, DFC	1954—Jun 1958	
W/Cdr J. G. Graham, DFC	Jun 1958—Mar 1959	
S/Ldr R. J. Badeni	Sep 1959—Nov 1961	
S/Ldr N. E. Taylor	Nov 1961—Dec 1963	
S/Ldr G. Stafford, BA	Dec 1963—Sep 1964	

Aircraft Insignia

No Squadron markings were carried until 1938 when the code letters 'TO' were allocated; it is not known whether these were ever carried. The letters were changed to 'DQ' in September, 1939 and these were used until 1943 when letters were dropped. In 1944 when letters were re-assumed on Coastal Command squadrons No. 228 now carried 'UE' on its Sunderlands. It is not known what, if any, markings were carried on the Liberators but the Shackletons at first carried the single-letter 'L'; this was replaced in 1955 by the Squadron number itself. No markings were carried on the Sycamores and Whirlwinds.

No. 230 SQUADRON

BADGE
In front of a palm tree eradicated, a tiger
passant

MOTTO
'Kita chari jauh'
('We seek far')

The badge and motto associate the Squadron
with Malaya where it served more than once.

The Squadron was formed at Felixstowe in August, 1918 by amalgamating Nos. 327 and 328 Flights into one Squadron. They were equipped with Felixstowe F.2A flying boats operating over the North Sea against German Zeppelins and surface vessels as well as U-boats. Later No. 487 Flight with Camels was added, the Flight in which Lt Culley had flown, off a lighter, and shot down Zeppelin *L.53* in August, 1918. The Squadron continued the patrols which had become notable under the RNAS War Flight until the Armistice and, in fact remained as one of the few flying-boat units in RAF servoce after the war. It moved in May, 1922 to Calshot and disbanded there on 1 April, 1923, being re-designated No. 480 Flight.

On 1 December, 1934 the Squadron was re-formed at Pembroke Dock but did not receive any aircraft until April, 1935 when the first Short Singapore IIIs arrived. A quick work-up with these was followed by a move to the Mediterranean in September as reinforcements because of the Abyssinian crisis. Many flights around the Med were flown until July, 1936 brought a return to Wales. But this was only for three months for in October the Squadron left on a tour of the Far East. After going as far as Hong Kong No. 230 Squadron returned to Singapore and set up base there. For a year it flew its Singapores in company with No. 205 Squadron then in 1938 it began to re-equip with Short Sunderlands in June, 1938. These it took on a tour to Ceylon after six months but was back in Singapore when war broke out. First wartime tasks were met flights but it soon became involved in anti-submarine and anti-sabotage patrols up and down the coastline. In October, 1939 there was a scare that the German cruiser *Admiral Scheer* was in the area and 230 began a fruitless search. A move to Ceylon followed and then on to India to cover the Indian Ocean. In May, 1940 No. 230 moved to Egypt as Italy was likely to enter the war and began flying anti-submarine patrols for the Med Fleet. On 21 June the CO was attacked by four Italian fighters whilst on patrol and shot one of them down; first action in World War II. A week later F/Lt Campbell sank an Italian submarine on the 28th and another on 29th landing and picking up four survivors from the latter. In July, 1940 it flew 40 sorties in the month, including fourteen transport trips to Malta. Another Italian submarine was sunk by bombing on 9th but on 28th two Sunderlands were attacked by Macchi MC.200s. The first (F/Lt Garside's crew) shot one down and damaged another; the

second (S/Ldr Ryley's crew) had a 57 min engagement in which one fighter was destroyed and another damaged. However the Sunderland (L5804) was also badly damaged, being holed in the wings but was kept flying by LAC Campbell who climbed into the wings and plugged the holes until overcome by petrol fumes. Operations continued unabated; in September another submarine was destroyed (F/L Atlington). In October No. 230's operational area was extended to Greece to assist the campaign there. In November it was almost entirely being used as a Greek airline, flying troops and passengers between Egypt and the forces there.

By January, 1941 its roles had been defined as a cover unit for the Aegean convoys and a support unit to the Med Fleet in its Ionian Sea actions. With the German invasion there was increased patrol activity off Greece and transport trips to Yugoslavia to evacuate their MPs. That same month the evacuation of Greece saw No. 230 flying many sorties, passengers including Greek Royalty, and this was followed by the shambles of Crete and evacuation flights from there. In May it sent one aircraft to Bahrein during the revolt in Iraq. The Squadron acquired eight new aircraft in June, Dornier Do 22 floatplanes from Yugoslavia with crews who flew with No. 230 until formed into a separate unit. That month the Squadron found a Vichy French destroyer and led a Swordfish squadron to destroy it.

A high intensity of A/S work followed on, with 80 sorties being flown in July. In October S/Ldr Garside found a submarine and bombed it and in January found and depth-charged three more, destroying one. He attacked two more in February and as 1942 went on the Squadron was making two or three attacks each month. As the year wore on, with the Squadron flying principally A/S patrols, its targets became scarcer and in January, 1943 the Squadron began a move to East Africa.

Its first task there was to fly a tour of the Indian Ocean islands to find suitable anchorages for Sunderlands. Operations began in March with convoy escorts and A/S patrols and the Squadron settled into a routine in which the boats flew tours of the islands, patrolling the Indian Ocean as they went. A change came in June when a detachment was sent through the Med to Bizerta to fly a Bizerta/Malta transport shuttle and this was continued for two months, ASR being also carried out when necessary. This transport work continued from Africa in November when a detachment at Kisumu flew a route to Khartoum and back.

Early in 1944 the whole Squadron moved to Koggala and concentrated on A/S and convoy work once more, without finding any action, and in May yet another transport role came No. 230's way when aircraft were detached to Assam to fly casevac sorties for the 3rd Indian Division: in June two aircraft flew out 500 casualties from Lake Indawgyi to the Brahmaputra river. The Squadron then returned to maritime activities solely. No enemy shipping or submarines were encountered but one Sunderland and crew was lost in

November, 1944. In February, 1945 a detachment went to Trombay from where it flew freight and supplies up to the Chidwin river. From here it moved to Akyab for offensive sorties but by now the war had moved too far away so it moved to Redhills Lake from where it flew armed recces to the Andaman Islands or over the Gulf of Siam, attacking suspicious ships. On 15 June F/Lt Holstein blew up one ship, damaged another and sank a motor launch and this set the pattern for similar attacks. With the war over the Squadron converted entirely to the transport role which was flown to Singapore, mainly to repatriate POWs. By October No. 230 was flying a Singapore Courier Service and the following month it moved into Singapore.

After four months of this work it flew back to the UK to join No. 201 Squadron in the Sunderland Wing at Calshot. The peacetime task was mainly co-operation with the Home Fleet, interspersed with international exercises and goodwill tours.

In 1947 such a tour took the Squadron to Norway and Denmark. July 1948 found the Squadron yet again flying transport work; this time it was on the Berlin Airlift in which 1,000 sorties were flown without any accidents in five months of operation.

Normal peacetime flying continued until August, 1952 when No. 230 moved to Young Sound to provide transport and support for the British North Greenland expedition. The following year it provided the only flying-boats in the Queen's Coronation Review of the RAF at Odiham. A month later it moved out to the islands in the Ionian Sea and provided transport duties to those islands damaged in the earthquake. It was back to Greenland in 1954 to evacuate the expedition and to carry out a photo survey of part of the area; in June 1955 the Squadron returned to Singapore briefly for a SEATO exercise. The days of the flying-boats were now numbered for no successor had been ordered for the Sunderland and, on 28 February, 1957 No. 230 Squadron was disbanded at Pembroke Dock.

It was re-formed in a completely different role, that of a light army transport support unit, by re-numbering No. 215 Squadron at Dishforth on 1 September, 1958. It now flew Scottish Aviation Pioneer aircraft and, two months after re-forming, moved to Cyprus to fly internal security patrols during the EOKA troubles there. These patrols involved reconnaissance tasks and No. 230 also flew communications flights. After a year there it returned to the UK and re-equipped with Twin Pioneers. These took to the Cameroons in September, 1960, once again flying internal security patrols. This type of work was being taken over by helicopters and in August, 1962 No. 230 re-equipped with Whirlwinds. With these it became part of RAF Germany for two years, beginning in January, 1963, where it provided front-line support to the BAOR. Whilst there it began a detachment to the United Nations Force in Cyprus, flying from Nicosia in support of the various forces keeping the peace there and this was continued for the whole period it flew Whirlwinds. With its base at Odiham the Squadron continued to move about the world, going to Labuan in February, 1965 to help with the Indonesian confrontation.

In December, 1971 No. 230 became the RAF's second Westland/Aérospatiale Puma squadron and used these as part of 38 Group's support force. It flew to action in Belize, where a recurring task is carried out; the Squadron has flown its share of operations supporting the Army in Northern Ireland.

Bases etc.

Formed from the Felixstowe War Flight (327 & 328 Flights) in August, 1918.

Felixstowe	Aug 1918—May 1922
Calshot	May 1922—Apr 1923

Disbanded at Calshot on 1 April, 1923. Re-formed at Pembroke Dock on 1 December, 1934.

Pembroke Dock	Dec 1934—Sep 1935
Aboukir and Alexandria	Sep 1935—Sep 1936
Pembroke Dock	Sep 1936—Oct 1936
Seletar	Oct 1936—Oct 1939
Penang	Oct 1939—Oct 1939
China Bay, det. Koggala, Galle	Oct 1939—May 1940
Alexandria, det. Scaramanga, Suda Bay, Bahrein	May 1940—Jun 1941
Aboukir	Jun 1941—Jan 1943
Dar-es-Salaam, det. Aboukir, Bizerta, Pamanzi, Mombasa, Kisumu	Jan 1943—Feb 1944
Koggala, det. Dibrugarh, Trombay	Feb 1944—May 1945
Akyab, det. Redhills Lake	May 1945—Jul 1945
Redhills Lake, det. Seletar	Jul 1945—Nov 1945
Seletar	Nov 1945—Apr 1946
Castle Archdale	Apr 1946—Sep 1946
Calshot, det. Hamburg	Sep 1946—Feb 1949
Pembroke Dock	Feb 1949—Feb 1957

Disbanded at Pembroke Dock on 28 February, 1957. Re-formed by re-numbering No. 215 Squadron at Dishforth on 1 September, 1958.

Dishforth	Sep 1958—Nov 1958
Nicosia	Nov 1958—Apr 1959
Upavon, det. El Adem	Apr 1959—May 1960
Odiham, det. Mamfi	May 1960—Jan 1963
Gütersloh, det. Nicosia	Jan 1963—Dec 1964
Odiham, det. Nicosia	Dec 1964—Feb 1965
Labuan	Feb 1965—Oct 1966
Odiham, det. Nicosia	Oct 1966—Mar 1969
Wittering, det. Nicosia	Mar 1969—Dec 1971
Odiham, det. Belize	Dec 1971—

Main Equipment

Curtiss H.12 (Aug 1918—   1918)
8661; 8663; 8677; 8683; 8689

Felixstowe F.2A (Aug 1918—   1919)
N4060, AX21; N4298, AM; N4302; N4482, B95; N4533; N4545, AM

Felixstowe F.5 (1919—   1923)
Believed N4044; N4838

Short Singapore III (Apr 1935—   1938)
K4578, X; K4579; K4581, 1; K4585; K6912; K6916; K6918

Short Sunderland I (Jun 1938—Jul 1942)
L2159, NM:W; L2161, MN:Y; L2164, NM:U; L2166, NM:U; N9029, NM:V; L5803, NM:T; L5804, NM:S; L5806, NM:Q; T9050, NM:Y

Dornier Do 22 (Jun 1941—Mar 1942)
157; 307; 308; 309; 311; 312; 313

Short Sunderland II (Dec 1941—Aug 1942)
W3987, NM:X

Short Sunderland III (Mar 1942—Jan 1945)
W4021, NM:W; W4022, NM:Z; W4023, NM:U; EJ132, X; EJ136, Y; EJ141, R; EJ143, S; DP180, O; DP189, L; EK595, Q; JM659, Q; JM673, P; JM711, M; ML846, W

Short Sunderland V (Jan 1945—Feb 1957)
DP200, B:Z; ML799, W; ML800, X; NJ264, 4X:R; PP117, 4X:W; PP147, V; PP152, W; PP158, T; PP164, 4X:X; RN270, 4X:O; RN299, 4X:P; RN304, B:B; SZ563, B:R; SZ577, 4X:Z; SZ581, B:Y; VB887, 4X:X

Scottish Aviation Pioneer CC.1 (Sep 1958—Mar 1960)
XK370; XL517; XL558, W; XL665, X; XL667, U; XL702, Y; XL703, Z

Scottish Aviation Twin Pioneer CC.1/CC.2 (Apr 1960—Aug 1962)
XL996, O; XM285; XM940, S; XM961, M; XN318; XP295

Westland Whirlwind HAR.10 (Aug 1962—Dec 1971)
XJ758; XK970, P; XL110; XP329, V; XP357, J; XP363, P; XP395, R; XP399, U; XP401, W; XR453, W; XR497, B; XS412, Y

Aérospatiale/Westland Puma HC.1 (Dec 1971—   )
XW202, DM; XW217, DA; XW220, DD; XW224, DH; XW227, DN, later DK; XW231, DO

Commanding Officers

W/Cdr C. E. Risk, DSO	Aug 1918—Dec 1920
W/Cdr I. T. Courtney	Dec 1920—Apr 1923
W/Cdr W. H. Dunn, DSC	Feb 1935—Nov 1938
W/Cdr G. M. Bryer, OBE, AFC	Nov 1938—May 1940
W/Cdr G. Francis	May 1940—Sep 1941
W/Cdr T. W. G. Eady	Sep 1941—Oct 1941
W/Cdr M. C. Collins	Oct 1941—Nov 1942
W/Cdr C. R. Taylor	Nov 1942—Aug 1943
W/Cdr D. K. Bednall	Aug 1943—Oct 1944
W/Cdr C. E. L. Powell	Oct 1944—Aug 1945
W/Cdr D. E. Hawkins, DFC	Aug 1945—Sep 1946
W/Cdr V. H. A. McBratney, AFC	Sep 1946—Jul 1947
S/Ldr G. A. Huxford	Jul 1947—Apr 1948
S/Ldr A. J. Payn, MBE	Apr 1948—Feb 1950
S/Ldr O. J. Wells	Feb 1950—Nov 1950
S/Ldr A. M. Campbell	Nov 1950—Jan 1952
S/Ldr J. G. Higgins, DFC, AFC	Jan 1952—Dec 1953
S/Ldr E. C. Bennett, DFM	Dec 1953—Jan 1955
S/Ldr C. M. Stavert, AFC	Jan 1955—Dec 1955
S/Ldr P. G. Adams, DSO	Dec 1955—Feb 1957
S/Ldr W. J. Simpson, DFC	Sep 1958—Jul 1960
S/Ldr H. J. West, DSO, DFC	Jul 1960—Oct 1962
S/Ldr D. H. Thomas	Oct 1962—
S/Ldr D. E. Too	
S/Ldr T. S. C. Jones	—Dec 1971
W/Cdr P. D. A. Austin	Dec 1971—Jan 1974

W/Cdr I. Horrocks	Jan 1974—Jun 1977
W/Cdr A. N. D. Parker-Ashley	Jun 1977—Jun 1979
W/Cdr B. A. Wright	Jun 1979—

Aircraft Insignia

As far as is known no specific squadron insignia was carried on the boats at Felixstowe though many individual colour schemes were devised. No known squadron markings were in fact carried until the onset of squadron code letters in 1938. No. 230 was originally allotted 'FV' but it is not known if this combination was carried. On the outbreak of World War II this was changed to 'NM' which was used until the Squadron went to East Africa when markings were dropped until 1945 when No. 230 Squadron returned to the UK. It now carried the letters '4X' and in addition the Squadron badge was painted on the sides of the forward hull. The code letters were changed to the single letter 'B' in 1951 and this was dropped in favour of the Squadron number '230' in 1956. The Pumas carried a two-letter code system, the first letter, 'D', denoting the Squadron; the emblem was also carried on the side door.

No. 231 SQUADRON

(No badge authorised)

No. 231 Squadron was first formed in August, 1918 as another squadron at the former RNAS Station at Felixstowe, flying F.3 and F.5 flying-boats on North Sea patrol until the war ended. It stayed at Felixstowe until disbanding on 7 July, 1919.

The Squadron was re-formed in World War II by the re-numbering of No. 416 Flight at Aldergrove on 1 July, 1940. Its role was now army co-operation and it was equipped with Westland Lysanders for this task. At first it flew anti-invasion coastal patrols each dawn and combined this with border recces along the Eire border. It saw little of the war in Northern Ireland and for a long time participated only in Army exercises, using a growing fleet of different types of aircraft.

In March, 1943 No. 231 moved to York where it equipped with Mustangs and in July began operations, flying *Lagoon* operations off the Dutch Coast. It moved south and in August flew operationally with regularity on weather recces and Channel patrols, forty sorties being flown in eleven days. In September it began photo recce with a sortie to Dunkirk and added *Rhubarbs* to its repertoire with a high success rate against trains in France. This became the pattern for the next few months, the Squadron claiming its first enemy aircraft destroyed when a Do 217 was shot down during a *Rhubarb* on Armistice Day. In the first fourteen days of 1944 it flew thirty *Popular* operations but was then disbanded on the 15th at Redhill.

On 8 September, 1944 No. 231 re-formed at Dorval in Canada within Transport Command. Its task was to fly long-range transport services across the Atlantic and soon it was maintaining regular schedules to Iceland and Prestwick. For this is used a variety of aircraft, Liberators, Dakotas, Hudson, Skymasters and Coronado flying boats. This was continued for a few months after the war in Europe ended and then the Squadron moved to Bermuda and flew transatlantic services to West Africa until the end of the year, disbanding there on 15 January, 1946.

That same month No. 231 re-formed at Full Sutton and began converting to the Avro Lancastrian for Transport Command routes. Before it could begin operating, however, it was again disbanded there in July, 1946.

Bases etc.

Formed from No. 416 Flight at Aldergrove on 1 July, 1940.

Aldergrove	Jul 1940—Jul 1940
Newtonards, det. Maydown	Jul 1940—Dec 1941
Long Kesh, det. Maghaberry	Dec 1941—Feb 1942
Maghaberry	Feb 1942—Nov 1942
Long Kesh	Nov 1942—Jan 1943
Nutt's Corner	Jan 1943—Mar 1943
York, det. Ballyhalbert	Mar 1943—Jul 1943
Dunsfold	Jul 1943—Jul 1943
Weston Zoyland	Jul 1943—Jul 1943
Woodchurch	Jul 1943—Oct 1943
Redhill	Oct 1943—Jan 1944

Disbanded at Redhill on 15 January, 1944. Re-formed at Dorval on 8 September, 1944.

| Dorval | Sep 1944—Sep 1945 |
| Bermuda | Sep 1945—Jan 1946 |

Disbanded at Bermuda on 15 January, 1946. Re-formed at Full Sutton in January, 1946.

| Full Sutton | Jan 1946—Jul 1946 |

Disbanded at Full Sutton in July, 1946.

Main Equipment

Westland Lysander II (Jul 1940—Aug 1941)
L4748; L4794; N1213; N1220; N1276; P9056, VM:A; P9075; P9097
de Havilland Tiger Moth II (Aug 1940—Apr 1943)
N6536; N9127; N9248; DE347
Westland Lysander III/IIIA (Nov 1940—Apr 1943)
R9132; V9408; V9736
Curtiss Tomahawk I/IIA/IIB (Oct 1941—Apr 1943)
AH754; AH798; AH822; AH855; AH911; AH947; AK140
North American Mustang I (Apr 1943—Jan 1944)
AG355; AG420; AG497; AG513; AG553; AG600; AG649; AL978; AM163; AM194; AM253; AP225
Consolidated Liberator II (Sep 1944—Jan 1946)
AL504; AL593; AM259, (LB.30A)
Douglas Dakota IV (Sep 1944—Jan 1946)
KN673; KP276
Consolidated Coronado I (Sep 1944—Jan 1946)
JX470; JX486; JX494; JX496; JX498; JX501
Avro Lancaster III (Dec 1945—Jan 1946)
RF199; RF261
Avro Lancastrian C.2 (Jan 1946—Jul 1946)
VL970; VL973; VL976; VL979; VM703; VM704; VM729; VM731; VM737

Commanding Officers

W/Cdr R. H. Humphries	Jul 1940—Aug 1941
W/Cdr E. D. Joyce	Sep 1941—Oct 1942
W/Cdr V. A. Pope	Oct 1942—Jul 1943
S/Ldr W. E. V. Malins	Aug 1943—Dec 1943
S/Ldr G. H. Nelson-Edwards	Dec 1943—Jan 1944

Aircraft Insignia

Upon formation No. 231 Squadron was allocated the code letters 'VM' which it used, probably up to re-arming with Mustangs in 1943. Thereafter there is no record of any unit insignia being carried.

No. 232 SQUADRON

BADGE
A dragon-ship under sail, oars in action
MOTTO
'Strike'

The dragon-ship comes from the arms of Lerwick and indicates the Squadron's association with Shetland and the Western Isles.

The Squadron first formed in August, 1918 when one of the flying-boat flights at Felixstowe was re-numbered No. 232 Squadron. It served there on anti-submarine patrols until disbanding on 5 January, 1919.

On 17 July, 1940 No. 232 was re-formed at Sumburgh in the Shetlands from B Flight of 3 Squadron and served as a fighter squadron in the UK, Singapore and the Mediterranean. It was disbanded at Gragnano, Italy, on 31 October, 1944.

No. 232 re-formed at Stoney Cross in Transport Command on 1 November, 1944. Here it began to work up on the Wellington XVI as a transport aeroplane but before embarking on the transport routes the aircrew were transferred to No. 243 Squadron in January, 1945 and the Squadron reduced to cadre. This unit moved to India where it equipped with Liberator transports in February and became operational in April. It flew a daily schedule from Delhi to Ceylon and also round trips to Australia (about 3 per month). Douglas C-54s were added in June, principally for the Sydney run. After VJ-Day a scheduled run was begun to Singapore and a 'special' took the C-in-C Transport Command to New Zealand. By the end of the year the frequency of schedules was reduced but a new Butterworth mail run was introduced. The C-54s were returned to the US, commencing in February, 1946 and the following month Avro Lancastrians arrived to replace them. However, in April all aircraft were inhibited and the few remaining routes were flown using No. 355 Squadron Liberator C.8s. On 15 August, 1946 the Squadron disbanded at Poona.

Bases etc.

Felixstowe	Aug 1918—Jan 1919
Disbanded Felixstowe 5 January, 1919. Re-formed at Stoney Cross on 1 November, 1944.	
Stoney Cross	Nov 1944—Feb 1945
Palam	Feb 1945—May 1946
Poona	May 1946—Aug 1946
Disbanded at Poona on 15 August, 1946.	

Main Equipment

Felixstowe F.2A (Aug 1918—Jan 1919)
  No serial numbers known
Felixstowe F.3 (Aug 1918—Jan 1919)
  No serial numbers known
Vickers Wellington XVI (Nov 1944—Jan 1945)
  R1710; R3225; DV617; DV704
Consolidated Liberator VII (Feb 1945—   1946)
  EW612; EW614; EW616; EW622; EW625; EW629; EW630; EW633
Douglas C-54D (Jun 1945—Feb 1946)
  KL977; KL978; KL981; KL984; KL985
Consolidated Liberator IX (Jul 1945—Aug 1945)
  JT979
Consolidated Liberator VI (Oct 1945—Aug 1946)
  BZ849; EW119; EW164; EW255; KH401; KH408; KH629; KL552
Avro Lancastrian C.2 (Mar 1946—Aug 1946)
  VM733; VM734

Commanding Officers

W/Cdr D. W. Balden	Nov 1944—Jan 1945
W/Cdr Sir R. H. Barlow, AFC	Feb 1945—Oct 1945
W/Cdr D. L. Prichard, DSO	Nov 1945—Aug 1946

Aircraft Insignia

As far as is known no unit insignia was carried, either during its period at Felixstowe, or whilst serving in Transport Command.
(See also *Fighter Squadrons of the RAF*, pp. 335–6)

No. 233 SQUADRON

BADGE
In front of a trident and sword in saltire, a star of eight points
MOTTO
'Fortis et Fidelis'
('Strong and faithful')

The first No. 233 Squadron was formed in August, 1918 by combining the RNAS units at Dover and Walmer. It flew coastal and cross-Channel patrols from then until the Armistice using D.H.9s from Dover and Sopwith Camels from Walmer providing fighter escort for them and other aircraft operating in the area. After the war it remained in existence until disbandment on 15 May, 1919.

The Squadron re-formed in the general reconnaissance role within Coastal Command at Tangmere on 18 May, 1937. It was equipped with Avro Ansons and worked up in its role, moving to its permanent station of Thornaby in July. By the time war broke out the Squadron had begun converting to Lockheed Hudsons and whilst this process went on operations were flown with the Ansons. On 5 September Sgt Mins in K8845 found a German submarine which he bombed but his own tanks were holed by shrapnel and the Anson had to ditch. Hudsons were brought into action in October and by the end of the year the Ansons had been phased out. In October a fourth flight (D Flight) was formed with fighter Blenheims but in December this moved to Birchams Newton to become No. 254 Squadron. By December the Squadron was flying over 130 sorties a month and its Hudsons were being fitted with ASV and IFF equipment; that month also another U-boat was bombed. In January, 1940 F/O McLaren found a He 111, exhausted his ammunition trying to shoot it down and then tried to bomb it. By the end of February three more U-boat attacks had been made. In April attention was concentrated on the Norwegian campaign with shipping searches and bombing raids on Stavanger and Bergen and attacks on German warships; three Hudson crews were lost. In May and June the Norwegian coast continued to occupy the Squadron's attention, much enemy shipping being bombed, including the *Scharnhorst*. Combats were now taking place with escorting Messerschmitts and although No. 233 had losses they also claimed some 109s shot down.

In August, 1940 the Squadron transferred to Northern Ireland and the protection of convoys leaving and entering the Liverpool and Clyde anchorages. This was only temporary before a return to the Norwegian coast patrols in September. On 25 October three aircraft attacked the Squadron's eighth U-boat and sank it; that month sortie rate went over the 150 mark. Towards the end of the year the Squadron attacked airfields in Norway before transferring again to the Atlantic operations in December. This brought much less in the way of action, most patrols being uneventful; the next fighting was not until 28 May when the CO shot down a He 111. June, however, brought two U-boat attacks which enabled 'damaged' claims to be made, and one FW 200 shot into the sea. In August a move south was made for Biscay operations and this produced a flurry of action with a motor vessel bombed, four U-boats depth-charged and one Hudson lost before September was out. U-boats continued to be No. 233s main pre-occupation although on 2 November six aircraft made a bombing attack on St. Nazaire docks. That month six U-boats attacks were made and five more in December. 1942 saw a change in operations. The Squadron moved to Thorney Island but established a detachment at Gibraltar and most operations were flown from there. This was a clumsy arrangement and by June the whole Squadron settled in at Gibraltar. Here its task was to cover the convoys up the Portuguese coast, look for U-boats there and also operate over the Western Mediterranean. With the North African invasion, the Squadron was heavily involved, flying 229 sorties in the November; the activity in the Straits attracted the enemy also and nine U-boat attacks were made by the Squadron, one of which was on a British submarine. The Squadron also lost six aircraft during this month. As soon as the invasion moved along the North African coast No.233 established a detachment at Agadir to extend its range. Both A/S and convoy patrols were the main task, interspersed with ASR and met flights. U-boats continued to present themselves as targets with one attack a month until March when six were found, depth-charged and in some cases, hit. Three more were attacked in April and two in May.

In June two combats with FW 200s took place (the Squadron was still operating over the Atlantic as well as in the Med). It began borrowing Beaufighters from other units for its more offensive activities and for anti-aircraft escort of convoys, enabling them to claim some FW 200s definitely destroyed. In October, 1943 the Squadron sent a detachment to the Azores for South Atlantic coverage and the widespread Squadron continued its anti-submarine activities into early 1944.

In February, 1944 No. 233 became non-operational and returned to the UK without aircraft. Base was established at Blakehill Farm where it began a new role, transport support duties. For this it received Dakotas and began intensive paratrooping exercises with the 1st Airborne Division. In April it began operations, flying *Nickel* raids over the Caen area. Intensive training exercises culminated, on 5 June, in the Squadron providing thirty aircraft for the invasion of France. Six of these towed Horsa gliders, the rest took 407 paratroops dropping them successfully; two Squadron Dakotas failed to return. On 6th twenty-one aircraft flew re-supply drops to the 6th Airborn Division and again two were lost. The Squadron was now assigned to close transport support and on 13th two aircraft landed at B.2 airstrip, the first Transport Command aircraft to land in France. After unloading they brought casualties home. This became a daily task; on 15th the Squadron took a whole 2nd TAF Fighter Wing to its new French base and, every trip, brought casualties back to UK. This became an intensive shuttle duty over the next few months, with a variation in August when two aircraft flew transport to Rome and ten aircraft dropped panniers to troops at Chambois; 259 sorties were flown that month. A similar figure was flown in September of which 75 sorties were on Operation Market, the fateful Arnhem operation, in which the Squadron flew glider-towing sorties for the first two days and then re-supply. Three aircraft were lost and twelve badly damaged in this activity. No. 233 Squadron then settled back into the short-range shuttle to the Continent and recorded a record total of 450 sorties in October, 1944. In January, 1945 a detachment was set up at Nivelles to provide supply routes within the Continent and in March the Squadron flew twenty-two sorties on Operation Varsity, the Rhine crossing. The intensity of flying was maintained until the war in Europe ended.

In July, 1945 the Squadron ceased flying and moved to Burma in August. Here it began flying rice and rations into the country in September, breaking its own record by making 461 sorties that month, and 676 in October, mostly short-range supply drops into the jungle. It continued this humanitarian task until the end of the year when it was disbanded at Tulihal on 15 December, 1945, being merged with No. 215 Squadron. It was re-formed once more, on 1 September, 1960, by taking the Valetta Flight of No. 84 Squadron and expanding it to squadron status. This was at Khormaksar and from here the Squadron both flew transport routes from Bahrein in the north to Kenya in the south and also flew support missions to the Army in the Aden Protectorate continuing its tradition of supply dropping to ground forces. Mercy flights were also flown when necessary, the Squadron operating just over three years in this role by which time the Vickers Valetta had come to the end of its RAF service. The Squadron was disbanded in Aden on 31 January, 1964.

Bases etc.

Formed at Dover and Walmer by combining Nos. 407, 471 and 491 Flights in August, 1918.

Dover, det. Walmer	Aug 1918	May 1919

Disbanded at Dover on 15 May, 1919. Re-formed at Tangmere on 18 May, 1937.

Tangmere	May 1937	Jul 1937
Thornaby	Jul 1937	Sep 1938
Leuchars	Sep 1938	Sep 1938
Gosport	Sep 1938	Sep 1938
Thornaby	Sep 1938	Jun 1939
Bircham Newton	Jun 1939	Sep 1939
Leuchars, det. Wick, Sumburgh	Sep 1939	Aug 1940
Aldergrove	Aug 1940	Sep 1940
Leuchars	Sep 1940	Dec 1940
Aldergrove	Dec 1940	Aug 1941
St. Eval, det. Gibraltar	Aug 1941	Jan 1942
Thorney Island, det. Gibraltar	Jan 1942	Mar 1942
St. Eval, det. Gibraltar	Mar 1942	Apr 1942
Thorney Island, det. Gibraltar	Apr 1942	Jun 1942
Gibraltar, det. Agadir, Blida, Lagens	Jun 1942	Feb 1944
en route to UK	Feb 1944	Mar 1944
Blakehill Farm, det. Nivelles	Mar 1944	Mar 1945
Birch	Mar 1945	Mar 1945
Blakehill Farm	Mar 1945	Jun 1945
Odiham	Jun 1945	Jul 1945
en route to Far East	Jul 1945	Aug 1945
Tulihal, det. Toungoo	Aug 1945	Dec 1945

Disbanded at Tulihal on 15 December, 1945 by merging into No. 215 Squadron. Re-formed on 1 September, 1960 at Khormaksar by expanding the Valetta Flight of 84 Squadron to squadron status.

Khormaksar	Sep 1960	Jan 1964

Disbanded at Khormaksar on 31 January, 1964.

Main Equipment

de Havilland D.H.9 (Aug 1918—May 1919)
No serial numbers known
Sopwith Camel (Aug 1918—May 1919)
No serial numbers known
Avro Anson I (May 1937—Dec 1939)
K6282, EY:S; K6298, EY:V; K8815, ZS:O; K8838, 233:C; K8845, ZS:N; N4958, ZS:A; N4961, ZS:Y
Lockheed Hudson I (Aug 1939—Sep 1941)
N7226, ZS:D; N7253, ZS:N; N7269, ZS:B; N7326, ZS:F; N7372, ZS:Y; P5117, ZS:S; P5156, T9248; T9270; T9284, ZS:J; T9313; T9317; T9365, ZS:K
Lockheed Hudson II/III (Aug 1940—Feb 1944)
T9378, ZS:U; T9430, ZS:E, later ZS:L; T9451, X; T9430, ZS:L; V9023, J; V9094, ZS:T; V9129, ZS:Z; V9168, V; V92222, E; AE535, ZS:F; AE591, ZS:E; AE606, ZS:M
Lockheed Hudson V (Aug 1941—Feb 1944)
AE641, ZS:A; AE650, ZS:E; AM555, ZS:N; AM558, ZS:R; AM575, ZS:S; AM603, ZS:G; AM735, ZS:Q
Lockheed Hudson IIIA (Jun 1942—Feb 1944)
FH260, Q; FH330, D; FH350, N; FH384, R; FH424, H; FK738, E; FK750, R
Douglas Dakota III (Mar 1944—Dec 1945)
FD878, V; FD931, G; FL526; FZ665, 5T:Z, later UX; FZ681, 5T:F; FZ692; KG313, 5T:UM; KG351, 5T:UB; KG403, 5T:UQ; KG447, 5T:AY; KG501, 5T:UD; KG561, 5T:UO; KG635, 5T:AK, later UP; KG700
Douglas Dakota IV (Mar 1945—Dec 1945)
KJ818, M; KJ844, T; KJ898, C; KJ903, N; KJ955, Y; KK169, Q; KK215, W; KN258, 5T:UJ; KN314, K; KN427, 5T:UZ, later AY; KN443, 5T:UR; KN559; 5T:UO; KN688, AB
Vickers Valetta C.1 (Sep 1960—Jan 1964)
VW149; VW162; VW195; VW198; VW200; VW821; VW837; VW851; VW860; VX542

Commanding Officers

S/Ldr J. B. M. Wallis	May 1937—	1939
W/Cdr W. C. P. Bullock	1939—Jun	1940
W/Cdr H. A. Purvis, DFC, AFC	Jun 1940—May	1941
W/Cdr E. C. Kidd, AFC, AFM	May 1941—Oct	1941
W/Cdr E. H. Clarke, AFC	Oct 1941—Mar	1942
W/Cdr T. W. T. McComb	Mar 1942—Nov	1942
W/Cdr H. G. D. Devey	Nov 1942—Dec	1943
W/Cdr M. E. Morrison, AFC	Nov 1943—Jun	1944
W/Cdr B. A. Miller	Jun 1944—Jul	1944
W/Cdr W. E. Coles, DFC, AFC	Jul 1944—Nov	1944
W/Cdr K. G. Mellor, DFC	Nov 1944—Jul	1945
W/Cdr E. Banthorpe	Jul 1945—Dec	1945
S/Ldr Perry	Sep 1960—	1962
S/Ldr D. W. Barnard	1962—Jan	1964

Aircraft Insignia

It is believed that no unit insignia was carried in World War I. The Ansons at first had the squadron number painted on the side and the emblem on a white six-pointed star on the fin. In 1938 this was changed to the code letter combination 'EY' which was retained until the outbreak of war when it was changed to 'ZS'. This latter was retained until shortly after moving to Gibraltar in mid-1942 when no markings were carried until the unit was re-equipped at Blakehill Farm with Dakotas in 1944. It now carried the code letters '5T' which remained, probably, until moving to India in August, 1945. It is not believed that any insignia was carried on the Valettas.

After spending most of World War II as a fighter squadron No. 238 re-formed in 1944 on transport duties and served in the Far East, both in the Burma campaign and on the Hump Route to China on which, presumably, KN247 here was engaged as the nose markings are Chinese characters.

No. 239 became an army co-operation squadron too late to see action before Dunkirk but its Lysanders were used for AA calibration, ASR work and intensive army support training in 1940 to 1942.

The Curtiss Tomahawk was the aircraft with which No. 239 Squadron became operational AH793 HB:Z being one of its Gatwick-based aircraft.

At Calshot the flying-boat Flights became No. 240 Squadron and continued anti-shipping patrols in the English Channel until the end of the war. Felixstowe F.3s are seen awaiting launching from the hard-standing early in 1919.

Although basically a maritime reconnaissance squadron operating from India, Ceylon and Indian Ocean island bases in 1944–45, No. 240 also had a Flight of its Catalina IBs, including FP225 P, permanently set aside for special duties which involved the setting down and picking up of agents in enemy territory all along the Burmese and Thai coastline.

No. 241 Squadron was a specialist fighter-reconnaissance unit which had fought throughout the North African and Sicilian campaign with Hurricanes and Spitfires and continued throughout the whole Italian campaign with Tac/R sorties as its primary task. Two of its Spitfire IXs are seen here flying past Mount Vesuvius.

No. 242 had become a long-range transport squadron in November, 1944 and by the end of the war was flying Avro Yorks all over the Empire. This was temporarily halted in 1949 when the Squadron flew into Gatow (MW267 KY:N seen here) in the Berlin Airlift.

K6363, this Vickers Vincent of No. 244 Squadron must have been one of the last operational biplanes in the RAF. It had seen service in the Habbaniya uprising in May, 1941 and continued in service well after that being eventually used for locust spraying in the Persian Gulf area.

From being a general purpose squadron in the Persian Gulf area No. 244 concentrated more and more on maritime reconnaissance as World War II progressed and eventually received Wellington XIIIs for this task. HZ712 F is seen here in the act of dropping a marker flare in 1945.

No. 246 Squadron will go down in RAF history as the only unit to operate Blackburn Kangaroo coastal patrol bomber. B9973 is seen here at the Squadron's base at Seaton Carew from which regular patrols over the North Sea were flown until the Armistice making eleven U-boat attacks and sinking one.

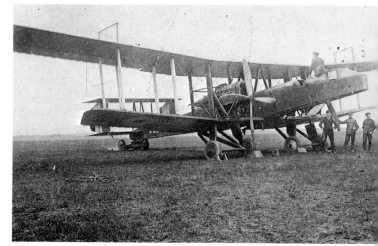

The Avro York C.1 had been principally designed for the RAF's Imperial routes and after World War II No. 246 Squadron, along with the others plied regularly through the Middle East to Singapore. MW203 VU:U is seen here.

Throughout its World War II existence No. 248 had been a coastal strike squadron flying Blenheims, Beaufighters and, latterly, Mosquitoes on Wing Strikes against enemy shipping from France to Norway. Immediately after the war there was a big Victory flypast over England, centring on London and many squadrons had to train to take part. It was no effort, however, for No. 248 which was used to low-level formation flying. This photograph was taken during the flypast and shows Mosquito RP.VI RF615 DM:S.

Towards the end of World War I many coastal Flights were established around the UK for shipping interception and reconnaissance. The D.H.6. trainer was employed in this role and could be flown from very small fields, including one at Padstow where No. 250 Squadron operated.

No. 252 had been formed as a coastal strike squadron within Coastal Command but with the great need for shipping strikes in the Mediterranean it moved to Egypt, being re-constituted there in 1942. Thereafter it spent the rest of the war using Beaufighters to attack shipping in the Mediterranean area. Mk. VIC X8077 F of 252 Squadron is seen here.

One of the most persistent performers of torpedo attacks on enemy shipping in World War II was No. 254 Squadron which for the most part flew Bristol Beaufighter Xs with the North Coates Wing. One of these, JM339 H is seen here during a visit to Linton-on-Ouse in August, 1944.

Another formidable anti-shipping weapon was the Mosquito XVIII, a version equipped with a 57 mm gun. This type was used by both Nos. 248 and 254 Squadrons (seen here) and several spectacular results were obtained in late 1944 and early 1945. The cannon barrel can be seen protruding below the nose.

During 1944 and 1945 the Indian Ocean was dotted with units flying Catalina flying-boats on long and usually fruitless maritime patrols. One such was No. 265 Squadron whose Catalin IB FP310 L is being boarded prior to start up here, at an unknown base.

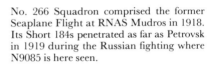

No. 266 Squadron comprised the former Seaplane Flight at RNAS Mudros in 1918. Its Short 184s penetrated as far as Petrovsk in 1919 during the Russian fighting where N9085 is here seen.

Anti-submarine patrols in the Mediterranean in World War I were based on Malta where the base at Kalafrana supported seaplanes and flying-boats. These became No. 267 Squadron in October, 1918, this Squadron remaining operative there until August, 1923. This is one of No. 267's Felixstowe F.2As.

No. 267 Squadron was re-formed out of the Comms. Flight at Heliopolis to fly transport and mail runs along the Western Desert. It received some of the first of the RAF's Dakota Is and IIIs. FD768 is seen here, wrongly painted FL768, in early 1943, probably at Bilbeis in the early RAF camouflage scheme.

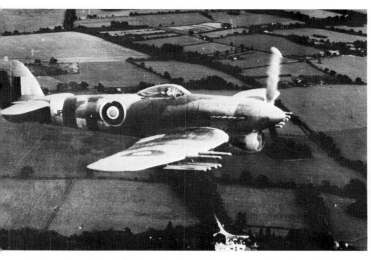

Only a handful of Hawker Typhoon IBs were used in the tactical reconnaissance role and No. 268 Squadron was one of the units that operated them, in this case flying from Odiham soon after D-Day.

No. 268 Squadron's principal mount in the last few months of the war was the Vickers Supermarine Spitfire FR.XIV, MV340 K seen here on the line at Mill.

No. 269 Squadron was one of the main operators of the Lockheed Hudson on anti-shipping duties, of which two years were flown from Iceland. Hudson I, T9256 UA:R is seen over the Atlantic.

The Handley Page Harrow bomber was converted to a transport and re-named the Sparrow; this type was used by No. 271 Squadron for transport duties and, in 1944, as an ambulance aircraft to bring wounded home from France. K6994 U is seen here on this task in Normandy on 12 September, 1944.

No. 269 Squadron's final task in World War II was as an ASR unit in the Azores. Warwick ASR.1 BV499 HK:D prepares for a sortie whilst standing on the PSP matting at Lagens in 1945.

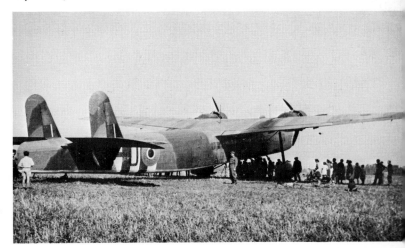

The Beaufighter proved a potent attack weapon, primarily for anti-shipping work but also in the Western Desert land battles. Foremost in such attacks from May, 1941 onwards was No. 272 Squadron whose Beaufighter IC T4892 T is seen at Edku in 1942.

From Harwell to Arnhem – Short Stirling IV LK 439 8Z:S of No. 295 Squadron takes a Horsa in tow for Operation Market on 17 September, 1944.

The Armstrong Whitworth Albemarle, originally a bomber, found its place as a troop transport and glider-tug, equipping No. 296 Squadron with whom it operated at D-Day. One of its aircraft, 9W:N is seen here above the clouds.

No. 297 Squadron also used the Albemarle on D-Day dropping paratroops near Caen and towing Horsa gliders there. V1823 P5:S was one of the Albemarles used.

After the war in Europe was over No. 298 Squadron went to India to fly airborne duties in Burma. In fact it flew route schedules and dropped food supplies to jungle tribes, remaining in the area until December, 1946, using Handley Page Halifax A.7s.

No. 301 Squadron re-appeared as a transport unit with Polish personnel just as World War II ended and eventually re-equipped with the Handley Page Halifax C.8 for transport duties. PP324 GR:V was one of its aircraft.

No. 304 Squadron which had been serving in Coastal Command during the war also flew on transport duties at its close, being based at Chedburgh with Warwick C.3s; HG306 is seen at dispersal there in 1946.

The orange triangle on the nose of Hudson I T9316 NO:A, taking off from Leuchars in 1941 shows it to be a Dutch aircraft belonging to No. 320 Squadron.

A second Dutch squadron, No. 321, was formed from escapees in 1940 and equipped with Avro Ansons for coastal recce, two of which are seen flying from Carew Cheriton in 1940. The nearest aircraft, K6285, still carries the code letters, MW, of No. 217 Squadron with which it previously served.

The Norwegians who had escaped in 1940 formed No. 330 Squadron for maritime recce duties, originally in Iceland with Northrop N-3PB float-planes but latterly with Short Sunderland IIIs, NJ188 seen here in February, 1945.

At the end of World War II No. 353 Squadron was using Warwick C.3s alongside its Dakotas. HG238 is seen here in February, 1945

EV848 was one of the Consolidated Liberator VIs flown by No. 354 Squadron in India in 1944–45.

The spy-dropping unit in the Far East operations was No. 357 Squadron which operated Hudsons, Dakotas, Catalinas, Liberators and Westland Lysander IIIAs of which V9289 C was one.

The first RCAF squadron to come to the UK in 1940 was No. 110, equipped with Westland Lysanders. It replaced these with Curtiss Tomahawks in April, 1941 at which time AH767 is seen on arrival at Odiham. By then it had been re-numbered No. 400 Squadron.

No. 400 Squadron really got into its operational stride with North American Mustang Is, flying Tac/R sorties in the main. AM251 0 is seen here at Dunsfold in 1943.

No. 234 SQUADRON

BADGE
A dragon rampant, flames issuing from the
mouth

MOTTO
'Ignem mortemque despuimu'
('We spit fire and death')

The dragon indicates the fighting role and the
flames associate with Spitfire.

The Squadron was formed from the RNAS coastal station in the
Isles of Scilly at Tresco in August, 1918. It had already seen action
dropping bombs on enemy submarines in the Western Approaches
with its flying-boats and it continued on such activities, mainly
convoy patrols, right up to the day before the Armistice, the last
patrol being flown, a convoy escort, on 10 November, 1918. It
continued at its base until disbandment on 15 May, 1919.

The Squadron re-formed on 30 October, 1939 at Leconfield as a
fighter unit and fought from the UK in the Battle of Britain and
subsequently in fighter sweeps over France, going on to cover the
Normandy landings in 1944 and long-range bomber escorts up to
the end of the war. After the war it re-equipped with Meteors and
was re-numbered 266 Squadron on 1 September, 1946. It re-formed
again in the fighter role in RAF Germany at Oldenburg on 1 August,
1952 and served there until 15 July, 1957 when it disbanded.
No. 234 lives on as one of the 'shadow numbers' of the Tactical
Weapons Unit at Brawdy where it uses BAe Hawk T.1s.

Bases etc.

Formed from the RNAS Tresco at Tresco in August, 1918.
Tresco   Aug 1918—May 1919

Disbanded at Tresco on 15 May, 1919.

Main Equipment

Curtiss H.12 (Aug 1918—May 1919)
  8652; 8654; 8656; 8658; 8674; 8675; N4341; N4343
Felixstowe F.3 (Aug 1918—May 1919)
  N4000; N4001; N4002; N4234; N4238; N4240; N4241; N4415
Short 184 (Aug 1918—May 1919)
  N1622; N2828; N2955
F.B.A (Aug 1918—   1918)
  N2727

Commanding Officers

S/Ldr Cox   Aug 1918—May 1919

Aircraft Insignia

There is no knowledge of any unit identity markings carried in World War I.
(See also *Fighter Squadrons of the RAF*, pp. 336–9)

No. 235 SQUADRON

BADGE
A double wyvern spouting fire

MOTTO
'Jaculamur Humi'
('We strike them to the ground')

No. 235 Squadron was formed in August, 1918 by giving this
number to the RNAS coastal station at Newlyn, Cornwall. This
seaplane base used Short floatplanes for convoy and anti-submarine
patrols over the Western Channel and these were carried on until the
Armistice in November, 1918. It remained in existence until disbanding on 22 February, 1919.

The Squadron re-formed at Manston on 30 October, 1939 as a
fighter unit equipped with Fairey Battles and Bristol Blenheims.
Before becoming operational it was transferred to Coastal Command in February, 1940 and began operations with Dutch coast
patrols in May, 1940. To these it added escort patrols to MTBs and
minelayers as well as shipping recces and escorting the Wellington
D.W.Is which were detecting and blowing up magnetic mines
around the coast. On 11 May No. 235 covered the landing of troops
at The Hague and was attacked by Messerschmitts. Two Blenheims
were lost but one 109 was destroyed and one claimed as probable.
Now, however, it turned its attention to the evacuation at Dunkirk,
flying beach patrols and escorting the 'small ships' fleets. The
Squadron also flew escort to Hudsons attacking targets such as
Borkum. All these operations were not without loss, six aircraft
being lost in enemy action in the month. In June the Squadron was
patrolling along the North French coast covering all the invasion
ports. A recce of the Zuider Zee on 27 June by six aircraft resulted in
four being lost. July and August were busy months along the
Channel; frequently Messerschmitt Bf 109s attacked and one or two
of them were shot down. On 15 August the Squadron was on a
Danish coast sweep when it met forty German bombers returning
from a raid on England. The aircraft attacked and shot down two
He 111s. In September 323 sorties were flown and on 11th,
although two Blenheims failed to return, two Bf 109s were shot
down while escorting Albacores raiding Calais and one destroyed
and one damaged in a raid on Boulogne. This type of work continued and in December the Squadron was given a boost when it
received Beaufighters, flying operation on 12th. But this was a false
start and the Squadron did not get any more, or fly any more on
operations for another year.

In 1941 the escorting, shipping recces, sweeps, Beaufort escorts
and bombing trips continued; in March a detachment went west to
cover the Biscay area and in June the whole Squadron moved north
to cover the North Sea and Norwegian coast. As the summer wore
on No. 235 began flying night intruders over Norway, having several inconclusive combats, and in December succeeded in putting a
Ju 88 into the sea. That month Beaufighter ops were resumed after
Christmas, being first used on Faeroes patrol.

In the first two months four Beaufighters were lost but in March,
1942 64 sorties were successfully flown (and a He 111 damaged)
without accident or loss. At the end of May a move enabled the
Squadron to operate off the Dutch and N. German coasts once
more, with a detachment also in the West Country. The main task
was now anti-aircraft escort to friendly convoys to counter the
increasing air attacks. In July it was fully based at Chivenor and
began flying escort to the Whitleys on patrol over Biscay. This
produced a crop of air combats in August when three Ar 196s were
shot down and two FW 200s damaged for no loss. September
proved a busy month with offensive sweeps providing groups of
Ju 88s to attack, five out of eight being destroyed plus another
Condor. One aircraft was lost that month but three in October. This
pattern of operations continued until 21 January when No. 235
moved north once more.

1943 now presented the Squadron with Norwegian coast patrols
and escorts to Hampden torpedo-bombers. Shipping recces were
added and on 1 March the Squadron escorted a Norwegian motor
vessel with escaping patriots during which one Ju 88 was shot down
and another damaged. Increasingly the torpedo-bombing escorts
met opposition from Bf 109s and FW 190s and savage fights
ensued. In May a detachment went to the South West once more for
Biscay patrols and this became the only part of the Squadron
operational in June, the rest working up on RPs. These they put to
use in July severely damaging a 2,500-ton motor vessel on 17th. At
the end of August No. 235 again moved into the Biscay area flying

anti-aircraft patrols under the direction of HMS *Bermuda*. Flying was at a high intensity, even the bad weather of December not preventing 101 sorties being flown.

These anti-aircraft patrols were continued off the West Coast of Ireland and in February a Ju 290 was shot down there. This type of work continued until June when the Squadron re-equipped with Mosquitoes which began operations on 16th. Despite the conversion 117 sorties were flown that month. The Squadron now went over to anti-shipping strikes in the course of which the CO shot down two Do 217s on 21 July. Two more were destroyed on 9 August and three days later one ship was sunk and another damaged, a similar result being achieved on 29th. In September the Squadron moved into the Banff Strike Wing with Nos. 144 & 404 Squadrons. It was back to Norway with anti-aircraft patrols and anti-submarine strikes, 150 sorties being achieved in October. Anti-shipping strikes continued with two ships being set on fire in Sognefjord on 14 November and eighteen ships hit in December. The intensity of operations now began to tail off but results were just as effective, two ships being destroyed at Helliso in February, 1945 and two U-boats destroyed in March as well as a steady score of enemy aircraft being shot down or damaged. The operations, most of which had been Wing strikes, ended on 31 May and the Squadron was disbanded on 10 July, 1945.

Bases etc.

Formed at Newlyn in August, 1918.

Newlyn	Aug 1918—Feb 1919

Disbanded at Newlyn on 22 February, 1919. Re-formed at Manston on 30 October, 1939.

Manston	Oct 1939—Feb 1940
North Coates	Feb 1940—Apr 1940
Bircham Newton, det. Detling, Thorney Island, St. Eval, Aldergrove	Apr 1940—Jun 1941
Dyce, det. Sumburgh	Jun 1941—Mar 1942
Sumburgh	Mar 1942—May 1942
Docking, det. Sumburgh	May 1942—Jul 1942
Chivenor	Jul 1942—Jan 1943
Leuchars	Jan 1943—Feb 1943
Sumburgh	Feb 1943—Feb 1943
Leuchars, det. Sumburgh, Predannack, St. Eval	Feb 1943—Aug 1943
Portreath	Aug 1943—Sep 1944

Banff	Sep 1944—Jul 1945

Disbanded at Banff on 10 July, 1945.

Main Equipment

Short 184 (Aug 1918—Feb 1919)
N1246; N1255; N1604; N1605; N1607; N1616; N1767; N1785; N2631; N2798; N2828; N2924; N2960; N2979; N2989

Fairey Battle II (Oct 1939—Feb 1940)
L5005; L5008; L5016; L5132; L5381; L5412; L5413

Bristol Blenheim IV (Feb 1940—Dec 1941)
L9189, LA:O; L9261, LA:M; L9324, LA:P; L9404, LA:A; N3523, LA:J; N3534, LA:X; N3543, LA:U; P4835, LA:H; P6957, LA:R; R2782, LA:X; R3965, LA:P; T1803, LA:D; T1869, LA:P; T1999, LA:S; V5430, LA:U; V5442, LA:S; V5642, LA:S; V5729, LA:D; Z5731, LA:B; Z5790, LA:L; Z5971, LA:B; Z6022, LA:B; Z6144, LA:Y

Bristol Beaufighter IC (Dec 1940 & Dec 1941—Sep 1942)
R2143; T3240, LA:L; T3292, LA:N; T4731, LA:V; T4759, LA:B; T4843, LA:K

Bristol Beaufighter VIC (Sep 1942—Jul 1943)
X7925, G

Bristol Beaufighter X (Sep 1943—May 1944)
LX401; LX817; LX933; LX944

Bristol Beaufighter XI (Apr 1944—Jul 1944)
JM106; JM107; JM113; JM117; JM280; JM281

de Havilland Mosquito VI (Jun 1944—Jul 1945)
HP887, LA:R; HP977, LA:J; HR113, LA:V; HR129, LA:D; HR137, LA:S; HR159, LA:Y; HR287, LA:Y; HR433, LA:L; PZ450; RF602, LA:P; RS523, LA:A; RS524, LA:S

Commanding Officers

S/Ldr R. I. G. McDougall	Oct 1939—May 1940
W/Cdr R. N. Clarke, DFC	May 1940—Dec 1940
S/Ldr I. M. T. de K. Bocock	Dec 1940—Jun 1941
S/Ldr A. G. Wincott	Jun 1941—Nov 1941
W/Cdr H. J. Garlick, DFC	Nov 1941—Aug 1942
W/Cdr G. H. B. Hutchinson	Aug 1942—Jul 1943
W/Cdr R. H. McConnell, DFC	Jul 1943—Apr 1944
W/Cdr J. V. Yonge	May 1944—Oct 1944
W/Cdr R. A. Atkinson, DSO, DFC	Oct 1944—Dec 1944
W/Cdr A. H. Simmonds, DFC	Dec 1944—Jul 1945

Aircraft Insignia

It is believed that no unit insignia was carried in World War I. The code letters 'LA' were used from Oct. 1939 until July 1945 with a probable break from the summer of 1943 until re-equipping with Mosquitoes in 1944.

No. 236 SQUADRON

BADGE
In front of a fountain a mailed fist grasping a sword

MOTTO
'Speculiate nuntiate'
('Having watched bring word')

No. 236 Squadron was formed in August, 1918 from the coastal flight at Mullion in Cornwall. It was equipped with D.H.6s which it used for anti-submarine patrols over the English Channel in co-operation with naval forces, its task being to find the submarines for the naval ships to destroy. Such patrols were flown until November when the war ended. The Squadron remained in existence until 15 May, 1919 when it was disbanded.

No. 236 was re-formed at Stradishall on 31 October, 1939 as a fighter squadron equipped with Blenheim Is and IVs and transferred into Coastal Command in February, 1940 before becoming operational. With serviceability problems it was June before No. 236 was declared operational flying convoy patrols over the Bristol and English Channels and also contributing to the patrols along the Havre/Cherbourg stretch of enemy coastline. In July it went over to night patrols in the Channel, on 17th finding three Ju 87s and damaging one. By day the Squadron escorted PR aircraft to France, losing three aircraft that month. These escorts continued; on 1 August the Squadron strafed Cherbourg airfield and lost two crews including the CO. A move to the west brought convoy patrols as the main task with occasional French coast recces. On 23

September three aircraft shot a He 111 into the sea and two days later F/O Russell did the same to a Do 18. From September to November the Squadron had A Flight at Aldergrove but on 19 November this became 272 Squadron. More and more the scene of No. 236's activities became the Brest-Ushant coast (known as *Bust* patrols) and out into Biscay. When Beauforts went torpedo-bombing No. 236 escorted them.

For most of 1941 the pattern was the same, *Bust* patrols, Fastnet patrols, escorts to DC-3s flying to Lisbon and back, and Brest recces. In June the Squadron flew 248 sorties, many of them convoy escorts. It began night intruder patrols in July to the Brest airfields and these were continued the following month as the Blenheims gave way to Beaufighters. First operations with the latter were in November. With these No. 236 detached to Sumburgh where, just after Christmas, one He 111 was shot down and another damaged. The final Blenheim operation was on 1 January, 1942 and then at the end of the month No. 236 came ops to send thirteen aircrews to the Middle East and the rest to 2 OTU. The Squadron itself moved to Wattisham and there received new crews in February and resumed operations in March with French coast recces. Two sorties were flown on 15th when one aircraft failed to return. Another Beaufighter was lost four days later but after that the new No. 236 got into its stride, damaging armed trawlers in an attack on 20th and providing cover for a secret force attacking St. Nazaire, during which a Ju 88 was shot down. Shipping searches now became the predominant task, then intruders on the midsummer nights (the Squadron now had detachments in Cornwall, Scotland and the

Shetlands). On 12 June F/Lt Gatward and Sgt Fern made a daring flight at low level (20-30 ft) to Paris, dropping a Tricolor on the Arc de Triomphe and shooting up the German Marine HQ. From that month on the Squadron's Beaus carried 2 x 250 lb bombs on their sorties for use against suitable targets. Shipping recces were sometimes eventful; three aircraft on 9 July were attacked by Bf 109s and only one returned. However at the end of the month a similar attack on one aircraft was countered by such violent evasive action as to cause a Bf 109 to fly into the sea. On 21 August the Squadron flew escort to Catalinas landing alongside Danish fishing vessels and in September No. 236 returned to its old area of Biscay, to provide escorts for the Whitleys on anti-submarine patrols. From here a detachment at Wick flew Norwegian coast patrols and found *Scharnhorst* in the Skaw in January 1943. Escorts to Hampden torpedo-bombers were also flown from Wick; losses were mounting, however, three aircraft missing in February.

Wing strikes now became the norm, No. 236 joining with Nos. 143 and 254 Squadrons as the North Coates Wing. On 1 May one such strike was on the cruiser *Nürnberg*; that same month No. 236 began training on RPs using these on 24th in a convoy strike in which two AFVs were sunk, and on 29th F/Sgt Hazell tried them against a U-boat; two days later F/Lt Bateman did the same and was able to claim a 'probably destroyed'. Now night Wing strikes were flown as well and the pattern stabilised on 60 to 80 sorties a month on such strikes with two or three crews missing a month. With the bad winter weather the Squadron mainly flew shipping searches but at the end of January, 1944 No. 236 was operating with the Wing once more on *Roadsteads*. One such on 7 March damaged eight vessels. 1944 was a busy year for the North Coates Wing, 236 flying over a hundred sorties each month. Before and during the invasion of France it was mainly employed on anti-E-boat patrols (known as *Con-E-Bo*) off the Dutch Coast.

On 15 June a most successful strike in this area sank an 8,000 ton merchant ship, an escort vessel and an M-Class minesweeper and set two other minesweepers on fire.

This operational activity was maintained for the rest of the war with shipping recces, armed *Rovers*, Wing strikes and, towards the end, strikes against midget submarines. Some *Percolate* sorties were flown with ASV Wellingtons directing the Beaufighters on to targets but these were none too successful. For the anti-submarine sorties the Beaus carried depth-charges and in the last few weeks of fighting there was great success: on 3 May a U-boat was blown up and many ships set on fire and on 4th two out of three U-boats were destroyed. Last sortie was flown on 11 May, and on 25 the Squadron disbanded at North Coates.

Bases etc.

Formed at Mullion on August, 1918 by numbering the RNAS Coastal Flight there.

Mullion	Aug	1918—May 1919

Disbanded at Mullion on 15 May, 1919. Re-formed at Stradishall on 31 October, 1939.

Stradishall	Oct	1939—Dec 1939
Martlesham Heath	Dec	1939—Feb 1940
North Coates	Feb	1940—Apr 1940
Speke	Apr	1940—May 1940
Filton	May	1940—Jun 1940
Middle Wallop	Jun	1940—Jul 1940
Thorney Island, det. St. Eval, Detling, Bircham Newton	Jul	1940—Aug 1940
St. Eval, det. Aldergrove	Aug	1940—Mar 1941
Carew Cheriton, det. St. Eval, Portreath, Bircham Newton, Sumburgh	Mar	1941—Feb 1942
Wattisham, det. Thorney Island, Predannack, Sumburgh, Leuchars	Feb	1942—Jul 1942
Oulton, det. Thorney Island, Wick	Jul	1942—Sep 1942
North Coates, det. Talbenny, Chivenor, Wick, Sumburgh, Grimsetter, Predannack, Tain, Manston	Sep	1942—May 1945

Disbanded at North Coates on 25 May, 1945.

Main Equipment

Airco D.H.6 (Aug 1918—May 1919)
No serial numbers known

Bristol Blenheim I (Oct 1939—Aug 1940)
K7135; K7143; L1119, FA:C; L1257, FA:F; L1301, FA:B; L6776, FA:K; L6797, FA:Q; L6815, FA:G; L6840, FA:Y; L8684, FA:D; L8718, FA:B

Bristol Blenheim IVF (Feb 1940—Feb 1942)
N3597, FA:Q; N3600, FA:R; N3603, FA:M; R2775, FA:O; R2799, FA:Q; R3878, FA:Z; T1810, FA:E; T1942, FA:J; V5432, FA:A; V5454, FA:V; Z5729, FA:H; Z5743, FA:Y; Z6031, FA:D

Bristol Beaufighter IC (Aug 1941—Jul 1942)
T4656, FA:B; T4724, FA:A; T4786, FA:E; T4796, ND:Z; T4826, FA:Y; T4827, ND:N; T4917, ND:V

Bristol Beaufighter VIC (Jun 1942—Jul 1943)
T5198, ND:Z; T5206, ND:D; T5258, ND:B; X8060, ND:E; X8088, ND:X; EL240, H; EL343, O; EL433, ND:T; JL421, ND:V; JL567, ND:R; JL778, ND:N; JL824, ND:O, later Y

Bristol Beaufighter X (Jul 1943—May 1945)
KW280, M; LX821, D; LX824, MB:G; LX934, B; LX974, C; LX981, MB:K; LZ187, H; LZ290, T; NE193, H; NE442, MB:P; NE575, MB:Q; NE756, O; NE799, MB:W; NT897, H; NT950, MB:T; NT991, MB:A; NV171, MB:Y; NV293, MB:G; NV797, MB:S; RD142, MB:D; RD457, MB:S

Commanding Officers

S/Ldr R. S. Booth	Aug	1918—May 1919
S/Ldr P. E. Drew	Oct	1939—Aug 1940
S/Ldr G. W. Montagu	Aug	1940—Dec 1940
S/Ldr F. Harrison	Jan	1941—May 1941
S/Ldr A. M. Glover	May	1941—May 1942
W/Cdr H. F. Wood	May	1942—Sep 1942
W/Cdr H. D. Fraser, OBE	Sep	1942—Nov 1942
W/Cdr H. N. G. Wheeler, DFC	Nov	1942—Sep 1943
W/Cdr W. H. Cliff, DSO	Sep	1943—Mar 1944
W/Cdr P. D. F. Mitchell	Mar	1944—Aug 1944
W/Cdr E. W. Tacon, DSO, DFC, AFC	Aug	1944—Sep 1944
W/Cdr D. G. Hall, DFC	Sep	1944—May 1945

Aircraft Insignia

From October, 1939 the Squadron carried the code letters 'FA' until ca. 1942 when they were changed to 'ND'. This probably took place when all the aircrew were posted away and the Squadron re-constituted at Wattisham in February, 1942. In mid-1943 however code letters were dropped and coloured markings introduced on the North Coates Wing aircraft, No. 236 having a horizontal yellow band along the side of the rear fuselage. In the summer of 1944, code letters were re-introduced, No. 236 Squadron carrying 'MB' until the disbandment in May, 1945.

No. 237 SQUADRON

BADGE
A lion passant guardant, charged on the shoulder with an eagle's claw and holding in the forepaw an elephant's tusk

MOTTO
'Primum agmen in caelo'
('The vanguard in the heavens')

The Squadron, primarily consisting of Rhodesian members and formed out of a Southern Rhodesian squadron carries a crest drawn from the arms of the British South Africa Company.

In August, 1918 one of the RNAS seaplane Flights at Cattewater was numbered 237 Squadron. Its task was anti-submarine patrols and escort work in the English Channel and this was continued until the war ended. The Squadron remained there until disbanding on 15 May, 1919.

No. 237 was re-formed on 22 April, 1940 by re-numbering No. 1 Squadron, Southern Rhodesian Air Force at Nairobi. It served in the Eritrean and Ethiopian campaigns, gradually becoming principally a fighter unit and moved on to the Western Desert serving there, in Iraq and Iran, then in Sicily, Italy and Southern France. It was disbanded at Rosignano on 15 September, 1945.

Bases etc.

Formed at Cattewater in August, 1918.
Cattewater   Aug 1918—May 1919
Disbanded at Cattewater on 15 May, 1919.

Main Equipment

Short 184 (Aug 1918—May 1919) The aircraft below served with either 237 or 238 Squadrons or both:

N1099; N1142; N1257; N1601; N1624; N1790; N1796; N2836

Commanding Officers

Not known

Aircraft Insignia

Believed nil.
(See also *Fighter Squadrons of the RAF* pp. 339–40)

No. 238 SQUADRON

BADGE
A three-headed hydra

MOTTO
'Ad finem'
('To the end')

No. 238 Squadron was formed at Cattewater (Plymouth) in August, 1918 at the RNAS seaplane station and flew anti-submarine patrols over the Channel until the Armistice with Short Floatplanes. It was eventually disbanded on 15 May, 1919.

No. 238 re-formed at Tangmere on 16 May, 1940 as a fighter squadron on the eve of the Battle of Britain. Through this period it fought with Fighter Command and after until going to Malta in June, 1941 and on to the Western Desert campaign. This was followed by the Italian and Southern France campaigns, having converted to Spitfires from Hurricanes in 1943. It was disbanded as a fighter Squadron at Gragnano on 31 October, 1944.

The Squadron again re-formed, this time as a transport unit at Merryfield on 23 November, 1944. It received no aircraft until January, 1945 due to a policy change as it had been intended to have Albemarles, but eventually it received Dakotas. Then No. 238 had an almost complete change of personnel (from Australians to British) so it was not until 14 February, 1945 that it could fly as a Squadron to India. A month later it began operations, flying supplies into the forward airfields and bringing casualties out; in the last fortnight of March it flew 331 sorties, and lost three aircraft, one due to enemy shellfire at Meiktela. In April 659 sorties were flown, supplying the troops fighting around Mandalay. In May it was concentrating on supplying Toungoo and evacuating casualties from Akyab and Ramree, also releasing POWs and bringing them back to Comilla. For the first week of June operations continued but then the Squadron began the move to South Australia, setting up base at Parafield in July. It began transport schedules within Australia and then began a shuttle Momote–Leyte–Guam–Eniwetok in August, supporting the British Pacific Fleet and a high rate of flying was continued until the war ended. The Squadron then stayed in Australia until disbanding on 4 January, 1946.

On 1 December, 1946 No. 525 Squadron at Abingdon was re-numbered 238 Squadron. Its equipment was again the Dakota which it flew both on army support and the various medium-range Transport Command routes until the beginnings of the Berlin Air-lift during which, on 5 November, 1948, it was disbanded by being re-numbered as No. 10 Squadron.

Bases etc.

Formed at Cattewater in August, 1918.

Cattewater	Aug 1918—May 1919

Disbanded at Cattewater on 15 May, 1919. Re-formed in the fighter role at Tangmere on 16 May, 1940. Disbanded at Gragnano on 31 October, 1944. Re-formed at Merryfield on 23 November, 1944 in the transport role.

Merryfield	Nov 1944—Feb 1945
en route to India	Feb 1945—Feb 1945
Raipur	Feb 1945—Mar 1945
Comilla	Mar 1945—Jul 1945
Parafield	Jul 1945—Jan 1946

Disbanded at Parafield on 4 January, 1946. Re-formed at Abingdon on 1 December, 1946 by re-numbering No. 525 Squadron.

Abingdon	Dec 1946—Nov 1948

Disbanded at Abingdon on 5 November, 1948 by re-numbering as No. 10 Squadron.

Main Equipment

Short 184 (Aug 1918—May 1919)
see No. 237 Squadron
Douglas Dakota C.3, C.4 (Feb 1945—Jan 1946 & Dec 1946—Nov 1948)
FZ671, FM:R; KG391, WF:G; KG397, FM:M; KG468, FM:V; KJ970, WF:U; KJ993; KK151, WF:B; KK193, WF:R; KN234, WF:Y; KN382, WF:Q; KN417, WF:G; KN520, WF:K; KN666, FM:KW; KP214, WF:L; KP227, FM:J; TJ170, FM:A

Commanding Officers

W/Cdr R. E. Bailey, DSO, DFC	Dec 1944—Jan 1945
W/Cdr H. Burton	Jan 1945—Jan 1946

Aircraft Insignia

It is believed that no insignia was carried on the Short floatplanes. The Dakotas carried the code letters 'FM' at some time during the first Dakota existence and 'WF' during the second.
(See also *Fighter Squadrons of the RAF*, pp. 340–1)

No. 239 SQUADRON

BADGE
A winged spur

MOTTO
'Exploramus'
('We explore')

This was the first squadron to work with an armoured division which included mechanised cavalry, with which the spur provided association.

In August, 1918 the coastal reconnaissance unit at Torquay was numbered 239 Squadron. It was equipped with floatplanes and flew coastal and anti-submarine patrols in the Channel until the Armistice. It was disbanded there on 15 May, 1919.

No. 239 was re-formed at Hatfield on 18 September, 1940 from Flights of Nos. 16 and 225 Squadrons equipped with Lysanders for operation with IV Corps. Its first task, however, was AA calibration for which it was detached to Gatwick. Another task it took on before the year was out was the training of glider personnel for which it used Magisters and Tiger Moths. Slowly it worked up in the army co-operation role, taking part in exercises in different parts of the UK. Tomahawks arrived in June, 1941 and the Lysanders were used for ASR work at Plymouth and Manston. In September, 1941 the Squadron began *Rhubarbs* from Manston over the Ostende area and these continued at the rate of about 20 sorties a month. In December *Populars* were also flown and in 1942 it equipped with Hurricanes, Battles, Masters and, eventually Mustangs which were used on the *Populars*. In the summer of 1942 the Squadron began standing patrols along the South Coast to intercept German fighter-bombers. On 19 August it took part in Operation Jubilee (Dieppe) flying fourteen low-level Tac/R sorties losing one aircraft. Standing patrols were maintained until January, 1943 when *Populars* were resumed once more. Operations continued until March when further tactical training took place until July, then No. 239 began *Rhubarbs* once more. July was a bad month, four pilots being lost on operations, and in August the Squadron flew recces with No. 501 Squadron as escort. The following month the Mustangs were allotted away as the Squadron was to be re-constituted as a night-fighter unit, the last operation being flown on 9th.

The Squadron then moved to Scotland and re-equipped with Mosquitoes which it flew in 100 (Bomber Support) Group until 1 July, 1945 when it was disbanded.

Bases etc.

Formed at Torquay in August, 1918.

Torquay	Aug 1918—May 1919

Disbanded at Torquay on 15 May, 1919. Re-formed at Hatfield on 18 September, 1940 from Flights of 16 and 225 Squadrons.

Hatfield, det. Teversham, Gatwick, Old Sarum	Sep 1940—Feb 1941
Gatwick, det. Detling, Manston	Feb 1941—Aug 1942
Twinwoods Farm, det. Snailwell, Gatwick	Aug 1942—Oct 1942
Cranfield	Oct 1942—Nov 1942
Odiham	Nov 1942—Dec 1942
Hurn	Dec 1942—Jan 1943
Stoney Cross	Jan 1943—Apr 1943
Gatwick	Apr 1943—Jun 1943
Fairlop	Jun 1943—Jun 1943
Martlesham Heath	Jun 1943—Jul 1943
Fairlop	Jul 1943—Aug 1943
Hornchurch	Aug 1943—Sep 1943

Transferred to night-fighter role and moved to Ayr, 30 September, 1943.

Main Equipment

Short 184 (Aug 1918—May 1919)
N2631; N2798; N2828; N2919; N2924; N2960; N2979; N9029
Westland Lysander II (Sep 1940—Mar 1941)
L4786, HB:U; L4802; L6850, HB:H; L6865, HB:H; N1254; N1265; P1674, HB:T; R2006, HB:F; R2007
Westland Lysander IIIA (Mar 1941—Jan 1942)
V9313; V9377; V9429; V9496; V9546; V9587
Curtiss Tomahawk I, II (Jun 1941—May 1942)
AH747; AH793, HB:Z; AH802; AH829, HB:F; AH846, HB:O; AH982, HB:T
Hawker Hurricane I, IIC (Jan 1942—May 1942)
T9519, HB:L; AG119, HB:E; BN373, HB:K; BN966, HB:X
Fairey Battle II (Jun 1942—Dec 1942)
L5025, HB:J; P5283; P6572, HB:G
Miles Master I, III (Mar 1942—Jul 1942)
T8382; T8568; DL646
North American Mustang I (May 1942—Sep 1943)
AG365, HB:T; AG439; AG544, HB:C; AG596, HB:X; AG614, HB:P; AM136, HB:A; AM181, HB:A; AM238, HB:V; AP170, HB:X

Commanding Officers

W/Cdr P. L. Donkin	Sep 1940—Sep 1942
W/Cdr P. Legge	Sep 1942—Sep 1943

Aircraft Insignia
It is believed that no insignia was carried on the Shorts in World War I. In World War II the code letters 'HB' were carried although it is likely that these were dropped early in 1943 and no unit markings carried until re-constituting with Mosquitoes.
(See also *Fighter Squadrons of the RAF*, pp. 341–2)

No. 240 SQUADRON

BADGE
In front of a hurt, a winged helmet

MOTTO
'Sjo Vordur Lopt Vordur'
('Guardian of the sea, guardian of the air')

The Icelandic helmet and motto relate to the Squadron's period in Iceland and activity in Icelandic waters.

The Squadron was formed in August, 1918 at Calshot by combining Nos. 345, 346 and 410 Flights of the RNAS, the former two being flying-boat units and the latter a seaplane Flight. The task was anti-submarine patrolling over the central English Channel and guarding the convoys in the area. After three months of such patrolling the war ended and 240 Squadron was eventually disbanded on 15 May, 1919.

No. 240 re-formed there on 30 March, 1937 by expanding C Flight, Seaplane Training Squadron up to full strength and was equipped with Supermarine Scapas.

Despite its number it operated as a training unit until November, 1938 when it re-equipped with Singapore IIIs and became operational on 1 January, 1939.

This lasted six months and again No. 240 became a training unit but in July it re-equipped once more and again worked up for operations with Saro Londons. On the outbreak of war it immediately began A/S patrols and convoy escorts, flying fifty sorties that month. It moved up to Sullom Voe in two stages for patrols in northern waters; there, on 19 December, it had its first action when K5258 had a fight with a He 111 in which the captain of the London was killed but the crew managed to return to base. This hard, dull work continued until May, 1940 when the Squadron moved to South Wales to re-equip. With Stranraers it returned to operations on 10 June and flew a hundred sorties from there before moving up to Scotland once more at the end of July. Patrolling continued without any sightings of the enemy; four Stranraers were lost, however, being sunk at their moorings in gales. In March, 1941 the

Squadron at last received modern equipment with the issue of Catalinas and operations began on the 21st, with a search for the *Scharnhorst*. On 29 April F/Lt Hayter found and depth-charged the Squadron's first U-boat and on 27 May P/O Goolden found and shadowed the *Bismarck* for four hours. In July the Icelandic detachment began and that month F/O Bradshaw took W8427 to Archangel and back on a clandestine operation. September was a productive month for No. 240; F/Lt Louw had two combats with a FW 200 whilst depth-charging a U-boat and F/O Goolden and F/Lt Porteous both attacked U-boats.

Operations continued without further action until February, 1942 when No. 240 Squadron began to move to the Far East. En route the aircraft flew shipping recces to Gibraltar and F/O Godber depth-charged a submarine in the Mediterranean on his way to India. It was a leisurely deployment and the Squadron established itself at Redhills Lake in July. On 1 August operations over the Indian Ocean began and soon the Squadron had detachments at other bases to spread the coverage. There was much less likelihood of enemy action here and month after month the convoy escorts, traffic patrols, submarine hunts and shopping patrols went on without action. In July, 1943 a detachment from Coconada flew 'Operation Breach', bombing attacks on Tavoya airfield. Otherwise there was no action until 23 January, 1944 when F/Lt Groves, whilst escorting a convoy, found a submarine and depth-charged it, resulting in a large oil patch. In 1944 the Squadron added meteorological recce flights to its repertoire; on 16 August S/Ldr Robinson found a tanker and attacked it but his aircraft was hit. About fifty sorties were being flown each month but this increased in October, 1944 when the Squadron began special operations dropping and picking up secret agents along the Burmese and Malayan coastline. Three complete crews and aircraft (SD Flight) were assigned specifically to this task and the work increased with the Thai coast being involved as well (Operation Siren). The method was for two aircraft to fly together, one with the agents and supplies, the other with depth-charges to drop near any enemy shipping to make it look like a mine-laying sortie.

In February, and March, 1945 the Squadron was busily engaged in these sorties, met flights, ASR trips, very long range survey PR trips (25 hrs) and leaflet-dropping, the maritime work consisting of a few convoy escorts. As the war rolled on the Squadron could use advanced bases further down the coast (Kyaukpyu, then Rangoon). On 1 July, 1945, the Squadron was disbanded at Redhills Lake and on the same day No. 212 Squadron, on the same base, was re-numbered No. 240, taking over also the SD Flight of the old No. 240. It now had Sunderlands and began phasing out the Catalinas (which were mainly used on the Special Duty flights). The Sunderlands were used for met flights, ferry flights and transport trips, latterly bringing home POWs from the Far East. In January, 1946 a move was made to Ceylon, flying regular schedules to Singapore, but on 13 March, 1946 No. 240 Squadron was disbanded.

It re-formed on 1 May, 1952 at St. Eval with Avro Shackletons, moving the following month to form part of the Ballykelly Wing. It participated in all the maritime exercises over the Atlantic area during the next few years, being one of the few Shackleton squadrons to retain Mk. 1s for most of its existence. In 1957 it sent aircraft to cover the nuclear tests, dropping leaflets on any ships that strayed into the danger zone. On 1 November, 1958 it was disbanded and re-numbered as No. 203 Squadron.

Bases etc.

Formed at Calshot in August, 1918 by combining Nos. 345, 346 and 410 Flights.

Calshot	Aug 1918—May 1919

Disbanded at Calshot on 15 May, 1919. Re-formed at Calshot from C Flight, Seaplane Training Squadron on 30 March, 1937.

Calshot	Mar 1937—Aug 1939
Invergordon, det. Sullom Voe	Aug 1939—Nov 1939
Sullom Voe	Nov 1939—Feb 1940
Invergordon, det. Sullom Voe	Feb 1940—Apr 1940
Sullom Voe	Apr 1940—May 1940
Pembroke Dock	May 1940—Jul 1940
Stranraer	Jul 1940—Mar 1941
Killadeas, det. Iceland	Mar 1941—Aug 1941
Castle Archdale	Aug 1941—Jun 1942
Redhills Lake, det. Koggala, Aden, Coconada, Kelai, Diego Guarcia, Addu Atoll	Jun 1942—Jul 1945

Disbanded at Redhills Lake on 1 July, 1945. Re-formed the same day at the same base by re-numbering No. 212 Squadron.

Redhills Lake, det. Rangoon	Jul 1945—Jan 1946
Koggala, det. Penang	Jan 1946—Mar 1946

Disbanded at Koggala on 13 March, 1946. Re-formed at St. Eval on 1 May, 1952.

St. Eval	May 1952—Jun 1952
Ballykelly	Jun 1952—Nov 1958

Disbanded at Ballykelly on 1 November, 1958 by re-numbering as No. 203 Squadron.

Main Equipment

Fairey Campania (Aug 1918—May 1919)
N2376; N2395

Short 184 (Aug 1918—May 1919)
N2985; N2999; N9018

Short 320 (1918—May 1919)
N1707; N1709

Felixstowe F.2A (Aug 1918—May 1919)
N4081; N4285; N4286; N4535

Curtiss H.12 (Aug 1918—May 1919)
N4334; N4337; N4349

Supermarine Scapa (Mar 1937—Nov 1938)
K4191; K4193; K4195; K4197; K4199; K7304

Short Singapore III (Nov 1938—Jul 1939)
K4579; K6909; K6919; K6920; K8566; K8568; K8856

Saro London II (Jul 1939—Jun 1940)
K5257; K5258, BN:H; K5261; K5263; K5910, BN:L; K5913

Supermarine Stranraer (Jun 1940—Mar 1941)
K7287, BN:B; K7292, BN:Y; K7295, BN:L; K7298, BN:A; K7299, BN:M; K7302, BN:Z

Consolidated Catalina I (Mar 1941—Mar 1943 & Apr 1945—Jul 1945)
W8405, BN:F; W8418, BN:U; Z2135, BN:A; Z2146, BN:W; Z2153, BN:K; AH546, BN:M; AH549, BN:F

Consolidated Catalina II (Mar 1941—Jul 1941)
AM264, BN:X; AM265; AM267; AM268; AM269, BN:K; AM270; AM281

Consolidated Catalina IB (Nov 1943—Dec 1945)
Z2146, B; FP165, K; FP182, W; FP225, P; FP233, A; FP304, Z

Consolidated Catalina IIA (Apr 1942—Mar 1945)
VA714, H; VA716; VA718, K; VA720, A; VA723, F; VA726, D; VA732

Consolidated Catalina IVB (Dec 1944—Aug 1945)
JX278, N; JX298, J; JX303, X; JX312, G; JX326, H; JX334, C; JX580, H; JX601, K

Short Sunderland GR.5 (Jul 1945—Mar 1946)
NJ272, B; NJ276, M; PP126, K; PP131, J; RN291, G; RN296, F; RN298, F

Avro Shackleton MR.1A (May 1952—Nov 1958)
VP287, 240:B; WB823; WB828; WB835; WB848; WB858, L:A; WB860, L:C; WG507, L:E, later 240:E; WG509, L:G; WG529

Avro Shackleton MR.2 (Mar 1953—Aug 1954)
WL739; WL749

Commanding Officers

Capt C. L. Scott	Aug 1918—
S/Ldr J. McFarlane, MC, AFC	Mar 1937—Oct 1937
S/Ldr M. W. C. Ridgway	Oct 1937—Aug 1939
W/Cdr R. H. Carter, OBE, DFC	Aug 1939—Sep 1940
W/Cdr A. W. Bates	Sep 1940—Feb 1941
W/Cdr C. A. Watt	Feb 1941—Oct 1941
W/Cdr C. A. V. Clayton, DFC	Oct 1941—Oct 1943
W/Cdr B. A. A. C. Wood	Oct 1943—Feb 1945
W/Cdr C. B. Gavin Robinson, AFC	Feb 1945—Jul 1945
S/Ldr L. F. Banks, DFC	May 1952—Apr 1954
S/Ldr A. P. Smallman	Apr 1954—May 1955
W/Cdr C. R. Alexander	Jul 1955—Aug 1957
W/Cdr W. D. Hodgkinson, DFC, AFC	Aug 1957—Jun 1958
W/Cdr H. R. Ken, MBE	Jun 1958—Nov 1958

Aircraft Insignia

It is not believed that any insignia was carried in World War I. No information is to hand concerning the markings carried in the thirties prior to the Munich crisis in September, 1938 when code letters were first allotted, No. 240's combination being 'SH'. This changed to 'BN' in September, 1939 which was used at least until the Squadron went to the Far East in 1942 after which no markings were used. At first the Shackeltons used the code letter 'L' but *ca.* 1956 this was replaced by the Squadron number.

No. 241 SQUADRON

BADGE
An eagle volant in front of two claymores in saltire

MOTTO
'Find and forewarn'

The claymores represent the Squadron's association with Scotland upon re-forming in 1940.

No. 241 Squadron was formed at Portland in August, 1918, taking over the former RNAS coastal Flight there and flying coastal patrol duties until November, 1918. It was finally disbanded there on 18 June, 1919.

The Squadron re-formed at Inverness on 25 September, 1940 from Flights of Nos. 4 and 614 Squadrons equipped with Lysanders in the army co-operation role. That same day it began coastal anti-invasion patrols. Its next task came in February, 1941 when it dropped supplies to snowbound farmers in its area. In addition it maintained army co-operation training continually. In April it moved south and began ASR duties and also took part in a photo survey of London as well as participating in army exercises. Tomahawks arrived for the army work, the Lysanders continued PR then in 1942 the Tomahawks were grounded and the Squadron received an Airacobra, AH651, for Tac/R trials followed by re-equipment with Mustangs in February. Before becoming operational the Squadron moved to Scotland where it converted to Hurricanes and prepared for overseas.

On 25 November, 1942 it landed at Maison Blanche airfield, Algiers, hot on the heels of the invading Allied armies. After settling in it began operations with a contact patrol on Christmas Eve. After Christmas the sorties rate began to build up with Tac/Rs and bombing attacks so that by the end of January it had flown 200 sorties. In February it converted to Spitfires without coming off ops, flying bombing sorties against enemy road transport and Tac/Rs wherever required. In March it made its fourth forward move to keep up with the armies and flew 256 sorties, the Hurricanes doing the strafing and bombing and the Spitfires the Tac/Rs. In April the ground attack work predominated and 515 sorties were flown on low-level attacks on enemy supply routes, airfields and road transport. This built up into the final push for Tunis in early May with 241 providing a continuous shuttle service bombing roads on the Cap Bon peninsula. In the five days up to 10 May 349 sorties had been flown; then the Squadron was stood down for a rest. It moved to Ariana and for a fortnight just flew shipping patrols. In June No. 241 began night bombing attacks on Pantellaria before coming off operations on 16th.

There now followed a period of rest and it was not until moving to Italy in December that it re-entered the operational area. Operations were resumed in January, 1944 with weather recces and shipping recces as far afield as Albania. The shipping recce sorties would land at bomber airfields so that attacks could be laid on as soon as possible. In February PR was added to the tasks and the occasional *Rhubarb*.

In March, 1944 the Squadron was operating for the American 57th Bomb Wing, finding shipping targets for them. The Squadron was split up with Flights operating both sides of the Apennines. In May the task was changed; No. 241 began Tac/Rs for the 8th Army attack on Cassino, completing all its sorties before 0630 each morning to give an up-to-date picture, 490 sorties being flown that month. Gradually the Squadron flew more and more bomber escorts due to a shortage of fighter squadrons and it began to build up a score (in July it claimed seven E/A destroyed, one damaged and forty-four barges damaged in the Po estuary). As the campaign moved on it returned mainly to strafing of roads and railways, flying 577 sorties in August, losing three pilots, destroying two aircraft, thirty-eight vehicles and twenty-eight locos and seven barges, with twenty-seven vehicles, twenty-four locos and thirty-five barges damaged.

As the winter moved in the heavy rains slowed down ground and air activity, but the Squadron maintained 300 or so sorties a month. In 1945 the predominance was on armed recces with bombing sorties, weather recces and ASR searches also on the list. Again the Squadron was called upon to provide escort duties and this became its main pre-occupation up to VE-Day. No. 241 remained in Italy until disbanding at Treviso on 29 August, 1945.

Bases etc.

Formed in August, 1918 from the RNAS Coastal Flight at Portland.

Portland	Aug 1918—Jun 1919

Disbanded at Portland 18 June, 1919. Re-formed from Flights of 4 and 614 Squadrons at Inverness on 25 September, 1940.

Inverness	Sep 1940—Apr 1941
Bury St. Edmunds	Apr 1941—Jul 1941
Bottisham	Jul 1941—May 1942
Ayr	May 1942—Nov 1942
Maison Blanche	Nov 1942—Dec 1942
Constantine	Dec 1942—Dec 1942
Souk-el-Arba	Dec 1942—Jan 1943
Souk-el Khemis	Jan 1943—Mar 1943
Thelepte	Mar 1943—Mar 1943
Souk-el-Khemis	Mar 1943—May 1943
Ariana	May 1943—Jun 1943
Bou Ficha	Jun 1943—Oct 1943
Phillippeville	Oct 1943—Jan 1944
Palata, det. Vesuvius, Madna, Pomigliano	Jan 1944—Apr 1944
Trigno, det. San Angelo	Apr 1944—Jun 1944
Sinello	Jun 1944—Jun 1944
San Vito	Jun 1944—Jun 1944
Tortoretto	Jun 1944—Jul 1944
Fermo	Jul 1944—Jul 1944
Falconara	Jul 1944—Aug 1944
Chiaravalle	Aug 1944—Aug 1944
Piagiolino	Aug 1944—Sep 1944
Cassandro	Sep 1944—Sep 1944
Rimini	Sep 1944—Nov 1944
Fano	Nov 1944—Dec 1944
Bellaria	Dec 1944—May 1945
Treviso	May 1945—Aug 1945

Disbanded at Treviso 29 August, 1945.

Main Equipment

Fairey Campania (Aug 1918—Jun 1919)
N2363
Short 184 (Aug 1918—Jun 1919)
N1259; N1758; N2833; N9007; N9008
Westland Lysander II (Sep 1940—Nov 1940)
N1204; N1219; N1249; P1677; P1712; P9099; R1990; R2026
Westland Lysander III, IIIA (Nov 1940—May 1942)
T1563; T1672, RZ:A; V9548; V9583; V9707, RZ:P
Curtiss Tomahawk I, II (Aug 1941—Apr 1942)
AH757; AH947; AK138, RZ:L; AK140
North American Mustang I (Feb 1942—Oct 1942)
AG355; AG381; AG405; AG512, RZ:A; AM125; AM145; AM177, RZ:V
Hawker Hurricane IIC (Oct 1942—Jan 1944)
BE350; BE651; BE689; BG951; HL780, T; HL964; HL973, G; HM140; HV368; HV674; HW556, K; HW664, R; HW748, C; HW889, Y; KW707, D; KW972, O; KX109, A; KX868, E; KX971, M
Vickers-Supermarine Spitfire VC (Feb 1943—Dec 1943)
AR551; BR365; EE867; ER220; ER495; ER617; ER723; ER979
Vickers-Supermarine Spitfire IX (Dec 1943—Oct 1944)
EN244; LZ831; MA425, RZ:V; MA580; MA767; MH320; MH599; MH608; MH924; MK425, RZ:R
Vickers-Supermarine Spitfire VIII (Jan 1944—Oct 1944)
JF278; JF422; JF517; JF582; JF659; JF700; JG162; JG541
Vickers-Supermarine Spitfire IXE (Oct 1944—Aug 1945)
MA451; MH529; MH773; MJ297; PL767; PT478; PT587; PT639; PT720; PV116; RR188

Commanding Officers

W/Cdr C. R. Lousada	Sep 1940—Aug 1941
W/Cdr J. L. Barker	Aug 1941—Jun 1943
W/Cdr O. D. E. Coe, DFC	Jun 1943—Jan 1944
S/Ldr E. H. C. Kee	Jan 1944—Apr 1944
S/Ldr M. H. Le Bas	Apr 1944—Nov 1944
S/Ldr A. J. Radcliffe, DFC	Nov 1944—Jun 1945
S/Ldr W. R. Turkington, DSO, DFC and Bar	Jun 1945—Jul 1945

Aircraft Insignia

The code letter combination 'RZ' was used from September, 1940 until going to North Africa and again in Italy 1944–45. It is unlikely it was used in between, probably being replaced by a single-letter code but this is not known.

No. 242 SQUADRON

BADGE
A moose's head erased

MOTTO
'*Toujours pret*'
('Always ready')

At the time the badge was awarded the officers serving with the Squadron were Canadian.

The Squadron was formed in August, 1918 from the RNAS Seaplane Flight at Newhaven and flew anti-submarine patrols there until the Armistice. It was disbanded on 15 May, 1919.

No. 242 re-formed at Church Fenton on 30 October, 1939 as a fighter squadron, originally with Canadian personnel and served in France in May/June 1940 and then in the Battle of Britain and with Fighter Command in 1941. At the end of that year it moved to the

Far East where it arrived for the final collapse in the Dutch East Indies and was re-formed in Fighter Command in April, 1942. At the end of 1942 it went to North Africa and fought through the Tunisian, Sicilian and Italian campaigns where it was disbanded, at Gregnano on 4 November, 1944.

No. 242 re-formed once more in the UK at Stoney Cross on 15 November, 1944 in the transport role equipped with Vickers Wellington XVIs. These were used for training purposes only and it converted to Short Stirling Vs with which it began freight operations to the Middle East that month; two aircraft were written off in March due to swinging on take-off otherwise operations proceeded without hitch. The route was continued to the Far East in April and the first Yorks arrived on the Squadron in the same month. By June it was flying over a thousand hours a month, passengers being carried in the Yorks as well as freight. However in July the Squadron had two setbacks; first all the Yorks and York crews were removed, then Stirling IVs arrived in place of the Vs; these had to be modified before use. However, in December it moved to Merryfield where it was completely equipped with Yorks. These it took to Oakington in May, 1946 and began scheduled route flying to India and the Azores. This continued as routine until 1948 when the Transport Command squadrons were called into the Berlin Airlift. The Yorks were sent forward in July, 1948 to Wunstorf from which they operated into Berlin. The Squadron flew 7,193 hours on the airlift in twelve months. On its return No. 242 re-equipped with Hastings and returned to the Far East route but this was short-lived for on 1 May, 1950 the Squadron was disbanded at Lyneham.

Bases etc.

Re-formed at Stoney Cross on 15 November, 1944.

Stoney Cross	Nov 1944—Dec 1945	
Merryfield	Dec 1945—May 1946	
Oakington, det. Wunstorf	May 1946—Jun 1949	
Lyneham	Jun 1949—May 1950	

Disbanded at Lyneham on 1 May, 1950.

Main Equipment

Short 184 (Aug 1918—May 1919)
8348; N1244; N1246; N2827
Vickers Wellington XVI (Nov 1944—Feb 1945)
Short Stirling IV (Jul 1945— 1945)
LJ669; LJ876; LK118; LK134; LK148; LK152; LK555
Short Stirling V (Feb 1945—Jan 1946)
PJ898, KY:V; PJ889, KY:W; PJ937, KY:T; PJ951, KY:O;
PJ991, KY:F; PK135, KY:N; PK157, KY:M
Avro York C.1 (Apr 1945—Jul 1945 & Dec 1945— 1949)
MW138, KY:V; MW179, KY:D; MW193, KY:AW, later KY:Z;
MW224, KY:Q; MW235, KY:J; MW241, KY:S; MW267, KY:W;
MW270, KY:R; MW286, KY:C; MW301, KY:B; MW321, KY:I;
MW330, KY:M
Handley Page Hastings C.1 (Jun 1949—May 1950)
TG526, H, later N; TG537, A; TG552, C; TG574, J; TG583, B;
TG604, W; TG613, K

Commanding Officers

S/Ldr M. C. B. Boddington	Nov 1944—Jan 1945	
W/Cdr H. Burton, DSO	Jan 1945—Feb 1945	
W/Cdr D. W. Balden	Feb 1945—Dec 1945	
W/Cdr D. M. Walbourn, DSO	Dec 1945—Aug 1946	
W/Cdr E. J. Wicht, DSO, DFC	Aug 1946—Jun 1947	
W/Cdr C. G. S. Rowan-Robinson, DSO, DFC	Jun 1947—Dec 1947	
W/Cdr B. D. Sellick, DSO, DFC	Dec 1947—Jan 1948	
S/Ldr E. W. Tarrant, DFC	Jan 1948—Feb 1949	
S/Ldr N. M. Maynard, DFC, AFC	Feb 1949—Apr 1950	
S/Ldr J. C. N. Cole	Apr 1950—May 1950	

Aircraft Insignia

The code letter combination 'KY' was carried on the Stirlings and the Yorks, otherwise no insignia was used.
(See also *Fighter Squadrons of the RAF*, pp. 342–4)

No. 243 SQUADRON

BADGE
A seahorse holding a sword erect
MOTTO
'Swift in pursuit'

No. 243 Squadron originally formed at Cherbourg in August, 1918 and flew anti-submarine patrols along the French coast with seaplanes, remaining there until 1 March, 1919 when it disbanded.

No. 243 re-formed in Singapore as a fighter squadron on 12 March, 1941 and was dispersed in March, 1942 after the fall of Singapore. It re-formed at Ouston on 1 June, 1942, again as a fighter squadron, and took part in the Tunisian campaign then on to Sicily, Italy and the Southern France landings, disbanding at Gragnano on 31 October, 1944.

The Squadron re-formed in a transport role at Morecambe on 15 December 1944 and its personnel immediately went overseas to Canada where it established at Dorval on 27 December and started ferry training on Dakotas. On 9 January, 1945 it began routeing itself to Australia and assembled at Camden by 9 February, from where it began surveying routes across Australia, to New Guinea and the Phillipines. Scheduled services began on 26 February; on 20 March KN343 ditched in the Coral Sea and crew and passengers were picked up the next day. Schedules to the Philippines began the same day. The Squadron grew in size so that by April it had forty-seven Dakotas on strength, some of which were fitted out for VIP flights. The Squadron's primary role became supporting the British Pacific Fleet until September then it switched to extended schedules such as the Mascot–Leyte–Hong Kong one. At the beginning of 1946 there began a gradual run-down as the Service traffic became less and national airlines sprang up and on 15 April, 1946 the Squadron was disbanded at Camden.

Bases etc.

Formed in August, 1918 from the RNAS Seaplane Flight at Cherbourg.

Cherbourg	Aug 1918—Mar 1919	

Disbanded at Cherbourg on 15 March, 1919. Re-formed in the transport role at Morecambe on 15 December, 1944.

en route to Canada	Dec 1944—Dec 1944	
Dorval	Dec 1944—Jan 1945	
en route to Australia	Jan 1945—Feb 1945	
Camden	Feb 1945—Apr 1946	

Disbanded at Camden on 15 April, 1946.

Main Equipment

Short 184 (Aug 1918—Mar 1919)
N1793; N1795; N2805; N2823; N2900; N2964; N9017; N9170
Wight Converted Seaplane (Aug 1918—Mar 1919)
9858; 9854
Douglas Dakota IV (Dec 1944—Apr 1946)
KJ995, AG; KK129, AC; KK147, AE; KK199, AJ; KN240, AY;
KN338, BC; KN347, AZ; KN364, BE; KN372, CL; KN528, BB

Aircraft Insignia

It is not believed that any markings were carried in World War I. The Dakotas carried their call signs on the fins, either the 'last two' as quoted above, or the complete call-sign, eg KN353 was VM-YBH.
(See also *Fighter Squadrons of the RAF*, pp. 344–6)

No. 244 SQUADRON

(No badge authorised)

No. 244 Squadron formed in August, 1918 as a coastal patrol squadron at Bangor in North Wales equipped with D.H.6s. It never became operational and was disbanded there on 22 January, 1919.

No. 244 re-formed on 1 November, 1940 by re-numbering S Squadron at Shaibah. This unit had been formed in August, 1939 with Vickers Vincents for patrol and communications duties. It flew PR and mail flights around the Gulf with detachments in Iraq at Habbaniya and Mosul. In January, 1941 it began working up in the bomber role and received Blenheims the following month. With the hostilities in Iraq it established its detachments at Bahrein and Sharjah and escorted the troop convoys bringing in troop reinforcements and then on 2 May began bombing operations with Vincents on the railways used by the enemy. One aircraft crashed on the first raid but its crew was picked up by the other. Ten sorties a day were being flown in the Vincents with leaflet dropping on the raids as well. Operations that month totalled 87 sorties, many being the transport of key personnel into beleaguered Habbaniya. In June it was back to training but in July operations were carried out in the brief fighting with Iran, 244 flying Tac/R sorties, twenty-two in all, losing one aircraft shot down in error by a Hurricane.

1942 found the Squadron flying anti-submarine patrols in the Gulf of Oman and also receiving Valentias on its strength. At last the Blenheims came more fully into service and were used for A/S patrols. On 25 October Sgt Chapple, in Blenheim V BA437, found a U-boat on the surface whilst on convoy escort and dropped two depth charges and two A/S bombs on it. The last Vincent operation was on 28 November.

By 1943 it was fully a maritime squadron flying convoy escorts and A/S patrols. It was hampered in June by the temporary grounding of the Blenheims and by August was using Hudsons, Wellesleys, Valentias and Vincents to supplement them. This, however was only a temporary expedient, the Blenheims taking over again.

At the beginning of 1944 the aircraft situation was bad but in February Wellington XIIIs arrived to replace the Blenheims and these began to take over in March. The Squadron built up on Wellingtons and maintained convoy escorts and A/S patrols until the war's end without sighting any further enemy shipping. No. 244 was disbanded at Masirah on 1 May, 1945.

Bases etc.

Formed at Bangor in August, 1918.

Bangor	Aug 1918—Jan 1919

Disbanded at Bangor on 22 January, 1919. Re-formed from 'S' Squadron at Shaibah on 1 November, 1940.

Shaibah, det. Bahrein, Sharjah, Dair-az-Azor, Habbaniya	Nov 1940— 1943
Sharjah, det. Masirah	1943—Feb 1944
Masirah, det. Khormaksar, Mogadishu, Santa Cruz	Feb 1944—May 1945

Disbanded at Masirah on 1 May, 1945.

Main Equipment

Airco D.H.6 (Aug 1918—Jan 1919)
No serial numbers known
Vickers Vincent (Nov 1940—Nov 1942)
K4121; K4702; K4733; K4738; K4741; K6337; K6350; K6359; K6363, V; K6366
Bristol Blenheim I (Feb 1941—Feb 1941)
L6656
Vickers Valentia I (Jan 1942—Aug 1943)
JR8063; K3599
Bristol Blenheim IV (Apr 1942—Jan 1943)
P6931; R3705, G; Z7418; Z7580; Z7629, L; Z9724; Z9735; Z9815
Bristol Blenheim V (Oct 1942—Mar 1944)
BA163, C; BA390, A, later L; BA430, X; BA481, F; BA540, P; BA677, H; BA862, M; BA938, R; EH337, K; EH348, N; EH404, O
Vickers Wellington XIII (Feb 1944—May 1945)
HZ658, W; HZ712, F; HZ897, C; HZ951, K; HZ979, M; JA149, W; JA182, B; JA267, N; JA406, G; JA482, B

Commanding Officers

S/Ldr H. V. Alloway	Nov 1940—Jan 1942	
S/Ldr F. L. Newall	Jan 1942—Apr 1942	
W/Cdr J. E. C. G. F. Gyll-Murray	Apr 1942— 1943	
W/Cdr R. C. Rotherham, DFC	1943—Jun 1944	
W/Cdr W. H. Hankin, DFC	Jun 1944—Mar 1945	
S/Ldr G. Burton	Mar 1945—May 1945	

Aircraft Insignia

As far as is known No. 244 never carried any squadron markings.

No. 245 SQUADRON

BADGE
In front of a fountain, an eagle volant

MOTTO
'Fugo, non fugio'
('I put to flight, I do not flee')

The eagle symbolises readiness to attack and the fountain the sea over which the Squadron flew many patrols.

The Squadron was formed in August, 1918 at Fishguard for anti-submarine patrols off the Welsh coast with seaplanes. This was continued until the Armistice after which the Squadron remained there until disbanding on 10 May, 1919.

No. 245 re-formed at Leconfield on 30 October, 1939 as a fighter squadron and fought with Fighter Command and 2nd TAF in this role throughout the war, disbanding at Schleswig on 10 August, 1945. It was re-formed the same day from No. 504 Squadron at Colerne, remaining a jet fighter squadron until July, 1957 when it disbanded again at Stradishall. On 21 August, 1958 it re-formed once more by re-numbering No. 527 Squadron at Tangmere. It now flew non-operationally as a radar calibration and signals squadron being once more re-numbered to 98 Squadron there on 18 April, 1963. (See Appendix)

Bases etc.

Formed at Fishguard in August, 1918.

Fishguard	Aug 1918—May 1919

Disbanded at Fishguard on 10 May, 1919.

Main Equipment

Short 184 (Aug 1918—May 1919)
N2657; N2659; N2843; N2940; N9015; N9032; N9033
Hamble Baby (Aug 1918—May 1919)
N1063; N1199

Commanding Officers

Not known.

Aircraft Insignia

It is unlikely that any squadron insignia was carried.
(See also *Fighter Squadrons of the RAF*, pp. 346–9).

No. 246 SQUADRON

(No badge authorised)

In August, 1918 the RNAS base at Seaton Carew was formed into two RAF squadrons Nos. 246 and 274. It is believed that No. 274 flew the seaplanes and No. 246 the landplanes. For this purpose No. 246 Squadron flew Blackburn Kangaroo twin-engined biplanes and used them on North Sea anti-submarine patrols. They first came into service in May, 1918 and between then and the Armistice flew 600 hours, attacking eleven U-boats of which one was sunk and four damaged. It also operated F.E.2b's on the same task of convoy escort and anti-submarine patrols. After the Armistice the Squadron remained at Seaton Carew until disbanding in May, 1919.

The Squadron re-formed at Bowmore on 1 September, 1942 as a general reconnaissance flying-boat unit equipped with Sunderlands. It began operations on 12 October with a convoy escort and maintained about fifteen operational sorties a month but for policy reasons was disbanded on 30 April, 1943.

No. 246 re-formed at Lyneham on 11 October, 1944 from the Liberator Flight of No. 511 Squadron. These it used on the UK/India schedule for which it took responsibility but at first it had to rely on many No. 511 Squadron crews. At the end of the year it formed a Halifax Development Flight to explore ways of using this as a transport, using them on a Cairo West route. It was also flying an Australian schedule and 'Specials' including one to Moscow in January, 1945 (via Italy and Greece), with ACM Tedder. By March, 1945 it had expanded its route mileage to include Iceland, the Azores and Ceylon with three Flights: A with Liberators, B with Yorks and C with Halifaxes. The following month it also acquired two Skymasters, which became part of its VVIP Flight, based at Northolt. It now had eight weekly schedules to fly and to do so the Halifaxes were relinquished in favour of further Yorks.

The end of the war initially increased the Squadron's commitment with so many troop movements to be made; a new route to Malta, Egypt, the Gulf and Burma was inaugurated purely for trooping, in November. By the end of 1945 No. 246 was primarily a York squadron. As the months went by one by one of the Squadron's services were reduced in frequency or cancelled and on 15 October, 1946 the Squadron was disbanded by merging into No. 511 Squadron.

Bases etc.

Formed at Seaton Carew in August, 1918.
Seaton Carew	Aug 1918—May 1919

Disbanded at Seaton Carew in May, 1919. Re-formed at Bowmore on 1 September, 1942.
Bowmore	Sep 1942—Apr 1943

Disbanded at Bowmore on 1 April, 1943. Re-formed at Lyneham from the Liberator Flight of 511 Squadron on 11 October, 1944.
Lyneham	Oct 1944—Dec 1944
Holmesley South, det. Northolt	Dec 1944—Oct 1946

Disbanded at Holmesley South 15 October, 1946; merged into 511 Squadron.

Main Equipment

F.E.2b (Aug 1918—May 1919)
  A5542; A6535
Sopwith Baby (Aug 1918—   1918)
  N2067; N2109; N2111
Blackburn Kangaroo (Aug 1918—May 1919)
  B9972; B9976; B9983
Short Sunderland II, III (Sep 1942—Apr 1943)
  W6050, A; W6057, B; W6060, D; W6066, F; DV978, E; DV980, G;
  EJ137, K; EJ139, L
Consolidated Liberator VII (Oct 1944—Sep 1945)
  EW612; EW617; EW622; EW626; EW631; EW633
Handley Page Halifax III (Dec 1944—Apr 1945)
  LW547; LW548; NA679; NA683
Avro York C.1 (Dec 1944—Oct 1946)
  MW108, VU:N; MW148, VU:O; MW165, VU:P; MW178, VU:C;
  MW192, VU:Y; MW208, VU:U; MW229, VU:B; MW231, VU:L;
  MW269, VU:V
Consolidated Liberator III (Feb 1945—Dec 1945)
  FL909; FL915; FL917; FL918; FL920
Consolidated Liberator VI (Apr 1945—Nov 1945)
  KH117; KH169; KH213
Douglas C-54A (Mar 1945—Nov 1945)
  KL977; KL978; KL982

Commanding Officers

W/Cdr L. M. Laws	Sep 1942—Apr 1943
S/Ldr P. H. L. Barclay	Oct 1944—Oct 1944
W/Cdr P. A. Lombard, DFC	Oct 1944—Sep 1945
W/Cdr S. P. Daniels, DSO, DFC	Sep 1945—Nov 1945
W/Cdr E. J. Wicht, DSO, DFC	Nov 1945—Jan 1946
W/Cdr S. P. Daniels, DSO, DFC	Jan 1946—May 1946
W/Cdr S. G. Baggott, DFC	May 1946—May 1946
W/Cdr J. J. K. Fleetwood, DSO	May 1946—Oct 1946

Aircraft Insignia

No distinguishing unit insignia was carried in World War I. The Sunderlands were identified by the number '2' during their brief service. In Transport Command service the Yorks carried the code letter combination 'VU' but it is not known whether this was applied to the other types.

No. 247 SQUADRON

BADGE
In front of a bezant, a demilion erased and crowned holding in the paws a scroll inscribed in Chinese characters 'Chu Feng'

MOTTO
'Rise from the East'

In World War II the Squadron was the China-British gift Squadron. It also served a long time in Devon and Cornwall. China is represented by the characters on the scroll and in the motto, Devon by the demi-lion and Cornwall by the sun.

No. 247 Squadron was formed in August, 1918 from one of the Flights at the RNAS Base at Felixstowe and flew anti-submarine patrols over the North Sea for three months until the war ended in November, 1918. It remained there until 22 January, 1919 when it was disbanded.

No. 247 re-formed at Roborough on 1 August, 1940 as a fighter squadron and fought in the Battle of Britain, going over to night fighting and intruding in 1941.

In 1942 it became a fighter-ground attack squadron with Typhoons, joining 2nd TAF later and going to the Continent. In August, 1945 it returned to the UK and in March, 1946 became the first RAF squadron with DH Vampire jet fighters. It remained as part of the UK defence until 31 December, 1957 when it disbanded at Odiham.

Bases etc.

Formed at Felixstowe in August, 1918.
Felixstowe	Aug 1918—Jan 1919

Disbanded at Felixstowe on 22 January, 1919.

Main Equipment

Felixstowe F.2A (Aug 1918—Jan 1919)
  No serial numbers known
Felixstowe F.3 (Aug 1918—Jan 1919)
  No serial numbers known

Commanding Officers

No record

Aircraft Insignia

The flying-boats carried no squadron markings.
(See also *Fighter Squadrons of the RAF*, pp. 350–2).

No. 248 SQUADRON

BADGE
A demi-sword in bend partly withdrawn from
the scabbard

MOTTO
'Il faut finir'
('It is necessary to make an end of it')

No. 248 Squadron was formed from the Seaplane Flight at Hornsea Mere in August, 1918, this Flight having been operative since September, 1917. It flew anti-submarine patrols from Blyth to Grimsby with Hamble Babys and Short 184s. It eventually disbanded on the 6 March, 1919 with a record of six U-boat's sighted, four attacked and one destroyed and one Zeppelin attacked.

No. 248 re-formed at Hendon on 30 October, 1939 as a twin-engined fighter squadron with Blenheims but before coming operational transferred to Coastal Command in February, 1940. First operations were flown at Dyce in June on fighter defence work then it moved to the Shetlands and began photo and recce patrols in the Trondheim area. On 3 August P/O Gane found a U-boat and attacked it but most of the work was recce, until September when shipping attacks were flown, two ships being bombed in the month. 105 sorties were flown in October for the loss of one crew, and this pattern was maintained until returning to the mainland in January, 1941. Recce patrols and convoy protection were the main tasks; several combats took place with enemy aircraft but it was not until May that the first confirmed victory, a Ju 88, was made. The following month No. 248 changed its operational area to the Dutch coast, flying sweeps, escorts and the occasional ASR.

In July, 1941 the Squadron began to re-equip with Beaufighters which at first it used on mine searches and convoy patrols until August when, on 22nd, its first Beaufighter shipping strike took place on armed trawlers and R-boats. At the end of October No. 248 moved to Cornwall where it flew Operation Milktrain, long-range interception patrols off the Scillies which produced the odd He 111 now and then. In addition met sorties were flown and a shipping attack on 27 December, during which two out of three Heinkels were shot down. After an attempted *Rover* to the *Scharnhorst* on 13 February, 1942 the Squadron moved to Scotland once more, flying *Stand* patrols off the Norwegian coast and escorting Beaufort shipping strikes. Added to these were convoy protection patrols and this pattern remained until July, during which several He 111s, He 115s and a BV 138 had been destroyed. In July the Squadron flew out to Malta where they provided air escort to Force Y, to Malta supply convoys and shot up Sardinian airfields.

On 21 August the Squadron gave fighter escort for Beauforts and Beaufighters attacking an enemy convoy off Corfu in which five enemy aircraft fell to 248's guns. Three days later the Squadron set off for UK once more.

In September it settled into the long-range fighter patrols over the Western Approaches once more. On these it acquired a steady score of Ju 88s destroyed or damaged and the occasional Beau lost; especially notable was a combat on 9 February, 1943 when three Beaufighters attacked four Ju 88s and shot down all of them. As the summer wore on the sortie rate went up to 120 per month until June when the Squadron came off operations to convert to Mk. X Beaufighters. Before the month was out it was back on operations once more and six aircraft went to Gibraltar for 'Folio' and 'Foolscap' operations. On 9 July two aircraft, escorting a Hudson out of Gibraltar found four FW 200s destroying one and damaging another; three days later a U-boat was attacked and set on fire. By September the home-based aircraft were flying anti-shipping sorties under Fighter Direction. By the end of the year No. 248 had received some Mosquitoes for conversion.

The last Beaufighter operations were flown in January, 1944; a month later No. 248 began operational patrols with Mosquitoes. The first shipping attack came on 10 March, an escort job to Mosquito XVIIIs attacking a convoy. The Mosquito XVIIIs were known as No. 248 Special Detachment, being ex-No. 618 Squad-

ron. The pattern would be for the XVIIIs to attack U-boats or shipping with their 57 mm guns whilst the FB.VIs attacked enemy air cover. The pace built up, soon a sortie rate of over 100 per month was being maintained whilst in June, 1944, due to the invasion, 274 sorties were flown, anti-shipping, anti-submarine and anti-Flak sorties. One U-boat was destroyed and one damaged and several aircraft shot down during this busy period. The attacks continued, in September five crews were lost in convoy attacks in the Gironde area before the Squadron moved north to join the Banff Wing. Here it flew *Rovers* over the Norwegian coast, concentrating on anti-submarine activities. This continued until the Mk. XVIIIs flew their last operation on 15 January, 1945, after which the Squadron concentrated on anti-shipping patrols with Mk. VIs all along the Norwegian coast. However, on 9 April the Squadron found two surfaced U-boats and, with RPs, damaged one and blew the other up. Ten days later another was sunk and another on 2 May. After VE-Day ASR patrols were flown in the Skaggerak.

In July it moved to Chivenor and began flying Operation Deadlight (strikes on captured U-boats for experimental purposes). The Squadron remained as one of the few Coastal strike squadrons until 1 October, 1946 when it was re-numbered 36 Squadron at Thorney Island.

Bases etc.

Formed at Hornsea Mere from the Coastal Flight there, August, 1918.

Hornsea Mere	Aug 1918—Mar 1919	

Disbanded at Hornsea Mere on 6 March, 1919. Re-formed at Hendon on 30 October, 1939.

Hendon	Oct 1939—Feb 1940	
North Coates	Feb 1940—Apr 1940	
Thorney Island	Apr 1940—May 1940	
Dyce, det. Montrose	May 1940—Jul 1940	
Sumburgh	Jul 1940—Jan 1941	
Dyce	Jan 1941—Jun 1941	
Bircham Newton, det. Portreath, Carew Cheriton, St. Eval	Jun 1941—Mar 1942	
Dyce, det. Sumburgh	Mar 1942—May 1942	
Sumburgh, det. Wattisham	May 1942—Jul 1942	
Gosport	Jul 1942—Jul 1942	
Ta Kali	Jul 1942—Aug 1942	
Dyce	Aug 1942—Sep 1942	
Talbenny, det. Chivenor	Sep 1942—Nov 1942	
Pembrey	Nov 1942—Dec 1942	
Talbenny	Dec 1942—Jan 1943	
Predannack, det. Gibraltar	Jan 1943—Feb 1944	
Portreath	Feb 1944—Sep 1944	
Banff	Sep 1944—Jul 1945	
Chivenor, det. Ballykelly	Jul 1945—May 1946	
Thorney Island	May 1946—Sep 1946	

Disbanded by re-numbering as No. 36 Squadron at Thorney Island on 1 October, 1946.

Main Equipment

Short 184 (Aug 1918—Mar 1919)
N1226; N1235; N2922; N2997; N9088
Hamble Baby (Aug 1918—Mar 1919)
N2099
Bristol Blenheim IF (Dec 1939—   1940)
L1212; L1226; L1336, WR:E
Bristol Blenheim IVF (Feb 1940—Jul 1941)
L9394, WR:O; L9450, WR:H; N6229, WR:L; N6233; P4831, WR:F; P6952; R3625, WR:A; T1870, WR:V; T2000, WR:Z; T2131, WR:P; V5429, WR:G; V5737, WR:H; Z5904, WR:X; Z5955, WR:B; Z6021, WR:F; Z6033, WR:M; Z6174, WR:L
Bristol Beaufighter IC (Jul 1941—Jul 1942)
T3326, WR:C; T3333, WR:R; T3351, WR:U; T4651, WR:F; T4670, WR:Y; T4721, WR:Q; T4752, WR:P; T4774, WR:M; T4843, WR:X
Bristol Beaufighter VIC (Jun 1942—Jun 1943)
T5100, WR:W; T5109, WR:P; T5149, WR:V; T5271, WR:Z; X7938, WR:F; X8089, WR:H; X8091, WR:A; EL264, WR:D; EL304, WR:C; EL362, WR:X
Bristol Beaufighter X (Jun 1943—Jan 1944)
LX806; LX818; JM334, B; JM335, L; JM342, H; JM397
de Havilland Mosquito VI (Dec 1943—Sep 1946)
HJ828, DM:R; HP866, DM:D; HP922, DM:U; HP988, DM:R; HR120, DM:G; HR261, DM:N; LR330, DM:J; LR378, DM:C;

LR413, DM:G; MM399, DM:S; MM431, DM:Z; RF387, DM:T;
RF615, DM:S; RF877, DM:C; RS610, DM:Y
de Havilland Mosquito XVIII (Mar 1944—Jan 1945)
HX903, DM:I; HX904, DM:E; MM424, DM:H; MM425, DM:L;
NT224, DM:E1; NT225, DM:O

Commanding Officers

F/Lt P. D. Robertson	Aug	1918—Mar	1919
S/Ldr J. H. Hutchinson	Oct	1939—Mar	1940
S/Ldr V. C. F. Streatfield	Mar	1940—Jan	1941
S/Ldr J. J. E. Coates	Jan	1941—Feb	1941
S/Ldr L. B. B. King	Mar	1941—Apr	1941
W/Cdr S. G. Wise, DFC	Apr	1941—Apr	1942
W/Cdr E. L. Hyde, DFC	Apr	1942—Apr	1942
W/Cdr J. M. N. Pike, DSO, DFC	May	1942—Oct	1942

W/Cdr A. Montagu-Smith	Oct	1942—Jul	1943
W/Cdr F. E. Burton, DFC	Jul	1943—Feb	1944
W/Cdr O. J. M. Barron, DFC	Feb	1944—Apr	1944
W/Cdr A. D. Phillips, DSO, DFC	Apr	1944—Jul	1944
W/Cdr G. D. Sise, DSO, DFC	Jul	1944—Mar	1945
W/Cdr R. K. Orrock, DFC	Mar	1945—Mar	1945
W/Cdr H. N. Jackson-Smith, DFC	Mar	1945—Oct	1945
W/Cdr J. V. Hoggarth	Oct	1945—Sep	1946

Aircraft Markings

From October, 1939 until the Squadron moved to Malta in July, 1942 the
aircraft used the code letter combination 'WR'. It is probably that from then
until the summer of 1944 no specific markings were carried, after which the
letters 'DM' were used until disbandment.

No. 249 SQUADRON

BADGE
In front of a bezant an elephant passant
MOTTO
'Pugnis et calcibus'
('With fists and heels')

Both the bezant and the elephant imply
associations with the Gold Coast, of which the
Squadron was one of the World War II gift
Squadrons.

No. 249 Squadron came into being on 18 August, 1918 at Dundee,
being formed from the flying-boat Flight there. It operated various
types of coastal patrols and anti-submarine patrols out over the
North Sea until the Armistice in November, 1918 and remained in
existence for another year, not disbanding until 8 October, 1919.

No. 249 re-formed on 16 May, 1940 as a fighter squadron with
Hurricanes and fought in the Battle of Britain. The following year it
moved to Malta where it fought in the defence of that island and
subsequently, with Spitfires, took part in the Sicilian and Italian
campaigns, also using Mustangs. It disbanded there on 16 August,
1945. No. 500 Squadron re-numbered 249 in Kenya on 23 October,
1945; now it was a light bomber squadron with Baltimores and then
Mosquitoes, moving to Iraq. Here it again became a fighter squad-

ron with Tempest F.6s, Vampires and then Venoms until 1956
when, in Cyprus, it converted to Canberras as a bomber squadron
once more and served there until disbanding at Akrotiri on February, 1969.

Bases etc.

Formed at Dundee on 18 August, 1918.
Dundee   Aug 1918—Oct 1919
Disbanded at Dundee on 6 October, 1919. Re-formed on 16 May, 1940 in
the fighter role.

Main Equipment

Short 184 (Aug 1918—Oct 1919)
N1276; N1661; N1831
Felixstowe F.2A (Aug 1918—Oct 1919)
N4287; N4290; N4291
Felixstowe F.3 (Aug 1918—Oct 1919)
No serials known
Felixstowe F.5 (1918—Oct 1919)
No serials known
Curtiss H.12B (Aug 1918—   1919)
N4336; N4345; N4350; N4352

Aircraft Insignia

As far as is known, no unit markings were carried in World War I.
(See also *Bomber Squadrons of the RAF*, p. 222 & *Fighter Squadrons of the
RAF*, pp. 353–4)

No. 250 SQUADRON

BADGE
A river eagle standing on a rock
MOTTO
'Close to the sun'

The river eagle is indigenous to the Sudan and
the Squadron was the Sudan gift squadron in
World War II.

The Squadron was first formed at Padstow in August, 1918 out of
the coastal Flight there. It used D.H.6s and D.H.9s for coastal
patrolling over the Bristol Channel and the Cornish and Devon
coasts, surviving until 15 May, 1919 when it was disbanded.

On 1 April, 1941 No. 250 re-formed at Aqir in Palestine as a
fighter squadron and fought in the Western Desert, Sicily and Italy
with Tomahawks, Kittyhawks and Mustangs, remaining in service
until disbanding at Treviso on 2 January, 1947.

Bases etc.

Formed at Padstow in August, 1918.
Padstow   Aug 1918—May 1919
Disbanded at Padstow on 15 May, 1919. Re-formed at Aqir on 1 April, 1941
as a fighter squadron.

Main Equipment

de Havilland D.H.9 (Aug 1918—May 1919)
B7611; C1301; D2965; H4284; H4287
de Havilland D.H.6 (Aug 1918—May 1919)
No serial numbers known

Aircraft Insignia

It is not thought that any unit insignia was carried on the aircraft.
(See also *Fighter Squadrons of the RAF*, pp. 355–7)

No. 252 SQUADRON

BADGE
A spartan shield
MOTTO
'With or on'

The Squadron was formed at Tynemouth in August, 1918 and flew D.H.6s and Short 184 seaplanes on coastal patrol duties to the Armistice. It remained there until disbandment on 30 June, 1919.

It re-formed at Bircham Newton on 21 November, 1940, moving to Chivenor ten days later where it received Bristol Beaufighter ICs. Work up was slow due to unserviceability but by the end of March No. 252 was declared operational and on 6 April began convoy AA patrols, from Aldergrove. Ten days later F/Lt Riley scored first blood by shooting a FW 200 into the sea but F/O Lane was lost the same day. The next month half the Squadron was detached to Malta where, again, convoy patrols were flown but in addition airfield strafing was begun in Sicily and Greece. In June the remainder of the Squadron in Northern Ireland joined with the remnants of No. 272 Squadron to form No. 143 Squadron. At the same time the crews in Malta appear to have moved on to Egypt and attached themselves to No. 272 Squadron at Edku and whilst so began building up again as a new No. 252 Squadron in December, 1941.

It flew its first operation as a new independent No. 252 Squadron on 16 January, 1942 with an escort to convoy *Boxer*, two days later claiming a Ju 88 in the sea on similar operations. In February the Squadron sent a detachment to Luqa once more and began providing continuous cover to convoys into Malta. More victories came the Squadron's way but these were matched by losses. The task was almost entirely convoy protection although occasional escorts were flown to aircraft transiting into and out of Malta. In March the Squadron began occasional shipping strikes on enemy convoys off the North African coast and in April this was extended to attacking road transport in the desert battles. On 12 May the Squadron found Ju 52s flying between Crete and Derna, shot down six and damaged three. As the summer progressed the work swung back towards shipping operations with frequent Malta detachments for convoy protection and flying escort to Beauforts on shipping strikes. A high rate of operations was flown, for example in September 201 sorties were made. This pattern ensued for the rest of the year, enlivened in November by the arrival of Beaufighter X7704 with a 40 mm cannon; little more is heard about it so presumably it was unsuccessful.

At this time operations tailed off to a few convoy escorts and it was not until May, 1943 that offensive sweeps over the Ionian Sea were introduced and livened up the Squadron's activities. The Squadron put bombs under the Beaufighter's wings and began more strikes, mainly on shipping. These were flown out of Cyprus from where most operations now took place. The pace increased so that by October the Squadron was flying 224 sorties a month, predominantly in the Aegean area. Mostly they were unopposed by German aircraft but occasional battles took place as on 31 January, 1944 when the Squadron attacked three Ju 88s, destroying one but being themselves attacked by Messerschmitt Bf 109s and losing two Beaufighters. This became more of a problem in February when three out of four Beaus on one strike fell to 109s. That month the Squadron began using RPs on moonlight shipping strikes. This type of operation became the norm for No. 252, flying over the Aegean arifields and attacking any likely targets. In June the Squadron mounted a strike on an enemy convoy with RPs in which one ship was sunk and another, and a destroyer, damaged for the loss of the CO, W/Cdr Meharg. This type of armed recce produced more ships sunk by the end of the year, becoming the predominant operation. On 15 October six aircraft made a rocket attack on the German garrison building at Naxia resulting in the surrender of the German troops there.

Shipping recces continued unabated into the New Year, the Squadron moving to Greece in February where operations were also flown against the insurgents there. The war being almost over No. 252 was flying primarily ASR sorties in April; the Squadron's last operations were rocket strikes aginst the coastal defence gun positions on Melos on 4 and 5 May, 1945. After the war in Europe ended the Squadron maintained an ASR alert, otherwise it flew training sorties, and met flights. Serviceability was badly affected by demobilisation and little flying took place in 1946. No. 252 remained in limited flying practice until 1 December, 1946 when it was disbanded at Araxos.

Bases etc.

Formed at Tynemouth in August, 1918.

Tynemouth	Aug 1918—Jun 1919

Disbanded at Tynemouth on 30 June, 1919. Re-formed at Bircham Newton on 21 November, 1940

Bircham Newton	Nov 1940—Dec 1940
Chivenor	Dec 1940—Apr 1941
Aldergrove, det. St. Eval thence Luqa	Apr 1941—Jun 1941
Nutt's Corner, det. Luqa	Jun 1941—Jun 1941

UK element disbanded into 143 Squadron 15 June, 1941. Malta crews moved to join 272 Squadron in Egypt, becoming separate unit again in January, 1942.

Edku, det. Luqa, Gambut, Paphos, St. Jean	Nov 1941—Jan 1943
Berka No. 3	Jan 1943—Feb 1943
Magrun, det. Bersis	Feb 1943—Aug 1943
Berka No. 3, det. Limassol, Lakatamia	Aug 1943—Dec 1943
LG.91	Dec 1943—Jan 1944
Mersa Matruh West	Jan 1944—May 1944
Mersa Matruh	May 1944—Jul 1944
Gambut	Jul 1944—Dec 1944
Mersa Matruh	Dec 1944—Feb 1945
Hassani	Feb 1945—Aug 1945
Araxos	Aug 1945—Dec 1946

Disbanded at Araxos on 1 December, 1946

Main Equipment

Short 184 (Aug 1918—Jun 1919)
  No serial numbers known
D.H.6 (Aug 1918—   1919)
  B3082; B3090; C2079
Bristol Blenheim IF (Dec 1940—Jan 1941)
  K7087; L1279; L6792
Bristol Blenheim IVF (Dec 1940—   1941)
  V5721; V5738; V5816; Z6245
Bristol Beaufighter IF (Dec 1941—Aug 1943)
  R2153, PN:W; R2198, PN:B; R2269, PN:C; T3231, PN:N;
  T3234, PN:P; T3242, PN:T; T4834, BT:C; T4840, BT:P;
  T4877, BT:R; T4893, A; T5028, H; T5045, G; T5110, C; T5137, F;
  V8321, J; V8347, A; X7713, X; X7819, N
Bristol Beaufighter VIC (Sep 1942—Apr 1944)
  X8103, K; X8144, E; X8158; EL270, R; EL309, Y; EL369, A;
  EL391, V; EL406, G; EL475, B; EL508, T; EL575, Z; JL512, E;
  JL523, F; JL765, J; JL896; JL911
Bristol Beaufighter X (Jan 1944—Dec 1946)
  LZ341, G; LZ377, S; LZ456, D; LZ492, Q; NE247, X; NE293, M;
  NE391, N; NE472, D; NE499, P; NE554, Q; NT895, H; NT993, V;
  NV207, I; NV239, S; NV373, A; NV485, N; NV590, G

Commanding Officers

S/Ldr R. G. Yaxley, MC	Dec 1940—Dec 1941
S/Ldr A. G. Wincott	Dec 1941—Sep 1942
W/Cdr P. H. Bragg	Sep 1942—Dec 1942
W/Cdr P. B. B. Ogilvie, DSO, DFC	Dec 1942—May 1943
W/Cdr D. O. Butler	May 1943—Dec 1943
W/Cdr P. H. Woodruff, DFC	Dec 1943—Mar 1944
W/Cdr B. G. Meharg, AFC	Mar 1944—Jun 1944
W/Cdr D. O. Butler	Jun 1944—Mar 1945
S/Ldr A. S. Hunter	Mar 1945—Apr 1945
S/Ldr C. M. Price-Owen	Apr 1945—Nov 1945
W/Cdr K. Gray	Nov 1945—Apr 1946
W/Cdr D. G. Hayward	Apr 1946—Dec 1946

Aircraft Insignia

The Squadron originally carried 'PN' on its aircraft during its brief stay in the UK. After re-forming in Egypt the code was changed to 'BT' but this was soon dropped and from late 1942 onwards no further squadron insignia was carried.

No. 253 SQUADRON

BADGE
The back of a dexter arm embowed fessewise in mogul armour, the head holding an Indian battle axe in bend

MOTTO
'Come one, come all'

The badge was suggested by the Nizam of Hyderabad, the Squadron being the gift squadron of Hyderabad in World War II.

In World War I No. 253 Squadron was formed at Bembridge in August, 1918 for coastal reconnaissance and U-boat spotting tasks. It flew seaplanes from there with a flight of D.H.6s detached at Foreland and continued on these duties until the Armistice after which it remained in existence until 5 May, 1919.

It re-formed at Manston as a fighter squadron on 30 October, 1939, flying Hurricanes over the Dunkirk beaches and fighting in the Battle of Britain. In 1942 it moved to North Africa taking part in that campaign and in Sicily and Italy, latterly with Spitfires, and disbanding in Austria in May, 1947. It re-formed once more as a night-fighter squadron at Waterbeach on 18 April, 1955 with Venoms, serving there until disbandment on 1 September, 1957.

Bases etc.

Formed at Bembridge in August, 1918.
Bembridge, det. Foreland   Aug 1918—May 1919
Disbanded at Bembridge on 5 May, 1919.

Main Equipment

Short 184 (Aug 1918—May 1919)
   N1798; N2646; N2928; N2975; N2980; N9003; N9060
Fairey Campania (1918—May 1919)
   N2385
Airco D.H.6 (Aug 1918—May 1919)
   No serial numbers known

Commanding Officers

Not known

Aircraft Insignia
No unit identity markings were carried in World War I.
(See also *Fighter Squadrons of the RAF*, pp. 357–9)

No. 254 SQUADRON

BADGE
A raven, wings endorsed and inverted

MOTTO
'Fljuga vakta ok Ijosta'
('To fly, to watch and to strike')

The Squadron first formed in World War I in August, 1918 at Prawle Point with D.H.6s and D.H.9s for coastal reconnaissance duties. It flew on this task for four months up to the end of the war and remained in being until disbandment there on 22 February, 1919.

No. 254 re-formed as a fighter squadron at Stradishall on 30 October, 1939 equipped with Bristol Blenheims but before becoming operational was transferred to Coastal Command and moved to Bircham Newton in January, 1940, beginning convoy escort duties on 29 February, 1940. Its primary task was patrolling the fishing fleet in the North Sea which was being attacked by German aircraft, first, inconclusive, combat taking place with a He 111 on 9 March. In that month No. 254 extended its range to the Norwegian coast and in April took the offensive, making a bombing attack on Stavangar airfield on 10th. It was now busily involved in escorting the naval forces involved in the Norwegian campaign, during which P/O Illingworth scored the first confirmed victory, a He 111. On 9 May No. 254 provided an escort to No. 806 Squadron of the Fleet Air Arm whose Skuas bombed Bergen successfully, two vessels being sunk. Hudsons were also escorted and the Squadron strafed Vaernes airfield. The Squadron saw this campaign out and continued in this area afterwards, attacking shipping; on 20 June three aircraft bombed a U-boat and then shot down a He 115 floatplane. However, on 6 July two Squadron aircraft were shot down by Bf 110s whilst escorting HMS *Cossack*.

In August No. 254 went on the defensive, flying anti-invasion patrols around the East Scottish coast and convoy escorts, these latter becoming the Squadron's principal task thereafter, until the New Year brought a fresh offensive on the Norwegian coast, escorting naval vessels and flying armed shipping recces, bombing a 4,000-ton motor vessel on 12 January and having a combat with He 111s and Bf 110s on 24th. Sortie rate was up to 133 per month by March and in April four crews were lost on these Norwegian patrols. The following month the operational area was moved to Northern Ireland, flying mainly convoy escorts which remained the Squadron's main task until June, 1942 when the Blenheims were replaced by Beaufighters. With Beaufighters it worked up in the torpedo attack role, a lengthy task which prevented operations before November when the first such attack was made on an enemy convoy of fifteen ships. No results were seen but one Beau was lost. The next strike was not until February, 1943 but this too was inconclusive. Shipping searches became the regular task now; losses were running at one or two crews a month so ASR sorties were also flown. The first success came on 18 April when nine aircraft damaged a large motor vessel. The area of operation was now the Dutch coast and No. 254 was flying three or four squadron strikes a month. On 2 April the whole Squadron attacked the German cruiser *Nürnberg*, three of the crews being shot down by the fighter escort. The Squadron was now flying as part of the North Coates Wing with two other Beaufighter Squadrons, 254 usually fulfilling the torpedo attack role. In August, 1943 it added *Night Rovers* to its operations which were now intense. In November another new task came No. 254s way; this type of operation was known as *Conebo*, being strikes on E-boats along the Continental coast and were usually highly successful with a proportion of boats sunk or on fire. The losses mounted also, for example when seventeen squadron aircraft attacked a convoy off Texel on 23 November only fourteen returned.

1944 saw yet another new type of shipping attack; these were *Gilbeys* in which the Squadron flew at night under the direction of ASV Wellingtons which led them to suitable targets, 415 Squadron being No. 254's Wellington guide. But most profitable anti-shipping work was the Wing Strike in daylight when the three squadrons would attack together, No. 254 concentrating on torpedo attack and usually suffering the highest losses. On 7 March a convoy was attacked off Nordeney and all the ships were left on fire. The pace increased as 1944 wore on, the Squadron concentrating on *Conebos* during the invasion period in June. A particularly successful attack was made on a convoy on 15th of that month when an 8000-ton motor vessel was sunk together with two other ships, a minesweeper was blown up and five ships left on fire. In July 171 sorties were flown on shipping strikes and armed night recces. September saw the strikes taken as far as the Norwegian coast again and also some land targets attacked such as the ground radar site at Terschelling. Enemy shipping was becoming scarcer but when convoys were found the destruction was usually effective, although one or two crews were lost on almost every strike.

A switch in February, 1945 came to anti-U-boat work, with depth-charges being carried, the midget submarines being particularly sought. These were elusive targets and although several were attacked it was not until 17 March when one was definitely damaged, and 25th when one was sunk. In April, as the war was nearly over, the Squadron received some Mosquitoes, including Mk. XVIIIs with the 57 mm (6 lb) gun. These were used in the submarine hunts, one being blown up by such a projectile. On 4 May a large ship and a destroyer were sunk by the Squadron then three U-boats were attacked on which one was damaged and one sunk. On 11 May six aircraft flew an ASR search and this was No. 254s last operation.

After the war No. 254 Squadron remained as the only torpedo Beaufighter squadron in the peacetime RAF, flying torpedo tactics development for some time until on 1 October, 1946 it was re-numbered as No. 42 Squadron at Thorney Island.

Bases etc.

Formed at Prawle Point in August, 1918.

Prawle Point	Aug 1918—Feb 1919	

Disbanded at Prawle Point on 22 February, 1919. Re-formed at Stradishall on 30 October, 1939.

Stradishall, det. Leuchars	Oct 1939—Dec 1939	
Sutton Bridge	Dec 1939—Jan 1940	
Bircham Newton, det. Lossiemouth	Jan 1940—Apr 1940	
Hatston	Apr 1940—Jun 1940	
Sumburgh	Jun 1940—Aug 1940	
Dyce	Aug 1940—Jan 1941	
Sumburgh, det. Dyce, Aldergrove	Jan 1941—May 1941	
Aldergrove, det. Carew Cheriton	May 1941—Dec 1941	
Dyce, det. Sumburgh, Wick	Dec 1941—Feb 1942	
Carew Cheriton, det. Angle	Feb 1942—May 1942	
Dyce, det. Wick, Abbotsinch	May 1942—Oct 1942	
Docking	Oct 1942—Nov 1942	
North Coates, det. Sumburgh, Skeabrae, Predannack, Wick, Tain, Thorney Island	Nov 1942—Jun 1945	
Chivenor, det. Turnberry	Jun 1945—Nov 1945	
Langham, det. Chivenor	Nov 1945—May 1946	
Thorney Island	May 1946—Oct 1946	

Disbanded 1 October, 1946 by being re-numbered No. 42 Squadron.

Main Equipment

Bristol Blenheim IF (Nov 1939—Jan 1941)
K7132; K7136; L1124; L1223; L6641; L8643
Bristol Blenheim IVF (Jan 1940—Jun 1942)
L8783, QY:K; L8842, QY:R; L9393, QY:L; L9406, QY:D; L9408, QY:F; N3528, QY:G; N3611, QY:F; R2779, QY:U; R3629, QY:P; R3888, QY:Q; T1941, QY:S; T2001, QY:N; V5735, QY:D; V5803, QY:D; V5935; Z5726, QY:N; Z5953, QY:U; Z6029, QY:L; Z6088, QY:O; Z6187
Bristol Beaufighter VIC (Jun 1942—Oct 1943)
T5106; T5162; T5185; X8087; X8099; EL225; EL291; JL756, H; JL833, O
Bristol Beaufighter XI (1943—Jan 1944)
JL828, QM:Q; JL852, QM:Z; JM211, V; JM215, QM:N
Bristol Beaufighter X (Jan 1944—Oct 1946)
JM338, QM:U; JM394, QM:X; LX806, QM:P; LZ217, QM:O; LZ267, QM:D; LZ416, QM:D; LZ436, QM:A; NE225, QM:T; NE481, QM:V; NE802, QM:K; NT921, QM:B; NV115, QM:Q; RD500, QM:N; RD578, QM:D; RD690, QM:B; RD779, QM:F; SR914, QM:Y
de Havilland Mosquito VI/XVIII (Apr 1945— 1945)
LR349, QM:Y; PZ468, QM:D

Commanding Officers

S/Ldr P. A. Hunter	Oct 1939—Jan	1940
S/Ldr G. K. Fairclough	Jan 1940—Jul	1940
S/Ldr Edwards	Jul 1940—Jul	1940
S/Ldr H. V. Hoskins	Jul 1940—Jul	1941
S/Ldr G. C. B. Bernard-Smith	Jul 1941—Dec	1941
W/Cdr R. H. McConnell, DFC	Jan 1942—Aug	1942
W/Cdr R. E. X. Mack, DFC	Aug 1942—Apr	1943
W/Cdr C. S. Cooper, DFC	Apr 1943—Sep	1943
W/Cdr A. W. D. Miller	Sep 1943—Jan	1944
W/Cdr R. E. Burns, DFC and Bar	Jan 1944—Sep	1944
W/Cdr D. L. Cartridge, DSO, DFC and Bar	Sep 1944—Mar	1946
W/Cdr Dinsdale	Mar 1946—	1946
S/Ldr P. C. Lemon, DSO, DFC	1946—Aug	1946
S/Ldr D. T. M. Lumsden	Aug 1946-Sep	1946
W/Cdr G. H. D. Evans, DSO, DFC	Sep 1946—Oct	1946

Aircraft Insignia

During the Blenheim period the aircraft carried toe code letters 'QY' on their aircraft. Having re-equipped with Beaufighters these were identified simply by a thin white band around the rear fuselage until early in 1944 when the code letters 'QM' were assumed, the white band being retained in addition at least until the end of 1945.

No. 255 SQUADRON

BADGE
A panther's face
MOTTO
'Ad auroram'
('To the break of dawn')

It formed in August, 1918 at Pembroke for coastal patrol duties over the Irish Sea for which it flew D.H.6s. In January, 1919 it was disbanded. The Squadron re-formed on 23 November, 1940 as a night-fighter unit at Kirton-in-Lindsey and served in this role until 31 March, 1946, fighting over the UK, in North Africa, Italy, the Balkans and Southern France. It was disbanded in Egypt.

Bases etc.

Formed at Pembroke in August, 1918.

Pembroke	Aug 1918—Jan 1919

Disbanded at Pembroke on 14 January, 1919.

Main Equipment

Airco D.H.6 (Aug 1918—Jan 1919)
No serial numbers known

Aircraft Insignia

As far as is known no identity markings were carried.
(See also *Fighter Squadrons of the RAF*, pp. 359–61)

No. 256 SQUADRON

BADGE
In front of an anchor, a ferret's head erased
MOTTO
'Adimus vim viribus'
('Strength to strength')

The Squadron existed from August, 1918 to June, 1919 as a coastal patrol unit at Sea Houses where it flew D.H.6s over the North Sea coast. It was disbanded there on 30 June, 1919. No. 256 re-formed on 23 November, 1940 at Catterick as a night-fighter squadron serving in the UK until 1943 when it moved to Malta, thence North Africa, Sardinia and Italy. With the war over it moved to Egypt and here it served until 12 September, 1946, with a detachment in Cyprus, using Mosquitoes for met observation work. It re-formed at Ahlhorn, Germany, on 17 November, 1952 again as a night-fighter squadron, serving there until 21 January, 1959 when it was re-numbered 11 Squadron.

Bases etc.

Formed at Sea Houses in August, 1918.
Sea Houses
Disbanded at Sea Houses on 30 June, 1919.

Aug 1918—Jun 1919

Main Equipment

Airco D.H.6 (Aug 1918—Jun 1919)
C5172; C7336

Aircraft Insignia

As far as is known no identity markings were carried.
(See also *Fighter Squadrons of the RAF*, pp. 361–3)

No. 257 SQUADRON

BADGE
A chinthe sejeant

MOTTO
'Thay myay gyee shin shwe hti'
('Death or glory')

The Squadron formed at Dundee in August, 1918 as a coastal reconnaissance seaplane Flight operating over the North Sea and the East Scottish coasts. It flew both seaplanes and flying boats and served there until 30 June, 1919. No. 257 was re-formed in World War II as a day-fighter squadron with Hurricanes, serving from 17 May, 1940 in the Battle of Britain, then on channel sweeps before converting to Typhoons and operating with 2nd TAF over the Continent towards the end of the war. It was disbanded there on 5 March, 1945 but was re-formed in Fighter Command with Meteors on 1 September, 1946 serving until 31 March, 1957 when it was again disbanded.

Bases etc.

Formed at Dundee in August, 1918.
Dundee
Disbanded at Dundee on 30 June, 1919.

Aug 1918—Jun 1919

Main Equipment

Fairey Campania (Aug 1918—Jun 1919)
N2366
Fairey Hamble Baby (Aug 1918—Jun 1919)
N1063
Felixstowe F.2A (Aug 1918—Jun 1919)
No serial numbers known

Aircraft Insignia

It is unlikely that any distinguishing markings were carried.
(See also *Fighter Squadrons of the RAF*, pp. 363–7)

No. 258 SQUADRON

BADGE
In front of wings elevated and conjoined at base, a panther's face

MOTTO
'In medias res'
('Into the middle of things')

The Squadron was formed at Luce Bay in August, 1918 with D.H.6s to fly coastal patrols over the Irish Sea. This was carried out until the Armistice in November, 1918. The Squadron remained there until disbandment on 5 March, 1919. No. 258 re-formed on 20 November, 1940 as a fighter squadron flying in the UK for a year before going to the Far East where it disbanded soon after the debacle in Sumatra. It re-formed in Ceylon on 30 March, 1942 and

fought in the Burma campaign eventually disbanding in Malaya on 31 December, 1945.

Bases etc.

Formed at Luce Bay in August, 1918.
Luce Bay
Disbanded at Luce Bay on 5 March, 1919.

Aug 1918—Mar 1919

Main Equipment

Airco D.H.6 (Aug 1918—Mar 1919)
No serial numbers known

Aircraft Insignia

It is believed that no identifying marks were carried.
(See also *Fighter Squadrons of the RAF*, pp. 367–9)

No. 259 SQUADRON

BADGE
On a terrestrial globe an eagle's head erased, facing to the sinister

MOTTO
'Haya ingia napigane'
('Get in a fight')

The original No. 259 Squadron formed at Felixstowe in August, 1918 from one of the RNAS Flights flying anti-submarine patrols over the North Sea. This task was continued until the Armistice after which the Squadron remained at Felixstowe until 13 September, 1919 when it was disbanded.

It re-formed at Beaumaris on 19 January, 1943 with Catalinas and immediately set out for East Africa, the aircraft flying there indi-

vidually. At first it was attached to No. 209 Squadron at Mombasa then 'officially' formed in its own right there (at Kipevu) on 16 February. It sent a detachment to Tulear in St. Lucia and began operations on 9 March with an anti-shipping patrol. Convoy patrols became the normal task, interspersed with U-boat searches when these were suspected in the Indian Ocean. On 20 August F/Lt Barnett on anti-submarine patrol from St. Lucia found a U-boat on the surface and depth-charged it, severely damaging it. He stayed with it, attacking now and then with gunfire for four hours until a No. 265 Squadron Catalina arrived and finished it off.

Operations averaged twenty to thirty sorties a month with detachments as far apart as Durban in the south and Aden and the Gulf in the North. Despite remaining continually operational all through 1944 no more action came No. 259s way. Early in 1945 it began converting to Short Sunderlands but after a month these were transferred to No. 35 SAAF Squadron and No. 259 Squadron began to run-down, disbanding at Dar-es-Salaam on 30 April, 1945.

Bases etc.

Formed at Felixstowe in August, 1918.

Felixstowe	Aug 1918—Sep 1919

Disbanded at Felixstowe on 13 September, 1919. Re-formed at Beaumaris on 19 January, 1943.

Beaumaris	Jan 1943—Feb 1943
Kipevu, det. Tulear, Congella, Langebaan	Feb 1943—Jun 1943
Congella, det. Langebaan	Jun 1943—Sep 1943
Dar-es-Salaam, det. Kipevu, Umm Rasas, Aden, Mauritius, Pamanzi, Tulear	Sep 1943—Apr 1945

Disbanded at Dar-es-Salaam on 30 April, 1945.

Main Equipment

Felixstowe F.2A (Aug 1918—Sep 1919)
No Serial numbers known

Felixstowe F.3 (Aug 1918—Sep 1919)
No serial numbers known

Consolidated Catalina IB (Jan 1943—Apr 1945)
FP111, J; FP118, Q; FP126, C, later L; FP133, F; FP192, Q; FP235, I, later P; FP247, O; FP256, A, later N; FP267, B; FP281, G; FP283, K, later L; FP310, N

Short Sunderland V (Mar 1945—Apr 1945)
NJ259; PP104; PP153; PP159

Commanding Officers

W/Cdr W. N. Bisdee	Jan 1943—Jan 1944
S/Ldr L. G. Virr	Jan 1944—Feb 1944
W/Cdr N. L. Smith	Feb 1944—Apr 1945

Aircraft Insignia

As far as is known no squadron identity insignia was carried by No. 259 Squadron in either war.

No. 260 SQUADRON

BADGE
A morning star and sword in saltire

MOTTO
'Celer et fortis'
('Swift and strong')

The Squadron was formed in August, 1918 at Westward Ho in Devon for coastal patrol duties equipped with D.H.6s. In this role it flew anti-submarine duties until the war's end, being disbanded on 22 February, 1919. The Squadron re-formed in the fighter role at Castletown on 22 November, 1940, moving to Egypt six months later where it fought over the Western Desert, moving to the Italian campaign later and eventually flying long-range fighter patrols over the Balkans. It was disbanded on 19 August, 1945.

Bases etc.

Formed at Westward Ho in August, 1918.

Westward Ho	Aug 1918—Feb 1919

Disbanded at Westward Ho on 22 February, 1919.

Main Equipment

Airco D.H.6 (Aug 1918—Feb 1919)
No serial numbers known

Aircraft Insignia

As far as is known no squadron insignia was carried.
(See also *Fighter Squadrons of the RAF*, pp. 369–72)

No. 261 SQUADRON

BADGE
In front of a sword erect, the point downwards,
a mullet, the whole in front of a Maltese Cross

MOTTO
'Semper contendo'
('I strive continually')

Formed in August, 1918 at Felixstowe this Squadron flew Felixstowe F.3s on North Sea patrols as part of the large force based at Felixstowe. It was disbanded there on 13 September, 1919. When No. 261 re-formed on 1 August, 1940 it was a fighter unit in Malta, providing the sole fighter defence of the island at first. It was disbanded there in May, 1941 and re-formed in the Persian Gulf on 12 July, 1941 by re-numbering No. 127 Squadron. It continued in a fighter role, fighting in Iran and Palestine until 1942 when it moved to the Far East Air Force fighting in Burma until the war ended, disbanding on 26 September, 1945.

Bases etc.

Formed at Felixstowe in August, 1918.

Felixstowe	Aug 1918—Sep 1919

Disbanded at Felixstowe 13 September, 1919.

Main Equipment

Felixstowe F.3 (Aug 1918—Sep 1919)
No serial numbers known

Aircraft Insignia

Nil.
(See also *Fighter Squadrons of the RAF*, pp. 372–4)

No. 262 SQUADRON

(No badge authorised)

The Squadron formed in name at Liverpool on 29 September, 1942 to sail for East Africa, arriving at Congella on 12 November (the official forming date was 29 September at Hednesford). Its first aircraft, a Catalina IB, did not arrive until 21 February, 1943 and two weeks later Sgt Lock flew the Squadron's first operation from St. Lucia on an anti-submarine convoy escort to Durban. This became the Squadron's sole task at first but shipping searches were added as the Squadron rose to full strength. On 19 May F/Lt Grant found a U-boat and depth-charged it, losing his port engine in the affray. Two months later F/O Roddick found another and attacked it. In November the Squadron was absorbed into the Union Defence Force, SAAF and began training SAAF crews. Operations continued and on 11 March F/Lt Roddick found his second U-boat and scored a probable with depth-charges and machine-guns. Although the Squadron was based at Durban all operations were flown at this time from St. Lucia. Another U-boat was damaged in an attack by F/Lt Fletcher on 5 July but this transpired to be No. 262s last action although patrols were continued on the basis of about ten sorties a month. By 1945 the Squadron was wholly SAAF personnel and on 15 February it was transferred to the SAAF to become No. 35 Squadron.

Bases etc.

Formed at Hednesford on 29 September, 1942. Moved to East Africa at once.

Congella, det. Tulear, Langebaan, Hermanus,
Umsingazi   Nov 1942—Feb 1945
Disbanded 15 February, 1945 by transferring to No. 35 Squadron, SAAF.

Main Equipment

Consolidated Catalina IB (Feb 1943—Feb 1945)
FP174, L; FP185, K; FP226, J; FP254, N; FP288, G; FP307, F; FP322, H
Consolidated Catalina IVB (Oct 1944—Feb 1945)
JX284, F2; JX319, A2; JX347, D2; JX348, C2; JX353, B2; JX367, G2

Commanding Officers

W/Cdr G. E. Wallace	Feb 1943—May 1943
W/Cdr K. W. Garside, DFC	May 1943—Dec 1943
W/Cdr D. B. Esmonde-White	Dec 1943—Jul 1944
LtCol R. D. Madeley	Jul 1944—Dec 1944
W/Cdr E. S. S. Nash, DFC, AFC	Dec 1944—Feb 1945

Aircraft Insignia

It is rumoured that the Squadron carried the code letters 'TR' *circa* May, 1944 but there is no confirmation of this and by the time of disbandment no identity markings were being carried.

No. 263 SQUADRON

BADGE
A lion rampant, holding in the fore paws a cross
MOTTO
'Ex ungue leonem'
('From his claws one knows the lion')

The Squadron was formed on 27 September, 1918 by combining Nos. 433, 436, 441 and 359 Flights at Otranto. These Flights were equipped with seaplanes and the Squadron used them to fly anti-submarine patrols covering the Otranto Straits until the war ended. It was eventually disbanded on 16 May, 1919. The Squadron re-formed at Filton on 2 October, 1939 as a fighter unit and fought in this role throughout World War II, in the Norwegian campaign, the Battle of Britain and the eventual attack on the Continent, disbanding in Germany on 28 August, 1945. No. 263 re-formed in Fighter Command by re-numbering No. 616 Squadron with Meteors and served on UK defence duties until 1 July, 1958 when it was re-numbered No. 1 Squadron.

Bases etc.

Formed at Otranto on 27 September, 1918.
Otranto, det. Sta. Maria de Leuca   Sep 1918—May 1919
Disbanded at Otranto on 16 May, 1919.

Main Equipment

Short 184 (Sep 1918—May 1919)
No serial numbers known
Fairey Hamble Baby (Sep 1918—May 1919)
No serial numbers known
Felixstowe F.3 (Sep 1918—May 1919)
No serial numbers known

Aircraft Insignia

Nil.
(See also *Fighter Squadrons of the RAF*, pp. 374–8)

No. 264 SQUADRON

BADGE
A helmet

MOTTO
'We defy'

No. 264 Squadron formed first at Suda Bay, Crete in August, 1918 from the seaplane Flight there and flew anti-submarine patrols with Short 184s until the war ended. It was disbanded on 1 March, 1919. Re-formed as a fighter Squadron on 30 October, 1939 it served in the UK, principally on night-fighter duties, throughout World War II, also moving to the Continent to support the advancing armies for a few months. It disbanded on 25 August, 1945 but was re-formed on 22 November and remained a night-fighter unit until re-numbering as No. 33 Squadron on 30 September, 1957.

Bases etc.

Formed at Suda Bay in August, 1918.
Suda Bay   Aug 1918—Mar 1919
Disbanded at Suda Bay on 1 March, 1919.

Main Equipment

Short 184 (Aug 1918—Mar 1919)
No serial numbers known

Aircraft Insignia

Nil.
(See also *Fighter Squadrons of the RAF*, pp. 378–82)

No. 265 SQUADRON

(No badge authorised)

No. 265 Squadron formed in August, 1918 at Gibraltar from Nos. 265, 266 and 364 Flights, RNAS and flew Short 184s and Felixstowe F.3s on anti-submarine patrols covering the Straits. It was disbanded in 1919.

It re-formed at Mombasa (Kipevu) on 11 March, 1943 equipped with Catalina IBs, moving to Diego Suarez at the end of the month, its first aircraft having arrived four days before. Some of its crews stopped off at Kisumu *en route* and finished their training there; consequently it was not until 6 May that the first operation was flown, an ASR search for Swordfish survivors. Slowly the Squadron built up flying mainly convoy escorts along the African coast. On 20 August, 1943 F/O Robin found a U-boat damaged by No. 259 Squadron and finished it off. The Squadron had detachments at St. Lucia, Mombasa and the Seychelles at this time and was flying about twenty sorties a month.

1944 began with intensive U-boat searches following two sinkings but to no avail. In May one aircraft was used for an island tour by the AOC, otherwise it was a routine of convoy escorts and anti-submarine patrols, one aircraft failing to return in August. The Squadron had done some photography of Mombasa in 1943; in October one aircraft went to Bassar da India (a coral reef) for survey photography and discovered the survivors of a ship torpedoed four months earlier. At the end of the year, however, the whole area quietened down and met observation flights took the place of some of the A/S work. In January, 1945 the Squadron began freight runs to Mauritius but in April a rundown began and the Squadron was disbanded at Diego Suarez on 18 April, 1945.

Bases etc.

Formed at Gibraltar in August, 1918.

Gibraltar	Aug 1918— 1919

Disbanded at Gibraltar in 1919. Re-formed at Mombasa on 11 March, 1943.

Kipevu	Mar 1943—Mar 1943
Diego Suarez, det. Kipevu, Pamanzi, Tulear, Mauritius, Seychelles, Masirah, Tulear, Congella	Mar 1943—Apr 1945

Disbanded at Diego Suarez on 18 April, 1945.

Main Equipment

Short 184 (Aug 1918— 1919)
No serial numbers known
Felixstowe F.3 (Aug 1918— 1919)
No serial numbers known
Consolidated Catalina IB (Mar 1943—Apr 1945)
W8428, P, later A; AH548, F; FP104, H; FP235, H; FP261, H; FP277, E; FP300, K, later B; FP311, O, later Z; FP323, A

Commanding Officers

W/Cdr H. J. Hobbs	Mar 1943—Jan 1944	
W/Cdr J. W. Louw, DFC	Jan 1944—Feb 1945	
LtCol Sheldon	Feb 1945—Apr 1945	

Aircraft Insignia

At least one of the Squadron's aircraft carried the code letters 'TR' in the summer of 1944 but it is not known whether this was universal throughout the Squadron or not.

No. 266 SQUADRON

BADGE
A bataleur eagle

MOTTO
'Hlabezulu'
('The stabber of the sky')

No. 266 Squadron was formed in August, 1918 from RNAS units at Mudros and, with seaplanes and flying-boats maintained anti-submarine patrols in that area until the Armistice. It was disbanded on 1 September, 1919.

It re-formed as a fighter squadron in the UK on 30 October, 1939 fighting with Fighter Command in the Battle of Britain and the channel sweeps, then transferring to 2nd TAF and moving to the Continent after D-Day. It disbanded on 31 July, 1945. It re-formed from No. 234 Squadron on 1 September, 1946, again in Fighter Command only to be re-numbered No. 43 Squadron on 11 Febru-ary, 1949. No. 266s final existence was in the ground attack role in Germany from 14 July, 1952 to 15 November, 1957.

Bases etc.

Formed at Mudros in August, 1918.

Mudros	Aug 1918—Sep 1919

Disbanded at Mudros on 1 September, 1919.

Main Equipment

Short 184 (Aug 1918—Sep 1919)
N1591; N9065
Felixstowe F.3 (Aug 1918—Sep 1919)
N4360

Aircraft Insignia

Nil.
(See also *Fighter Squadrons of the RAF*, pp. 382–4)

No. 267 SQUADRON

BADGE
A pegasus

MOTTO
'Sine Mora'
('Without delay')

The Squadron was first formed at Kalafrana in October, 1918 from Flights at the RNAS seaplane base. It was equipped with both seaplanes and flying-boats and provided aerial support for the Mediterranean Fleet, remaining there long after most other such Flights had disbanded. Eventually the Squadron itself was dis-banded on 1 August, 1923.

On 19 August, 1940 it was re-formed at Heliopolis out of the Communications Flight there, its first task being to fly Western Desert mail runs and VIP flights, Wavell, Longmore and Collishaw being regular users of the Squadron. At first it had Ansons, Magisters and Proctors but Q6s, Hudsons and Lockheed 12As were added and other types as times went on. In 1941 the mail run was flown by Lysanders and it even acquired a Met Flight of four Gladiators. On 11 April, 1941 one of its Lodestars took Prince Paul and Princess Olga of Greece to Egypt and then No. 267 began regular evacuation flights from Athens to Egypt, 91 passengers being flown in three days. In June more royalty used the Squadron when King Peter of Yugoslavia was flown in. New types were being added all the time and in August the fleet of Lysanders were turned to anti-malarial spraying around Egypt and local PR work. By the end of the year the Lodestars were providing navigational escorts to forma-tions of Tomahawks to the Turkish coast *en route* for other users. The Squadron also provided pilots for ferrying on the trans-Sahara route.

1942 saw no let up in the types acquired, the Squadron at one time flying a captured Messerschmitt Bf 109F. By June the tentative Malta runs had become a scheduled service and the Squadron began rationalising its fleet on Lodestars and Hudsons. Both the Duke of Gloucester and Winston Churchill were amongst the passengers flown by No. 267 that year. In October, 1942 it was included in 216 Group's Mobile Operations Force which involved Western Desert support and casevac and especially the support of two Hurricane squadrons based in enemy territory behind the German lines at the end of 1942. The main task, however, was the freight and passenger route in and out of Malta and this extended into 1943. That year it began, in March, Operation Helpful, intensive flights to Castel Benito with army personnel, averaging eleven round trips a day. At this time Dakotas began to replace the Hudsons which had all gone by July. In June a detachment was set up at Ouina to support the Sicilian invasion, one hundred and thirty-four sorties being flown that month. This Sicilian support also involved diversionary flights, dropping dummy paratroops and pyrotechnics on the island. Two Dakotas were lost within three days on this task. Another task No. 267 took on was to transport the stores and ground personnel of DAF Wings moving into Sicily. Monthly hours now topped the 3,000 mark. In October the Squadron began supply-drops to troops on Kos and Leros and, in the other direction, transport trips to Nairobi and Lagos. In November it moved to Bari and set up regular schedules to Tunis, Foggia, Naples and Algiers. By the beginning of 1944 it had four daily regular schedules and in addition flew 'specials', some such in February, 1944 were *Nickel* raids over Yugoslavia. This was followed by forty-four special sorties in March dropping supplies to insurgents in Greece. This led on to similar night drops over Yugoslavia. On 16 April F/Lt Harrod in Dakota FD919 flew Operation Wildhorn, taking agents into a field near Warsaw and picking up five passengers including the deputy GOC of the Polish Home Army. This pattern was maintained by No. 267 over the next few months with about half the sorties being transport and half supply-drops (350 total per month).

In July the Squadron was regularly landing in Yugoslavia to pick up wounded partisans; one aircraft was lost doing this. Further Operation Wildhorns were flown, and in September a special mission was flown to Bucharest by five aircraft. In October the Squadron was busy flying troops into Greece behind the enemy lines, and more sorties into Romania. An amusing episode took place on 4 November: a Squadron Dakota was followed into its secret strip in Yugoslavia by a Junkers Ju 52, intent on capturing the crew. However, the Ju 52 became bogged down and instead the German crew were captured by the partisans. First trips into Albania were flown that month as well. By the end of the year the Squadron was flying 300 special ops sorties a month and only thirty-nine routine flights.

But this ended in 1945 for in February the Squadron was transferred by air to India. There it began glider-towing training and then moved up to Tulihal for operations, commencing these on 1 March flying thirty tactical drops a day, aircraft being damaged by ground fire on many of them. At the end of the month a move to Akyab Island brought a change; No. 267 now flew routine trips to Meiktela as well as tactical drops around the area. This formed the pattern for the next few months until August, 1945 brought a change with the Karachi–Rangoon route to fly and then a move to Rangoon brought with it mercy drops with food, clothing and medical supplies to POW camps. This was followed by flights to Bangkok to repatriate POWs released there.

In September a Singapore shuttle service began and one to Saigon soon after; the Squadron was now flying regular routes all the time, adding Hong Kong, Delhi and Java to its schedules. In January, 1946 No. 267 flew 472 sorties on the routes and twenty-six 'specials' in addition. This pace continued until May, 1946 when the demobilisation began to cut down personnel. From July onwards the Squadron began running down and was disbanded about 21 July, 1946 at Mingaladon.

No. 267 re-formed once more as a communications and army support unit on 15 February, 1954 at Kuala Lumpur. It was equipped with Pioneers, Pembrokes and a few Dakotas fitted up with loud-speaking equipment to pass messages to the terrorists in the jungle. For three years it flew into and out of jungle strips on support and casevac trips until being re-numbered No. 209 Squadron on 1 November, 1958.

Four years later to the day it was re-formed at Benson in the transport role with Argosies. It flew these, both on Transport Command routes and in its roles as 38 Group army support for the next eight years until it fell foul of the defence cuts at the end of the decade. The Squadron was disbanded at Benson on 1 June, 1970.

Bases etc.

Formed at Kalafrana in October, 1918.

Kalafrana	Oct 1918	Aug 1923

Disbanded at Kalafrana on 1 August, 1923. Re-formed by expanding the Heliopolis Communications Flight at Heliopolis on 19 August, 1940.

Heliopolis	Aug 1940	Aug 1942
Bilbeis East	Aug 1942	Nov 1942
El Adem	Nov 1942	Jan 1943
Marble Arch, det. El Adem	Jan 1943	Apr 1943
Cairo West, det. Ouina, San Francesco, Catania	Apr 1943	Nov 1943
Bari	Nov 1943	Feb 1945
Bilaspur	Feb 1945	Feb 1945
Tulihal	Feb 1945	Mar 1945
Mawnubyin	Mar 1945	May 1945
Akyab Main	May 1945	Aug 1945
Mingaladon	Aug 1945	Jul 1946

Disbanded at Mingaladon on 21 July, 1946. Re-formed at Kula Lumpur on 15 February, 1954.

Kuala Lumpur	Feb 1954	Nov 1958

Disbanded at Kuala Lumpur on 1 November, 1958 by re-numbering as No. 209 Squadron. Re-formed at Benson on 1 November, 1962.

Benson	Nov 1962	Jun 1970

Disbanded at Benson on 1 June, 1970.

Main Equipment

Felixstowe F.2A (Oct 1918— 1919)
N4089; N4092; N4436; N4438; N4488; N4490
Short 184 (Oct 1918— 1921)
9053; N1096; N1097; N1823
Felixstowe F.3 (1919— 1922)
No serial numbers known
Fairey IIID (1921—Aug 1923)
N9454; N9465; N9486; N9489; N9494; N9499
Avro Anson I (Aug 1940— 1942)
L7974; L7992
Miles Magister I (Aug 1940— 1941)
P2453; R1953; R1954; P2450; N3844
Percival Q6 (Aug 1940— 1941)
P5640; W6085; HK838
Percival Proctor I (Aug 1940—Jul 1942)
P6114; P6116; P6119; P6123; P6126
(Gull Six)
AX698
Lockheed Hudson III (Aug 1940—Jul 1943)
V9093; V9227; AE624; AE633
Lockheed Lodestar IA/II (Feb 1941—Oct 1942)
AX685; AX723; EW977; EW982; EW992; EW995; HK852; HK855
Westland Lysander I/II (Feb 1941—May 1942)
L4677; L4720; L4727; L6880; P1737; R1987; R1994; P9191
Gloster Gladiator I/II (Mar 1941— 1941)
K7893; K7963; L8003; N5825
Lockheed Hudson VI (Jul 1942—Jul 1943)
EW884, KW:B; EW889; EW937; EW943; EW961, KW:H; FK454; FK476; FK504, KW:S; FK507; FK526; FK575; FK580; FK619
Douglas Dakota I (Aug 1942— 1943)
42-5650; 42-5656; FD774; FD775; FD780; FD815; FD818
Douglas Dakota III (Apr 1943—Jul 1946)
FD841, G; FD849; FD857, S; FD883; FD926, B; FD955; FD965, G; FL551; FL567, D; FL589, A; FL619; FZ551, K; KG466, P; KG472, Y; KG496, Al; KG511, Cl; KG523, H; KG546, J; KG754
Douglas Dakota IV (Jan 1945—Jul 1946)
KJ883, U; KJ920, R; KJ937, Y; KJ998, Q; KK178; KK208; KN205; KN302; KN396; KN458; KN540; KN591; KN626; KN686,U
Scottish Aviation Pioneer CC.1 (Feb 1954—Nov 1958)
XE512; XE513; XE514; XE515; XG562; XJ466
Hunting Pembroke C.1 (1956—Nov 1958)
XK885
Hawker Siddeley Argosy C.1 (Nov 1962—Jun 1970)
XN815; XN847; XN853; XP441; XR105; XR109; XR133; XR137; XR143

Commanding Officers

W/Cdr C. S. Wynne-Eaton, DSO	Aug 1940	Jul 1942
W/Cdr J. A. P. Harrison	Jul 1942	Aug 1942
W/Cdr J. P. S. Smyth	Aug 1942	Oct 1942
W/Cdr C. S. Wynne-Eaton, DSO	Oct 1942	Feb 1943
W/Cdr E. W. Whittaker, DFC	Feb 1943	May 1944
W/Cdr A. N. Francombe, MBE	May 1944	Mar 1945
W/Cdr W. S. Hillary, DFC, DFM	Mar 1945	Aug 1945
W/Cdr R. A. R. Chalmers	Aug 1945	Jul 1946
S/Ldr M. E. J. Hickmott	Feb 1954	1955
S/Ldr T. W. G. Godfrey, DFC	1955	1957
S/Ldr M. L. Hamilton	1957	Nov 1958
W/Cdr A. Steedman	Nov 1962	
W/Cdr S. A. Price	Dec 1968	Jun 1970

No regular markings were carried on World War I aircraft although the F.2As were at one time given the names of planets. As far as is known, the first identity markings carried in World War II were the code letters 'KW' which seem to have only been used on the Hudsons *ca* 1942–1943. With the arrival of the Dakotas this was dropped but instead a Pegasus emblem was carried on the nose, at least until moving to India. No markings were carried whilst in Malaya, but the Argosies carried the Pegasus emblem once more, this time on a white disc on the fin top.

No. 268 SQUADRON

BADGE
A swallow soaring, holding in the claws a tomahawk

MOTTO
'*Adjidaumo*'
('Tail in the air')

The original No. 268 Squadron was formed at Kalafrana, Malta in August, 1918 from one of the ex-RNAS seaplane Flights there. It flew anti-submarine patrols in the Central Mediterranean for the remainder of the war and was eventually disbanded there on 11 October, 1919.

It was re-formed in the army co-operation role at Bury St. Edmunds on 30 September, 1940 from a Flight each of Nos. 2 and 26 Squadrons, equipped with Westland Lysanders. Its immediate task was anti-invasion coastal patrols at dawn each morning and these were continued into 1941. It also despatched a Flight to Gatwick for AA calibration flying in November. Army exercises took up an increasingly large proportion of its time in 1941 and, with the arrival of Tomahawks in May, the dawn patrols and the AA calibrated ceased as it worked up on Tac/R duties with these. On 19 October the CO and a wingman flew No. 268's first operations with a Dutch coast *Rhubarb*; more were scheduled but a few days later the Tomahawks were grounded. Next operations were from Ibsley in December, flying convoy patrols with No. 501 Squadron and these continued intermittently until 21 February when F/O Hoskins was shot down in error by Spitfires. Further troubles with Tomahawks resulted in their being replaced by Mustangs in April.

At the end of June, 1942 No. 268 became operational once more with *Jim Crows* (shipping recces) and in July flew 42 sorties on this task. By September the work had extended to the Dutch coast and also included some daylight bomber escorts. *Rhubarbs* in October produced a score of four locomotives damaged and a tugboat in flames on the first one and subsequent ones produced similar results. No. 268s first enemy aircraft was a Ju 52 shot down by P/O Bethell on 26 November. But it was not all one way for in November one pilot had been lost and in January, 1943 two went down. In February no less than six trains were destroyed in *Rhubarbs* whilst in March the Squadron attacked an SS HQ at Amersfoort. This pattern was maintained into the summer of 1943, *Night Rangers* being added in June and a detachment was at Tangmere for interception duties against German fighter-bombers. Thereafter the Squadron flew an increasing number of low-level PR sorties over Northern France until moving north and coming off operations temporarily in November.

These were resumed from North Weald in January, 1944, the PR being the main task with *Noball* sorties added. On one such two aircraft were jumped by FW 190s but F/Lt Brees managed to fly through trees and his pursuing 190 crashed into them. The pressure built up to over one hundred sorties a month with Tac/Rs and PR of France and Belgium being made in preparation for the Second Front. On D-Day itself the Squadron flew with the RN monitoring the shooting of the naval bombardment against the shore batteries then switched to Tac/Rs over the bridgehead in the subsequent days, 395 sorties being flown that month. In July Typhoons were added to its complement and these were used operationally on Tac/Rs in August. On 10th of that month the Squadron moved to France itself to keep up with the advancing armies and flew intensive Tac/R and PR work amassing 534 sorties. Four moves took place in September to keep up with the advance and on into October, with weather reducing the number of ops to under three hundred a month by November. In that month the Typhoons were withdrawn.

As fighting opened up more in 1945 so the Squadron's work increased; in April it began operating with 'contact cars' directing its work and that month received some Spitfire XIVs to complement the Mustangs. It was now flying shipping recces off Holland and Tac/R against road transport and trains in NW Germany. However, the war was now all but over and its last operation was on 8 May, a Tac/R of Sylt and the Danish coast. It moved into Germany after VE-Day and flew PR of German harbours and airfields in the next few months. In September, 1945 the Spitfire XI Flight from No. 16 Squadron joined No. 268 and it was officially re-numbered 16 Squadron on 19 September but the change did not take place until 1 October, 1945.

On 16 October, 1945 No. 487 Squadron was advised that it had been officially re-numbered No. 268 Squadron on 19 September, 1945. It was now flying Mosquito FB.6s at Cambrai/Epinoy. However, it was itself disbanded there on 31 March, 1946.

Bases etc.

Formed at Kalafrana in August, 1918.

Kalafrana	Aug 1918—Oct 1919

Disbanded at Kalafrana on 11 October, 1919. Re-formed from Flights of Nos. 2 & 26 Squadrons at Bury St. Edmunds on 30 September, 1940.

Bury St. Edmunds, det. Gatwick	Sep 1940—Apr 1941
Snailwell, det. West Raynham, Penshurst, Ibsley, Docking, Wing, Bottisham	Apr 1941—May 1943
Odiham, det. Tangmere	May 1943—Oct 1943
Funtington	Oct 1943—Oct 1943
Odiham	Oct 1943—Oct 1943
Thruxton	Oct 1943—Nov 1943
Turnhouse, det. Kinnell	Nov 1943—Jan 1944
North Weald	Jan 1944—Mar 1944
Sawbridgeworth	Mar 1944—Mar 1944
Gailes	Mar 1944—Apr 1944
Gatwick	Apr 1944—Apr 1944
Odiham, det. B.10	Apr 1944—Aug 1944
Plumetot (B.10)	Aug 1944—Aug 1944
Beny sur Mer (B.4)	Aug 1944—Sep 1944
Boisney (B.27)	Sep 1944—Sep 1944
Fresney Folney (B.31)	Sep 1944—Sep 1944
Fort Rouge	Sep 1944—Sep 1944
St. Denis-Westrem (B.61)	Sep 1944—Oct 1944
Deurne (B.71)	Oct 1944—Nov 1944
Gilze-Rijen (B.77)	Nov 1944—Mar 1945
Mill (B.89)	Mar 1945—Apr 1945
Twente (B.106)	Apr 1945—May 1945
Celle (B.118)	May 1945—Jun 1945
Hustedt (B.150)	Jun 1945—Sep 1945
Celle (B.118)	Sep 1945—Oct 1945

Re-numbered 16 Squadron on 1 October, 1945, at Celle. Re-formed by re-numbering No. 487 Squadron at Cambrai/Epinoy on the same day in the light bomber role.

Main Equipment

Short 184 (Aug 1918—Oct 1919)
No serial numbers known
Short 320 (Aug 1918—Oct 1919)
No serial numbers known

Westland Lysander II (Sep 1940— 1942)
  L4776; L4780; L4816; N1209; N1268; N1319; P1742; P9067; P9107;
  P9177; R1989; R1997, NM:L
(Mk. III)
  T1736
Curtiss Tomahawk I, IIB (May 1941—May 1942)
  AH769; AH775, NM:P; AH834; AH852; AH856; AH998, NM:V
North American Mustang I (Apr 1942—Jul 1943)
  AG412; AG433; AG465; AG474; AL994; AM104; AM131; AM147;
  AM193; AM253; AP200; AP219; AP232; AP256, U; AP260
North American Mustang IA (Jun 1943—Apr 1945)
  FD434; FD441, A; FD471; FD488; FD495; FD503; FD535, X;
  FD544, V; FD563
Hawker Typhoon IB (Jul 1944—Nov 1944)
  EK135; EK180; EK240; EK372; EK428; JP373; JP389
North American Mustang II (Nov 1944—Aug 1945)
  FR894; FR903; FR906; FR915; FR927; FR931; FR938
Vickers-Supermarine Spitfire XIVB (Apr 1945—Oct 1945)
  MV273; MV313; MV340, K; MV369; NH643; NH652; NH807; NH836

Vickers-Supermarine Spitfire XI (Sep 1945—Oct 1945)
  No serial numbers known

Commanding Officers

W/Cdr P. de G. H. Seymour	Sep 1940	Dec 1940
W/Cdr A. F. Anderson, DFC	Dec 1940	Nov 1942
W/Cdr P. W. A. Dudgeon, DFC	Nov 1942	Apr 1943
W/Cdr C. W. M. Ling	Apr 1943	Jun 1943
S/Ldr A. G. Pallot	Jun 1943	1943
S/Ldr A. S. Mann, DFC	1943	1945
S/Ldr C. T. P. Stephenson, DFC, and Bar	1945	Oct 1945

Aircraft Insignia

The code letters 'NM' were carried until early 1943, after which no squadron identity markings were used.
(See also *Bomber Squadrons of the RAF*, p. 223)

No. 269 SQUADRON

BADGE
An ancient ship in full sail
MOTTO
'Omnia videmus'
('We see all things')

On 6 October, 1918 No. 269 Squadron was formed from the Seaplane Flight at Port Said which had Short 184s, Sopwith Baby, Felixstowe F.3, D.H.9s and B.E.2c's. With these it flew coastal patrols in the Eastern Mediterranean as it had been doing since January, 1916. The Squadron remained at Port Said until 15 September, 1919 when it moved to Alexandria where it was disbanded exactly two months later.

It was re-formed from C Flight of No. 206 Squadron at Bircham Newton on 7 December, 1936 with Avro Ansons for general reconnaissance duties. Its permanent base became Abbotsinch to cover the Clyde and Forth areas; in September, 1938 it moved to Thornaby, its war station for the Munich crisis, but returned in October. In June, 1939 it had the sad task of searching for HM submarine *Thetis* which was lost with all hands off Liverpool. On 25 August, 1939 it moved to Montrose from where it began line patrols and searches on the outbreak of war. On 15 September Sgt Smith found, and bombed, a U-boat in the North Sea and four days later P/O Burrell had a combat with a Do 18 in which he was killed but his navigator flew the Anson back.

In October it moved to Wick and flew out over the Atlantic as well as the North Sea; two U-boats were attacked in November and one, probably destroyed, in December and one Anson was lost.

By January, 1940 the Squadron was flying one hundred and fifty patrol sorties a month and in February the Squadron made six attacks on U-boats, one being claimed as probably destroyed. In March the rate went up to two hundred sorties and the first Hudsons arrived on the Squadron, first operation with these taking place on 21 April. By now the Squadron was involved in the Norwegian campaign, attacking shipping and U-boats in the fjords and carrying out a bombing attack on Stavanger airfield in May, losing one crew on it. Raids continued on Norway and 11 June a twelve aircraft attack was made on the *Scharnhorst* at Trondheim, two Hudsons being shot down. That month was a busy one for No. 269 and the activity continued in July; P/O Weightman managed to destroy a U-boat on 21st and on 23rd four combats were fought with Do 18 flying-boats, one being shot down. In August one of three U-boats attacked was destroyed; the pressure kept up with 204 sorties in September but the weather in October and November reduced the number of operations possible. The Norwegian coast remained No. 269's operational area until the summer of 1941 when it moved to Iceland and began to patrol the Atlantic Gap. Within the

first month (June) the Squadron had four U-boat attacks as it flew A/S patrols and convoy escorts. August was another busy month with seven attacks on one of which S/Ldr Thompson, in UA:S managed to secure the surrender of *U-570*. Another five attacks took place in September then came a period of patrols without successes. Ice reconnaissances were also part of No. 269's duties in Iceland, keeping an eye on the extent of the icebergs for shipping information. For the first part of 1942 bad weather hindered operations and it was not until July that the next U-boat attack took place, a successful one claimed as a probable. Then came a flood of activity once more with six attacks in eight days and the pressure kept up in August also. In September three U-boats were found and attacked but two Hudsons and crews were lost. The winter weather now closed down on operations somewhat, although on 5 October F/O Markham destroyed the U-boat he attacked.

Despite the weather one hundred and fifty-nine sorties were flown in January, 1943, the Squadron sending a detachment to Greenland to endeavour to close the gap still further. The weather there was treacherous, however, and two aircraft were lost on 1 March when trying to get back into Bluie West One; the detachment returned in April. May became a record month for U-boat sightings, no fewer than thirteen attacks being made. The summer was a busy time for No. 269 and an increasing number of ASR sorties came its way as well. In August the Squadron began working up with RPs under the Hudsons' wings and this bore fruit on 5 October when F/Sgt Allsop sank a U-boat with rockets. As the year drew to a close so the Squadron began to run down and in January 1944 it returned to the UK, a new No. 269 forming at the same time at Davidstow Moor.

In March, 1944 the Squadron moved to the Azores where it took on a composite role of anti-submarine, met recce and ASR tasks. For these it was equipped with Walrus amphibians, Hudsons and Spitfires. The met recces were the primary function and were all flown in the Hudsons, the Spitfires being used for U-boat hunts! The Hudsons also carried airborne lifeboats and one was successfully dropped to Liberator survivors on 26 July. In October Warwicks replaced the Hudsons for the ASR work and also flew A/U sorties, the Spitfires now taking on twice daily met ascents, which continued into 1945. By the time the European war was over the Squadron, due to lack of spares, was down to one Hudson and one Warwick but this was remedied during the summer. Because of the amount of transatlantic air traffic at this time the Squadron remained on ASR and met duties until 10 May, 1946 when it was disbanded at Lagens.

The Squadron re-formed after the war in the maritime recce role once more at Ballykelly with Avro Shackletons on 10 March, 1952 and served in this role for six years with various detachments, mostly for exercises although in 1958 it went to Christmas Island to monitor the nuclear tests. On its return to Ballykelly it was disbanded by re-numbering as No. 210 Squadron on 1 December, 1958.

Bases etc.

Formed at Port Said on 6 October, 1918.

Port Said	Oct 1918—Sep 1919
Alexandria	Sep 1919—Nov 1919

Disbanded at Alexandria on 15 November, 1919. Re-formed from C Flight, 206 Squadron at Bircham Newton on 7 December, 1936.

Bircham Newton	Dec 1936—Dec 1936
Abbotsinch	Dec 1936—Sep 1938
Thornaby	Sep 1938—Oct 1938
Abbotsinch	Oct 1938—Aug 1939
Montrose	Aug 1939—Oct 1939
Wick, det. Kaldadarnes	Oct 1939—Jun 1941
Kaldadarnes, det. Bluie West One	Jun 1941—Mar 1943
Reykjavik	Mar 1943—Jan 1944
Davidstow Moor	Jan 1944—Mar 1944
Lagens	Mar 1944—Mar 1946

Disbanded at Lagens 10 March, 1946. Re-formed at Ballykelly on 10 March, 1952.

Ballykelly, det. Bodo, Christmas Island	Mar 1952—Dec 1958

Disbanded at Ballykelly on 1 December, 1958 by re-numbering as No. 210 Squadron.

Main Equipment

Short 184 (Oct 1918—Nov 1919)
N2643; N2657
Sopwith Baby (Oct 1918—Nov 1919)
N2132
Felixstowe F.3 (Oct 1918—May 1919)
N4330
Airco D.H.9 (Oct 1918—Nov 1919)
No serial numbers known
B.E.2c (Oct 1918—   1919)
No serial numbers known
Avro Anson I (Dec 1936—Jun 1940)
K6204, UA:I; K6240, 269:A; K6247, 269:C; K6258, 269:B, later UA:B; K6259, KL: ; K6286, UA:E; K6316, UA:O; K8742, UA:C; K8751, 269:H; K8760, UA:Q; K8838, UA:A; N4859, UA:T; N5317, UA:R; N9535, UA:L; N9672, UA:F; N9679, UA:W; R9817, UA:
North American Hudson I (Mar 1940—   1942)
N7276, UA:X; N7303, UA:R; N7331, UA:D; N7361, UA:G; N7376, UA:W; P5118, UA:R; P5129, UA:E; P5147, UA:Q; P5161, UA:A; T9275, UA:W; T9294, UA:P; T9299, UA:Y; T9349, UA:Q

Lockheed Hudson II, III (Mar 1941—Jul 1945)
T9374, UA:W; T9389, UA:A; T9420, UA:X; T9436, UA:M; V8977, UA:O; V9028, UA:S; V9047, UA:S; V9051, UA:W; V9096, UA:N; V9118, UA:C; V9185, UA:P; FH363, UA:M; FH423, UA:O; FH521, UA:Y; FK738, U; FK747, C; FK777, D; FK799, Q; FK807, B
Vickers-Supermarine Walrus II (Jan 1944—   1944)
No serial numbers known
Vickers-Supermarine Spitfire VB (Jan 1945—Mar 1946)
P8781; AB936; AD253; BL939; EN823; EP175, J
Vickers Warwick ASR.1 (Oct 1944—Mar 1946)
BV356, HK:E; BV483; BV499, HK:D; BV508, HK:B; BV519, HK:A
Vickers Warwick ASR.6 (Sep 1945—Mar 1946)
HG136; HG142; HG156; HG171; HG192; PN862
Avro Shackleton MR1/MR.1A (Mar 1952—Dec 1958)
VP255, B:D; VP284, 269:F; VP291, B:C; WB820, B:S; WB851, B:H; WB852, B:R; WG529
Avro Shackleton MR.2 (Mar 1953—Aug 1954 & Oct 1958—Dec 1958)
WL739; WL746; WL748; WL750; WL795

Commanding Officers

S/Ldr P. L. Holmes	Oct 1918—Nov 1919
S/Ldr J. A. Dixon	Dec 1936—May 1937
S/Ldr N. S. Allinson	May 1937—Jul 1937
W/Cdr H. W. Evens	Jul 1937—Jun 1939
W/Cdr F. L. Pearce, DSO, DFC	Jun 1939—Aug 1940
W/Cdr R. A. McMurtrie, DSO, DFC	Aug 1940—Jul 1941
W/Cdr M. H. Kelly, OBE	Jul 1941—Mar 1942
W/Cdr J. G. Davis	Mar 1942—Feb 1943
W/Cdr J. Riley	Feb 1943—Dec 1943
W/Cdr R. H. Warcup	Dec 1943—Dec 1944
W/Cdr G. A. B. Cooper	Dec 1944—May 1945
W/Cdr H. C. Bailey	May 1945—Jan 1946
W/Cdr J. S. Dinsdale, DSO, DFC	Jan 1946—Mar 1946
S/Ldr G. F. Morley-Mower, DFC	Jan 1952—Mar 1952
S/Ldr E. D. Pennington, AFC	Mar 1952—Apr 1954
S/Ldr J. Quinn, DFC	May 1954—Aug 1955
W/Cdr P. Norton-Smith	Aug 1955—Nov 1956
W/Cdr A. P. Morgan	Nov 1956—Dec 1958

Aircraft Insignia

No identity markings were carried in World War I. The Ansons at first had the Squadron number painted on the rear fuselage and the emblem on a six-pointed white star on the fin. From the time of Munich code letters succeeded such markings and 'KL' was carried up to the outbreak of World War I after which 'UA' was used, probably until the Squadron returned from Iceland. During its Azores period the Warwick aircraft carried 'HK' letters at one time but whether this was used by the other types is not known. The Shackletons originally carried the letter 'B' on the rear fuselage but this was replaced, ca 1956, by the Squadron number in the same location.

No. 270 SQUADRON

(No badge authorised)

The Squadron was formed at Alexandria in August, 1918 from the coastal Flight there, flying anti-submarine patrols off the Egyptian Coast. It also had a Flight of D.H.9s. When No. 269 Squadron moved to Alexandria on 15 September, 1919 it was disbanded into No. 269 Squadron.

No. 270 re-formed at Jui in November, 1942 as a general recce squadron, equipped with Catalinas and began patrolling the mid-Atlantic in December. It started the New Year well when Sgt Evans found a U-boat and depth-charged it. Slowly it built up its operations from twenty a month at the beginning of the year to thirty and then forty in the summer. The tasks were varied, with the customary A/S patrols and convoy escorts interspersed with reconnaissances, ASR trips and patrols to find ships running the blockade of the Vichy French ports. Another U-boat was attacked on 27 April, 1943. At the end of the year it began supplementing its Catalinas with Sunderlands which began operations in February, 1944. On 16 April it flew Exercise Filto, dropping food supplies to African troops. No more U-boats were found, the patrols becoming pure routine. In October met recce flights were commenced and these

soon formed the major part of No. 270 Squadron's task. These operations were maintained without further action until the Squadron disbanded at Apapa on 30 June, 1945.

Bases etc.

Formed at Alexandria in August, 1918.

Alexandria	Aug 1918—Sep 1919

Disbanded into 269 Squadron at Alexandria on 15 September, 1919. Re-formed at Jui in November, 1942.

Jui	Nov 1942—Jul 1943
Apapa, det. Banana, Abidjan, Jui	Jul 1943—Jun 1945

Disbanded at Apapa on 30 June, 1945.

Main Equipment

Short 184; Felixstowe F.3; Sopwith Baby (Aug 1918—Sep 1919)
No serial numbers known
Consolidated Catalina IB (Nov 1942—May 1944)
FP152, A; FP161, B; FP173, J; FP192, E; FP224, C; FP229, Y; FP253, Q; FP304, D
Short Sunderland III (Dec 1943—Jun 1945)
DW108, Y; DW109, Q; EK584, D; EK589, V; EK593, A; ML849, K; ML867, N; ML874, L

Aircraft Insignia

As far as is known No. 270 Squadron never carried any identity insignia.

No. 271 SQUADRON

BADGE
A gauntlet holding a cross
MOTTO
'Death and life'

The original No. 271 Squadron formed in September, 1918 from the coastal recce Flight at Otranto with Short 184s and Felixstowe F.3s for anti-submarine patrols covering the Otranto Barrage. It served there until the end of the year when it was disbanded on 9 December, 1918.

The Squadron re-formed on 1 May, 1940 at Doncaster being No. 1680 Flight expanded to Squadron strength. Its particular task was to move the men and equipment of fighter squadrons from station to station and for this it was equipped in the main with Handley Page Harrows although augmented with other types. In May a detachment was sent to Hendon specifically for supporting the evacuation of squadrons in France and whilst on this task it acquired other aircraft: Bristol Bombays, a Ford Trimotor, some Handley Page HP.42s temporarily and four Savoia-Marchetti SM.73Ps which it had picked up from the disintegrating Belgian airline SABENA. May and June were hectic months with aircraft flying in and out of France under the noses of the Germans and not all the aircraft returned safely.

With that campaign over the detachment at Hendon began to convert the bomber-transports into more satisfactory transport aircraft which were nicknamed Sparrows, this becoming a semi-official nomenclature. The Squadron now extended its activities to cover Coastal Command squadrons as well and was busy ferrying throughout the UK for the rest of the year by which time it was virtually standardising on the Harrows. Early in 1941 an intensive period of flying between Wick and the Shetlands ensued as well as the normal runs and by March it was flying about 240 sorties a month. It still had a D.H.91 at this time and it began to use this on regular scheduled flights to the new bases in Iceland, being augmented by Hudsons later in the year. This service was continued until April, 1942, after which the Squadron began 'Islands and Highlands' services in the north-west of Scotland with Dominies. As more Harrows became available the Squadron took on extra work, flying many sorties in the autumn of 1942 out of Netheravon giving airborne troops air experience and map-reading and doing air sickness research with them.

In 1943 the Squadron took on airborne work regularly and also flew many ENSA shows about the country. In August the first Dakotas arrived but the Squadron was still flying mainly Harrows, until February, 1944 when it moved to Down Ampney to become a regular Dakota squadron with a Harrow Flight. It began airborne training, glider-towing and paratroop dropping and flew some *Nickel* raids over France in April, 1944. On 3 June, 1944 its Dakotas had black and white striping painted on and two days later it flew in Operation Tonga dropping 165 men of the 3rd Para Brigade in France. Each aircraft also dropped some 20 lb bombs ahead of the troops to keep the Germans' heads down. At the same time another seven squadron aircraft took Horsa gliders to Dropping Zone V and a further ten aircraft took more paratroops (altogether twenty-six successful sorties). On D-Day itself another fifteen aircraft towed Horsas successfully to LZ N and over that night eleven aircraft flew night supply drops to the troops already dug in. From 13 June, when bridgehead airstrips had been established, No. 271 began flying into these with supplies and flying casualties out.

It also reverted to its original task of flying squadrons across to their new, French bases. In July it was heavily involved in flying in and out of the beached strips and the Harrows were now formed into the Sparrow Ambulance Flight, commencing regular schedules into B.15 strip. In September came Arnhem (Operation Market) when nineteen Dakotas took off with Horsas to tow over there. Four were lost in bad weather over Oxfordshire but the rest landed successfully. The following day twenty-four Horsas were landed successfully. On 19th a re-supply drop was flown to DZ V but this was already in German hands; two aircraft were lost including the one in which F/Lt Lord won his VC for gallantry in pressing on with a blazing aircraft. Re-supply missions were flown each day and the opposition became fiercer, three aircraft being lost on 21st.

In that month (September) the Sparrow Flight moved to the Continent to enable casevac flights to be flown more expeditiously and support flying to continue as the armies advanced. Thus the pattern continued for the rest of 1944. On New Year's Day the Sparrow Flight was virtually wiped out in the German raids of that morning. The Dakotas were now flying scheduled services to and from the Continent and one or two more Sparrows were found and put into service. In March the Squadron's part in Operation Varsity was to tow twelve Horsa gliders across the Rhine. The remaining Sparrows finally left the Ambulance Flight in April, 1945, Dakotas taking over the task.

With the end of the war in Europe the Squadron began flying to open up routes within the Continent and was detached to Croydon which became an UK terminal for passenger services. By 1946 the Squadron had transferred to Middle East services, mainly Italy and Southern France and these were continued at a lower frequency throughout 1946. On 1 December, 1946 the Squadron was disbanded at Broadwell by re-numbering as No. 77 Squadron.

Bases etc.

Formed at Otranto in September, 1918.

Otranto	Sep 1918—	Dec 1918

Disbanded at Otranto on 9 December, 1918. Re-formed from No. 1680 Flight at Doncaster on 28 March, 1940.

Doncaster, det. Hendon, Errol	Mar 1940—	Feb 1944
Down Ampney, det. Netheravon, Hampstead Norris, Blakehill Farm, B.15, Coulombs, Evere, Northolt, Croydon	Feb 1944—	Aug 1945
Odiham	Aug 1945—	Oct 1945
Broadwell	Oct 1945—	Dec 1946

Disbanded at Broadwell 1 December, 1946 by re-numbering as No. 77 Squadron.

Main Equipment

Short 184 (Sep 1918—Dec 1918)
No serial numbers known
Felixstowe F.3 (Sep 1918—Dec 1918)
No serial numbers known
Handley Page Harrow/Sparrow (Mar 1940—Apr 1945)
K6937, BJ:C; K6949; K6970; K6983, BJ:L; K6984, BJ:E; K6987, BJ:P; K6988, BJ:N; K7009; K7011, BJ:P; K7024; K7031
Bristol Bombay I (May 1940—Jan 1941)
L5817; L5832; L5833; L5853; L5855
Savoia-Marchetti S.M.73P (May 1940—Jun 1940)
OO-AGO; OO-AGS
Handley Page H.P.42 (May 1940—Apr 1941)
AS981; AS982; AS983
Ford Trimotor (May 1940—Nov 1940)
X5000
de Havilland Albatross (Nov 1940—Apr 1942)
AX903; AX904, BJ:W
Lockheed Hudson V (Dec 1941—Apr 1942)
AM816
de Havilland Dominie I (Apr 1942—Feb 1944)
X7351, YS:A; X7378; X7411; X7519
Douglas Dakota III (Aug 1943—Dec 1945)
FD904; FD939; FZ549; FZ601, YS:L; FZ613, YS:Q; FZ628, YS:Y; FZ668, YS:J; KG340, YS:LL; KG358, YS:V; KG378, YS:H; KG515, YS:UP; KG545, YS:KB; KG562, YS:D; KG621, YS:DM
Douglas Dakota IV (Aug 1945—Dec 1946)
KJ866, YS:R; KJ874, YS:F; KJ881, YS:K; KJ910, YS:B; KJ974, YS:F; KK153, YS:D; KN276, YS:C; KN313, YS:Q; KN330, YS:M; YN55S, YS:O; KN625, YS:A; KN662, YS:Q

Commanding Officers

S/Ldr B. V. Robinson	Mar 1940—	Sep 1940
W/Cdr J. N. Glover	Sep 1940—	Mar 1943
W/Cdr K. J. D. Dickson, AFC	Mar 1943—	Sep 1943
W/Cdr M. Booth, DFC, and Bar	Sep 1943—	Jan 1945
Lt. Col J. S. Joubert, AFC	Jan 1945—	Aug 1945
W/Cdr P. Peters, DFC	Aug 1945—	Dec 1946

Aircraft Insignia

The code letter combination 'BJ' was used from *ca* early 1941 onwards on the Squadron's aircraft until the end of 1943 when it was changed to 'YS' although this was never used, as far as is known, on the Harrow/Sparrows.

No. 272 SQUADRON

BADGE
A man in armour, couped at the shoulders
MOTTO
'On, on!'

No. 272 Squadron had a brief and uneventful existence in World War I, being formed at Macrihanish in August, 1918 and equipped with D.H.6s which it used for coastal patrols over the Clyde Estuary and Inner Hebrides. It was disbanded in December, 1918.

It re-formed from a Flight of No. 236 Squadron at Aldergrove on 19 November, 1940 as a coastal fighter/reconnaissance unit with Blenheim IVs. Five days later it began operations with convoy escort duties and lost one aircraft that day. This type of task was the Squadron's main routine over the next few months, an intensive duty with convoys in and out of Liverpool and the Clyde and in February, 1941 234 sorties were flown. In April it moved up to the Shetlands for patrol work but later that month it moved south to Chivenor to convert to Beaufighters which it flew out to the Middle East.

On 29 May the CO flew the first operation from Egypt – the task was similar in that it now flew convoy escort to the ships evacuating Crete. This produced more action and within a few days the Squadron was in combat with Ju 88s. It also began offensive action by strafing oil tanks at Beirut on 3 June. At this stage it was joined by aircrews from 252 Squadron who flew with No. 272 until rebuilding as a separate squadron. Soon it had detachments in Palestine, Cyprus and Malta flying convoy escorts, fighter patrols and recces over a wide area of Mediterranean. At the end of July F/Lt Campbell found five Ju 87s bombing a convoy and shot down two, opening the Squadron's score of enemy aircraft. Airfield strafing came into vogue in the Western Desert, too, with useful results. The Malta detachment also set about airfields in Sicily as well as protecting incoming convoys. Also, when the land battle required it, the Squadron attacked motor transport along the desert roads. On 18 November an especially successful raid took place on Tmimi airfield: an Hs 126 and four SM.79s on the ground were destroyed and five Ju 52s, just taking off, were all shot down; two other Ju 52s were shot down the same day. The Squadron now concentrated on these airfields and destroyed a large number of aircraft, continuing until March, 1942 when it returned to convoy work. This was expanded into attacks on enemy convoys, the Squadron concentrating on the escorting aircraft. After a very busy period on this work the Squadron took a ten day break in June to bring serviceability up to date. Then it was back to Malta convoys, one sortie being disastrous when seven Squadron aircraft were lost due to inadequate fighter direction.

There followed another few weeks of strafing in the Western Desert and then a return to convoy escort work. This continued until November when the whole Squadron moved to Malta. Here it actively attacked airfields in Tunisia and flew patrols in the Cap Bon area to intercept the aircraft flying the Tunis/Sicily channel. The Beaufighters now carried bombs and both shipping and aircraft were attacked, resulting in forty-one aircraft being destroyed, thirty-four damaged and three ships damaged in the month. No. 272 Squadron continued in this vein until February, 1943 when a brief rest was followed by Malta convoy patrols and the beginning of intruder sorties on airfields on the toe of Italy. These took place at night; by day the Squadron resumed offensive shipping sweeps and in April indulged in dive-bombing Lampedusa airfield. It did not come out of these operations unscathed, losing six crews in May.

The Squadron's task now was to provide fighter cover for the convoys landing troops in Sicily and this brought a crop of attacks on Do 18s and He 115s. For these it returned to the African mainland in September, then to Catania the following month. From here and Alghero it roamed far over the convoy routes around Italy and provided anti-Flak escorts for shipping strikes by 39 Squadron. This became a significant task over the next few months, the two

Squadrons often flying as a Wing. In June, 1944 intruders were flown as far north as Florence and Rome; the Squadron was now fitting RPs to its aircraft and the following month used these on anti-shipping *Rovers* to good effect. It also acquired two AI radar equipped Beaufighters for leading night attacks on shipping and enemy airfields. In September it moved to Italy, first as a detachment (which took part in the attack on the *Rex*) and then the whole Squadron moved into Foggia. From here it operated over the Adriatic where coastal shipping became the main target. For example, in November it destroyed fourteen barges, three schooners, one 1400-ton ship and a 13,000-ton motor vessel and damaged many more. This pace was maintained into the New Year, an increasing number of armed recces being flown at night. Final operations came on 18 April and two days later No. 272 moved to Catania where it was disbanded on 30 April, 1945 having destroyed 185½ aircraft, probably destroyed 9, damaged 177, sunk 12 motor vessels over 1000 tons, plus a half-share of the *Rex*, sunk 56 smaller vessels, damaged 318 others, destroyed 12 trains and 832 M/T vehicles.

Bases etc.

Formed in August, 1918 at Machrihanish.

Machrihanish	Aug 1918	Dec 1918

Disbanded at Machrihanish in December, 1918. Re-formed from a Flight of 236 Squadron at Aldergrove on 19 November, 1940

Aldergrove	Nov 1940	Apr 1941
Sumburgh	Apr 1941	Apr 1941
Chivenor	Apr 1941	May 1941
en route to Middle East	May 1941	May 1941
Abu Sueir, det. Maaten Bagush	May 1941	Jun 1941
Edku, det. Nicosia, Lydda, Luqa, Ras Gharib, Gerawla, Tmini, Berka, LG.143, LG.104	Jun 1941	Jul 1942
Khanka	Jul 1942	Jul 1942
Heliopolis	Jul 1942	Jul 1942
Edku, det. Paphos	Jul 1942	Nov 1942
Ta Kali	Nov 1942	Jun 1943
Luqa, det. Gardabia West	Jun 1943	Sep 1943
Bo Rizzo	Sep 1943	Oct 1943
Catania, det. Gibraltar	Oct 1943	Jan 1944
Alghero, det. Reghaia, Borgo, Falconara	Jan 1944	Sep 1944
Foggia, det. Falconara	Sep 1944	Mar 1945
Falconara	Mar 1945	Apr 1945
Catania	Apr 1945	Apr 1945

Disbanded at Catania 30 April, 1945.

Main Equipment

Airco D.H.6 (Aug 1918—Dec 1918)
No serial numbers known
Bristol Blenheim IVF (Nov 1940—Apr 1941)
L9252; L9415; N3526; N3542; P4845; V5754, XK:A
Bristol Beaufighter IC (Apr 1941—Jul 1943)
T3242, T; T3290, A, later B; T3304, H; T3313, R; T4708, P; T4708, P; T4713, G; T4829, V; T4832, U; T4866, X, later L; T4892, T; T4980, F; T4986, C; T5038, V; T5079, G; X7633, K; X7677, Z
Bristol Beaufighter VIC (Nov 1942—Dec 1943)
V8373, B; X8031, S; X8079, M, later K; X8105, S; X8158, G, later M; EL227, X; EL274, T; EL323, M; EL385, D; EL470, C; EL521, H; JL623, U; JL646, L; JL706, N
Bristol Beaufighter XI (Sep 1943—Apr 1944)
JL901, B; JM229, K; JM231, C; JM263, A
Bristol Beaufighter X (Feb 1943—Apr 1945)
JM382, B; JM402, E; LX709, V; LX787, S; LX879, L; LX909, V; LX999, N; LZ121, J; NE491, F; NE544, B; NE732, T; NT891, P; NT971, V; NV120, G; NV203, A; NV270, E; NV388, U; NV470, B; NV499, F; NV568, M; NV586, E; NV609, G; NV620, A; RD165, D

Commanding Officers

S/Ldr A. W. Fletcher, DFC and Bar	Nov 1940	Oct 1941
W/Cdr R. C. Yaxley, DSO, MC, DFC	Oct 1941	Feb 1942
S/Ldr Moggarth	Feb 1942	Feb 1942
S/Ldr Lydall	Feb 1942	Mar 1942
S/Ldr C. V. Ogden	Mar 1942	Sep 1942
W/Cdr J. M. White	Sep 1942	Oct 1942
S/Ldr A. Watson, DSO, DFC	Oct 1942	Nov 1942
W/Cdr J. K. Buchanan, DSO, DFC and Bar	Nov 1942	Jun 1943
W/Cdr W. A. Wild	Jun 1943	Jan 1944
W/Cdr D. H. Lowe	Jan 1944	Sep 1944
W/Cdr G. R. Park, DFC	Sep 1944	Oct 1944
W/Cdr R. N. Lambert, DFC	Nov 1944	Dec 1944

Aircraft Insignia

During its period in the UK the Squadron carried the code letters 'XK' on its aircraft but overseas no markings were carried.

No. 295 SQUADRON

BADGE
A hand manacled and couped at the wrist holding a sword in its scabbard in bend sinister

MOTTO
'In caelo auxilium'
('Help from the skies')

The Squadron was formed on the 3 August, 1942 at Netheravon and immediately began training in dropping paratroops with Whitleys. In October it began a ferry service to Ireland, towing Hotspur gliders to Nutt's Corner and also commenced operations flying *Nickel* raids over France. These continued and the Squadron's first casualty was P/O Wood and crew on 12 December. In the New Year Halifaxes joined the Whitleys and both types flew bombing raids on Distre on 19 February, when two out of fourteen aircraft failed to return. The *Nickel* raids were continued with the Whitleys until May by which time the Squadron was concentrating on airborne exercises. Glider towing on an operational basis was another task the Squadron began at this time and in September the Halifaxes began an overseas ferry service towing gliders but this was short-lived for in October both types were replaced by Albemarles.

It now concentrated on working-up with this new type and began operations on 3 February, 1944. These consisted of supply-drops to the SOE groups in France, eleven sorties being flown that month. These were continued right up to the end of May. In the meantime, the Squadron was also engaged in intensive airborne exercises and collecting Horsas for future operations. These came on the evening of the 5 June when 23 aircraft of No. 295 Squadron took off from Harwell, eleven with paratroops, twelve towing Horsas, to begin the invasion of France. Apart from two gliders, all forces reached their DZs and LZs successfully. The next day nineteen aircraft took a further force of gliders across (one aborting into Ford), then on 7 June two aircraft flew in Operation Cooney dropping SAS men behind the enemy lines to disrupt communications.

No. 295 then returned to SOE drops which were flown with greater regularity, forty-four being made in July; the Squadron also began converting to Stirlings that month. August, 1944 was a good month for No. 295 with 60 SOE drops and 18 sorties on Operation Ditcher, arming the Maquis in Southern France to foil escaping Germans. That month it achieved 87.5% successful drops, the highest in 38 Group. September found the Squadron busy with Operation Market, taking twenty-two gliders to Arnhem on 17th (three releasing prematurely). The following day nineteen re-supply missions were flown, two aircraft, plus one glider, being shot down. On 19th the Flak was so heavy that all seventeen aircraft on re-supply were hit, two had to turn back and one was shot down. Similar results happened on the next two days as the Squadron valiantly tried to support the doomed paratroopers.

In October, 1944 the Squadron moved base and now turned its attention to supply sorties to the Norwegian Resistance forces, returning to its SOE runs over the Continent soon afterwards. These were supplemented in February, 1945 with tactical bombing sorties by night. In March came Operation Varsity, the Rhine crossing; No. 295 contributing thirty Horsa gliders to the attack, one Stirling being lost. For the last few weeks of the war No. 295 was busy dropping supplies to Resistance forces in Holland and

Norway. In May came Operation Doomsday, taking liberating troops to Oslo and Operation Useful bringing back troops and POWs from Brussels. In the immediate peace the Squadron began 'milk run' sorties to and from Brussels and maintained its airborne capability with exercises. In July regular schedules were flown to Brussels, Hamburg, Aldergrove, Oslo and Copenhagen, extending to Prague in August and as far as Mauripur in September. These schedules were flown until 14 January, 1946 when No. 295 Squadron was disbanded at Rivenhall.

The Squadron existed again for two short periods; it re-formed at Tarrant Rushton on 1 February, 1946 with Halifax VIIIs but was disbanded again on 31 March, 1946. It re-formed again at Fairford on 10 September, 1947 with Halifax A.9s and served for a year on airborne duties until disbanding once more on 1 October, 1948.

Bases etc.

Formed at Netheravon on 3 August, 1942.

Netheravon, det. Hurn	Aug 1942—May 1943
Holmesley South	May 1943—Jun 1943
Hurn	Jun 1943—Mar 1944
Harwell, det. Ayr	Mar 1944—Oct 1944
Rivenhall	Oct 1944—Jan 1946

Disbanded at Rivenhall on 14 January, 1946. Re-formed at Tarrant Rushton on 1 February, 1946.

Tarrant Rushton	Feb 1946—Mar 1946

Disbanded at Tarrant Rushton on 31 March, 1946. Re-formed at Fairford on 10 September, 1947.

Fairford	Sep 1947—Oct 1948

Disbanded at Fairford on 1 October, 1948.

Main Equipment

Armstrong-Whitworth Whitley V (Aug 1942—Nov 1943)
BD445; BD497; BD501; BD537, XH:A; BD582, V; EB289, N; EB303, XH:R; EB311; LA790, L; LA793, P; LA823; LA870; LA883, K

Handley Page Halifax V (Feb 1943—Oct 1943)
DG388, WW; DG391, RR; DG396, QQ; DJ989, MM; DJ994, UU; DK124, HH; DK131, VV; EB130, SS; EB139, NN; EB153, AA

Armstrong-Whitworth Albemarle I (Oct 1943—Jul 1944)
P1369; P1397, 8Z:M; P1404, B; P1436, O; P1445; V1601; V1656; V1723, E; V1740, 8Z:A; V1764; V1787; V1809; V1820

Short Stirling IV (Jul 1944—Jan 1946)
LJ884, 8Z:L; LJ890, 8E:L; LJ951, 8E:W; LJ976, 8E:Q; LK129, 8Z:B; LK141, 8E:K; LK246, 8E:X; LK288, 8Z:G; LK300, 8Z:A; LK346, 8Z:H; LK425, 8Z:N; LK439, 8Z:S; LK543, 8Z:K; LK555, 8Z:S; PK226, 8Z:R; PW439, 8E:U

Handley Page Halifax A.7 (Feb 1946—Mar 1946)
NA400

Handley Page Halifax A.9 (Sep 1947—Oct 1948)
RT796; RT898

Commanding Officers

W/Cdr G. P. Marvin	Aug 1942—Mar 1943
W/Cdr B. R. Macnamara	Mar 1943—Sep 1944
W/Cdr H. E. Angell	Sep 1944—Nov 1945
W/Cdr R. N. Stidolph	Nov 1945—Jan 1946

Aircraft Insignia

It is almost certain that the Whitleys originally carried 'XH' code letters but about mid 1943 the Squadron dropped identity markings altogether until early 1944 when two sets of codes were allotted, '8E' and '8Z'. These were used by both Albemarles and Stirlings. It is not believed that the post-war Halifaxes carried any identity markings.

No. 296 SQUADRON

BADGE
In front of a sword in pale, the point downwards, a scroll

MOTTO
'Prepared for all things'

On 25 January, 1942 the Glider Exercise Unit at Ringway was re-named No. 296 Squadron. At first it flew Hawker Harts and Hectors towing Hotspur gliders in the training role and giving air experience to the growing numbers of airborne forces. In June, 1942 it received its first Whitleys and slowly began to work up as an airborne squadron with paradropping and glider-towing exercises. In October it became operational, flying *Nickel* raids over Lille, Paris and other French cities. In November it towed Horsa gliders to move the ground personnel and equipment of No. 168 Squadron from Bottisham to Odiham.

In 1943 the Squadron re-equipped with Albemarles with which it continued the leaflet raids and embarked on some tactical night bombing raids on specific targets. It continued to be a transport unit to Army co-operation squadrons when they moved base and in May the Squadron began *Rebecca* training. June was spent in moving to North Africa where the Squadron flew practice drops in its new environment and also practised towing Waco CG-4A gliders. On 9 July, twenty-five Squadron aircraft set off for Sicily putting seventeen of their gliders into the Landing Zone at Syracuse. Three days later four aircraft dropped a SAS unit into Sicily, one aircraft failing to return (the CO). The following day eight aircraft towed CG-4As to capture a bridge in Sicily and four of them were shot down. It then flew some more *Chestnuts* (SAS drops) until 19th when it reverted to a training role in North Africa. At the end of August it again became operational, dropping dummy paratroops in the heel of Italy for spoofing and in September was employed dropping SAS units at Genoa and Spezia. In addition it flew a mail run into Grottaglie on behalf of the British forces there. On 2 October the Squadron was busily involved with the first daylight paratroop dropping on various DZs on the east coast of Italy after which the Squadron began to transit back to the UK.

After dis-embarkation leave it resumed training and in February, 1944 began dropping to Resistance forces in France right up to D-Day. On 5 June F/Lt Whitty, as pathfinder, and two other aircraft, dropped the 22nd Independent Parachute Coy into Normandy to secure a DZ, followed 30 mins later by eight other aircraft with men of the 5th Para Brigade. Two hours later eight Horsas were taken over with the 6th Landing Brigade. At midday on 6th nineteen aircraft, taking part in Operation Mallard, towed nineteen Horsas to Caen with the 6th Airborne Division, followed the next day by four aircraft dropping the French 4th Para Brigade in the Brest Peninsula. The assault having been successful 296 returned to drops to SOE groups behind the lines for a couple of months then began marshalling Horsa gliders to Manston for Operation Market.

This took place on 17 September and No. 296 towed twenty Horsas and seven CG-4As to Arnhem, followed up the following day by another nineteen Horsas. October was spent converting to Halifaxes, ferrying Horsas and delivering the Albemarles to 22 Heavy Glider Conversion Unit. Operations were resumed in December with more SOE drops.

These were continued spasmodically in the New Year and in addition the Squadron began flying transport sorties to the Middle East and indulging in tactical bombing over the Ruhr. The Rhine crossing came in March, thirty of the Squadron's aircraft taking part

without loss or trouble. After this SOE drops continued until the war was over. Then followed general transport flights, principally to Norway, Belgium and Denmark. These were eventually expanded as far afield as Greece and India but on 23 January, 1946 it came to an end with the Squadron's disbandment at Earl's Colne.

Bases etc.

Formed at Ringway on 25 January, 1942 out of the Glider Exercise Unit.

Ringway	Jan 1942	Feb 1942
Netheravon, det. Hurn	Feb 1942	Aug 1942
Hurn	Aug 1942	Oct 1942
Andover	Oct 1942	Dec 1942
Hurn	Dec 1942	Jun 1943
Froha	Jun 1943	Jun 1943
Goubrine II, det. Cassibile, Torrente Communelli	Jun 1943	Oct 1943
Hurn, det. Ayr	Nov 1943	Mar 1944
Brize Norton	Mar 1944	Sep 1944
Earl's Colne	Sep 1944	Jan 1946

Disbanded at Earl's Colne on 23 January, 1946.

Main Equipment

Hawker Hector I (Jan 1942—Aug 1942)
K8099; K8112; K8146; K8154; K9689; K9696; K9711; K9727; K9746; K9757; K9768; K9781
Hawker Hart T (Jan 1942—Aug 1942)
K5819; K5861; K6467; K6476; K6478; K6534
Armstrong-Whitworth Whitley V (Jun 1942—Apr 1943)
Z9228, W; BD415, C; BD422, K; BD436, H; BD493, A; BD531, C; BD541, J; EB298, N; EB304, B; EB312, A; LA828
Armstrong-Whitworth Albemarle I (Jan 1943—Oct 1944)
P1373, C; P1389, AE, later K; P1427, AA; P1434, G; P1446, PM; P1468, D; P1474, V; P1501, W; P1528, AF; P1551, B; V1630, T; V1695, R; V1704, C; V1739, J; V1785, N1; V1813, L1; V1821, D; V1866, C1; V1699, 9W:H
Handley Page Halifax V (Oct 1944—Mar 1945)
LL278, 9W:R; LL278; LL325; LL330, 9W:N; LL384; LL411, 9W:X; LL441, 9W:N
Handley Page Halifax III (Feb 1945—Jan 1946)
LV691, 7C:P; LW446; MZ688, 9W:Y; NA129, 7C:M; NA290, :B; NA613, 9W:J; NA614, 7C:K; NA657, 7C:S; NA686, 9W:P; NA700, 9W:D

Commanding Officers

S/Ldr P. B. N. Davis	Jan 1942	Oct 1942
W/Cdr P. R. May, AFC	Oct 1942	Jul 1943
W/Cdr L. C. Bartram	Jul 1943	Aug 1943
W/Cdr D. I. McInnies	Aug 1943	Oct 1944
S/Ldr R. W. Jamieson	Oct 1944	Feb 1945
W/Cdr T. C. Musgrave	Feb 1945	Jan 1946

Aircraft Insignia

It is not known what identity markings, if any, were carried by the unit until the advent of the Albemarles. These at first carried no such markings but on return from North Africa started carrying code letters '9W' and, presumably, '7C' as well although the latter are not confirmed on this type. Both letter combinations were used on the Halifaxes.

No. 297 SQUADRON

(No badge authorised)

The Squadron was formed on the 22 January, 1942 from the Parachute Exercise Squadron at Netheravon. It was initially equipped with Tiger Moths but Whitleys arrived in February and these were used for paratroop training duties. These grew in intensity followed by more realistic airborne exercises and by October the Squadron became operational, flying leaflet raids over Northern France by night. About twenty such sorties were flown a month then in February, 1943 the Squadron began night bombing on a tactical basis. In April, 1943 the Squadron began using gliders for transport work, taking ground personnel and equipment of bomber squadrons from one base to another. Such flying was the pattern over the next few months until August when conversion to Albemarles began.

In September, 1943 the Squadron used its Whitleys for a paradrop when, on the 2nd, they placed the 12th Commando at St. Valerie en Caux. From then on, however, it was more and more airborne exercises. In February, 1944 the Squadron began operational dropping sorties to SOE groups until 5 June, 1944. That night four Albemarles set out for the east bank of the River Orne near Caen where they dropped the 22nd Independent Para Coy, then nine aircraft dropped troops and containers on the same DZ. After this nine Horsas were towed across. The next day (D-Day) twenty Horsas were towed to the same DZ, now turned into a LZ, one Albemarle being lost. On 7th two aircraft dropped French troops to contact the Resistance (Operation Cooney). This done the Squadron returned to SOE drops in greater intensity until September when the Squadron took two trains of Horsas to Arnhem on 16th and 18th but did not enter into the re-supply flying. It moved at the end of the month and began conversion to Halifaxes.

With these No. 297 resumed operations in February, 1945 flying more SOE sorties and some night tactical bombing behind the German lines. The final mass airlift of World War II was Operation Varsity on 24 March when the Squadron towed thirty Horsas to LZ P over the Rhine. SOE drops continued in April then in May the Squadron was busy flying troops into Norway and Denmark. These were followed by establishing scheduled runs to the various liberated capitals. In November, 1945 it began route flying to India and remained on this task as well as keeping in training on airborne duties as one of the few, peacetime, airborne units.

At the end of 1948 No. 297 converted to the Handley Page Hastings and used this type on the Berlin airlift, being detached to Schleswigland for this purpose. Soon after the airlift was over the Squadron was disbanded on 15 November, 1950 at Topcliffe.

Bases etc.

Formed at Netheravon on 22 January, 1942 from the Parachute Exercise Squadron.

Netheravon	Jan 1942—Jun 1942
Hurn	Jun 1942—Oct 1942
Thruxton	Oct 1942—Aug 1943
Stoney Cross	Aug 1943—Mar 1944
Brize Norton	Mar 1944—Sep 1944
Earl's Colne	Sep 1944—Mar 1946
Brize Norton	Mar 1946— 1948
Fairford	1948—Oct 1948
Dishforth	Oct 1948—Dec 1948
Schleswigland	Dec 1948—Nov 1949
Topcliffe	Nov 1949—Nov 1950

Disbanded at Topcliffe on 15 November, 1950.

Main Equipment

de Havilland Tiger Moth II (Jan 1942—Mar 1942)
  N5445; T5608; T5974; T7848; DE158; DE251; DE303

Armstrong Whitworth Whitley V (Feb 1942—Sep 1943)
  Z9218; Z9313; Z9319; Z9431; AD670; BD199; BD211; BD294; BD421; BD440; BD560; BD668; EB293, P; LA872, S; LA940, V
Armstrong-Whitworth Albemarle I (Aug 1943—Nov 1944)
  P1399, A; P1409, E; P1471, P5:N; P1626, Y; P1645, Z; V1700, W; V1716, Y; V1772, R; V1812, B; V1823, P5:S; V1845, J; V1860, L
Handley Page Halifax V (Sep 1944—Feb 1945)
  LK988, H; LL217, P5:M; LL275, P5:Z; LL295, W; LL309, P5:L; LL331, P5:V; LL412, P5:G
Handley Page Halifax III (Feb 1945—Feb 1946)
  LW467, L5:U; LK848, P5:K; MZ569, L5:N; MZ637; MZ745; MZ973, P5:L; NA104, L5:V; NA128, P5:J; MA141, P5:N; NA294, L5:J; NA673, P5:C; NA688, L5:X
Handley Page Halifax A.7 (Dec 1945— 1947)
  NA400, L5:L; NA461
Handley Page Halifax A.9 (1947—Oct 1948)
  RT762, Z; RT875; RT992A
Handley Page Hastings C.1 (Oct 1948—Nov 1950)
  TG514, C; TG572, F; TG586, B; TG601, T; TG605, A; TG607, V; TG609, Z

Commanding Officers

W/Cdr B. A. Oakley	Jan 1942—Apr 1942
W/Cdr R. B. Wardman	Apr 1942—Feb 1943
W/Cdr G. F. Donaldson, AFC	Feb 1043—Aug 1943
W/Cdr R. W. G. Kitley	Aug 1943—Nov 1943
W/Cdr P. B. M. Davis	Nov 1943—Dec 1943
W/Cdr J. G. Minifie	Dec 1943—Sep 1944
W/Cdr J. R. Grice	Sep 1944—Dec 1944
W/Cdr E. G. Dean	Dec 1944— 1946

Aircraft Insignia

Markings up to the end of 1943 are not known. It is believed that the code letter combination 'P5' was used then and the additional combination 'L5' came into use in 1944. These were both retained until the advent of the Halifax A.9 in 1947 after which no markings were carried.

No. 298 SQUADRON

BADGE
A hand holding a dagger in bend sinister
thrusting to the dexter
MOTTO
'Silent we strike'

The Squadron was originally formed at Thruxton on 24 August, 1942 with Whitleys. This was a false start, however, and it was disbanded again on 19 October, 1942. It did not re-form again until a year later, on 4 November, 1943 at Tarrant Rushton with Halifax Vs, from A Flight of No. 295 Squadron. It immediately began working up for the Second Front, carrying out Hamilcar towing exercises, paradropping and successive exercises. On 29 February, 1944 it became operational with container drops to SOE forces in France. These continued for the next few months but in June, 1944 it was involved in the airborne landings in Normandy. On the evening of 5th it flew Operation Coup de Main with three Horsa tows to France, followed by 'Tonga', towing fifteen Horsas and two Hamilcars, taking off at 0100 on 6th and landing back at 0500 hrs. One Halifax was shot down and two Horsas fell off en route, otherwise all went well. This was immediately followed up by 'Mallard' when fifteen Hamilcars and one Horsa were taken across the Channel; the gliders arrived safely but one Halifax ditched on the return. On 10 June three aircraft dropped Jeeps by parachute to the troops below then the Squadron returned to SOE work apart from some Hamilcar retrieving trips from France in July. In addition to 147 SOE sorties in August six Hadrians were towed to a LZ at Lorient on the 5th; three crews were lost that month. In September the Squadron took part in the Arnhem drops taking seven Hamilcars and thirteen Horsas on the first day (17th) and eight of each on 18th. On 19th another ten Horsas were safely delivered then the Squadron returned to night SOE drops once more.

This remained the Squadron's task until supplemented with tactical bombing in January, 1945. On 24 March the Squadron was active in Operation Varsity towing six Horsas and twenty-five Hamilcars for the Rhine crossing. Five Hamilcars dropped off en route and one Halifax was shot down over the target. The Squadron returned to dropping containers to agents until the war ended when it began flying troops into Oslo and out of Brussels, with POWs returning home. In June it started a protracted move to India to join No. 1341 Flight. It began various route schedules, including the 'Hump' route to China, and also maintained an airborne support role for the Army in India. This became its sole task in January, 1946, the route flying ceasing. It worked with the 2nd Indian Airborne Division, then in March it spent a month at Meiktela flying Operation Hunger II dropping rice supplies to starving tribes in the jungle. It carried one thousand tons of rice in one month. Later that year it took part in mass airborne exercises at Quetta. Towards the end of the year its establishment was reduced and on 30 December, 1946 it was disbanded at Mauripur.

Bases etc.

Formed at Thruxton on 24 August, 1942.

Thruxton	Aug 1942—Oct 1942

Disbanded at Thruxton on 19 October, 1942. Re-formed at Tarrant Rushton on 4 November, 1943.

Tarrant Rushton	Nov 1943—Mar 1945
Woodbridge	Mar 1945—Mar 1945
Tarrant Rushton	Mar 1945—Jun 1945
Raipur, det. Akyab, Alipore	Jun 1945—Dec 1945
Digri, det. Negombo, Chaklala, Meiktela	Dec 1945—May 1946
Baroda	May 1946—Jul 1946
Mauripur, det. Risalpur	Jul 1946—Dec 1946

Disbanded at Mauripur on 30 December, 1946.

Main Equipment

Armstrong Whitworth Whitley V (Aug 1942—Oct 1942)
  EB285; EB287; EB337

Handley Page Halifax V (Nov 1943—Oct 1944)
DG384, TT; DG388, KK; DJ993, X; DK197, XX; DK199, SS;
EB159, EE; LK651, JJ, later 8I:F; LK966, 8A:C; LK988, CC,
later 8A:C; LL129, NN; LL147, BB, later 8T:O; LL198, D;
LL273, VV, later 8T:Y; LL302, DD; LL336, 8A:V; LL353, 8A:L;
LL361, 8T:F
Handley Page Halifax III (Oct 1944—May 1945)
MZ955, 8T:F; MZ970, 8A:P; MZ979, 8A:V; MZ989, 8T:J;
NA103, 8T:M; NA116, 8A:W; NA146, 8A:V; NA163, 8T:A;
NA296, 8T:N; NA613, 8A:Z; NA667, 8T:C
Handley Page Halifax VII (May 1945—Dec 1946)
NA310, 8A:M; NA341, 8A:L; NA408, 8A:O; NA465, R; PN245, Y;
PN252, BB; PN258, M; PN260, V; PN266, K; PN292, O; PP372, W

Commanding Officers

S/Ldr L. C. Bartram	Sep 1942—Sep 1942
S/Ldr C. H. Briggs	Nov 1943—Dec 1943
W/Cdr D. H. Duder, DSO, DFC	Dec 1943—Jan 1945
W/Cdr H. Law-Wright, DSC, DFC	Jan 1945—Apr 1945
W/Cdr Stewart, DFC	Apr 1945— 1945
W/Cdr A. G. Norman, DFC	1945—Jan 1946
W/Cdr W. G. Gardiner, DFC, AFC	Mar 1946—Dec 1946

Aircraft Insignia

No markings were carried to identify the Squadron until 29 May, 1944 when the letters '8A' were allotted to 'A' Flight and '8T' to 'B' Flight. These were retained until the Squadron moved to India in June, 1945 when markings were dropped once more.

No. 299 SQUADRON

(No badge authorised)

On 4 November, 1943 the Squadron was formed at Stoney Cross from C Flight of No. 297 Squadron. It initially flew Lockheed Ventures but in January, 1944 began to convert to Stirling IVs in the airborne role. It worked up intensively and on 5 April flew its first operations: drops to SOE agents in France. These were continued until early June when the Squadron was readied for D-Day. It flew twenty-three aircraft in Operation Tonga dropping paratroops on the night of 5th; seven were hit by Flak and one failed to return. Operation Mallard followed on D-Day itself, the Squadron towing sixteen Horsas across the Channel; again one Stirling was shot down, and two Horsas released prematurely. Re-supply drops were flown on 8 and 10 June (Operation Robroy) then No. 299 built up its SOE operations until in August 195 sorties were flown in the month.

The Squadron was heavily involved in Operation Market (Arnhem) taking twenty-five Horsas on the first day, twenty-two on the second and seven on the third, with seventeen re-supply sorties also flown that day. Fierce opposition was encountered and three crews, including the CO, were shot down in flames. After a day's break eleven missions were flown with one crew lost on 21st and fourteen on 23rd, one aircraft crash-landing.

299 Squadron then re-couped and returned to agent supply sorties at night over Holland and Norway into the New Year. Most of these operations were mail runs but some were non-scheduled 'Specials'. The Squadron's existence came to a close on 15 February, 1946 when No. 299 disbanded at Shepherd's Grove.

Bases etc.

Formed at Stoney Cross on 4 November, 1943.

Stoney Cross	Nov 1943—Mar 1944
Keevil	Mar 1944—Oct 1944
Wethersfield	Oct 1944—Jan 1945
Gosfield	Jan 1945—Jan 1945
Shepherd's Grove	Jan 1945—Feb 1946

Disbanded at Shepherd's Grove on 15 February, 1946.

Main Equipment

Lockheed Ventura I, II (Nov 1943—Jan 1944)
AE733, A
Short Stirling IV (Mar 1944—Feb 1946)
EE996, X9:F, later 5G:T; EF272, 5G:N; EF321, X9:A; EF323, 5G:F;
EH950, X9:E; LJ572, X9:T; LJ594, 5G:L; LJ669, 5G:M;
LJ821, 5G:G; LJ879, 5G:W; LJ893, 5G:Y; LJ942, X9:I;
LJ996, X9:N; LK124, X9:B; LK153, 5G:O; LK239, X9:C;
LK284, 5G:V; LK428, X9:G; LK439, 5G:J; LK544, 5G:L;
PJ609, 5G:I; PW443, 5G:Q; PW448, X9:P

Commanding Officers

W/Cdr R. W. G. Kitley	Nov 1943—Dec 1943
W/Cdr P. B. N. Davis, DSO	Dec 1943—Sep 1944
W/Cdr C. B. R. Colenso, DFC	Sep 1944—Dec 1944
W/Cdr P. N. Jennings	Dec 1944—Sep 1945
W/Cdr R. N. Stidolph	Sep 1945—Nov 1945

Aircraft Insignia

From soon after receiving its Stirlings the Squadron carried two sets of code letters, 'X9' and '5G'. They both remained in use until the Squadron was disbanded in 1946.

No. 301 SQUADRON

(No badge authorised)

The Squadron stated its existence as the second bomber squadron in the RAF formed from Polish personnel. It was formed at Bramcote on 22 July, 1940 and began night bombing operations with Wellingtons from Swinderby in September.

For two and a half years it flew continually on this task but on 7 April, 1943 it was disbanded, its personnel being dispersed to No. 300 and No. 305 Squadrons and a proportion going to No. 138 Squadron for Special Duties.

On 7 November, 1944, however, No. 1586 (Polish) (Special Duties) Flight, based at Brindisi, was re-numbered No. 301 Squadron. It was equipped with Halifaxes and was engaged in flying supplies to the Polish Home Army and resistance groups in other countries, principally Crete, Northern Italy and Yugoslavia. It also acquired Liberators and flew these alongside the Halifaxes. In December 71 sorties were flown of which 35 were known to be successful. January's weather prevented most operations but in

February no fewer than 86 trips were flown by the Squadron for the loss of one Liberator. This was the end of No. 301s operations, though and in March the personnel returned to the UK, leaving the aircraft in Italy.

The Squadron re-constituted at Blackbushe in April and began working up as a transport squadron with Warwick IIIs. Its first freight trip was to Gardermoen, Oslo on 22 June, 1945. The next month it moved to North Weald and on 21st began freight schedules to Oslo, Istres and Athens. The Warwick unfortunately was having engine troubles and during August the Squadron had aircraft forced-landed in Denmark, France and Italy. Another move took place in September and the aircraft were grounded for eleven days. In October only thirteen route flights were flown but the rate increased to 41 in November although three aircraft were written off in the process. This manner of operation went on until January, 1946 when No. 301 started converting to Halifax C.8s. It began route-flying with these in March but in April the Polish squadrons were restricted to flights within the UK only. Eventually the Squadron was disbanded on 10 December, 1946.

Bases etc.

Re-formed at Brindisi out of No. 1586 (Polish) (Special Duties) Flight on 7 November, 1944.

Brindisi, det. Rosignano	Nov 1944	Mar 1945
en route to UK	Mar 1945	Apr 1945
Blackbushe	Apr 1945	Jul 1945
North Weald	Jul 1945	Sep 1945
Chedburgh	Sep 1945	Dec 1946

Disbanded at Chedburgh 10 December, 1946.

Main Equipment

Handley Page Halifax II and II Srs. 1A (Nov 1944—Mar 1945)
BB440, GR:G; JN898, GR:K; JP231, GR:A; JP252, GR:L;
LL118, GR:C; LL359, GR:B; LL534, GR:M
Consolidated Liberator VI (Nov 1944—Mar 1945)
BZ965, GR:V; KG834, GR:U; KG994, GR:R; KH151, GR:S;
TW766, GR:F; TW769, GR:X

Vickers Warwick C.3 (May 1945—Jan 1946)
HG226, GR:S; HG275, GR:S; HG281, GR:C; HG296, GR:B;
HG298, GR:M; HG327, GR:H
Handley Page Halifax C.8 (Jan 1946—Dec 1946)
PP218, GR:F; PP225, GR:W; PP324, GR:V; PP332, GR:A;
PP335, GR:G; PP342, GR:A

Commanding Officers

S/Ldr K. Kaczmarczyk	Nov 1944—	1945
W/Cdr E. Arcuszkiewicz	1945—May 1945	
W/Cdr T. Pozyczka	May 1945—Dec 1946	

Aircraft Insignia

The aircraft carried the code letters 'GR' throughout No. 301 Squadron's service.
(See also *Bomber Squadrons of the RAF*, p. 225)

No. 304 SQUADRON

(No badge authorised)

No. 304 Squadron had formed in Bomber Command as the third Polish squadron in that Command. Formation had taken place at Bramcote on 22 August, 1940 and the Squadron began operating over the Continent at night in April, 1941. Just over a year later, on 7 May, 1942, it transferred to Coastal Command. Here it was based at Tiree in the Hebrides equipped with Wellington ICs with which it began anti-submarine sweeps. Before the month was out S/Ldr Buczma had bombed a suspected U-boat wake and Sgt Jonski had ditched successfully. The following month F/Lt Hirsz damaged a U-boat with his depth-charges before the Squadron moved to South Wales from where A/S sweeps were resumed, resulting in two U-boat attacks and a combat with an Arado Ar 196 in July. Ninety-two sorties were flown in August, all A/S except for a seven aircraft attack by night on shipping at La Pallice; night A/S sweeps were also begun that month. September saw another U-boat attacked; now the Squadron aircraft were being attacked by Ju 88s, at first without losses, although one crew was lost the following month and one in November.

U-boat attacks continued into 1943, Sgt Bakanacz attacking two on one sortie on 5 January. Sortie rate kept up to 70 or 80 per month as the Squadron maintained patrols over Biscay and the Western Approaches. On 26 March the Squadron was able to claim Sgt Targwski's U-boat as its first confirmed destruction (after nine previous attacks) and within ten days two more attacks had been made. Many moves took place in 1943 but still the main emphasis was on the SW Approaches. That summer No. 304 had a bad patch in which six aircraft were lost in two months. In October the Squadron began working up on Leigh Lights (it now had Wellington XIVs) and from then on it flew almost all sorties at night. Sorties went over the hundred per month in February, 1944 with approximately two U-boat attacks each month – hardly ever was it possible to see the results at night though.

As the invasion of Normandy approached the Squadron concentrated on preventing U-boats transitting the Channel and five attacks were made in May-June, one of which resulted in the destruction of a U-boat on 18 June. The pressure was maintained until September when the Squadron returned to the Hebrides. From here it turned its attention to the North Atlantic and the convoys coming into Liverpool and the Clyde, flying longer sorties but still finding U-boats. Through the winter of 1944—45 this was its pattern then in March, 1945 it moved to Cornwall from where its last operations in Coastal Command were flown on 30 May. The Squadron had flown 2,439 sorties in Coastal Command, made 61 U-boat attacks, had 15 air combats and operationally lost 18 aircraft.

It now changed over to sonobuoy-equipped Wellingtons but within a month or two transferred to 301 Wing, Transport Command, settling in at North Weald in July, 1945. Here it re-equipped with Warwick IIIs and had a protracted work-up on this type

beginning operations in December with special flights to Italy. In January, 1946 No. 304 began regular freight flights to Naples and Athens but in April the Polish squadrons were restricted to flights within the UK only. In May it converted to Halifax C.8s. No. 304 Squadron was disbanded on 10 December, 1946.

Bases etc.

Transferred to Coastal Command duties at Tiree on 7 May, 1942.

Tiree	May 1942	Jun 1942
Dale	Jun 1942	Nov 1942
Talbenny	Nov 1942	Dec 1942
Dale	Dec 1942	Apr 1943
Docking, det. Dale, Davidstow Moor, Thorney Island	Apr 1943	Jun 1943
Davidstow Moor	Jun 1943	Feb 1944
Chivenor	Feb 1944	Sep 1944
Benbecula, det. Limavady	Sep 1944	Mar 1945
St. Eval	Mar 1945	Jul 1945
North Weald	Jul 1945	Sep 1945
Chedburgh	Sep 1945	Dec 1946

Disbanded at Chedburgh 10 December, 1946.

Main Equipment

Vickers Wellington IC (May 1942—May 1943)
R1230, E; R1413; R1657; R1704; W5718; Z1072; Z1112; DV558;
DV594; DV671; DV781; DV920; HF836, E; HF894, A; HX384
Vickers Wellington X (Feb 1943—Aug 1943)
HE304; HE576; HZ577
Vickers Wellington XIII (Jul 1943—Sep 1943)
HZ551; HZ573; HZ635; HZ698; HZ700; HZ723; HZ762
Vickers Wellington XIV (Sep 1943—Jan 1946)
HF121, 2:V; HF188, 2:A; HF202, 2:G; HF268, 2:U; HF330, 2:N,
later QD:N; HF386, 2:W; HF419, 2:D; HF451, 2:S, later QD:S;
MP721, QD:A2; NB767, 2:L, later QD:L; NC178, QD:G;
NC830, QD:U; NC888, QD:D; NC907, QD:N; PF821, QD:W
Vickers Warwick C.3 (Aug 1945—May 1946)
HG233, QD:A; HG276, QD:Q; HG298, QD:T; HG306, QD:Y;
HG335, QD:H; HG340, QD:M
Handley Page Halifax C.8 (May 1946—Dec 1946)
PP232; PP270, QD:G; PP293, QD:H

Commanding Officers

W/Cdr S. Poziomek	May 1942	Jul 1942
W/Cdr K. Czetowicz	Jul 1942	Jan 1943
W/Cdr M. Pronaszko	Jan 1943	Nov 1943
W/Cdr C. Korbut	Nov 1943	Apr 1944
W/Cdr J. M. Kranc	Apr 1943	Jan 1945
W/Cdr S. J. Zurek	Jan 1945	Oct 1945
W/Cdr W. J. Piotrowski	Oct 1945	Dec 1946

Aircraft Insignia

It is not known what squadron identity markings were carried by No. 304 Squadron from its entry into Coastal Command until late in 1943. It then carried the identity number '2' at least during its stay at Chivenor, until mid 1944 when it was allocated the code letters 'QD' which it used until disbandment.
(See also *Bomber Squadrons of the RAF*, p. 226)

No. 309 SQUADRON

(No badge authorised)

This Squadron was formed from Polish personnel at Abbotsinch on 8 October, 1940 in the army co-operation role. It was equipped with Lysander IIIs and worked up slowly, beginning to exercise with the Polish Army in Scotland, specifically with the 10th Polish Armoured Brigade from September onwards. In November, 1941 it was declared operational.

In August, 1942 the Squadron converted to Mustangs and at the end of 1942 sent a detachment to Gatwick for operations, flying PRs of the French coast and *Rhubarbs*. In January, 1943 it began regular convoy patrols along the Scottish coast and after moving south in June, 1943 began operating *Lagoon*'s along the Dutch coast, flying fifty-two sorties during July. This increased to sixty-eight in August, mostly *Jim Crows* and *Lagoons* but after this operations tailed off and in January, 1944 its aircraft were grounded because of engine failures. At this point it was decided that No. 309 would transfer to Fighter Command where it was equipped first with Hurricanes and later with Mustang IIIs which it flew on long-range bomber escort missions. It was eventually disbanded at Coltishall on 6 January, 1947.

Bases etc.

Formed at Abbotsinch on 8 October, 1940.

Abbotsinch	Oct 1940—Nov 1940
Renfrew, det. Scone	Nov 1940—May 1941
Dunino	May 1941—Nov 1942
Findo Gask, det. Gatwick, Peterhead	Nov 1942—Mar 1943
Kirknewton, det. Peterhead	Mar 1943—Jun 1943
Snailwell	Jun 1943—Nov 1943
Wellingore	Nov 1943—Nov 1943
Snailwell	Nov 1943—Feb 1944

Transferred to Fighter Command ca February, 1944.

Main Equipment

Westland Lysander III (Oct 1940—May 1941)
T1423; T1425; T1468; T1521; T1523; T1550; T1572
Westland Lysander IIIA (May 1941—Aug 1942)
V9314, V; V9425; V9435; V9503; V9608
North American Mustang I (Aug 1942—Feb 1944)
AG423, L; AG435, D; AG561, K; AG628, M; AG648, E; AL964, N; AM119, H; AM165, P; AM221, A; AP217, F; AP249, T

Commanding Officers

W/Cdr N. W. F. Mason	Oct 1940—Nov 1941
W/Cdr Z. Pistl	Nov 1941—Feb 1943
W/Cdr W. J. Piotrowski	Feb 1943—Oct 1943
W/Cdr M. Piotrowski	Oct 1943—Feb 1944

Aircraft Insignia

From formation to 1943 the letters 'AR' were carried. Thereafter no markings were carried on the Mustangs. On transferring to Fighter Command the Squadron used 'WC'.
(See also *Fighter Squadrons of the RAF*, p. 395)

No. 311 SQUADRON

BADGE
A thresher and a morning star in saltire, the hafts fracted

MOTTO
'Na mnozstvi nehledte'
('Never regard their numbers')

A combination of these ancient weapons was successfully used by the Czechs in the past and was considered suitable as a badge.

No. 311 Squadron was formed from Czech personnel at Honington on 29 July, 1940 as a bomber unit flying Wellingtons in 3 Group, Bomber Command and commencing night operations in September. It continued on this task until April, 1942 when it transferred to Coastal Command at Aldergrove.

Here it worked up in the coastal role becoming operational on 22 May with an A/S sweep by five aircraft. In June it moved to South Wales and, apart from a brief return to bomber operations for the '1000 bomber' raid on Bremen on 25 June, the Squadron continued on maritime tasks, flying 83 sorties in July. On 11th Sgt Dostal's crew had a fight with a Ju 88 which they damaged but four days later the same crew failed to return from ops. However, on that day, 15 July, F/O Baba found a U-boat, attacked and destroyed it. Before the month was out another U-boat had been attacked and a combat with two Arado Ar 196s had resulted in one almost certainly being shot down. In August six U-boats were attacked, one damaged and one probably sunk but two Wellingtons were lost. The pace continued until the autumn weather cut down operations in October. By now interceptions by Ju 88s were frequent, sometimes with packs of up to eight aircraft, the Wellingtons generally giving as good as they received in combat.

In 1943 the Squadron began turning its attention to surface ships as well as submarines with a bombing raid on Bordeaux in January and attacks on ships in Biscay subsequently. These were made at night and were attempts to catch blockade runners. But U-boats were still the main target; in June Liberators replaced the Wellingtons and after two months conversion first Liberator operations were on 21 August when the CO (W/Cdr Br Breitcetl went missing on an A/S patrol. These Liberators were equipped with rocket projectiles which were first used by F/O Irving on a U-boat on 27 September. On 10 November another submarine was successfully attacked and sunk with them by F/Sgt Zanta and crew. At the end of December P/O Dolzal found the blockade runner *Alsterufer* and sank it.

The Squadron intensified its anti-submarine activities in 1944, concentrating on the western end of the Channel and flew 131 sorties in the June period. In August it moved north having attacked six U-boats and made three shipping attacks up till then in 1944. It now turned its attention to the Norwegian coastal shipping encountering fierce Flak which shot down one Liberator and damaged two others. No. 311 then engaged in training to make Schnorchel attacks; it also had a bad period with three fatal take-off crashes at the end of the year. It was not until March, 1945 that the Squadron was operating successfully once more and in that month five U-boats and several surface vessels were attacked. In April 92 sorties were flown off Norway and 82 in May, W/O Benes finishing off No. 311s war by destroying a U-boat on 5th. After VE-Day it escorted surrendered U-boats to ports. The following month it transferred to Transport Command and, fittingly, opened up the routes to Czechoslovakia once more. It disbanded from the RAF at Milltown on 15 February, 1946.

Bases etc.

Transferred to Coastal Command on 30 April, 1942 at Aldergrove.

Aldergrove	Apr 1942—Jun 1942
Talbenny	Jun 1942—May 1943
Beaulieu	May 1943—Feb 1944
Predannack	Feb 1944—Jun 1945
Milltown	Jun 1945—Feb 1946

Disbanded at Milltown on 15 February, 1946.

Main Equipment

Vickers Wellington IC (Apr 1942—Jun 1943)
R1147, Q; R1155, F; R1497, D; R1531, M; R1600, T; T2564, T;

W5711, G; X9664, K; X9745, S; X9827, F; DV477, G; DV507, W; DV664, A; DV738, C; DV799, Z; DV886, X; HD988, U; HE113, B; HF859, R

Consolidated Liberator V (Jun 1943—Feb 1945)
BZ763, O; BZ775, G; BZ787, E; BZ795, H; BZ872, E; BZ882, Q

Consolidated Liberator VI (Feb 1945—Feb 1946)
EV943, PP:F; KG867

Commanding Officers

W/Cdr Snajdr, DFC	Apr 1942—Jan 1943
W/Cdr J. Breitcetl, DFC	Jan 1943—Aug 1943
W/Cdr V. Nedved, MBE, DFC	Aug 1943—Jan 1944
W/Cdr J. Sejbl, DFC	Jan 1944—Aug 1944
W/Cdr J. Kostohryz, DSO	Aug 1944—Feb 1946

Aircraft Insignia

It is not known whether the Squadron retained the code letters 'KX' which it had used on its Wellingtons in Bomber Command during its Coastal service. It is fairly certain that at first no insignia was carried on the Liberators but in 1945—46 the code letters 'PP' were used.
(See also *Bomber Squadrons of the RAF*, pp. 227–8)

No. 318 SQUADRON

.(No badge authorised)

No. 318 Squadron was formed of Polish personnel on 20 March, 1943 at Detling as a tactical recce unit and was given Hurricane I aircraft to work up in this role. This continued until August when the Squadron moved to Egypt and re-equipped with Hurricane IIBs. Here it worked up with the Polish Army, specifically with the II Corps, for the rest of the year. The work-up was prolonged into 1944 and morale dropped with no action. However, in May, 1944 the Squadron moved to Italy with Spitfires, flying its first operations under 208 Squadron's guidance on 2 May.

This was what the Squadron needed and by the end of the month it had flown 326 tactical recce sorties. This was but a start and in the next few months the Squadron was flying very intensively on artillery observation, tactical recce and sweeps over the battlefield, topping the 500 sorties a month in August. Losses were surprisingly low and the pressure was kept up into the winter although the shorter hours and bad weather reduced operations to some extent.

With the spring of 1945 the Squadron again opened up, moving forward with the advancing armies until VE-Day brought an end to hostilities. Thereafter No. 318 Squadron remained in Italy until 16 August, 1946 when the personnel left for the UK without aircraft; the Squadron was disbanded at Coltishall on 31 August, 1946.

Bases etc.

Formed at Detling on 20 March, 1943.

Detling, det. Weston Zoyland, Snailwell	Mar	1943—Aug 1943
en route to Egypt	Aug	1943—Sep 1943
Muquebeila	Sep	1943—Oct 1943
Gaza	Oct	1943—Apr 1944
Amriya	Apr	1944—Apr 1944
Madna	Apr	1944—May 1944
Trigno	May	1944—Jun 1944
San Vito, det. Torturetto	Jun	1944—Jul 1944
Fermo	Jul	1944—Jul 1944
Falconara, det. Castiglione	Jul	1944—Aug 1944
Chiaravalle, det. Malignano	Aug	1944—Aug 1944
Piagiolino	Aug	1944—Sep 1944
Cassandro	Sep	1944—Sep 1944
Rimini	Sep	1944—Nov 1944
Bellaria	Nov	1944—Feb 1945
Forli	Feb	1945—May 1945
La Russia	May	1945—May 1945
Treviso	May	1945—Mar 1946
Tissano	Mar	1946—Aug 1946
Treviso	Aug	1946—Aug 1946
en route to UK	Aug	1946—Aug 1946
Coltishall	Aug	1946—Aug 1946

Disbanded at Coltishall on 31 August, 1946.

Main Equipment

Hawker Hurricane I (Mar 1943—Aug 1943)
L1572; L1742; N2647; P2826; P3524; P3776; V6544; V6947

Hawker Hurricane IIB (Sep 1943—Dec 1943)
No serial numbers known

Vickers-Supermarine Spitfire VB, VC (Dec 1943—Mar 1945)
EE810; EE867; EF730; EN843; EP777; EP828; EP893; ER138; ER639; ER675; ER886; ES116; ES190; ES233; JG749; JG869; JG918; JK173; JK512; JK988, X; JL186; JL313; LZ923; MA859

Vickers-Supermarine Spitfire IX (Jul 1944—Aug 1946)
EN186; EN460; MA238; MA423; MA706; MH412; MH599; MH877; MJ226; MJ426; MJ838; MK145; NH262; PL353; PT676, LW:T; PT717; PV211; RR251; SM138; SM177; TA864

Commanding Officers

W/Cdr A. Wojtyga	Mar 1943—Jan 1944
W/Cdr L. Wielochowski	Jan 1944—Dec 1944
W/Cdr Z. S. Mosczynski, DFC	Dec 1945—May 1946
S/Ldr W. Berezcki	May 1946—Aug 1946

Aircraft Markings

By the end of the war the Squadron's aircraft carried the code letters 'LW' on its Spitfires but whether this had been used all through is not known.

No. 320 SQUADRON

BADGE
In front of a fountain an orange tree fracted and eradicated

MOTTO
'Animo libero dirigimur'
('We are guided by the mind of liberty')

This Squadron was formed at Pembroke Dock on 1 June, 1940, being composed of members of the Royal Netherlands Naval Air Service who had escaped from Holland when Germany invaded and who brought with them a collection of twenty-six aircraft. Of these

nine (8 Fokker T-VIIIWs and one C-XIVW) became 320s immediate equipment. These were put to good use, the Squadron carrying out convoy patrols and anti-shipping sorties in the South-Western Approaches. During these two crews were lost and gradually the Squadron was inhibited by lack of spares. As a result, in October the Squadron was transferred to Leuchars and re-equipment with Ansons and Hudsons began. One final sortie with the Fokkers took place on 15 October when Lt Schaper flew to a lake in Friesland to make contact with Dutch agents but was fired on by Germans and had to retreat.

The Squadron now became linked with No. 321 Squadron, the second Dutch unit which was already flying Ansons and provided crews for No. 320. This cross-transferring delayed a return to operations until 19 February, 1941 when 320 set off in Hudson T9362 to resume operational flying with an ASR sortie. However, the main task of No. 320 was to be patrolling the Norwegian coastline on shipping reconnaissance and flying armed *Rovers* to attack U-boats and surface vessels transitting into the North Atlantic via the coast. The first such *Rover* was on 30 August and out of four aircraft engaged only one returned. This operational area continued to occupy the Squadron's attention until April, 1942 when it moved to Norfolk and began operating over the Dutch coastline, attacking shipping at high cost for the Hudson was not the ideal aircraft for operations in such a highly-defended area. The Squadron fought on at this task throughout the remainder of 1942 and into the first few months of 1943 but it was withdrawn from operations early in March of that year and transferred to Bomber Command on 15th.

Here it became part of 2 Group and was re-equipped with North American Mitchells with which it began daylight bombing sorties in August. Thereafter No. 320 maintained a consistent bomber offensive with 2 Group, going to the Continent in October, 1944 and fighting on until, on 2 August, 1945, it transferred once more to the Royal Netherlands Navy.

Bases etc.

Formed at Pembroke Dock on 1 June, 1940.

Pembroke Dock	Jun 1940	Oct 1940
Leuchars, det. Carew Cheriton, Silloth	Oct 1941	Apr 1942
Bircham Newton	Apr 1942	Mar 1943

Transferred to Methwold (Bomber Command) on 15 March, 1943.

Main Equipment

Fokker T-VIIIW (Jun 1940—Oct 1940)
AV958; AV959; AV960; AV961; AV962; AV964; AV965
Avro Anson I (Aug 1940—Jul 1941)
K8706, NO:W; N5064, NO:O; N5202, NO:E; R9827, NO:A; W1672, NO:R; W1789, NO:S
Lockheed Hudson I (Oct 1940—   1941)
N7208; N7288; N7396, NO:V; T9279, NO:L; T9316, NO:A; T9339, NO:C; T9362, NO:E
Lockheed Hudson II, III (Jul 1941—Aug 1942)
T9381, NO:K; T9396, NO:P; T9435, NO:R; T9440, NO:Q; V8982, NO:D; V9033, NO:K; V9041, NO:X; V9063, NO:M; V9122, NO:N; AE525, NO:H
Lockheed Hudson V, VI (Apr 1942—Mar 1943)
AM686, NO:C; AM939, NO:E; EW893, NO:X; EW899, NO:G; EW905, NO:A; EW914, NO:M; EW924, NO:D; FK402, NO:R; FK450, NO:B; FK458, NO:S

Commanding Officers

LtCdr J. M. van Olm	Jun 1940	Oct 1940
LtCdr W. van Lier	Oct 1940	Mar 1943

Aircraft Insignia

Apart from the Dutch orange triangle on the nose the Fokkers carried no distinguishing insignia. The Ansons and Hudsons carried the code letters 'NO' in addition to the triangle.
(See also *Bomber Squadrons of the RAF*, pp. 228–9)

No. 321 SQUADRON

(No badge authorised)

On 1 June, 1940 the Squadron formed at Pembroke Dock from the second group of Dutch Naval personnel to have escaped to the UK after the invasion of Holland. It soon moved to Carew Cheriton where it received Avro Ansons and began convoy escort duties over the Irish Sea on 28 July, 1940. These continued until January, 1941 when No. 320 Squadron became a Hudson unit, No. 321 disbanding to provide No. 320 with crews. 18 January, 1941 was the date on which it was combined with 320 Squadron. It re-formed on 15 August, 1942 at Koggala with Consolidated Catalina flying-boats which it used for anti-submarine patrols over the Indian Ocean. The crews and aircraft had escaped from the Japanese when Java and Sumatra were overrun and they could begin operations immediately. In October the Squadron moved to China Bay with a detachment at Mombasa.

By 1943 additional detachments had been sent to Capetown, Durban and Ratmalana and the Squadron was flying shipping searches, photo recce sorties, the occasional 'Special' involving the landing or picking-up of agents, as well as the normal convoy and anti-submarine duties. On 24 May Lt Vonk sighted a submarine but was wrongly placed to attack and it submerged; forty minutes later he sighted a periscope, dropped depth-charges and damaged it. The next attack took place on 22 January, 1944 and Lt Haman claimed the submarine probably destroyed. Only eight days later another submarine was found and attacked. After this the Squadron rephased into long and uneventful sorties once more.

At the end of 1944 No. 321s Catalinas were supplemented by Liberators and these were used for transport flights as well as maritime work. By May a large proportion of the duties, both of Catalinas and Liberators were on transport flights but in July a detachment went to the Cocos Islands from where armed recces flew out and attacked surface vessels over a wide area and these produced several sinkings and heavily-damaged ships before the war ended. Thereafter it immediately began parachuting supplies to POWs and civilian internees in the Dutch East Indies and then to resistance troops there. The intention was to move the Squadron back into

Sourabaya but the Indonesian uprising delayed this. When a move was made in October, 1945 the first aircraft came under fire and had to withdraw, and it was not until 8 December, 1945 that the Squadron eventually re-settled into Java under the control of the Royal Netherlands Naval Air Service once more.

Bases etc.

Formed at Pembroke Dock on 1 June, 1940.

Pembroke Dock	Jun 1940	Jun 1940
Carew Cheriton	Jun 1940	Jan 1941

Combined into No. 320 Squadron 18 January, 1941. Re-formed at Koggala on 15 August, 1942 from a detachment of the Royal Netherlands Naval Air Service which had escaped there from the Netherlands East Indies.

Koggala, det. Mombasa	Aug 1942	Oct 1942
China Bay, det. Capetown, Durban, Ratmalana, Masirah, Socotra, Cocos Islands	Oct 1942	Oct 1945
Cocos Islands, det. Kemajoran	Oct 1945	Dec 1945

Transferred to Royal Netherlands Naval Air Service at Sourabaya on 8 December, 1945.

Main Equipment

Avro Anson I (Jun 1940—Jan 1941)
K6285; K8823; N5064; N5105; N5202; N5237; N5357; N9535
Consolidated Catalina II (Aug 1942—Dec 1944)
Y-49; Y-55; Y-56; Y-63, FF; Y-69; Y-71; Y-83, RR
Consolidated Catalina III (Dec 1943—Aug 1945)
Y-74, JJ; Y-76, LL; Y-79, OO; Y-80, PP; Y-82, QQ; Y-85, TT
Consolidated Liberator VI (Dec 1944—Dec 1945)
EV824, L, later X; EV834, K; EV869, H; EW317, F; EW321, E; KG847, D; KG852, A; KG991, c; KH194, V; KH296, J; KH299, Z
Consolidated Catalina VA (Aug 1945—Dec 1945)
No identities known
Consolidated Catalina IVB (Dec 1945—Dec 1945)
Y-91, G; Y-92, S; JX272; JX294; JX315; JX365, N

Commanding Officers

LtCdr H. Kolff	Jun 1940	Aug 1940
LtCdr M. G. Smalt	Aug 1940	Oct 1940
LtCdr W. van Lier	Oct 1940	Jan 1941
LtCdr W. van Prooyen	Jul 1942	1945

Aircraft Insignia

No identity markings for No. 321 Squadron are known, although the Catalinas could be identified by double aircraft letters.

No. 330 SQUADRON

BADGE
In front of a sun in splendour a Viking ship in
full sail
MOTTO
'Trygg havet'
('Guarding the seas')

On 25 April, 1941 the Squadron was formed from Norwegian personnel who had escaped and trained in Canada; it was based at Reykjavik in Iceland and equipped with Northrop seaplanes ordered by the Norwegian Government. Until they arrived the aircrew flew with RAF crews on Sunderlands but by the end of May the first Northrops arrived and work-up commenced. First operation took place on 23 June, a night convoy escort. The build up was quite rapid, B Flight forming and moving to Akureyri in July and by August over 40 operations a month were being flown (and the Squadron had lost its first aircraft and crew). At the end of the month Qm Helgesen found a submarine and depth-charged it and the next day Qm Holdö did the same and had the satisfaction of seeing it surrender to a destroyer; he then found another which he attacked. C Flight formed in September and moved to Budareyri. Patrols continued and one more U-boat was attacked before the year was out.

1942 saw operations intensify so that by May No. 330 logged 118 sorties in the month. The next month two Catalina IIIs arrived for the Squadron, supplementing the Northrops and extending the range of operations. During the summer several combats took place inconclusively with FW 200s and two more U-boats were attacked with DCs. In addition the Squadron began mercy flights with Icelandic civilians in need of hospital treatment. These operations continued until January, 1943 when the Squadron ceased operations and moved to Oban to re-equip.

At Oban it received Sunderland IIIs, working-up and resuming operations on 20 April with a convoy escort. In May a detachment went to the Shetlands and two months later the Squadron moved there. It flew anti-submarine patrols to North Norway and beyond to cover Russian convoys. No action was forthcoming though the Squadron put up again forty sorties a month. In fact it was not until

29 February, 1944 that No. 330 again found a U-boat but was unable to attack due to losing it in a snowstorm. However, on 16 May Lt Johnson had a fight with a U-boat on the surface. His front gunner was killed, the U-boat was damaged as was the Sunderland which returned on two engines. Another U-boat was damaged in July then the operations continued with no visible results. The Squadron flew continuously on patrols from Sullom Voe until May, 1945 when the war ended, only one other U-boat attack being made. At the end of that month No. 330 moved to Norway and was taken over by the Royal Norwegian Air Force.

Bases etc.

Formed at Reykjavik on 25 April, 1941		
Reykjavik, det. Akureyri, Budareyri	Apr 1941	Mar 1943
Oban, det. Sullom Voe	Jan 1943	Jul 1943
Sullom Voe	Jul 1943	May 1945
Transferred to the Royal Norwegian Air Force 21 November, 1945.		

Main Equipment

Northrop N3 PB (Mar 1941—Mar 1943)
  8, GS:A; 11, GS:B; 15, GS:L; 16, GS:G, later GS:S; 17, GS:M; 18, GS:T; 20GS:U; 22, GS:F
Consolidated Catalina III (Jun 1942—Dec 1942)
  FP525, Y; FP526, Z; FP528, W; FP529, X; FP531, P; FP533; FP534, O; FP535, V; FP536, R
Short Sunderland III (Jan 1943—May 1945)
  W6053, E; W6061, X; W6067, T; DD843, S; DD856, G; DP181, U; DP184, F; EJ133, W; EJ155, O; ML780, WH:A; ML819, WH:V; NJ178, WH:H; NJ181, WH:Z; PP140, WH:V
Short Sunderland V (May 1945—Nov 1945)
  EJ138, WH:Y; ML758, WH:O; ML814, WH:A; ML824, WH:Z, later WH:T; NJ178, WH:L

Commanding Officers

Cdr H. A. Bugge, AFC	Apr 1941	Apr 1942
Cdr Brinch	Apr 1942	Jan 1943
Cdr T. Diesen	Jan 1943	Oct 1944
Cdr C. R. Kaldager	Oct 1944	Nov 1945

Aircraft Insignia

The Northrops carried the code letters 'GS' during their service in Iceland. At first on receiving Sunderlands no markings were carried but from 1944 onwards the letters 'WH' were used.

No. 333 SQUADRON

BADGE
In front of a pair of wings elevated and
conjoined at base a Viking ship affrontee
MOTTO
'For Konge, federland og flaggets heder'
('For King, Country and the honour of the
flag')

On 10 May, 1943 No. 1477 (Norwegian) Flight was expanded to full squadron strength and numbered No. 333 Squadron. It was a dual purpose squadron in that part of it functioned at Leuchars with Mosquitoes and part at Woodhaven with Catalina flying-boats. Both parts, however, operated in the same area, flying shipping reccs, convoy escorts and anti-submarine patrols over the North Sea and Norwegian coastline. In addition, the Catalinas flew 'Specials' to Norway, co-operating with agents in Norway itself. The Squadron began to build up a score of enemy aircraft whilst engaged on these tasks, a Do 24 being shot into the sea in June, and two Ju 88s in July. In December another Ju 88 and a FW 190 fell to No. 333's cannon.

In 1944 three more enemy aircraft were destroyed before the Squadron lost its first aircraft. The pace increased with U-boats now becoming targets and several running fights with submarines on the surface ensuing, with damage to both U-boats and aircraft. The Mosquitoes were now carrying depth-charges which they used to

good effect against the U-boats; three such craft were attacked in June, 1944, one being destroyed for the loss of two Mosquitoes. July brought six attacks with one U-boat definitely damaged but one Mosquito lost; during that month the Catalinas moved to the Shetlands. In September, 1944 the Mosquito element moved to Banff where it joined the Strike Wing, increasing its shipping reccs and armed *Rovers*, sixty-three sorties being flown in October.

Mines became one of the weapons the Mosquitoes used in 1945, being dropped in Norwegian fjords; strikes were also made on navigation aids up the coast to disrupt enemy shipping traffic. The Catalinas were now operating special flights to Grasnaya in northern Russia. This type of operational pattern was maintained until VE-Day brought an end to hostilities.

The Squadron eventually returned to Norway and came under control of the Royal Norwegian Air Force on 21 November, 1945.

Bases etc.

Formed at Leuchars on 10 May, 1943 out of No. 1477 (Norwegian) Flight.		
Leuchars and Woodhaven, det. Sullom Voe	Oct 1943	Sep 1944
Banff, det. Sullom Voe	Sep 1944	1945
Transferred to the Royal Norwegian Air Force 21 November, 1945.		

Main Equipment

Consolidated Catalina IB (Oct 1943—Jan 1945)
  W8424, B; FP121, C; FP183, D; FP222, B; FP314, A

de Havilland Mosquito II (Oct 1943— 1944)
  DZ711, L
de Havilland Mosquito VI (Oct 1943—Nov 1945)
  HP859, M; HP862, KK:K; HP864, H, later KK:H; HP904, KK:E;
  HP910, KK:L; HR116, KK:F; HR126, KK:S; HR262, KK:N;
  LR560, KK:C; RF769, KK:P
Consolidated Catalina IV (Aug 1944— 1945)
  JV933, C; JX224, KK:B; JX265, KK:B; JX582, KK:A

Commanding Officers

Cdr F. Lambrechts	May 1943—	1945

Aircraft Insignia

No squadron identity markings were carried until 1944 when the letters 'KK' were allocated and used on both Mosquitoes and Catalinas.

No. 353 SQUADRON

BADGE
A Bengal tiger rampant
MOTTO
'Fear nought in unity'

The Squadron was formed at Calcutta (Dum Dum) on 1 June, 1942 with Lockheed Hudson IIIs in the general reconnaissance role. On 13 July it became operational, flying shipping recces down the Cheduba Straits and over Ramree Island. It had an Indian Air Force component and these flew this Air Force's first operations in World War II. Six more sorties were flown that month then the Squadron increased to a normal forty or so sorties each month with shipping and airfield searches predominating but also convoy escorts and anti-invasion patrols being flown. On 18 August P/O Smith found a Japanese flying-boat near the convoy he was escorting, attacked and damaged it.

In September the Squadron became much more a general purpose unit flying, in addition to its maritime task, airfield recces, leaflet drops, internal security patrols (for which it received Blenheims), weather recces and supply dropping sorties. To these were added in early 1943 an increasing number of attacks on river shipping behind the enemy lines with some success. But as the year progressed it returned almost completely to its maritime recce duties.

All this changed in August, 1943 when No. 353 came off operations and moved to Palam, Delhi to convert to a transport squadron. In September it began a scheduled route from Delhi through to Calcutta with mail, flying forty-eight trips a month. Four aircraft were lost in accidents before 1943 was out. In January, 1944 the rate was up to seventy-three trips and in March No. 353 Squadron began re-equipping with Dakotas. These were used over the 'Hump' to Kunming, setting up a new scheduled route from Dum Dum via Dinjan. In May the routes were re-scheduled, the Hudsons flying six routes out of Palam and the Dakotas four out of Dum Dum. In July, however the two Dakota Flights (C & D) were re-numbered No. 52 Squadron, No. 353 remaining as the Palam-based unit, changing to Dakotas from Hudsons that same month. With these two new routes were introduced, one to Colombo in Ceylon, one to Mauripur. In August it began supply drops once more. In October the Squadron lost two Dakotas to birds, one to a vulture and one to a hawk.

At the end of 1944 some Warwick IIIs supplemented the Dakotas but these were not found to be suitable and lasted only three months. Ansons had arrived in September, 1944 and these were augmented by Beechcraft Expediters in January, 1945 for local communications work. The Squadron maintained a high rate of scheduled flying throughout 1945 although the work began to fall off from August onwards. With the war over the routes were re-scheduled, the Squadron continuing in this role until 1 October, 1946 when it disbanded at Mauripur.

Bases etc.

Formed at Dum Dum on 1 June, 1942.

Dum Dum, det. Cattack	Jun 1942—Feb 1943
Dhubalia, det. Jessore	Feb 1943—Mar 1943
Tanjore, det. St. Thomas Mount	Mar 1943—Aug 1943
Palam, det. Dum Dum	Aug 1943—Jul 1944
1 July, 1944 C & D Flights re-numbered 52 Squadron at Dum Dum.	
Palam, det. Jiwani	Jul 1944—May 1946
Mauripur	May 1946—Oct 1946
Disbanded at Mauripur on 1 October, 1946.	

Main Equipment

Lockheed Hudson III (Jun 1942—Aug 1943)
  V9176, V; V9192, R; AE514, J; FH241, W; FH254, G; FH286, J;
  FH291, X; FH364, K; FH370, D; FH409, V; FH411, B; FH444, H;
  FH461, A
Lockheed Hudson VI (Aug 1943—Aug 1944)
  EW902; EW963; EW972; FK477; FK493; FK498; FK576; FK607;
  FK636
Douglas Dakota III (Mar 1944— 1945)
  FD787; FD864; FD887; FD912; FL541; FL577; FL600; FL623;
  FL642; FZ608; FZ616; FZ627; FZ673; KG492; KG542; KG641;
  KG692; KG716
Avro Anson X (Sep 1944—Feb 1945)
  DJ821; NK352; NK356; NK369
Vickers Warwick III (Dec 1944—Mar 1945)
  HG243; HG249
Beech Expediter I, II (Jan 1945—Jun 1945)
  HB149; HB193; KJ507; KJ514; KJ550; KJ551; KJ553
Douglas Dakota IV (Dec 1944—Oct 1946)
  KJ905; KJ923; KJ946; KJ963; KK112; KK119; KN316; KN322

Commanding Officers

W/Cdr L. G. W. Lilly	Jun 1942—Jul 1944
W/Cdr C. E. Slee, MVO, AFC	Jul 1944—Feb 1945
S/Ldr F. M. Biddulph	Feb 1945—Mar 1945
W/Cdr A. H. Harding, DFC	Mar 1945—Oct 1945
W/Cdr P. B. Wood	Oct 1945— 1946

Aircraft Insignia

As far as is known no squadron identity markings were carried by No. 353 Squadron's aircraft.

No. 354 SQUADRON

(No badge authorised)

No. 354 Squadron was formed at Drigh Road on 6 July, 1943 as a general reconnaissance unit but received no aircraft until the end of August by which time it had moved to Cuttack. After a month of working up on the Liberator it began flying operationally on convoy escort patrols which it maintained for the rest of the year. In December it began flying *Maxim* patrols; these were armed recces of the Arakan coast, attacking any enemy shipping that could be found. As 1944 opened up these sorties became No. 354s major task and many sampans and similar craft were attacked and destroyed. Several times the Liberators were attacked by Japanese Mitsubishi Ki-21 'Sally' patrol bombers but none were lost. In March, 1944 there was a submarine in the Squadron's area and a 'Hunt to exhaustion' was carried out; ninety sorties were flown that month and in April night *Maxims* were begun. The Squadron's first loss was on 7 May when F/O Banks' crew went missing on a *Maxim*. By the end of July the Squadron turned from *Maxims* to traffic patrols, keeping a continuous watch on the shipping lanes. These and convoy escorts became the staple diet of the Squadron until January, 1945 when the Squadron again went on the anti-shipping offensive with some success.

On 13 February three aircraft attacked an enemy force, destroying a sub-chaser and two coasters, then on 26 March F/Lt W. G. McRae made a courageous attack on the transport *Risui Maru* with great success (sinking it) but was shot down in the process. This work was continued in April off the Tennaserim coastline and at the beginning of May seven strikes were made on Moulmein Harbour. This brought No. 354s operations to an abrupt end for the Squadron was disbanded at Cuttack on 18 May, 1945.

Bases etc.

Formed at Drigh Road on 6 July, 1943.

Drigh Road	Jul 1943—Aug 1943
Cuttack, det. Sigirya	Aug 1943—Oct 1944
Minneriya, det. Kankesanturai	Oct 1944—Jan 1945
Cuttack	Jan 1945—May 1945

Disbanded at Cuttack on 18 May, 1945.

Main Equipment

Consolidated Liberator IIIA (Aug 1943—Apr 1944)
FK227, T; FL912, H, later K
Consolidated Liberator V (Aug 1943—Jul 1944)
BZ805, V; BZ862, A; BZ865, C; BZ886, P; BZ888, S; BZ938, L
Consolidated Liberator VI (Jan 1944—May 1945)
BZ988, Z; BZ991, C; EV829, H; EV834, Z; EV848, M; EV856, K; EV942, N; EV950, T; EV972, K; EW319, A; KG822, P; KG850, Y; KG863, J; KH138, W; KH187, H; KH296, D

Commanding Officers

W/Cdr K. J. Mellor, DFC	Jul 1943—May 1944
W/Cdr D. T. MacPherson	May 1944—Mar 1945
W/Cdr F. G. Paisey	Mar 1945—May 1945

Aircraft Insignia

It is believed that no squadron identity markings were carried on the Liberators.

No. 357 SQUADRON

BADGE
A crocodile

MOTTO
'Mortem hostibus'
('We bring death to the enemy')

The Squadron was formed on 1 February, 1944 from No. 1576 (Special Duties) Flight at Digri, India. It comprised two Flights, A Flight with Liberators and Hudsons and B Flight at Redhills Lake, with Catalinas. Most of its operations consisted of dropping supplies to insurgent groups behind the Japanese lines in the Burma jungle. These involved accurate navigation and expert piloting to drop the supplies at the right place, often in narrow valleys. The Liberators were also used over the 'Hump' to China, very often ferrying petrol to Kunming and by July the Squadron was also operating over the French Indo-China border. Between twenty and thirty drops were made each month behind the lines. The Catalinas were used to land and pick up agents on rivers and inlets in enemy hinterland along the Burma and Malayan coasts.

At the turn of the year the Squadron replaced the Hudsons with Dakotas and the sortie rate went up to 105 in January, 1945. The work involved dropping and supplying agents, saboteurs; dropping patrols ahead of Allied troops (Z Force) and keeping them supplied, faking parachute drops and arranging for the escape of POWs in Japanese hands. It also flew some sorties for the OSS, the American saboteur agency. By now the Squadron was working Burma, Siam, Malaya, China and Indo-China. That same month a C Flight was formed from the Lysander Flight which had left 161 Squadron in the UK in November. It began to work up with Stinson L-5s, Harvards and Austers until the Lysanders had been uncrated, erected and test-flown. On 25th F/O Churchill flew the Squadron's longest sortie in a Liberator of 21 hrs 55 mins over Malaya. By March the sortie rate had soared to 149 in the month, many of them now over Indo-China due to the Japanese take-over there. A new feature of most sorties now had become the dropping of leaflets. In March S/Ldr T. P. O'Brien flew into Dien-Phu under the Japanese noses and evacuated French personnel. That same month the Lysanders started training agents and working up.

The Squadron now concentrated on Burma in April and May, the Dakotas taking the preponderance of the operations and the Lysanders beginning operations on 3rd, F/Lt P. Arkell flying food and ammunition into a strip at Mewaing and evacuating two casualties. Three days later two Lysanders dropped into Mingaladon airfield with infiltrators. In June the Dakotas began pick-up operations in Burma. Meanwhile the Lysanders were suffering accidents due to inadequate strips but found a successful one at Lipyekhi where they were able to operate and two further strips (Kowaing and Tidemata) where they flew about two trips a day. By July the Lysander Flight alone was flying 87 sorties per month and the Dakotas 84 (the Liberators having been reduced). The Dakotas were now principally involved over Siam and the Catalinas flew 21 trips in the month. In August the Dakotas again concentrated on Siam, some sorties bringing POWs back, while the few remaining Liberators flew over Malaya, dropping a medical team and supplies to POWs in Japanese hands. The Lysanders flew similar sorties, taking doctors into POW camps and flying POWs out (Operation Mastiff). Even though the war ended in September the Dakotas kept up a steady flow of trips into Siam whilst the Lysanders continued 'Mastiff', flew to a crashed Dakota and rescued the crew and also looked for lost lightships for the Navy. At the end of September some 'Lizzies' were detached to Bangkok to fly liaison duties for the Army there.

There was now little call for special duty flying so on 15 November, 1945 the Squadron was disbanded at Mingaladon, C Flight being attached to the Burma Communications Squadron to complete its commitment to Force 136.

Bases etc.

Formed 1 February, 1944 from No. 1576 (SD) Flight at Digri, detached Redhills Lake. C Flight formed 23 January, 1945 at Jessore ex Lysander Flight of 161 Squadron.

Digri, det. Redhills Lake, Dum Dum	Feb 1944—Sep 1944
Jessore, det. Cox's Bazaar, Minneriya, China Bay, Toungoo, Drigh Road, Meiktela, Mingaladon	Sep 1944—Sep 1945
Mingaladon, det. Don Muang	Sep 1945—Nov 1945

Disbanded at Mingaladon on 15 November, 1945.

Main Equipment

Lockheed Hudson IIIA (Feb 1944—Dec 1944)
V9176; FH231; FH333; AE518
Consolidated Liberator III (Feb 1944—Dec 1944)
BZ847; BZ901, U; BZ902; BZ909; BZ923, W; BZ952; BZ954, Y; BZ959
Consolidated Catalina IB (Feb 1944— 1945)
No serial numbers known
Consolidated Liberator VI (Sep 1944—Oct 1945)
BZ998; EV876; EV911; EV960; EW119; EW164, Q; EW242; KH160, W; KH166, S; KH216, Z; KH257, Q; KH273, R; KH313, V; KH320, D; KH391, Y; KL552, R
Douglas Dakota III, IV (Dec 1944—Nov 1945)
KG490, N; KJ913, B; KJ919, F; KJ922, J; KJ926, M; KK180, A; KN304, H
Westland Lysander IIIA (Mar 1945—Dec 1945)
T1532, G; V9289, C; V9303; V9494; V9665; V9818; V9867, K

Commanding Officers

W/Cdr J. R. Moore   Feb 1944—Dec 1944
W/Cdr L. M. Hodges, DSO, DFC   Dec 1944—Jul 1945
W/Cdr P. R. Gaskell, DFC   Jul 1945—Nov 1945

Aircraft Insignia

No specific squadron markings appear to have been carried by No. 357 Squadron aircraft.

No. 400 SQUADRON

BADGE
In front of two tomahawks in saltire an eagle's head erased

MOTTO
'Percussuri vigiles'
('On the watch to strike')

The eagle's head indicates the reconnaissance role and the tomahawks one of the types the Squadron flew in World War II.

On its arrival in England on 25 February, 1940 No. 110 Squadron, (Auxiliary) of the Royal Canadian Air Force settled into Old Sarum equipped with Westland Lysanders IIs, moving to Odiham in June where it was too late to see action. It worked up with frequent army exercises and was also used for AA battery ranging over London, Surrey and Hampshire in the summer of 1940. This continued into the New Year when, on 1 March, 1941, it was re-numbered No. 400 Squadron. The next month it began to re-equip with the Tomahawk; however it was not until November, 1941 that the Squadron became operational when it began *Rhubarbs* over Northern France out of Tangmere. These were quickly followed by *Populars* in the Channel, twenty-two sorties being flown that month. These continued into December, when on 13th two members were shot into the Channel returning from a *Popular*.

Operations ceased early in the New Year and were not resumed until May, 1942; two months later Mustangs came into the Squadron and these were used on Operation Jubilee on 19 August, the Squadron making twenty-four deep low-level reconnaissances during the Canadian assault on Dieppe; one Squadron member failed to return. By October No. 400 was fully worked-up on Mustangs and resumed *Rhubarbs* and *Populars* regularly. On 7 November F/O Hanton began the Squadron's score when he was attacked by German fighters and scored one probably destroyed. By the end of the year the Squadron was averaging forty sorties a month comprising *Jim Crows*, *Insteps*, *Lagoons* and *Rhubarbs* and using Portreath as an Advanced Landing Ground. An unfortunate occurrence took place in January, 1943 when F/O Ferris was shot into the sea by an RAF Typhoon. *Rhubarbs* became the staple task of early 1943 until April when the Squadron began *Night Rangers* and, immediately, F/O Grant caught and destroyed a Do 217. By then, No. 400 was flying operationally by day and by night, four pilots being lost during the summer when a Fi 156 Storch and another Do 217 were destroyed. In September more photo recce sorties were being flown and in October the Squadron score began to mount with a FW 190 and a Hs 126 shot down on 24th and a Me 210 on 11 November, together with another probably destroyed and one damaged.

1944 brought a change of equipment, the Squadron receiving Spitfires and Mosquitoes. It now converted to photo recce sorties entirely, concentrating on *Noball* targets. As the spring came the targets were more and more mapping tasks in preparation for the invasion, rivers and railways featuring high in the list. In May 103 sorties were flown on airfields, AA positions, *Noballs*, enemy HQs, bomb assessment and the completion of a mosaic of the Caen area. June saw both high-altitude PR sorties and low-level action over the beaches, once the invasion started. On 1 July the Squadron moved B Flight into the beachhead itself, the whole Squadron moving across in August; that month 251 sorties were flown. For the next few weeks the Squadron was on the move to keep in touch with the advancing armies, most of its sorties still being high-level tactical PR. The winter slowed down the number of operations but the Squadron continued its tasks into the New Year; it lost five aircraft in the New Year's Day raids by the Luftwaffe. As the weather

improved so No. 400 built up its operations once more. April and May saw several forward moves but it flew its last operations on 8 May. On the following day on a non-operational flight, F/Lt L. McMillan, DFC was hit by AA from a German ship and crashed into the sea. The Squadron remained in Germany until August, 1945, being disbanded at Lüneburg on 7th.

No. 400 re-formed again as the City of Toronto Auxiliary Squadron on 15 April, 1946, becoming an Air Reserve Squadron on 1 February, 1968.

Bases etc.

Arrived Liverpool 25 February, 1940 as No. 110 Squadron, RCAF, and moved to Old Sarum on 26th.

Old Sarum	Feb 1940	—Jun 1940
Odiham	Jun 1940	—Mar 1942
Thruxton	Mar 1942	—Mar 1942
Odiham	Mar 1942	—May 1942
Gatwick	May 1942	—May 1942
Odiham	May 1942	—Oct 1942
Middle Wallop	Oct 1942	—Feb 1943
Dunsfold	Feb 1943	—Jul 1943
Woodchurch	Jul 1943	—Oct 1943
Redhill	Oct 1943	—Feb 1944
Odiham	Feb 1944	—Jul 1944
Sommervieu (B.8)	Jul 1944	—Aug 1944
St. Honorine de Ducy (B.21)	Aug 1944	—Sep 1944
Avrilly (B.34)	Sep 1944	—Sep 1944
Blankenburg (B.66)	Sep 1944	—Oct 1944
Eindhoven (B.78)	Oct 1944	—Mar 1945
Petit Brogel (B.90)	Mar 1945	—Apr 1945
Rheine (B.108)	Apr 1945	—Apr 1945
Wunstorf (B.116)	Apr 1945	—May 1945
Soltau (B.154)	May 1945	—May 1945
Lüneburg (B.156)	May 1945	—Jul 1945
Kastrup (B.160)	Jul 1945	—Aug 1945
Lüneburg (B.156)	Aug 1945	—Aug 1945

Disbanded at Lüneburg 7 August, 1945.

Main Equipment

Westland Lysander II (Jun 1940—Aug 1940)
  L4788; L4789; N1209; N1220; N1265; N1301; P1695
Westland Lysander III (Aug 1940—Dec 1941)
  R9001; R9008; R9113; R9117; R9123; T1434; T1460; T1564
Curtiss Tomahawk I, IIA, IIB (Apr 1941—Jul 1942)
  AH756, SP:Z; AH789, SP:L; AH806, SP:W; AH817, SP:S;
  AH841, SP:K; AH895, SP:B; AK324, SP:S; AK481, SP:S;
  AK526, SP:Y
North American Mustang I (Jul 1942—Feb 1944)
  AG488, SP:B; AG520, SP:B; AG587, SP:L; AG615, SP:Q;
  AG641, SP:V; AG659, SP:U; AL971, SP:S; AM126, SP:D;
  AM184, SP:N; AM237, SP:E; AP191, SP:O
de Havilland Mosquito XVI (Jan 1944—May 1944)
  MM277; MM284; MM307; MM353; MM356
Vickers-Supermarine Spitfire XI (Jan 1944—Aug 1945)
  EN332; EN683; MB941; MB947; PA871; PA894; PA900; PA927;
  PA942; PA961; PL797; PL828; PL836; PL903; PL975; PM136

Commanding Officers

W/Cdr W. D. Van Vliet	Feb 1940	—Sep 1940
W/Cdr E. H. Evans	Sep 1940	—Nov 1940
W/Cdr R. M. McKay	Nov 1940	—Aug 1941
W/Cdr H. W. Kerby	Aug 1941	—May 1942
W/Cdr R. C. A. Waddell, DSO, DFC	May 1942	—Jul 1943
S/Ldr W. B. Woods, DFC	Jul 1943	—Sep 1943
W/Cdr R. A. Ellis, DFC	Sep 1943	—Nov 1944
S/Ldr M. G. Brown, DFC and Bar	Nov 1944	—Jul 1945
S/Ldr J. A. Morton, DFC	Jul 1945	—Aug 1945

Aircraft Markings

From some time in 1941 until early 1943 the Squadron's aircraft carried the code letters 'SP'. Early in its existence the Lysanders carried a motif comprising winged dice under the cockpit window. Otherwise no insignia was carried.

No. 404 SQUADRON

BADGE
A buffalo's head
MOTTO
'Ready to fight'

The buffalo is a fierce and powerful fighter.

No. 404 Squadron was formed at Thorney Island with RCAF personnel on 1 May, 1941 as a coastal fighter squadron equipped with Blenheim IVs. The following month it moved to Scotland and commenced operations on 22 September with convoy escort duties. These, together with shipping recce sweeps over the North Sea, took up No. 404s time during the winter. Over Christmas the Squadron was detached to Wick where it provided fighter escort for the Vaagso raid, during which it fought with Messerschmitt Bf 109s and scored one probably destroyed. In January, 1942 72 sorties were flown and two German aircraft attacked; it was not established on a patrol over the Faeroes as well as its other tasks. The North Sea and Norwegian coastline continued to be No. 404s pre-occupation all through 1942, re-equipping in September with Beaufighters. These commenced operations in November and in January, 1943 the Squadron moved to Devon.

From Chivenor the Squadron operated over the Western Approaches and the French Atlantic coast, flying convoy fighter patrols, fishery patrols and Biscay patrols. In April, however, it returned to Scotland and the North Sea. *Rovers* along the Norwegian coast and shipping recces became the tasks, together with escort duties to the strikes made by Hampden torpedo-bombers on German coastal convoys. These brought occasional combats with enemy aircraft, two Ju 88s and a BV 138 being probables in May and two BV 138s being shot into the sea in July. By September the Squadron was flying as part of the Tain Wing, large formation strikes and escorts becoming the pattern for the months thereafter. At the end of the year the Squadron's aircraft were equipped with RPs; now it was flying in about four large strikes a month.

In 1944 the operations increased to about 75 sorties a month. In May the Squadron moved to Cornwall to cover the Western Channel during the invasion of Normandy. On D-Day the Squadron attacked three German destroyers, damaging two and probably sinking the third; three days later another destroyer was beached after a Squadron attack; 218 sorties were flown that month. The next month the Squadron moved again to concentrate on the Dutch coast, operating in conjunction with the North Coates Wing. This was a time for large formations roaming in search of coastal convoys and was continued until September when the Squadron moved to the Banff Wing to work against Norwegian coastal shipping once more. This was a busy month, an especially effective attack being made on 14th with one motor vessel blown up and another left in flames for the loss of one Beaufighter crew. Further attacks were made and on 9 October three ships were sunk. A similar score was recorded on 18 November.

In January, 1945 two ships were sunk but on 9 February, in an attack on destroyers and minesweepers, the Squadron came off badly losing six crews. This type of action continued until April when the Squadron began to convert to Mosquitoes. It managed to accomplish forty-seven sorties in May before the war ended and the Squadron was disbanded at Banff on 25 May, 1945.

Bases etc.

Formed at Thorney Island on 1 May, 1941.

Thorney Island	May 1941	Jun 1941
Castletown	Jun 1941	Jul 1941
Skitten	Jul 1941	Oct 1941
Dyce, det. Sumburgh	Oct 1941	Dec 1941
Sumburgh, det. Dyce	Dec 1941	Mar 1942
Dyce, det. Sumburgh, Leuchars, Wick	Mar 1942	Aug 1942
Sumburgh	Aug 1942	Sep 1942
Dyce, det. Sumburgh, Wick	Sep 1942	Jan 1943
Chivenor	Jan 1943	Apr 1943
Tain	Apr 1943	Apr 1943
Wick, det. Sumburgh	Apr 1943	May 1944
Davidstow Moor	May 1944	Jul 1944
Strubby	Jul 1944	Sep 1944
Banff	Sep 1944	Oct 1944
Dallachy	Oct 1944	Mar 1945
Banff	Mar 1945	May 1945

Disbanded at Banff 25 May, 1945.

Main Equipment

Bristol Blenheim I (May 1941—Jul 1941)
K7031; K7120; L1102
Bristol Blenheim IV (May 1941—Mar 1943)
L9337, EE:O; L9454, EE:G; N3525, EE:H; N3600, EE:J, later, EE:K; P4847, EE:A; T1808, EE:N; T1869, EE:O; T1949, EE:M; V5430, EE:V; V5729, EE:R; V5765, EE:K; Z5728, EE:T; Z5736, EE:Q; Z5963, EE:J; Z5972, EE:X; Z6035, EE:M; Z6181, EE:B; Z6279, EE:X; Z6341, EE:Z; Z6343, EE:W
Bristol Beaufighter IIF (Sep 1942—Mar 1943)
T3155, EE:N; T3169, EE:U; T3436, EE:J; T3440; V8131, EE:T; V8144, EE:S; V8157, EE:P; V8189, EE:F; V8202, EE:L; V8214, EE:G
Bristol Beaufighter XIC (Mar 1943—Oct 1943)
JL947, EE:D; JM105, EE:B; JM111, EE:T; JM119, EE:E; JM124, EE:S; JM132, EE:U; JM160, EE:Q; JM166, EE:K; JM173, EE:N; JM174, EE:R
Bristol Beaufighter X (Aug 1943—Mar 1945)
LX940, EE:Y; LZ173, EE:W; LZ179, EE:J; LZ289, EE:R; LZ297, EE:A; LZ314, 2:P; LZ403, EE:D; LZ439, EE:O; LZ446, 2:L; LZ451, EE:M; NE198, 2:R; NE318, 2:G; NE339, 2:U; NE355, 2:H; NE425, 2:G; NE669, 2:A; NE800, 2:N; NE825, EO:P; NT890, EO:F; NT991, EO:E; NV173, EO:X; NV191, EO:R; NV292, EO:O; NV416, EO:J; NV427, EO:L; RD331, EO:J; RD427, EO:O
de Havilland Mosquito VI (Mar 1945—May 1945)
RF777, EO:L; RF842, EO:C; RF853, EO:N; RF857, EO:Q; RF875, EO:R; RF880, EO:X; RF882, EO:Z

Commanding Officers

W/Cdr P. H. Woodruff	May 1941	Jun 1942
W/Cdr J. A. Dixon	Jun 1942	Jul 1942
W/Cdr E. H. McHardy, DFC and Bar	Jul 1942	Oct 1942
W/Cdr G. G. Truscott	Oct 1942	Sep 1943
W/Cdr C. A. Willis	Sep 1943	Mar 1944
W/Cdr A. K. Gatwood, DSO, DFC and Bar	Apr 1944	Aug 1944
W/Cdr E. W. Pierce	Aug 1944	May 1945

Aircraft Insignia

From its inception until mid 1943 the Squadron carried the code letters 'EE'. When such letters were dropped in Coastal Command the Squadron used the number '2' until the Spring of 1944 when code letters were again used, initially 'EE', then this was changed to 'EO'.

No. 407 SQUADRON

BADGE
A winged trident piercing the shank of an anchor
MOTTO
'To hold on high'

The badge represents the blows struck against enemy shipping by the Demon Squadron.

The Squadron was formed at Thorney Island with RCAF personnel on 8 May, 1941 with Bristol Blenheim IVs as interim equipment. In June it re-equipped with Lockheed Hudsons and moved to North Coates in July for operations. On 15 August it flew as ASR sortie and was declared operational in September, flying over the southern North Sea on *Rovers* and anti-E-boat patrols; in its first month it flew 75 sorties. On 10 October an attack was made on an armed trawler and the Squadron lost its first crew. November was a heavy month and twenty-two ships attacked for the loss of only two crews. Three more failed to return from operations in December.

In January, 1942 No. 407 became a night bombing unit, attacking German ships off the Dutch and German coasts and further along the Channel in February when it came off operations for a rest until the end of March. Its first task then was to send a detachment to St. Eval to escort the force attacking St. Nazaire. Then it moved back to Bircham to resume its attacks along the Dutch, N. German and Danish coasts. This was costly, four crews being lost in April. In May 83,000 tons of shipping were attacked by the Squadron, one particularly hard-fought action being on 15th when eleven aircraft took part in a night attack on a convoy when three ships were set on fire but four aircraft were missing and two crashed on landing. With the Squadron depleted few attacks were made until mid-June when two ships were set on fire; on 25th No. 407 took part in the '1000 bomber' raid on Bremen. Shipping attacks continued but there was a continual changing of aircraft, Hudson Mk. IIIs, IIIAs, Vs and VIs. In the autumn the Squadron began a spell over the Western Approaches and Biscay, then back to the Channel and Dutch coast, mainly operating anti-E-boat patrols.

This was a difficult time for the Squadron but in January, 1943 a successful strike brought morale up again. The Squadron now began converting to Wellingtons and resumed operations in March. It was now flying almost entirely on anti-submarine patrols over the Western Approaches; on 22 April F/Lt D. Pickard attacked the Squadron's first U-boat with depth-charges then machine-gunned a second. Another was attacked before the month was out. Two attacks in May and two in June set the pattern as the Squadron operated over the Western Approaches. On the other side of the coin roughly one crew was going missing a month at this time. By August over a hundred sorties a month were being flown and day operations commenced. Two U-boats were attacked in September but two crews lost also, including the CO.

Early in 1944 the Squadron moved area, flying from N. Ireland out over the Atlantic where it found more U-boats available for attack. The sorties were longer but two attacks were being made regularly each month until mid-1944 when targets were more difficult to find. At the end of August 407 moved to Wick to cover the Northern Transit Area. Three U-boats were depth-charged in October then the Squadron returned to the south-west again in November where it maintained about one hundred sorties a month up to the end of the European war. In the latter months its prime targets were the midget submarines operating along the Dutch and Channel coasts. With the war over No. 407 was soon disbanded, at Chivenor, on 4 June, 1945, having definitely sunk four U-boats and damaged a further three, losing forty-two aircraft in the process.

Bases etc.

Formed at Thorney Island on 8 May, 1941.

Thorney Island	May 1941	Jul 1941
North Coates	Jul 1941	Feb 1942
Thorney Island	Feb 1942	Mar 1942
Bircham Newton, det. St. Eval	Mar 1942	Sep 1942
St. Eval, det. Thorney Island	Sep 1942	Nov 1942
Docking	Nov 1942	Feb 1943
Skitten	Feb 1943	Mar 1943
Chivenor	Mar 1943	Sep 1943
St. Eval	Sep 1943	Dec 1943
Chivenor	Dec 1943	Jan 1944
Limavady	Jan 1944	Aug 1944
Wick	Aug 1944	Nov 1944
Chivenor, det. Langham	Nov 1944	Jun 1945

Disbanded at Chivenor 4 June, 1945.

Main Equipment

Lockheed Hudson I (Jun 1942—   1941)
    P5116, RR:D; T9357, RR:F
Lockheed Hudson III (Jun 1941—   1942)
    V9095, RR:G; V9102, RR:X; V9107, RR:W
Lockheed Hudson V (Jun 1941—Feb 1943)
    AE649, RR:R; AM551, RR:C; AM562, RR:B; AM586, RR:T;
    AM597, RR:F; AM602, RR:M; AM619, RR:Q; AM626, RR:K;
    AM646, RR:J; AM684, RR:O; AM718, RR:V; AM732, RR:S;
    AM811, RR:H; AM878, RR:B
Lockheed Hudson VI (Oct 1942—Mar 1943)
    No serial numbers known
Vickers Wellington XI (Feb 1943—Apr 1943)
    MP520; MP522; MP523; MP531; MP534, 1:E; MP544
Vickers Wellington XII (Mar 1943—Apr 1944)
    HF115, 1:P; HF115, 1:W; HF116; MP541, 1:O; MP578, 1:D;
    MP587, 1:A; MP596, 1:B; MP634, 1:F; MP652, 1:S; MP688, 1:D;
    MP756, 1:S
Vickers Wellington XIV (Jul 1943—Jun 1945)
    HF124, 1:Q; HF134, 2:M, later 2:L; HF148, 1:P; HF169, 1:F;
    HF187, 1:S; HF207, 1:O, later 2:O; HF228, 1:N; HF286, 2:L;
    HF302, 2:J; NB821, 2:B; NB828, 2:P, later 2T; NB838, 2:J;
    NB856, 2:X; NB910; NC513, G; NC610; NC677; NC755, F; NC798;
    NC848, P; NC884; PF834

Commanding Officers

W/Cdr H. M. Styles, DSO	May 1941	Jan 1942
W/Cdr A. C. Brown, DSO, DFC	Jan 1942	Sep 1942
W/Cdr C. F. King	Sep 1942	Nov 1942
W/Cdr J. C. Archer	Nov 1942	Sep 1943
S/Ldr D. G. Pickard	Sep 1943	Oct 1943
W/Cdr R. A. Ashman	Oct 1943	Nov 1944
W/Cdr K. C. Wilson	Nov 1944	Jun 1945

Aircraft Insignia

From its formation until the re-equipment with Wellingtons the Squadron carried the code letters 'RR' on its Blenheims and Hudsons. The arrival of the Wellingtons coincided with the transfer, in Coastal Command, to station number codes and at first they carried the number '1', later the number '2'. In mid-1944 Coastal Command reverted to code letters and it is not certain what letters were carried by No. 407 Squadron although the combination 'C1' has been quoted.

No. 413 SQUADRON

BADGE
In front of a maple leaf an elephant's head affrontee

MOTTO
'Ad vigilamus undis'
('We watch the waves')

The elephant's head represents the squadron's operations from Ceylon while the motto suggests its function.

No. 413 Squadron, RCAF, was formed at Stranraer on 1 July, 1941 and immediately equipped with Consolidated Catalina I's. During its work-up period it flew the C-in-C Western Approaches to Iceland in September and began operations on 7 October with an escort task to an oil tanker. That month it flew twenty-three sorties including a special recce of Tromso, on 22nd. It settled into the routine of convoy escorts and anti-submarine patrols over the North Atlantic, with occasional recces of the Norwegian coast. This continued until March, 1942 when the Squadron left its aircraft in the Shetlands and began the long trek out to Ceylon.

At Koggala the first aircraft arrived on 2 April, 1942 and the Squadron began recce patrols with it that day. Two days later S/Ldr L. J. Birchall sighted and reported a large enemy force 350 miles south of Ceylon, only to be shot down by fighters from a Japanese carrier. Four days later F/Lt R. Thomas also found the same force and failed to return. In May and June the Squadron was largely occupied in flying anti-invasion patrols, establishing a detachment at Addu Atoll in July to extend its coverage.

On 3 August S/Ldr Randall was persistently attacked by RN Fulmars, the rudder and aileron controls were shot away, flight engineer killed, three others wounded and the tanks holed. Despite these handicaps he returned to base. At the end of the month and in early September the Squadron was much involved with an enemy submarine which sank several ships; the only time it was sighted the depth-charges on the Catalina concerned hung up. At that time the Squadron also had a detachment at Aden. By the end of the year the Squadron was flying the occasional offensive recce to Sumatra, a 2000 mile round trip.

The pattern into 1943 was much the same with anti-submarine patrols, convoy escorts, ASR searches and some surveying and anti-invasion work. In May the Squadron began a round freight trip to Australia once every two weeks. All this was without action until 3 November when F/O Gowans found a surfaced U-boat which he attacked and damaged, receiving some damage in return. On 27 December P/O Grandin found a submerging U-boat which he attacked; the amount of debris indicated that it was probably destroyed and survivors from it were found. In January, 1944 the Catalinas were fitted with Leigh Lights for A/S work. March brought intensive U-boat searches and also a task of photo recce of the Cocos Islands. It was a busy year for No. 413 and in July it flew as many as eighty sorties. However, there was no more action that year and in January, 1945 the Squadron ceased operations to return to the UK for conversion. On its return, however, it was disbanded at Bournemouth on 23 February, 1945.

Bases etc.

Formed at Stranraer on 1 July, 1941.

Stranraer	Jul 1941—Oct 1941	
Sullom Voe	Oct 1941—Mar 1942	
en route to Ceylon	Mar 1942—Apr 1942	
Koggala, det. Addu Atoll, Aden, Langebaan, Tulear, Diego Guarcia	Apr 1942—Jan 1945	
en route to UK	Jan 1945—Feb 1945	

Disbanded at Bournemouth 23 February, 1945.

Main Equipment

Consolidated Catalina I (Jul 1941—   1944)
W8412, QL:B; W8421, QL:D; W8434, QL:F; Z2135, QL:H; Z2149, QL:K, later QL:V; AH549, QL:F, later QL:W; AH550, QL:Z; AH561, QL:Y; AH567, QL:C; AJ155, QL:A; AJ161, W; FP282, Y; FP306, D, later Z; FP323,A
Consolidated Catalina IV (1944—Jan 1945)
JX276, Z; JX292, B; JX299, V; JX311, C; JX321, D; JX333, F; JX336, C; JX357, V

Commanding Officers

W/Cdr V. H. A. McBratney	Jul 1941—Aug 1941	
W/Cdr R. G. Briese	Aug 1941—Oct 1941	
W/Cdr J. D. Twigg	Nov 1941—Mar 1942	
W/Cdr J. L. Plant	Mar 1942—Oct 1942	
W/Cdr J. C. Scott, DSO	Oct 1942—Jun 1943	
W/Cdr L. H. Randall, DFC	Jun 1943—Sep 1944	
W/Cdr S. R. McMillan	Sep 1944—Feb 1945	

Aircraft Insignia

From formation until the end of 1942 the Squadron's aircraft carried the code letters 'QL'. Thereafter no insignia was carried.

No. 414 SQUADRON

(No badge authorised)

This RCAF Squadron was formed at Croydon on 12 August, 1941 in the army co-operation role, equipped with Lysander and Tomahawk aircraft. At this time there was little operational activity for such squadrons and for a long time it was engaged in a continuous series of army exercises. In June, 1942 it began re-equipment with the North American Mustang I and took this type into action at Dieppe on 19 August, flying eighteen Tac/R missions, losing two aircraft shot down by FW 190s, one pilot being rescued. Just over a month later the Squadron began *Populars* and in October also added anti-*Rhubarb* patrols, flying 75 sorties that month. These included six *Rhubarbs* over France which accounted for two locomotives destroyed. In November double this number of operational sorties were flown, mostly on coastal and convoy protection operations, these generally being in the area between Shoreham and St. Catherine's Point (on the Isle of Wight).

Initially it was off operations in 1943 until March when *Rhubarbs* were resumed, to which were added *Roadsteads*, anti-*Rhubarbs* and shipping recces in April. This year was a period of many moves, from Surrey to Cornwall; eighty to one hundred sorties were flown each month and about one aircraft was lost a month. In August the Squadron began operations at night on *Rangers* and it was at this that F/Lt Stover shot down a Ju 88. In September two Squadron aircraft were shot down into the sea by FW 190s and another pilot was lost on a night intruder sortie. By the end of the year No. 414 was flying exclusively on *Populars*. Early 1944 saw the Squadron transitting between Hampshire and Scotland until returning to operations at Gatwick in March. It was now busy flying Tac/R and PR sorties against the *Noball* bases in Northern France. The pressure built up as D-Day approached. On D-Day itself the Squadron provided spotting for the Naval bombardment, followed by continuous Tac/R sorties for the army on the Continent flying up to thirty sorties a day and accomplishing fifty sorties on 14th. Despite all this activity (470 sorties in the month) only four aircraft and two pilots were lost. The Squadron was using a coastal airstrip as forward base and this continued throughout July and early August. On 15 August

No. 414 Squadron moved to France and at the same time began converting to Spitfires.

As the armies moved across into Belgium and Holland No. 414 went with them, flying intensively (493 sorties were clocked up in October, 1944), almost all its work being tactical recces. At the close of the year, however, it was flying more long-range PR sorties into Germany and these were also continued into the New Year. On New Year's Day five Squadron aircraft were destroyed in the Luftwaffe raids but twenty sorties were flown and a FW 190 destroyed and a Bf 109 damaged. In addition the CO attacked twenty-plus aircraft raiding Eindhoven airfield and shot down two 109s and damaged a FW 190. As the spring came on the sortie rate increased once more, the Squadron maintaining a high-level of Tac-R up to the end of the war in Europe. Soon after it ended the Squadron was disbanded, at Lüneburg, on 7 August, 1945.

Bases etc.

Formed at Croydon on 12 August, 1941.

Croydon	Aug 1941—Dec 1942
Dunsfold, det. Tangmere	Dec 1942—Feb 1943
Middle Wallop, det. Predannack	Feb 1943—Feb 1943
Dunsfold	Feb 1943—Apr 1943
Middle Wallop	Apr 1943—May 1943
Harrowbeer	May 1943—Jun 1943
Portreath	Jun 1943—Jun 1943
Dunsfold	Jun 1943—Jul 1943
Gatwick	Jul 1943—Aug 1943
Ashford	Aug 1943—Oct 1943
Woodchurch	Oct 1943—Oct 1943
Redhill	Oct 1943—Nov 1943
Gatwick	Nov 1943—Feb 1944
Peterhead	Feb 1944—Feb 1944
Odiham	Feb 1944—Feb 1944
Dundonald	Feb 1944—Mar 1944
Gatwick	Mar 1944—Apr 1944
Odiham	Apr 1944—Aug 1944
St. Honorine de Ducy (B.21)	Aug 1944—Aug 1944
Illiers l'Eveque (B.26)	Aug 1944—Sep 1944
Poix (B.44)	Sep 1944—Sep 1944
Evere (B.56)	Sep 1944—Sep 1944
Blankenburg (B.66)	Sep 1944—Oct 1944
Eindhoven (B.78)	Oct 1944—Mar 1945
Petit Brogel (B.90)	Mar 1945—Apr 1945

Rheine (B.108)   Apr 1945—Apr 1945
Wunstorf (B.116)   Apr 1945—Apr 1945
Soltau (B.154)   Apr 1945—May 1945
Celle (B.118)   May 1945—May 1945
Lüneburg Heath (B.156)   May 1945—Aug 1945
Disbanded at Lüneburg Heath 17 August, 1945.

Main Equipment

Westland Lysander IIIA (Aug 1941—May 1942)
V9381, RU:W; V9445, RU:X
Curtiss Tomahawk I, II (Aug 1941—Aug 1942) (Apr 1943—Jul 1943)
AH902, RU:Z; AH935, RU:A; AH936, RU:H; AK185, RU:V;
AK219, RU:F
North American Mustang I (Jun 1942—Aug 1944)
AG376, RU:R; AG416, RU:S; AG444, RU:H; AG527, RU:H;
AG543, RU:E; AG612, RU:B; AG655, RU:X; AL984, H;
AM160, RU:T; AM248, L; AM251, O; AP197, Z; AP204, X;
AP211, V
Vickers-Supermarine Spitfire IX (Aug 1944—Apr 1945)
MJ351, S; MJ518, O; MJ553, G; MJ617, W; MJ633, F; MJ746, V;
MJ780, B; MJ871, C; MJ896, A; MJ910, F; MJ966, J; MK127, K;

MK183, T; MK202, Q; MK249, C; MK290, U; MK359, X;
MK924, L
Vickers-Supermarine Spitfire XIV (Apr 1945—Aug 1945)
MV269; MV299; MV314; MV348; MV382; NH648; NH797; NH808;
NH899; NH903; NM821; NM896, B

Commanding Officers

W/Cdr D. M. Smith	Sep 1941	Jul 1942
W/Cdr R. F. Begg	Jul 1942	Jun 1943
S/Ldr J. M. Godfrey	Jun 1943	Jul 1943
S/Ldr H. P. Peters, DFC	Jul 1943	Nov 1943
S/Ldr G. H. Stover, DFC	Nov 1943	Jun 1944
S/Ldr R. T. Hutchinson, DFC	Jun 1944	Oct 1944
S/Ldr G. Wonnacott, DFC and Bar	Oct 1944	Mar 1945
S/Ldr F. S. Gilbertson, DFC	Mar 1945	Apr 1945
S/Ldr J. B. Prendergast, DFC	Apr 1945	Aug 1945

Aircraft Insignia

The code letters 'RU' were used from August, 1941 to early 1943 after which no specific squadron insignia was carried.

No. 415 SQUADRON

BADGE
A swordfish

MOTTO
'Ad metam'
('To the mark')

Both badge and motto indicate the squadron's
duties in attacking shipping.

On 20 August, 1941 No. 415 Squadron, RCAF, was formed as a torpedo-bomber unit at Thorney Island. It was initially equipped with Bristol Beauforts and Blenheim IVs and worked up with these but never became operational with them. In January, 1942 it re-equipped with Hampden Is and flew its first operation on 27 April. These comprised anti-shipping patrols over the Bay of Biscay which became the mainstay of its task. It also undertook offensive shipping strikes, its first, in May, on a 6000-ton motor vessel in which it was damaged and one of the three Hampdens was lost. In June the Squadron moved to North Coates and operated over the North Sea, losing four aircraft that month, two in an attack on a convoy near Borkum. On 1 July an attack resulted in one ship being set on fire, encouraging the Squadron to continue its attacks along the German North Sea coast. It moved north in August and from then on operated over the North Sea to the Norwegian coast, striking at the shipping moving up and down *en route* to the Atlantic. Before the year ended, however, it was back to operating both over Biscay and along the Dutch coast.

By 1943 the Hampden was outclassed as a torpedo-bomber and although most sorties were now flown at night the losses increased. The Squadron still had successes as on 14 April when good hits were obtained on a 6000-ton ship. A high rate of sorties was flown that summer, 70 or 80 individual trips being made each month. Although primarily an anti-shipping unit the CO found a U-boat on 2 August and disabled it, enabling a Liberator to destroy it. In September operations ceased and the Squadron began converting to Wellington XIIIs and Fairey Albacore biplanes. These it used, when it resumed operations on 3 November, for Operation Deadly (anti E-boat patrols), the system being for the Leigh Light Wellingtons to find and illuminate the E-boats and the Albacores to attack them. The Squadron roamed up and down the Dutch and Channel coasts attacking any enemy shipping it could find with some success. In January, 1944 Operation Gilbey was also flown (directing Beaufighters). On 20 January two Albacores attacked two destroyers and set one on fire, although one aircraft was lost. In February the pace increased again and in March 121 sorties were

flown with a high success rate, the targets ranging from barges to ocean-going tankers. This pace was maintained up to the end of May, 1944 when the Squadron handed its aircraft to 119 Squadron and was transferred to 6 Group, Bomber Command, serving as a Halifax bomber squadron until disbanding at East Moor on 15 May, 1945.

Bases etc.

Formed at Thorney Island on 20 August, 1941.

Thorney Island, det. Detling	Aug 1941	Jun 1942
North Coates	Jun 1942	Aug 1942
Wick, det. Tain, Leuchars	Aug 1942	Sep 1942
Leuchars, det. St. Eval	Sep 1942	Nov 1942
Thorney Island, det. Predannack, Tain	Nov 1942	Nov 1943
Bircham Newton, det. Manston,		
Thorney Island, North Coates, Winkleigh	Nov 1943	May 1944

Transferred to No. 6 Group, Bomber Command at East Moor May—July, 1944.

Main Equipment

Bristol Beaufort I (Aug 1941—Feb 1942)
L9802, GX:R; L9819, GX:Q; L9896, GX:R; N1082, GX:A;
N1102, GX:S; AW219, GX:C
Bristol Blenheim IV (Aug 1941—   1941)
L9476, GX:Y; T2397; Z5740
Handley Page Hampden I (Jan 1942—Oct 1943)
L4084; P1157, O; P1310; P2065; X3140, T; AD762, GX:J;
AE360, GX:H; AT152, GX:S; AT229, GX:V; AT232, GX:A;
AT245, GX:U; AT248, GX:J; AT250, GX:K
Vickers Wellington XIII (Sep 1943—Jul 1944)
HZ644, NH:O; HZ653, NH:L; HZ721, NH:J; HZ756, NH:G;
JA638, NH:R; JA635, NH:A; MF231, NH:D; MF634, NH:K;
MF640, NH:F; NC507, NH:C; NC626, NH:E
Fairey Albacore I (Oct 1943—Jul 1944)
L7080; L7173, NH:C1; X9130, NH:X1; X9169; X9222, NH:A1;
BF588, NH:M

Commanding Officers

W/Cdr E. L. Wurtele	Aug 1941	Aug 1942
W/Cdr R. R. Dennis	Aug 1942	Nov 1942
W/Cdr W. W. Bean	Nov 1942	Mar 1943
W/Cdr G. H. D. Evans	Mar 1943	Aug 1943
W/Cdr C. G. Ruttan, DSO	Aug 1943	Jul 1944

Aircraft Insignia

The Squadron was allotted the code letters 'GX' from its inception and used these on Blenheim IVs, Beauforts and Hampdens. In the Spring of 1943 code letters were discontinued in Coastal Command and no insignia was carried. However, in early 1944 code letters were used once more and now the Squadron carried 'NH' on its aircraft until transfer to Bomber Command.

No. 422 SQUADRON

BADGE
A cubit arm holding in the hand a tomahawk
MOTTO
'This arm shall do it'

The painted arm indicates that the Red Indian brave is at war. The motto, from Shakespeare, refers to the Squadron's striking power.

No. 422 was formed from Canadian personnel as the RCAFs fifth coastal squadron in World War II. The date was 2 April, 1942 and the base was Lough Erne. It was originally equipped with Saro Lerwick flying boats but these were only used for work-up and training as they had been found unsatisfactory for operations and by August were being superseded by Catalinas. Becoming operational with these the Squadron's first task was to fly transport sorties between Invergordon and Grasnaya in the Soviet Union, taking Hurricane spares for the Soviet Air Force. This was soon linked with convoy patrols for convoys in and out of Soviet ports up to 24 September when 422 came off operations, its Catalinas and Lerwicks being removed. In October the crews went to the USA and began ferrying Catalinas across the Atlantic; at last it received four of its own and with these and Sunderlands worked up for operations. However its new task began in January, 1943 with ferrying overseas mail down the West African coast to Lagos, combining these with coastal recces. It was not until 25 February that the Squadron's first official Coastal Command sortie was flown, a convoy escort. From them on it flew regularly on anti-submarine and convoy escort tasks, working up to 53 sorties a month by July. It was now entirely Sunderland-equipped. On 17 October the Squadron's first U-boat attack was made by F/Lt P. T. Sargent in JM712 but the aircraft was shot down by the U-boat and only seven survivors recovered.

The monotonous pattern continued with little change until 10 March, 1944 when W/O Martin and crew found a U-boat (*U-625*) and attacked it under heavy return fire. They damaged it so severely that the crew abandoned it and it sank. Another ten months went by before further attacks were made, most of the Squadron's work being over the Western Approaches although a detachment was operating out of the Shetlands. A flurry of activity took place in March, 1945 with four depth-charge attacks on U-boats between the 5th and 8th. From then on it was a run down in Squadron activity until the war in Europe ended. On 24 July, 1945 the No. 422 left Pembroke Dock and its Sunderlands and moved to Bassingbourn to become a transport squadron with Liberators, the intention being to support 'Tiger Force' in the Far East. However, with the end of hostilities this was not needed and No. 422 Squadron disbanded there on 3 September, 1945.

Bases etc.

Formed at Lough Erne on 2 April, 1942.

Lough Erne, det. Invergordon	Apr 1942	Nov 1942
Oban	Nov 1942	May 1943
Bowmore	May 1943	Nov 1943
St. Angelo	Nov 1943	Apr 1944
Castle Archdale	Apr 1944	Nov 1944
Pembroke Dock	Nov 1944	Jul 1945
Bassingbourn	Jul 1945	Sep 1945

Disbanded at Bassingbourne 3 September, 1945.

Main Equipment

Saro Lerwick I (Jul 1942—Oct 1942)
L7250, U; L7256, V; L7259, Q; L7264, N; L7266, Y; L7267, Y
Consolidated Catalina IB (Aug 1942—Oct 1942)
FP103, A; FP105, B; FP106, C; FP240; FP245; FP248
Short Sunderland III (Nov 1942—Jul 1945)
W6026, 2:A; W6028, 2:C; W6032, 2:H; W6066, 2:F; DD831, 2:K; DD846, 2:D; DD854, 2:P; DP178, 2:L; DV910, 2:T; DV988, 2:D; EJ151, DG:H; EK576, 2:Q; EK594, 2:W; JM679, 2:E; JM712, 2:S; ML773, 2:R; ML816, DG:X; ML871, DG:Q; ML884, DG:Z; NJ172, DG:O; NJ189, DG:V
Consolidated Liberator C.VI/C.VIII (Aug 1945—Sep 1945)
No serial numbers known

Commanding Officers

S/Ldr J. S. Kendrick	Jun 1942	Jul 1942
W/Cdr L. W. Skey, DFC	Jul 1942	Oct 1943
W/Cdr J. R. Frizzle	Oct 1943	Oct 1944
W/Cdr J. R. Sumner	Oct 1944	Sep 1945

Aircraft Insignia

It is not known what code letters were originally carried by No. 422 Squadron on the Lerwicks and Catalinas, although 'DG' has been quoted for this period. In 1943 Coastal Command dropped letters, using base numbering systems and under this system the Squadron carried the number '2'. When code letters were again introduced in 1944 the Squadron then used 'DG'.

No. 423 SQUADRON

BADGE
A bald-headed eagle volant
MOTTO
'*Quaerimus et petimus*'
('We search and strike')

The bald-headed eagle is a powerful bird of prey from across the Atlantic.

This Squadron formed as an RCAF unit at Oban on 18 March, 1943. By July it began to receive Sunderland flying boats and this type formed its equipment for its entire operational existence in Coastal Command. Its first operation was flown by F/Lt Musgrave on 23 August searching for a submarine over the Atlantic. At first it only made a few sorties a month but as more aircraft and crews became operational so its output increased so that by March, 1943 it was flying thirty sorties a month. That month two crews made attacks on U-boats, F/O Howell's crew on 20th attacking two submarines and seeing debris coming from the first. On 5 April F/Lt Bradley attacked another which blew up with much debris. More attacks followed, with *U-456* being shared between F/Lt Musgrave and two destroyers. On 4 August F/O A. A. Bishop and crew attacked *U-489*; the Sunderland was shot down and five of the crew lost but the U-boat crew abandoned ship, which blew up. All survivors were rescued. In the autumn of 1943 the Squadron was flying Biscay patrols by going to and from Gibraltar; two Sunderlands were lost before the year was out.

The ocean patrols continued into 1944, more sightings coming in April. In June, the month of the invasion of France, the Squadron flew a record 89 sorties, bettering this in September with 100. Eight attacks were made that year and only one Sunderland was lost on operations. The pressure continued into 1945, three attacks occurring in January alone. This continued right up to the end of the war in Europe, the last U-boat fight taking place on 4 May, 1945. In June the Squadron abandoned Coastal Command, joining 301 Wing Transport Command. On 7 August it moved to Bassingbourn and there received Liberators for its new role. This was forestalled by the end of hostilities and No. 423 Squadron disbanded on 3 September, 1945.

Bases etc.

Formed at Oban on 18 May, 1942m
Oban   May 1942—Nov 1942
Castle Archdale (Lough Erne), det.
   Pembroke Dock   Nov 1942—Aug 1945
Bassingbourn   Aug 1945—Sep 1945
Disbanded at Bassingbourn on 3 September, 1945.

Main Equipment

Short Sunderland II (Jul 1942—May 1943)
  W3990; W6000, AB:A; W6001, AB:B
Short Sunderland III (Jul 1942—Jun 1945)
  W6006, AB:F; W6052, AB:D; W6061, AB:K; W6068, AB:N;
  DD828, AB:A; DD859, 3:G; DD862, 3:A; DD867, 3:G; DP181, 3:D;
  DP191, 3:L; DV978, 3:NP; DW111, :S; EJ157, YI:K; EK581, 3:D;
  JM666; ML784, YI:L; ML742, YI:P; ML825, YI:D; NJ182, YI:N;
  NJ185, YI:E
Consolidated Liberator C.VI/C, VIII (Aug 1945—Sep 1945)
  No serial numbers known

Commanding Officers

W/Cdr F. J. Rump	May 1942—	Jul 1943
W/Cdr L. G. G. J. Archambault	Jul 1943—	Jul 1944
W/Cdr P. J. Grant	Jul 1944—	Feb 1945
W/Cdr S. R. McMillan	Mar 1945—	Sep 1945

Aircraft Insignia

From formation until mid-1943 the Squadron carried the code letters 'AB'. These were replaced, for a year, by the station number '3', only to be replaced itself by the letters 'YI' from mid-1944 to June, 1945. It is not believed that the Liberators carried any insignia.

No. 430 SQUADRON

(No badge authorised)

This RCAF Squadron was formed at Hartford Bridge on 1 January, 1943 with Curtiss Tomahawks in the army co-operation role. It soon re-equipped with Mustangs, working up to start operations on 26 May with *Rhubarbs* against railway targets in Northern France. In June sixty-three sorties were flown with weather recces, *Rhubarbs* and *Populars* on the Cherbourg Peninsula area. This became the pattern for the Squadron through to the autumn when, for a while, it was more concerned with anti-*Rhubarb* sorties covering the coast from North Foreland to Beachy Head. Both offensive and defensive sorties were flown through to the spring of 1944, though various detachments for exercises intertered; in the New Year the targets were increasingly *Noball* targets in Northern France.

With the build-up to the Second Front in 1944 the Squadron's activity increased as it became involved in the preparation for the invasion. In May, 1944 it was flying with the Typhoon fighter-bombers to photograph the results of their bombing attacks as well as on PR, Tac/R and *Popular* tasks. 140 sorties were flown in May and 270 in June, the month of Operation Overlord. On D-Day itself it concentrated on PR sorties of the roads around Caen, losing one pilot only. In subsequent days its task was reconnaissance to check on enemy M/T movements behind the battle area.

By the end of the month three more pilots had been lost and the Squadron had moved to France itself. Now it was able to increase its operations, flying 558 sorties in July and 608 in August, all in and just behind the battle area. September saw it moving eastwards to keep up with the advancing armies and flying Tac/R sorties as it went. By November it was in Holland and here it re-equipped with Spitfire XIVs. The task was the same with this type, Tac/R and artillery recce predominating.

Weather restricted operations during the winter but as the spring of 1945 came the Squadron became increasingly involved in the final push into Germany, flying 477 sorties in April. With the end of the war the Squadron was soon disbanded, to allow its Canadian personnel to be re-patriated, at Lüneburg Heath on 7 August, 1945.

Bases etc.

Formed at Hartford Bridge on 1 January, 1943.

Hartford Bridge	Jan 1943—	Jan 1943
Dunsfold, det. Ouston	Jan 1943—	Jul 1943
Gatwick	Jul 1943—	Aug 1943
Ashford	Aug 1943—	Oct 1943
Gatwick, det. Peterhead	Oct 1943—	Feb 1944
Clifton	Feb 1944—	Feb 1944
Gatwick	Feb 1944—	Apr 1944
Odiham	Apr 1944—	Jun 1944
Sommervieu (B.8)	Jun 1944—	Aug 1944
St. Honorine de Ducy (B.21)	Aug 1944—	Sep 1944
Avrilly (B.34)	Sep 1944—	Sep 1944
Diest (B.66)	Sep 1944—	Oct 1944
Eindhoven (B.78), det. Y.25	Oct 1944—	Mar 1945
Petit Brogel (B.90)	Mar 1945—	Apr 1945
Rheine (B.108)	Apr 1945—	Apr 1945
Soltau (B.154)	Apr 1945—	May 1945
Lüneburg Heath (B.156)	May 1945—	Aug 1945

Disbanded at Lüneburg Heath 7 August, 1945.

Main Equipment

Curtiss Tomahawk, I, III (Jan 1943—Jun 1943)
  AH905; AH909; AH910; AK189
North American Mustang I (Jan 1943—Dec 1944)f AG349, A; AG355, R;
  AG424, N; AG455, F; AG522, P; AG552, M; AG627, C; AG664, M;
  AL966, E; AL986, T; AM125, W; AM139, P; AM191, R; AM226, C;
  AM253, A; AP188, A
Vickers-Supermarine Spitfire XIV (Nov 1944—Aug 1945)
  RM783, F; RM794, T; RM807, L; RM850, O; RM866, T; RM874, L;
  RM910, Y; RM927, X; RM929, S; RN114, W; RN116, C; RN202, S

Commanding Officers

W/Cdr E. H. G. Moncrieff, AFC	Jan 1943—	Jul 1943
S/Ldr R. A. Ellis, DFC	Jul 1943—	Sep 1943
S/Ldr F. H. Chesters	Sep 1943—	Oct 1944
S/Ldr J. Watts	Oct 1944—	Mar 1945
S/Ldr C. D. Bricker, DFC	Mar 1945—	May 1945
S/Ldr H. W. Russell	May 1945—	Aug 1945

Aircraft Insignia

It has been reported that this Squadron used the code letters 'G9', on the Spitfire XIVs only. It is almost certain that the Tomahawks and Mustangs carried no identity markings.

No. 435 SQUADRON

BADGE
A chinthe on a plinth
MOTTO
'Certi provehendi'
('Determined on delivery')

The chinthe is a legendary monster which guards the temples in Burma where this Squadron operated.

This RCAF Squadron was formed officially at Gujarat on 20 August, 1944 but it was not until 1 October that ground crew began arriving and the end of the month before the Squadron was really a going concern. In December it moved to Tulihall for operations which commenced on 20th with supply drops to the 14th Army, 304 sorties being flown by the end of the month. The task involved comparatively short flights from base to the forward troops, sometimes operating behind the Japanese lines, dropping supplies on

DZs cut out of the Jungle. In January, 1945 2325 sorties were flown in this way; on 12 January, while five aircraft were in the circuit dropping supplies at Shwebo they were attacked by Japanese Oscars (Nakajima Ki.43) and two Dakotas were shot down. As a result of this the Squadron went over to largely night drops until it could be arranged for fighter escorts. In February, 1945 the Squadron flew just over 1000 sorties, mainly into landing strips in the Shwebo area and across the Irrawaddy bridgehead; one aircraft was lost that month. In March operations were doubled and No. 435 transferred to the Meiktela area. Operation Dracula came in May with many sorties dropping over the Rangoon area which the monsoon interfered with operations for some time. Increasingly in June and July the Squadron was flying rice into North Burma to alleviate the starvation there, then in August the Squadron began running down in India, the crews staging through to England.

No. 435 Squadron was re-constituted at Down Ampney in Gloucestershire on 29 August, 1945 and after a brief work-up began operating as part of 120 (RCAF) Wing on Transport Command's schedules to the Continent, maintaining a detachment at Croydon for this purpose, this latter airport becoming the immediate post-war terminal for London. This type of operation was continued through until early 1946, the last flight taking place on 14 March, 1946. The Squadron officially disbanded at Down Ampney on 1 April, 1946.

Bases etc.

Formed at Gujarat on 20 August, 1944.

Gujarat	Aug 1944—Dec 1944
Tulihall	Dec 1944—Mar 1945
Sentinel Hill	Mar 1945—Aug 1945
en route to UK	Aug 1945—Aug 1945
Down Ampney, det. Croydon	Aug 1945—Apr 1946

Disbanded at Down Ampney on 1 April, 1946.

Main Equipment

Douglas Dakota III (Oct 1944—Apr 1946)
FD821, C; FD915, O; FZ658, Q; FZ665; FZ671, R; KG317, A; KG397, D; KG414, G; KG486, H; KG557, U; KG587, T; KG659, W; KG713, Y

Douglas Dakota IV (Oct 1944—Apr 1946)
KJ821, C; KJ883, N; KK106, O; KK169, Q; KN261, Y; KN413, F; KN511, Z; KN655, LW; KN666, KW; KP227, J; KP241, V; TS425, C

Commanding Officers

W/Cdr R. W. Goodwin	Oct 1944—Nov 1944
W/Cdr T. P. Harnett	Nov 1944—Aug 1945
W/Cdr C. N. McVeigh, AFC	Aug 1945—Apr 1946

Aircraft Insignia

The Squadron was allotted the Transport Command call-sign code 'ODM' and this was carried, together with the aircraft letter, on the aircraft, usually as an abbreviated two-letter symbol, and often on the extreme nose.

No. 436 SQUADRON

BADGE
An elephant's head couped carrying a log

MOTTO
'Onus portamus'
('We carry the load')

The badge symbolises the Squadron's role as a transport squadron in India.

No. 436 Squadron was officially formed at Gujarat on 20 August, 1944 but it was not until October, 1944 that RCAF personnel began arriving. Dakotas followed in November and the Squadron worked up, becoming operational early in December, its first task being to transport No. 117 Squadron from Bikram to its operational base at Hathazari. Full operations, however, did not begin until the New Year after moving to Kangla and consisted of taking No. 42 Squadron into Ye-U and then food and petrol for XXXIII Corps there. Thereafter the pressure built up so that by March the Squadron was flying 1600 sorties a month, flying supplies into little strips or dropping them on to DZs in the jungle. In April most of the operations were directed towards Meiktela and they were hazarded by many engine failures due to the use of wrong oil. Ramree Island became the focus in May and June, despite the monsoon 1388 sorties being flown that month. A similar total came in July and that month the Squadron's first fatal accident took place. In August operations began running down as repatriation hit the Squadron but after VJ-Day in nevertheless began casevac sorties to Chittagong and as far as Hong Kong.

At the end of August, 1945 it handed over its schedules to No. 48 Squadron and began routing back to the UK, re-forming itself at Down Ampney on 26 September. Here it worked up for flying in the European scene. In October it began freight schedules within Europe and the following month began trooping to Norway, Germany and Czechoslovakia. It settled into regular European schedules as well as flying army commitments when they arose. This work continued until 22 June, 1946 when the last Dakotas left Odiham and the Squadron officially disbanded.

Bases etc.

Formed at Gujarat on 20 August, 1944.

Gujarat	Aug 1944—Jan 1945
Kangala	Jan 1945—Mar 1945
Mawnubyn	Mar 1945—May 1945
Kyaukpyu, det. Kinmagon	May 1945—Sep 1945
en route to UK	Sep 1945—Sep 1945
Down Ampney, det. Biggin Hill, Odiham	Sep 1945—Apr 1946
Odiham	Apr 1946—Jun 1946

Disbanded at Odiham 22 June, 1946.

Main Equipment

Douglas Dakota III (Aug 1944—Jun 1946)
FD844; FD856; FD878; FL532; FL569; FL578; FZ607, Z; FZ658, S; FZ671, R; KG317, A; KG350, BW; KG441, N; KG565; KG587, L; KG635, P; KG790

Douglas Dakota IV (Aug 1944—Jun 1946)
KJ799; KJ844; KJ893; KJ904; KJ964; KK107; KK143, A; KK181; KN208; KN225; KN277, Q; KN305; KN458; KN665, W; KP224, L; TS422

Commanding Officers

W/Cdr R. A. Gordon, DSO, DFC	Oct 1944—Aug 1945
W/Cdr R. L. Denison, DFC	Aug 1945—Jun 1946

Aircraft Insignia

The Squadron was allotted the Transport Command call-sign code 'ODN' and this was carried in abbreviated form on the nose of the aircraft, usually just the 'N' plus the aircraft letter. It has also been quoted that the Squadron carried the identity code letters 'U6' whilst in the UK but no confirmation of this is to hand.

No. 437 SQUADRON

BADGE
A husky's head affronte erased

MOTTO
'Omnia passim'
('Anything anywhere')

Nicknamed the 'Husky' Squadron this unit adopted as its badge a husky's head indicative of its function of glider-towing and freighting.

This RCAF Squadron formed on 4 September, 1944 at Blakehill Farm as a transport unit with Douglas Dakotas. With RCAF personnel drawn from other Dakota squadrons it was almost immediately operational, flying into the Arnhem operation on 17 September, fourteen aircraft towing gliders there safely. The following day another six took part in a glider tow to Arnhem and the Squadron now began flying the Continental shuttle with the other transport squadrons; mail, passengers, freight and petrol going in and mail and wounded coming back. On 21 and 23 September two Arnhem re-supply missions were flown in intense opposition and four Dakotas failed to return from these. Thereafter No. 437 Squadron flew exclusively on the shuttles to Continental bases. In November Ansons were added to the fleet and scheduled services were established across the Channel, between two and three hundred flights being made each month.

These normal transport duties were maintained until early March when No. 437 was withdrawn to work-up for Operation Varsity. This, the airborne crossing of the Rhine, took place on 24th, the Squadron towing twenty-four Horsa gliders safely across. The Squadron then returned to cross-Channel runs until 7 May when it moved to Belgium and began schedules within Europe itself. This involved shorter trips, the Squadron was averaging about 420 flights a month.

With the war over No. 437 concentrated on POW flights both ways (to and from the Continent) and with repatriating the Canadian Army to the UK. In July a detachment went to Oslo to open up-air services there, staying until November. In August another detachment moved to Odiham so now the Squadron was operating from bases in Belgium, Norway and the UK. To this was added a detachment at Berlin in October. A grand total of 676 sorties was flown at this time. In November the whole Squadron moved to Odiham, with a small detachment at Evere in Belgium. In 1946 it operated increasingly out of Croydon airport, flying more and more on regular schedules and maintained this pattern until 16 June, 1946 when it was disbanded at Odiham.

Bases etc.

Formed at Blakehill Farm on 4 September, 1944.

Blakehill Farm, det. Broadwell, Down Ampney	Sep 1944—May 1945
Nivelles (B.75)	May 1945—Jun 1945
Melsbroek (B.58), det. Fornebu, Odiham	Jun 1945—Sep 1945
Evere (B.56), det. Fornebu, Odiham, Gatow	Sep 1945—Nov 1945
Odiham, det. Evere, Croydon, Hamburg (B.188)	Nov 1945—Jun 1946

Disbanded at Odiham 16 June, 1946.

Main Equipment

Douglas Dakota III (Sep 1944—Jun 1946)
FZ639, Z2:NS; FZ692, Z2:DB; FZ695, Z2:OA; KG310, Z2:DD; KG345, Z2:DV; KG395, Z2:DY; KG409, Z2:DK; KG425, Z2:DM; KG501, Z2:OD; KG529, Z2:DJ; KG577, Z2:OAW; KG600, Z2:DC; KG634, Z2:OBW; KG634, Z2:OT; KG692, Z2:DR
Avro Anson I, XI (Nov 1944—   1945)
NK487; NK651; NK700, Z2:NW; NL140; NL199, Z2:NY
Douglas Dakota IV (Feb 1945—Jun 1946)
KJ808, Z2:OM; KK211, Z2:ND; KN256, Z2:OL; KN269, Z2:OU; KN278, Z2:OL; KN291, Z2:OI

Commanding Officers

W/Cdr J. A. Sproule, DFC	Sep 1944—Sep 1945
W/Cdr A. R. Holmes	Sep 1945—Jun 1946

Aircraft Insignia

The aircraft carried the Squadron identity code letters 'Z2' during its entire existence. In addition the last two letters of the four-letter Transport Command code were carried on each aircraft. At first these comprised two-letter combinations beginning with 'D' and 'N' (short for 'ODD' and 'ODN') then after the War this was changed to 'O' with the code becoming 'ODO'; in each case the last letter was the individual aircraft letter.

No. 455 SQUADRON

BADGE
In front of two battle axes in saltire a winged helmet

MOTTO
'Strike and strike again'

The helmet and battle axes are indicative of much of the Squadron's operational activity – rapid strikes across the North Sea.

No. 455 Squadron formed in Britain at Swinderby on 30 June, 1941 as the first Australian bomber squadron in Britain, later absorbing the original No. 455 Squadron party formed at Williamston in New South Wales. Equipped with Hampdens it began night operations on 29 August, 1941 and continued on night bomber operations until April, 1942 when it moved to Leuchars, on 26th, on transfer to Coastal Command.

At first it continued similar bombing and mining activities along the Norwegian coast on behalf of Coastal Command but at the same time it began receiving Hampden Is equipped for torpedo-dropping and much of its time was devoted on torpedo training. Operations and training continued during the summer (much time was spent in July searching for the *Tirpitz*) until on 14 September the first torpedo strike was flown. This was from Vaenga in the Soviet Union, whence a detachment of the Squadron had gone. Nothing came of this strike, and the Squadron then concentrated on teaching the Russians to fly the Hampden, leaving their aircraft there and returning to the UK by HMS *Argonaut* in October.

The Squadron worked-up again to full strength, now flying mainly anti-submarine patrols in northern waters; on 27 October P/O Ethell attacked a U-boat without result. At last, in January, 1943, the torpedo training bore fruit. On 22nd a 2000-ton motor vessel was hit by No. 455s torpedoes, five days later a U-boat was torpedoed and on 29th a 6000-ton MV was hit and sunk. The next success came on 4 April when two crews hit a 5000-ton MV whilst themselves being attacked by enemy aircraft. On 30th F/Sgt Freeth depth-charged a U-boat and destroyed it. May brought sixty-one

sorties flown and two more ships hit, one of which sank. This was the pattern throughout the summer with shipping *Rovers* and anti-U-boat patrols predominating. Activity declined in the autumn as most crews were tour-expired and the Hampden was becoming too old for the task.

In December, 1943 the Squadron re-equipped with Beaufighters, the last Hampden operation being flown on 10th. A lengthy work-up followed and no operations took place until March, 1944 by which time No. 455 had become an integral part of the Leuchars Strike Wing with No. 489 Squadron, RNZAF. On 6 March operations began with No. 455 flying as strike escort to No. 489's torpedo-equipped Beaufighters. This was the pattern as the Wing flew many operations over the spring months of 1944. In April it moved to Langham for work along the Dutch coast, rendering the eastern end of the Channel impassable for E-boats. These operations, for which No. 455 carried 250 lb bombs, were known as *Conebos*; later 500 lb bombs were also used. Over the period of the D-Day landings the Squadron was detached to Manston for 'channel-bottling' purposes and found many targets amongst E-boats, armed trawlers and coastal convoys. One strike on 15 June was particularly successful with a 4000-ton MV sunk, an 8000-ton MV beached, one minesweeper sunk and four set on fire for no loss. One hundred and seventy-nine sorties were flown that month. In August the Squadron began operating at night on Purblind sorties under the direction of 524 Squadron's Wellingtons. During the day most of No. 455s Wing attacks saw the Squadron in the anti-Flak role and for this it began to use RPs in August. The level of sorties remained just under the 200 mark all through the summer and autumn, losses varied, coming back unscathed from many strikes but increasingly one or two Beaufighters would be lost.

With the Channel increasingly clear and Holland being occupied the Squadron moved to Scotland in October, becoming part of the Dallachy Wing and starting Norwegian coast *Rovers* once more. This became the Squadron's main occupation through the winter of 1944—45, operations being reduced in number by the short day-light hours. In March, 1945, however, the Squadron began night sorties as well as by day and these were continued right up to beyond

VE-Day, the last operation being on 21 May, 1945 when two aircraft flew an anti-U-boat patrol looking for submarines which had not surrendered. Four days later the Squadron was disbanded at Dallachy.

Bases etc.

Formed at Swinderby on 30 June, 1941 in Bomber Command. Transferred to Coastal Command at Leuchars on 26 April, 1942.

Leuchars, det. Vaenga (USSR), Sumburgh, Wick, Skitten	Apr 1942—Apr 1944	
Langham, det. Manston	Apr 1944—Oct 1944	
Dallachy	Oct 1944—May 1945	

Disbanded at Dallachy on 25 May, 1945.

Main Equipment

Handley Page Hampden TB.1 (May 1942—Dec 1943)
L4038, UB:R; P1207, P; P1287, UB:B; P1346, T; P2078, UB:P; P2126, UB:S; P4312, Z; P5315, UB:K; P5390, UB:O; X2904, UB:Q; X3116, R; X3150, UB:O; AD743, UB:F; AD976, E; AE194, UB:P; AE307, UB:M; AE378, UB:G; AE384, F; AN148, UB:K; AN163, K; AT109, UB:C

Bristol Beaufighter X (Dec 1943—May 1945)
LZ192, H; LZ407, UB:F; KW277, D; NE196, P1; NE200, UB:A; NE204, C1; NE207, UB:N; NE223, Y; NE325, D1; NE342, UB:G; NE543, UB:N; NE668, Z; NE777, UB:T; NE798, UB:Q; NT914, M; NT923, UB:Z; NT954, UB:A; NT987, W; NV199, O; NV423, W later UB:H; NV432, UB:D; RD329, UB:X; RD332, UB:C; RD427, UB:G

Commanding Officers

W/Cdr G. M. Lindeman	Dec 1941—Jan 1943	
W/Cdr R. Holmes	Jan 1943—Dec 1943	
W/Cdr J. N. Davenport, DSO, DFC and Bar	Dec 1943—Oct 1944	
W/Cdr C. G. Milson, DSO and Bar, DFC and Bar	Oct 1944—May 1945	

Aircraft Markings

The Squadron markings 'UB' were carried from the time of transfer from Bomber Command through until mid-1943 when codes on Coastal Command were disused. They were re-assumed in mid-1944 and carried until the war ended.
(See also *Bomber Squadrons of the RAF*, pp. 252–3)

No. 458 SQUADRON

(No badge authorised)

No. 458 Squadron personnel began to exist at Williamtown, New South Wales, from 8 July, 1941 but the Squadron did not fully form until the crews had come to the UK from Australia and gathered at Holme-on-Spalding Moor by 1 September, 1941. Equipped with Wellington IVs it served on the night bomber offensive for just over three months from the end of October. The Squadron was withdrawn from operations at the end of January, 1942 for posting overseas. The ground crew arrived in Egypt at the end of May and the aircrews began flying Wellingtons out. The CO was shot down *en route* but those crews that arrived in the Middle East were immediately posted to make up losses in other Wellington squadrons and it was not until 1 September, 1942 that the Squadron existed once more as a whole unit. This was at Shallufa; here it equipped with Wellington ICs and VIIIs for maritime operations over the Mediterranean. After a work-up period it began operations on 1 November, 1942 with night shipping strikes over the Central Mediterranean. The following night it scored successes with two destroyers being hit. It also flew anti-submarine patrols and mining sorties, using Berka as an ALG. In December thirty-three sorties were flown as the Squadron became fully in action.

With 1943 the Squadron sent a detachment to Malta and, operating from there, hit two ships before January was out. The Squadron grew as the year wore on, flying a variety of Wellingtons (termed 'Goofingtons', 'Snoopingtons', 'Fishingtons' or 'Bombingtons' according to their roles) both over the Aegean from Egypt or the Central Mediterranean from Malta and toting between sixty and seventy sorties a month. On 11 April F/O Hailstone suceeded in sinking a 3000-ton motor vessel and four days later the squadron led naval ships to two destroyers which were then sunk. At the same time three crews were lost that month. In April No. 458 began re-equipping with Mk. XIII Wellingtons with better engines and radar equipment. Various moves soon after resulted in the Squadron being wholly based in North Africa with its HQ at Blida. It maintained a standing strike force ready to attack shipping and flew regular shipping searches in the Sicily and Corsica/Sardinia areas. On 18 June a tanker was torpedoed and sunk and a month later a 9000-ton motor vessel was similarly despatched. That month (July) nine attacks were made. The Squadron was now regularly flying over 130 sorties a month, losing on average two or three crews in that period.

Towards the end of the year the Squadron was more and more involved in the war against U-boats and this became part of the pattern in 1944. Leigh Light Wellingtons came in January and these enabled night attacks on submarines to be made more easily. In March more than 150 sorties were flown for the first time, the type of operations remaining as before. In September the Squadron moved to Italy and concentrated on attacking coastal convoys and ports, these being flown as armed recces, attacking any suitable targets that came up on the radar. In January, 1945 No. 458 moved to Gibraltar and from there maintained regular patrols until the war ended, with enemy targets becoming few and far between. It was disbanded there on 8 June, 1945.

Bases etc.

Transferred to maritime duties at Shallufa on 1 September, 1942.

Shallufa det. Luqa	Sep 1942—Mar 1943	
LG.91, det. Blida	Mar 1943—May 1943	
Blida, det. LG.91	May 1943—Jun 1943	
Protville	Jun 1943—Oct 1943	
Bone, det. Bo Rizzo, Grottaglie, Ghissonaccia, Luqa	Oct 1943—Jun 1944	
Alghero	Jun 1944—Sep 1944	
Foggia, det. Ancona, Le Vallon, Rosignano	Sep 1944—Jan 1945	
Gibraltar, det. Rosignano	Jan 1945—Jun 1945	

Disbanded at Gibraltar — June, 1945.

Main Equipment

Vickers Wellington IC (Oct 1942— 1943)
BB457, MD:U; HX445, MD:M; HD964, MD:D; HX508, MD:Q; HX516, x; HX569, D; HX606, MD:P; HX639, MD:D; HX688, MD:S; HX714, MD:A; HX739, MD:N; HX767, T
Vickers Wellington VIII (Oct 1942—May 1943)
BB771. E; HX509, F; HX519, M:L; HX570, S; HX594, MD:X; HX605, MD:S; HX630, O; HX677, W; HX722, MD:J; HX747, MD:U; LA979, X; LA991, MD:B; LB134, MD:G; LB155, W; LB180, J; LB238, Q
Vickers Wellington XIII (Apr 1943—Sep 1944)
HE124, HF114; HF233; HF271; HZ587; HZ690; HZ882, A; JA104, B; JA277; JA299; JA338; MP537, V; MP584, P; MP684; MP749
Vickers Wellington XIV (Feb 1944—Jun 1945)
HF114; HF243; HF265; HF281; HF351; HF400, M; HF417; MP797; MP810; NB768; NB804; NB853, R; NB885; NB890; NC490

Commanding Officers

W/Cdr L. L. Johnston	Sep 1942—Jun 1943	
L/Col. B. R. McKenzie (SAAF)	Jun 1943—Oct 1943	
W/Cdr J. Dowling	Oct 1943—Jul 1944	
W/Cdr R. C. MacKay, DFC	Jul 1944—Jun 1945	

Aircraft Insignia

From the arrival of its first aircraft in Egypt the code letters MD' were adopted and were carried until some time in 1943. After that they fell into general disuse although possibly they were again used spasmodically from time to time.
(See also *Bomber Squadrons of the RAF*, pp. 253–4)

No. 404 (RCAF) Squadron spent almost its entire existence on shipping strikes around the UK coast, its Beaufighters wreaking great havoc. Beaufighter RP.X NE355 2:H awaits its crew, with rockets already loaded, probably at Wick or Sumburgh in early 1944.

Successfully moored at Stranraer in 1941 is Consolidated Catalina I W8434 QL:F of No. 413 Squadron.

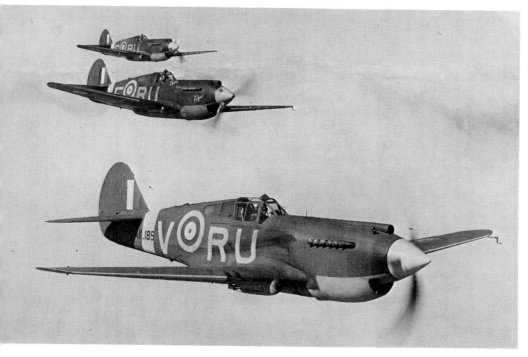

Three Curtiss Tomahawk IIBs of No. 414 Squadron, RCAF, flying above the clouds from Croydon in 1941.

No. 415 Squadron's Wellington XIIIs were used, not only to attack U-boats themselves but also to search out E-boats and R-boats and home other strike squadrons on to them.

Entering the water from the slipway in early, 1944 with outer engines turning to make steerage way is Sunderland III EK575 2:C of No. 422 (RCAF) Squadron.

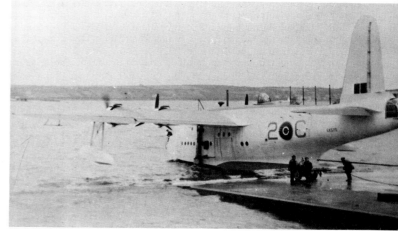

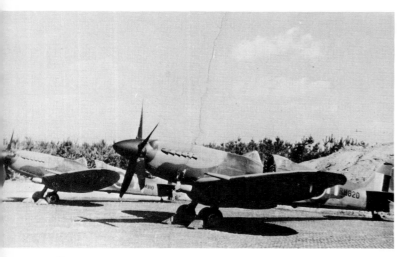

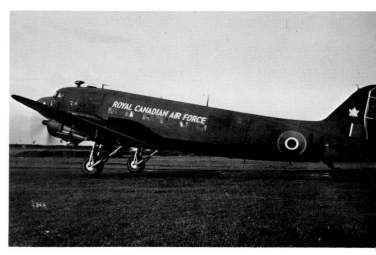

Pausing in between sorties at Petit Brogel are two Spitfire FR.XIVs of No. 430 Squadron.

The Maple Leaf on the fin endorses that this Douglas Dakota IV was part of the RCAF's Transport Wing in the UK.KN665 actually belonged to No. 436 Squadron.

One of No. 437 Squadron's Dakota IVs airborne over the UK just after the close of World War II.

The RAAF Handley Page Hampden squadron, No. 455, transferred from Bomber to Coastal Command in April, 1942, operating out of Leuchars.

Taxying out for a shipping strike is Beaufighter TF.X NE444 of No. 455 Squadron in mid-1944. The base is probably Langham in Norfolk.

At Kabrit in early 1943 is Vickers Wellington VIII HX602 P of No. 458 (RAAF) Squadron. Note the deletion of the nose turret.

No. 459 Squadron was formed from RAAF personnel in Egypt with Lockheed Hudsons for general reconnaissance duties over the Eastern Mediterranean and its aircraft briefly carried the code letters GK as seen here on V8998.

No. 461 (RAAF) Squadron flew all its operations with RAF Coastal Command over Atlantic and Western Approaches with Short Sunderlands. Mk.III ML747 JT:N taking off from Pembroke Dock.

Seen here at Thorney Island is AN127, one of No. 489 (RNZAF) Squadron's torpedo-dropping Hampden TB.1s in July, 1942.

BD572, a Whitley VII of No. 502 Squadron, patrolling over the Western Approaches in 1942.

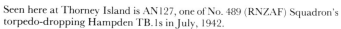

HR686 J2, a Handley Page Halifax II Srs. Ia of No. 502 Squadron operating over the English Channel from Holmesley South in the summer of 1943.

All its existence No. 511 was a long-range transport squadron. In the fifties it flew Handley Page Hastings C.1s and C.2s on all Transport Command's overseas routes. Photo shows Hastings C.1 TG529, displaying the Squadron's yellow fin diamond.

Seen over Brussels in June, 1945 is this Dakota of No. 512 Squadron whilst flying European schedules before the resumption of airline services.

The RAF only acquired a few Martin Mariner flying boats and these were operated briefly by No. 524 Squadron at Oban where this photograph was taken.

On 9 August, 1944 Flt Lt Richards set out for a photo recce sortie over Danzig in de Havilland Mosquito IX LR435. The Record Book relates 'FTR – Failed to Return.' This photograph shows what happened; the starboard propeller is feathered revealing one engine failure and the locale is Sweden where the aircraft force-landed.

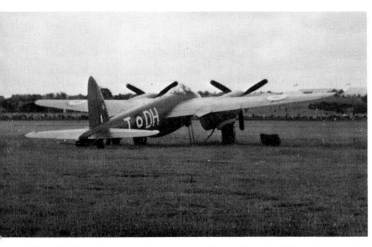

No. 540 Squadron continued to use Mosquitoes for PR duties into the fifties. This PR.Mk.34 of the Squadron, PF662, is at Farnborough in July, 1950 on the occasion of the RAF Display there.

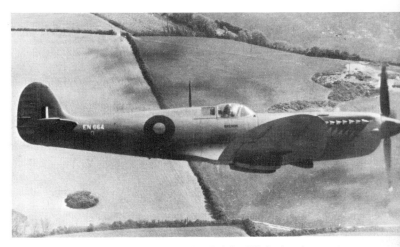

No. 541 Squadron used the Supermarine Spitfire XI for its photo recce sorties from January, 1943 until September, 1946, EN664 Q being on the Squadron in 1943-44.

In the fifties the Gloster Meteor entered service in the photo recce role. This was the PR.Mk.10 version and it served in RAF Germany with No. 541 Squadron at Bückeburg and Laarbruch. VS985 is seen here in its blast pen at Bückeburg – the band round the fuselage is an exercise marking, the letter A denotes No. 541 Squadron.

The high-level long-range photo reconnaissance role was continued after World War II by No. 543 Squadron, its ultimate type being the Handley Page Victor SR.2 which served until No. 543's disbandment in May, 1974. XM715 shown here.

The second Mosquito PR squadron operating from the UK during World War II was No. 544, based at Benson. This Mosquito XVI, NS502 M, was with No. 544 at the time of the Invasion of Normandy.

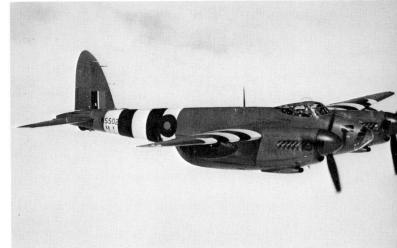

No. 547 Squadron was engaged all through its existence on anti-submarine and anti-shipping patrols and convoy escorts, chiefly over the Atlantic. This Liberator GR.VI, KG869 is seen in typically dirty Atlantic weather in 1945.

The Stirling IVs of No. 570 Squadron (LK117 V8:F here) were used for the Arnhem and Rhine crossing airborne assaults and for general transport work as well as dropping supplies to SOE forces on the Continent.

Anson I N5361 of No. 608 Squadron climbs out over the North Sea on a convoy patrol in 1940.

No. 612 Squadron was another of the Coastal Command units that used the Armstrong Whitworth Whitley extensively for anti-submarine searching and attack. Much of this time it was flying in northern waters as is this Mk.VII BD622 WL:U setting course out of Wick in 1942.

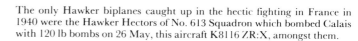

The only Hawker biplanes caught up in the hectic fighting in France in 1940 were the Hawker Hectors of No. 613 Squadron which bombed Calais with 120 lb bombs on 26 May, this aircraft K8116 ZR:X, amongst them.

No. 614, the County of Glamorgan Auxiliary Squadron, mobilised to its war station at Odiham in September, 1939 and there received Westland Lysander IIs, N1241 seen here in March, 1940.

Although predominantly a fighter squadron, No. 615 (County of Surrey) Squadron began life at Kenley with Hawker Hector Is. K8116 is shown here in 1938.

During its preparation for operations as a special mine-laying unit in the Pacific, No. 618 Squadron flew deck-landing trials on HMS *Implacable* in October, 1944. Mosquito IV, DZ542, is just beginning its take-off run.

After the war most of the airborne forces squadrons disbanded but No. 620 moved to Palestine with its Halifax A.7s (PN295 at Wastina, March, 1946) and served there until September, 1946.

The only auxiliary transport squadron was No. 622, formed at Blackbushe in December, 1950 with Vickers Valetta C.1s.

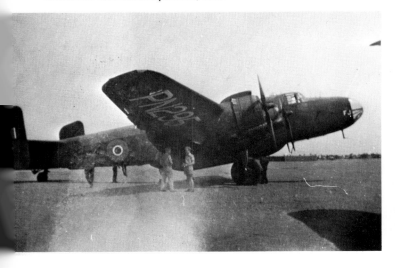

The calm before the storm. Handley Page Halifax V LL312 9U:T waits at Tarrant Rushton as part of No. 644 Squadron for its next glider-towing sortie over the Normandy beachhead.

No. 680 Squadron maintained the long-range photo recce sorties on the Mediterranean and Italian fronts. Latterly, its Mosquito XVIs (RF987 here), carried red and white striped rudders for identification purposes.

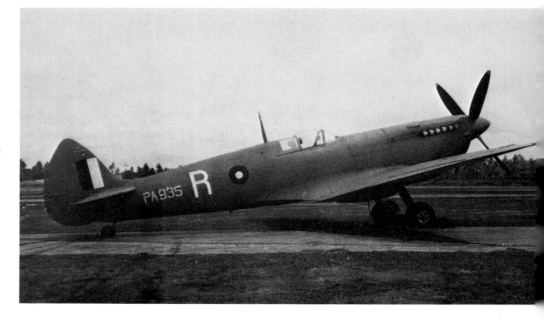

Sitting on Mingaladon is Supermarine Spitfire XI PA935 of No. 681 Squadron.

A *rara avis*, indeed. Avro Lancaster PR. 1 PA379 of No. 683 Squadron at Fayid in the early fifties.

Alipore on 8 April, 1944 and Mosquito XVI MM332 of No. 684 Squadron lands after another sortie deep into Japanese-held territory.

No. 459 SQUADRON

(No badge authorised)

This RAAF Squadron was formed at Burg-el-Arab (LG.39) in Egypt on 10 February, 1942 for coastal reconnaissance duties. It was equipped with Blenheim IVs for work-up and Lockheed Hudsons for operational use and four days after forming it flew its first patrols over the Mediterranean. Such anti-shipping patrols became the Squadron's routine flying and in addition, in March and April, it flew escort duties to formations of Hurricanes flying to Malta, the Hudsons providing the navigation. All this was done with only two Hudsons. However, in May more aircraft arrived on strength and in June it was able to set up standing coastal patrols between Mersa Matruh and Sidi Barrani. That month fifty-two sorties were flown; P/O Cowan Hunt was attacked by three Ju 88s and managed to shoot one down; he was killed in a fatal accident on 1 July. In July the Squadron went on the offensive, bombing enemy convoys; one such attack on 10th resulted in three out of the nine aircraft being lost. In August most operations were against F-boats operating out of Tobruk, the Squadron sinking sixteen and damaging three for the loss of four aircraft. The following month No. 459 sent detachments west to St. Jean and east to Aden for convoy escort duties. P/O Beaton scored a victory on 4 September by bombing a destroyer and setting it on fire and four days later P/O Proctor severely damaged a large motor vessel. Most of the flying, however, was routine escort and patrol work and resulted in no enemy being sighted. Each month for the rest of the year the Squadron was flying well over a hundred sorties a month.

In 1943 the routine patrolling continued, by night as well as by day, with Cyprus being another base for detachment. It was not until 12 June that more action appeared, S/Ldr W. Allsopp depth-charging a submerging U-boat. F/Sgt Barnard went one better four days later by sinking one. In September the Squadron began bombing enemy coastal installations as well and airfields in Greece and Crete. The principal area of operation was now the Aegean where surface craft in particular were the targets. Over a hundred sorties a month were flown against shipping, ports and airfields until the year's end.

In December, 1943 the Squadron began to re-equip with Ventura Vs. With these it began night operations in January, 1944, mostly convoy escorts, building up to 45 sorties in February and 97 in March and losing about one aircraft a month. In March the last Hudson sortie was flown; by May the Venturas were largely used for bombing and this predominated until Martin Baltimores came to replace the Venturas in July. By August conversion was complete and the Squadron was back on anti-shipping sorties and shipping recces; these latter were largely to find shipping for the Beaufighter squadrons to attack. The Squadron continued with the routine

round of shipping recces ASR sorties, U-boat searches, an increasing number of *Nickels* (leaflet raids), bombing in the Dodecanese area and the occasional PR sorties until January, 1945. In February, 1945 it came off operations and moved to the UK where it reassembled at Chivenor on 14 March. Before it could be equipped with new aircraft policy decisions were changed and the Squadron was disbanded on 10 April, 1945.

Bases etc.

Formed at Burg-el-Arab on 10 February, 1942.

Burg-el-Arab (LG.39)	Feb 1942	May 1942
LG.40, det. Sidi Barrani (LG.05)	May 1942	Jul 1942
Gianaclis, det. St. Jean, Khormaksar, LG.100	Jul 1942	Sep 1942
LG.208	Sep 1942	Nov 1942
Gianaclis, det. Gambut	Nov 1942	Dec 1942
Gambut 3, det. Nicosia, LG.91, Berka, St. Jean, Ramat David	Dec 1942	Apr 1944
Ramat David, det. Mersa Matruh	Apr 1944	May 1944
St. Jean	May 1944	Aug 1944
Berka	Aug 1944	Feb 1945
Chivenor	Mar 1945	Apr 1945
Disbanded at Chivenor 10 April, 1945.		

Main Equipment

Lockheed Hudson III, IIIA (Feb 1942—Mar 1944)
T9397; V8992, GK:B; V8998, GK:O; V9027, GK:H; V9052, GK:D; V9101, GK:G; V9187, GK:C; AE510, GK:F; AM853, J; AM950, GK:N; FH227, GK:Y; FH246, GK:X; FH302, GK:C; FH352, V; FH388, O; FH428, R; FH478, Y
Lockheed Hudson VI (1943—Feb 1944)
EW937, N; EW967, A; EW971, P; FK381, C; FK455, B; FK579, F; FK613, Q
Lockheed Ventura V (Dec 1943—Jul 1944)
FN997, S; FP537, E; FP556, O; FP592, A; FP604, H; FP612, F; FP631, Z; JS899, P; JS916, G; JS937, B; JS980, U; JT824, E; JT838, A; JT892, H
Martin Baltimore IV (Jul 1944—Feb 1945)
FA421, E; FA429, Q; FA444, S; FA494, D; FA655, E; FA671, H; FA603, R
Martin Baltimore V (Jul 1944—Feb 1945)
FW314, H; FW388, B; FW412, O; FW442, U; FW485, G; FW520, N; FW609, V

Commanding Officers

S/Ldr P. W. Howson	Feb 1942	Apr 1942
W/Cdr K. S. Hnnock	Apr 1942	Sep 1942
W/Cdr P. W. Howson	Sep 1942	Oct 1943
W/Cdr A. D. Henderson	Oct 1943	Nov 1944
W/Cdr C. E. Payne	Nov 1944	Apr 1945

Aircraft Insignia

The Hudsons of this Squadron carried the code letter combination 'GK' from inception until some time in 1943 when code letters were dropped and it is believed that no other insignia was carried thereafter.

No. 461 SQUADRON

BADGE
A demi-shark couped, pierced by a harpoon
MOTTO
'They shall not pass unseen'

By 1942 sufficient RAAF Sunderland crews were in the UK to form a second squadron and on 25 April, 1942 a nucleus from No. 10 Squadron, RAAF was detached at Mount Batten to form No. 461 Squadron. By June it was operational on ASR duties and on its first such operations on 12th a Sunderland was attacked ineffectually by Messerschmitts. In July it was declared operational for anti-submarine operations and immediately began patrols over the Bay of Biscay. After a week the CO found the crew of a ditched Whitley

and went on to the sea and picked them up. On 30th P/O Manger was dropping leaflets to French fishing vessels when he was attacked by three Ar 196s and his crew shot one into the sea. On 2 August, however, the CO was lost but on 6th another Whitley crew was picked out of the sea, this time by F/O B. Buls. September brought two attacks on U-boats but in October operations ceased and the Squadron was used for transit flights to and from Gibraltar in preparation for the North African landings. The following month operations were resumed with Biscay patrols.

In January, 1943 the Squadron lost its third Sunderland on operations, only twenty sorties were flown. This was repeated in February but in this month a U-boat was attacked with depth-charges and F/Lt C. Walker's crew tackled with two Ju 88s and two FW 190s and escaped. On 29 April F/O R. de V. Gipps crew claimed a U-boat destroyed as a result of their attack; six days later another U-boat was sunk by F/Lt E. C. Smith and the following day a further attack was made. On 28 May a Sunderland piloted by F/Lt S. E. Dods attempted to land on the sea to pick up a crew in a dinghy, but the aircraft crashed and the captain was killed; the rest of the crew escaped in their own dinghy. The next day F/O G. E. Singleton picked them up but his aircraft was holed on take-off and he eventually landed the aircraft on Angle airfield, near the Squadron's base. On 2 June F/Lt Walker's crew had a running battle with eight Ju 88s for 45 minutes; one of the gunners was killed but three Ju 88s were shot down, two more were probables and three more damaged. The Sunderland had to be beached immediately on landing due to combat damage. In July three more U-boats were attacked, one of which was destroyed. In August two of the Sunderlands were lost in fights with Ju 88s and one U-boat was 'shared' with No. 228 Squadron. On 16 September F/Lt Marrows' crew fought with six Ju 88s and eventually ditched successfully after being reduced to flying on one engine.

And so the battle continued, sometimes the Ju 88s being the victors, sometimes the Sunderlands. On 28 January, 1944 F/Lt R. D. Lucas' crew had the satisfaction of seeing the U-boat they had depth-charged blow up. At the end of that month No. 461 transferred its area of operations from Biscay to the Western Approaches. Even here they were subject to enemy air attack and F/O H. Bunce's crew were shot down on 23 March by nine Ju 88s, seven of the crew escaping. As D-Day approached the operation became more intense and in June seventy-eight sorties were flown to keep enemy shipping out of the Channel, three U-boats being attacked. No further attacks were made until August when P/O I. F. Southall's crew damaged the *U-385* at night and surface vessels finished it off. Two days' later another U-boat was sunk by F/O D. A. Little and the day after another attacked.

In September, 1944 a detachment was sent to the Shetlands for operations off Norway, more sorties being flown there than at Pembroke Dock. This detachment returned at the end of October

and the Squadron spent the rest of the war over the Western Approaches. Here there was much less activity as the French U-boat bases were captured and the crews flew some special operations in support of naval forces attacking pockets of enemy resistance on the French Atlantic coast. The Squadron did not long survive the end of the war in Europe, being disbanded at Pembroke Dock on 20 June, 1945.

Bases etc.

Formed at Mount Batten on 25 April, 1942 from a nucleus from No. 10 Squadron, RAAF.

Mount Batten	Apr 1942—Aug 1942
Hamworthy Junction	Aug 1942—Apr 1943
Pembroke Dock, det. Sullom Voe	Apr 1943—Jun 1945

Disbanded at Pembroke Dock 20 June, 1945.

Main Equipment

Short Sunderland II (Apr 1942—May 1943)
 T9085, UT:A; T9109, UT:D; T9111, UT:C; T9115, UT:K; W6050, UT:L
Short Sunderland III (Aug 1942—Jun 1945)
 W6077, UT:U; DD866, B; DP196, UT:K; DV960, UT:H; DV989, F; EJ133, T; EJ142, S; EJ154, T; EK577, UT:D; EK579, C; JM676, P; JM683, W; JM686, Y; ML735, A; ML744, UT:B; ML758, E; ML771, UT:G; ML827, UT:C; ML831, UT:H
Short Sunderland V (Feb 1945—Jun 1945)
 ML747, UT:N; NJ193, UT:F; NJ264, UT:G; NJ268, UT:M; PP113, UT:D; PP119, UT:E; PP162, UT:C; RN282, UT:N

Commanding Officers

W/Cdr N. A. R. Halliday	May 1942—Aug 1942
W/Cdr R. C. O. Lovelock	Aug 1942—Jan 1943
W/Cdr D. L. G. Douglas, DFC	Jan 1943—Feb 1944
W/Cdr J. M. Hampshire, DFC	Feb 1944—Feb 1945
W/Cdr R. E. Oldham	Feb 1945—Jun 1945

Aircraft Insignia

The code letter combination 'UT' was used on No. 461 Squadron's Sunderlands throughout its existence except for a period of about a year between mid 1943 and mid 1944 when no identity markings were carried.

No. 489 SQUADRON

BADGE
Standing on a torpedo, a kiwi

MOTTO
'Whakatanagata kia kaha'
('Quit ye like men, be strong')

The torpedo in the badge indicates the Squadron's role and the kiwi relates to its being a Squadron of the Royal New Zealand Air Force

On 12 August, 1941 No. 489 Squadron formed at Leuchars equipped with Bristol Beaufort Is. It had a very slow work-up and two months later only had four aircraft on strength. In January, 1942 all the Beauforts left and it made do with Blenheim fighters until April when Hampden torpedo-bombers arrived. First 'action' came from friendly forces, one Hampden being attacked by a Spitfire and another by AA fire. However, in May a detachment went to St. Eval from where anti-submarine patrols began. By June nearly forty sorties a month were being flown and two combats had taken place with German aircraft. In July another detachment went to Wick for special recces of Trondheim fjord. Whilst doing these a torpedo attack was launched on three motor vessels and a Blohm & Voss BV 138 flying boat was damaged when it attacked the Hampdens. The Squadron consolidated at Skitten in August, flying shipping *Rovers* over the North Sea. A notable action took place on 17 September when two ships were attacked and three torpedo hits obtained on them, one ship being left on fire. Another ship was hit on 21 October and another on 15 November. By the end of the year three more ships had been torpedoed.

Bombs were used as well as torpedoes and two ships were sunk in January, 1943, one with bombs and the other by torpedo, but two crews were lost. By March the Squadron was operating with No. 455 Squadron, crews inter-changing. In April 83 sorties were flown, two ships were torpedoes (one sunk) and four crews lost on ops. May was much the same but fewer encounters were made in June and July, the next ship attack being in August. Most activity was now monotonous patrolling and this continued until November when operations ceased for No. 489 to convert to Beaufighters.

The Squadron was declared operational again on 8 January, 1944. On 14th eight aircraft found a 4000-ton motor vessel and torpedoed it. Before the month was out another ship had been hit and a minelayer sunk. The Squadron now began operating by day and night and this produced three more ship victims in February. In March four convoys were sighted and attacked on two days. On 11 April the Squadron moved south and transferred its operations to the Dutch and North German coastline where it flew *Conebos*, amassing 118 sorties in May. This continued at the same intensity in June, covering the French coast and Dunkirk to Hook of Holland to protect the invasion fleets. In a Wing strike on 15 June an E-boat depot ship and a 8000-tonner were sunk together with four minesweepers. In July the sortie rate went up to 189, with intensive anti-E-boat operations and *Gilbeys*. Nine anti-shipping Wing strikes were flown with highly successful results. This pattern continued until October when the Wing moved north to Dallachy and operated against Norwegian coastal shipping lanes for the rest of the war. The winter weather cut the sortie rate but on average one ship a month was still being destroyed by No. 489 Squadron. A spectacular strike was made on 26 February when three aircraft torpedoed the *Alsterufer*, loaded with mines, which blew up. Losses were running at one or two aircraft a month. Activity increased as the spring came but in May the war in Europe ended. The following month No. 489 Squadron moved and re-equipped with Mosquitoes but it was disbanded at Banff on 1 August, 1945 before becoming operational on them.

Bases etc.

Formed at Leuchars on 12 August, 1941.

Leuchars	Aug 1941—Mar 1942
Thorney Island, det. St. Eval, Wick	Mar 1942—Aug 1942
Skitten	Aug 1942—Oct 1943
Leuchars	Oct 1943—Apr 1944
Langham	Apr 1944—Oct 1944
Dallachy	Oct 1944—Jun 1945
Banff	Jun 1945—Aug 1945

Disbanded at Banff on 1 August, 1945.

Main Equipment

Bristol Beaufort I (Aug 1941—Jan 1942)
    N1075; N1089; N1105; N1106
Bristol Blenheim IVF (Jan 1942—Mar 1942)
    No serial numbers known
Handley Page Hampden I (Mar 1942—Dec 1943)
    L4144, T; L4145, XA:L; P1159. K; P1214, X; P1337, XA:M;
P2084, XA:B; P2133, XA:J; P5335, XA:R; T4347, XA:C; X2905, T;
AD795, XA:K; AD852, XA:N; AD929, L; AE116, K; AE261, XA:C;
AE422, A; AN123, XA:D; AN156, XA:K; AN164, R; AN249, W;
AT111, XA:Z; AT147, XA:X; AT238, O; AT256, G
Bristol Beaufighter X (Nov 1943—Jun 1945)
    KW277, C; LZ419, D; LZ435, A; LZ531, P6:K1; LZ543, Y;
NE209, J; NE213, P6:H; NE325, P6:C; NE427, V; NE433, P6:W;
NE518, P6:E; NE691, P6:G; NE741, P6:E; NE803, P6:M;
NT888, P6:Y; NT909, P6:E; NT961, P6:Q; NV175, P6:D1;
NV312, P6:T; RD228, P6:H1; RD330, P6:G1; RD352, P6:K1;
RD428, P6:H1
de Havilland Mosquito FB.6 (Jun 1945—Aug 1945)
    No serial numbers known

Commanding Officers

W/Cdr J. A. S. Brown	Aug 1941—Oct 1942
W/Cdr V. C. Darling	Oct 1942—Aug 1943
W/Cdr J. S. Dinsdale, DSO, DFC	Aug 1943—Aug 1944
W/Cdr L. A. Robertson	Aug 1944— 1945
W/Cdr D. H. Hammond, DSO, DFC and Bar	1945—Aug 1945

Aircraft Insignia

From inception the Squadron was allocated the code letters 'XA' but it is not known whether these were used on any aircraft but the Hampdens. In mid-1943 all identity markings were dropped and not resumed until a year later when No. 489s Beaufighters carried 'P6' for the rest of their service.

No. 490 SQUADRON

BADGE
An arm couped below the elbow, holding in the hand a Patu
MOTTO
'Taniwha kei runga'
('The taniwha is in the air')

Seventh and last of the New Zealand squadrons formed within the RAF, No. 490 Squadron was formed at Jui, in West Africa, on 28 March, 1943 for maritime patrols duties over the South Atlantic. It received its first Catalinas in June and became operational in July, its first sortie, a convoy escort, being flown on 6th. In August F/O Grant found the survivors of the torpedoed *Fernhill* and four days later the CO attacked a U-boat with depth-charges and damaged it. The Squadron flew up to thirty operations a month and the next excitement was in October when some more survivors were found at sea. Towards the end of the year intense U-boat hunts increased the monthly sortie rate to over forty.

For the most part the Squadron flew long patrols with nothing to show for it. In May, 1944 Sunderlands replaced the Catalinas. One of these, ML852 had a double engine failure on 14 July and ditched in a 30 knot wind; two crew were killed and five injured. These and the rest of the crew were 22 hours in their dinghy before rescue.

From then on routine patrols and U-boat hunts were flown as required until May, 1945 but no more action came No. 490 Squadron's way and when the European war ended the Squadron prepared for the end, disbanding eventually at Jui on 1 August, 1945.

Bases etc.

Formed at Jui on 28 March, 1943.

Jui, det. Fisherman's Lake, Apapa	Mar 1943—Aug 1945

Disbanded at Jui on 1 August, 1945.

Main Equipment

Consolidated Catalina IB (Jun 1943—Jul 1944)
    FP108, A; FP112, M; FP123, P; FP242, W; FP258, N; FP278, O;
FP299, H; FP324, F
Short Sunderland III (May 1944—Aug 1945)
    EJ135, N; EJ169, Y; JM717, O; ML810, W; ML835, Z; ML852, P;
ML863, X; ML869, V

Commanding Officers

W/Cdr D. W. Baird, DFC	Jun 1943—Dec 1943
W/Cdr B. S. Nicholl	Dec 1943—Oct 1944
W/Cdr T. F. Gill	Oct 1944—Aug 1945

Aircraft Insignia

As far as is known no squadron identity markings were carried on No. 490 Squadron's aircraft although the individual Catalinas had their own names.

No. 500 SQUADRON

BADGE
A horse forscene
MOTTO
'Quo fata vocent'
('Whither the fates may call')

The white horse of Kent was adopted as the badge to commemorate the Squadron's association with that county.

No. 500 Squadron was formed as a Special Reserve Squadron at Manston on 16 March, 1931 as a night-bomber squadron with Vickers Virginia aircraft. In 1936 it became an Auxiliary squadron and on 7 November, 1938 changed its role to general reconnaissance, having moved to Detling in September. It was now part of 16 Group, Coastal Command and in March, 1939 began to receive Avro Ansons for this task.

By the outbreak of World War II the Squadron was operational and began coastal patrols along the line Great Yarmouth to South-end. Convoy escorts and anti-Submarine patrols were added, the Squadron averaging seventy sorties per month but losing about one aircraft a month. In January, 1940 attention was switched to Dover patrols and to escorting the leave boats from France and in March the Squadron also flew photo sorties covering naval installations. By May the Squadron was busily involved with patrols off the French and Belgian coasts and, as the Dunkirk disaster took place flew patrols covering the escaping forces. On 25 May an enemy MTB was bombed by MK:N whilst U and F dive-bombed some more, Anson MK:U being shot into the sea. Three more Ansons were lost before the month was out but on 1 June P/O Peters' crew re-dressed the balance; he was attacked by nine Messerschmitts, his rear gunner shot down one, he shot down a second with his front gun, and a third was damaged. The fighting continued over the Channel and three more Ansons were lost in June, although 147 sorties were flown. In July the Squadron added a Heinkel He 111 and Messerschmitt Bf 110 to its score of enemy aircraft shot down by Ansons. Thereafter the Squadron turned more to coastal convoy work as the Anson was outclassed for more vigorous operations, even though the Squadron's Ansons had a unique installation on its aircraft: a free-moving 20 mm cannon positioned to fire through the floor. During the autumn and winter of 1940 the Squadron's Ansons were also used to fly over London in the early evening to check on the efficiency of London's blackout.

In the early months of 1941 it flew convoy patrols almost exclusively although in March some Operation QDs were flown – these were night recces of the Ostende area.

In April it came off operations to convert to Blenheims, resuming convoy patrols on 15 May and building up to 100 sorties in June. These included more and more ASR tasks as the summer wore on. In September the Squadron began night intruder operations over Holland and night bombing raids on docks, Donges, St. Nazaire, La Rochelle and Nantes all being visited. Increasingly the Squadron was taking the offensive so that in October it was almost entirely flying night strikes on the Dutch and Britanny coasts, on 9th managing to sink a 3000-ton motor vessel in a convoy off Holland.

In November, 1941 Blenheims were replaced by Hudsons and these were first used on ASR sorties but by 1942 shipping searches and *Armed Rovers* were being flown. There were a number of casualties, mainly due to accidents, six aircraft being lost in two months. In March No. 500 Squadron moved to Scotland and Ireland and flew anti-submarine patrols over the Atlantic. The following month F/O Ensor found, and attacked, the Squadron's first U-boat, followed by F/Lt McKenzie damaging a second one the day after. Ensor attacked his second submarine in July, then in August the Squadron changed its operational area to the SW Approaches. This was short-lived for in November it moved to Gibraltar to cover all the convoys moving in for the North African landings. It arrived there on 5 November; on 6th three U-boats had been attacked, one of which was destroyed and one aircraft was lost. On 7th three more U-boats were depth-charged, one being damaged and another destroyed and on 8th the Squadron was patrolling the assault beaches as the troops went in. On 11th the Squadron established an ALG on the African coast at Tafaroui from where W/O Obee shot down a Ju 52. The pressure was maintained, one U-boat on 12th, five on 13th and two on 14th being set on by the Squadron, one of the latter being beached. Four more were attacked on 15th one of which blew up and so badly damaged the attacking Hudson that it crashed into Algiers Bay. On 17th a submarine was so battered by the Squadron that it surrendered whilst three more were attacked in two days. December, 1942 saw the Squadron flying 236 sorties, attacking six U-boats and shooting down a Cant Z.1007 bomber but losing two Hudsons, one to a U-boat.

Into 1943 the pace only slowly eased off with three submarine attacks in January and two in February. However, several aircraft

were lost during the next few months as enemy aircraft and sub-marines fought back. In May the Squadron began working up with RPs and transferred most of its activities to night anti-submarine patrols, regularly flying 250 sorties a month. Throughout the whole of the year the Squadron followed along the North African coast providing A/S cover and moving on to Sicily at the end of the year to keep cover with the forces moving on into Italy. Here it re-equipped with Lockheed Venturas in December, 1943 using them for *Swamp* operations to drive U-boats out of its area. It also began shipping recces north of Corsica to interfere with enemy coastal shipping. The Squadron now ranged over most of the Western Mediterranean on A/S and convoy work. On 19 May, 1944 W/O Mundy destroyed a U-boat in the first attack for many months. Two months later the Squadron was disbanded, No. 17 Squadron, SAAF being formed from it, on 11 July at La Senia.

Two days later the Squadron was re-formed at La Senia with Baltimores in the bomber role, surviving until 23 October, 1945 when it was re-numbered No. 249 Squadron at Eastleigh, Kenya. After the war it re-formed on an auxiliary basis once more at West Malling in June, 1946 as a fighter squadron and served in this role with Mosquitoes and Meteors until the RAuxAF was disbanded in 1957.

Bases etc.

On 7 November, 1938 the Squadron transferred to the general reconnaissance role at Detling.

Detling	Nov 1938	May 1941
Bircham Newton, det. Carew Cheriton	May 1941	Mar 1942
Stornoway, det. Limavady	Mar 1942	Aug 1942
St. Eval	Aug 1942	Nov 1942
Portreath	Nov 1942	Nov 1942
Gibraltar, det. Tafaroui, Blida	Nov 1942	May 1943
Tafaroui, det. Blida, Bone	May 1943	Dec 1943
Montecorvino	Dec 1943	Jan 1944
Grottaglie	Jan 1944	Jan 1944
La Senia, det. Ghisonaccia, Borizzo, Blida, Bone	Jan 1944	Jul 1944

Disbanded into No. 17 Squadron, SAAF, at La Senia on 11 July, 1944. Re-formed in the bomber role at La Senia on 13 July, 1944.

Main Equipment

Avro Anson I (Mar 1939—May 1941)
K6246; K6300; K8706; N4890; N4893; N5051, MK:P; N5066; N5220, MK:N; N5228, MK:D; N5225, SQ:M; N5233, MK:Q; N5354; N5356; N9732, MK:V; N9907, MK:S
Bristol Blenheim IV (Apr 1941—Dec 1941)
L4899; V5538; Z6050; Z6161, MK:T
Lockheed Hudson III, V (Dec 1941—Apr 1944)
V9094, MK:W; AE568, L11; AM527, E; AM532, C; AM582, N1; AM610, H; AM631, D; AM732, L; AM785; AM826, F; AM857, D; AM882, E; FH410; FK500, T; FK565, O; FK627, V; FK661, V; FK681, D; FK706, P; FK813
Lockheed Ventura V (Dec 1943—Jul 1944)
FN978, N11; FN983; FP540; FP594; FP600; FP633, R; FP672; JS930; JS952; JS964, X

Commanding Officers

S/Ldr V. G. Hohler	Oct 1936	Oct 1939
S/Ldr W. K. Le May	Oct 1939	Feb 1940
S/Ldr R. E. X. Mack	Feb 1940	Jul 1940
W/Cdr C. H. Turner	Jul 1940	Mar 1941
W/Cdr G. I. Pawson	Mar 1941	Apr 1942
W/Cdr D. F. Spotswood, DFC	Apr 1942	Apr 1943
W/Cdr D. G. Keddie	Apr 1943	Feb 1944
W/Cdr C. K. Bonner	Feb 1944	May 1944
W/Cdr C. E. A. Garton	May 1944	Jul 1944

Aircraft Insignia

When the Ansons arrived they were adorned with the code letter combination 'SQ' which was changed to 'MK' in September, 1939. This was retained until the Squadron went to Gibraltar after which no markings were carried. (See also *Bomber Squadrons of the RAF*, pp. 262–3, and *Fighter Squadrons of the RAF*, pp. 453–5)

No. 502 SQUADRON

BADGE
A red hand erased

MOTTO
'Nihil timeo'
('I fear nothing')

The red hand is taken from the arms of Ulster,
502 being the Ulster Auxiliary Squadron.

The Squadron originally formed at Aldergrove on 15 May, 1925 as a Special Reserve Squadron in the bomber role with Vickers Vimy aircraft. It became an Auxiliary Squadron in July, 1937 and the following year transferred to the general reconnaissance role. This took place in November, 1938 and two months later it began to replace its Hind bombers with Avro Ansons. It was fully operational with these by the time war broke out and began patrolling and escorting convoys from 5 September onwards. Its first enemy submarine was found off the Scottish coast on 24 September when S/Ldr Buggs attacked it with A/S bombs with no observed result. From then it soldiered on unspectacularly, receiving Tiger Moths in November for inshore anti-submarine patrols and sending a detachment to Hooton Park in November. It was flying between thirty and forty sorties a month and losing about one aircraft a month at this period, but as the spring of 1940 came this increased to about ninety sorties a month, and two hundred and fifty by July. Several oil slicks were bombed in hopes of hitting a U-boat and a periscope was also attacked with no result but generally the Squadron shepherded its convoys with little action.

In October, 1940 No. 502 became the first Coastal Command unit to use Armstrong Whitworth Whitleys, converting to these for longer-range oversea recce. That same month it was a No. 502 Squadron crew that found the liner *Empress of Britain* on fire in the Atlantic and three days later another crew found a U-boat and bombed it. Several Whitleys were lost or crashed in accidents through the winter but the pressure was maintained; for example, in January, 1941 one hundred and three sorties were flown. On 10 February F/O Walker damaged a U-boat in his attack, and in June F/O Holdsworth made two attacks on U-boats in four days. On 17 July W/Cdr Shore had a combat with a FW 200 and had to ditch afterwards. Two more attacks took place in August and three in September as the Squadron maintained its regular anti-submarine patrols over the NW Approaches.

From November, 1941 the Squadron maintained a detachment in the south-west, reaching out into the Biscay area and at the same time began to receive Whitleys equipped with ASV radar. Just after Christmas the whole Squadron moved to St. Eval. Biscay was to be its operational area throughout 1942, predominantly flying A/S sorties as the submarine war intensified. Two such craft were bombed in March, six in April, though two Whitleys failed to return. In May the Squadron turned its attention to fishing vessels. In July the Squadron recorded one U-boat definitely sunk as a result of F/Sgt Hunt's attack on 17th; the same crew also had a combat with an Arado Ar 196 on 6 July. September was the busiest month: three U-boats were attacked, an oil tanker was bombed, one crew was shot down by a friendly convoy, three others failed to return and one crashed on take-off. October produced more attacks, both on submarines and surface vessels and in November, as well as four U-boat attacks No. 502 was engaged in bombing shipping at Bordeaux.

In January, 1943 a welcome change of equipment brought Handley Page Halifaxes to the Squadron which consolidated on these at Holmesley South, becoming operational in March, then moving back to St. Eval. The first Halifax U-boat attack came on 1 April but the crew had to bale out owing to the weather being below limits on return. Five U-boats were attacked in May, and in June the Squadron began shipping searches with three aircraft in formation (Operation Musketry). The U-boats, likewise seemed to hunt in threes now for F/O Davey found three together on 15 April and on 30 July two

Halifaxes found three and attacked them, destroying one. Enemy opposition was getting fiercer; on 16 July F/O Grant and crew had been attacked by four Ju 88s and shot down, and more attacks came after this. On 2 August F/O Bigger found three destroyers and bombed them ineffectually. U-boats were still to be found and attacked. At the end of the year eight aircraft set out on a daylight shipping strike on an enemy convoy of twelve ships, all of which were attacked; night shipping strikes were also undertaken. In December a move was made to St. David's in South Wales.

This brought fresh targets, it seemed, for in January, 1944 four U-boats were found and depth-charged, two in one day. Surface vessels were also attacked, cargo ships, destroyers and E-boats all receiving No. 502s bombs. On 25 April another confirmed destruction of a submarine was made by F/Lt Holderness. It was now most important for the Squadron to participate in bottling the Channel from U-boat infiltration from the French Atlantic ports and this became the Squadron's chief task as D-Day approached. In June three U-boats were attacked, one in Guernsey harbour; July produced four U-boat attacks and seven surface-vessel attacks for the Squadron, the north and west coasts of France being the target area. Then in September a change of scene came with the Squadron's move to the Hebrides. From here it flew both A/U patrols and attacks on shipping off the Norwegian coast. On one such F/Lt Hornand bombed a motor ship near the Swedish coast but his Halifax was set on fire; despite it being almost uncontrollable he coaxed it back to base. No. 502 was now operating mainly in the Skaggerak, attacking both surface and submarine shipping where ever it could be found. Most of these sorties were at night; in November out of forty-four sorties in the month nineteen attacks were made, one aircraft being shot down.

In the New Year (1945) Hercules-engined Halifaxes arrived and continued the offensive in the Skaggerak with many ships being badly damaged. This was maintained up to VE-Day but then the need for the Squadron evaporated and it was disbanded at Stornaway on 25 May, 1945.

No. 502 re-formed as part of the Auxiliary Air Force once more at Aldergrove on 17 July, 1946 and served there as a fighter squadron until the RAuxAF was dismantled in 1957 when it was finally disbanded.

Bases etc.

Transferred to the general reconnaissance role at Aldergrove in November, 1938.

Aldergrove, det. Hooton Park	Nov 1938	Jan 1941
Limavady, det. Wick, Chivenor, St. Eval	Jan 1941	Dec 1941
St. Eval	Dec 1941	Jan 1942
Docking, det. St. Eval	Jan 1942	Feb 1942
St. Eval	Feb 1942	Mar 1943
Holmesley South, det. St. Eval	Mar 1943	Mar 1943
St. Eval	Mar 1943	Jun 1943
Holmesley South, det. St. Eval	Jun 1943	Dec 1943
St. David's	Dec 1943	Sep 1944
Stornoway, det. Wick	Sep 1944	May 1945

Disbanded at Stornoway on 25 May, 1945. Re-formed at Aldergrove on 17 July, 1946 as a fighter squadron in the Auxiliary Air Force.

Main Equipment

Avro Anson I (Jan 1939—Nov 1940)
N5049, YG:A; N5063, YG:N; N5105, YG:D; N5109, YG:P; N5216, YG:S; N5237, YG:V; N5374, YG:W; N9629, YG:E; N9631, YG:Z; N9899, YG:H; N9918, YG:B; R3335, YG:N

Armstrong Whitworth Whitley V (Oct 1940—Nov 1941)
P5041, YG:C; P5054, YG:C; P5090, YG:L; P5107, YG:H; T4142, YG:N; T4168, YG:E; T4219, YG:P; T4223, YG:G; T4277, YG:J; T4320, YG:L; Z6501, YG:S; Z6553, YG:E; Z6632, YG:Q; Z6733, YG:O

Armstrong Whitworth Whitley VII (Nov 1941—Feb 1943)
Z6967, YG:U; Z9124, YG:T; Z9136, YG:R; Z9190, YG:B; BD572, YG:R; BD677, YG:C; EB332, YG:G

Handley Page Halifax II Srs. IA (Jan 1943—Mar 1945)
DT692; HR688, K; HR693, O; HR782; HR815, U; HX223; JB901; JD245; JP166; JP271, F

Handley Page Halifax IIIA (Dec 1944—May 1945)
RG364, V9:D; RG369, V9:R

W/Cdr L. R. Briggs	Nov 1937—Dec 1940
W/Cdr T. B. Cooper	Dec 1940—Nov 1941
W/Cdr F. C. Richardson	Nov 1941—Sep 1942
W/Cdr J. C. Halley	Sep 1942—Aug 1943
W/Cdr N. M. Bayliss	Aug 1943—May 1944
W/Cdr C. A. Maton, DSO	May 1944—Oct 1944
W/Cdr K. B. Corbould, DFC	Oct 1944—Nov 1944
W/Cdr H. H. C. Holderness, DFC, AFC	Nov 1944—May 1945

Aircraft Insignia

It is not known whether the Ansons carried any markings pre-war although the code letters 'KQ' had been allotted. From September, 1939 until early 1943 the letters 'YG' were used then, roughly coincident with the arrival of the Halifaxes, all identity markings were dropped. However, in early summer 1944 a new set of code letters 'V9' was allotted and used on the Halifaxes.

(See also *Bomber Squadrons of the RAF*, pp. 264–5 and *Fighter Squadrons of the RAF*, pp. 458–9)

No. 511 SQUADRON

BADGE
In front of a compass card, an eagle volant affrontee, the head lowered to the dexter, holding in the claws a chain of five links

MOTTO
'Surely and quickly'

The badge symbolises the unit's function as a link between the different parts of the world.

The Squadron was formed on 1 October, 1942 by expanding No. 1425 Flight to squadron strength. This Flight had been formed for the purpose of maintaining a transport service between England and Gibraltar and had been running since November, 1941. It was equipped with Albemarles and Liberators and very soon expanded the service on to LG.224 in Egypt. In November, 1942 a further route was established from Lyneham to Malta, aircraft being detached to Gibraltar to fly the shuttle to Malta.

On 13 January, 1943 the Squadron flew the Prime Minister and Chiefs of Staff to the Casablanca conference and provided VIP transport there during the period of the conference (known as Operation Static). In February Lancaster W4114 was used to assess its suitability on the routes, these trials lasting three months. With the formation of C Flight to use the Albemarles the Squadron concentrated this type on general freighting runs to the forces in North Africa. Three Albemarles were lost in crashes in April in that area. In July, a No. 511 Squadron Liberator carrying General Sikorsky crashed inexplicably shortly after take-off from Gibraltar, and another Albemarle went missing off Gibraltar in August.

In September, 1943 Dakotas joined the strength and immediately began to take over the Gibraltar and North African runs from the Albemarles which were phased out in February, 1944. In November, 1943 the first York arrived for service with No. 511 and this was used, together with a Liberator, to provide special flights out of Cairo for the Heads of State conference at Teheran. At the same time the Squadron's route flying was extended to Karachi in India. As 1944 progressed the Squadron was more and more involved in 'Specials', rapidly becoming the VIP Squadron for long-distance transport; Liberator crews were detached to Montreal and York crews to Northolt for this purpose. By June the Squadron had a route established as far as Colombo in Ceylon.

The Dakotas were transferred to No. 525 Squadron in July, being replaced by Convair C-87s which took over their routes. These expanded to Italy as the armies advanced; the Squadron also flew trips to the Soviet Union in September, 1944 supporting Nos. 9 and 617 Squadrons during their detachment there for *Tirpitz* attacks. The following month nine Liberators were transferred to No. 246 Squadron together with two of the scheduled routes. The Squadron began concentrating on the Far East routes and 'Specials', being wholly York equipped in 1945. Trooping continued to take up most of No. 511s energies and this was maintained even after the war ended. In fact it was not until July, 1948 that the Squadron was involved elsewhere when it was switched in to the Berlin Airlift, operating out of Wunstorf for a year. It then came off operations to

convert to Hastings and with these it reverted to the Far East routes once more.

Other trooping flights involved a series to Kenya in 1952 to support the anti-Mau Mau operations and to Korea to assist the Commonwealth troops fighting there. Mercy flights also came within No. 511's scope, flying sandbags to the East Coast of England during the flooding and bringing survivors of the sunken troopship *Empire Windrush* back from Gibraltar in 1954.

In 1956 the Squadron built up a shuttle service to Cyprus in support of the British forces in the Suez operation and, in November, flew paratroop dropping and *Nickel* raids over Port Said.

After fifteen years at Lyneham No. 511 Squadron moved to Colerne in May, 1957 and was disturbed there on 1 September, 1958 by re-numbering as No. 36 Squadron. However, a new No. 511 Squadron re-formed at Lyneham once more on 15 December, 1959 when the second squadron in the RAF's Britannia long-range transport force was formed. Its task from 1960 onwards was to maintain scheduled services to the Near and Far East as part of the trunk routes of Air Support Command. No. 511 also responded to emergency calls during the military crises in Kuwait, Cyprus and the Radfan. In 1966 it took part in the Zambian oil lift and was also involved in the many withdrawals of the period as Great Britain shrugged off its responsibilities in the Far and Middle East. In June, 1970 the Squadron moved base to Brize Norton and continued to fly on the RAF's routes until the Defence cuts brought about the elimination of the Britannia Force and No. 511's disbandment at Brize Norton in January, 1976.

Bases etc.

Formed out of No. 1425 Flight at Lyneham on 1 October, 1942.

*Lyneham, det. Gibraltar, Dorval, Northolt	Oct 1942—May 1957
Colerne	May 1957—Sep 1958

Disbanded by re-numbering as No. 36 Squadron at Colerne on 1 September, 1958.
Re-formed at Lyneham on 15 December, 1959.

Lyneham	Dec 1959—Jun 1970
Brize Norton	Jun 1970—Jan 1976

Disbanded at Brize Norton January, 1976.
* The Squadron ceased to exist for nine days in 1946. It was disbanded at Lyneham on 7 October and re-formed there on 16 October, still with Avro Yorks.

Main Equipment

Armstrong Whitworth Albemarle I (Oct 1942—Feb 1944)
P1433; P1449; P1453; P1472; P1500; P1520; P1561; P1564
Consolidated Liberator I (Oct 1942—Jun 1944)
AM259; AM911; AM912; AM913; AM914; AM922
Consolidated Liberator II (Oct 1942—Jun 1944)
AL504; AL516; AL529; AL547; AL561; AL584; AL616; AL635
Douglas Dakota I/III (Sep 1943—Jul 1944)
FD869; FD902; FD939; FD945; FL517; FL546; FL585; FL649
Avro York I (Nov 1943—Aug 1949)
MW100; MW101; MW112; MW128; MW138; MW174; MW187; MW208; MW231; MW253; MW269; MW294; MW302
Consolidated Liberator VII (Jul 1944—Dec 1944)
EW613; EW618; EW624; EW629; EW634
Handley Page Hastings C.1 (Sep 1949—Sep 1958)
TG509; TG516; TG531; TG536, GAU; TG553, GAK; TG577; TG587, JAZ

Handley Page Hastings C.2 (1951—Sep 1958)
WD475, GAQ; WD486; WD497, GAO; WJ329; WJ333, GAY;
WJ338, GAC; WJ341
Bristol Britannia C.1, C.2 (Dec 1959—Jan 1976) (Aircraft shared with 99
Squadron)
XL635; XL638; XL657; XL660; XM489; XM496; XM517
(C.2)
XN404

Commanding Officers

W/Cdr W. J. Pickard	Oct 1942	Mar 1943
W/Cdr J. N. Glover	Mar 1943	Jun 1943
W/Cdr C. E. Slee, MVO, AFC	Jun 1943	Jun 1944
W/Cdr E. W. Whitaker, DFC, AFC	Jun 1944	Aug 1945
W/Cdr S. W. R. Hughes, OBE	Sep 1945	Oct 1946
W/Cdr R. J. Burrough, DFC	Oct 1946	Jan 1948
S/Ldr G. H. Smith	Jan 1948	Jan 1950
S/Ldr M. C. S. Haycroft	Jan 1950	Apr 1952

S/Ldr Langdon	Apr 1952	—
S/Ldr R. E. Dyson, DFC	May 1954	Jun 1956
S/Ldr G. W. Turner	Jun 1956	May 1958
S/Ldr W. L. Green	May 1958	Sep 1958
W/Cdr A. W. G. Le Hardy	Dec 1959	—
W/Cdr J. H. Lewis		
W/Cdr P. A. Ward		—Jun 1972
W/Cdr R. J. Hutchings	Jun 1972	Jul 1974
W/Cdr R. G. Robertson	Jul 1974	Jan 1976

Aircraft Insignia

Little is known about markings of the aircraft operated by No. 511 Squadron from 1942 to 1944. The Yorks carried the last two letters of their Transport Command four-letter code, usually on a black nose-cap. With the Hastings, apart from three-letter markings on the aircraft, denoting the aircraft call-sign, not the unit, they latterly had a yellow diamond at the top of the fin with a black '511' on it. The Britannias were pooled and carried no insignia.

No. 512 SQUADRON

BADGE
In front of a horse's head couped, a sword
erect, the point upwards

MOTTO
'Pegasus militaris'
('Pegasus at war')

No. 512 Squadron was formed at Hendon on 18 June, 1943 out of the Dakota element of No. 24 Squadron. Just over a month later it became operational, flying transport routes to Gibraltar and Maison Blanche as its main task with subsidiary internal UK and North African sorties as well. Once established the route was extended east to Bombay and west to the Azores before the end of the year.

This type of flying was continued until February, 1944 when No. 512 transferred from 44 Group to 46 Group to become a tactical airborne squadron. It began to work up in the glider-towing and paratrooping roles, as well as concentrating on cross-country work. On 24 April it flew its first operations, *Nickel* raids over Northern France, but its main task was to work-up to operational efficiency by 1 June, 1944. Accordingly, on the evening of the 5 June thirty-three Dakotas of the Squadron took the 9th Battalion of the 3rd Para Brigade to Normandy, flying in three Vics of eleven aircraft each. This was Operation Tonga; Operation Mallard followed on 6th when eighteen aircraft towed gliders to LZ N, all of which landed successfully although one Dakota was hit by Flak and had to ditch. The final operation on D-Day was a five aircraft re-supply mission to DZ N but the formation was caught in cross-fire from naval vessels and two Dakotas were shot down.

On 17 June the Squadron took No. 124 Typhoon Wing from Holmesley South to their Normandy landing strip (B.5) and brought 138 casualties home on return. Similar sorties were made on successive days and this cross-Channel shuttle became No. 512s daily task. As the armies moved forward so the routes varied and by September the Squadron was using Brussels as its continental base, flying 321 sorties that month. These included participation in Operation Market, the ill-fated airborne landing at Arnhem. Twenty-two gliders were towed there successfully on 17th, another twenty-four on 18th, one Dakota being lost. Fourteen aircraft participated on 19th and another Dakota was lost. During a re-supply flight on 20th two Squadron Dakotas were shot down. In October, 1944 the Squadron flew 398 sorties on Continental supply runs and casevacs and this pace continued through the winter; in addition ADLS services were flown by Ansons from Northolt to Brussels and back.

The work eased off a little in 1945 and the Squadron re-trained on glider-towing which it put to good use on 24 March, twenty-four aircraft participating in Operation Varsity (the Rhine crossing) and the Squadron leading the whole airborne force. One aircraft was

lost. In August the Squadron moved to Evere in Belgium for its base and principally flew services within the continent. With the war over it started scheduled services on the continent. In July, 1945 512 Squadron began Operation Chancery, flying troops to Lydda, Shaibah and Mauripur and very soon all its time was spent on route-flying to India. In October it moved to Palestine and began opening up Middle East routes. At the end of the year No. 512 Squadron was transferred to Bari in Italy from where it flew routes to Greece, Romania, Egypt, Austria, UK and within Italy. This pattern of flying was maintained until February, 1946 when the Squadron began to fly itself back to the UK where it disbanded officially on 14 March, 1946.

Bases etc.

Formed at Hendon on 18 June, 1943 from the Dakota element of No. 24 Squadron.

Hendon	Jun 1943	Feb 1944
Broadwell	Feb 1944	Mar 1945
Evere (B.56)	Mar 1945	Aug 1945
Holme-on-Spalding Moor	Aug 1945	Oct 1945
Castina	Oct 1945	Oct 1945
Gianaclis	Oct 1945	Dec 1945
Bari	Dec 1945	Feb 1946
en route to UK	Feb 1946	Mar 1946

Disbanded on return to the UK on 14 March, 1946.

Main Equipment

Lockheed Hudson IIIA (Jun 1943—Sep 1943)
V9177; AM850; FH167; FH369; FH455; FH460
Douglas Dakota I, III (Jun 1943—Mar 1946)
FD795; FD826; FD873; FD905; FD939, HC:F; FL518; FL547;
FL586; FZ647, HC:AH; FZ651, HC:AJ; FZ696, HC:AQ;
KG323, HC:UI; KG347, HC:SI; KG377, HC:S; KG418, HC:UT;
KG486, HC:UA; KG544, HC:UV; KG582, HC:AA; KG616, HC:AF;
KG641, HC:AC
Douglas Dakota IV (Apr 1945—Mar 1946)
KK193, HC:K; KN291, HC:A; KN499, HC:AW; KN523, HC:EW;
KN641, HC:BW; KN657, HC:DW
Avro Anson I (Aug 1944—   1945)
NK491; NK488; NK533; NK699

Commanding Officers

W/Cdr M. Booth, DFC	Aug 1943	Sep 1943
W/Cdr K. J. D. Dickson	Sep 1943	Dec 1943
W/Cdr R. M. Blennerhassett	Dec 1943	Feb 1944
W/Cdr B. A. Coventry, DFC	Feb 1944	Jan 1945
W/Cdr R. G. Dutton, DSO, DFC and Bar	Jan 1945	Jul 1945
LtCol P. G. McA. Murdock	Jul 1945	Dec 1945
S/Ldr W. A. Mostyn-Brown	Dec 1945	Mar 1946

Aircraft Insignia

The code letter combination 'HC' was carried by the Dakotas of No. 512 Squadron.

No. 524 SQUADRON

(No badge authorised)

The Squadron was formed at Oban on 20 October, 1943 to operate the small number of Martin Mariner flying-boats entering the RAF. It worked up and became operational by the end of the year but policy changed, the aircraft were withdrawn in January, 1944 and the Squadron disbanded on 29 January.

No. 524 Squadron re-formed at Davidstow Moor on 7 April, 1944 with Wellington XIIIs for anti-E-boat and anti-submarine patrols off the North French coast at night, illumination of night targets for Beaufighter strikes and occasional E-boat strikes. Its first operation was on 30 April and the Squadron carried out forty E-boat patrols in May. Strikes with Beaufighters began in June as it was concerned with stopping enemy channel movements. On 1 July the Squadron moved to East Anglia and absorbed No. 415 Squadron, flying eighty sorties that month, beginning bombing E-boats on its own account. It was now operating off the Dutch coast and found shipping of all descriptions there which it bombed with regularity. One crew was lost that month and one the following month in which ninety sorties were flown, many out of Thorney Island on Operation Purblind which involved leading the North Coates Beaufighter Wing to enemy convoys and laying marine markers on the shipping for them to attack.

These attacks improved in efficiency and the Squadron continued to work with Beaufighters or to attack on its own account throughout the autumn of 1944, keeping up ninety sorties a month until the weather reduced operations. A detachment at Dallachy extended the area of operations into the Skagerrak. As the New Year came the Squadron tended to fly Box patrols searching for shipping and then attacking any targets that came up, losing about one crew a month. The methods were refined so that by April No. 524 Squadron was

directing RN surface forces on to enemy shipping (Operations Taboo & Physic). The last sortie was flown on 11 May and thereafter the Squadron flew a few trips along the enemy coastline to show their ground crews where the action had been. A month later, on 25 June, 1945, No. 524 Squadron was disbanded at Langham.

Bases etc.

Formed at Oban 20 October, 1943.

Oban	Oct 1943	Jan 1944

Disbanded at Oban 29 January, 1944. Re-formed at Davidstow Moor on 7 April, 1944.

Davidstow Moor	Apr 1944	Jul 1944
Docking	Jul 1944	Jul 1944
Bircham Newton, det. Docking, Langham, Dallachy	Jul 1944	Nov 1944
Langham, det. Dallachy	Nov 1944	Jun 1945

Disbanded at Langham on 25 June, 1945.

Main Equipment

Martin Mariner I (Oct 1943—Jan 1944)
  JX100; JX105; JX106; JX110
Vickers Wellington XIII (Apr 1944—Jun 1945)
  HF276, 7R:D; HF283, 7R:B; HZ644, 7R:T; MF176, 7R:J; MF319, 7R:D; MF234, 7R:L; MF335, 7R:H; MF374, 7R:K; MF442, 7R:A; MF444, 7R:B; MF577, 7R:X; NB854, 7R:K

Commanding Officers

W/Cdr W. E. M. Lowry	Oct 1943	Jan 1944
S/Ldr A. W. B. Naismith	Apr 1944	Jul 1944
W/Cdr R. G. Knott, DSO, DFC	Jul 1944	May 1945
S/Ldr G. E. Willis, DFC	May 1945	Jun 1945

Aircraft Insignia

The Mariners carried no squadron identity markings. The Wellingtons used the code letter combination '7R'.

No. 525 SQUADRON

(No badge authorised)

The Squadron was formed on 2 September, 1943 to operate the Vickers Warwick as a transport aircraft. By November No. 525 had worked up sufficiently to begin a route schedule to Gibraltar flying RAF passengers. By March, 1944 it had extended these flights to various points in North Africa, but in April it suffered two accidents and at the end of the month the Warwicks were withdrawn. In May it began converting to Dakotas, had a Stirling delivered and resumed Warwick flying on freight duties only. However, by July it was a fully-Dakota squadron, flying four routes to the Mediterranean area. Two months later No. 525 switched to the northern European scene flying in support of the armies there but in October it divided its activities between this type of flying and the longer routes, going as far as Karachi. By the end of the year there had been a considerable change of personnel and it was now predominantly a RCAF-manned unit. In January, 1945 No. 525 sent a detachment to the Crimea to provide support for the Yalta conference; it was also using some crews for secret missions as well as flying about seventy services a month. This was maintained into the summer of 1945 when it switched to trooping flights to India but another change in September sent a detachment to Cairo to fly troops into Greece. Services now had to be cut down as a speedy repatriation of the Canadians ensued, the last leaving 525 in October.

The trooping flights ended in February, 1946, the Squadron having suffered two fatal accidents during that winter. No. 525 now began European mail and newspaper services to various points on the Continent, flying six routes by March. As the summer came so intensity built up again, one hundred and seventy four services being flown in June, 1946 but this began falling off quite rapidly in

the autumn. On 1 December, 1946 the Squadron was disbanded at Abingdon by re-numbering as No. 238 Squadron.

Bases etc.

Formed at Weston Zoyland on 2 September, 1943.

Weston Zoyland	Sep 1943	Feb 1944
Lyneham	Feb 1944	Jul 1945
Membury, det. Almaza	Jul 1945	Oct 1946
Abingdon	Oct 1946	Dec 1946

Disbanded at Abingdon on 1 December, 1946 by re-numbering as No. 238 Squadron.

Main Equipment

Vickers Warwick I (Sep 1943—Jun 1944)
  BV244; BV247; BV249; BV252; BV253; BV254; BV256
(C.3)
  HG219
Douglas Dakota III (Jun 1944—Jun 1945)
  FD869; FD940; FD945; FL517; FL547; FL585; FL649; KG733; KG741; KG751; KG773; KG787; KG808
Douglas Dakota IV (Dec 1944—Dec 1946)
  KJ829; KJ861; KJ966; KJ970, WF:U; KK156; KK193, WF:R; KN234, WF:Y; KN285, WF:A; KN383; KN417, WF:G; KN497, WF:C; KN500; KN582; KN637, X; KN661, WF:Q

Commanding Officers

W/Cdr C. E. F. Riley	Oct 1943	Sep 1944
W/Cdr D. R. Miller	Sep 1944	Jun 1945
W/Cdr R. G. Dutton, DSO, DFC	Jun 1945	Mar 1946
W/Cdr H. D. Newman	Mar 1946	Dec 1946

Aircraft Insignia

The Squadron code letters 'WF' were carried latterly on the Dakotas of the Squadron. It is not known what, if any, markings were carried previously.

No. 540 SQUADRON

BADGE
A mosquito
MOTTO
'Sine qua non'
('Indispensable')

The badge indicates the Squadron as the first operational user of the de Havilland Mosquito. When the Photographic Reconnaissance Unit had expanded to a considerable extent so that it had Flights in many parts of the UK these were merged into larger units and the PR Squadrons came into existence. This took place on 19 October, 1942 and on that day H and L Flights of the PRU were amalgamated to form No. 540 Squadron at Leuchars.

The Squadron's primary task was to keep a photo watch on the movements of ships of the German Navy and as most of these transitted the Norwegian coastline the Squadron flew most of its sorties there. One of its principal pre-occupations was the battleship *Tirpitz* and her moves from fjord to fjord. Within a few days of forming it sent a detachment to Gibraltar to provide coverage for the North African landings and this detachment also flew bomb-damage assessment sorties over Italy whilst there. Although the German Navy was the primary target the Squadron roamed all over Europe and in early 1943 was losing about two crews a month (out of approx fifty sorties). In April the Squadron concentrated on the Cherbourg peninsula but with the longer evenings the Squadron wandered as far as the Italian Adriatic coast. One of the special targets regularly visited was the German research centre at Peenemünde and it was No. 540 Squadron Mosquitoes that obtained the first pictures of V1s in November, 1943.

As the spring of 1944 came the Squadron began concentrating on Northern France both looking for V1 sites and also preparing for the invasion; No. 540's particular task was to keep up a photographic record of railway movements there. Eighty to ninety sorties a month were flown during the summer of 1944 as the invasion took place and the armies moved across France and Belgium. These sortie figures were doubled in July and August, France being the main target area and losses running at two or three crews a month. The Squadron was spread abroad again in September with a detachment at Gibraltar once more for a survey of the Canary Islands and another at Yagodnik in the Soviet Union to cover the 5 Group operations against the *Tirpitz*. Thereafter No. 540 was back to its old area of Scandinavia and Northern Germany and this was the centre of activities until the war ended.

At the end of March, 1945 the Squadron had moved to France and now its main task was a photo survey of France. This was completed by November and the Squadron returned to the UK where it remained on survey tasks until disbanding at Benson on 30 September, 1946.

No. 540 re-formed there on 1 December, 1947, again with Mosquitoes, to maintain a PR capability and to fly survey sorties. Converting to Canberras in December, 1952, No. 540 maintained this task until 31 March, 1956 when it disbanded at Wyton.

Bases etc.

Formed from H&L Flights of No. 1 PRU at Leuchars on 19 October, 1942.		
Leuchars, det. Benson, Gibraltar	Oct	1942—Feb 1944
Benson, det. Gibraltar, Agadir, Lossiemouth, Yagodnik (USSR), Dyce, Leuchars	Feb	1944—Mar 1945
Coulommiers	Mar	1945—Nov 1945
Benson	Nov	1945—Sep 1945
Disbanded at Benson 30 September, 1946. Re-formed there on 1 December, 1947.		
Benson	Dec	1947—Mar 1953
Wyton	Mar	1953—Mar 1956
Disbanded at Wyton on 31 March, 1956.		

Main Equipment

de Havilland Mosquito IV (Oct 1942—Sep 1943)
   W4051; W4059; W4061; DK284; DK311; DK315; DK320; DK342;
   DZ383; DZ419; DZ438; DZ473; DZ480; DZ517
de Havilland Mosquito IX (Jun 1943—Dec 1944)
   LR405; LR412, A; LR422, O; LR435; LR467
de Havilland Mosquito XVI (Jun 1944—Sep 1946)
   MM276, N; MM299; MM300; MM351; MM358; MM397; NS525;
   NS571; NS588
(**PR.32**) NS640; NS643; NS658; NS693; NS800; RF970; RF980; RG128;
   RG139; RG158
de Havilland Mosquito VI (Nov 1944—   1945)
   PZ345; RS502, Y; RS512, H
de Havilland Mosquito PR.34 (Dec 1947—Mar 1953)
   PF662, DH:T; PF679, DH:A; RG181, DH:F; RG215, DH:S;
   RG236, DH:C; RG245, DH:S; RG290, DH:N; RG302, DH:B;
   VL613, DH:X; VL625, DH:D
English Electric Canberra PR.3 (Dec 1952—Mar 1956)
   WE136; WE141; WE145; WE148; WE167
English Electric Canberra PR.7 (1956—Mar 1956)
   WH795; WJ815, G

Commanding Officers

W/Cdr M. J. B. Young, DFC	Oct	1942—May 1943
W/Cdr Lord Douglas-Hamilton, OBE	May	1943—Mar 1944
W/Cdr J. R. H. Merrifield, DSO, DFC and Bar	Mar	1944—Sep 1944
W/Cdr A. H. W. Ball, DSO, DFC	Sep	1944—

Aircraft Insignia

No. 540 Squadron's aircraft carried no squadron insignia until the 1947 period when it used the code letters 'DH' and carried the squadron badge on the fin. With the Canberras the badge was carried on the nose.

No. 541 SQUADRON

BADGE
A bird's eye speedwell
MOTTO
'Alone above all'

On 19 October, 1942, when No. 1 PRU was expanded into squadrons, No. 541 Squadron formed at Benson from B and F Flights of No. 1 PRU. It was equipped with Spitfire IVs, its primary task being regular photographic coverage of all enemy ports from Spain to the Baltic. Many other types of sorties were flown and the Squadron was regularly preparing pinpoint photos of targets for Bomber Command and then bomb-damage assessment pictures after the raids. It flew weather recces also and some low-level sorties, though most of its operational flying was at high-level. Most of its activity concentrated on the Channel ports although in January,

1943 No. 541 sent a detachment to Leuchars to provide Norwegian cover. With the arrival of Mark XI Spitfires it began to attempt to fly above 39,000 ft to avoid leaving vapour trails. In February, 1943 out of 71 sorties three pilots were lost but there was one outstanding effort when, on 19th, F/O J. R. Breen, DFC spent 45 minutes over Berlin obtaining coverage of the whole city. The Squadron was now operating five different versions of the Spitfire for high and low level work. Germany and Northern France continued to take most of No. 541's efforts that year although sorties over Spain and North Africa were also flown. The Möhne and Eder dams were covered before and after No. 617's famous raid. Towards the end of the year the Squadron began on its next important task which was to photograph, and keep updated, the whole French coast from Bordeaux to the River Scheldt in preparation for the invasion.

This was stretched inland as well to cover the *Noball* sites which became an even greater priority. When the invasion came the Squadron was augmented by some SAAF pilots flying Mustang IIIs at low level who covered targets which were obscured by cloud. No. 541 was operating intensively, 262 sorties being flown in August, 1944; in September Arnhem was the prime target in preparation for the airborne landings. F/Lt Garvey managed to score an enemy aircraft destroyed on 6 October, though his Spitfire was unarmed; he was attacked by two FW 190s at 9000 feet, dived to ground level followed by them, when one FW 190 flew into a tree and blew up. By now the Squadron was working over Holland and Germany and more and more involved in Bomber Command's damage assessment programme.

With the war over a new task was found for the PR Spitfires and No. 541 began flying diplomatic mail both to Bordeaux and to Gatow in Berlin. It also received some Meteor F.3s for evaluation. In February, 1946 the Squadron was re-organised, A Flight becoming the Spitfire Flight and B Flight re-equippped with Lancaster PR.1s which it took to Takoradi for a survey of the Gold Coast in March, 1946. At home the flying dropped to almost a standstill due to a lack of electricians and on 30 September, 1946 No. 541 Squadron was disbanded at Benson, B Flight being re-numbered 82 Squadron. The Squadron was re-formed once more at Benson on 1 November, 1947 with Spitfire PR.19s and continued in its previous role until 1951 when it was re-equipped with Gloster Meteor PR.10s. With these it joined BAFO in Germany in June, 1951 and flew as part of the 2nd TAF there until final disbandment at Laarbruch on 6 September, 1957.

Bases etc.

Formed at Benson from 'B' & 'F' Flights of No. 1 PRU.
Benson, det. Mount Farm, Leuchars,
    St. Eval, Gibraltar, Lübeck, Takoradi   Oct 1942—Sep 1946
Disbanded at Benson on 30 September, 1946, B Flight being re-numbered 82 Squadron at Takoradi. The Squadron re-formed at Benson on 1 November, 1947.

Benson	Nov 1947—Jun 1951
Bückeburg	Jun 1951—Jun 1955
Laarbruch	Jun 1955—Sep 1957

Disbanded at Laarbruch on 6 September, 1957.

Main Equipment

Vickers-Supermarine Spitfire IV (Oct 1942—Nov 1943)
  R7041; R7044; R7211; AA790; AA807; AB125; AB309; AB428; BP879; BP881; BP926; BR658; BR670; BS499, L
Vickers-Supermarine Spitfire IX (Nov 1942—Dec 1943)
  BS338; BS437; EN149; EN154; EN410; EN503
Vickers-Supermarine Spitfire VB (Jan 1943—   1943)
  No serial numbers confirmed
Vickers-Supermarine Spitfire XI (Jan 1943—Sep 1946)
  EN342; EN662; EN664, Q; EN666; EN683, D; MB787, T; MB903, E; MB907, Z; PA856; PA868, H; PA942, G; PA943, V; PL715; PL789; PL856; PL882; PL919; PL952; PL966; PM139; PM154
Vickers-Supermarine Spitfire X (May 1944—Jan 1945)
  MD191; MD195; MD198; MD199; SR395
North American Mustang III (Jun 1944—May 1945)
  FB182; FX855; FX952
Vickers-Supermarine Spitfire XIX (Sep 1944—Sep 1946 and Dec 1947—   1951)
  PM580, WY:G; PM609, WY:N; PM623, ES:B; PM658, WY:D; PM659, ES:G; PS832; PS858, WY:H; PS887, ES:B, later WY:B; PS921, WY:E; PS934, WY:R; RM638
Gloster Meteor F.3 (Jul 1945—Apr 1946)
  EE409; EE410; EE411
Avro Lancaster PR.1 (Feb 1946—Sep 1946)
  PA434; PA439, D; TW884, B; TW899, F; TW901; TW904, E
Gloster Meteor PR.10 (Jan 1951—Sep 1957)
  VS973, WY:A; VS975, A:N; VS985, WY:B, later A:T; VW378, WY:D; WB156, A:B; WB181, A:X; WH571, A:Y; WH573

Commanding Officers

S/Ldr D. W. Steventon, DSO, DFC	Oct 1942	—Jul 1943
S/Ldr E. A. Fairhurst, DFC	Jul 1943	—Nov 1943
S/Ldr J. H. Saffey, DSO	Nov 1943	—Sep 1944
S/Ldr E. A. Fairhurst, DFC	Sep 1944	—Oct 1945
S/Ldr T. D. Calnan	Oct 1945	—Mar 1946
W/Cdr Edwards, DFC	Mar 1946	—Sep 1946

Aircraft Insignia

No identity markings were carried by No. 541 Squadron until the war ended when its Spitfires received 'ES' code letters until disbandment. Upon re-forming the letters 'WY' were used until 1951 when the Meteors received the letter 'A' instead. The Squadron badge was carried on the nose of the Meteors.

No. 542 SQUADRON

BADGE
Within an orle of seven mullets, a terrestrial globe
MOTTO
'Above all'

No. 542 Squadron formed on 19 October, 1942 from A & E Flights of No. 1 PRU at Benson, using Mount Farm as the operating base for its Spitfires. Nine sorties were flown in the remainder of that month. It was mainly involved in covering the Northern France coastline from Cherbourg to Calais but also flew some sorties over Norway. The workload was built up so that by February, 1943 it was flying 75 sorties per month, within northern Europe ports being the main targets. By and large the Spitfires flew too high for interference but about one pilot a month was lost on average through one cause or another.

In May, 1943 the Squadron began to switch its activities to co-operating with Bomber Command, photographing targets before a raid for briefing purposes, and after for damage assessment. For the rest of the year its duties were divided between this type of work and the coastal watch. Early in 1944 the most urgent task became the monitoring of the *Noball* (V1) in Northern France and this took priority. With the coming invasion of Normandy the Squadron became under great pressure and during June, 1944 flew 225 sorties, mainly in connection with the invasion and with the *Noballs*. For the next few months the tactical situation on the Continental took up most of the Squadron's capacity, working ahead of the fighting line, building up a picture of movements and suitable targets in Holland, Belgium and North Germany.

Frequently the Squadron's activities were limited by cloud cover. However in December the Squadron evolved a new method of dealing with this by using a GEE-equipped Mosquito to escort a Spitfire near the target; the Spitfire would then descend through the cloud, take the photographs, climb up and away. These sorties were repeated in the New Year when the emphasis switched to German transportation systems, railways, ports, oil targets and U-boat pens. By the time the war in Europe ended in May, 1945 the Squadron had flown 2458 operational sorties. It was then switched to flying diplomatic mail until normal channels had been established once more amongst the liberated nations. The Squadron was disbanded at Benson on 27 August, 1945.

No. 542 re-formed again in the PR role at Wyton on 17 May, 1954, equipped with English Electric Canberras but this period was short-lived, the Squadron disbanding again there on 1 October, 1955. Exactly a month later No. 1323 Flight at Wyton was re-numbered No. 542 Squadron; again it was equipped with PR Canberras but had a specific task, which was to provide high-level monitoring for the nuclear tests in Australia. This it did in early 1956/57, returning to the UK in April, 1957. The Squadron now served in the PR role in the UK until being re-numbered as No. 21 Squadron at Upwood on 1 October, 1958.

Bases etc.

Formed at Benson on 19 October, 1942 by combining A&E Flights of No. 1 PRU.
Benson, det. Mount Farm, Leuchars   Oct 1942—Aug 1945
Disbanded at Benson on 27 August, 1945. Re-formed at Wyton on 17 May, 1954.

Wyton	May 1954—Oct 1955

Disbanded at Wyton on 1 October, 1955. Re-formed there by re-numbering No. 1323 Flight on 1 November, 1955.

Wyton	Nov 1955—Dec 1955
Weston Zoyland	Dec 1955— 1956
Laverton, Australia	1956—Apr 1957
Hemswell	Apr 1957—Jul 1958
Upwood	Jul 1958—Oct 1958

Disbanded at Upwood on 1 October, 1958 by re-numbering as No. 21 Squadron.

Main Equipment

Vickers-Supermarine Spitfire IV (Oct 1942—Mar 1943)
P9565; X4335; AA785; AA811; AA918; AB124; AB303; AB430; BP884; BP917; BP929
Vickers-Supermarine Spitfire IX (Feb 1943—Jul 1943)
BS497; BS501; BS502; EN149; EN141; EN413; EN417
Vickers-Supermarine Spitfire XI (Feb 1943—Aug 1945)
EN652; EN658; EN667; EN684; MB771; MB793; PA885; PA912; PA941, H; PA948; PL766; PL785; PL825; PL886; PL896; PL900, L; PL921; PL963; PM127; PM147; PM150
Vickers-Supermarine Spitfire X (Jun 1944—May 1945)
MD194; MD198; MD213; SR396; SR398; SR402

Vickers-Supermarine Spitfire XIX (May 1944—Aug 1945)
RM628; RM632; RM634; RM636; RM646
English Electric Canberra PR.7 (May 1954—Oct 1955 & Nov 1955—Oct 1958)
WH779; WH795; WH799
English Electric Canberra B.2, B.6 (Nov 1955—Oct 1958)
WH701; WH884; WH887; WH909
English Electric Canberra PR.3 (May 1954— 1955)
WE136; WE150; WE151; WE166; WE194

Commanding Officers

S/Ldr D. Salwey, DFC	Oct 1942—Jun 1943	
S/Ldr E. D. L. Lee, DFC	Jun 1943—Jul 1943	
S/Ldr D. M. Furniss, DFC	Jul 1943—Dec 1943	
S/Ldr D. B. Pearson, DFC	Dec 1943—Mar 1944	
S/Ldr A. H. W. Ball, DSO, DFC	Mar 1944—Sep 1944	
S/Ldr G. B. Singlehurst, DSO, DFC	Sep 1944—Aug 1945	
S/Ldr A. J. Picknett, DFC	May 1954—Oct 1955	

Aircraft Insignia

As far as is known no aircraft of No. 542 Squadron carried any distinguishing squadron markings.

No. 543 SQUADRON

BADGE
A crane's head, the crane carrying an open padlock, with key, in its beak
MOTTO
'Valiant and vigilant'

The Squadron was formed at Benson on 19 October, 1942 with Spitfire IVs for photo recce duties. A Flight was detached to St. Eval where it flew operationally whilst B Flight was established at Mount Farm and served as an OTU for PR pilots going overseas.

The operational A Flight covered the Atlantic coast of France and the Iberian Peninsula, with the occasional sortie to the Channel Isles or Holland. This was maintained throughout most of 1943. In September, 1943 a detachment went to Grasnaya in the Soviet Union and flew thirty-one sorties over the northern Norwegian fjords, photographing the movements of *Altmark. Lützow, Scharnhorst* and *Tirpitz*. On 18 October, 1943 the Squadron was disbanded, A Flight transferring to No. 541 Squadron and B Flight continuing in its non-operational role.

No. 543 Squadron re-formed at Gaydon on 24 September, 1955 with Vickers Valiants equipped for recce duties and took up the photo recce role actively once more. For nearly twenty years it maintained this task, re-equipping with Victors when the Valiants were grounded in 1965 until eventually disbanding at Wyton on 24 May, 1974.

Bases etc.

Formed at Benson on 19 October, 1942.

Benson, det. St. Eval, Mount Farm, Grasnaya (USSR)	Oct 1942—Oct 1943

Disbanded at Benson on 18 October, 1943, A Flight transferring to No. 541 Squadron. Re-formed at Gaydon on 24 September, 1955.

Gaydon	Sep 1955—Nov 1955
Wyton	Nov 1955—May 1974

Disbanded at Wyton on 24 May, 1974.

Main Equipment

Vickers-Supermarine Spitfire IV (Oct 1942—Oct 1943)
N3111; R7139; X4786; AA803; AB128; AB306; AB424; AR420; BR412; BR658
Vickers-Supermarine Spitfire IX (Nov 1942—Oct 1943)
EN385; EN424; EN426
Vickers Valiant B(PR)K.1 (Sep 1955—May 1965)
WP217; WP223; WZ380; WZ382; WZ391; WZ393; WZ394; WZ399
Handley Page Victor SR.2 (Jan 1966—May 1974)
XH672; XH674; XL161; XL165; XL193; XL230; XM715; XM716

Commanding Officers

S/Ldr A. E. Hill, DSO, DFC and Bar	Oct 1942—Oct 1942	
S/Ldr G. E. Hughes, DFC	Oct 1942—Oct 1943	
W/Cdr R. E. Havercroft, AFC	Aug 1955—Aug 1957	
W/Cdr R. Berry, DSO, OBE, DFC	Aug 1957—	
W/Cdr C. G. St. D. Jeffries		

Aircraft Insignia

During World War II service no particular squadron markings were carried. The Valiants carried the Squadron's crane emblem on the underwing tanks and this was painted on the Victor's fins above the fin stripes.

No. 544 SQUADRON

BADGE
A gannet volant, the head lowered
MOTTO
'Quaero' ('I seek')

On 19 October, 1942 No. 544 Squadron formed at Benson with two separate Flights at two bases far apart: A Flight was at Benson with Ansons and Wellingtons and B Flight at Gibraltar with Spitfires. Only the latter was operational, providing PR coverage for the North African landings and keeping an eye on Spanish airfields as well. A Flight was engaged in experimental night photography and

this began over France with the Wellingtons in January, 1943. In the meantime B Flight had also received a Maryland which it detached to Agadir to cover a secret operation in that area. The Wellingtons were succeeded by Mosquitoes in April, 1943, and these were more successful except when DZ600 was shot down by British night fighters just six miles from Benson on 28 July, 1943.

In October, 1943 B Flight at Gibraltar was transferred to No. 541 Squadron and a new B Flight formed at Benson with Mosquitoes. The Squadron now concentrated on day and night operations over Germany and Western Europe generally, building up to about 40 sorties a month in January, 1944. In February, 1944 the Squadron began long-range sorties to South France, Southern Germany and Austria by shuttling through to San Severo in Italy. B Flight moved to Leuchars in February to concentrate on Norway whilst A Flight turned its attention to Eastern Germany and Poland. The sortie rate went up to nearly 70 per month in May, then the Squadron switched to Northern France for the Second Front landings, covering the hinterland behind the bridgehead. However, in July, 1944 it returned to its long-distance sorties once more finding an increasing number of interceptions by enemy aircraft, with losses going up accordingly. In October, 1944 the Squadron's Mosquitoes began transitting into Moscow (Vnukovo) for operating over Eastern Germany and Poland. These became 4 hour 30 mins round-trips for the crews. Others were flown via the Crimea, Cairo and Italy. In December some of the Squadron's aircraft were stripped of cameras and used to carry diplomatic mail to Hassani in Greece and this, known as Operation Haycock, was extended to Italy and Egypt in early 1945.

On 16 March, 1945 F/O RM Hays had a harrowing flight in Mosquito NS795. Over Leipzig he was intercepted by three Me 163s but managed to throw them off by a 480 mph dive in which his starboard engine caught fire. After feathering the prop it went out so he set course for the Allied lines, flying through violent frontal conditions, was set on by a Messerschmitt Bf 109 which he threw off by diving to ground level and eventually landed at Lille, still on one engine. For this he received the DFC. As the war ended the Squadron was allocated to 'Tiger Force' for operations in the Far East but in the meantime flew courier trips across Europe. This was followed by a survey task covering Dutch and Belgian communications systems. With the Far East war over the end came for No. 544, it disbanding at Benson on 13 October, 1945.

Bases etc.

Formed at Benson on 19 October, 1942
Benson, det. Gibraltar, Agadir, Leuchars   Oct   1942—Oct   1945
Disbanded at Benson on 13 October, 1945.

Main Equipment

Vickers Wellington IV (Oct 1942—Apr 1943)
Z1417; Z1418
Vickers-Supermarine Spitfire IV (Oct 1942—Oct 1943)
BR666; BR668; BR669; BR925; BS491
Vickers-Supermarine Spitfire XI (May 1943—Oct 1943)
EN423
Martin Maryland I (Dec 1942—Feb 1943)
AR744
de Havilland Mosquito IV (Mar 1943—Sep 1943)
DZ494; DZ538; DZ596; DZ600
de Havilland Mosquito IX (Sep 1943—Mar 1945)
LR411; LR417; LR425; LR432, L1; MM231; MM239; MM242; MM247
de Havilland Mosquito XVI (Mar 1944—Aug 1945)
MM272; MM283; MM307; MM352; MM396; NS502, M; NS525; NS587 (**Mk. 32**); NS633; NS652, O; NS682, K; NS795; NS803; RF981; RG115; RG133
de Havilland Mosquito PR.34 (Jun 1945—Oct 1945)
RG195; RG198

Commanding Officers

S/Ldr W. R. Acott	Oct 1942—	Jul 1943
S/Ldr J. P. H. Merrifield, DFC	Jul 1943—	Oct 1943
W/Cdr D. C. B. Walker	Oct 1943—	Nov 1943
W/Cdr D. W. Steventon, DSO, DFC	Nov 1943—	Sep 1945
S/Ldr F. L. Dodd, DSO, DFC, AFC	Sep 1945—	Oct 1945

Aircraft Insignia

As far as is known no squadron identity insignia were carried by No. 544 Squadron aircraft.

No. 547 SQUADRON

BADGE
A kingfisher diving

MOTTO
'Celer ad caedendum'
('Swift to strike')

The Squadron was formed at Holmesley South on 21 October, 1942 as a maritime reconnaissance unit and received its first Wellington VIIIs the following month. Its first operations came on 17 December when it flew ASR searches and then some convoy escorts in January, 1943. This was followed by a period of operations for exercises in Scotland. In April it started offensive work more fully; on 10th five aircraft made a strike on an enemy convoy in Biscay and further *Rover* sorties followed. Torpedo training began but the Squadron's first action came whilst on patrol on 14 June when W/O Hornington found three U-boats and dropped his depth-charges on one of them. Two more attacks followed before the month was out. Fifty-five patrols were flown in July, mostly anti-submarine sorties known as *Musketry*, and on one of these F/O J. Whyte destroyed a U-boat, the crew abandoning it. By contrast August was a bad month with three crews lost. Patrols continued until October, 1943 when the Squadron moved to Thorney Island with a detachment at Aldergrove to convert to Liberators.

Operations were resumed from St. Eval in January, 1944 with long-range anti-submarine patrols and by March sorties were up to over sixty per month; that month two U-boats were attacked. One U-boat, the crew abandoning it. By contrast August was a bad month with three crews lost. Patrols continued until October, 1943 claimed damaged, and another crew never returned. Anti U-boat patrols continued as the mainstay of the Squadron, together with the occasional attack but in September the Squadron began also co-operating with the SOE in France and flying special reconnaissance missions. This came to an end when No. 547 moved to Scotland and began operating off the Norwegian coast. In October

two crews were lost and another in November but one U-boat was attacked also. Weather severely hampered operations over the turn of the year but in February, 1945 three different U-boat attacks were made and depth-charges were also dropped on a large motor vessel and a tanker. Six more U-boats suffered from the Squadron's depth-charges in March, all along the Norwegian coast whilst on 26th F/Lt Sharp made five depth-charge attacks on enemy shipping in one sortie. Three other crews attacked other surface vessels and two more attacked destroyers and R-boats. This was a productive month with 102 sorties flown on offensive anti-shipping work. The pace slackened in April and May and then the war ended, not before one U-boat had had its own revenge by shooting down F/Lt Hill's Liberator. With the end of hostilities the Squadron was quickly disbanded at Leuchars on 4 June, 1945.

Bases etc.

Formed at Holmesley South on 21 October, 1942.

Holmesley South	Oct	1942—	Dec 1942
Chivenor	Dec	1942—	Jan 1943
Tain	Jan	1943—	Mar 1943
Chivenor	Mar	1943—	Jun 1943
Davidstow Moor	Jun	1943—	Oct 1943
Thorney Island, det. Aldergrove	Oct	1943—	Jan 1944
St. Eval, det. Tain	Jan	1944—	Sep 1944
Leuchars	Sep	1944—	Jun 1945

Disbanded at Leuchars on 4 June, 1945.

Main Equipment

Vickers Wellington VIII (Oct 1942—Apr 1943)
HX687; HX733; HX743; HX774; HX777; LB118; LB122; LB192
Vickers Wellington XI (Apr 1943—Dec 1943)
HZ252; HZ351; HZ359; HZ361; HZ404; HZ406; HZ409; MP504
Consolidated Liberator V (Nov 1943—Oct 1944)
BZ723, V; BZ745, E; BZ754, A; BZ797, M; BZ821, D; BZ874, B; FL937, H; FL941, F; FL960, C; FL979, U
Consolidated Liberator VI (May 1944—Jun 1945)
BZ986, 2V:P; BZ995, 2V:N; EV897, 2V:E; EV933; EV996, 2V:U; EW296, 2V:F

Consolidated Liberator VIII (Apr 1945—Jun 1945)
KK327, 2V:M

W/Cdr D. McKenzie   Feb 1945—Jun 1945

Commanding Officers

S/Ldr H. N. Garbett	Nov 1942—May 1943
W/Cdr R. N. McKern	May 1943—Apr 1944
W/Cdr C. F. C. Wright, DFC	Apr 1944—Feb 1945

Aircraft Insignia

It is not known what code letter combination the Squadron used in its early days. It is likely that from mid-1943 to mid-1944 no unit markings were carried but from mid-1944 to June, 1945 the Squadron's Liberators carried the combination '2V'.

No. 570 SQUADRON

BADGE
A winged chariot

MOTTO
'Impetum deducimus'
('We launch the spearhead')

On 15 November, 1943 personnel from Nos. 295 and 296 Squadron combined at Hurn to form No. 570 Squadron. The new unit was equipped with Armstrong-Whitworth Albemarles in the airborne role and immediately began paratroop and glider-towing training. This continued into the New Year intensively and in February the Squadron began its operational service, dropping loads to SOE forces in France. This continued through April, only one crew being lost in 57 sorties. As D-Day approached the work-up became intensive until 5 June when ten aircraft set off to drop the pathfinding paratroops at dawn. Two more aircraft towed off two close-support gliders but the towropes parted and the gliders landed in the sea off the French coast. Another ten aircraft towed a second wave of gliders. By now it was light on the 6th and No. 570's next duty was to tow twenty gliders to Caen as part of Operation Mallard. The next day came Operation Cooney when two aircraft dropped SAS troops behind the lines in France. Thereafter the Squadron returned to supporting the SOE forces in France, dropping supplies at Tours, Dijon, Arras, Brest and Paris, one more crew being lost on this task.

In July No. 570 began to convert to Stirlings and these were brought on to the SOE work in August. In September the Squadron was all set for Operation Market and on 17th twelve aircraft took members of the 1st Airborne Division to Arnhem in Horsa gliders while another eight took the 1st Airborne HQ to another LZ. In Phase 2 another ten aircraft towed reinforcements for the Division, one aircraft and glider being shot down by Flak at Overflakkee. Fifteen aircraft dropped supply containers into Arnhem, one Stirling being shot down on this task, and another over the Dutch coast. In Phase 3 seventeen aircraft flew re-supply sorties to Arnhem, three being shot down by intense Flak; the next day sixteen aircraft followed in on re-supply and all returned safely. This was repeated on the next two days, four Stirlings being lost on the final sortie. After this tragic action was finished the Squadron returned to SOE drops and, towards the end of the year, assisted in ASR searches over the North Sea.

With the advent of 1945 the Squadron trained for and began tactical bombing sorties at night, beginning at Grevenboich on 1 February but SOE sorties were flown as well. In March came Operation Varsity, the Rhine airborne crossing. No. 570s part was

to tow thirty Horsas successfully across without loss to the gliders or tugs. Early the next month came Operation Amherst, the dropping of paratroops into Groningen blind at night; this was carried out most successfully. By now the Squadron was flying its supply-drops to subversive organisations in Denmark and two crews were lost on this task in April. These operations also marked the end of the Squadron's war activities.

Immediately after VE-Day No. 570 took part in Operation Doomsday flying the 1st Airborne Division to Gardermoen airfield at Oslo, at the same time beginning to fly troops back from the Continent to the UK. It now began regular continental and Norwegian runs on behalf of Transport Command, reaching as far as Prague in August. In September it began scheduled mail and newspaper runs to Brussels, Handorf and Cologne, started a service to Cairo and also continued glider-towing training. This pattern was maintained until 8 January, 1946 when the Squadron was disbanded at Rivenhall.

Bases etc.

Formed at Hurn on 15 November, 1943.

Hurn, det. Stoney Cross	Nov 1943—Mar 1944
Harwell, det. Ayr	Mar 1944—Apr 1945
Rivenhall, det. East Fortune	Apr 1945—Jan 1946

Disbanded at Rivenhall on 8 January, 1946.

Main Equipment

Armstrong-Whitworth Albemarle I, II, V (Nov 1943—Jul 1944)
P1371, V8:O; P1379, DD, later V8:D; P1441, XX; P1653, V8:I; V1602, V8:U; V1617, V8:S; V1627, KK; V1645, BB; V1694, V8:Z; V1703, YY, later V8:Y; V1746, RR; V1783, V8:W; V1785, V8:F; V1816, E7:Z; V1842, V8:O

Short Stirling IV (Jul 1944—Jan 1946)
EF275, E7:Y; EF306, E7:Y; EH897, E7:Z; LJ596, V8:K; LJ615, V8:H; LJ636, E7:N; LJ647, V8:U; LJ883, V8:K; LJ913, V8:P; LJ992, E7:K; LK122, V8:R; LK154, E7:P; LK203, V8:E; LK286, E7:T; LK364, V8:O; LK555, V8:S; PK234, V8:E; PW446, V8:M

Commanding Officers

W/Cdr R. J. M. Bangay	Nov 1943—Jun 1945
W/Cdr K. R. Slater	Jun 1945—Aug 1945
W/Cdr R. E. Young, DSO, DFC	Aug 1945—Dec 1945
W/Cdr J. Blackburn, DSO, DFC	Dec 1945—Jan 1946

Aircraft Insignia

No Squadron identity markings were originally carried by No. 570 Squadron but just before D-Day the Squadron was allotted the code letter 'V8' with 'E7' as a back-up as it had too many aircraft for just one combination. These two markings were carried until the Squadron disbanded.

No. 575 SQUADRON

BADGE
A hand couped at the wrist, supporting a terrestrial glove

MOTTO
'The air is our path'

The Squadron was formed at Hendon on 1 February, 1944 from a nucleus of 512 Squadron. Two weeks later it moved to Broadwell where it began glider-towing training with Dakotas. In April it began *Nickel* raids on the Cherbourg peninsula as well as increasing the tempo of its training so that by June, 1944 it was ready for airborne action. On the night of 5 June, as part of Operation Tonga, it took twenty-one aircraft across the Channel and dropped the 5th Parachute Brigade successfully on its DZ. This was followed on D-Day itself by towing twenty-one gliders across and dropping panniers with supplies and equipment, one aircraft crashing on the runway on take-off and delaying the remainder but, fortunately, without harm.

On 17 June the Squadron began casevac flights out of B.5 strip in France, then it became involved in transporting 2nd TAF fighter and fighter-bomber Wings to their landing strips in France and bringing casualties out on the return trips. July, August and September were busy months shuttling across the Channel with supplies and casualties, 215 sorties being flown in August. But September also brought the Arnhem tragedy where No. 575 was heavily involved. On 17th it took men of the Border Regiment across in nineteen Dakotas towing Horsa gliders. The next day twenty-three more gliders were towed off for Arnhem, two force-landing *en route*; one pilot was killed by Flak but his crew returned. On 19th nineteen Dakotas flew a re-supply mission and two were lost, one crash-landing back in the UK. A similar mission was flown on 20th without loss. On 23 September the Squadron was detached to Brussels for Arnhem support missions but by then it was virtually over. On 26th one Dakota flew into a Landing Zone at Grave and picked up glider-pilots from Arnhem, then the Squadron returned to the Continental shuttle, establishing a detachment at Antwerp (Deurne).

This pattern continued until March, 1945 when the Squadron put up twenty-four aircraft to two gliders successfully across the Rhine; this operation was in addition to 273 Continental shuttle sorties. This total went up to 397 in April, the Squadron now flying sorties within the Continent itself. With the war over continental flying continued for a while but in August the Squadron moved and was held for the India route which it began to fly in October, this carrying on until January, 1946. Then No. 575 moved to Italy and began route-flying within and from Italy opening up regular schedules about the Mediterranean. This was continued until the Squadron disbanded at Bari on 15 August, 1946.

Bases etc.

Formed at Hendon from 512 Squadron personnel on 1 February, 1944.

Hendon	Feb 1944—Feb 1944
Broadwell, det. Evere, Deurne	Feb 1944—Aug 1945
Melbourne	Aug 1945—Nov 1945
Blakehill Farm	Nov 1945—Jan 1946
Bari	Jan 1946—Aug 1946

Disbanded at Bari 15 August, 1946.

Main Equipment

Douglas Dakota III (Feb 1944—   1946)
  FD945, I9:X; FZ518; FZ593, I9:UI; FZ636, I9:O; FZ662, I9:X; FZ695, I9:B; KG328, I9:P; KG348, I9:M; KG361, I9:O; KG432, I9:UG; KG442, I9:DH; KG511, I9:M; KG550, I9:NN; KG567, I9:F; KG602, I9:V; KG620, I9:Q; KG695
Avro Anson I (Jun 1944—   1944)
  NK492; NK605; NK674, I9:M; NK766
Douglas Dakota IV (Mar 1945—Aug 1946)
  KK154; KN258, I9:W; KN272, I9:DO, later I9:L; KN290, I9:B; KN431, I9:F; KN636, I9:BW; KN663, I9:FW

Commanding Officers

W/Cdr T. A. Jefferson, AFC	Feb 1944—Dec 1944
W/Cdr E. C. Deanesly, DFC	Dec 1944—Jul 1945
W/Cdr B. L. Duigan, DSO, DFC	Jul 1945—Aug 1946

Aircraft Insignia

The only identity markings carried by No. 575 Squadron, throughout its existence, were the code letters 'I9'.

No. 608 SQUADRON

BADGE
A falcon's leg, erased, belled and fessed

MOTTO
'Omnibus ungulis'
('With all talons')

The falcon's leg was chosen to indicate the Squadron's readiness to go into the air at any time and fight tooth and nail.

Amongst the auxiliary Squadron No. 608 (North Riding) Squadron changed its role twice before World War II began. Starting as a bomber squadron between formation on 17 March, 1930 and January, 1937 it then replaced its Wapitis by Demons and became a fighter squadron for two years. Then, on 20 March, 1939 it was transferred, at its base of Thornaby, to Coastal Command and began to work up on Avro Ansons. Soon after the outbreak of war it began operations with an anti-submarine patrol over the North Sea on 21 September, 1939. Most of its work became East Coast convoy protection and it suffered its first casualty on 8 October when Anson N5204 was shot down by an over-eager Hurricane. Thereafter the aircraft were re-painted with Type A roundels and told to fly with their undercarriages down. The Squadron maintained a continuity of convoy and anti-submarine patrols, sixty-four sorties being flown in November. It was not until March, 1940 that further action came No. 608s way when F/O A. Brown found three He 111s attacking a convoy and scattered them without result. That month 96 sorties were flown and the following month this total went up to 131. These included ASR work as well and coastal patrols, looking for signs of German invasion forces.

In June the operations were maintained at full strength although A Flight was away at Silloth converting to the Blackburn Botha and this type was introduced into operations on 10 August. Just prior to that P/O Reeve had attacked a Ju 88 over a convoy but, with its superior speed, it escaped. Through September and October the Squadron largely flew its operations on Bothas, being the only squadron to use this type operationally, but it was found to have serious deficiencies and in November all the Squadron's Bothas were withdrawn and it was back to Ansons again. Two combats with He 115s took place that month but without any results.

It was now urgent to replace the Ansons so in February, 1941 the Squadron began to fly Blenheim IVs, using them operationally in March, the Ansons finally disappearing in April. With the Blenheim the task was just the same – convoys, anti-submarine patrols and ASR duties over the North Sea. In July the Blenheims began to be replaced by Hudsons, giving No. 608 a more offensive capability and in September the first bombing attack on an enemy convoy was carried out. On 10 September the Squadron claimed its first enemy aircraft damaged, a Ju 88. With the greater range available the Squadron began operating over Denmark, dropping leaflets in *Nickel* raids. More offensively it bombed the port of Aalborg on 3 October and Esbjerg on 13th. The Squadron was now principally engaged in this area with shipping *Rovers* and attacks on ports. In November three large ships were bombed and two Hudson crews lost, including the CO.

In January, 1942 the Squadron moved to the north of Scotland and from there operated over the Norwegian coast, bombing Bergen on 7th. As it settled in and the spring came No. 608s intensity of operations increased again, becoming mainly shipping strikes in the fjords (Operation Bluebeard). Mostly surface ships were attacked but some U-boats were found for which depth-charged were carried and dropped. This pattern of operation continued until August, 1942 when the Squadron was deployed south to prepare for overseas.

Between September and November, 1942 the Squadron was moving to, and establishing itself, at Gibraltar from where it became busily engaged in providing anti-submarine cover for the large convoys bringing the invasion forces to North Africa in November. On 11 November a U-boat was attacked and another two days later. Then on 13th there were three such attacks, two on 14th and four on 15th. Three more were made before the end of the month. 157 sorties were flown in December and 177 in January, 1943 as the Squadron maintained overall coverage of the Straits and Western Approaches at this vital period. Four U-boats were attacked in January, one being definitely damaged, and two in February and March respectively. By May the sortie rate had topped the two hundred mark, an average of two U-boats being depth-charged each month. The Squadron had been operating from Algerian bases since November, 1942 moving eastwards in spring to extend cover and to try to interfere with the German supply routes into Tunisia, operating in Sicilian waters to do this.

In October, 1943 it moved into Sicily itself and from now on No. 608 returned to the more prosaic task of convoy escort as the troop convoys moved in for the onslaught on Italy. This task became particularly arduous in January, 1944 when the Squadron provided a constant anti-submarine patrol for the convoys in and out of the Anzio beach-head and four crews were lost that month on the Anzio patrol. In March the flow of operations was halted by volcanic activity, the aircraft being covered in ash. Operations, mainly convoy work, were maintained up to 7 July when No. 608 was withdrawn to be disbanded on 31 July, 1944 at Montecorvino.

A new No. 608 Squadron was re-formed at Downham Market in the UK on 1 August, 1944 as a light bomber squadron in Bomber Command, serving in this role until 24 August, 1945 when it again disbanded. It re-formed on an Auxiliary basis at Thornaby on 31 July, 1946, becoming a fighter squadron with Mosquitoes, Spitfires and later Vampires. It eventually disbanded at Middleton St. George on 10 March, 1957.

Bases etc.

Transferred to Coastal Command at Thornaby on 17 March, 1939.

Thornaby, det. Bircham Newton, Dyce	Mar 1939—Jan 1942
Wick	Jan 1942—Aug 1942
Sumburgh	Aug 1942—Aug 1942
Gosport	Aug 1942—Sep 1942
en route to Gibraltar	Sep 1942—Nov 1942
Gibraltar	Nov 1942—Nov 1942
Blida, det. Bone	Nov 1942—Aug 1943
Protville	Aug 1943—Sep 1943
Bo Rizzo, det. Grottaglie	Sep 1943—Oct 1943
Montecorvino	Oct 1943—Dec 1943
Grottaglie, det. Guado	Dec 1943—Feb 1944
Montecorvino, det. Bo Rizzo	Feb 1944—Jul 1944

Disbanded at Montecorvino on 31 July, 1944. Re-formed at Downham Market on 1 August, 1944, in the bomber role and disbanded there on 24 August, 1945. It re-formed once more as an Auxiliary squadron on 10 May, 1946 and finally disbanded, after nine years as a fighter squadron at Middleton St. George, on 10 March, 1957.

Main Equipment

Avro 652A Anson I (Mar 1939—Apr 1941)
N5053, UL:A; N5067, UL:L; N5104, UL:W; N5198, UL:D; N5207, UL:P; N5216, UL:A; N5357, UL:R; N5362, UL:S; N9742, UL:U; N9918, UL:X; R9687, UL:S; R9773, UL:P; R9819, UL:F

Blackburn Botha I (Jun 1940—Dec 1940)
L6170, UL:F; L6191, UL:M; L6195, UL:R; L6208, UL:N; L6215, UL:Q; L6239, UL:Z; L6380; L6382

Bristol Blenheim IV (Feb 1941—Jul 1941)
V5526, UL:G; V5572, UL:K; V5682, UL:B; V5726, UL:S; V5733, UL:A; V5763, UL:E; V5873, UL:L; Z5982, UL:U; Z5986, UL:R; Z6043, UL:H

Lockheed Hudson V (Jul 1941—Jul 1944)
V9108, W; AE642, H, later V; AM571, A; AM599, H; AM610, L; AM638, K; AM657, D; AM686, D; AM739, O; AM744, B; AM791, P; AM818, R; AM853, W; AM882, P

Lockheed Hudson IIIA (Jun 1943—Jul 1944)
FH345, Z; FK733, O; FK749, W; FK772, F; FK798, D; FK801, J; FK809, Z; FK813, L

Lockheed Hudson VI (Mar 1943—Jul 1944)
EW925, Z; FK444, P; FK520, J; FK543, M; FK640, M; FK677, N; FK684, R; FK708, U

Commanding Officers

W/Cdr G. Shaw, DFC	Mar 1939—May 1941
W/Cdr R. S. Derbyshire	May 1941—Nov 1941
W/Cdr P. D. R. Hutchings, AFC	Nov 1941—Feb 1943
W/Cdr C. M. M. Grece, DFC	Feb 1943—Dec 1943
W/Cdr D. Finlay, OBE	Dec 1943—Jul 1944

Aircraft Insignia

In 1939 the code letters 'PG' were allotted to No. 608 Squadron but it is not known whether these were carried. In September, 1939 these were changed to 'UL' which were carried at least until 1942. From its move overseas until disbandment in 1944 the Hudson carried no markings to identify the unit. (See also *Bomber Squadrons of the RAF*, p. 278 and *Fighter Squadrons of the RAF*, pp. 491–2)

No. 612 SQUADRON

BADGE
In front of a trident and harpoon in saltire, a thistle dipped and leaved

MOTTO
'Vigilando Custodimus'
('We stand guard by vigilance')

The trident and harpoon signify the Squadron's anti-submarine role whilst the thistle relates to the Squadron's basis as the County of Aberdeen Auxiliary Squadron.

This auxiliary Squadron was formed at Dyce, Aberdeen, on 1 June, 1937 as an army co-operation squadron and by the end of that year had equipped with Hawker Hectors. It worked up in this role but in November, 1938 was re-designated a general reconnaissance unit although the equipment for this task, Avro Ansons, did not arrive until July, 1939. Despite a short work-up No. 612 began coastal patrols in September, 1939 with the outbreak of war and on 5th F/O J. P. Smythe dropped two 100-lb bombs on a U-boat and claimed to have damaged it. Slowly the Squadron built up its task, flying part of the time with No. 269 Squadron at Leuchars, and in December another U-boat attack was made. In 1940 it also flew counter-invasion patrols in borrowed Tiger Moths, checking that no inva-

sion forces were landing along the Scottish coast. Its main task, however, was the usual convoy escort and anti-submarine patrols. By June, 1940 it was flying over 280 sorties a month and made two attacks on suspected U-boats that month and two more in July; in addition one crew had an inconclusive combat with a Do 17. A detachment of No. 612 had been flying at Bircham Newton in May/June, now a similar one went to Stornoway for the rest of the year.

In November, 1940 the first Whitleys arrived for the Squadron. At first these were used in a temporary transport role to move No. 254 Squadron, then in the New Year No. 612 came off operations to convert. It was not until 22 February when operations were resumed with patrols off the Faroes and Shetlands. The Squadron's start with Whitleys was faltering with five bad crashes but in March P/O Harrop's crew bombed a submerged U-boat. A transfer to Wick at the end of March enabled the Squadron to move ahead; even so many of its sorties at this stage were abortive due to the ASV equipment being unserviceable. Seventy to eighty sorties were being flown each month, mainly on convoy escort. On 21 May the Squadron sent six aircraft to bomb the *Bismarck* and *Prinz Eugen* in Bergen Harbour but were frustrated by bad weather. This was repeated more successfully on the night of 5/6 June. Subsequent operations also brought a succession of losses, two crews being killed in August. In September a detachment went to Iceland and four U-boat attacks took place, one being definitely damaged by F/O Riddell's crew. The Iceland detachment returned in October when a further detachment went to Cornwall for operations in the Biscay area until early November. At the end of the year the Squadron moved completely to Iceland. Here its task was anti-submarine patrols out into the middle of the Atlantic and also ice patrols; it acquired a flight of Fairey Battles, remnants from No. 98 Squadron.

In February, 1942 two U-boats were found and attacked, though one aircraft subsequently crashed in Iceland. For the most part the patrols produced little action. A small detachment again went to St. Eval for Biscay operations for two months. This continued until August when the Squadron began to move to Thorney Island by two's and three's. Here it became non-operational to re-equip with modified aircraft. Its new task, begun in September, was to attack shipping in the Cherbourg to Le Havre area flying T.I. sorties as well as bombing. On 13 September four aircraft bombed and sank the tanker *Solglimt* in Cherbourg harbour. However, before the end of the month No. 612 had moved back to Wick and from there was finding more U-boats to attack. It also put much effort into escorting Russian convoys. In November a detachment went to Skitten to convert to Leigh Light Wellingtons, and the first Wellington operations were flown on 13 December.

With these the Squadron flew shipping recces along the Norwegian coast as they gradually replaced Whitleys. However, in February all the Wellingtons went to Nos. 172 and 179 Squadrons and No. 612 had to soldier on with Whitleys until April when it moved to Davidstow Moor for conversion. In May three U-boats were attacked and one Whitley was lost. By June the Wellingtons were in the ascendant and the last Whitley ops took place that month. With the Wellingtons most sorties were night patrols over the Bay of Biscay; in August two crews failed to return, in September also two, but six U-boats were found and three attacked. This pattern continued for the rest of the year, and into 1944. By March the Squadron was attacking E-boats as well as submarines, about 90 sorties a month being flown. In April three U-boats were attacked, F/O C. Punter's attack resulting in the destruction of the U-boat concerned.

In June the Squadron concentrated on 'Channel Stops', sorties to ensure that no enemy shipping entered the western end of the Channel to interfere with the invasion fleets. These were continued until September when No. 612 moved to Ireland for Atlantic patrols until December. All of these were unsuccessful in terms of targets.

In December the Squadron moved to Norfolk from where it operated at night along the Dutch coast attacking E-boats and destroying two in the first six sorties. The run of success continued into 1945 with a steadily mounting score of E-boats, sorties running at the one hundred a month mark. These operations were continued right up to the end of the war, after which No. 612 flew a few transport sorties to Holland before disbanding at Langham on 9 July, 1945.

It re-formed at Dyce on an Auxiliary basis on 1 November, 1946 in the fighter role and flew Spitfires and Vampires until disbanding at Edzell on 2 March, 1957.

Bases etc.

Formed at Dyce on 1 June, 1937.

Dyce, det. Bircham Newton, Stornoway, Wick	Jun 1937—Mar 1941	
Wick, det. Limavady, Reykjavik, St. Eval	Mar 1941—Dec 1941	
Reykjavik, det. St. Eval	Dec 1941—Aug 1942	
Thorney Island, det. Wick, St. Eval	Aug 1942—Sep 1942	
Wick, det. St. Eval, Skitten	Sep 1942—Apr 1943	
Davidstow Moor	Apr 1943—May 1943	
Chivenor, det. Davidstow Moor	May 1943—Nov 1943	
St. Eval	Nov 1943—Dec 1943	
Chivenor	Dec 1943—Jan 1944	
Limavady	Jan 1944—Mar 1944	
Chivenor, det. Limavady	Mar 1944—Sep 1944	
Limavady	Sep 1944—Dec 1944	
Langham	Dec 1944—Jul 1945	

Disbanded at Langham 7 July, 1945.

Main Equipment

Hawker Hector (Dec 1937—Nov 1939)
K8100; K8104; K9757; K9763; K9786
Avro Anson I (Jul 1939—Dec 1940)
N5219, WL:J; N5272, WL:F; N5345, WL:N; N5369, WL:S; N5373, WL:X; N9722, WL:E; N9741, WL:Z; N9875, WL:K; N9917, WL:D; R3333, WL:M; R3409, WL:B; R9825, WL:Y; W1651, WL:T
Armstrong Whitworth Whitley V (Nov 1940—   1941)
P5070, WL:B; P5083, WL:N; T4139, WL:V; T4262, WL:J; T4272, WL:A; T4286, WL:M; T4295, WL:H; T4321, WL:P; T4329, WL:U; Z6475, WL:D; Z6631, WL:B; Z6652, WL:L; Z6720, WL:K; Z6736, WL:K; Z6764, WL:M; Z6806, WL:W; Z6832, WL:R
Armstrong Whitworth Whitley VII (May 1941—Jun 1943)
Z6961, WL:W; Z6965, WL:E; Z9120, WL:V; Z9138, WL:R; Z9196, WL:L; Z9364, WL:T; Z9376, WL:M; Z9383, WL:P; Z9520, WL:F; BD565, WL:K; BD622, WL:U; BD675, WL:J; BD680, WL:N; BD697, WL:E; EB330, WL:J
Vickers Wellington VIII (Nov 1942—Feb 1943)
HX444, WL:K; HX575, WL:Z; HX629, WL:L; HX690, WL:U; HX771, WL:W; LB178, WL:X; LB194, WL:D
Vickers Wellington XII (May 1943—Jun 1943)
MP628, F; MP654, J; MP682, G
Vickers Wellington XIV (Jun 1943—Jul 1945)
HF126, M; HF133, T; HF173, H; HF177, E; HF190, J; HF206, B; HF250, C; HF268, 8W:A; HF269, S; MP752, K; MP758, N; MP763, R; NB623, 8W:B; NB823, 8W:Y; NB874, 8W:N; NB933, 8W:E; NB999, 8W:A; NC420, 8W:O; NC544, 8W:T; NC786, 8W:L; NC800, 8W:J; NC906, 8W:O; ND130, 8W:D

Commanding Officers

W/Cdr F. Crerar	Jun 1937—Jun 1940
W/Cdr J. B. M. Wallis	Jun 1940—Jul 1941
W/Cdr D. R. Shore	Jul 1941—Jan 1942
W/Cdr R. T. Corry	Jan 1942—Jul 1942
W/Cdr R. M. Longmore, CBE	Jul 1942—Apr 1943
W/Cdr J. S. Kendrick	Apr 1943—Jun 1943
W/Cdr J. B. Russell, DSO	Jun 1943—Jan 1944
W/Cdr D. M. Brass, DSO	Jan 1944—Feb 1945
W/Cdr A. M. Taylor	Feb 1945—May 1945
W/Cdr G. Henderson	May 1945—Jul 1945

Aircraft Insignia

The Squadron was allotted the code letters 'DJ' before World War II and these may have been carried on the Hectors and Ansons. For the first four years of the War the Squadron's aircraft carried 'WL' code letters. Between mid-1943 and mid-1944 no letters were carried then the Squadron used the combination '8W' on its Wellingtons.
(See also *Fighter Squadrons of the RAF*, pp. 500–1)

No. 613 SQUADRON

BADGE
In front of two wings conjoined at base a fleur de lys

MOTTO
'Semper parati'
('Always prepared')

The design of the badge is based on that of the Manchester Regiment.

No. 613 the City of Manchester Auxiliary Squadron, formed at Ringway on 1 March, 1939 as an army co-operation squadron at Ringway. It was equipped with Hawker Hind bombers as an interim measure and it was not until after the outbreak of war that it received its proper equipment, Hawker Hectors. These it flew from its War Station of Odiham until replaced by Westland Lysanders in April, 1940. With the outbreak of the fighting in France, however, the Hectors were held for a short while and flown to Hawkinge and from there both types were used, with 120-lb bombs, to attack the field gun emplacements at Calais on 26 May. The next day the Lysanders dropped supply containers to the beleagured Calais garrison, the Hectors acting as fighter escort. A daily standby was maintained at Hawkinge thereafter until 3 June when No. 613 returned to Odiham for normal routine exercises. However, later that month a detachment went to Doncaster for East coast anti-invasion patrols, then the whole Squadron moved to Netherthorpe to concentrate on these dawn and dusk coastal patrols which were maintained until 18 November, 1940.

In 1941 the Squadron was engaged in radar calibration, air firing, gas spraying training and army exercises all over England. In August the Lysanders began to be replaced by Tomahawks. Both types were retained into 1942 and in June Mustangs arrived, but it was not until the end of the year that the Squadron standardised on this type and began operations, flying *Populars* (PR sorties along the French coast) from 5 December. First casualty was two days later when F/Lt Usher Smith was lost on such an operation. Soon after *Rhubarbs* were flown as well, on all these tasks the aircraft being operated in pairs.

These operations were continued in January, 1943 but then No. 613 was moved north for more army exercises in the spring and it was not until April that operations were resumed. These were flown from East Anglia and comprised *Lagoons*, anti-shipping sorties along the Dutch Coast in company with Coastal Command Beaufighters. Thirty-four sorties were flown in April and sixty-six in May, with *Ranger* sorties as well. On one of these on 11 May the Squadron's first claim for an enemy aircraft destroyed came when F/O Townsend shot down a FW 190 and F/O Bodington damaged another.

June saw a different type of operation – *Insteps*: escorting Mosquitoes over the Bay of Biscay. In July a move to East Anglia saw No. 613 flying *Distil* operations, patrols over the Frisian Islands looking for Ju 52 magnetic mine detectors. *Lagoons* were also flown and on one of these four Bf 109Gs jumped four Mustangs of the Squadron on 18 July resulting in one Messerschmitt destroyed and two damaged. That same day four other aircraft attacked a convoy off Egmond and were jumped by eight enemy aircraft. This time only one Mustang returned, having shot a Messerschmitt into the sea.

The Squadron then transferred to Jim Crow sorties in August and September. In October it was withdrawn from operations and moved to Lasham where it re-equipped with Mosquito FB.VIs in the light bomber role. Here No. 613 formed part of 2 Group and fought with them on daylight raids throughout the rest of the war, moving to a French base in November, 1944. It disbanded there on 8 August, 1945 by re-numbering as No. 69 Squadron. It re-formed as the City of Manchester Auxiliary Squadron at Ringway on 1 November, 1946. It now flew in the fighter role and equipped with

Spitfires and then Vampires, maintained this status until disbandment on 10 March, 1957.

Bases etc.

Formed at Ringway on 1 March, 1939.

Ringway	Mar 1939	Oct 1939
Odiham, det. Weston Zoyland, Hawkinge	Oct 1939	Jun 1940
Netherthorpe	Jun 1940	Sep 1940
Firbeck	Sep 1940	Jul 1941
Doncaster	Jul 1941	Sep 1941
Andover	Sep 1941	Apr 1942
Twinwoods Farm	Apr 1942	Aug 1942
Ouston, det. Odiham	Aug 1942	Mar 1943
Wing	Mar 1943	Mar 1943
Bottisham	Mar 1943	Mar 1943
Ringway	Mar 1943	Mar 1943
Wellingore, det. Coltishall	Mar 1943	May 1943
Clifton	May 1943	Jun 1943
Portreath	Jun 1943	Jul 1943
Snailwell	Jul 1943	Oct 1943

12 October, 1943 moved to Lasham on transfer to No. 2 (Bomber) Group, 2nd TAF.

Main Equipment

Hawker Hind (May 1939—Feb 1940)
K5273; K5406; K5433; K5478; K5490; K6666
Hawker Hector (Nov 1939—Jun 1940)
K8108; K8111; K8116, ZR:X; K8127; K8138; K9689; K9706; K9717; K9732; K9781
Westland Lysander II (Apr 1940—Jan 1941)
L4791; L4799, ZR; L6855; L6872; N1269; P1670; P1693; P1724, ZR:L; P9079; P9176; R1998; R2003 (**Mk. III**); T1438, ZR:F
Westland Lysander IIIA (Jan 1941—Jun 1942)
V9324, ZR:B; V9347, ZR:A; V9373, ZR:P; V9374, ZR:F; V9402; V9433; V9579, ZR:L; V9679, ZR:G; V9680, ZR:C; V9720
Curtiss Tomahawk II (Aug 1941—Jun 1942)
AH771; AH926; AH939; AH950; AK118; AK124; AK156; AK190
North American Mustang I (Jun 1942—Oct 1943)
AG450; AG487; AG522, SY:L; AG567; AG599; AG602; AG646; AL967; AM152; AM175; AM209; AM254; AP177; AP230

Commanding Officers

S/Ldr E. Rhodes	Mar 1939	Jan 1940
S/Ldr A. F. Anderson	Jan 1940	Jul 1940
W/Cdr J. N. T. Stephenson	Jul 1940	Jun 1941
W/Cdr Viscount Acheson	Jun 1941	Sep 1942
S/Ldr C. L. Page	Sep 1942	Dec 1942
W/Cdr C. B. E. Burt-Andrews	Dec 1942	Oct 1943

Aircraft Insignia

The Squadron was allotted the code letters 'ZR' prior to the outbreak of war and these were not changed on the outbreak of war being used on Hinds, Hectors and Lysanders. At some stage, probably early in 1942, the combination was changed to 'SY' which was certainly used on the Mustangs up to mid-1943.
(See also *Bomber Squadrons of the RAF*, p. 280 and *Fighter Squadrons of the RAF*, pp. 501–2)

No. 614 SQUADRON

BADGE
On a demi-terrestrial globe, a dragon passant

MOTTO
'*Codaf I geislo*'
('I rise to search')

The red dragon shows the Squadron's connection with Wales, as County of Glamorgan Squadron.

This, the only Auxiliary Squadron formed in Wales, came into being at Cardiff Airport (Llandow) on 1 June, 1937 as an army co-operation squadron. As an interim measure it was equipped with Hawker Hinds but at the end of the year Hawker Hectors were added to the complement. On the outbreak of war it took these to

Odiham and there re-equipped with Westland Lysanders. After working up on this type it sent a detachment to Amiens on 3 May as a back-up to the squadrons in France ready for the German breakthrough. It did not fight itself but provided aircraft there for replacement to the other units. In June it moved to the East coast of Scotland where it maintained dawn and dusk coastal patrols as a counter-invasion measure. Its area stretched from Inverness to Berwick, for which purpose A Flight was detached to Inverness and became No. 241 Squadron in September.

On 19 November the coastal patrols ceased and the Squadron continued to work-up in the army co-op role, being attached to the Polish Army. In June, 1941 a detachment was sent to Tangmere and flew ASR sorties over the Channel. The following month the Squadron converted to Blenheim IVs, still in the army co-op role. In addition to this work, flying many army exercises, it was attached to

No. 114 Squadron at West Raynham in May, 1942, flying night bombing sorties over the occupied countries.

On 19 August the Squadron was successfully operating over the Dieppe landings, laying a smoke screen over the proceedings although sustaining casualties. Later that month the Squadron moved to Odiham and re-equipped with the Blenheim V preparatory to serving as a bomber squadron in North Africa.

It took part in the North African landings and was involved in tactical bombing throughout that campaign until May, 1943 when it assumed a coastal recce role at Tafaroui. While working up in the anti-shipping task No. 614 began convoy escort patrols on 6 June, adding anti-shipping and then ASR sorties to its duties. These largely uneventful patrols continued until F/Lt Holloway failed to return in September after which the aircraft flew in pairs for mutual protection. Between eighty and ninety sorties were flown each month up to the end of 1943 when operations ceased and in February, 1944 the Squadron was disbanded.

On 3 March, 1944 it was re-formed as a bomber squadron in Italy at Celone by re-numbering No. 462 Squadron. It flew Halifaxes and Liberators on night bomber raids until the war in Europe ended, being disbanded on 27 July, 1945. Ten months later No. 614 re-formed at Llandow on 10 May, 1946 as a fighter squadron in the Auxiliary Air Force flying Spitfires and Vampires until disbandment on 10 March, 1957.

Bases etc.

Formed at Llandow on 1 June, 1937.

Llandow	Jun 1937	Sep 1939
Odiham	Sep 1939	Jun 1940
Grangemouth, det. Inverness	Jun 1940	Mar 1941
Tranent, det. Inverness, Tangmere, Odiham, West Raynham	Mar 1941	Aug 1942
Thruxton	Aug 1942	Aug 1942
Macmerry	Aug 1942	Aug 1942

Moved to Odiham 26 August, 1942 to transfer to bomber duties.

Transferred from bomber to coastal reconnaissance duties at Tafaroui June, 1943.

Tafaroui	Jun 1943	Aug 1943
Bo Rizzo	Aug 1943	Feb 1944

Disbanded at Bo Rizzo February, 1944.

Main Equipment

Hawker Hind (Jun 1937—   1938)
K5379; K5478; K5493; K6735; L7239, (T)
Hawker Hector (Dec 1937—Nov 1939)
K8109; K8111; K9727; K9729; K9735; K9742; K9748; K9762
Westland Lysander II (Nov 1939—Oct 1940)
L4761; L6851; L6853; L6863; L6872; N1214; N1226; N1241; N1247; N1253; N1273; P1677 (**Mk. I**); P1690 (**Mk. I**); P1731; P9076; P9100; P9121; P9194; R1991
Westland Lysander III, IIIA (Oct 1940—Aug 1941)
R9022; R9071; R9124, LJ:P; T1430; V9380; V9547; V9588
Bristol Blenheim IV (Aug 1941—Aug 1942)
L9381; N3536; N6143; R3758; T1848; T2288; V5398; V5451; V5487; V5534, LJ:K; V5625; V5752; V5808; Z5882; Z6104
Bristol Blenheim VA (Jun 1943—Feb 1944)
BA812, L; BA825, J; BB140, N; BB175, B; BB182, Q; EH334, S; EH340, H; EH377, X

Commanding Officers

S/Ldr R. E. C. Cadman	Jun 1937	Nov 1939
S/Ldr W. R. Wills-Sandford	Nov 1939	Jan 1940
S/Ldr A. N. Malan	Jan 1940	Jun 1940
W/Cdr D. J. Eayrs	Jun 1940	Feb 1940
W/Cdr H. M. Mulliken	Feb 1940	Aug 1941
W/Cdr R. E. S. Skelton	Aug 1941	Jun 1942
W/Cdr H. T. Sutton	Jun 1942	Aug 1942
W/Cdr C. K. Bonner	Jun 1943	Feb 1944

Aircraft Markings

Originally the aircraft carried the code letters 'YX' which was the pre-war allocation for No. 614 Squadron. At some stage, probably late 1940 or early 1941 this was changed to 'LJ' but this was dropped from August, 1942 onwards.
(See also *Bomber Squadrons of the RAF*, pp. 280–1 and *Fighter Squadrons of the RAF*, pp. 502–3).

No. 615 SQUADRON

BADGE
On a star of six points, an oak sprig fructed
MOTTO
'Conjunctis viribus'
('By our united force')

The county of Surrey's Auxiliary Squadron was formed at Kenley on 1 June, 1937 for army co-operation duties and first equipped with Hawker Audaxes in this role. These were replaced with Hawker Hectors later in the year and for nearly a year No. 615 worked-up at weekends in this role. However on 7 November, 1938 the Squadron was transferred to Fighter Command and the Hectors were replaced by Gauntlets. Thereafter it served in this role, entering the war with Gloster Gladiators and using these in France as part of the BEF Air Component. By the time of the German onslaught in May, 1940 the Squadron had Hurricanes and fought with these in France and then through the Battle of Britain with 11 Group mainly. It flew on offensive sweeps in 1941 then set out for India. From there it moved into the Burma campaign, remaining operational from 1942 to the

end, latterly flying Spitfires. It was eventually disbanded there on 10 June, 1945, only to be re-formed at Biggin Hill on 31 July, 1946 as a fighter squadron in the Auxiliary Air Force once more.

Bases etc.

Formed at Kenley on 1 June, 1937.

Kenley	Jun 1937	Nov 1938

Transferred to Fighter Command at Kenley on 7 November, 1938.

Main Equipment

Hawker Audax (Jun 1937—   1938)
K3061; K7381
Hawker Hector (Nov 1937—Nov 1938)
K8102; K8115; K8127; K8129; K9785

Commanding Officers

S/Ldr A. V. Harvey	Jun 1937	Nov 1938

Aircraft Insignia

No unit identity markings were carried on the Audaxes and Hectors.
(See also *Fighter Squadrons of the RAF*, pp. 503–8)

No. 618 SQUADRON

(No badge authorised)

This Squadron formed at Skitten on 1 April, 1943 with Mosquito IVs, the intention being that this unit should use the 'skip bomb', developed by Barnes Wallis for the dambusting operation, in a

modified form for attacks on enemy warships. Primary targets were the enemy shipping in the fjords in Norway and particularly the battleship *Tirpitz*. By the end of April six fully-modified Mosquitoes arrived from Weybridge and the first trials were flown from Manston from 13 to 29 April. As a result modifications were made to the

Highball weapons and further trials flown from Turnberry in May and again at Manston in June. The weapon was still not satisfactory so in the interim it was decided that No. 618 would use the present stock as depth charges against U-boats. However, before any attacks were made the Squadron was grounded on 13 September and aircraft and personnel dispersed to await a suitable weapon, the cadre of the Squadron moving to Benson.

In December, 1943 some further drops were made in Loch Striven, in the meantime the aircrews being attached to No. 248 Squadron at Predannack for operations with Mosquito VIs and XVIIIs. It was soon realised that by the time the weapon had been perfected for use with Mosquitoes most of the suitable targets in Europe would be destroyed so in July, 1944 the Squadron was re-constituted for Operation Oxtail. This was to be as a special mine-laying unit in the Pacific. It was now at Wick and it worked up on Mosquito VIs, at the same time doing ADDL's (Aerodrome Dummy Deck Landings) flying Barracudas at Crail, following these up with practice deck-landings on HMS *Rajah*.

In September, 1944 it received a full complement of modified Mosquito IVs and began Mosquito deck-landing on HMS *Implacable* until the end of October. It then boarded HMSs *Fencer* and *Striker* for Australia. On arrival it took up residence at Fisherman's Bend in January, 1945, moving to Narrowmine the following month. By now, though, there was a shortage of Japanese shipping in the area covered by the British Pacific Fleet and after many conferences no operational use could be found for the Squadron. As a result No. 618 remained in Australia until 14 July, 1945 when a signal was received to disband.

Bases etc.

Formed at Skitten on 1 April, 1943.

Skitten, det. Manston, Turnberry	Apr 1943—Sep 1943
Benson, att. Predannack	Sep 1943—Jun 1944
Wick, det. HMS *Implacable*	Jun 1944—Oct 1944
en route to Australia	Oct 1944—Jan 1945
Fisherman's Bend	Jan 1945—Feb 1945
Narromine	Feb 1945—Jul 1945

Disbanded at Narromine 14 July, 1945.

Main Equipment

de Havilland Mosquito IV (Apr 1943—Sep 1943 & Sep 1944—Jul 1945)
DK293; DZ355; DZ423; DZ468; DZ489; DZ520/G, A; DZ537/G; DZ547, VY; DZ558, G; DZ579, M; DZ639, P; DZ652, O
Bristol Beaufighter II (Apr 1943—Jun 1943)
R2401; R2458; T3034; T3380
de Havilland Mosquito VI (Feb 1944—Sep 1944)
HR373; PZ274, S; PZ282, H1; PZ295, G1; PZ297, R1; PZ303, Q1
de Havilland Mosquito Mk XVIII
HX903; MM424
de Havilland Mosquito XVI (Sep 1944—Oct 1944)
NS572; NS577

Commanding Officers

S/Ldr C. T. Rose, DFC, DFM	Apr 1943—Apr 1943
W/Cdr G. H. B. Hutchinson	Apr 1943—Sep 1943
F/O H. B. Mcready	Sep 1943—Jul 1944
W/Cdr G. H. B. Hutchinson	Jul 1944—Oct 1944
G/Cdr R. C. Keary	Oct 1944—Jul 1945

Aircraft Markings

As far as is known no specific squadron insignia was carried.

No. 620 SQUADRON

BADGE
In front of a demi-pegasus couped a flash of lightning
MOTTO
'Dona ferentes adsumus'
('We are coming bearing gifts')

No. 620 was formed at Chedburgh on 17 June, 1943 as a bomber squadron in 3 Group, Bomber Command equipped with Stirling IIIs. Its first raid took place on 19 June against Le Creusot in France. Thereafter it remained on the night bomber offensive until November, 1943 when, on 27th, it transferred to 38 Group, Transport Command at Leicester East.

Here it began working up in its airborne role, towing gliders and practising para-drops. It re-equipped with Stirling IVs in February, 1944 and began supply drops over France to SOE forces that same month, losing one crew almost immediately and another in April. These nightly sorties to deliver supplies to the Maquis and other partisans carried on until June when, on 5th, the Squadron used twenty-three aircraft to drop the 6th Airborne Division at Caen, three crews failing to return. Later as D-Day developed, eighteen aircraft towed loaded Horsa gliders to Caen, then the Squadron returned to its SOE drops. In July it flew one hundred and eleven such sorties for the loss of only one crew, and nearly two hundred in August; that month it also flew a few low-level night bombing sorties against tactical targets in Southern France. September saw the Arnhem debacle in which No. 620 Squadron took part with twenty-five aircraft on 17th, towing gliders or dropping the advance paratroops. The following day eighteen aircraft towed in Horsa gliders then from 19 to 24 September the Squadron was involved in the hectic re-supply of the beleagured forces, losing five crews in the process.

After this operations were at a low level for a month or two, October being chiefly occupied in towing gliders to Italy whilst November saw the extension of SOE sorties to Holland and Nor-

way. The New Year ushered in further tactical bombing sorties into Germany and this and the supply drops formed the Squadron's task until the Rhine crossing in March, thirty aircraft dropping thirty gliders successfully.

In May the Squadron converted to Halifaxes and then took part in Operation Doomsday to Oslo, flying in troops. With the end of the war the task was troop movements to and from the Continent. The sphere of operation was changed to Greece in August with Operation Hellas and by September/October the Squadron was flying regular runs to Czechoslovakia, Egypt, Italy and Palestine. In December the Squadron moved to Egypt where it began airborne exercises with the Middle East forces together with meteorological flights and troop runs to Italy and mail runs to the UK. In August, 1946 it began searches for illegal shipping to Palestine. On 1 September, 1946 No. 620 was re-numbered No. 113 Squadron at Aqir.

Bases etc.

Formed at Chedburgh on 17 June, 1943 as a bomber squadron; transferred to Transport Command at Leicester East on 27 November, 1943.

Leicester East, det. Hurn	Nov 1943—Mar 1944
Fairford	Mar 1944—Oct 1944
Great Dunmow	Oct 1944—Dec 1945
El Aouina	Dec 1945—Jan 1946
Aqir	Jan 1946—Mar 1946
Cairo West	Mar 1946—Apr 1946
Shallufa	Apr 1946—Jun 1946
Aqir	Jun 1946—Sep 1946

Disbanded by re-numbering as No. 113 Squadron at Aqir on 1 September, 1946.

Main Equipment

Short Stirling III (Jun 1943—Jun 1944)
BF576, QS:F; BF580; BK713, QS:E; BK801; EE878; EF197, QS:Z; EF203, QS:Q; EF336; EF503; EH894, QS:E; EH931, QS:O; EH946, QS:P; LJ440, QS:V; LJ459, QS:E; MZ264, QS:A
Short Stirling IV (Feb 1944—Jun 1945)
LJ566, D4:Y; LJ627; LJ849; LJ873, QS:H; LJ892, QS:T; LJ917; LJ930; LJ946; LJ970; LK116; LK250; LK294; LK304, D4:W; LK410; LK432; LK509; LK554

Handley Page Halifax III (May 1945— 1945)
MZ588; MZ650; NA135; NA296
Handley Page Halifax VII (May 1945—Sep 1946)
NA343, D4:O; NA364, QS:G; NA372, QS:C; NA420, D4:S;
NA450, D4:Q; NA468, QS:M; PN295, QS:J; PN316, D4:V;
PP340, D4:R; PP342, D4:Y; PP346, QS:L; PP348, D4:O

Commanding Officers

W/Cdr D. H. Lee, DFC   Jun 1943—Oct 1944

W/Cdr G. T. Wynne-Powell, DFC	Oct 1944—	Jul 1945
W/Cdr G. H. Briggs, DFC	Jul 1945—	Sep 1945
W/Cdr R. I. Alexander, DFC	Sep 1945—	1946
W/Cdr M. Thomas	1946—	Sep 1946

Aircraft Insignia

From inception the Squadron carried the code letter combination 'QS' on its aircraft and to this was added 'D4' when the Squadron establishment was expanded on becoming a Transport Command unit.

No. 621 SQUADRON

(No badge authorised)

No. 621 Squadron was formed at Port Reitz in Kenya on 12 September, 1943 as a general reconnaissance unit equipped with Wellington XIIIs. That same month it began operations with a U-boat search by P/O Grover who ran out of fuel and crash-landed. The rest of the Squadron began searching for his aircraft locating it three days' later when one aircraft landed and picked up the crew. The following month No. 621 moved to Mogadishu where it began regular escort flights to the convoys up and down the east coast of Africa. By November it was flying nearly fifty sorties a month including two overland recces on behalf of the Army looking for four thousand stolen camels!

At the end of 1943 No. 621 moved to Aden with detachments around the southern Arabian coast, flying convoy escorts, anti-submarine patrols, ASR, shipping searches and recces. This continued to be the Squadron's duty month after month. On 13 March an ASR search located seventy survivors from a sinking ship in lifeboats and rafts and on 1 May F/O Mitchell found a U-boat (the *U-852*) and attacked it. The next day F/O Read added his depth-charges to the same submarine, followed by W/O Ryall and then the CO who re-fuelled and made a further attack. They were followed by attacks from F/O Wade and Doyle. On 3 May Wade found the U-boat burning and surrounded by wreckage and blazing oil. There was no further excitement until September when a Wellington ditched with four crew members lost. Another aircraft was lost in December, 1944.

With the New Year the Squadron was reduced from sixteen aircraft to eight and operations ceased in May. Gradually the Squadron went over to transport flying with regular schedules starting in September, 1945. In November the Squadron moved to Egypt and re-equipped with Warwicks the following month. It now began Operation Sunburn from Aqir, flying sorties to search for illegal immigrants into Palestine. It also flew several desert searches for missing vehicles and aircraft. In April it moved to Palestine where it

re-equipped with Lancasters for the ASR role, mainly being used on *Sunburns*. On 1 September, 1946 it was re-numbered No. 18 Squadron at Ein Shemer.

Bases etc.

Formed at Port Reitz on 12 September, 1943.

Port Reitz, det. Mogadishu	Sep 1943—	Oct 1943
Mogadishu, det. Port Reitz, Scuiscuiban	Oct 1943—	Dec 1943
Khormaksar, det. Scuiscuiban, Riyan,		
Socotra, Bender Kassim	Dec 1943—	Nov 1945
Mersa Matruh, det. Aqir, Benina	Nov 1945—	Apr 1946
Aqir	Apr 1946—	Jun 1946
Ein Shemer	Jun 1946—	Sep 1946

Disbanded at Ein Shemer by re-numbering as No. 18 Squadron on 1 September, 1946.

Main Equipment

Vickers Wellington XIII (Sep 1943—Jan 1945)
HZ705; HZ712, F; HZ799, D; HZ804, Q; HZ870, D; HZ940, T;
HZ956, A; HZ968, B; JA107, E; JA149, C; JA184, Y; JA205, H;
JA259, R; JA315, E; JA389, B; JA400, U; JA420, R; JA513, C;
JA537, O; JA564, U; JA645, A; ME887, H; ME911, E; MF156, E;
MF265, B; MF312, R; MP790, Q
Vickers Wellington XIV (Jan 1945—Dec 1945)
NB923, F; NB967, C; NB969, N; NB981, W; NC772, A; NC833, G;
NC828, H
Vickers Warwick GR.5 (Nov 1945—Sep 1946)
LM778, D; LM786, A; LM814, A; LM835, L; LM840, Z; LM843, G;
PN753, K; PN763, N; PN817, V; PN824, T
Avro Lancaster ASR.3 (Apr 1946—Sep 1946)
RF313; RF320, B; RF322; RF323

Commanding Officers

W/Cdr P. Green, OBE, AFC	Sep 1943—	Dec 1944
W/Cdr F. T. Gardiner, DFC	Dec 1944—	Nov 1945
S/Ldr G. Schofield	Nov 1945—	Feb 1946
W/Cdr B. E. Peck, DFC	Feb 1946—	Sep 1946

Aircraft Insignia

As far as is known no squadron identity insignia was carried by No. 621 Squadron.

No. 622 SQUADRON

BADGE
A long-eared owl volant affrontee, carrying in
the claws a flash of lightning
MOTTO
'Bellamus noctu'
('We wage war by night')

No. 622 was formed as a bomber squadron in 3 Group, Bomber Command at Mildenhall on 10 August, 1943. Throughout its war service it flew on the night bomber offensive over Germany and the Occupied Countries, at first with Stirlings and, from December, 1943 onwards with Lancasters. It was disbanded at Mildenhall on 15 September, 1945.

In 1950 the Squadron was re-formed as part of the Royal Auxiliary Air Force at Blackbushe on 15 December. The idea was to provide an auxiliary transport force by forming squadrons attached

to air charter companies and No. 622 was the first and only such squadron, being attached to Airwork Ltd. Its aircraft, Vickers Valettas, were compatible with the Vikings that Airwork operated so that all the members of the Squadron had to learn were the more military types of operation such as supply-dropping, paratrooping and glider-towing. The experiment was not a success, however, and the Squadron disbanded at Blackbushe on 30 September, 1953.

Bases etc.

Formed at Blackbushe on 15 December, 1950.
Blackbushe   Dec 1950—Sep 1953
Disbanded at Blackbushe on 30 September, 1953.

Main Equipment

Vickers Valetta C.1 (Dec 1950—Sep 1953)
VL271, B; VX527, A; VX542

Aircraft Insignia
No squadron identity markings were carried by No. 622 Squadron's Valettas.
(See also *Bomber Squadrons of the RAF*, pp. 286–7)

No. 624 SQUADRON

(No badge authorised)

No. 624 Squadron was formed at Blida on 22 September, 1943 by re-numbering No. 1575(SD) Flight. Its task was dropping agents and supplies to the underground forces in Europe. To do this No. 624 flew principally Halifax IIs although it also possessed a few Venturas. It ranged over Corsica, Yugoslavia, Southern France, Czechoslovakia and Northern Italy flying up to one hundred sorties a month depending on weather. In 1944 it added Albania and Greece to its area of operations. Occasionally an aircraft was lost, usually due to flying in low hilly terrain rather than to enemy action.

In March and April, 1944 it devoted all its attention to Southern France in preparation for the invasion there and was flying over one hundred and fifty sorties a month to build up the local partisans. In June it lost two aircraft and a further one in July as it began to convert to Stirlings for the same task. The work over France continued until September, 1944 when the Squadron's task was done and it disbanded at Blida on 24 September, 1944.

Three months later, on 28 December, 1944, it was re-formed at Grottaglie as a mine-spotting squadron equipped with Walrus amphibians. It was not until February, 1945 that it became operational, flying mine reconnaissances in the Adriatic from Foggia. For the rest of the year it continued on this task, flying from a variety of bases in Greece, Italy, Malta and North Africa. However, with the war over in Europe and the reduction of flying over Italy its operational tasks ran down and eventually No. 624 was disbanded at Littorio on 13 November, 1945.

Bases etc.

Formed at Blida on 22 September, 1943 by re-numbering No. 1575(SD) Flight.

Blida, det. Protville	Sep 1943	Dec 1943
Brindisi	Dec 1943	Feb 1944
Blida	Feb 1944	Sep 1944

Disbanded at Blida on 24 September, 1944. Re-formed in the mine-spotting role at Grottaglie on 28 December, 1944.

Grottaglie	Dec 1944	Feb 1945
Foggia, det. Hassani, Pisa	Feb 1945	Apr 1945
Falconara, det. Treviso	Apr 1945	Jul 1945
Rosignano, det. Sedes, Hal Far	Jul 1945	Aug 1945
Littorio	Aug 1945	Nov 1945

Disbanded at Littorio on 13 November, 1945.

Main Equipment

Handley Page Halifax II Srs. I (Sep 1943—Jul 1944)
BB386; BB429, N; BB444, D
Handley Page Halifax V (Sep 1943—Jul 1944)
DG357; EB140; EB154, A; EB179, W; EB188, A; EB197
Handley Page Halifax II Srs. IA (Feb 1944—Jul 1944)
JN888; JN896, R; JN941, C; JN945, G; JN958, H; JN960, L; JP159, Q; JP160, Y; JP205, K; JP246, U; JP291; LW272
Short Stirling IV (Jul 1944—Sep 1944)
LJ927, S; LJ953; LJ974, Q; LJ987, X; LK175, R; LK179, M; LK184, Y
Supermarine Walrus (Dec 1944—Nov 1945)
K8850; L2172; L2201, B; L2263, O; P5667, D; R6543; W2741, E; W2797; W3020, G; W3072, C; X9521, D; X9522, J; Z1754; Z1769, A
Hawker Hurricane IIB (Mar 1945—Nov 1945)
KW975; LB897
Avro Anson I (Apr 1945—Nov 1945)
MG679; MH103
Lockheed Ventura II (Sep 1943—   1943)
AE948

Commanding Officers

S/Ldr J. B. Austin, DFC	Sep 1943	Jan 1944
W/Cdr C. S. G. Stanbury, DSO, DFC	Jan 1944	Sep 1944
S/Ldr G. M. Gallagher	Dec 1944	Nov 1945

Aircraft Insignia

As far as is known no squadron identity markings were carried on No. 624 Squadron aircraft during either period of service.

No. 644 SQUADRON

BADGE
In front of an increscent, a pegasus rampant

MOTTO
'Dentes draconis serimus'
('We sow the dragon's teeth')

The Pegasus signifies the Squadron's association with the Parachute Brigade.

The Squadron was formed at Tarrant Rushton on 23 February, 1944 from No. 298 Squadron personnel and equipped with the Halifax V. It worked up in the airborne role in company with No. 298 and began supply drops to SOE forces in France on 30 March, having completed forty-six such trips by the end of April. These were continued in May when one Halifax was attacked by enemy aircraft on 5th and damaged. On 5 June twenty aircraft flew on Operation Tonga towing two Hamilcar and fifteen Horsa gliders across the Channel. The other aircraft dropped bombs on an explosives factory at Caen. On return sixteen aircraft re-fuelled and then took fifteen Hamilcars and one Horsa across to the LGs already occupied; they all landed safely, despite some Flak damage. On 10 and 13 June three *Rob Roy* re-supply sorties were flown each day then the Squadron returned to its normal duties of supply drops to

agents and para-military forces in occupied France, Belgium and Holland. On 31 August the Squadron had its first operational loss when F/O W. Calverley and crew failed to return.

September, 1944 brought Operation Market (the Arnhem assault). On the first day (17th) the Squadron towed fourteen Horses and seven Hamilcars there, one releasing prematurely, and the next day eight Horsas and seven Hamilcars, one being lost in the Channel. On 19th a similar operation took ten Horsas and one Hamilcar of which two released prematurely and one glider's tail was shot off. The Squadron was not employed in the dangerous re-supply missions to Arnhem, resuming SOE drops. As well as these it flew Operation Quaver in October, a special mission dropping two paratroops, six containers and six packages into Norway. Thereafter it was this type of supply drop of agents in occupied countries which was the Squadron's main task, supplemented in January and February, 1945 with tactical bombing, also by night. On 24 March the Squadron put up thirty aircraft on Operation Varsity, the Rhine crossing, losing two crews shot down. From then on the supply drops were principally into those parts of Europe not yet liberated. In April two more crews were lost on these sorties, one in France and one in Denmark. With the war coming to a close No. 644 took part in transporting troops to Oslo for the liberation and then began Continental shuttle flying on transport duties. In

August it flew twenty-eight sorties on Operation Hellas to Greece and at the end of the year moved out to Palestine.

In 1946 it worked-up in the paratroop role there as well as flying a mail run to the UK and Met flights. In May it flew Exercise Gordon, towing gliders all the way to the Sudan, and in July maintained photo reconnaissance cover of Cyprus. On 1 September, 1946 it was disbanded by re-numbering as No. 47 Squadron.

Bases etc.

Formed at Tarrant Rushton on 23 February, 1944 from 298 Squadron personnel.

Tarrant Rushton, det. Woodbridge	Feb 1944—Nov 1945
Qastina, det. Bilbeis	Nov 1945—Sep 1946

Disbanded by re-numbering as No. 47 Squadron at Qastina on 1 September, 1946.

Main Equipment

Handley Page Halifax V (Feb 1944—Nov 1944)
DK121, Q; DK198; LK641, 9U:N; LK655, 2P:B; LL146, E;
LL198, 2P:D; LL217, 9U:M; LL309, 9U:S; LL326, 9U:N; LL338, 9U:J; LL357, 9U:P; LL405, 2P:M

Handley Page Halifax IIIA (Aug 1944—Mar 1945)
MZ959, 2P:T; MZ964, 9U:G; MZ967, 9U:K; MZ970, 2P:P; MZ981, 9U:H; NA122, 2P:W; NA127, 9U:D; NA549, 9U:Q; NA614, 2P:Z; NA656, 2P:R; NA662, 9U:Z; NA676, 2P:Y

Handley Page Halifax VII (Mar 1945—Sep 1946)
NA314, 9U:R; NA336, 9U:C; NA346, 2P:K; NA353, 9U:S; NA366, 9U:C; NA388, 2P:Z; NA3999, U:O; PN262, 2P:X; PN305, 9U:W; PN312, 2P:B; PP365

Handley Page Halifax IX (Aug 1946—Sep 1946)
RT784; RT790; RT882

Commanding Officers

S/Ldr A. G. Norman, DFC	Feb 1944—Mar 1944
W/Cdr V. A. Pope	Mar 1944—Nov 1944
W/Cdr E. L. Archer, AFC	Nov 1944—Jun 1945
W/Cdr W. H. Ingle	Jun 1945—Sep 1946

Aircraft Insignia

The Squadron used two code letter combinations, '2P' and '9U', throughout its existence.

No. 680 SQUADRON

(No badge authorised)

On 1 February, 1943 No. 2 Photographic Reconnaissance Unit at LG 219 was re-numbered No. 680 Squadron. It was equipped with Spitfires and Beaufighters flying PR sorties over the Greek islands and had A Flight detached at Castel Benito for covering Gabes and the Mareth Line. The latter unit flew most of the sorties (53 as opposed to 10 from LG 219 in March). In April B Flight went to Cyprus to cover the Dodecanese Islands, and A Flight moved up to cover Cap Bon and Pantellaria. This continued until the end of May when the Flights again consolidated at LG 219, apart from C Flight which now went to Cyprus. It had flown all the sorties with Spitfires, the Beaufighters departing soon after the Squadron formed. During the summer the Squadron was mainly operating from Derna but in August the entire operational area became Greece and the Dodecanese Islands. On 25 September P/O Bray discovered a destroyer at Rhodes, enabling the Navy to go in and deal with it, typical of the immediate benefits of PR apart from the more strategic value. In October no fewer than 196 sorties were flown, each designated target ranging from Italy to Turkey being covered four times per day. On these operations the Squadron was losing an average of one pilot a month all through 1943.

The accent increasingly became shipping recces during the next few months and this continued into 1944. In February, 1944 the Squadron began converting to twins with Blenheims, Baltimores and Mosquitoes arriving, together with a few Hurricanes. The Spitfires remained in service until June, by which time the Squadron was a predominantly Mosquito unit. It was still concentrating on Greece, and the Aegean area, flying 130 to 140 sorties a month, losses now being negligible.

In August, 1944 it moved to Italy and from here A Flight with Mosquitoes flew sorties over Yugoslavia and Hungary whilst B Flight, which still had a few Spitfires in addition to its Mosquitoes concentrated on shipping PR in the Greece/Salonika area. By November it was reaching into Germany with its PR sorties. From late 1944 onwards the Squadron became more and more involved in mapping and survey duties around Italy. In February, 1945 it was withdrawn to Egypt and here it flew largely survey work, including covering all Palestine. It remained in this role after the war was over and eventually was disbanded on 13 September, 1946 by re-numbering as No. 13 Squadron at Ein Shemer.

Bases etc.

Formed at LG 219 by re-numbering No. 2 PRU on 1 February, 1943.

LG 219, det. Castel Benito, Senem, Nicosia, Monastir	Feb 1943—May 1943
LG 219, det. Nicosia, Derna, Tocra	May 1943—Dec 1943
Matariya, det. Lakatamia	Dec 1943—Aug 1944
San Severo, det. Matariya	Aug 1944—Feb 1945
Deversoir, det. Aleppo, Aqir	Feb 1945— 1946
Aqir	1946— 1946
Ein Shemer, det. Aqir, Habbaniya	1946—Sep 1946

Disbanded at Eim Shemer on 13 September, 1946 by re-numbering as No. 13 Squadron.

Main Equipment

Vickers Supermarine Spitfire IV (Feb 1943—May 1944)
AA780; AA815; AB421; BP885; BP909; BP936; BR410; BR427; BR644; BR663; BS362; BS473; BS133, (**Mk. VI**); BS149, (**Mk. VI**)

Bristol Beaufighter IC (Feb 1943—Feb 1943)
T3301; X7741

Lockheed Electra (Feb 1943—Sep 1944)
AX701, *Cloudy Joe*

Hawker Hurricane I, II (Feb 1943— 1945)
P2915; V6738; V7404; W9225; W9242; Z4604; Z5132; AG153; BN354; BP510; BP652; HV295; HV479; HW663; LD204

Vickers-Supermarine Spitfire IX (Feb 1943— 1945)
EN155; EN264; EN388; EN412

Vickers-Supermarine Spitfire XI (Aug 1943— 1946)
EN655; EN661; PA843; PA845; PA850; MB785

Martin Baltimore IIIA, V (Feb 1944—May 1944)
FA343; FA372; FW525

Bristol Blenheim IV (Feb 1944—Jul 1944)
V5586; V6089

de Havilland Mosquito IX/XVI (Feb 1944—Sep 1946)
LR444; MM284; MM289; MM291; MM297; MM330; MM335; MM347, N; MM348; NS469; NS496; NS530; NS534; NS683; NS705; RF987, O; RG117; RG316

Commanding Officers

W/Cdr J. R. Whelan, DFC and Bar	Feb 1943—Oct 1944
W/Cdr J. C. Paish	Oct 1944—

Aircraft Insignia

The only known insignia carried by No. 680 Squadron aircraft was towards the end of the war when its Mosquitoes had red/white diagonally-striped rudders for identification purposes.

No. 681 SQUADRON

(No badge authorised)

No. 681 Squadron was formed by re-numbering No. 3 PRU at Dum Dum on 2 January, 1943. It was equipped with Hurricane IIs and Spitfire IVs while a Dutch element in C Flight was flying North American Mitchells which belonged to the Dutch Air Force. The Squadron roamed across Burma on photographic reconnaissance duties flying between fifty and ninety sorties a month depending on weather conditions. During 1943 Rangoon, Mandalay and the Andaman Islands were amongst the most frequent targets; on 8 June W/O Brown had a fortunate escape when his Spitfire (AB318) disintegrated in rough air. In July, 1943 some Mosquitoes were added for longer-range sorties to supplement the Mitchells in C Flight. This was relatively short-lived, however, for in October the twin-engined aircraft were hived off into the newly-formed 684 Squadron and No. 681 remained entirely equipped with Spitfire XIs.

The end of 1943 found the Squadron flying mainly special recces for the army in Mandalay. On 13 December the Squadron lost its first member on operations, F/O Gordon-White, over Mandalay. In 1944 the monthly sortie total went regularly over the one hundred mark. Three pilots were lost in the first quarter as the Squadron first concentrated far afield on oilfields and then, more tactically, kept up a close watch on airfields and railways behind the fighting areas. Two more pilots were lost in July-August. Towards the end of 1944 the Squadron turned its main attention to river and coastal traffic on the Irrawaddy and other rivers. In December it was busy preparing for the assault on Akyab Island and early in 1945 Rangoon became the most visited target, two hundred and thirteen sorties being flown in March.

As the offensive moved on so No. 681 flew farther afield and in July was photographing Bangkok and the Burma/Siam railway. With the war at an end, it was switched to roads and Japanese escape routes, then airfields and POW camps in what had been enemy territory. In September operations were switched to cover Hong Kong in preparation for its liberation. At the end of the year the Squadron, now based in Malaya, sent detachments to Batavia for the Indonesian campaign, providing tactical PR during it. Another detachment went to Saigon for operations over Indo-China. Soon afterwards the Squadron's tasks ran down and by early 1946 morale was low as, particularly ground crew, chaffed at not being able to get

demobilisation. The detachment continued operations until May when the Squadron returned to India and on 1 August, 1946 was re-numbered No. 34 Squadron at Palam.

Bases etc.

Formed at Dum Dum on 25 January, 1943 by re-numbering No. 3 PRU.

Dum Dum, det. Alipore	Jan 1943—Dec 1943
Chandina	Dec 1943—Jan 1944
Dum Dum	Jan 1944—May 1944
Alipore, det. Imphal, Kalemyo, Monywa, Mingaladon	May 1944—Jun 1945
Mingaladon, det. Alipore	Jun 1945—Sep 1945
Kai Tak	Sep 1945—Dec 1945
Kuala Lumpur, det. Kemajoran, Tan Son Nhut	Dec 1945—Jan 1946
Seletar, det. Don Muang, Mingaladon, Kemajoran	Jan 1946—May 1946
Palam, det. Kohat	May 1946—Aug 1946

Disbanded by re-numbering as No. 34 Squadron at Palam on 1 August, 1946.

Main Equipment

North American B-25C Mitchell II (Jan 1943—Nov 1943)
N5/144, B; N5/1145, C; N5/148, M; MA956, E; MA957, K
Hawker Hurricane II (Jan 1943—Nov 1943)
Z5594, Z; AP891, N; BG814, R; BG952, Y; BM969, Q; BN125, U; BN224, V; HV481, X
Vickers-Supermarine Spitfire IV (Jan 1943—Dec 1944)
AA793, F; AA799, M; AB311, R; AB315, H; AB319, J; BP911, T; BP935, Y; BR431, P
Vickers-Supermarine Spitfire XI (Oct 1943— 1946)
EN679, B, later G; MB891, A; MB898, J; MB904, D; MB911, I; PA841, U; PA856, U; PA862, W; PA890, B; PA908, E; PA913, P; PA926, J; PA940, N; PA951, F; PL769, A; PL773, D; PL784, M; PL791, C; PL838, G; PL852, M; PL884, L; PL898, N; PL907, V; PL951, K; PL969, X; PL982, Y; PL997, S; PM129, H
de Havilland Mosquito IV, IX (Aug 1943—Nov 1943)
DZ696, S; DZ697, J; HJ730, Y; HJ759, W; LR440, V; LR441
Vickers-Supermarine Spitfire PR.19 (Aug 1945—Aug 1946)
PM508, Y; PM510, U; PM514; PM538; PM545; PM552; PM574; PS918, Z

Commanding Officers

W/Cdr S. G. Wise, DFC and Bar	Jan 1943—Dec 1943
W/Cdr F. D. Proctor, DFC	Dec 1943—Apr 1945
W/Cdr D. B. Pearson	Apr 1945—May 1946
S/Ldr H. Roberts	May 1946—Aug 1946

Aircraft Insignia

As far as is known no squadron identity markings were carried by No. 681 Squadron aircraft.

No. 682 SQUADRON

(No badge authorised)

The Squadron formed at Maison Blanche on 1 February, 1943 by re-numbering No. 4 Photographic Reconnaissance Unit there. It was equipped with Spitfire IVs, IXs and XIs flying sorties in support of the Army in Tunisia and, further afield, strategically over Italy. In April it acquired some Mosquitoes for longer-range operations using them first on 20 May with a sortie over the French Alps. By July it was flying exclusively over Italy, 145 sorties being flown that month, most of the targets being airfields. By August the Mosquitoes had been withdrawn and from then on all sorties were again flown on Spitfires. As the year wore on it was increasingly used for shipping recces around Italy and in October it put a detachment to Foggia in Italy, following it with a move there at the end of the year.

It was now busily involved in photographing Yugoslavia and Albania. A break came in March, 1944 to cover the 5th US Army front at Anzio and on 21 March a particularly accurate PR, flown by the CO, of Solta Island on the Dalmation coast enabled a Com-

mando raid to be made there which wiped out the entire garrison. It also flew damage assessment sorties up into Austria. In April, 1944 the Squadron concentrated on Southern France in preparation for the invasion there, and a detachment was kept at Alghero and Borgo for this purpose up to and over the event. This was B Flight which moved into France on 1 September and followed the armies north-wards whilst A Flight continued to provide PR facilities on the Italian fronts. The two Flights came together in Italy again in March, 1945 and concentrated on the final fighting there. Both Flights remained operational to cover Greece when the insurgents began a civil war there. After the hostilities No. 682 Squadron was detailed for aerial survey tasks and sent a detachment to Malta for Naval calibration work. The Squadron disbanded at Peretola on 14 September, 1945.

Bases etc.

Formed out of No. 4 PRU at Maison Blanche on 1 February, 1943.

Maison Blanche	Feb 1943—Jun 1943
La Marsa, det. Foggia	Jun 1943—Dec 1943

San Severo, det. Vasto, Pomigliano,
  Alghero, Voltone, Borgo Biguglia,
  Follonica, Cecina, Malignano, Le Luc,
  Valence, Lyon   Dec 1943—Sep 1944
Peretola, det. Dijon, Nancy, Hal Far   Sep 1944—Sep 1945
Disbanded at Peretola on 14 September, 1945.

Main Equipment

Vickers-Supermarine Spitfire IV (Feb 1943—May 1943)
  AA803; AB426; BP930; BR361; BR421; BR664; BS361; BS473
de Havilland Mosquito IV, VI (Apr 1943—   1943)
  DZ549; DZ553; HJ668; HJ672
Vickers-Supermarine Spitfire XI (Apr 1943—Sep 1945)
  EN337; EN422; EN432; EN504; EN656; EN672; EN675; MB777;
  MB787; MB888; MB897; MB934; MB940; PA854; PA867; PA895;
PA911; PA932; PA960; PL760; PL771; PL842; PL857; PL864; PL918;
  PL949; PL980; PM126
Vickers-Supermarine Spitfire PR.19 (Sep 1944—Sep 1945)
  RM630; RM639; RM640; RM645, I

Commanding Officers

S/Ldr A. H. W. Ball, DSO, DFC   Feb 1943—Jul 1943
S/Ldr J. T. Morgan, DSO   Jul 1943—Jul 1944
S/Ldr R. C. Buchanan, DFC   Jul 1944—Mar 1945
S/Ldr H. B. Oldfield   Mar 1945—Aug 1945
S/Ldr B. R. Kenwright, DFC   Aug 1945—Sep 1945

Aircraft Insignia

As far as is known no identity markings were carried on No. 682 Squadron's aircraft.

No. 683 SQUADRON

BADGE
In front of a mullet of six points, a telescope in bend
MOTTO
'Nihil nos latet'
('Nothing escapes us')

No. 683 Squadron formed at Luqa, Malta on 8 February, 1943 from B Flight of No. 69 Squadron. It was equipped with Spitfire IVs and was immediately operational flying PR sorties over Sicily and Italy, concentrating on Sicilian airfields and shipping movements. Seventy-two sorties were flown in March, there were several interceptions but only one Spitfire (and pilot) was lost. In May the first Mosquito came on strength and the sortie went up to 157 in the month. This was exceeded in June as the Squadron was busily engaged in preparing for the invasion of Sicily. That same month the Mosquitoes were withdrawn and No. 683 became solely a Spitfire unit. In July the Squadron was at its most hectic with 288 sorties flown during the Sicilian assault and the following month it was using a base in Sicily as an Advanced Landing Ground. By September it was flying farther afield, Dubrovnik, Scutari and targets in Albania coming up but the Squadron was by then reduced to seven aircraft. It was now concentrating almost entirely on the Balkans until 9 October when it began a nin-day period off operations then flew two sorties a day on the 5th US Army front out of Montecorvino. When it resumed full operations in November it now concentrated on targets in north-west Italy.

Rome, Venice, Trieste and the Po Valley were the areas for No. 683 in early 1944 and then in February, a detachment on the east coast at Trigno allowed sorties over Yugoslavia. By April it was flying as far afield as Toulon, Belgrade, Vienna and Budapest using Mk. XI Spitfires in place of the Mk IVs. As it built up to over 200 sorties a month again by July it was going even farther afield into France and Southern Germany. It also had one Flight which was flying solely Tac/Recce sorties with the army in Italy. In September it began to receive Spitfire PR.19s which initially gave poor serviceability and, combined with the weather, reduced operations for a while. By the end of the year this was remedied and at this time the Squadron was concentrating on Greece and flying some special missions as well. Only five pilots had been lost during 1944 but in January, 1945 two went within a fortnight. This, however, was not typical and for the rest of the War no more losses occurred. After VE-Day the Squadron continued to fly PR over Yugoslavia due to the strained relations with Tito; then it settled into mapping Austria followed by a complete survey of the coastline of Italy, Sicily, Corsica, Greece, Albanian and the islands around Italy for the Italian Government. In the summer of 1945 it also put a detachment in Greece to cover the Greek Islands and railways for the new Greek Government. It eventually disbanded at San Severo on 22 September, 1945.

The Squadron re-formed at Fayid on 1 November, 1950 with Avro Lancaster PR.1s for survey and mapping duties in the Middle East. For this purpose it sent detachments to East Africa and Arabia until January, 1952 when it moved to Aden to concentrate on Aden and Somaliland. Four months later it moved to Habbaniya where it flew similar tasks over the Arabian Gulf until 30 November, 1953 when it disbanded there.

Bases etc.

Formed at Luqa on 8 February, 1943 from B Flight, No. 69 Squadron.
Luqa   Feb 1943—Nov 1943
El Aouina   Nov 1943—Dec 1943
San Severo, det. Trigano, Aquino, Osa,
  Falerium, Orvieto Main, Castiglione,
  Malignano, Chiavarelle, Piogiolino, Cassandro,
  Rimini, Bellaria, Forli, Ferrara, Treviso,
  Tissano, Hasani   Dec 1943—Sep 1945
Disbanded at San Severo on 22 September, 1945. Re-formed at Fayid on 1
November, 1950.
Fayid   Nov 1950—   1951
Kabrit   1951—Jan 1952
Khormaksar   Jan 1952—May 1952
Habbaniya   May 1952—Nov 1953
Disbanded at Habbaniya 30 November, 1953.

Main Equipment

Vickers-Supermarine Spitfire IV (Feb 1943—   1943)
  AB310; BP905; BP932; BR646; BR656, L; BS358; BS364; BS496
Vickers-Supermarine Spitfire XI (1943—Sep 1945)
  EN153; EN338; EN414; EN430; EN637; EN676; MB772; MB777;
  MB786; MB897, F; MB938; PA844; PA866; PA904; PA923; PA939;
  PA950; PL760; PL788; PL835; PL846; PL885; PL955; PL986
de Havilland Mosquito VI (May 1943—Jun 1943)
  HJ672, A
Vickers-Supermarine Spitfire PR.19 (Sep 1944—Sep 1945)
  RM626; RM641
Avro Lancaster PR.1 (Nov 1950—Nov 1953)
  PA379; RA626, S; RA629; TW652, P

Commanding Officers

W/Cdr A. Warburton, DSO and Bar, DFC and Bar Feb 1943—Oct 1943
S/Ldr H. S. Smith, DFC   Oct 1943—Aug 1944
S/Ldr R. T. Turton, DFC   Aug 1944—Apr 1945
S/Ldr E. R. Pearson, DFC   Apr 1945—Sep 1945
S/Ldr I. D. N. Lawson   Nov 1950—   1952
S/Ldr N. N. Ezekiel   1952—Nov 1953

Aircraft Insignia

As far as is known no squadron identity markings were carried on No. 683 Squadron's aircraft.

No. 684 SQUADRON

BADGE
A mask
MOTTO
'Invisus videns'
('Seing through unseen')

On 29 September, 1943 No. 684 Squadron was formed at Dum Dum from the twin-engined components of No. 681 Squadron. It was thus equipped with Mitchells and Mosquitoes for phot-reconnaissance duties and was immediately in action flying recces over Rangoon and the Andaman Islands. These proved to be the 'bread-and-butter' runs for the Squadron. With the range of its aircraft it also flew as far afield as Thailand. Hint of the troubles that beset Mosquitoes in the Far East came on 23 December when F/O A. Orr, in HJ760, crashed on take-off after structural failure. Despite this operations were maintained at a high level and in January No. 684 visited the Burma–Siam railway, Andamans, targets in Burma, the Shan States, Irrawaddy, Thailand, Akyab and special areas on behalf of the army. In February it was back at Calcutta to re-organise on the Mk IX and XVI Mosquitoes solely. Whilst there it carried out a quantity of survey flying before moving up to the front-line again in May. Even there it carried out a proportion of survey flights made with a view to offensive actions and beach-heads. For the latter beach gradient photographs were taken, at selected points, on the west coast of Burma. In August a detachment went to Ceylon (including the Mitchells) for survey duties. With the monsoon coming on the aircraft would position at an ALG before first light and then climb out early to avoid the worst of the thunderstorm build-up.

By the end of 1944 the Squadron was being hit by a lack of serviceability but this improved again in 1945, allowing 73 sorties to be made in January over a wide area. In April it received Beaufighters for flying a courier service with photos and other needed things; generally speaking the aircraft returned scot-free from their sorties, but in April two were lost in one week. By July the Squadron had a detachment in the Cocos Islands which put up the highest number of sorties. By August the Squadron was covering French Indo-China. After the end of hostilities No. 684's first task was to transport film of the Japanese surrenders at Rangoon, Singapore and Penang; afterwards it flew mainly high-speed courier flights. In October it began a survey of French Indo-China, Thailand and the Kia Isthmus. In December it took over some Spitfires XIs from No. 681 Squadron.

In January, 1946 it moved to Bangkok with a detachment at Baigachi on a survey task for the Indian Government. These duties continued until 1 September, 1946 when it was re-numbered No. 81 Squadron at Bangkok.

Bases etc.

Formed at Dum Dum on 25 September, 1943 from the twin-engined element of 681 Squadron.

Dum Dum	Sep 1942—Dec 1943
Comilla	Dec 1943—Jan 1944
Dum Dum	Jan 1944—Apr 1944
Alipore, det. Yelahanka, China Bay, Cocos Island, Mingaladon	Apr 1944—Oct 1945
Saigon, det. Seletar	Oct 1945—Jan 1946
Don Muang, det. Seletar, Baigachi	Jan 1946—Sep 1946

Disbanded at Don Muang 1 September, 1946 by re-numbering as No. 81 Squadron.

Main Equipment

de Havilland Mosquito II, VI (Sep 1943—Dec 1943)
    DZ696; HJ730, U; HJ759, W; HJ760, Y
de Havilland Mosquito IX (Sep 1943—   1944)
    LR440, V; LR445, F, later R; LR462, G; LR464, J; LR473, P;
    LR481, M; MM228, D; MM244, H; MM253, H
North American B-25C Mitchell II (Sep 1943—Sep 1945)
    MA956, E; MA957, Z; N5/144, B; N5/145, C, later Z
de Havilland Mosquito XVI (Feb 1944—Sep 1946)
    MM296, M; MM343, W; MM367, U; MM392, K, later W; NS497, J;
    NS499, N; NS503, Y; NS524, V; NS622, X; NS629, W; NS646, I;
    NS655, G; NS675, Z; NS688, Q; NS692, D; NS704, O; NS779, K;
    NS807, R; RF994, J; RG119, B; RG127, L; RG132, D
Bristol Beaufighter VI, X (Apr 1945—Apr 1946)
    EL364; KV907; KW319; JL967; NE548; NV371; RD155, A; RD746, B
de Havilland Mosquito PR.34 (Jun 1945—Sep 1946)
    RG186, G; RG203, E; RG213, O; RG249, U; RG254, M; RG263, P
Vickers-Supermarine Spitfire XI/XIX (Dec 1945—   1946)
    PL781; PL920; PL982; PM508; PM510

Commanding Officers

S/Ldr B. S. Jones	Sep 1943—Dec 1943
W/Cdr W. B. Murray	Dec 1943—Nov 1944
W/Cdr W. E. M. Lowry, DFC	Nov 1944—Nov 1945
W/Cdr K. J. Newman, DFC and Bar	Nov 1945—Apr 1946
W/Cdr J. R. H. Merrifield, DSO, DFC and Bar	Apr 1946—Sep 1946

Aircraft Insignia

As far as is known no squadron identity markings were carried on No. 684 Squadron's aircraft.

APPENDIX 1
Squadron Identity Code letters

Note: This unavoidably incomplete list has been painstakingly compiled over many years from often fragmentary information due to the destruction of most official documents relating to the squadron code allocations during World War II. Apart from that many RAF Coastal Command, Photographic Reconnaissance, Army Co-operation and various support squadrons did not carry any squadron identification codes throughout their service, and Coastal Command officially abolished squadron codes for almost a year in 1943–44 before re-introducing them again.

A	No. 8 (1944–45)	EY	No. 78 (1945–50)	L9	No. 190 (1944–45)
	No. 72 (1970–82)		No. 233 (1938–39)	LA	No. 235 (1939–45)
	No. 120 (1951–57)			LD	No. 117 (1942–43)
	No. 201 (1951–57)	FA	No. 236 (1939–42)	LJ	No. 614 (1941–42)
	No. 202 (1951–57)		No. 281 (1942–45)	LW	No. 318 (1943–46)
	No. 541 (1952–56)	FH	No. 53 (1944–46)	LX	No. 225 (1939–42)
AB	No. 423 (1943)	FK	No. 209 (1938–39?)		
AD	No. 251 (1944–45)	FM	No. 238 (1945–46)	M4	No. 587 (1943–46)
AN	No. 13 (1938–39)	FS	No. 148 (1943–45)	MA	No. 161 (1942–44)
AQ	No. 276 (1941–45)	FV	No. 205 (1939–42)	MB	No. 236 (1944–45)
AR	No. 309 (1940–43)		No. 230 (1938–39)	MD	No. 458 (1942–43)
AW	No. 42 (1939–43)	FY	No. 4 (1938–39)		No. 526 (1943–45)
AX	No. 202 (1941–43)			ME	No. 280 (1943–46)
		G5	No. 190 (1944–45)	MF	No. 280 (1943–44)
B	No. 2 (1951–54)	G9	No. 430 (1944–45)	MH	No. 51 (1946–50)
	No. 18 (1970–82)	GA	No. 208 (1938–39)	MK	No. 500 (1939–42)
	No. 203 (1951–56)	GE	No. 58 (1942–44)	MP	No. 76 (1945–46)
	No. 206 (1952–57)	GK	No. 459 (1942–43)	MW	No. 217 (1939–42)
	No. 217 (1952–56)	GR	No. 301 (1944–46)	MY	No. 278 (1941–45)
	No. 224 (1951–56)	GR	No. 301 (1944–46)		
	No. 269 (1952–56)	GS	No. 330 (1941–43)	ND	No. 236 (1942–43)
B4	No. 282 (1943–45)	GX	No. 415 (1941–43)	NE	No. 143 (1944–45)
BA	No. 277 (1941–45)			NF	No. 138 (1941–44)
BF	No. 28 (1941–42)	HB	No. 239 (1940–43)	NH	No. 20 (1939–42)
BG	No. 660 (1945–?)	HC	No. 512 (1943–46)		No. 119 (1944–45)
BJ	No. 271 (1941–43)	HK	No. 269 (1944–46)		No. 415 (1944)
BN	No. 170 (1942–43)	HL	No. 26 (1938–39)	NM	No. 230 (1939–41)
	No. 240 (1939–42)	HN	No. 20 (1939–43)		No. 268 (1940–43)
BS	No. 120 (1946–51)	HO	No. 143 (1941–43)	NO	No. 320 (1940–43)
	No. 160 (1945–46)	HU	No. 220 (1938–39)	NQ	No. 24 (1943–53)
BT	No. 252 (1941–42)			NR	No. 220 (1939–43)
BX	No. 86 (1940–42)	12	No. 48 (1944–46)	NS	No. 201 (1944–51)
	No. 666?(1945–?)	14	No. 567 (1943–46)	NT	No. 203 (1939–40)
BY	No. 58 (1944–45)	19	No. 575 (1944–46)	NW	No. 286 (1941–45)
	No. 59 (1945–50)	II	No. 116 (1941–45)		
				OA	No. 22 (1939–42)
C	No. 33 (1971–82)	JN	No. 30 (1947–53)	OE	No. 168 (1942–43)
C1	No. 407 (1944–45)	JR	No. 161 (1944–45)		No. 661 (1944–47)
CB	No. 31 (1948–55)	JU	No. 202 (1938–39)	OG	No. 172 (1944–45)
CJ	No. 203 (1944–51)	JV	No. 6 (1939–42)	OH	No. 120 (1941–43)
CX	No. 14 (1944–46)			OI	No. 2 (1945–51)
		KG	No. 204 (1939–43)	OO	No. 13 (1939–42)
D4	No. 620 (1943–46)	KJ	No. 16 (1938–39)	OQ	No. 5 (1939–41)
DA	No. 210 (1939–43)	KK	No. 333 (1944–45)	OS	No. 279 (1941–44)
DF	No. 221 (1940–42)	KL	No. 269 (1938–39)	OT	No. 58 (1946–51)
DG	No. 422 (1942–43; 1944–45)	KM	No. 205 (1938–39)	OY	No. 48 (1939–42)
DH	No. 540 (1947–53)	KN	No. 77 (1945–46)	OZ	No. 179 (1944–46)
DJ	No. 612 (1938–39)	KO	No. 2 (1938–42)		No. 210 (1946–51)
DM	No. 36 (1946–47)	KQ	No. 502 (1939)		
	No. 248 (1944–46)	KU	No. 47 (1942; 1944–46)	P5	No. 297 (1943–47)
DQ	No. 228 (1939–43)	KW	No. 267 (1942–43)	P6	No. 489 (1944–45)
DT	No. 192 (1943–45)	KX	No. 311 (1942–43)	PG	No. 608 (1939)
			No. 529 (1943–45)	PJ	No. 59 (1938–39)
E7	No. 570 (1944–46)	KY	No. 242 (1944–50)	PL	No. 144 (1942–45)
EE	No. 16 (1939)	KZ	No. 287 (1941–46)	PN	No. 252 (1940–41)
	No. 404 (1941–43; 1944)			PP	No. 203 (1938–39)
EK	No. 168 (1942)	L	No. 210 (1951–56)		No. 311 (1945–46)
EO	No. 404 (1944–45)		No. 228 (1954–55)	PQ	No. 206 (1944–46)
ES	No. 541 (1945–46)		No. 240 (1952–56)	PU	No. 53 (1946–49)
ET	No. 662 (1944–?)	L5	No. 297 (1944–47)		No. 187 (1945–46)

PV	No. 275 (1941–45)		
PW	No. 224 (1938–39)		
PZ	No. 53 (1939–42)		
QD	No. 42 (1938–39)		
	No. 304 (1944–46)		
QL	No. 413 (1941–42)		
QM	No. 42 (1946–48)		
	No. 254 (1944–46)		
QN	No. 5 (1939–41)		
QO	No. 167 (1953–58)		
QS	No. 620 (1943–46)		
QX	No. 224 (1939–43)		
QY	No. 254 (1939–42)		
RF	No. 204 (1938–39)		
RG	No. 208 (1939–45)		
RL	No. 38 (1946–47)		
	No. 279 (1944–46)		
RM	No. 26 (1939–43)		
RP	No. 288 (1941–46)		
RR	No. 407 (1941–43)		
RU	No. 414 (1941–43)		
RW	No. 36 (1944–45)		
RZ	No. 241 (1940–42; 1944–45)		
SE	No. 95 (1941–42)		
SH	No. 216 (1939–42)		
	No. 240 (1938–39)		
SP	No. 400 (1941–43)		
SQ	No. 500 (1939)		
SY	No. 613 (1942–43)		
T	No. 36 (1953–54)		
	No. 79 (1951–52)		
	No. 204 (1954–57)		
	No. 220 (1951–55)		
TB	No. 51 (1945–46)		
TE	No. 53 (1938–39)		
TH	No. 20 (1949–51)		
TJ	No. 202 (1944–45)		
TO	No. 228 (1938–39)		
TQ	No. 202 (1939–43)		
TR	No. 59 (1939–42)		
	No. 262 (1944?)		
	No. 265 (1944)		
TS	No. 657 (1945–?)		
TV	No. 4 (1938–39; 1939–43)		
U4	No. 667 (1943–45)		

U6	No. 436 (1944?)		
UA	No. 269 (1939–43)		
UB	No. 455 (1942–45)		
UE	No. 228 (1944–45)		
UG	No. 16 (1939–42)		
UL	No. 608 (1939–42)		
US	No. 28 (1939–41)		
UT	No. 17 (1949–51)		
	No. 461 (1942–43; 1944–45)		
V8	No. 570 (1944–46)		
V9	No. 502 (1944–45)		
VG	No. 210 (1938–39)		
	No. 285 (1941–45)		
VM	No. 231 (1940–43)		
VQ	No. 201 (1938–39)		
VR	No. 22 (1938–39)		
VS	No. 31 (1948–54)		
VT	No. 216 (1938–39)		
VU	No. 36 (1938–39)		
	No. 246 (1944–46)		
VX	No. 206 (1939–42)		
WC	No. 309 (1944–47)		
WD	No. 206 (1938–39)		
WE	No. 59 (1944–45)		
WF	No. 238 (1946–48)		
	No. 525 (1944–46)		
WH	No. 330 (1944–46)		
WL	No. 612 (1939–43)		
WN	No. 172 (1942–43)		
	No. 527 (1943–45)		
WQ	No. 209 (1939–42; 1945–51)		
WR	No. 248 (1939–42)		
WU	No. 225 (1942; 1943–47)		
WY	No. 541 (1947–51)		
X6	No. 290 (1943–45)		
X9	No. 299 (1944–46)		
XA	No. 489 (1941–43)		
XB	No. 224 (1944–51)		
XC	No. 26 (1944–46)		
XH	No. 295 (1942–43)		
XK	No. 46 (1945–50)		
	No. 272 (1940–41)		
XM	No. 652 (1945–?)		
XQ	No. 86 (1945–46)		
XV	No. 2 (1941–43)		
Y3	No. 202 (1946–51)		

	No. 518 (1943–46)		
YE	No. 289 (1941–45)		
YF	No. 280 (1942–43)		
YG	No. 502 (1939–43)		
YI	No. 423 (1944–45)		
YQ	No. 217 (1938–39)		
YS	No. 77 (1946–49)		
	No. 271 (1943–46)		
YX	No. 614 (1938–41)		
Z2	No. 437 (1944–46)		
Z9	No. 519 (1943–46)		
ZA	No. 10 (1945–47)		
ZE	No. 293 (1943–46)		
ZK	No. 24 (1939–43)		
ZM	No. 201 (1939–43)		
ZO	No. 196 (1942–46)		
ZR	No. 613 (1938–42)		
ZS	No. 233 (1939–42)		
ZW	No. 48 (1938–39)		
	No. 140 (1941–42)		
ZZ	No. 220 (1944–46)		
2M	No. 520 (1943–46)		
2P	No. 644 (1944–46)		
2V	No. 547 (1944–45)		
3M	No. 679 (1943–45)		
3Y	No. 577 (1943–46)		
4M	No. 695 (1943–49)		
4X	No. 230 (1945–51)		
5G	No. 299 (1944–46)		
5O	No. 521 (1942–46)		
5S	No. 691 (1943–49)		
5T	No. 233 (1944–45)		
6D	No. 631 (1943–49)		
6Y	No. 171 (1944–45)		
7B	No. 595 (1943–49; 1949–51)		
	No. 5 (1949–51)		
7C	No. 296 (1944–46)		
7R	No. 524 (1944–45)		
7T	No. 196 (1942–46)		
8A	No. 298 (1944–45)		
8D	No. 220 (1945–46)		
8E	No. 295 (1944–46)		
8Q	No. 34 (1949–51)		
8T	No. 298 (1944–45)		
8W	No. 612 (1944–45)		
8Z	No. 295 (1944–46)		
9U	No. 644 (1944–46)		
9W	No. 296 (1944–46)		

APPENDIX 2
The Rescue Squadrons

One of the parts of the Royal Air Force which most prominently hits the public eye in these days is the activities of the Search and Rescue Squadrons, with their yellow-painted helicopters and whilst not operational squadrons in the sense of active participation in warfare their tasks are very operational in flying terms, involving some of the most hazardous flying, both in peacetime and in war.

In Royal Air Force terms they are a relatively recent occurence, having been originally formed during World War II. As so often their formation arose out of an unfulfilled need; in this case the serious loss of valuable aircrew who had baled out of their aircraft, landed in the sea and then died in their dinghies through exposure and not being picked up. The first move came when the fleet of RAF Rescue Launches was doubled towards the end of 1940 and at the same time aircraft were brought into the team for the purpose of finding the lost aircrew, and if necessary, dropping dinghies, supplies and survival equipment to them. There happened to be a source of aircraft available with crews who were hanging around with little to do. These were the Lysander squadrons of Army Co-operation Command for the fighting in France had proved beyond doubt that the Lysander was of little use in its primary role of battlefield reconnaissance and army co-operation. So before 1940 was out most of these squadrons had Flights detached to airfields on the coast, predominantly in the south and south-east where they flew out to find the unlucky who had fallen into the sea during the sweeps and bomber raids that were beginning to take place over France, as well as those fighter pilots who were still countering the Luftwaffe's final offensive over the UK. This quickly made a difference and in January, 1941 an Air Sea Rescue Directorate was set up to expand this organisation to cover the whole of the UK. It is significant that within six months of setting up this organisation the percentage of ditched aircrew who were saved rose from 20 to 33 per cent. Other aircraft were pressed into service for search duties, principally squadrons who were not heavily operationally committed, and the Fleet Air Arm units ashore also became involved. From them came the idea of using Walrus amphibians to actually land and pick up the survivors, given a reasonable sea state, an activity which very often saved hours of time, a valuable commodity with wounded or hypothermic victims. Experiment in methods and equipment was encouraged and, very often on a station basis, new equipment was devised which eventually became standard; most significant of these was the 'Lindholme Gear', an elaborate system of liferafts which could be dropped to survivors providing a wide range of necessities. During 1941 the 'trade' grew steadily and by the autumn had outgrown the basis of detached flights of squadrons whose basic role was something quite different. These Flights were removed from the Army co-operation squadrons and formed into squadrons themselves, whose sole task was Air Sea Rescue. This meant better and more direct organisation and training and the addition of more diverse types, principally the acquisition of Walrus amphibians from the Navy. It also enabled expansion into the longer range tasks of rescuing bomber and coastal crews out over the North Sea and for this task squadrons were equipped with Lockheed Hudsons and Vickers Warwicks. At the same time much development went into the designing of airborne lifeboats which could be dropped by parachute from these latter types of aircraft.

So the ASR organisation expanded and diversified during the war. Other types were brought into play, Spitfires and Defiants for the search role, Ansons for medium-range supply and dinghy drops and in 1945 the Sea Otter, descendant of the Walrus, as the sole amphibian. ASR squadrons had moved farther afield, too, as will be seen from the squadron briefs at the end of this Appendix, with the South Atlantic, Mediterranean and Indian Ocean having their own units.

With the end of the war the requirements largely disappeared. Aircraft were no longer subject to enemy action and what little call there was for rescue duties was made part of the tasks of the maritime reconnaissance squadrons just re-equipping with Lancasters. These were well able to carry out the search and dropping tasks and, with modifications, to carry an airborne lifeboat, thus fulfilling the role completely. However, the advent of the helicopter in the early fifties, and their application to rescue roles in the Korean War, highlighted the possibilities of their use for a wider range of rescue duties around the UK. This coincided with the RAF expansion of the mid-fifties, the increased use of jet fighters, the increasing cost of the modern warplane and the training of the aircrew and the possible social benefits of having a force of trained rescue helicopterists in the country. So in 1953 an ASR unit was again formed in the RAF, given the number 275, of the first such unit formed in 1941 and equipped with Sycamore helicopters to develop the helicopter in rescue roles within the Service, drawing to some extent on the earlier pioneer work carried out by 705 Squadron of the Fleet Air Arm using Dragonfly helicopters.

Having pioneered the use of helicopters for Search and Rescue in the RAF, No. 275 was expanded in March 1959 to fly Whirlwinds and then re-numbered 228 Squadron. By that time No. 22 Squadron had been re-formed with Whirlwinds and was fully operational in this role. Since then the Rescue Squadrons have carried numbers perpetuating some of the more famous Coastal Command squadrons and reference to the individual units will be found in the body of the book. Little has to be said about the development of these squadrons for their activities have become well known to the British public. Although primarily maintained for the rescue of Service aircrew in distress, they have made the largest and most dramatic contribution to the rescue services within Great Britain for very many years and most of their time and energies are in fact taken up with rescues of civilians around the British coasts, from ships at sea, from mountain climbing accidents and in rushing critically ill patients to specialist hospitals.

THE SQUADRONS

Nos. 22, 72, 84, 103, 202, 228, 269 Squadrons have their ASR period covered in their respective passages in the body of the book.

No. 275 Squadron
Formed at Valley from Detachments at Valley and Andreas on 15 October, 1941.

Bases etc.

Valley, det. Andreas, Eglinton	Oct 1941	Apr 1944
Warmwell	Apr 1944	Aug 1944
Bolt Head, det. Portreath	Aug 1944	Oct 1944
Exeter, det. Portreath, Bolt Head	Oct 1944	Jan 1945
Harrowbeer, det. Portreath, Bolt Head	Jan 1945	Feb 1945

Disbanded at Harrowbeer 15 February, 1945. Re-formed at Linton-on-Ouse on 13 April, 1953.

Linton-on-Ouse	Apr 1953	Nov 1954
Thornaby	Nov 1954	Oct 1957
Leconfield	Oct 1957	Sep 1959

Disbanded by re-numbering as No. 228 Squadron at Leconfield on 1 September, 1959.

Main Equipment

Westland Lysander IIIA (Oct 1941—Aug 1943)
  V9737; V9738; V9749, N
Supermarine Walrus II (Dec 1941—Feb 1945)
  L2207, PV:Z; HD923, PV:S; HD929, PV:Z; W2746, PV:K
Boulton Paul Defiant I (May 1942—Aug 1943)
  N3423; T3920
Avro Anson I (Mar 1943—Aug 1944)
  AX645; EG492, PV:F; LT592, PV:O
Supermarine Spitfire VB (Jan 1943—Apr 1943 & Apr 1944—Feb 1945)
  BL294; BM448
Bristol Sycamore HR.14 (Apr 1953—Sep 1959)
  XD197, A; XG506, F; XG509, J; XL823
Westland Whirlwind HAR.4 (Mar 1959—Sep 1959)
  XJ761

No. 276 Squadron

Formed at Harrowbeer from Detachments at Harrowbeer, Fairwood Common, Perranporth, Roborough and Warmwell on 21 October, 1941.

Bases etc.

Harrowbeer, det. Fairwood Common,			
Perranporth, Portreath Warmwell	Oct	1941—Apr	1944
Portreath, det. Querqueville (A.23)	Apr	1944—Sep	1944
Querqueville, det. Portreath	Sep	1944—Sep	1944
Amiens-Glisy (B.48), det. Portreath	Sep	1944—Sep	1944
St. Denis-Westrem (B.61), det. Portreath	Sep	1944—Oct	1944
St. Croix (B.63), det. Ursel (B.67)	Oct	1944—Dec	1944
Knocke-le-Zoute (B.83)	Dec	1944—Jun	1945
Andrews Field	Jun	1945—Aug	1945
Kjevik, det. Sola	Aug	1945—Aug	1945
Vaernes, det. Sola	Aug	1945—Sep	1945
Gardemoen	Sep	1945—Nov	1945
Dunsfold	Nov	1945—Nov	1945

Disbanded at Dunsfold on 14 November, 1945.

Main Equipment

Westland Lysander IIIA (Oct 1941—May 1943)
T1620, AQ:F; V9710, AQ:K; V9743, AQ:L; V9820
Supermarine Walrus II (Oct 1941—Nov 1945)
L2271, AQ:X; P5638, AQ:N; W3026, AQ:N; X9522, AQ:W
Boulton Paul Defiant I, II (May 1942—May 1943)
N3372, AQ:T; T3929; T4051, AQ:N; AA296
Supermarine Spitfire IIA (Apr 1942—May 1943)
P7366; P8131, AQ:C
Supermarine Spitfire VB (Apr 1943—Jun 1945)
P8565; BL495; EN841
Hawker Hurricane II (Dec 1941—   1942)
Z3672; BE510
Avro Anson I (Mar 1943—May 1944)
R3443, AQ; EG499; EG505, AQ
Vickers Warwick I (Apr 1944—Oct 1944)
BV353; BV530; HF938

No. 277 Squadron

Formed from Detachments at Hawkinge, Martlesham Heath, Shoreham and Tangmere at Stapleford Tawney on 22 December, 1941.

Bases etc.

Stapleford Tawney, det. Hawkinge,			
Martlesham Heath and Shoreham	Dec	1941—Dec	1942
Gravesend, det. Hawkinge,			
Martlesham Heath, Shoreham	Dec	1942—Apr	1944
Shoreham, det. Hawkinge, Hurn, Warmwell	Apr	1944—Oct	1944
Hawkinge, det. Portreath	Oct	1944—Feb	1945

Disbanded at Hawkinge 15 February, 1945.

Main Equipment

Westland Lysander IIIA (Dec 1941—Feb 1945)
V9288, BA:X; V9431, BA:S; V9545, BA:C
Supermarine Walrus II (Dec 1941—Feb 1945)
L2313, BA:T; W3077; X9563, BA:A; HD867, BA:F; HD917, BA:U
Boulton Paul Defiant I (May 1942—May 1943)
N1561; V1117; AA254; AA312
Supermarine Spitfire IIA (Dec 1942—May 1944)
P8030; P8179, BA:T
Supermarine Spitfire VB (May 1944—Feb 1945)
P8705, BA:C; AD366, BA:Z; BM510
Supermarine Sea Otter II (Nov 1943—Apr 1944)
JM796
Vickers Warwick I (Nov 1944—Feb 1945)
BV527; HF940; HF960

No. 278 Squadron

Formed from No.3 ASR Flight at Matlaske on 1 October, 1941.

Bases etc.

Matlaske, det. North Coates	Oct	1941—Apr	1942
Coltishal, det. N. Coates,			
Woolsington, Acklington,			
Hutton Cranswick, Ayr, Drem,			
Castleton, Peterhead, Sumburgh	Apr	1942—Apr	1944
Bradwell Bay, det. Martlesham Heath,			
Hornchurch	Apr	1944—Feb	1945
Thorney Island, det. Hawkinge,			
Beccles, Exeter	Feb	1945—Oct	1945

Disbanded at Thorney Island on 14 October, 1945.

Main Equipment

Westland Lysander IIIA (Oct 1941—Feb 1943)
V9431; V9541; V9817, E
Supermarine Walrus II (Oct 1941—Oct 1945)
K8549; L2268, MY:A; L2307, MY:G; R6548, MY:E; HD917, MY:AA
Avro Anson I (Feb 1943—Jul 1944)
DG809; EF985, MY:F; LT592, MY
Supermarine Spitfire VB (Apr 1944—Feb 1945)
R6965, MY:P; AD562, MY:V
Vickers Warwick I (May 1944—Feb 1945)
BV478, Y; BV529; HF961; HF976
Supermarine Sea Otter II (May 1945—Oct 1945)
JM826, MY:O; JM885, MY:U, JM957, MY:M

No. 279 Squadron

Formed at Bircham Newton on 16 November, 1941.

Bases etc.

Bircham Newton, det. Reykjavik,			
St. Eval	Nov	1941—Oct	1944
Thornaby	Oct	1944—Sep	1945
Beccles	Sep	1945—Mar	1946

Disbanded at Beccles on 10 March, 1946 by re-numbering as No. 38 Squadron.

Main Equipment

Lockheed Hudson III, V, VI (Nov 1941—Nov 1944)
T9406, OS:L; V9158, OS:T; AE534, OS:O; AM700, OS:C; EW914, OS:D; FH356, OS:A; FK757, OS:G
Vickers Warwick I, II (Nov 1944—Sep 1945)
BV288; BV392; BV516; HF948; HF963; HF981; HG212, RL:G
Hawker Hurricane IIC, IV (Apr 1945—Jun 1945)
KX180, RL:K; KX878, RL:U; KZ322, RL:S; KZ383, RL:N; LB651
Supermarine Sea Otter II (Jul 1945—Sep 1945)
JM861
Avro Lancaster ASR.3 (Sep 1945—Mar 1946)
RF272, RL:A; RF310, RL:A; RF320, RL:N; SW295, RL:C; TX269, RL:N

No. 280 Squadron

Formed at Thorney Island on 10 December, 1941.

Bases etc.

Thorney Island	Dec	1941—Feb	1942
Detling	Feb	1942—Jul	1942
Langham	Jul	1942—Nov	1942
Bircham Newton	Nov	1942—Sep	1943
Thorney Island	Sep	1943—Oct	1943
Strubby	Oct	1943—Sep	1944
Langham	Sep	1944—Oct	1944
Beccles	Oct	1944—Nov	1945
Langham	Nov	1945—Jan	1946
Thornaby, det. St. Eval, Thorney Island,			
Lossiemouth, Aldergrove, Reykjavik	Jan	1946—Jun	1946

Disbanded at Thornaby on 21 June, 1946.

Main Equipment

Avro Anson I (Feb 1942—Oct 1943)
AX607, YF:Y; AX623, YF:G; AX645, YF:F; DG877, YF:J; DG917, YF:A
Vickers Warwick I (Oct 1943—Jun 1946)
BV304, YF:P; BV333, F3; HG145, ME:U; HG188, ME:H; HG211, ME:X

No. 281 Squadron

Formed at Ouston on 29 March, 1942.

Bases etc.

Ouston	Mar	1942—Jun	1943
Woolsington	Jun	1943—Oct	1943
Drem	Oct	1943—Nov	1943

Disbanded at Drem on 22 November, 1943, being absorbed by No. 282 Squadron. Re-formed on 22 November, 1943 at Thornaby.

Thornaby	Nov	1943—Feb	1944
Tiree	Feb	1944—Feb	1945
Mullaghmore	Feb	1945—Mar	1945
Limavady, det. Tiree	Mar	1945—Aug	1945
Ballykelly, det. Tiree	Aug	1945—Oct	1945

Disbanded at Ballykelly on 24 October, 1945.

Main Equipment

Boulton Paul Defiant I (Apr 1942—Jun 1943)
N1613; N3481; T4036

Supermarine Walrus II (Feb 1943—Nov 1943)
X1758
Avro Anson I (Apr 1943—Nov 1943)
EG467, FA:F; EG560; NK589
Vickers Warwick I (Nov 1943—Oct 1945)
BV404, FA:A4; BV411, FA:B; HG151, FA:V; HG183, FA:N
Supermarine Sea Otter II (Apr 1944—Oct 1945)
JM808
Vickers Wellington XIV (Sep 1945—Oct 1945)

No. 282 Squadron
Formed at Castletown on 1 January, 1943.

Bases etc.

Castletown	Jan 1943—Jan 1944	

Disbanded into 281 Squadron on 31 January, 1944. Re-formed at Davidstowe Moor on 1 February, 1944.

Davidstowe Moor	Feb 1944—Sep 1944	
St. Eval	Sep 1944—Jul 1945	

Disbanded at St. Eval on 19 July, 1945.

Main Equipment

Supermarine Walrus II (Jan 1943—Jan 1944 & Mar 1945—Jul 1945)
L2036, B4:Q; W2741, X
Avro Anson I (Mar 1943—Jan 1944)
DJ617; EG540; EG555; EG583
Vickers Warwick I (Feb 1944—Jul 1945)
BV411, B4; HF978, B4:H
Supermarine Sea Otter II (Mar 1945—Jul 1945)
JM745, B4:T

No. 283 Squadron
Formed at Algiers in February, 1943.

Bases etc.

Algiers	Feb 1943—May 1943	
Maison Blanche	May 1943—May 1943	
Tingley	May 1943—May 1943	
La Sebala, with dets.	May 1943—Aug 1943	
Palermo, with dets.	Aug 1943—Dec 1943	
Ajaccio	Dec 1943—Dec 1943	
Borgo, with dets.	Dec 1943—Apr 1944	
Hal Far, with dets.	Apr 1944—Mar 1946	

Disbanded at Hal Far on 31 March, 1946.

Main Equipment

Supermarine Walrus II (Apr 1943—Apr 1944)
X9471; X9498, B
Hawker Hurricane II
KW980
Supermarine Spitfire IX (1944— 1945)
MK433, I
Vickers Warwick I (Mar 1944—Mar 1946)
BV451, B

No. 284 Squadron
Formed at Gravesend on 7 May, 1943.

Bases etc.

Gravesend	May 1943—May 1943	
Martlesham Heath	May 1943—Jun 1943	
en route to Mediterranean	Jun 1943—Jul 1943	
Hal Far	Jul 1943—Jul 1943	
Cassibile	Jul 1943—Aug 1943	
Lentini East	Aug 1943—Sep 1943	
Scanzano	Sep 1943—Oct 1943	
Gioia del Colle	Oct 1943—Nov 1943	
Brindisi	Nov 1943—Mar 1944	
Alghero, det. Ramatuelle, Bone	Mar 1944—Sep 1944	
Elmas, det. Ramatuelle, El Aouina	Sep 1944—Nov 1944	
Bone, det. El Aouina, Elmas, Istres, Pomigliano	Nov 1944—Apr 1945	
Pomigliano	Apr 1945—Sep 1945	

Disbanded at Pomigliano on 21 September, 1945. Re-formed at Nicosia on 15 October, 1956.

Nicosia	Oct 1956—Aug 1959	

Disbanded at Nicosia on 1 August, 1959 by re-numbering as No. 103 Squadron.

Main Equipment

Supermarine Walrus II (Jul 1943—Sep 1944)
W2705; W3012, W
Vickers Warwick I (Mar 1944—Sep 1945)
BV460, L
Hawker Hurricane II (Sep 1944—Mar 1945)
HW249
Bristol Sycamore HR.14 (Oct 1956—Jul 1959)
XF269, 6; XG547, 5; XJ335, 2; XJ384; XL824
Westland Whirlwind HAR.2 (Nov 1956—Aug 1959)
XJ766

No. 292 Squadron
Formed at Jessore on 1 February, 1944.

Bases etc.

Jessore	Feb 1944—Feb 1945	
Agartala	Feb 1945—Jun 1945	

Disbanded at Agartala on 14 June, 1945.

Main Equipment

Supermarine Walrus II (Feb 1944—Jun 1945)
HD808
Vickers Warwick I (Apr 1944—Jun 1945)
HF970, Q; HG125
Supermarine Sea Otter II (Nov 1944—Jun 1945)
JM766
Consolidated Liberator VI (Dec 1944—Jun 1945)
KH311; KH319, F

No. 293 Squadron
Formed at Blida on 28 November, 1943.

Bases etc.

Blida	Nov 1943—Dec 1943	
Bone, dets. in Italy	Dec 1943—Mar 1944	
Pomigliano	Mar 1944—Mar 1945	
Foggia	Mar 1945—Jun 1945	
Pomigliano	Jun 1945—Apr 1946	

Disbanded at Pomigliano on 5 April, 1946.

Main Equipment

Vickers Warwick I (Nov 1943—Apr 1946)
BV234, ZE:L; BV270, ZE:T; BV315, ZE:H
Supermarine Walrus II (Apr 1944—Apr 1946)
L2217, ZE:P; Z1813

No. 294 Squadron
Formed at Berka on 24 September, 1943.

Bases etc.

Berka	Sep 1943—Oct 1943	
Amriya South, dets. Libya, Cyprus, Palestine	Oct 1943—Mar 1944	
Idku, dets. as above and Greece	Mar 1944—Jun 1945	
Basra, dets. Persian Gulf, Arabian Sea	Jun 1945—Apr 1946	

Disbanded at Basra on 8 April, 1946.

Main Equipment

Supermarine Walrus II (Sep 1943—Apr 1946)
W3018; W3050, G
Vickers Wellington IC & XI (Sep 1943—Nov 1944)
N2812, Q; MP588, L; MP600
Vickers Wellington XIII (May 1944—Apr 1946)
HF720; HZ315; JA574; ME941, U
Vickers Warwick I (Nov 1944—Apr 1946)

APPENDIX 3
The Meteorological Squadrons

Weather has always been a vital factor in the operation of aircraft, both civil and military, and it was not long after the establishment of British military air arms that it became the practice on most stations on anything but the finest of days for the first flight of the day to be the 'Weather Flight', one pilot taking off early for a local 'look-see'. In the thirties this rather basic way of doing things was supplemented by the establishment of two Meteorological Flights, one at Duxford and one at Aldergrove. Equipped with Gloster Gauntlets these Flights flew twice daily climbs to 20,000 ft taking readings of temperature, pressure and humidity which was then passed through the meteorological service to the operational stations. With the outbreak of war the weather became a matter of national secrecy and so these Flights proliferated at home and overseas; these Flights were numbered in the 1400 series. In 1943–44 six Flights were expanded to sufficient size to be re-constituted as squadrons and given squadron numbers. They provided a vital service for the operational squadrons and the land and sea forces in addition but with the end of the war all but one were disbanded, the final one becoming No. 202 Squadron where its subsequent history will be found.

THE SQUADRONS

No. 251 Squadron
Formed originally in August, 1918 for coastal anti-submarine patrol duties along the Yorkshire coast. It was an amalgamation of Nos. 504, 505 & 506 Flights.

Bases etc.

Hornsea, det. Atwick, Greenland Top & Owthorne	Aug 1918—Jun 1919

Main Equipment

D.H.6 (Aug 1918—Jun 1919)
F3393

It was disbanded at Hornsea on 30 June, 1919 and re-formed on 1 August, 1944 at Reykjavik, Iceland. Previously it had been No. 1407 Flight and its primary task was meteorological reconnaissance in the mid-Atlantic and Iceland area; it also had a secondary role as an ASR unit, some of its Hudsons being fitted for dropping airborne lifeboats. These tasks were continued until disbandment on 30 October, 1945.

Bases etc.

Reykjavik	Aug 1944—Oct 1945

Main Equipment

Lockheed Hudson IIIA (Aug 1944—Aug 1945)
FH361; FK743, AD:L; FK757; FK807
Boeing Fortress II, IIA (Mar 1945—Oct 1945)
FA701; FK197, AD:E; FK210, AD:W; HB791 (Mk. III)
Lockheed Ventura I (Aug 1944—Oct 1944)
AE714; AE779
Vickers Warwick I (Aug 1945—Oct 1945)
HG174; HG179; HG184

No. 517 Squadron
Formed from No. 1404 Met. Flight at St. Eval on 11 August, 1943 and was responsible for met. sorties over the Western Approaches. It was also involved in anti-submarine patrols from time to time during 1944–45 to help out the normal anti-submarine squadrons of Coastal Command. It was disbanded at Chivenor on 21 June, 1946.

Bases etc.

St. Eval	Aug 1943—Nov 1943
St. David's	Nov 1943—Feb 1944
Brawdy	Feb 1944—Nov 1945
Chivenor	Nov 1945—Jun 1946

Main Equipment

Handley Page Hampden I (Aug 1943—Oct 1943)
AD724
Boeing B-17F (Sep 1943—Nov 1943)
Serials not known
Lockheed Hudson III (Aug 1943—Sep 1943)
V9123
Handley Page Halifax V (Nov 1943—Jun 1946)
DT642; LL216, A
Handley Page Halifax III (Feb 1945—Jun 1946)
NA247; NA231

No. 518 Squadron
Formed at Stornoway on 9 July, 1943 and flew operational met. patrols into the Atlantic from September onwards. It also operated as a stand-by anti-submarine unit, keeping a watching brief for U-boats during these sorties and being equipped to attack them. On 19 September, 1945 it also absorbed No. 1402 Flight on its move to N. Ireland. On 1 October, 1946 it was re-numbered No. 202 Squadron (q.v.) and remained as the only met. squadron in existence in the peacetime RAF.

Bases etc.

Stornoway	Jul 1943	Sep 1943
Tiree	Sep 1943	Sep 1945
Aldergrove	Sep 1945	Oct 1946

Main Equipment

Handley Page Halifax V (Jul 1943—Aug 1945)
DG304, H; LK682, Y3:N; LL221, Y3:S; LL517, Y3:C
Handley Page Halifax IIIA (Mar 1945—Oct 1946)
MZ462, Y3:Y; NA223; RG390, Y3:A1
Vickers-Supermarine Spitfire IX (Sep 1945—Oct 1946)
MB181
Hawker Hurricane IIC (Sep 1945—Oct 1946)
PZ815
Handley Page Halifax VI (1945—Oct 1946)
RG780, Y3:M; RG843, Y3:O; ST798, Y3:L; ST809, Y3:V

No. 519 Squadron
Formed from No. 1406 Met. Flight at Wick on 15 August, 1943. Its sphere of operation was to cover the North Atlantic, North Sea and up towards the Arctic Sea, using both short-range and long-range aircraft. It was disbanded at Leuchars on 31 May, 1946.

Bases etc.

Wick	Aug 1943	Dec 1943
Skitten	Dec 1943	Nov 1944
Wick	Nov 1944	Aug 1945
Tain	Aug 1945	Nov 1945
Leuchars	Nov 1943	Oct 1943

Main Equipment

Handley Page Hampden I (Aug 1943—Oct 1943)
P1209, Z9:N; P5395, Z9:F; X3122, Z9:G
Vickers-Supermarine Spitfire VI (Aug 1943—Jan 1945)
BR307, Z9:X
Lockheed Hudson III, IIIA (Sep 1943—Mar 1945)
V9118, Z9:R; V9195, Z9:L; AE509, Z9:C; FK744, Z9:C
Lockheed Ventura V (Oct 1943—Oct 1944)
FN962, Z9:B; FP568, Z9:M; JS940, Z9:K; JT853, Z9:J
Vickers-Supermarine Spitfire VII (Oct 1944—Dec 1945)
EN297, Z9:W; EN506, Z9:V; MD141, Z9:T; MD160, Z9:U
Boeing Fortress II (Nov 1944—Sep 1945)
FA695, Z9: FK213, Z9:G; FL450
Handley Page Halifax IIIA (Aug 1945—May 1946)
HX344, Z9:O; MZ390, Z9:K; NA165; RG385, Z9:A

No. 520 Squadron
Formed from the Gibraltar detachment of No. 1402 Met. Flight on 20 September, 1943 and served from 'The Rock' on met. duties throughout its existence, being finally disbanded on 25 April, 1946. It also had a small Flight of Martinets for target-towing duties from September, 1944.

Bases etc.

Gibraltar	Sep 1943—Apr 1946

Main Equipment

Lockheed Hudson III (Sep 1943—Oct 1945)
  FH357
Handley Page Halifax V (Feb 1944—Jun 1945)
  DG344, 2M:G; LL518, 2M:K
Vickers-Supermarine Spitfire VB (Feb 1944–Jun 1944)
  EP412
Hawker Hurricane IIC (Jun 1944—Apr 1946)
  PZ830, 2M:D
Handley Page Halifax IIIA (Apr 1945—Apr 1946)
  PN190
Vickers Warwick VI (Aug 1945—Apr 1946)
  HG114; HG135; HG179; PN828

No. 521 Squadron

Established on 1 August, 1942 as the earliest of the Met. squadrons, it was formed from No. 1401 Flight at Bircham Newton to cover the North Sea and also used Spitfires and Mosquitoes to fly over enemy-held territory. It disbanded on 31 March, 1943, being broken down into Nos. 1401 and 1409 Flights but was re-formed again at Docking on 1 September, 1943 to cover the same area. It was finally disbanded at Chivenor on 1 April, 1946.

Bases etc.

Bircham Newton	Aug 1942—Mar 1943
Docking	Sep 1943—Oct 1944
Langham	Oct 1944—Nov 1945
Chivenor	Nov 1945—Apr 1946

Main Equipment

Lockheed Hudson III, V (Aug 1942—Mar 1943 & Sep 1943—Mar 1945)
  FH380; FK740
Vickers-Supermarine Spitfire VA/VB (Aug 1942—Mar 1943)
  N3270; AB131; BR287
de Havilland Mosquito IV (Aug 1942—Mar 1943)
  DK328; DK329; DZ316; DZ359; DZ406
Gloster Gladiator I, II (Aug 1942—Mar 1943 & Sep 1943—Apr 1945)
  K7972; N2307
Handley Page Hampden I (Sep 1943—Dec 1943)
  L4204; AT225, E
Lockheed Ventura V (Dec 1943—Oct 1944)
  FP571; JT894, W
Hawker Hurricane IIC (Aug 1944—Feb 1946)
  PZ803
Boeing Fortress II, III (Aug 1944—Feb 1946)
  FA710; FL450; HB786
Handley Page Halifax VI (Dec 1945—Apr 1946)
  RG787
Some of its aircraft carried the squadron code letters '5O'.

No. 628 Squadron

Formed at Redhills Lake on 21 March, 1944 from B Flight of 357 Squadron and was employed on Indian Ocean Met. flights for six months, being disbanded on 1 October, 1944. It also flew several ASR flights.

Bases etc.

Redhills Lake	Mar 1944—Oct 1944

Main Equipment

Consolidated Catalina IB, IV (Mar 1944—Oct 1944)
  FP134, U; FP191, T; FP225, T; JX347, V
No markings were carried to identify the Squadron.

APPENDIX 4
The Anti-aircraft Co-operation Squadrons

Up to the outbreak of World War II ground-based anti-aircraft weaponry was fairly basic and what little practice was afforded the AA batteries was accomplished by the occasional sortie by regular squadrons. One or two miscellaneous units had been formed in the second half of the thirties to provide target aircraft and to tow drogue targets for live firing. With the immense expansion of the armed forces in 1939–45 the need for a supply of continuous practice aircraft wherever the Army, and the Navy, were land-based grew to such an extent that a whole series of AAC (Anti-Aircraft Co-operation) Flights were formed to furnish targets and drogues not just for AA guns but also to fly simulated low-level and dive-bombing attacks on ground troops and installations and to provide many other services required by the forces on the ground. By the end of 1941 these Flights had expanded to squadron strength and were given squadron numbers although they were non-operational units; this practice has continued until today. The Squadrons concerned over the past forty years have been:

(*NB* Most of these Squadrons had detachments at other airfields; these are not listed below).

No. 5 Squadron
Re-formed in this role on 11 February, 1949 by re-numbering No. 595 Squadron at Pembrey and served until disbanding on 25 September, 1951.

Bases etc.

Pembrey	Feb 1949—Oct 1949
Chivenor	Oct 1949—Sep 1951

Main Equipment

Vickers-Supermarine Spitfire LF.16E (Feb 1949—Sep 1951)
RW388, 7B:D; SL600, 7B:E; TD339, 7B:B; TE390, 7B:F
Airspeed Oxford T.1 (Feb 1949—Sep 1951)
X7187; PH318, 7B:T
Bristol Beaufighter TT.10 (Jan 1950—Sep 1951)
RD566, 7B:O; RD577, 7B:P; RD812, 7B:N
de Havilland Vampire F.3 (Aug 1950—Sep 1951)
VG693; VT815; VV205
The aircraft were identified by the letter combination '7B'

No. 7 Squadron
Re-formed at St. Mawgan in this role on 1 May, 1970 providing target facilities largely for coastal units until 12 December, 1981 when it was disbanded.

Bases etc.

St. Mawgan, det. Lossiemouth	May 1970—Dec 1981

Main Equipment

English Electric Canberra B.2 (May 1970—Mar 1976)
WH869; WJ611; WJ677; WK119; WK145
English Electric Canberra T.19 (Mar 1976—Jul 1978)
WH904, K; XA536, L
English Electric Canberra TT.18 (May 1970—Dec 1981)
WH718; WH856; WJ629; WJ682; WJ715; WK118

No. 17 Squadron
Also served at Chivenor as an AAC squadron, being re-formed there by re-numbering No. 691 Squadron on 11 February, 1949. It continued to serve the Bristol Channel, S. Wales and Western Approaches area until disbandment on 13 March, 1951.

Bases etc.

Chivenor	Feb 1949—Mar 1951

Main Equipment

Vickers-Supermarine Spitfire LF.16E (Feb 1949—Mar 1951)
SL549, UT:N; SM406, UT:H; TB758, UT:X; TE380, UT:C
Bristol Beaufighter TT.10 (Feb 1949—Mar 1951)
RD751, UT:10; RD771, UT:7; RD807, UT:5; RD867, UT:H; SR919, UT:6

Miscellaneous Types (Feb 1949—Mar 1951)
Airspeed Oxford T.1
NJ296, UT:Y
N.A. Harvard T.2B
FX222, UT:M

No. 20 Squadron
Entered this role on 7 February, 1949 by re-numbering No. 631 Squadron at Llanbedr. It served the Irish Sea area until disbandment there on 16 October, 1951.

Bases etc.

Llanbedr	Feb 1949—Oct 1951

Main Equipment

Vickers-Supermarine Spitfire LF.16E (Feb 1949—Oct 1951)
RW351; SL614; TB380, TH:B; TD264, TH:U; TE448, TH:E
Miscellaneous Types (Feb 1949—Oct 1951)
Beaufighter TT.10
RD546, TH:N
Miles Martinet TT.1
HN884; NR637
N. A. Harvard T.2B
KF561, TH:Z
de Havilland Tiger Moth T.2
T8072, TH:E
Airspeed Oxford T.1
PH467
de Havilland Vampire F.1, F.3 (1950—Oct 1951)
TG444; VF283; VT797; VT866; VT872

No. 34 Squadron
Provided AAC facilities for the East Coast after its re-formation at Horsham St. Faith on 11 February, 1949 by re-numbering No. 695 Squadron. It continued on this role until disbandment there on 20 July, 1951.

Bases etc.

Horsham St. Faith	Feb 1949—Jul 1951

Main Equipment

Vickers-Supermarine Spitfire LF.16E (Feb 1949—Jul 1951)
SL542, 8Q:2; TD248, 8Q:T; TE356, 8Q:Z; TE450, 8Q:R
Bristol Beaufighter TT.10 (Feb 1949—Jul 1951)
RD544, 8Q:G; RD767, 8Q:E; RD809, 8Q:A; RD855, 8Q:C
Airspeed Oxford T.1 (Feb 1949—Jul 1951)
HM808, 8Q:N; LW795, 8Q:Q; MP354, 8Q:M; PH418, 8Q:L
Miscellaneous Types (Feb 1949—Jul 1951)
N.A. Harvard T.2B
KF155, 8Q:6
Miles Martinet TT.1
EM575, 8Q:N
Hawker Hurricane IIC
PZ751, 8Q:W
Vultee Vengeance IV
HB519, 8Q:C

No. 85 Squadron
Re-formed at West Raynham on 1 April, 1963 from the Target Facilities Squadron there. It was largely used for fighter interception training during its twelve years of service in this role, disbanding at West Raynham on 19 December, 1975.

Bases etc.

West Raynham	Apr 1963—Apr 1963
Binbrook	Apr 1963—Jul 1971
Scampton	Jul 1971—Sep 1971
Binbrook	Sep 1971—Jan 1972
West Raynham	Jan 1972—Dec 1975

Main Equipment

Gloster Meteor F.8 (Apr 1963—Jul 1970)
WF654, Z; WH291, T; WH364, U; WK887, Y

English Electric Canberra B.2 (May 1963—Dec 1975)
  WD966, M; WH641, S; WH878, A; WJ620, W; WK116, H
English Electric Canberra T.11, T.19 (May 1963—Dec 1975)
  WH714, K; WH903, B; WJ975, E (**T.11**); WH724, C; WJ640, F;
  WH903, B (**T.19**)

No. 100 Squadron

Has also served as a target facilities unit, primarily for fighter interception since it was re-formed at West Raynham on 1 February, 1972. It has continued on this duty ever since and is the last remaining RAF squadron serving in this role.

Bases etc.

West Raynham	Feb 1972—Jan 1976	
Marham	Jan 1976—Jan 1982	
Wyton	Jan 1982—	

Main Equipment

English Electric Canberra B.2 (Feb 1972—)
  WE113, H; WH670, B; WH703, S; WJ728, R
English Electric Canberra T.19 (Dec 1975—)
  WH903, P
English Electric Canberra E.15 (Feb 1976—)
  WH964, W; WH972, X

No. 285 Squadron

Formed from No. 9 Group AAC Flight at Wrexham on 1 December, 1941 and served in the Mersey and North Midlands area until moving south in 1944. It was disbanded at Weston Zoyland on 26 June, 1945.

Bases etc.

Wrexham	Dec 1941—Oct 1942	
Honiley	Oct 1942—Aug 1943	
Woodvale	Aug 1943—Nov 1944	
Andover	Nov 1944—Jan 1945	
North Weald	Jan 1945—Jun 1945	
Weston Zoyland	Jun 1945—Jun 1945	

Main Equipment

Westland Lysander II, III, IIIA (Dec 1941—Jun 1942)
  L4737; R2638; V9484; V9727
Lockheed Hudson III
  V9038
Bristol Blenheim I (Dec 1941—Mar 1942)
Boulton Paul Defiant I, III (Mar 1942—Jan 1944)
  N1706, VG:K; T3923, VG:M; V1134, VG:O; AA353, VG:Z
Airspeed Oxford I, II (Mar 1942—Jun 1945)
  V3149, VG:E; BG156, VG:V; EB950, VG:C; HN845, VG:A;
  LX463, VG:D
Miscellaneous Types
Miles Martinet I (Jul 1943—Dec 1943)
  MS507
Bristol Beaufighter I (Sep 1943—Nov 1944)
  R2076
Hawker Hurricane IIC (Jan 1944—Jun 1945)
  LF600
N.A. Mustang I (Mar 1945—Jun 1945)
  AP168

No. 286 Squadron

Served the Bristol Channel and West Country, being formed from No. 10 Group AAC Flight at Filton on 17 November, 1941, remaining in this area until disbanding at Weston Zoyland on 16 May, 1945.

Bases etc.

Filton	Nov 1941—Jan 1942	
Lulsgate Bottom	Jan 1942—Mar 1942	
Colerne	Mar 1942—Apr 1942	
Lulsgate Bottom	Apr 1942—May 1942	
Zeals	May 1942—Sep 1942	
Colerne	Sep 1942—Oct 1942	
Locking	Oct 1942—Nov 1943	
Weston Zoyland	Nov 1943—Apr 1944	
Culmhead	Apr 1944—May 1944	
Colerne	May 1944—Jul 1944	
Zeals	Jul 1944—Sep 1944	
Weston Zoyland	Sep 1944—May 1945	

Main Equipment

Westland Lysander II (Nov 1941— 1942)
  R2042
Airspeed Oxford I, II (Nov 1941—May 1945)
  X6850, NW:K; HM774, NW:W; HN138, NW:F; LB471, NW:D;
  LW889, NW:F
Boulton Paul Defiant I, III (Nov 1941—Jul 1944)
  N1735; N3477; AA628, NW:V; DR877
Hawker Hurricane I, IIC, IV (Nov 1941—May 1945)
  AG101; KX829; PG488
Miles Martinet I (Jul 1943—Dec 1944)
  MS509
Miles Master III (Nov 1944—Mar 1945)
  W8833

No. 287 Squadron

Formed at Croydon on 19 November, 1941 from No. 11 Group AAC Flight and provided AAC facilities in the Metropolitan area and South-East England throughout the rest of the war and for a year beyond, disbanding at West Malling on 15 June, 1946.

Bases etc.

Croydon	Nov 1941—Jul 1944	
North Weald	Jul 1944—Aug 1944	
Gatwick	Aug 1944—Jan 1945	
Redhill	Jan 1945—May 1945	
Hornchurch	May 1945—Jun 1945	
Bradwell Bay	Jun 1945—Sep 1945	
West Malling	Sep 1945—Jun 1946	

Main Equipment

Bristol Blenheim IV (Nov 1941—Feb 1942)
  T2291
Westland Lysander I, II, III, IIIA (Nov 1941—May 1942)
  N1222; N1313; R2034; V9540
Hawker Hurricane I, IIB, IV (Nov 1941—Feb 1944)
  P2754; P5172; W9294
Lockheed Hudson III (Nov 1941—Apr 1942)
  V9160
Miles Master III (Feb 1942—Sep 1942)
  W8839
Boulton Paul Defiant I, III (Apr 1942—Oct 1943)
  L6955; N1569, KZ:G; N1581, KZ:Q; N1699; N3310; DR961
Airspeed Oxford I, II (Apr 1942—Jun 1946)
  T1005; HN146, KZ:O; PG926, KZ:E
Miles Martinet I (Sep 1943—Jun 1946)
  JN673, KZ:A; MS528, KZ:B
Bristol Beaufighter I, VI, X (Nov 1944—Jul 1946)
  V8159, KZ:F; X7626
Hawker Tempest V (Nov 1944—Jun 1945)
  JN764, KZ:R; JN769
Vickers-Supermarine Spitfire VB, IX, LF.16E (Nov 1943—Jun 1946)
  EN765; NH547; TB625, KZ:A

No. 288 Squadron

Formed from No. 12 Group AAC Flight at Digby on 18 November, 1941 serving in the Lancashire/Yorkshire area until June, 1946, disbanding at East Moor on 15 June, 1946. It re-formed in the target facilities role at Middle Wallop for training night-fighter radar operators on 16 March, 1953 and served there until 12 September, 1957 when it again disbanded.

Bases etc.

Digby	Nov 1941—Dec 1942	
Wellingore	Dec 1942—Jan 1943	
Digby	Jan 1943—Nov 1943	
Coleby Grange	Nov 1943—Nov 1943	
Digby	Nov 1943—Jan 1944	
Collyweston	Jan 1944—Nov 1944	
Church Fenton	Nov 1944—Aug 1945	
Hutton Cranswick	Aug 1945—May 1946	
East Moor	May 1946—Jun 1956	
Middle Wallop	Mar 1953—Sep 1957	

Main Equipment

Bristol Blenheim IV (Nov 1941—Dec 1941)
  L8837
Westland Lysander II, III (Nov 1941—Mar 1942)
  P1695; P9060; P9100
Hawker Hurricane I, IIC (Nov 1941— 1944)
  P2983; KX200, RP:V; KZ576, RP:P; LE836, RP:W

Boulton Paul Defiant I. III (Mar 1942—Jul 1943)
  N1697; N1702; N3312; N3455; T4069
Airspeed Oxford I, II (Mar 1942—May 1945)
  X7104, RP:M; HN694, RP:H; HN706, RP:H
Lockheed Hudson III (Dec 1941—Mar 1942)
  AE606
Bristol Beaufighter I (Mar 1944—Nov 1944)
  R2137
Vickers-Supermarine Spitfire VB, IX, LF.16E (Mar 1944—Jun 1946)
  AB832, RP:S; AR517, RP:N; BM271, RP:C; SL669, RP:K,
  TB744, RP:Z
Vultee Vengeance II (May 1945—Jun 1946)
  HB368, RP:K; HB461, RP:E; HB517, RP:O; HB528, RP:J
Boulton Paul Balliol T.2 (Jun 1953—Sep 1957)
  WG147, C; WG185, P; WG216, L; WN145, A; WN508, V; WN522, P

No. 289 Squadron

Originated in No. 13 Group AAC Flight and was formed at Kirk-
newton on 20 November, 1941. It covered the Lowlands and
north-east England until after the war ended in Europe then moved
south to disband at Andover on 26 June, 1945.

Bases etc.

Kirknewton	Nov 1941—May 1942	
Turnhouse	May 1942—May 1945	
Acklington	May 1945—May 1945	
Eshott	May 1945—Jun 1945	
Andover	Jun 1945—Jun 1945	

Main Equipment

Bristol Blenheim IV (No 1941—Jan 1942)
  N6141; Z5880
Westland Lysander II, IIIA (Nov 1941—Mar 1942)
  N1226; P9099; P9104; P9187; V9319
Hawker Hurricane I, IIC, IV (Dec 1941—Jun 1945)
  N2558; P3621; LF580, YE:W; LF626, YE:N; LF676, YE:M
Airspeed Oxford I, II (Mar 1942—Jun 1945)
  X6801, YE:E; V3170, YE:G; AS973; EB973, YE:F; HN170, YE:G;
  LB475, YE:P
Boulton Paul Defiant I, III (Mar 1942—Jul 1943)
  N1536; N1569; N1750; N3316; V1125; DR875
Miles Martinet I (Jun 1943—Apr 1945)
  EM445, YE:10; JN512, YE:11; JN670, YE:12; JN672, YE:16
Vultee Vengeance II, IV (Mar 1945—Jun 1945)
  FD335, YE:M; HB359, YE:A; KG815, YE:9

No. 290 Squadron

Formed for the Northern Ireland AAC duties from Nos. 1480 and
1617 Flights at Newtonards on 1 December, 1943. It moved to
Scotland in August, 1944 (where it already had detachments) and to
Belgium in January, 1945 for the defences of the forces occupying
the Low Countries. It disbanded at Knocke on 27 October, 1945.

Bases etc.

Newtonards	Dec 1943—Mar 1944	
Long Kesh	Mar 1944—Aug 1944	
Turnhouse	Aug 1944—Jan 1945	
Knocke-le-Zoute (B.83)	Jan 1945—Oct 1945	

Main Equipment

Airspeed Oxford I, II (Dec 1943—Oct 1945)
  L4579; HN840
Miles Martinet I (Dec 1943—Oct 1945)
  EM522, X6:D; MS827, X6:S
Hawker Hurricane IIC (Dec 1943—Jan 1945)
Vickers-Supermarine Spitfire VB (Dec 1944—Oct 1945)
  W3641, X6:H; BM356

No. 291 Squadron

Formed from Nos. 1613, 1629 & 1634 Flights at Hutton Cranswick
on 1 December, 1943 and was purely a target-towing squadron
serving the AA guns along the Yorkshire and Lincolnshire coasts
until 26 June, 1945 when it disbanded.

Bases etc.

Hutton Cranswick	Dec 1943—Jun 1945	

Main Equipment

Miles Martinet I (Dec 1943—Jun 1945)
  EM616; MS731, B
Hawker Henley III (Dec 1943—   1944)
  L3258; L3343; L3353; L3395

Vultee Vengeance II (Nov 1944—Jun 1945)
  HD442

No. 516 Squadron

Formed from No. 1441 (Combined Operations) Flight and its task
was to provide low-level attacks of various types on units training in
Combined Operations assaults. It was based at Dundonald from its
formation on 28 April, 1943 until disbandment on 2 December,
1944.

Bases etc.

Dundonald	Apr 1943—Dec 1944	

Main Equipment

N.A. Mustang I (Apr 1943—Feb 1944)
  AG419; AG458; AG517; AG642; AM181; AP234
Avro Anson I (Apr 1943—Dec 1944)
  MG843; MG858
Westland Lysander II, IIA (Apr 1943—Dec 1943)
  L4800; P9105; V9311
Bristol Blenheim IV (May 1943—Dec 1944)
  L9301
Hawker Hurricane II (Dec 1943—Dec 1944)
  LE999; LF160; LF180; LF207; LF534

No. 567 Squadron

Formed on 1 December, 1943 from No. 1624 Flight and provided
AAC facilities over the Kent and Thames Estuary areas until 15
June, 1946 when it was disbanded at West Malling.

Bases etc.

Detling	Dec 1943—Nov 1944	
Hornchurch	Nov 1944—Jun 1945	
Hawkinge	Jun 1945—Aug 1945	
Manston	Aug 1945—Apr 1946	
West Malling	Apr 1946—Jun 1946	

Main Equipment

Miles Martinet I (Dec 1943—Jul 1945)
  EM462, I4:M; JN293, I4:C; JN673, I4:E; MS528, I4:B; NR597, I4:A
Airspeed Oxford I, II (Dec 1943—Jun 1946)
  V3240, I4:L; V4262, I4:N; NM332, I4:M; PH129
Hawker Hurricane I, IIC, IV (Dec 1943—Jun 1945)
  V7056, I4:X; V7075, I4:J; LF584, I4:X
Vickers-Supermarine Spitfire VB (Jun 1945—Sep 1945)
  AR518
Vultee Vengeance IV (Apr 1945—Jun 1946)
  FD308, I4:C; HB364, I4:Q
Vickers-Supermarine Spitfire LF.16E (Jul 1945—Jun 1946)
  RW349, I4:F; SM243, I4:G; TE155, I4:O

No. 577 Squadron

Formed on 1 December, 1943 from detachments from Nos. 6, 7 & 8
AACUs at Castle Bromwich to serve the defences in the Midlands. It
was disbanded there on 15 June, 1946.

Bases etc.

Castle Bromwich	Dec 1943—Jun 1946	

Main Equipment

Airspeed Oxford I, II (Dec 1943—Jun 1946)
  N1194; N6340; P1814; V3151, 3Y:N; HN705, 3Y:P
Hawker Hurricane IIC, IV (Dec 1943—Jul 1945)
  KZ325
Bristol Beaufighter I, X (Nov 1944—Jul 1945)
  LX957, 3Y:J; NE716, 3Y:F; RD713, 3Y:R
Vickers-Supermarine Spitfire VB, LF.16E (Jun 1945—Jun 1946)
  BM569, 3Y:F; SM199, 3Y:B; SM417, 3Y:Z; SM511, 3Y:J

No. 587 Squadron

Formed for AAC duties from three Flights, Nos. 1600, 1601, 1623,
at Weston Zoyland on 1 December, 1943 and covered the South-
West and Bristol Channel areas. It finally disbanded at Tangmere on
15 June, 1946.

Bases etc.

Weston Zoyland	Dec 1943—Apr 1944	
Culmhead	Apr 1944—Oct 1944	
Weston Zoyland	Oct 1944—Jun 1946	
Tangmere	Jun 1946—Jun 1946	

Main Equipment

Hawker Henley III (Dec 1943—May 1944)
  L3247; L3307; L3315; L3383; L3396
Airspeed Oxford I, II (Dec 1943—Dec 1944)
  V4148; HN132, M4:
Hawker Hurricane IIC, IV (Dec 1943—Jun 1945)
  No known serials
Miles Martinet I (Dec 1943—Dec 1944)
  EM412; HP216, M4:16
N.A. Harvard T.2B (1945—Jun 1946)
  FS767, M4:R; FS770, M4:S
Vickers-Supermarine Spitfire LF.16E (Jul 1945—Jun 1946)
  TB304, M4:V

No. 595 Squadron

Formed at Aberporth on 1 December, 1943 from Nos, 1607, 1608 and 1609 Flights and served the Welsh region through until 1949 when, on 11 February, it was re-numbered No. 5 Squadron at Pembrey.

Bases etc.

Aberporth	Dec 1943—Apr 1946
Fairwood Common	Apr 1946—Oct 1946
Pembrey	Oct 1946—Feb 1949

Main Equipment

Hawker Henley III (Dec 1943—Jun 1944)
  L3248; L3274; L3311; L3327; L3335; L3369; L3409
Miles Martinet I (Dec 1943—Feb 1949)
  EM697, 7B:Z; HP200, 7B: NR633, 7B:M; PX126, 7B:W;
  RG897, 7B:V
Hawker Hurricane I, IIC, IV (Dec 1943—Dec 1944)
  P2887; KW792; KX829; KZ910; LB650; LE755
Airspeed Oxford I, II (Jun 1944—Feb 1949)
  X7187, 7B:; HN773; NJ296, 7B:; PH318, 7B:T
Vickers-Supermarine Spitfire VB (Nov 1944—Jul 1945)
  AD506, 7B:P; BM581, 7B:R; BM628, 7B:M; EN992, 7B:K
Vickers-Supermarine Spitfire XII (Dec 1944—Jul 1945)
  MB804, 7B:N; MB837; MB848
Vickers-Supermarine Spitfire IX, LF.16E (Jul 1945—Feb 1949)
  ML247, 7B:F; PT753, 7B:G; RW388, 7B:D; SL600, 7B:E;
  TD151, 7B:H
de Havilland Vampire F.1 (Dec 1946—Oct 1948)
  VF278; VF283; VF300; VF310

No. 631 Squadron

Formed at Towyn on 1 December, 1943 from Nos, 1605 and 1628 Flights to serve the Welsh gunnery ranges for target-towing and gun-laying purposes. It remained in service after World War II and was re-numbered No. 20 Squadron at Llanbedr on 7 February, 1949.

Bases etc.

Towyn	Dec 1943—May 1945
Llanbedr	May 1945—Feb 1949

Main Equipment

Hawker Henley II (Dec 1943—Feb 1945)
  L3243; L3251; L3268; L3315; L3325; L3337; L3386; L3438
Hawker Hurricane IIC (Mar 1944—Jul 1945)
  KX829, 6D: LF910
Miles Martinet I (Sep 1944—Oct 1944 & Jan 1947—Feb 1949)
  EM524; HN884, 6D:K
Vultee Vengeance IV (May 1945—May 1947)
  No serials known
Vickers-Supermarine Spitfire VB, LF.16E (Jun 1945—Feb 1949)
  AA930, 6D:H; AB186, 6D:J; AB275, 6D:V; AD295, 6D:R, **(Mk. VB)**;
  RW351, 6D:L; SL614, 6D:A; TB380, 6D:B; TE328, 6D:Z, **(Mk LF.16E)**
de Havilland Vampire F.1 (Aug 1948—Feb 1949)
  TG444; TG447; VF273; VF283; VF301

No. 639 Squadron

Formed on 1 December, 1943 by the amalgamation of Nos. 1602, 1603 and 1604 Flights at Cleave. It remained at this base serving the Cornish area on AAC duties until disbanded there on 30 April, 1945.

Bases etc.

Cleave	Dec 1943—Apr 1945

Main Equipment

Hawker Henley III (Dec 1943—Apr 1945)
  L3247; L3254; L3268; L3300; L3315; L3335; L3388
Hawker Hurricane IIC, IV (Aug 1944—Apr 1945)
  KX829; LD976

No. 667 Squadron

Formed at Gosport on 1 December, 1943 from Nos. 1631 and 1662 Flights from where it flew AAC and fleet co-operation duties until 20 December, 1945, disbanding at Gosport on that date.

Bases etc.

Gosport	Dec 1943—Dec 1945

Main Equipment

Boulton Paul Defiant I, III (Dec 1943—Jun 1945)
  N1553, U4:7; N3431, U4:J; N3440, U4:6; AA296, U4:J; DR875
Hawker Hurricane I, IIC (Apr 1944—Aug 1945)
  L1706; L1934; P3151
Fairey Barracuda II (May 1944—Jun 1945)
  No serials known
Airspeed Oxford I, II (Jun 1944—Dec 1945)
  P8981; HM706
Vultee Vengeance IV (Oct 1944—Dec 1945)
  HB361, U4:B; HB406, U4:L; HB529, U4:E
Vickers-Supermarine Spitfire LF.16E (Jul 1945—Dec 1945)
  TB392; TE283, U4:7

No. 679 Squadron

Formed at Ipswich on 1 December, 1943 from Nos, 1616 & 1627 Flights for AAC work in East Anglia. It remained there until 26 June, 1945 when it was disbanded.

Bases etc.

Ipswich	Dec 1943—Jun 1945

Main Equipment

Hawker Hurricane IIC, IV (Dec 1943—Jun 1945)
  KZ339, 3M:G; KZ661, 3M:V; KZ708, 3M:H; KZ907, 3M:C
Miles Martinet I (Dec 1943—Jun 1945)
  EM413, 3M:S; HN874, 3M:U; HN958, 3M:G; MS629, 3M:G
Westland Lysander II (Dec 1943—   1944)
  R2639
Fairey Barracuda II (Mar 1944—Jun 1945)
  DR154
Vultee Vengeance IV (Apr 1945—Jun 1945)
  FD315

No. 691 Squadron

Formed at Roborough on 1 December, 1943 from No. 1623 Flight. It served in the Devon and Cornwall area for most of its existence and remained in operation until 11 February, 1949 when it was re-numbered as No. 17 Squadron.

Bases etc.

Roborough	Dec 1943—Feb 1945
Harrowbeer	Feb 1945—Aug 1945
Exeter	Aug 1945—Apr 1946
Weston Zoyland	Apr 1946—Jul 1946
Fairwood Common	Jul 1946—Oct 1946
Chivenor	Oct 1946—Feb 1949

Main Equipment

Boulton Paul Defiant I, III (Dec 1943—Apr 1945)
  N1568; N1624; N1728, 5S:G; N3434; V1108
Airspeed Oxford I (Dec 1943—Feb 1949)
  LW868, 5S:B; NJ296, 5S:Y; NM302, 5S:X; PH456, 5S:O
Hawker Hurricane I, IIC (Dec 1943—Aug 1945)
  L1715; L2064; P2575; LF638
Vultee Vengeance IV (Apr 1945—May 1947)
  FD193, 5S:R
Miles Martinet I (Aug 1945—Feb 1949)
  HP524, 5S:; JN513, 5S:S; NR637, 5S:2; PW981, 5S:J
Vickers-Supermarine Spitfire LF.16E (Aug 1945—Feb 1949)
  SM189, 5S:M; TB759, 5S:A; TB993, 5S:Q; TD151, 5S:D;
  TE354, 5S:K

No. 695 Squadron

Formed at Bircham Newton from Nos. 1611 & 1612 Flights on 1 December, 1943, operating on AAC duties in the Norfolk area throughout the remainder of the war and through to 11 February, 1949 when it was disbanded by re-numbering as No. 34 Squadron.

Bases etc.

Bircham Newton	Dec 1943—Aug 1945
Horsham St. Faith	Aug 1945—Feb 1949

Main Equipment

Westland Lysander I, II (Dec 1943—Jan 1944)
  No serials known
Hawker Henley III (Dec 1943—Jun 1944)
  L3256; L3313, G; L3320; L3378; L3388; L3421
Hawker Hurricane IIC (Dec 1943—Sep 1945)
  No serials known
Miles Martinet I (Dec 1943—May 1945 & Dec 1946—Jan 1949)
  HN958, 4M:C; HP218, 4M:A; JN543, 4M:J; NR661, 4M:D; PX173, 4M:H
Vickers-Supermarine Spitfire VB, LF.16E (Sep 1944—Feb 1949)
  SL666, 4M:S; SM254, 4M:U; SM418, 4M:K; TB592, 4M:K; TD344, 4M:H
Vultee Vengeance IV (Mar 1945—May 1947)
  FD131, 4M:C; FD176, 4M:Z; FD203, 4M:D; HB478, 4M:W; HB545, 4M:A
Airspeed Oxford I, II (Jun 1946—Feb 1949)
  BG261, 4M:U; HM688, 4M:O; LB477, 4M:M; NJ360, 4M:N; PH458, 4M:C
N.A. Harvard T.2B (Dec 1946—Feb 1949)
  FX219; KF155; KF331, 4M:Q
Bristol Beaufighter TT.10 (Dec 1948—Feb 1949)
  RD767, 4M:E; RD802, 4M:D; RD855, 4M:C; SR911, 4M:G

APPENDIX 4A
The Air Observation Post Squadrons and Glider Assault Squadrons

The Air Observation Post Squadrons were formed from August, 1941 onwards being operated by RAF personnel on behalf of the Army. They flew light aircraft, in the main variants of the Taylorcraft Auster, and were used as scouting run-abouts by Army units to keep track of enemy positions and as light liaison and communications organisations. The Squadrons were numbered between No. 651 and 666 Squadrons and these numbers have been taken up and used by the post-war Army Air Corps squadrons. In view of their predominantly Army involvement within the Army organisational structure no attempt is made here to chronicle their histories; this must await a volume devoted to Army aviation.

The same must apply to Nos. 668 to 673 Squadrons which were formed in India for airborne assault having a mixture of RAF and Glider Pilot Regiment personnel. The intention was that they should be used for airborne assaults and their main equipment consisted of Xaco Hadrian gliders but they were never operational being largely used, from the RAF point of view, to occupy personnel for which there were not other postings at the time. They were in existence between November, 1944 and July, 1946.

APPENDIX 5
The Calibration Squadrons

The arrival of radar in the early 1940s brought about an entirely new task for the RAF which added to the complexity of the radio calibration duties undertaken by small units within the RAF. A growing need for means of air calibration of the defence radars around the UK meant that aircraft were specifically required to fly over the areas concerned checking the accuracy of the systems. This was extended to other radio and radar systems such as blind-landing and homing devices and this task has continued ever since and has spread to the surveillance of other people's devices as well. Originally this was a task for the Westland Lysander crews in 1940–41, for they were at a loose end, their aircraft being unfit for operations. As the war progressed many other aircraft types were used in the task. Squadrons involved in this, and allied, tasks at some time in their existence were:

No. 97 Squadron
Re-formed at Watton on 25 May, 1963 by re-numbering No. 151 Squadron. It was largely involved in development work within Signals Command and was disbanded again there on 2 January, 1967.

Bases etc.

Watton	May 1963—Jan 1967

Main Equipment

English Electric Canberra B.2 (May 1963—Jan 1967)
  WH739
Vickers Varsity T.1 (May 1963—Jan 1967)
  WJ911, X; WL687, Y; WL690, Z
Handley Page Hastings C.2 (May 1963—Jan 1967)

No. 98 Squadron
Became a Signals squadron on 19 April, 1963 at Tangmere by the re-numbering of No. 245 Squadron there. It served on calibration duties with Canberras for thirteen years before disbanding at Cottesmore on 27 February, 1976, some of its aircraft being taken over for the same task by No. 100 Squadron.

Bases etc.

Tangmere	Apr 1963—Oct 1963
Watton	Oct 1963—Apr 1969
Cottesmore	Apr 1969—Feb 1976

Main Equipment

English Electric Canberra B.2 (Apr 1963—   1968)
  WD955; WE122, J; WH681; WH869; WK144
English Electric Canberra E.15 (1968—Feb 1976)
  WH948, 8; WH964, 4; WH972, 2; WH983, 3; WJ756, 6

No. 115 Squadron
Another long-standing bomber squadron, was re-formed in the calibration role on 21 August, 1958 by re-numbering No. 116 Squadron at Watton. It flew in a complementary role to No. 98 Squadron, the latter fulfilling the high-level calibration and No. 115 Squadron the low-level role. To do this it flew Vickers Varsity T.1s, later HS Argosies and, finally HS Andover E.3s, being the main calibration squadron in action today.

Bases etc.

Watton	Aug 1958—Aug 1958
Tangmere	Aug 1958—Oct 1963
Watton	Oct 1963—Apr 1969
Cottesmore	Apr 1969—Feb 1976
Brize Norton	Feb 1976—date

Main Equipment

Vickers Varsity T.1 (Aug 1958—Aug 1970)
  WF371, L; WF389, Q; WF424, F; WJ887, J; WJ947, K; WL678, C
Hawker Siddeley Argosy E.1 (Feb 1968—Jan 1978)
  XN816; XN855; XP439; XP448; XR137; XR143
Hawker Siddeley Andover C.1, E.3 (Nov 1976—date)
  XS603, (E.3); XS605, (E.3); XS640, (C.1); XS641, (C.1)

No. 116 Squadron
The original calibration squadron, formed from No. 1 Anti-Aircraft Calibration Flight at Hatfield on 17 February, 1941 flying Westland Lysanders. The Squadron maintained one headquarters with very many detached Flights across the UK for the calibration of mainly AA gun radars and used a variety of types of aircraft. The work was continued until VE-Day, soon after which No. 116 Squadron was disbanded at Hornchurch on 26 May, 1945. It re-formed again, from the Calibration Squadron of the Central Signals Establishment at Watton, on 1 August, 1952 and resumed calibration duties, mainly with Varsities, until becoming No. 115 Squadron on 21 August, 1958.

Bases etc.

Hatfield	Feb	1941—Apr	1941
Hendon	Apr	1941—Apr	1942
Heston	Apr	1942—Dec	1943
Croydon	Dec	1943—Jul	1944
North Weald	Jul	1944—Aug	1944
Gatwick	Aug	1944—Sep	1944
Redhill	Sep	1944—May	1945
Hornchurch	May	1945—May	1945
Watton	Aug	1952—Aug	1958

Main Equipment

Westland Lysander II, III, IIIA (Feb 1941—Jan 1943)
  L4776; P9111; T1515; T1430, II:O; T1651; V9619, II:R
Hawker Hurricane I, IIA (Nov 1941—May 1945)
  P2681; V7112, II:F; AG205
de Havilland Tiger Moth II (Jun 1942—May 1945)
  T5623; DE564
Airspeed Oxford I (Nov 1942—May 1945)
  L4637; N4582; P6817; ED218
Avro Anson I (Mar 1945—May 1945)
  N5145
Avro Lincoln B.2 (Aug 1952—Apr 1954)
  RE311, 48; WD124, 46
Avro Anson C.19 (Aug 1952—Aug 1958)
  TX232; VM313, 34; VM332, 27
Vickers Varsity T.1 (Jan 1954—Aug 1958)
  WJ940; WJ945; WL622, R; WL636, D; WL685, S

No. 151 Squadron
Predominantly a fighter squadron, this unit entered briefly into the calibration world, being re-formed from the Signals Development Squadron at Watton on 1 January, 1962 and being re-numbered No. 97 Squadron there on 25 May, 1963.

Bases etc.

Watton	Jan 1962—May 1963

Main Equipment

Avro Lincoln B.2 (Jan 1962—May 1963)
  RA685, M; RF398; RF505, K; WD132, C
Vickers Varsity T.1 (Jan 1962—May 1963)
  WF376; WJ940; WL686
English Electric Canberra B.2 (Jan 1962—May 1963)
  WH642; WH945; WJ984

No. 245 Squadron
This Squadron was re-formed by re-numbering No. 527 Squadron at Watton on 21 August, 1958. It carried out high-level calibration work for five years before being re-numbered No. 98 Squadron at Tangmere on 18 April, 1963.

Bases etc.

Watton	Aug 1958—Aug 1958
Tangmere	Aug 1958—Apr 1963

Main Equipment

English Electric Canberra B.2 (Aug 1958—Apr 1963)
  WD955; WE113; WH670; WH840; WJ611; WJ860; WK130

No. 360 Squadron

Although not strictly a calibration unit this Squadron is included here because of its link with Signals Command. It is an ECM training unit, formed at Watton on 1 April, 1966 and is a unit comprising both RAF and Fleet Air Arm personnel. It flies Canberra T.17 aircraft for these duties. Another Squadron, No. 361, also formed at Watton on 2 January, 1967 for service in the Far East but was disbanded before going there on 14 July, 1967.

Bases etc.

Watton	Apr	1966—Apr 1969
Cottesmore	Apr	1969—Jul 1975
Wyton	Jul	1975—date

Main Equipment

English Electric Canberra B.2, T4 (Oct 1966—Aug 1967)
WH665; WT488, Y (T.4)
English Electric Canberra T.17 (Dec 1966—date)
WD955, Q; WF916, P; WH665, J; WH872, W; WJ565, C; WJ981, S;
WK111, B

No. 526 Squadron

Formed at Inverness on 15 June, 1943 for calibration duties in Northern Scotland. It used various aircraft for this but predominantly Bristol Blenheim IVs. It was also equipped with Dominies for communications and provided a comms. service for other RAF units in the region. It was absorbed by No. 527 Squadron on 1 May, 1945.

Bases etc.

Inverness	Jun	1943—May 1945

Main Equipment

Bristol Blenheim IV (Jun 1943—May 1945)
L9271; L9303; T2001, MD:B; Z6166
Airspeed Oxford I (Jun 1943—May 1945)
N4847, MD:L; X7200, MD:N; AP482, MD:F
de Havilland Dominie I (Aug 1943—May 1945)
R5934, MD:X; X7327
de Havilland Hornet Moth (Jun 1943—May 1945)
W5781; W9388, MD:R

No. 527 Squadron

Formed on 15 June, 1943 at Castle Camps as an amalgamation of the various calibration Wings in the south of England and East Anglia. From 1944 onwards the calibration needs began to dwindle so 527 absorbed No. 528 Squadron on 1 September, 1944 and No. 526 on 1 May, 1945. It was itself disbanded at Watton on 15 April, 1946. However, it was re-formed for high-level calibration out of N & R Squadrons of the Central Signals Establishment at Watton on 1 August, 1952 and served there until 21 August, 1958 when it was re-numbered No. 245 Squadron.

Bases etc.

Castle Camps	Jun	1943—Feb 1944
Snailwell	Feb	1944—Apr 1944
Digby	Apr	1944—Nov 1945
Watton	Nov	1945—Apr 1946
Watton	Aug	1952—Aug 1958

Main Equipment

Bristol Blenheim IV (Jun 1943—May 1945)
L9295, WN:A; N3598, WN:E; R3615, WN:Y; T2227, WN:G;
Z7950, WN:L
Hawker Hurricane I, IIB (Jun 1943—Apr 1945)
P2992, WN:P; V7922, WN:M; AG209, WN:D; BP672
Vickers-Supermarine Spitfire VB (Jul 1944—Apr 1946)
AA915, WN:Y; AB910, WN:S; AD227
Airspeed Oxford I (Sep 1944—Apr 1946)
LX116, WN:O; LX122, WN:P
Miscellaneous Types: **Hornet Moth** W9391; **Wellington X** HZ616, WN:M;
Dominie I HG721
Avro Lincoln B.2 (Aug 1952—Mar 1957)
SX942, L; SX948, B; SX980, R; WD141
Avro Anson C.19 (Aug 1952—Mar 1954)
VL312, 25
English Electric Canberra B.2 (? 1955—Aug 1958)
WH877; WK144; WK145

No. 528 Squadron

Formed at Filton on 28 June, 1943 for calibration tasks in the West Country, transferring to Lincolnshire in May, 1944 and being absorbed into No. 527 Squadron in September, 1944 at Digby.

Bases etc.

Filton	Jun	1943—May 1944
Digby	May	1944—Sep 1944

Main Equipment

Bristol Blenheim IV (Jun 1943—Sep 1944)
R3615; T2219
de Havilland Hornet Moth (Jun 1943—Sep 1944)
W5751

No. 529 Squadron

Formed from No. 1448 Flight at Halton on 15 June, 1943. This Flight had pioneered radar calibration with autogyros and light aircraft and continued to do this until after World War II, disbanding at Henley-on-Thames on 20 October, 1945. It was the first RAF squadron to use a helicopter operationally.

Bases etc.

Halton	Jun	1943—Aug 1944
Henley-on-Thames	Aug	1944—Oct 1945

Main Equipment

Cierva C.30 Rota IA (Jun 1943—Oct 1945)
K4233, KX:F; K4239, KX:J; V1187, KX:O; AP507, KX:H;
DR624, KX:L
de Havilland Hornet Moth (Jun 1943—Oct 1945)
W5750, KX:Y; W5779, KX:S; AV952, KX:T
Cierva C.40 (Jun 1943—Jul 1944)
L7594
Airspeed Oxford I (Sep 1944—Oct 1945)
T1210
Vought-Sikorsky Hoverfly I (May 1945—Oct 1945)
KK993, KX:R

APPENDIX 6
The Communications Squadrons

Right from the beginnings of military aviation the aeroplane has been used as a means of communication; flying people of importance from place to place. At the end of World War I certain units were set aside for this very purpose and in the twenties and thirties this was exemplified by the career of No. 24 Squadron, the specialist in this field. Since then other units have taken up the mantle of Communications duties, flying short-range routes and individual flights with governmental and service chiefs as and when needed. Most of the squadrons involved in this necessary, but rather pedestrian, duty are recorded elsewhere in this book for at various phases in their existence they have served in other roles. Those that are not thus recorded are listed below:

No. 32 Squadron

For most of its existence No. 32 has been a fighter squadron but then a strike squadron but re-formed in the communications role on 3 February, 1969 at Northolt by the re-numbering of the Metropolitan Communications Squadron. Since then it has been the premier squadron in this role, flying all dignitaries below royal status (who are taken care of by the Queen's Flight). It has three Flights, one of which is equipped with HS.125 fast jets (and manned by Royal Navy personnel as well as RAF), one of helicopters and one of larger aircraft (Andovers) for longer-distance or greater numbers.

Bases etc.

Northolt   Feb   1969—date

Main Equipment

Beagle Basset CC.1 (Feb 1969—Jan 1975)
   XS769; XS772; XS781
Bristol Sycamore HC.14 (Feb 1969—Aug 1972)
   XG502; XG544; XL829; XL918
HS. Andover CC.2 (Feb 1969—date)
   XS791; XS792; XS794; XS597, (C. Mk. 1)
Westland Whirlwind HC.10, HCC.12 (Jan 1970—date)
   XJ407; XJ763; XP328; XP399; XR488 (HCC. 12)
HS.125 CC.1 (May 1971—date)
   XW788; XW789; XW790; XW791
HS.125 CC.2 (Apr 1973—date)
   XX507; XX508
Westland/Aerospatiale Gazelle HC.1 (1976—date)
   XW855; XZ935

No. 152 Squadron

No. 152 has spent most of its existence as a fighter squadron but on 29 September, 1958 it was re-formed from No. 1417 Flight at Muharraq and flew on communications duties in the Arabian Gulf area until disbandment on 9 December, 1967. It had two Flights, A with Hunting Pembroke C.1s and B with Scottish Aviation Twin Pioneer CC.1s. An interesting facet is that its aircraft carried the fighter squadron markings hitherto used on its Meteors.

Bases etc.

Muharraq   Sep   1958—Dec 1967

Main Equipment

Hunting Pembroke C.1 (Sep 1958—Dec 1967)
   WV700; WV706; WV743, J; WV747, L; XL955
Scottish Aviation Twin Pioneer CC.1 (Sep 1958—Dec 1967)
   XL966; XL996; XM285, M; XM291, Q; XM939; XM958

No. 163 Squadron

Re-formed at Suez on 10 July, 1942 and almost immediately moved to Eritrea where it was based and flew a mail and communications service throughout central North Africa, connecting with Sudan, Ethiopia, Nigeria, Madagascar and Egypt. Five months later it was reduced to cadre and disbanded eventually on 16 June, 1943.

Bases etc.

Suez   Jul   1942—Jul   1942
Asmara   Jul   1942—Jun   1943

Main Equipment

Lockheed Hudson III, VI (Jul 1942—Dec 1942)
   EW884; EW935; EW960; FH279; FK397; FK411

No. 173 Squadron

Formed at Heliopolis on 9 July, 1942 out of part of No. 267 Squadron for communications duties in the Egypt and Western Desert general area. A Flight was equipped with Lockheed Lodestars for the longer runs, B Flight had a miscellany of light types, predominantly Percival Proctors. It flew on these duties, carrying many famous people, until 29 February, 1944 when it became the Middle East Communications Squadron. It was re-formed briefly on 1 February, 1953 at Hawarden by the re-numbering of No. 4 (Home) Ferry Unit and flew ferrying duties until disbandment on 1 September, 1957. It had a small fleet of aircraft for ferry pilot transport.

Bases etc.

Heliopolis   Jul   1942—Feb 1944
Hawarden   Feb   1953—Sep 1957

Main Equipment

Lockheed Lodestar (Jul 1942—Feb 1944)
   AX685; AX723; EW989; EW990; EW996
Lockheed 10 Electra (Aug 1942—   1942)
   AX700
Percival Proctor I, III (Jul 1942—Feb 1944)
   P6112; P6116; P6122; P6152; P6177;
   HM371; HM395; HM415; HM458
Westland Lysander I, II (Jul 1942—   1943)
   N1294; P9051; P9191; R1994
Hawker Audax I, Hart variants (Jul 1942—   1943)
   K3124; K4909; K6421; K7525
Hawker Hurricane I (Jul 1942—   1943)
   L1700; V6939; Z4700; Z4912; V7679
Miles Magister I (Nov 1942—   1943)
   L8067; P2453; R1882; V1064
Miscellaneous Types (Jul 1942—Feb 1944)
Douglas Boston III Z2193; **Percival Q6** HK838; **Percival Gull** AX698;
   D.H. Moth HK839
Vickers Varsity T.1 (Feb 1953—Sep 1957)
   WF382; WJ912, C; WL683
Vickers Valetta C.1 (Feb 1953—Sep 1957)
   VW806; VX494
Avro Anson C.19 (Feb 1953—Sep 1957)
   VM370; VP513; VP522

No. 207 Squadron

No. 207 has served exclusively as a bomber squadron throughout its existence, re-formed in the comms. role at Northolt on 3 February, 1969 by re-numbering the Southern Comms. Squadron. Detachments at Turnhouse and Wyton provide coverage for the entire UK and the Squadron was equipped with Beagle Bassets, Hunting Pembrokes and de Havilland Devons. The first two types dropped out of service in the seventies leaving the Squadron with the entire RAF fleet of Devons to carry on this work.

Bases etc.

Northolt, det. Turnhouse, Wyton   Feb   1969—date

Main Equipment

Beagle Basset CC.1 (Feb 1969—May 1974)
   XS774; XS777; XS780; XS784
Hunting Pembroke C.1 (Feb 1969—Jun 1976)
   WV735; WV746; WV754; XK884; XL929
de Havilland Devon C.2 (Feb 1969—date)
   VP952; VP957; VP962; VP971; VP977; WB534

No. 60 Squadron

Re-formed in the comms. role after a lifetime of bombing and fighting on 3 February, 1969 at Wildenrath by the re-numbering of the RAF Germany Comms. Squadron. Since then it has fulfilled the role of supplying the short-range transport needs of the RAF in Germany using Hunting Pembrokes and, for a while, de Havilland Herons.

Bases etc.

Wildenrath   Feb   1969—date

Main Equipment

de Havilland Heron C.2, C.4 (Feb 1969—Jul 1972)
   XM296; XR391
Hunting Pembroke C.1 (Feb 1969—date)
   WV701; WV720; WV746; XF796; XK884; XL953

No. 510 Squadron

Formed at Hendon on 15 October, 1942 when No. 24 Squadron concentrated its role on transport flying. All its light communications aircraft were put into the new 510 Squadron and for eighteen months the Squadron maintained the UK communications task formerly flown by 24 Squadron. It was mainly using Ansons and Proctors together with a variety of impressed civil types. On 8 April, 1944 it was re-named the Metropolitan Communications Squadron.

Bases etc.

Hendon   Oct   1942—Apr 1944

Main Equipment

Percival Proctor I, III, IV (Oct 1942—Apr 1944)
   P6194; P6200; DX231; MX451
Avro Anson I (Oct 1942—Apr 1944)
   EG224
de Havilland Dominie I (Oct 1942—   1943)
   R5925; R5931
Miscellaneous Types (Oct 1942—Apr 1944)
de Havilland Puss Moth AX868; **G.A. Cygnet** HM495; **Percival Q6** X9363; de Havilland Gipsy Moth MX463; **Hawker Hart** K2452; **Curtiss Mohawk III** AR633; **Airspeed Oxford I** L4635, etc.

APPENDIX 7
Squadron Locations

A.12 (Balleroy) 16
Aalborg West 19
Abbotsinch 224, 225, 254, 269, 309
Abeele 4, 6, 10, 33, 42
Aberporth 595
Abingdon 18, 24, 27, 30, 40, 46, 47, 51, 52, 59, 238, 525
Ablainzeville 12
Aboukir 39, 204, 228, 230
Abscon 42
Abu Sueir 13, 203, 208, 272
Accra 82
Acklington 140, 202, 228, 278, 289
Addu Atoll 205, 217, 240, 413
Aden 240, 259, 413
Afrikanda 144
Afuleh 142
Agaba 14
Agadir 48, 179, 233, 540, 544
Agartala 28, 31, 62, 117, 194, 216, 292
Agroma 208
Aire 10, 16
Aix le Chateau 52
Ajaccio 283
Akab 63
Akrotiri 13, 70, 84, 208
Akureyri 330
Akyab 31, 62, 194, 203, 211, 230, 267, 298
Aldergrove 2, 4, 42, 48, 59, 86, 118, 120, 143, 202, 206, 220, 224, 231, 233, 236, 252, 254, 272, 280, 311, 502, 518, 547
Aleppo 680
Alexandria 204, 228, 230, 269, 270
Algiers 283
Alghero 36, 39, 272, 284, 458, 682
Ali Gharbi 30
Alipore 28, 52, 298, 681, 684
Allonville 4, 9, 53, 82
Ambala 5, 20, 28, 31
Amberkoj 17
Amiens 2, 3, 4, 5, 9, 24
Amiens/Glissy 16, 69, 140, 276
Amman 14
Amriya 47, 318
Amriya South 294
Ancona 458
Andover 2, 13, 16, 21, 42, 53, 59, 81, 105, 169, 170, 225, 289, 296, 613
Andreas 275
Andrews Field 276
Angle 254
Apapa 270, 490
Aqir 162, 208, 216, 620, 621, 680
Aqsu 208
Aquino 208, 683
Arab Village 30
Arawali 28
Araxos 252
Argenvilliers 9, 82
Argos 208
Ariana 225, 241
Ark Royal (HMS) 4
Arzew 209, 210
Asansol 28, 62
Ascq 4, 5, 6, 42
Ashford 414, 430
Asmara 163
Aspelaere 4

Assiut 17
Aston Down 4, 187
Athies 9
Atwick 251
Auchel 3, 18
Auchey 16
Aulnoy 5, 42, 52
Authrie 26
Auxi-le-Chateau 6, 8
Avesnes 8, 12, 52
Avret Hisar 17
Avrilly 400, 430
Ayr 26, 241, 278, 295, 570
Azaziyah 30

B.10 268
B.15 271
B.21 163
Baghdad 30, 63
Bahrein 84, 114, 230, 242
Bailleul 1, 4, 5, 6, 7, 42, 53, 69
Baizieux 4, 18
Baldonnel 4
Balleroy (A.12) 16, 140
Bally 212
Ballyhalbert 26, 63, 231
Ballykelly 53, 59, 86, 120, 203, 204, 210, 220, 240, 248, 269, 281
Banana 270
Banff 14, 143, 144, 235, 248, 333, 404, 489
Bangor 244
Bannu 18, 31
Bapaume 15
Baqubah 30
Barce 208
Barford St. John 169
Bari 117, 187, 208, 216, 267, 512, 575
Baroda 298
Barurah Reach 30
Basra 30, 31, 63, 203, 294
Bassal 31, 62, 194, 215
Bassingbourn 24, 40, 51, 59, 422, 423
Bathurst 95, 204, 228
Batoum 17
Beaugnatre 59
Beaulieu 53, 224, 311
Beaumarais 259
Beccles 278, 279, 280
Bekesbourne 2
Beketovka 47
Belize 42, 230
Bellaria 241, 318, 683
Bembridge 253
Benbecula 36, 179, 206, 220, 304
Bender Kassim 621
Benina 38, 162, 221, 621
Benson 2, 21, 30, 58, 63, 82, 105, 114, 140, 168, 170, 215, 267, 540, 541, 542, 543, 544, 618
Beny-sur-Mer 2, 4, 268
Berca 38, 39, 203, 221, 227, 252, 259, 272, 294
Berlimont 2
Bernes 69
Bersis 252
Bertangles 2, 6, 9, 16, 18, 21, 52, 82
Bertry West 6

Bethune 2
Beverley 47, 86
Bevinco 216
Bhatpara 211
Bicester 2, 5, 48
Bickendorff 7, 12, 59
Bienfay 3
Biferno 39, 227
Biggin Hill 436
Bikram 117
Bilaspur 10, 267
Bilbais 31, 117, 162, 267, 644
Binbrook 85
Birch 233
Bircham Newton 21, 42, 48, 53, 59, 119, 168, 200, 206, 217, 220, 221, 233, 235, 236, 248, 252, 254, 269, 279, 280, 320, 407, 415, 500, 521, 524, 608, 612, 695
Bir el Gubi 208
Bisseghem 7, 82
Bizerta 230
Blida 13, 36, 144, 233, 293, 458, 500, 608, 624
Blackbushe 24, 167, 301, 622
Blake Hill Farm 233, 271, 437, 575
Blandford 26
Blankenburg (B.66) 168, 400, 414
Bluie West One 269
Bodo 269
Boiry St. Martin 8, 12
Boisdinghem 21, 53
Boisney 2, 4, 268
bologna 208, 225
Bolt Head 275
Bone 36, 225, 284, 293, 458, 500, 608
Bonneuil 52, 82
Borgo 272, 283, 682
Borizzo 36, 52, 272, 458, 500, 608, 614
Boscombe Down 217, 224
Bottisham 2, 4, 168, 169, 241, 268, 613
Bou Ficha 241
Boulmer 202
Bourincourt 69
Bourlon 52
Bovelles 5, 6
Bowmore 19, 246, 422
Bradwell Bay 278, 287
Bramham Moor 47
Brawdy 22, 202, 517
Bray Dunes 52
Breighton 78
Brindisi 148, 284, 301, 624
Brize Norton 53, 99, 115, 296, 297, 511
Broadwell 10, 77, 271, 437, 512, 575
Brooklands 1, 8, 9, 10
Bruay 3, 16, 18, 35
Brüggen 2, 17, 80
Brunei 10
Bückeburg 2, 79, 541
Buckheim 7
Budareyri 330
Buka 203
Burg-el-Arab 39, 47, 208, 459
Burgh-el-Mair 47
Bushire 63
Bustan 30
Butterworth 47, 52, 81, 110

Mourlaincourt 9
Moyenville 4, 5
Mudros 47, 266
Muharraq 30, 84, 105, 152
Mullaghmore 281
Murree 31
Musanoaq Bend 30
Mustabig 14
Mustapha Pasha 17
Mullion 236
Mumfi 230
Muquebella 318
Mssindye 26
Mtoa 26
Mtonia 26
Mtua 26
Mwembe 26

Nahungu 26
Nairobi 21
Nancy 682
Narborough 35, 59
Narromine 618
Nasriyah 30
Negombo 298
Netheravon 1, 3, 4, 5, 6, 7, 10, 12, 13, 17, 18, 21, 26, 27, 35, 42, 48, 52, 53, 187, 271, 295, 296, 297
Netherthorpe 613
New Delhi 28, 31
Newlyn 235
Newmarket 138, 161
Newport 210
Newtonards 13, 231, 290
Nicosia 18, 70, 84, 103, 114, 162, 208, 216, 227, 230, 272, 284, 459, 680
Nivelles 233, 437
Njombe 26
North Coates 22, 42, 53, 59, 86, 143, 224, 235, 236, 248, 254, 278, 407, 415
North Creake 171
Norfolk 53
Northolt 4, 16, 18, 24, 32, 48, 69, 140, 207, 246, 271, 511
North Weald 2, 4, 26, 63, 116, 168, 268, 285, 287, 301, 304
Norwich 18
Novorossisk 47
Nurlu 9
Nutts Corner 120, 220, 231

Oban 95, 209, 210, 228, 330, 422, 423, 524
Oakington 10, 18, 24, 27, 30, 46, 62, 86, 206, 242
Oatlands Hill 169
Odiham 2, 4, 13, 16, 18, 26, 33, 53, 59, 63, 66, 72, 168, 171, 225, 230, 233, 239, 268, 271, 400, 414, 430, 436, 437, 613, 614
Okehampton 16, 225
Old Lassiti 26
Old Sarum 13, 16, 53, 59, 225, 239, 400
Omagh 105
Oosthaven 205
Orah 30
Oranmore 2, 105
Orljak 17
Orvieto Main 208, 683
Osa 208, 683
Ostende 6
Otranto 263, 271
Oulmene 13

Oulton 236
Ouston 430, 613
Ovina 267
Owthorne 251
Oxelaere 8

Padstow 250
Palam 31, 62, 76, 77, 194, 353, 681
Palata 241
Palermo 283
Pallazzo 225
Palms 26
Pamanzi 230, 259, 265
Paphos 252, 272
Parachinar 20, 31
Parafield 238
Patenga 48
Pecq 5, 6
Pembrey 5, 225, 248, 595
Pembroke Dock 95, 119, 201, 209, 210, 228, 230, 240, 255, 320, 321, 422, 423, 461
Penang 28, 209, 230, 240
Penshurst 268
Peretola 225, 682
Peronnes 7
Perranporth 276
Peshawar 20, 28, 31
Petah Tiqua 208
Petanga 117, 215
Peterhead 26, 63, 278, 309, 414, 430
Petit Brogel (B.90) 400, 414, 430
Pezearches 2, 3, 4, 5
Phaphamau 211
Pharsala 208
Phillipopolis 17
Phillippeville 241
Piagiolino 241, 318, 683
Pisa 624
Plivot 53
Plumetot 2
Pocklington 76
Poggio Renatico 42
Poix (B.44) 53, 59, 414
Pomigliano 241, 284, 293, 682
Poona 10, 31, 76, 232
Poperinghe 4, 6
Port Blair 28
Port Ellen 48
Port Etienne 95, 200, 204
Portland 24
Port Reiz 621
Port Said 269
Poulainville 8, 35, 52
Prawle Point 254
Predannack 179, 235, 236, 248, 254, 311, 414, 618
Premont Farm 9, 69
Pronville 5
Protville 13, 36, 39, 47, 52, 144, 148, 458, 608, 624
Provene 7, 9, 82
Proyart 9, 69

Qasaba 208
Qastina 49, 512, 644
Quatre Vents Farm 15
Quelmes 82
Querqueville (A.23) 276
Quetta 5, 20, 28, 31, 114
Queveuvillers 9, 82
Quonset Point 53

Rabigh 14
Rabovo 17
Railhead 26
Raipur 238, 298
Ramadi 30, 63
Ramat David 38, 208, 216, 459
Ramatuelle 225, 284
Ramleh 14, 142, 208
Ramree 15, 117, 160
Ranchi 28, 47, 211
Raneffe 53
Rangoon 209, 240
Ras-el-Tin 202
Ras Gharib 272
Ratmalana 22, 160, 203, 217
Ratnap 28
Rawalpindi 31
Rayak 162, 208
Rebais 5
Reckem 10
Redhill 16, 116, 231, 287, 400, 414
Redhills Lake 191, 212, 230, 240, 357, 628
Reghaia 36, 39, 272
Rely 6, 42
Renfrew 309
Reumont 53
Reykjavik 53, 59, 86, 119, 120, 204, 210, 221, 251, 269, 279, 280, 330, 612
Rheims 24
Rheine (B.108) 400, 414, 430
Rimini 241, 318, 683
Ringway 4, 296, 613
Risalpur 5, 20, 31, 117, 298
Rivenhall 295, 570
Riyan 621
Roborough 16, 225, 276, 691
Rosignano 38, 301, 458, 624
Rufisque 200

Sadaung 28
Saigon 81, 684
St. Andree-aux-Bois 6, 21, 35
St. Angelo 208, 241, 422
St. Croix 119, 276
St. David 53, 58, 220, 502, 517
St. Denis-Westrem 2, 4, 276
St. Eval 22, 42, 48, 53, 59, 86, 120, 140, 143, 161, 179, 203, 206, 210, 217, 220, 221, 224, 228, 233, 235, 236, 240, 248, 279, 280, 282, 304, 407, 415, 489, 500, 502, 517, 541, 543, 612
St. Honorine de Ducy (B.21) 400, 414, 430
St. Inglebert 21
St. Jean 38, 47, 221, 252, 459
St. Leger-Leyaume 18
St. Marie-Cappel 35
St. Mawgan 7, 10, 22, 42, 201, 206, 213, 220, 228
St. Omer 1, 2, 3, 4, 5, 6, 7, 9, 10, 12, 13, 15, 16, 18, 35, 42, 53, 59, 82
St. Pol 6
St. Quentin 3, 4, 5
St. Thomas Mount 200, 203, 211, 353
Salerno 225
Samarra 63
Samlesbury 225
San Francesco 267
San Lucia 3, 4, 5
San Severo 680, 682, 683
San Stefano 17, 208
Santa Cruz 22, 203, 217, 244